TIMELINE OF
HEDVIG SAMUELSON
AND
WINNIE RUTH JUDD

TIMELINE OF
HEDVIG (SAMMY) SAMUELSON
AND
WINNIE RUTH JUDD

1860-2001

by

SUNNY LYNN WOREL

Worel Publications

ISBN-13: 978-1523481989
ISBN-10: 1523481986

Dedicated to the memory of:
Sunny Lynn Worel

Sunny died before this could be published

TABLE OF CONTENTS

FOREWORD

In 1931, two young women were murdered in Phoenix, Arizona by Winnie Ruth Judd. One of the victims was Hedvig (Sammy) Samuelson, the great aunt of Sunny Lynn Worel. Sunny became fascinated with this crime at a young age. However, the family knew little about Sammy's life; only that she had been murdered and that her body had been dismembered and packed into a trunk. Sunny set out on a quest to find out the true identity of her great aunt. Her journey was documented in her earlier book, *Sammy and Sunny*, 2015.

Sunny intensely researched the crime and the lives of the principals involved; Sammy, Winnie and the other murdered woman, Anne LeRoi. As she collected the emerging facts, she methodically placed them into a timeline in accordance with their occurrence. The timeline begins in 1875 and ends in 2001, a few years after the death of Winnie Ruth Judd. The early lives of Sammy and Winnie are detailed, their chance meeting in Phoenix, extensive details surrounding the time of the crime, as well as Winnie's life following this event are included. The long legal drama that followed as well as seven escapes of Winnie from a mental hospital are portrayed. All events are carefully recorded along with sources. This results in a rather disjointed document which follows these people and events day by day and year by year. Since many events happened to the various characters on the same days, the document skips around and is not easily read unless one is already knowledgeable regarding these happenings. Still, it presents extensive information to those who are enthusiasts, completists and scholars of this subject and who have the patience to read through this extensive timeline.

As with the book, *Sammy and Sunny,* this timeline is being self-published for Sunny posthumously. Sunny's mother, Janet V. Worel, inherited this body of research after Sunny's death from colon cancer on July 1, 2014. She was aware that this was an important part of her daughter's life work and that it had never been published as had been Sunny's intent. In the hope that this work will be preserved, it is hereby also presented to the public in the hope that it might be helpful and interesting to some readers.

Section 1

1860-1919

1860, March 26
Reverend Harvey McKinnell is born in Illinois.[1]

1866, January 20

Carrie B. McKinnell is born in Illinois. Her father's name was Niswonger.[2] Her maiden name was Joy.[1]

1889
Captain Lathrop leaves Ashland, Wisconsin to go the Pacific Northwest arriving first in Seattle.[3]

1900
The Samuelson family lives at 645 Washington St. in Milwaukee. Anders is unemployed for 5 months.[4]

1903, June 12
Agnes Anne LeRoi is born on a homestead at Three Rivers, Oregon near Tillamook.[5]

1903, June 17
Dr. Judd's first wife, Lillie Lee Colwell was born in Oklahoma.[6]

1903, November 17
Sarah Hedvig Samuelson (Sammy) is born in Milwaukee, Wisconsin at Washington Street between old Ninth and Tenth Streets. Attendant: , Carrie Gabrielson; Health Office, F.M. Shulz [7] [8]

1904, June 12
Anne LeRoi (Imlah) is born in Dolph, Oregon.[9] (conflict with above date)

1904, September 4
Anders Samuelson files for a homestead in ND in Minot and paid $14.[10]

1905, January 29
Winnie Ruth Judd (McKinnell) is born in Indiana [11] She was born in a tiny parsonage during a blizzard and had double pneumonia at two weeks of age.[12]

1905, February 8
Thomas Frelinghuysen is born.[13]

1905
Dr. WC Judd (Winnie's husband) graduates from Willamette Medical School in Oregon. He grew up in Salem Oregon.[14] Lothar Whitman was said to have been a classmate of his. He was a Saratoga rancher whose name was mentioned in letters of Winnie and William C. Judd.[15]

1905, April
Anders moves to White Earth, ND.[16] Anders learns of a mistake in the homestead filing.[10]

1905, May or June
Samuelson family moves to homestead at White Earth ND.[16]

1905, July
Anders files an amendment for a mistake in his homestead application.[10] Carrie and Reverend McKinnell take Ruth to a church in Pine Village. Ruth was baptized following the ceremony. A silver collection was taken up, and Carrie carried Ruth in her arms to the pulpit. She had given the baby a silver dollar for the collection. The Bishop tried to take the coin from Ruth but she wouldn't let go and clutched it even more tightly. Ruth cried and the Bishop took the coin by force. "She is just like the older people", he said. "She is a poor giver." Another incident at this time was when Carrie was dusting and cleaning. Ruth was playing on the kitchen floor. Ruth started imitating her by mopping the floor with an old rag. They laughed and thought that she might grow up to be a scrub woman.[17]

1906

Anders produces 60 broken acres, 20 acres of crop; threshed 8 or 9 bushels flax.[10]

1907

The Samuelson farm produces 15 acres of crop [10] Dr. Judd was licensed in Oregon.[18]

1908

The Samuelson farm produces 25 acres of crop; threshed 200 bushels grain.[10] Dr. Judd was licensed to practice medicine in Texas.[18]

1909

The Samuelson farm in White Earth produces 50 acres of crop; threshed about 600 bushels wheat.[10]

1909, July 15

Robert Andrew Bowie killed himself in Bisbee, Arizona by gunshot. He is buried at Bisbee. He was 27. He is listed as a widower. HJ McKinnell stated that this was his sister's son. The McKinnell's raised him as a child from about the age of 2 years. He remained with them until he was 16. He said that he seemed queer. He wouldn't stay in school. He would run off from school and play hooky. At the time of his death, his sister's family asked them to bury him in Bisbee decently and send them the bill. They paid the cost of the burial. He stated that his father and mother took care of him until he was married to his first wife. They took him in and took care of him until he decided to leave home. The 1880 Bon Pas census confirms that he lived with his parents and he was two at the time. His first wife's name was Malinda J Martin. They were married in the 1900 census.[19]

1906

Reverend HJ McKinnell came to Peoria accepting the pastorate of the Free Methodist Church at Underhill and Windom Streets in Peoria, IL. He stayed until 1911. During this time, he and his family made their home at 604 Windom Avenue. He was considered a "supply" pastor and not a member of the conference.[20]

1912, February 6

Arnold Samuelson, brother of Sammy, was born at White Earth, ND.[16]

1912

The Samuelson family lived in White Earth N.D.[21]

1912

Ruth Judd tells the entire neighborhood that her mother had a new baby at home and gave specific details regarding the baby's antics. She knew this was untrue and was punished by her parents for lying.[22]
Ruth and her family were living at West Salem, Illinois. Neighbors came over to see and said that Ruth stated that there was a new baby in the house.[23]

1912-1919

The Samuelson family lived in Williston, N.D. at 611 Seventh Ave West. Hedvig attended the Westlawn School in Williston from 1912-1919, had an average record and was extremely proficient in penmanship.[24] However, from the next records, they were not in Williston during this entire time period.

1913, January 29

This might have been in 1912. Ruth states that on her 7th or 8th birthday the little farmer boys and girls came dressed in their Sunday best and would come and bring some little presents for her. On this birthday a boy brought her a calf. It was a very expensive present and "I was thrilled to tears. I didn't know whether my father would let me keep it or not. Father wasn't at home while we were having the party. He came back as early as he could in the afternoon and I met him at the front gate. We were not living on a farm and he said there was no place to keep it. I remember bursting into tears and pleading with him. One of the farmers, who was a deacon at the church, had come as far as the gate with him and saw the whole thing. He said, 'That's all right parson, I'll keep the calf out in my barn. I got plenty of room. Winnie can come out there whenever she wants to.'"[25]

1913-1914 Winter

The Samuelson's spent the winter in Williston.[26]

1914, June 30

A. Samuelson and family return from Williston.[26]

1914, August
A. Samuelson and his family were business and social callers in White Earth near the end of the month.[26]

1915
Joseph Carlson of 1155 Harrison Street who was a salesman in San Francisco stated in 1931 that he went to school with Hedvig Samuelson in 1915. Although, he states he lived in Grafton, ND which is on the opposite side of the state. He states that she was a quiet very studious girl. "She didn't have much to do with the other pupils at the school, but was bright and pleasant. She had no boyfriends as I remember. Her parents, fine people, owned a farm about four miles from Grafton."[27] ?

1915, Summer
Captain Lathrop arrives in Anchorage Alaska.[3]

1915, October 14
Captain Lathrop opens his movie theater in Seward. It has 300 seats, and showed "The Sea Wolf".[3]

1916
Ruth Judd runs away from home. She is said to have walked back and forth in a cornfield while she was trying to decide what to do.[28] When Ruth is 11 she told Dr. Bowers that she fell and hurt the lower end of her spine. This was followed by convulsive movements immediately thereafter.[29] Carrie, her mother stated that she ran away at the age of 10 (same time?). They lived at Pine Village, Indiana at the time. She took a notion that she would make her own living and decided to run away to Chicago. She visited a member of the church to say goodbye and said that she was leaving for Chicago. She left and the congregation member told them and HJ went out to get her. He traced her through the cornfields. Ruth was found going back and forth through the cornfields like she did not know whether to go on or come back. She would first start one way and then start back. He followed her tracks as near as he could. He did not see her there, and so he went back to a house where a girl friend of hers lived and she was there. It was about 2.5 miles from the field. He brought her home with him. She was gone only a few hours.[23] Carrie (I believe) stated that she was more or less active in Sunday School and the church, but that influence

was either helpful or a hindrance according to the mood she was in. She said she was moody and depressed at times. She said it was either exaltation or depression, depending on the mood she happened to be in at a given time. (This testimony may have been Rev. Niswonger, a relative of Carrie's)[23]

1917, February 14
In White Earth, Hedvig won a testament at a church contest for singing a chorus from memory after the pastor sang a verse on the previous evening.[30]

1917, June 27
Hedvig graduates from eighth grade at the White Earth School.[31]

1917, November
Members of the Excelsior Literary Society at the White Earth School are mentioned. Hedvig is listed as the treasurer. They meet every other Friday afternoon.[32]

1917, November 28
Sammy participated in a combined program of the literary societies for Thanksgiving.[32]

1918
Ruth Judd (McKinnell) starts menstruation at the age of 13. She is highly irregular having one period at 13, then skipped a year, one at 14, and then skipped a year and one at 15.[33] Another doctor stated that she was always irregular, often missing 6-10 months at a time. Then sometimes when she did menstruate, she would continue to flow for two months as she did at least one time.[28] Her mother stated that she had an issue with bed wetting until the age of 12.[23]

1918, February
Sammy joined the Red Cross in White Earth. She is listed as a new member.[34]

1918, March
Sammy was elected Secretary for the new semester for the "Excelsior" Literary Society. The program for the literary society had a Washington Theme on 2-8-18.[35]

1918, April 17
William C. Judd is wounded at the Chateau-Thierry sector. There may be details of "conspicuous conduct under fire". This is how Dr. Judd first became addicted to morphine.[36] Dr. Judd fought in battles at Verdun, St. Michel and Argonne Forest.[37] According to Ruth, Dr. Judd was attached to a field hospital unit. He received a bullet shot to the leg out on the line of battle while away from the hospital. He did not report it. The big drive came along. He was in pain and he had an infection. They gave him heroin to stop the pain and to keep going.[38] A record of his admission to a military home in 1933 gives this date as April 17, 1918. Other sources have pointed to September 18th instead.[39]

1918, May 6
Anna Samuelson starts teaching for a period of 7 months in ND in Mountrail County.[10]

1918, September 27
The deed at 2929 North Second Street in Phoenix is transferred to Jennie R Detwiler and Stella J Rittenhouse.[40]

1919, January 17
Hedvig was listed as making "No average standing in any branch below 90 per cent" at the White Earth School.[41]

1919, February
Sammy was not absent or tardy from school (room IV) during this month.[42]

1919, February 11
Sammy sang a song at the literary society program, Lincoln Theme.[41]

1919, February 15
Sammy spent Saturday at the home of her parents?[43] (Where else would she be?) (or did she board in town during the week?)

1919, February 21
Sammy participated in an all school program about Washington and Lincoln, Friday night, 7:30. She delivered a speech called Our Washington.[43]

1919, March 7-14

Sammy became a member of a new class called "Bacteria Yeast and Molds".[44]

1919, March

Sammy made a mark above 90 percent in every school subject.[45]

1919, March 17

A St. Patrick's Day party was given by the high school girls at White Earth.[45]

1919, April first week

Marie and Anna return to White Earth after spending the winter in Chicago and Milwaukee.[46]

1919, April 8

The deed of the house at 2929 N 2nd Street, Phoenix, is transferred from Jennie R and JR Detwiler h/w and Stella J and CH Rittenhouse h/w to HS Prince.[40]

1919, May 14

George Wilson died at Bartonville, Illinois in a hospital for the insane. He died when he was 21 or 22. He was Winnie Ruth Judd's second cousin. He formerly was hospitalized at Kankakee. He died of TB. His insanity was caused by hard work and hard study on wrecked nerves. One symptom that he developed was a failure on his part to recognize and speak to his acquaintances. He grew into a condition of despondency. He was also dizzy much of the time. He gradually grew weak physically and more nervous. Just before he was judged insane he had a desire to possess a gun, and said he would kill his schoolmate whom he claimed had offended him. He did get three guns, and tried to hide them from the officers since the guns had been stolen. He did not suffer with any physical illness prior to his mental disorder. Dora Peters stated that she did not know if Ruth was acquainted with him.[47] HJ stated that they visited him at Bartonville 8-10 times. Carrie visited him no less than 8 or 10 times and took him a dinner occasionally. When they visited him a year before his death he was chained to a chair. He seemed to have "no reason hardly whatever."[19] His card from Peoria stated that his occupation had been a farmer and that the assigned cause of admission was "over study and self-abuse" – Dementia, Praecox, Catatonic [48]

8

1919, June 29
Sammy performed a vocal solo for the graduation exercises. She did not graduate this year.[49]

1919, July 11
Dr. Judd was discharged from the army since he was "not needed".[39]

1919
Ruth received her diploma from the Danville Public School system in Vermillion County Illinois. Her marks averaged about 85.[50] Carrie stated that Ruth liked to read but she never read anything much since they never had any books around the house. Everything she got of that was at school. Carrie mentioned that when Ruth was a girl she wrote a little poem on time. The teacher wanted them to write poems and bring them in. Ruth wrote a verse or two and brought it back to school. (Not sure of date)[23]

1919, Fall
Ruth attends the College at Greenville, Illinois.[51] Ruth stated that until she went away to boarding school she was afraid to sleep without a light burning in her room. Ruth stated that her parents were so anxious that she marry a missionary or a minister and keep in the church work that they sent her to this college. She stated that many of her classmates were twice her age.[12] It was the nearest Free Methodist school.[50] She was said to be of highly nervous temperament and prone to do XXXX(unreadable) things.[52] Ruth disappeared shortly after starting school there. Her parents hurried to the school and started a search for her. Finally, she returned. Apparently she had been to Springfield with a party of students, taken there by the county superintendent. Her explanation was, "I wanted to go, but I was afraid I couldn't get permission. So, I didn't take a chance, but went anyway.[50] Ruth was "campused" as punishment in that she was ordered to remain on the campus for some months. She was given a penance, a thick book to read. At the end of sixty pages, she hurled the book across the room and refused to read another line.[50] There is some evidence that Ruth had an exaggerated opinion of her ability in English composition. Apparently, mathematics was difficult and she made only passing marks in that subject.[22] Ruth stated that the men at the school were all very, very much older than her. She said that men as old as 40 were in her classes, but they did not interest her. She said there was one boy,

the son of the professor of theology and homiletics who was 17 years of age. He was the nearest boy of her age. They went together. He brought her home from church and he would come up and they would go for walks in the early evening. His name was Paul Ladue. They went together off and on for a year and a half. He told her at the time that his mother had just died. He told her, "Ruth, I promised Mother on her death bed that I would never go with a girl until" ...... I don't know whether he said of age or 18 years of age, but he said, "I am sure that if Mother could see you, she would be glad we are going together." He only held her hand and they sat on the school steps and talked. They went without lunch so that they could stay in the auditorium and talk. This boy visited her with Burton at La Vina Sanatorium in 1928. He may have called her in the LA jail. [53]

Sept 9, 1919-June 1920
Sammy attended the South Division High School in Milwaukee as a sophomore in High School. She lived in Milwaukee with Helma Nelson at 655 Twenty-Seventh Ave.[54] Ida Nelson, her cousin said that "Hedvig was strong for outdoor sports. She liked to skate, ride horseback, hike and picnic. She liked other sports too, and dancing, but she cared most for the outdoors. Her favorite pastime was skating."[7]

1919, December 27- 1920, February 21
Dr. WC Judd was hospitalized at the Oregon State Hospital as a narcotics addict after returning from the war.[55]

1.　　Arizona State Department of Health, *Harvey J. Mckinnell Death Certificate*, in *Arizona Vital Records*. July 16, 1942: Phoenix. http://genealogy.az.gov/
2.　　Arizona State Department of Health, *Carrie B. McKinnell Death Certificate*, in *Arizona Vital Records*. November 8, 1953: Phoenix. http://genealogy.az.gov
3.　　Tower, Elizabeth A., *Mining, media, movies : Cap Lathrop's keys for Alaska's riches*. 1991, Anchorage, Alaska (6761 Roundtree, Anchorage 99516): E.A. Tower. [v], 110 p.
4.　　*US Census*. 1900, United States Government.
5.　　*Murdered Woman Native of Oregon: Mrs. Leroi without Enemy, Says Sister, of Aurora*, in *The Morning Oregonian*. October 21, 1931: Portland. 8.

6.   Arizona State Board of Health, *Lillie Lee Judd Death Certificate*, in
      Arizona Vital Records. August 14, 1920: Phoenix.
      http://genealogy.az.gov

7.   *Samuelsen Woman was Born Here*, in *Wisconsin News*. October 22,
      1931: Milwaukee, WI. 1.

8.   *Birth Certificate*. December 14, 1903, 1903: Milwaukee.

9.   State of Arizona and State of California Department of Public Health,
      Agnes Alexandria Leroi Smith Death Certificate, in *Arizona Vital
      Records*. October 16, 1931: Phoenix, Arizona.
      http://genealogy.az.gov

10.   Peterson, Phyllis, *Anders Severin Samuelson*. August 23, 1998:
      Carpinteria, CA.

11.   *Mrs. Judd Formerly Was Telephone Operator*, in *Los Angeles Times*.
      October 21, 1931: Los Angeles. 9.

12.   Judd, Winnie Ruth, *Judd Reminiscences*, in *Arizona Historical Society,
      Southern Arizona Division*. 1941: Tucson, AZ.

13.   *List of US Citizens arriving on the Olympic sailing from
      Southhampton to New York, September 18, 1928*. 1928.

14.   *Dr. Judd Ex-Salem Man*, in *The Morning Oregonian*. October 21,
      1931: Portland.

15.   *Clues Spur Search Here*, in *San Francisco Examiner*. October 21,
      1931: San Francisco. 4.

16.   Anderson, Anna Johanna Samuelson and Kathy Ginter, *Anders
      Severin Samuelson*. received on August 20,1999, 1999.

17.   McKinnell, Reverend H. J., *Ruth Precocious Child Pastor Father
      Writes*, in *Los Angeles Examiner*. October 31, 1931: Los Angeles.

18.   *Medical Examiners Receive Data on Dr. Judd Report*, in *Los Angeles
      Evening Express*. October 30, 1931: Los Angeles. 16.

19.   *Testimony of HJ McKinnell*, in *State Vs Judd: Arizona State Archives
      and Public Records*. 1932: Phoenix, AZ.

20.   *Trunk Murder Woman once Lived in Peoria*, in *Peoria Journal*.
      October 21, 1931: Peoria, IL.

21.   *T.B. Sufferer and Nurse Brutally Slain in Arizona by Woman
      Companion; Motive Remains Mystery*, in *Tioga Gazette*. October 22,
      1931: Tioga, ND.

22.   Unknown author at the Arizona State Hospital, *Ruth Judd:
      Summary, June 25, 1947*, in *Personal Collection of Jerry Leukowitz*.
      June 25, 1947: Phoenix. 3.

23.   *Testimony of Carrie McKinnell in State vs Judd*. 1932, Arizona State
      Archives and Public Records.

24. *Slain Teacher Lived Here*, in *Williston Herald*. October 22, 1931: Williston, ND.

25. Judd, Winnie Ruth, Burton Joy McKinnell, and Relman Morin, *Ruth Judd's Life Story: Chapter II*. October 26, 1931: Los Angeles Record. 1.

26. *Notes and News About Town*, in *White Earth Record*. July 3, 1914: White Earth, ND.

27. *Miss Samuelson Quiet Girl, Says S. F. Schoolmate*, in *San Francisco Call Bulletin*. October 20, 1931: San Francisco.

28. *Testimony of Dr. Clifford Wright*. Feb 2, 1932, Arizona State Library and Public Records: Phoenix, AZ.

29. *Testimony of Paul E Bowers*, in *State Vs Judd*. 1932: Phoenix, AZ.

30. School Notes in *White Earth Record*. February 16, 1917: White Earth, ND.

31. School*Notes...* in *White Earth Record*. June 21?, 1917: White Earth, ND.

32. *School Notes*, in *White Earth Record*. November 23, 1917, 1917: White Earth, ND. 1.

33. *Testimony of Edward Huntington Williams MD*. 1932, Arizona State Archives and Public Records: Phoenix.

34. *Red Cross Notes*, in *White Earth Record*. February 13, 1918: White Earth, ND.

35. *School Notes*, in *White Earth Record*. March 8, 1918: White Earth, ND.

36. Judd, William C, *My Life with Winnie Ruth Judd - Part 1*, in *Intimate Detective Stories*. March, 1940. 2-7, 52.

37. Swent, Eleanor, *Marian Lane: Mine Doctor's Wife in Mexico*. Western Mining in the Twentieth Century Oral History Services. 1996, Berkeley. 121.

38. Judd, Winnie Ruth, *Killer Shies at Word Murder*, in *San Francisco Examiner*. October 29, 1931: San Francisco. 10.

39. US National Homes for Disabled Volunteer Soldiers, *William Craig Judd Admission Record*. 1933. www.ancestry.com

40. *Lot 9, Block 1, La Belle Place, 4/42 Deed Recordings*. Phoenix, Arizona.

41. *School Notes*, in *White Earth Record*. February 14, 1919: White Earth, ND.

42. Hansen, Agnes, *School Notes*, in *White Earth Record*. February 28, 1919: White Earth, ND.

43. Hanson, Agnes, *School Notes*, in *White Earth Record*. February 21, 1919: White Earth, ND.

44. Dolan, Gladys, *School Notes*, in *White Earth Record*. March 14, 1919: White Earth, ND. 1.

45. Strom, Lottie, *School Notes*, in *White Earth Record*. March 21, 1919: White Earth, ND.

46. *Local News*, in *White Earth Record*. April 11, 1919: White Earth, ND.

47. *Deposition of Dora A Peters, 440 Harvard Place, Indianapolis, IN*, in *State Vs Judd: Arizona State Archives and Public Records*. 1932: Phoenix, AZ.

48. *Hospital card from Peoria Illinois regarding George Wilson*, in *State vs Judd: Arizona State Archives and Public Records*. 1932: Phoenix, Arizona.

49. *Commencement*, in *White Earth Record*. July 4, 1919: White Earth, ND. 1.

50. McKinnell, Reverend H. J., *Refusal to read flung book away: Slayer but Average Student; liked, however, to be biggest toad in puddle at school activities*, in *Unknown Newspaper Clippings of Lloyd Andrews*. 1931.

51. West, Nathaniel, *Legendary 'Trunk Murderess,' Who Once Lived Here, Dead at Age 93*, in *Greenville Advocate*. October 29, 1998: Greenville, IL. 1.

52. *Girl's Abduction Story is Attacked.*, in *Olney Daily Mail*. November 16, 1922.

53. Judd, Ruth, *Ruth Judd's Life Story in her Own Words*, in *Los Angeles Examiner*. October 28, 1931: Los Angeles.

54. *Woman Murdered in Trunk Mystery Once Lived Here*, in *Milwaukee Journal*. 1931: Milwaukee. 1.

55. *Judd Formerly in Salem*, in *Morning Oregonian*. October 22, 1931: Portland. 15.

Section 2

1920-1929

1920, February
Dr. Judd moved to Menard, Texas with Dr. Longino intending to open a hospital there. He practiced medicine there for about 5 months.[1]

1920, June
Dr. Judd performed on operation on Miss Lillian Colwell for appendicitis.[1]

1920, July 10
Dr. Judd marries Lillian Colwell in Junction near Menard. She is 17 years-old. Dr. Judd stated that he could "cure" her if he had her with him. They soon left Menard for Phoenix.[1] She was the daughter of Mrs. Collie Colwell of Menard, Texas.[1] Her father was Lee Colwell.[2] They lived on East Van Buren.[3]

1920, August 14
Dr. Judd's first wife, Lillian Lee Colwell, died in Arizona of TB. (I thought it was a morphine overdose)[4] Dr. Judd informed her mother that Lillian had died of heart disease and acute indigestion.[1] Her death certificate stated that she died of an accidental morphine poisoning.[2] She was 17 years old, 1 month and seven days. She is listed as married and a housewife. She is buried in Los Angeles, California.[2] Ruth Judd stated that she gave up and committed suicide. In another account she stated that she died from falling off a horse in 1916.[3]

1921, March
Austin Cap. Lathrop serves on the following committees in the legislature in Juneau. He was territorial representative from the 3rd division: Banks, Banking and Corporation, Fisheries, Fish, Game and Agriculture, Municipal Affairs, Transportation, Commerce, and Navigation and Ways and Means.[6]

1921, April

Carrie leaves Ruth at boarding school alone for 2 months. (This could be 1922) This is the only time Ruth had been apart from her. She had stayed at Greenville with her.[7]

1921, Summer

Ruth returns from school where she had been away from Carrie for the first time between April and June.[7] Ruth had a job in a real estate office and coughed constantly all summer.[5] Carrie testified that she was going to school at Greenville and school was out in June. She came home and Frank Hull was at the church and wanted to bring her home. Ruth declined saying that they had company and had to go home with who she came with. He asked a third time while she was with the other young man for her company and she refused. He said, maybe another time. He made it a point to try to go with her, and he would come and go with her to church sometimes, and sometimes he would take her to shows, and sometimes go out car riding, and Mr. McKinnell followed him out to the car one night and said, "Frank, be good to my little girl, she is all the little girl I have". He took her car riding and went way off quite a distance and came to a turn off place that led into the woods. He stopped and asked her to get out. Ruth wouldn't get out. He took a hold of her and tried to put her out, and she held to the car, and she just asked God to let some car come along so that he would let her alone. Carrie said that was what Ruth told her. She also made the statement, "She went with a young man and we think that he was indiscreet".[7] Ruth told Carrie that she asked the Lord to let somebody go by so that He would break that up so they could go on home. She stated that at the time Ruth said that he had what he desired at that point. She didn't remember exactly what Ruth said. He ended up saying, "Ruth, you are an angel and I am a devil" and said he cried or pretended to cry. He brought her home.[7] Ruth stated that she became acquainted with him while she was gathering zoological specimens. He used to help her go out and help her catch butterflies and get specimens for her collection.[8]

1921, Fall

Ruth has some sort of breakdown at boarding school. She claimed she was taking a heavy course load at school. She was also helping in the church in inviting new acquaintances to the Sunday school. She built up the class from 5 to 28 pupils, but she had never professed any salvation or sanctification. She attended a revival at the church. They told her that God was going to shake hell until she repented. She sort of freaked out but cooperated and went to the "mourning bench". She claimed the evangelist from the pulpit prayed to God to shake her over hell until she saw what she was doing by refusing to go to the mourner's bench, claiming that she was a stumbling block. If she went to the altar first the other young people would follow. Then the Evangelist fell under the power and lay there rigid for hours with his arms uplifted. Ruth described the mourning bench one time as "people would go to the Mourner's bench and fall under the power, go into trances and sing and cry and shout sometimes until midnight. When I would fall asleep it was frightening to suddenly awaken by shouts when someone received sanctification and started singing songs like, "He takes me as I am, Salvation is free for you and me and He takes me as I am, How the fire fell or I've got that old time religion".[5] Ruth refused and went home. However, she wanted to please her father so she went back. She claimed that this whole event did something horrible to her.[5] Greenville police described Ruth as "highly emotional" and that she had "fantastic ideas".[9]

1922, January
Ruth stated that she left Greenville because her parents couldn't afford the high tuition.[8] Ruth stated that she went with a boy by the name of Raymond Cullison. This caused quite a bit of jealously from a girl in Olney. She was fond of him. They split up, so, she started going with the girl's cousin, Frank Hull. He told her stories about France and she thought this was very romantic.[8] Ruth has some sort of relationship with Frank Hull.[10] Frank Hull was born on Oct 20, 1898. In 1918 he was an RFD carrier in Claremont Illinois. His home was in Calhoun.[11] In 1918, he was considered slender and tall with gray eyes and light hair. His middle name was Leroy.[11] Ruth stated that at some point they had split up. She was furious. She said that his girlfriend was the cause. SheRuth stated that her friend Joy Yelch (I hated her, I always will) crowed. Ruth had taken the boy Raymond Cullison from her. They later got married. Frank was interested in her friend Beulah and she asked him not to go with Beulah. Frank thought she was doing it for meanness. She said that since so many unmarried girls in that part of the woods were having babies, she conceived of stating that she was and make Frank marry her. She stated Frank never touched her. She had never had intercourse with him or any man until she met Dr. Judd.

Frank cried and cried and told her father that he had never touched her. He told her that she was crazy. Ruth told him that he should quit going with Beulah or she would send him to the pen. She stated that she would not be tormented by Joy Yelch. She said she was doing well in her English class. She made a 90 in Botany and Zoology. Her stories were published in the school paper and the Olney paper. She stated that she was popular at school and popular with her teachers. She got so worked up that Frank told her that she was crazy. Ruth stated that she knew it but if I started this thing I would have to finish it.[12] Ruth told in the examiner that they had broken up since Frank had decided that he liked Beulah better. She said that she didn't mind but that Frank's cousin started "Twitting" at her that Beulah had taken him from her. She went to Frank and told him that she couldn't stand being tormented. That he needed to stop seeing Beulah until at least she went back to school. If he didn't agree, she would charge that he had attacked her. He laughed at her since their lovemaking hadn't gone very far. He said, "Go ahead kid, hop to it." He didn't think she really would. Because he had dared her, she wrote him a note and hid it in the clock. Her parents found it. Her father summoned the boy and confronted him.[13] Carrie stated that since the incident in the woods from the previous summer that Frank Hull ought to marry her. Although, she said something about this being a month or so before January or February. Carrie thought that there was something wrong since she found Ruth making little clothes for a baby; baby clothes. She took her to see Dr. Weber at the Sanitarium in Olney. It was known as the Weber Sanitarium at Olney. There were several Dr. Weber's. They were brothers. She took her there for an examination to see if she was pregnant. He said that he thought she was not. He did not state on whether she had sexual relations or not. Ruth did not return to school. She was making baby clothes until July. Carrie stated that she gave part of them away. She gave a little girl a little dress for her doll since she had a pretty big doll at that time.[7] Carrie agreed that Frank quit going out with Ruth and was with another young lady in Olney. She said Ruth was jealous and that she seemed to care a great deal for the young man.[7] Carrie stated that Ruth was "pretty quick tempered and she would say what she wanted to say and was pretty cutting with it".[7] Carrie also said that she always kept Ruth close to her at home. She never allowed her to go anywhere unless she felt that it was safe for her to go. She watched her very close and kept her pretty close at home. She never went out because she would not permit it until she became about 16 years of age.[7]

4

1922, January 18
In the complaint against Frank Hull, the date of the seduction is listed as January 18. There are four counts: January 18th, January 25th, January 29th and February 5th. On January 18th, the complaint states that Frank Hull obtained carnal knowledge of her and had elicit carnal intercourse by deceit and promise of marriage. The Grand Jury is set for the November term of the Richland County Circuit Court.[14]

1922, January 25
Another count of seduction was claimed against Frank Hull.[14]

1922, January 29
Another count of seduction was claimed against Frank Hull.[14]

1922, February 5
This complaint regarding Frank Hull differed in that she was persuaded by the gift of a diamond finger ring and promise of marriage and he unlawfully and maliciously seduced and obtained carnal knowledge of her and had elicit carnal sexual intercourse.[14]

1922, June 1
Sammy graduated from high school from White Earth. She gave the class Salutatory. Class Motto: Finished, yet Beginning; Class Colors: Red and White; Class Flower: Red Rose.[15] One of her friends from the Minot Normal School stated that the principal at White Earth dissuaded her from becoming a nurse and urged her into teaching. He said to her, "with your personality you belong in a school room".[16]

1922, June
Mildred Keaton graduates from the St. Peter's School of Nursing in Olympia Washington.[17] Ruth continues to make baby clothes and is at home with her mother.[7]

1922, September 2
Ruth appeared before GA Keller, Justice of the Peace and signed a complaint that called for the arrest of Frank Hull for the seduction charge. This is the date the state warrant is signed by the Justice of the Peace, GA Keller.[14]

1922, November 3

Ruth mails a letter to the mother of Frank Hull from Claremont RFD. One section of the letter states: The most people have given me the most expensive dainty baby clothes. People in Olney have given me the best wool shirts, stockings, dainties, dresses, laces, gowns, beautiful baby blankets and the prettiest expensive cap and coat. Frank Maxine Hull has the most elaborate dainty clothes of any baby I've ever seen. You'd feel quite elated if I'd change my name to Hull wouldn't you? I think maybe I will, so I can keep our baby. It doesn't cost over several hundred dollars and I'd rather keep the baby than let even a multi-millionaire keep it. One wealthy Dr.'s wife worth thousands of dollars wants it so bad. One banker's wife who has no children wants to adopt it so bad too and another family not far from Olney would like to keep it so if Frank don't love his helpless little bit of humanity, oceans of others do. Must close. Hope Frank Maxine can soon write to you.[18] In the drainpipe letter she said she had a baby girl after she had run away.[12]

1922, November 6 or so

Ruth said that she had worked herself up into such a nervous state over her trouble with the young man involved that her mother had taken her early in the week to the James Jones home in Bonpas township where she could be away from it all.[19] Although, in trial HJ stated that he took her to a farm about fourteen miles from Olney. In some other excerpts it sounds like they are near Browns.[20] In her trial one of the doctors stated that Ruth kept up the act that she was pregnant until her mother took her away.[21] Ruth stated that she was quite ill and crying most of the time. Her parents took her away out in the country.[5] There were a multitude of subjects racing through her head.[5] This lasted until she had double pneumonia when the multitude of subjects stopped racing through her head.[5] Carrie testified that she took her out in the country with her and they were at the place where we went until I thought it was time if she was pregnant for the child to be born. She went to a doctor over there at Berryville, "when we went over and told Jim...." Interrupted. "The doctor at Berryville came to see her and he touched her feet to see if her feet were swollen, or normal, anything like that but he didn't make any examination to know whether she was pregnant or not."[7]

1922, November 7

Ruth states that Tuesday night (although says Nov 8) they were aroused by what they thought was someone prying at the window of the room where she said her mother was sleeping.[19] Ruth decided that she needed to do something drastic, so she hopped out of the window one night in her gown and grabbed a few gunny sacks and over shoes and ran away and said she was kidnapped. She planned to say that Frank had her kidnapped.[12] Carrie stated that one morning when she woke up, Ruth was gone. She thought perhaps she had just gotten up early. She was dressing and noticed that Ruth's clothes were lying there that she had taken off the night before. So, she didn't have her clothes with her. Carrie hurried up and dressed. She went to find her. She went to the front door to see if she had gone with Mrs. Jones to help her with the feeding and milking. Jim Jones was gone. He had gone that same night to be at his son's to be there early to husk corn. When Carrie asked her where Ruth was, she replied that she did not know. Carrie ran out in the yard and looked around to see if she could find her. She called for her, but she didn't answer and she thought she had gone. She ran out to the grove that was close by and looked over the grove to see if she could find her. She was screaming and crying since she was gone. She then went to one of the neighbors and looked in the well to see if she could find her. She saw a straw stack in another field. Some of the neighbors ran around to see if they could see her anywhere. She was gone all that day and the following night and the next day. They were looking for her the whole time. She ended up closer to Olney than the Jones' farm. I think this means, it was interrupted, but it sounds like they went home to Olney.[7] Newell Wilson, father of Benjamin Wilson was called by his brother WL Niswonger of Champaign to go to Olney to assist HJ McKinnell in locating his daughter. He was a retired blacksmith and wood worker. He knew Ruth as a child between the ages of 5-10. He knew her from camp meetings and other religious gatherings. He saw her about 4 times a year. He never thought she was a normal child. There were times when she was very emotional, sensitive, and imaginative.[22] HJ said that his wife telephoned him that first morning when she was gone. They searched for two days, went to various towns, one called Vincennes, Indiana, twenty- seven miles away.[20] In regard to Benjamin Wilson, HJ stated that his mind failed when he was at Greenville College.[20]

7

1922, November 8

Ruth stated that she was abducted. Ruth claimed that while she and her mother were asleep at Calhoun, she was chloroformed by two men which was administered by a sponge.[10] She said she was taken through a window of the bedroom, gagged and bound head and foot and placed in a one-seated car. Ruth said she went to sleep about 11 o'clock and thinks her abduction took place about midnight. She says she remembers nothing of a definite nature until she came to herself, bound and gagged in the car inthe road. After she was safely in the car she says they displayed a pair of scissors. One of the men said, "_____, did you cut the wires?" They had some conversation about cutting the wires to Berryville to prevent the alarm being spread, and one of the men left the car and shortly returned. Ruth describes one of the men as wearing a mask over the lower part of his face all the time he was around her. The other man was unmasked, but he wore a moustache. Ruth says she lost track of directions but described points and turns in the road. She remembered especially a sign which read, "Three miles to Parkersburg". This sign has been located as being 3 miles south of Parkersburg. This sign was about half the distance to the house where she was imprisoned, she says.[19]

1922, November 9

It was nearing daylight Thursday morning when the house was reached. There was a woman of about 60 years, a little stooped shouldered, and also a younger woman. Ruth heard men's voices that seemed other than her abductors.[19] Carrie testified that Ruth was taken to a house near Brown Station and she was there for a whole day. There was two women and she heard voices of men.[7] She was at this time clad only in her night dress and was nearly frozen. There was only a bed and stand in the room. To keep warm, she remained in bed. Her bonds had been loosened. Either the old or young woman remained in the room during the entire day. One time when she tried to fight one of her abductors, he told her he would teach her a lesson and he took a whip and lacerated her legs until they bled. She said she was still further frightened when she heard one of the men say they "had better take her to St. Louis". During that day she was offered but refused food. She says she heard noises in a room next to the adjoining room, but could not tell what was being said. During the evening she was left alone when the others were gathered in the other room. She had seized the scissors the men had and secreted them in the bed. She found a gunny sack and cut holes to make a vest. It was about 8:30 o'clock Thursday night as near as she can tell which she escaped from the house though a window she pried open.[19]   Carrie testified that Ruth went to a window and opened it and tore off the mosquito bar, that there wasn't a wire screen, it was just a screen and slipped out. She said she just asked the Lord to direct her the way home, and she started the right way and came down to the railroad tracks.[7] She started on the road and in about a half mile came to a railroad track. Afraid to apply to any one, fearing she would be recaptured by her enemies, she says she began to walk the track.[19] At places where there was fine gravel and sand in the track, she walked in that to ease her feet. Not knowing just what direction she was going, she says she passed through three towns and at last came in sight of Calhoun. She declares she was still afraid to apply to any house she passed for fear she would again fall into the hands of her abductors.[19] As she walked the 23 miles, she stated that her feet hurt from walking on the stones and that she was so tired that she stopped to sleep along the railroad track.[22] HJ said that she kneeled down and prayed to the Lord to show her what way to go and she took the road towards Olney. He seems to indicate she was near Brown's Crossing. (way more than 14 miles from Olney)[20]

1922, November 10
Ruth walks along the tracks at night. She says when she was making this weary journey in the dead of night; no passenger trains passed but there were two freights. One of them nearly ran over her. She said she sat down on the rails to rest and evidently had fallen asleep. She was awakened by a roar and flashing lights and rolled off the track just in advance of the passing freight. At places where there was fine gravel and sand on the track, she walked in that to ease her feet. Not knowing just what direction she was going, she says she passed through three towns and at last came in sight of Calhoun. She declares she was still afraid to apply to any house she passed for fear she would again fall into the hands of her abductors.[19] At Calhoun, which she at first thought was Olney, she did not know what to do. Nearly dead with cold and exhaustion, she finally found refuge in Rev Lawler's barn, deciding to continue her trip on to Olney when night came.[19] Carrie stated that she went and got up into a loft of a garage so that she would not be seen in her nightclothes and the gunny sack. She stated that she made the gunny sack outfit so she would not be seen out in her night clothes.[7] Ruth spends the night in a corn crib where she clothed herself in a gunny sack and an old sweater.[23] In one version of the story,

she stated that she did not remember what happened until she awoke Friday morning in a deserted house entirely divested of clothing. She said she found a gunny sack and cut holes in it to cover herself. She also secured an old sweater.[10] She was discovered by Rev. Lawler about 2 pm of that day, having been asleep in the meanwhile.[19] When Reverend Lawler finds her she said, "You get away from here" and he told her that he was not going to hurt her. He asked her why she was there. She must not have replied so he went into the house and told his wife that there was a girl down there in the garage loft.[7] Ruth is discovered by Reverend Lawler in his garage in Calhoun, Illinois.[23] The paper stated the next day that she was in the hayloft of his stable.[10] Rev. Lawler said she had on a sweater which she had pulled down over her limbs. From his daughter, who took out the clothing, it was learned that the girl had a gown of some sort in addition to the gunny sack and sweater. She was bare foot. The girl gave a false name to Rev. Lawler and explained her presence in the garage by saying that she was visiting in the neighborhood and become lost..Reverend Lawler had his daughter take her clothing and afterwards drove her to her mother.....She is found in the afternoon.[23] She was wearing no shoes. She told Rev. Lawler that she was staying in the area and had become lost.[10] Another account stated that he was on his way to Olney and decided to turn her into the authorities and then she confessed to whom she was. He dropped her off at her father's home.[10] Rev Lawler provided her with clothing and brought her to her home in this city late Friday afternoon.[19] Carrie stated that she came home in the evening, the second evening. She came by herself to the house, but she was brought from Calhoun by the Methodist preacher there. She asked him to take her to another house since she thought that they wouldn't be there. He said to the woman, "I have brought your daughter home." And the woman replied, "I am glad". Later, she saw a light on over at the house and she knew somebody was home and she came back home by herself. She was not wearing the gunny sack. She was wearing the clothes that the preacher had his wife take her to dress.[7] Carrie stated that she never saw Rev. Lawler since she wasn't brought to their home, but to a neighbor. She said it wasn't far and Ruth could see when they lit the lamp from there. They had no electric lights in the house but used a lamp.[7] She had scratches on her lower limbs, indicating that she had been walking through brush and briers. Ruth claimed that she had been whipped by her alleged abductors.[22] HJ claimed that where she was found in Calhoun was about 8 miles from her starting place, the farmhouse. She claimed she was 14 miles away to start. (?) [20]

1922, November 14

There is much talk around Olney about the story of Ruth being abducted. Ruth claimed to have been taken by two men as she was visiting near Calhoun with her mother. She claimed they took her into the woods and horribly mistreated and beat her. Ruth's father visited, states attorney Lewis in the afternoon, but they were interrupted and he did not get the full story.[23]

1922, November 16

People around town are wondering if Ruth's story is true. Frank Hull was brought to town from Montezuma, Indiana on a charge related to Ruth Judd with his connection to her that dated to January 1922. He was provided with bond for his appearance. His friends claimed that they would show that he had had no connection to Ruth for more than 10 months. Ruth is at home on Jasper Street and was said to be too ill to leave her home.[10] Court documents on the bond schedule seem to indicate that Frank Hull posted a 1000-dollar bond and agreed to appear before a Justice of the Peace on November 20th.[14] Interestingly, even when Ruth says it was made up in 1931, Carrie made the statement on the stand, "She said she didn't know who it was; she said one of the men was masked and the other one she did not know. They tried to find out but they didn't know how to go at it. They never found them."[7]

1922, November 18

The Olney Daily Mail printed Ruth's story. They stated "Ruth McKinnell, 17-year-old daughter of Rev and Mrs. H. J. McKinnell, undoubtedly went thru a harrowing experience Thursday and Friday of last week. Even if half of what she tells is the result of her imagination there remains the ground work for a serious criminal offense which may involve a number of persons. Since her return to her home at 313 South Jasper Street in East Olney last Friday night Miss McKinnell has been confined to her bed." To a representative of the Daily Mail, Sheriff Craig detailed her experiences this morning. Ruth had written this note to the Daily Mail in the morning to facilitate this interview. "If you wish to print the truth about my abduction, send a reporter down. I will give him some material. I am aware in such a serious case as this, the XXXX demands it, but I have been too ill. I have made several attempts to write some but it exhausted me. Decided XXXX fate fiends of hell are absolutely untrue and very absurd. As to Hull's having any connection in this affair, although his friends claim he can readily XXXX, yet

Hull is on the verge of being proven at the bottom of this trouble as he made me just such desperate threats and doubled fists and curses. If I dare, I'll expose him to authorities as to the things as they have occurred. One object in keeping this silent has been the fact that detectives are working on this case and have found valuable clues as to the criminals. Different statements made in the papers are decidedly untrue and the general tone in the Nov 16th story was contemptible. Rev. Lawler had no such intention (ask him) as was printed. Of course rumors told you have been misleading, so if you send a reporter; I will tell him the truth."[19] The story concluded, "Rev. McKinnell has been engaged since her abduction in trying to substantiate her story. He was assisted by several others and it is said with the details supplied about her journey to and from the house where she was held has been substantiated at least in part. The location of this house from her story must be south and near Bone Gap. In telling her story Miss McKinnell attributes plausible reasons for not asking aid at the houses she passed. Fear of the designs of her abductors, however heightened by her imagination, made her fear to come in contact with any one and her sole object was to get to Olney. 'I thought if I could only get back home, I would be willing to die the next minute', the girl said. Miss McKinnell is large for her age and a comely and intelligent girl. One who hears her story will not doubt that she has passed thru a harrowing experience even if she is not revealing all she knows about the purposes of her alleged abductors. Frank Hull, arrested at Mohezuma,Ind., on a complaint in connection with this case, had given bond. As the grand jury meets next week the preliminary was dispensed with. The charges against young Hull are for seduction of Miss Ruth McKinnell on or about January 15, 1922. The complaint was filed before Justice Keller. Miss McKinnell declared that the threat of this proceeding in court is the cause of the attempt to abduct her."[19]

1922, November 12-14
Ruth disappears for several days. She was a student at Olney and was found on November 14 in the hayloft of Rev E. L. Lawler, a Methodist pastor at Olney. He found her unclothed in the hayloft of his barn. She told officers that she had been chloroformed by two men when she was asleep. She said she had been held captive two days in a deserted house somewhere south of Olney. After her abduction, she told officers of her escape. Ruth told them she escaped from the two men, without her clothing and sought refuge in the hayloft. She also stated that a fellow Indiana youth was the father of her unborn child. Mr.

Lawler took Ruth home. Ruth was considered a neurasthenic at the Time.[24] She told her parents during this time that she had been kidnapped and raped, claimed to be pregnant, etc. in an attempt to force a neighbor boy (ten years older than herself) to marry her. This episode was carried to the point of medical examination and disproval of the accusations, after her father had filed a complaint against the lad.[25] Ruth quit school at the time of her supposed pregnancy.[25] Carrie stated that she went with Ruth when she filed the complaint against Frank Hull.[7] HJ stated that he was away from home when Ruth swore the warrant out for his arrest.[20]

November 13, 1922
Construction starts on a 7000 square foot moving picture studio in downtown Anchorage as directed by Cap. Austin Lathrop.[6]

November 20, 1922
The original bond schedule stated that Frank Hull should appear at the courthouse on this date.[14]

November 21, 1922
The grand jury in Olney was having a large number of witnesses in the case for Ruth McKinnell. Ruth testified as did her mother in the afternoon. Ruth was carried up the court house steps.[26]

November 23, 1922
Ruth was given the opportunity to testify to confirm her account of abduction and detention by force in a house thought to be in the neighborhood of Bone Gap. Ruth was before the Grand Jury again as she was on Tuesday for 2 hours. She told her story of the abduction. The paper states, "While the attitude of the jury is not known, the investigation today is thought to be in line with suggestions of that body. Former Sheriff Ed Houser, as special bailiff, Page Whitaker, and Mrs. HJ McKinnell and Rev McKinnell formed a search with the intention to start from the Jone's house taking Miss McKinnell's recorded statements as a guide for the route. When the house where she claims she was imprisoned is reached, her story will be further verified." The paper also made the statement that the seduction against Frank Hull is not affected by the attempt to solve the abduction case.[27] GA Keller provides a summary of the Hull case. He states that Frank Hull waives examination and enters into bond in the sum of 1000

Dollars for his appearance before the Grand Jury. He states his mother Mary Hull and Bruce Collusion are his sureties and Frank Hull is discharged from the court.[14]

November 25, 1922
Court documents appear to indicate that Frank Hull was arrested and posted bond of $500. The documents seem to indicate that he will appear the following third Monday of April (1923?). There is nothing in the court documents that anything occurred after this. It seems like Wm Knight might have put up his farm to cover the $500 bail.[14] The grand jury "returned an indictment against Frank Hull for seduction on the complaint of Miss McKinnell". No indictments were returned in the Ruth McKinnell abduction case. The paper reports the results of the trip the officers took over the route of Ruth McKinnell. They reported results were mixed. "The route was transversed and her recorded description of places was followed and took the party to a house near Brown's. At the house indicated there was a girl whom Miss McKinnell identified as the girl at the place of her imprisonment. Miss McKinnell declared the house was not the one she was detained in. The old lady of the house was said to be at Brown's and the party went to hunt her up. Miss McKinnell identified a small bent woman as the old lady of the prison house. The woman denied that she had ever seen Miss McKinnell before.[28] HJ McKinnell said that they went in a "machine" down to Browns Crossing, 16 miles south of Olney by the Illinois Central Railroad and went to the house that Ruth claimed was the one. She pointed out a young woman who was there when she was there.(?) The mother of the other woman was up at Browns at Bone Gap. When asked what woman, he explained the young woman; the older woman of the two was at Bone Gap, five miles north. They went to Bone Gap and Ruth pointed out that she was the other woman who had been in charge.[20] The younger woman at the house was the one Ruth pointed at. The woman denied it. He claimed that after that they were not certain that the evidence was sufficient. They went to Bone Gap. They took her to the house where the other woman was stopping. The first woman told them how to find the house. When the woman came out in the yard, Ruth declared that she was the other woman that had charge of her. The woman denied it. After that they just left. The woman denied that she knew the other woman. She said that it wasn't true.[20] Ruth claims the doctors her parents took her to when they knew she wasn't pregnant, didn't talk to her to find out how ill she was at the time. She wrote letters to a friend who was four years older than

her. She saved the confused jumbled up mess of ideas and sent those letters to attorneys. She claimed the letters were an exaggerated effort of words, phrases of no connection which took Ruth's fancy with literary articles, parts of speeches of various Presidents, Orators, and Poets intermingled with religious ideas and confused and even contradictory stories at times of motherhood.[5] Ruth stated that she had brought a suit against Frank Hull and as soon as Joy moved, she dropped the charges and that was the end of it. She said that she had never told anybody of this and she wished that she would have apologized to Frank Hull. Frank thought it was funny until she had him arrested for rape and kidnapping.[12] HJ stated that he attended a session of the Grand Jury. He stated that the young man had been arrested. He was placed under bond. He stated that there was no trial. "I know the Grand Jury brought in a true ill against him and he was placed under bond."[20]

March 8, 1923
The Anchorage paper announced that the cast of actors (recruited in Portland, New York and Hollywood) were in route to Alaska from Portland for the beginning of filming of the "Cheechakos".[6]

March 15, 1923
1000 people in Anchorage greet the cast of the "Cheechakos", the first film produced in Alaska. There was a free dance and jollification at the movie dome.[6]

Early May, 1923
Shooting for the "Cheechakos" is filmed inside the steamship Alameda.[6]

1923 Summer
William Judd meets Ruth at the State Hospital at Evansville, Indiana. Ruth found because of the wages and not having to pay board she could save more money by working there.[5] Ruth started there as an attendant, but later relieved the night supervisor and matron. She took care of the superintendent's wife who was ill and did just about anything she could do for her. Dr. Judd was a staff surgeon and Ruth was working there for the summer.[5] Ruth stated that she was taking care of the superintendent's wife and that the state paid her.[29] Ruth stated their romance started when she was taking some ice cream to a patient. It was against the rules to bring food to a patient. So, she stood there and talked to him with her hands

15

behind her back. The ice cream melted and dripped down the back of her dress.[30] Ruth was cutting up a water melon as Dr. Judd passed by and asked her for some. Ruth approached him out of concern for a patient who was wounding himself because of his restraints. Dr. Judd said he would help her out, but also asked her to dinner at the Elk's Club.[5] Ruth stated that he asked her this on the 4th of July when she was out on the lawn with some patients. Dr. Judd came out and talked to her.[30] Ruth had never been to a restaurant before. At the end of the summer, Ruth returned to Lafayette where her family was. She stated that she wanted to start college at Purdue that fall, but stated that she did not because her parents couldn't afford it. She asked Dr. Judd to visit her at Lafayette. Dr. Judd planned not to visit her (because of his age and drug addiction), but her letters persuaded him.[31] Her family moved up to Lafayette (from Olney) at the time, so Ruth moved to be near them.[5] During this time, the son of one of the members in her father's church owned the lumber yard in a small town close to the hospital. He and his whole family wanted Ruth to marry him. He was nearer to her age and the family tried to tell her how well off she would be one day, but she liked her work at the hospital and "worshiped" her future husband.[5]

1923, August 31
Samuel Samuelson, Sammy's brother, graduates from the Minot Normal School.[32]

1923, November
The Cheechakos has completed final editing. Captain Lathrop personally took charge of the distribution of the film.[6]

1923, November 11
The first Alaskan presentation of the Cheechakos.[6]

1923, December
Dr. Judd visits Ruth at Lafayette and meets her parents. Ruth confesses that she didn't enter Purdue, but was working as a telephone operator. He kisses her and her parents catch them. He didn't know what to say, so he says "I want to marry your daughter" and they were engaged. But, he wasn't serious about marrying her and made up some ways to get out of it.[31] Carrie stated that Ruth worked as a telephone girl until up to the time that she got married.[7]

1923, December 15
Mildred Keaton leaves for Kake Alaska on Kupreanof Island on the steamship Jefferson to be the first nurse ever stationed there.[17]

1923, Christmas
Dr. Judd spends the holidays with Ruth and her parents. He is offered a job at the American Smelting and Refining Company at Matehuala in Mexico. He loved Ruth but planned to make this job into a long engagement. However, when he arrived at the McKinnell's, Ruth was ill with two bright spots on the side of her face. Dr. Judd knew that it was TB. Dr. Judd felt that she had less than two years to live. He didn't say anything to Ruth or her parents. He decides to take Ruth to Mexico and marry her in hopes that the warm dry climate would heal her TB. He stresses their age difference and tells her about his drug addiction. Ruth says that it doesn't matter.[31]

1924, January 31- February 1, 1924
Minot Mid-Winter Festival at the Minot Normal School. "Chimes of Normandy" was a play presented. Hedvig played the role of Suzanne, one of the Village Maidens.[33]

1924, April 22
The Cheechakos shows at the Ritz Carlton Hotel in New York to the producers only. Afterwards, the movie played in several other locations in the United States.[6]

1924, April 18
Winnie Ruth McKinnell marries William C. Judd. [34] When he proposed he asked her, "How would you like to marry me and live in a dirty little mining town out in Arizona?"[35] Ruth's father would not give Ruth permission to marry Dr. Judd; he felt she was too young and the doctor was 20 years her senior. Ruth was too young to get married in Indiana without consent. She planned to go to the elders of the church to get their permission. Then, her dad relented and went with Dr. Judd to get the permit. However, he would not marry them and another person did.[35] A minister by the name of Johnson married them.[35] Her father thought that they wouldn't be happy, not because Ruth was too young, but because Dr. Judd was much older. He felt that he was a "man of the world".[35] Burton stated that they hustled and bustled at the house when they received the news, decorating. Burton decorated the living room in pink and white. He said that it was a

happy affair with the big cake and the guests. Burton wanted to stage a charivari which is a custom out in the country. It means that he and a group of friends would gather outside with tin pans, horns and all kinds of noise machines and keep up the racket until they fed them the wedding cake. Then they would ride them on a rail or make the groom trundle the bride through town on a wheel barrow. Ruth said she would not mind but stated that the Doctor objected.[36] Carrie said that Ruth moved away within a few days to a few weeks after she married. They wrote letters every week; sometimes 2 or 3.[7] They went to New Orleans for their honeymoon. Ruth states that she had never been on a Pullman, never had stayed at a hotel, and had never seen a glass of liquor or a full deck of cards until then.[5] Ruth states that they have a lovely room and that she would see the clock in the tower. It was the first time she had ever stayed in a hotel.[37] They were in route to Mexico. Ruth says she is interested in having a baby. Dr. Judd tells her that his condition prohibited that. He was really worried about her condition at the time and this was an easy lie for him to tell her.[31] They stayed in New Orleans for a few days. From New Orleans they ferried on the train across the Mississippi. Then, they went down to Laredo through Monterey to San Luis Potosi, and on to Matehuala. They stayed at this place for 2 years. When they crossed the border at Laredo her husband wanted to go up to the casino to have a drink. Her husband had two beers and Ruth was worried that maybe she had married a drunk. Ruth had never seen any liquor before in her life. She had lemonade.[35] They at first planned to go to Jerome, Arizona, but in El Paso, Dr. Judd sent an application to Asarco (American Smelting and Refining Company in Mexico) and so they went to Maehuala instead.[35]

1924, May 5
Ruth is on her honeymoon. She writes this letter from New Orleans from the Hotel DeSota. "Having a wonderful time. New Orleans is beautiful and quaint. We have a lovely room here. New Orleans is the largest city in this area in the U. S. Of the 405,000 inhabitants, 7% are foreign born and 26% Negros. Beautiful palm trees and everything. Gee, this is exciting. Doctor is so kind and good to me. I'll write later and maybe send you some money, Love Ruth."[37]

1924, May 7
Dr. and Ruth Judd move to Chihuahua Mexico for 4 years.[38] Matehuala? Ruth's condition improves rapidly. She learned Spanish quickly.[31] Ruth stated that they came down on the train to a place called Venegas. They

had to change trains there to go to Matehuala where the mines were; the American Smelting and Refining Company. The main train goes on, past Catorce, on down to Mexico City.[35] Ruth writes to her parents about the time she and doctor Judd move to Mexico. She writes the following at 11:35 A.M. from Vanegas Mexico. "Dear Folks, Guess we'll be at our destination tomorrow – Mexico! We are eating in the queerest Mexican restaurants. I'm trying to learn Spanish. The Mexicans are very nice and polite. I like them very much. Such a wonderful country. So cool at night. This a.m. I awoke about 4 AM and watched the first ray of daylight creep over the chain of high mountains and old volcanos. Great shapes of? and cactus in bloom grow at their feet. I dozed back to sleep but soon was awakened by shooting, yelling, and beautiful music. This was about 6 AM. A Mexican general was coming on our train in his special car. I love Mexico. They have beautiful music and the upper classes of Spaniards are so nice and refined. All Mexicans are polite, but I am proud to associate with the cultured Spanish upper class. Doctor and I are going to go broke if we don't quit meeting poor, blind, and crippled beggars. I hate to look at the poor things. We have given them a few cents apiece. It isn't nearly so hot here as Laredo where we crossed the Rio Grande. Oodles of little Mexicans were running naked on shore and swimming. Women are beating washings on rocks in the river. Men were hauling muddy water in barrel carts. Some of their houses are mud domes. Their nicer homes are built of adobe or mud which is dug, molded and baked into blocks similar to our cement blocks at home. Their ovens are mud domes outdoors. Pigs, goats, and chickens live with them. I will write again when I get there. I am well and happy. Lovingly Ruth."[37]

1924, May 8

In Matehuala they met the Hendersons. They called Dr. Judd Doctor Williams. Mrs. Henderson kissed Ruth. They had tea with lemon and mint leaves. Ruth was wearing a lavender hat and the new grey coat Dr. Judd had given her. They rode up in the car to the mountain with Casiano. Ruth snuggled up to Dr. Judd in the back seat and stated that she was happy (Dr. Williams) we are going to our home in the mountains.[37] On the day they arrive it was Don Amelmo's Birthday who was the foreman at the mine. There was a big party and everyone was drinking. Ruth was shocked. She had never had a glass of liquor in her life. She had never seen a deck of cards before or been to a dance.[35] Ruth later referred to this as Don Antonio's Saint's Day. She stated the Reyers welcomed them there on the mountain side. Doctor

Wilkinson scared Ruth. She stated that he had wine and women that night. All of the Americans had to drop in and salute. They all kissed Ruth on both cheeks, knowing that she was a bride.[37] Ruth loved the children and gave them lots of money at first until Dr. Judd instructed her to give them candy instead.[31] They were given a five-room house to live in with hardwood floors, a yard, and a fireplace. They had servants. There were old men that could no longer work in the mines. He gave them jobs as servants and watchmen instead of putting them on a pension. They brought in the wood, kept the yard mowed and ran errands. The watchman at night met the doctor when he had night calls. The cars would come in, lower down the mountainside. He would run down and meet him with a lantern and help him walk up or carry his little medical satchel on up the mountain.[35] They didn't have electricity for the first year. They did not have running water. It came up on the railroad track. The Mexican women brought up water in large oil cans for themselves.[35] The home was away up in the mountains seven miles from Matehuala. The other families were lovely, well educated people. Dr. Judd showered Ruth with lovely things. Dr. Judd sent for his books stored in California. They had Encyclopedias, old classic complete sets, works of Mark Twain, Alexander Dumas, O'Henry, Joseph Conrad, Tolstoy, Balzac, Maufessaunt, Oscar Wilde, Sax Rohmer, Poe, and Shakespeare. Ruth said she learned to read more and learned to play bridge.[5] Ruth stated that everything in the house was new. They had tinted it in all of the colors she wanted. She had new pans and kettles. She had a pet named Bruno who ate cheese, walked 7 miles, ate oranges as well as fought with a goat. It was a pup. They had a rabbit named Hop.[37] Ruth told one of the alienists that they had many pets in Mexico; 4-5 cats, a couple of dogs, a horse, and some birds. Dr. Judd was jealous of her affection for them and got rid of several of them.[21]

1924, June
Sammy is chosen to participate as a returning member of the Glee Club during summer session.[39] The yearbook shows her in the Glee Club. They are wearing sweaters with a diamond on the front with wide collars. The yearbook states, "If a visitor, listening to the first Glee Club practice in October has been asked to define that "concord of sweet sounds" he would probably have called it "an attempt to express the emotions that are beyond speech." However, Mr. Bland has proved himself worthy of much praise for his untiring efforts with his group of warblers, and now the girls might even be able to "sooth the savage

beast" if it weren't more ferocious than a lap-dog or a kitty. The Glee
Club, one of the oldest organizations in the school has advanced in long
strides under the direction of Mr. Bland, in spite of the fact that he was
handicapped by being new here. The object of the club is to promote
an interest in music through the school and from the work of the
singing chorus in "Wake Miss Lindy", one would be led to believe that
they had accomplished their aim.[40]

1924, June 8

Sammy participated in Graduation exercises (The Senior Sermon). She
performed in a sextet which sang "I will Exalt Thee".[33] Sometime
during her time at the Minot Normal School, Sammy knew Corrine
Babcock who was from Westhope and later lived in San Francisco.[41]
Corinne was the former daughter-in-law of Asst. District Attorney G.
A Rogers of Los Angeles involved in the Judd case. She stated
"Although she was a senior, and had taught school for two terms and I
was a sophomore, our courses threw us together in several classes. She
was exceptionally bright and always among the honor students. I never
knew or heard of her going out with a boy, although she was beautiful
with rich red hair, lovely coloring and fine features. It seemed to me
that Hedvig, raised on a North Dakota farm, working her way by
helping in a cafeteria, winning student honors, just didn't have time for
such things. She was always frank about her finances. I remember that
once I handed her a note in a class, asking her to go somewhere and she
scribbled in one of my textbooks; 'I haven't the cash'. We knew each
other well. I lived, when not at school, with an aunt in Westhope. Sammy
lived six miles away at Landa. Often we went home together on the
same train for the weeends. It is terrible to think of her meeting such
a death. Everyone who knew her loved her. I think that it was Mrs.
Judd who killed her. It was because of jealousy over Hedvig's friendship
with Mrs. LeRoi."[42] Marion Vrem said that they were classmates together in
Minot. She talked about her beauty, popularity, and her eagerness that
others should escape the suffering of tuberculosis. She described Sammy as
one of the best ice skaters at Minot and a splendid horsewoman."[43] She
said "after graduation we wrote to each other frequently. I called her
Sammy as all her friends did."[44] There is a photo of Sammy skating near a
bridge overpass. She is with an unidentified friend. Mouse River near
Minot? It's not Juneau. [45] There is a photo of Sammy and two friends
standing in a fountain with heavy winter coats on. It is Minot in Riverside,
now Roosevelt Park. It seems to match the coats in another picture of

Sammy and friend with a child standing next to a rabbit hutch and another of them sitting by a railroad bridge or depot.[46] These pictures are also Minot at Riverside Park. The building is a picnic pavilion that was located next to a bridge going over the Mouse River. The other picture is of the zoo that was and is located in Roosevelt Park. The woman is currently unidentified.[47]

1924, June 12
Sammy is listed in the graduation program as finishing the Elementary Course.[33] In the 1924 yearbook, *The Magician*, below her name read, "When she has left, she will leave a place no one can fill."[48,49] She is listed as being in the Glee Club and the Mecca for Pep.[49]

1924, July
Mildred Keaton's nurse friend, Thelma and her brother Buster Keaton visit her in Kake. Thelma later married Mildred's older brother Ralph.[17]

1924, August 11
Anne LeRoi marries William Mason, automobile salesman in Portland, Oregon while she is training to become a nurse at the Good Samaritan Hospital. They were married in Kelso and lived together 18 months. They did not fight, but "it was a case of incompatibility" and decided to divorce [50,51,52,53] He stated that Anne could not keep the marriage a secret and was forced to leave the hospital. After they were divorced, she returned to hospital work.[54] She later married Dowell LeRoi Smith, an organist who was living in Ocean View, Oregon in 1931.[55]

1924, Fall
Mary Reep comes to Kake to teach. She lives with Mildred Keaton in the Manse. She sang and played the piano well. Her health was not good and so she left Kake in December.[17] Anne LeRoi begins her hospital training at Good Samaritan Hospital[56] on September 1.[57] Sometime, 6-7 years before her death, she worked as a technician for a Dr. Brachvogal. (a dentist?) She meets Dr. James O'Dell who later is her physician and identifies her body. Dr. O'Dell's office is adjacent to this office in Portland OR.[58] Ann LeRoi is the nurse of Portland Aviator and Jewelry manufacturer, Hugh Angle. He gives her a picture (at her request) with the inscription, Hugh Angle, Christmas 1923, 20 years old. This picture was found in one of the trunks at the time of her death.[57]

1924, September 27

Philip Harold Bisch and his wife Esther have a son, Philip III. Their first son Philip died in infancy.[59]

1924, October

It is the beginning of the new season for the Glee Club at Minot. Sammy is listed as a soprano. The group meets at 3:30 on Wednesdays.[60]

1924, December

Donie Taylor comes to Kake to replace Mary Reep. Donie played the guitar and sang with the girls in the school.[17]

1924, Christmas

Winnie Ruth Judd spends her first Christmas in Mexico. Ruth claimed that the doctor had so many packages for her. Ruth made him handkerchiefs, pajamas he could never wear, and a shirt. Dr. Judd ate up all of the fruit cake before Christmas. so they made more. Bruno was so careful of the tree. Dr. Judd made light fixtures for the tree. Ruth painted the bulbs. Dr. Judd got a wire and fastened each one on the wire and connected it to a battery down in the garage. They had a real lit up tree then.[37]

1925 January

Sammy was a Glee Club member at the Minot Normal School. However, she is listed as new. (?)[61]

1925, March 15

Revolution has broken out in Mexico. Ruth writes to her parents and tells them she shall be home soon. The mine where they were was 90 miles from the railroad. The trip was over a narrow pass that could only be passed by mule.[62]

1925, April

Ruth stated that she tried and tried to get the doctor to beat his narcotic's habit. There was one night when the power went out at Matehuala. He was very sick. You could see him suffering. Ruth felt so sorry for him. He would filter his hypodermic syringe with solutions through a cotton filter. He would boil the spoon. He would boil it and filter it through this so it was sterile. He was having terrible convulsions one night. He was vomiting and the bed was just shaking. Ruth was there and she went in and boiled up all those little cotton wads. She prayed that it would be the last dose he would ever have. The next day, the manager from the mine came down and said, "Doctor, we had doctors here in the past that we couldn't trust with the narcotics here. So, I kept the narcotics up at my house. My little boy four years old climbed up and got into the medicine cabinet the other day and I don't want to have the responsibility of this morphine up there any longer. So, I am bringing it down to you." Ruth cried and cried. Ruth went up the hill to the manager's house. The manager's wife was so good to her. The manager wasn't home yet. Ruth just sat there. She showed her some pictures of her parents. Ruth cried. The woman thought it was a little spat that she and Dr. Judd had. She sat there until supper time and just cried and cried. Mr. Reyer came home and it was getting dark. So, she ate supper with them. She ate a bite or two and she couldn't get the courage to tell them not to bring the narcotics. She felt that she could not betray her husband. Mr. Reyer walked her home. There was a great big rock there and they sat on that rock. Ruth cried and cried. It was April. He said, "Only at this time of year can you see the Southern Cross and the Northern Star at the same time." He sat and showed her where they were. Ruth couldn't tell him. And she didn't tell him.[35] Sometime during 1925, Dr. Leff was in Mexico and met Ruth Judd there. He took Dr. Judd's place for two weeks while he was preparing and taking medical examinations. He lived in the same camp as Ruth and they had all of their meals together.[63] He said that he was very close to Mrs. Judd then as they lived in the same camp. He said he saw her almost constantly. Dr. Leff knew Ruth when she lost her first baby, how sick she was, and what she went through trying to get the Doctor off of narcotics.[64] Dr. Leff stated that Ruth enjoyed outdoor sports at that time. She often went horseback riding over the barren country. She was also a very good hostess. He said that she said she spent time with the Mexicans in their hovels and would teach the mothers how to cook decent meals. She often scrubbed and cleaned their houses.[65] He stated that Ruth would drink when others drank, but never heard her ask for a drink.[65] He stated that Ruth was a level-headed woman of considerable intelligence. He said, "I have known Mrs. Judd for some time and never regarded her as being the least bit insane. She visited us in Glendale on several occasions and always seemed perfectly normal. I could scarcely believe it when I read she was suspected of having committed the murders."[66]

1925, July 23
Sammy plays Yum-Yum in the *Mikado* at the Minot Normal School. Daily rehearsals were during the previous month.[67] Note: Hedvig did

not perform *Madame Butterfly* since this was the first opera to be attempted in years, the last being *City of Dreams*.[68] Mr. Trotter has a voice of pleasing quality, and his solos, and duets with Yum-Yum were among the entertaining features of the evening. Miss Hedvig Samuelson was a delectable Yum-Yum, having vivacity and a small, but sweet voice.[69] One of Sammy's school mates says of her, "I remember her standing in the curve of the grand piano long after classes were over, singing difficult passages again and again for the music director, an exceptionally irritable and temperamental man. But Sammy could get along with him, and he swore by her. She got along with everybody in the entire school, faculty and students alike. There was probably no better liked girl in the college whatever may have happened or whatever she may have become in the intervening years. She was always smiling and always sincere. I never remember her saying an unkind or a catty thing about anyone, no matter what the provocation. She was extremely attractive, rather than beautiful by the accepted standards." She also stated that her lovely soprano voice immediately took her to the front in the school's and the city's amateur music circles. She also says she remembers her rehearsing "One Fine Day" from *Madame Butterfly* wearing the same dress she wore to have her picture taken that appears in the paper (her school picture). She said they wore their skirts long that year (1925) and Sammy's frock of black velvet with a band of ermine at the neck stunningly contrasted with her Norse fairness and her queer greenish-grey eyes. Although, she probably never played in *Madame Butterfly*, Lucy Doles stated, "It seems strange that her favorite operatic character Cho Cho San who killed herself to release her American lover, should find such a gruesome comparison in her own life."[16]

1925, July 24
Sammy graduates from the standard course at the Minot Normal School.[48] Sammy is listed in the Advanced Curriculum. The music included, "Send out Thy Light", "Triumph Polka", and "Old Sweet Song." It is held in the gymnasium with President George A. McFarland presiding. Miss J. Nielson, State Superintendent of Public Instruction, gave the address and conferred the diplomas.[70] Sammy is wearing the black shirt with the ermine collar that was later printed in newspapers several times taken from her yearbook photo. The quote next to her photo says, "How music, that stirs all one's devout emotions, blends everything into harmony!"[49] Sammy was a member of the

Mecca for Pep, Glee Club, and the Home Economics Club.[48] Sammy
was described as "a young woman of pleasing presence, happy
disposition, and most excellent character".[48] The picture in the
yearbook shows the Glee Club members with dark shirts with sailor
type collars. Sammy seems to be wearing a tie. "Under the competent
direction of Mr. Bland, the Girls' Glee Club has progressed greatly.
Much local recognition has been accorded to them. On several
occasions the assembly has been entertained by the 'Wonderful
Warblers'."[49] Sammy is also listed as being a part of the YWCA.
"The YWCA has been a great factor in the life of the school. The
weekly devotional meetings feature a speaker or present group
discussion with regard to conduct or ideals. The YWCA aims to give
opportunity for the development of religious interests and noble ideals.
Several pageants depicting the YWCA work in home and foreign fields
have been staged during the year."[49]

1925-1926
Sammy teaches in Landa, North Dakota before going to Whitehall.[71]
She sometimes took the train from Minot to Landa with Corinne
Babcock who was a fellow student at Minot who often went to Westhope
on the weekends.[42] Sammy lived with the Louis Bogstie family in Landa,
ND while teaching.[72] In 1930, this family consisted of: Louis Bogstie, 45,
who was a grain buyer at the grain elevator in Landa. His wife's name was
Clara B. who was 36 in 1930. Their children were as follows: Doris O,
Thelma C, Lois A. They were ages 16, 14, and 8 in 1930 (11, 9, and 3 in
1925). They were of Norwegian descent. [73] Only two pages of people were
in Landa, including the Hagens listed in the 1930 census. (Sammy wrote to
Howard who later moved to Georgia.[41]) That family consisted of Martin H,
33, Anne A, 30, and Grace A, 17. Howard must have been younger? Or one
of Sammy's students, or was this his brother's family? [73] The other teachers
in 1930 in Landa include Charlotte Risley, and Beth Lenors who lived with
the Hagens as boarders. The other boarders at the Hagen's included Pearl
Roosevelt, a bank teller, and William Goda, a truck driver.[73]

1925, August
Mildred Keaton brings a patient to Juneau. Mildred stays with her brothers,
Bob and Ted, who now lived there and worked at the AJ Mine.[17]

1925, October
Ruth becomes pregnant in Mexico. She is extremely happy about it.[31]

Dr. Judd testified that he had his photo taken with a baby in Delores, State of San Luis Potosi in about 1925. He said it was a baby. The mother was a sister of the wife of the general manager of the company. She came there to be confined. He took care of her in confinement and sometime afterward they wanted some pictures and among them they wanted a picture of me holding their baby which was taken.[74]

1925, December 31
The deed of the house at 2929 North 2nd Street in Phoenix was transferred to HR Harrison, a widower from HS and Jane A. Prince h/w.[75]

1926, March
Dr. Judd was frantic when Ruth tells him she is pregnant. However, even though Ruth's TB was better in Mexico, the Doctor felt that she should not go through with the pregnancy. He first tells her that because of his drug wrecked body that they should not have a child. Then, in the end, he finally tells her about her own condition; that she had TB. Ruth wept bitterly. Ruth agrees to terminate the pregnancy. Dr. Judd calls an American colleague in an adjoining mining smelter to take care of it the next day. Ruth does not recover quickly from the ordeal. She was grieving for the baby. Her spirit was gone and she was not trying to get well. She was weakened after that strain on her frail constitution and she recovered extremely slowly. She wasn't trying to get well and she had lost her spirit. Dr. Judd told her to be patient. Dr. Judd said he would never be well. He told her that she must have a younger man for the father of her baby, a healthy man. She was hysterical for hours.[31] Ruth recounts it a bit differently; that the Doctor was furious when she became pregnant. He was using an enormous amount of morphine and heroin at that time and he told her that the child couldn't possibly be normal as the children of an addict were often idiotic or as he cited to her, several medical cases of babies being born with enormous heads. Ruth was very upset and walked the floor and cried and wondered what she was going to do.[5] She wanted the child badly. She couldn't decide whether it was a greater wrong to have an abortion or bring a child into the world who would most likely be an idiot. She was vomiting and weighed less than 90 pounds. Finally, the Doctor promised her that if she would have an abortion he would go to a sanatorium and take the cure and then they could try to have a child. However, afterwards he simply kept her from getting pregnant. The smelter doctor told her that she was so run down that she

couldn't possibly continue with the pregnancy. She was then five months pregnant.[5]

1926, April or so
Ruth states that after she had been in Matehuala for about two years, Dr. Judd was transferred to the largest unit of the American Smelting and Refining Company in Santa Barbara, Chihuahua. There was five mines there. There was one big hospital. There were two doctors there. They had one American nurse. The other doctor there had hurt feelings because he didn't get the top job, and he quit. Dr. Judd was working day and night. He got back to using narcotics again. Eventually, he lost this job. They gave him another chance and sent him to Los Charcos (? When). This was within driving distance from where he was in Matehuala.[35] Ruth was so unhappy that the Dr. thought that a change of scenery might be good for her.[31] Sometime in 1926, Ruth went back to Indiana to visit her parents.[76] HJ stated that she came back to Indiana once about 4 or 5 years ago, (1926 to 1927?). She stayed about three months, but he was not certain about that. At that time she was extremely nervous. She had a degree of impatience and worry.[20] Burton stated that she visited them in Darlington for 3 weeks. She was kind to him, buying him soda and candy since she had her own money then from the doctor. She stated that she wished she could have taught a Sunday school class during this visit.[36]

1926, Summer
At McKinley Park, a 12-mile-long stage coach road was started to the head of Savage River from the Savage River Tourist Camp. It was completed in 1927.[77] Sammy attends the summer term at the Minot Normal School[72] She gets a letter from Howard Hagen, three weeks after she leaves Landa. His middle name is Morten and his date of birth is June 8, 1897. His draft card describes him as having gray eyes and brown hair with a slender build. He worked for his father in Landa. His father is from Norway.[78] In another letter he writes from "our house" in Landa. He writes of Sammy's departure and "roping her trunk". "Up at 10, went down and roped your trunk, expressed it to White Earth. I think you must be out in the other room taking a nap. I'm going out to make sure pretty soon. If you're there I'll kiss you-but really, Sam, it's awfully lonesome around here-I'm going to wish you back for an hour at least. So they took away your public, Sammy. That's certainly too bad, for now I'll be able to beat you in an argument or at least talk the loudest-but if all that fails I'm the best wrestler and

I'll spank you- no, I wouldn't do that-somehow or another I wouldn't want to anymore and besides, you'd never be unreasonable, would you dear? If it hadn't rained so much I think I would have seen you by this time, maybe this week sometime, surely by next week. But if so, don't wear that new dress. Soon you'll have to wear it first for me. How will that be? But I suppose you'll be afraid of me busting it someplace. I think you will have to wear that Jack Dempsey sweater. Three weeks ago today we took you to Minot and you're taking your exercises every night since. That's the girl. I'll kiss you for every one of them soon. Maybe even establish a little credit to go on, or rather, I mean pay in advance. I had a very vivid dream of you last night; a perfect replica of many occasions, waking was such a disillusion. Good night, Sam. Lovingly, Howard."[79] Howard Hagen of Landa North Dakota writes to Sammy and writes to her for five years regularly.[41] One of his letters that was published in the paper was on stationary of the Farmer's Elevator Co, from Landa. "Dear little girl: I was tremendously touched by your letter, Sammy (tonight). I hardly know how to begin. I've lost my usual spontaneity and don't know how to begin. (Read that over and found proof of that statement in the repetition) Anyway, Sam, you're a sweet little girl and I am so pleased that you didn't let him kiss you or put your arms around him. Damn it Sam, a girl is at such a decided disadvantage if she is honest with her affections. With a boy, he can do just what he wants because they always take the initiative, but as you say, the girl has to follow the boy's mood if she wants to go out and it is what the majority wants as you say. And yet, Sammy, dear, I think your ideals and intentions will pay, because it would cheapen you, especially in your own mind, and that is terrible. I know that down in my heart that if I knew you were otherwise I wouldn't care for you anything like I do. Don't you think those things are revealed very easily in a person and they mean so much to me. I'll argue those points with Joe time and time again and his final thrust is always, 'Well, but you can't find them like that'. And sometimes I've though he was right. How disgusted he would get last summer when I wouldn't enjoy myself with the various girls we went out with. I haven't been any good, Sam, but I haven't on the other hand been insincere, and never promiscuous. Your own experience can bear that out a little. Since you left I haven't taken the Nash out once. I haven't had the slightest desire to go to Bottineau. (Don't think that propaganda) You ask me if you should go swimming with Gus. I knew I'll be terrible jealous of you in swimming with him. He'll see so much that is mine. I hope I outdistance this letter. I've got to see that dress first. Howard. P.S. I'm so anxious to see that dress, especially what's in it."[79]

1926, June
According to Ruth, she gave birth to a son.[80] Dr. Judd said that Ruth became pregnant in the autumn of 1925, but persuaded her to give up the baby on account of her poor health. (This equals nine months)[31]

1926, August
Donie Taylor and Mildred Keaton are transferred from Kake to Juneau. They arrived on the Admiral Rogers. Mildred was to be a nurse in the Juneau district and Donie was to teach in the schools. They were shocked to discover when they got onto the boat that women were now wearing their skirts between their knees and their ankles. The others on the boat thought they were missionaries because of their long skirts. They arrived in the evening and lights were seen in town and from the AJ mine on the side of Mount Roberts. It was a lovely orange glow. Mildred's brother met them and took them to the Gastineau Hotel where they had electricity and running water for the first time in years. They spent the evening hemming their skirts and went for a shopping spree the next day at the shop of Christine Halverson. They went up to the home of Judge and Mrs. Paine to press the new hems the next day. They had visited Mildred regularly in Kake since they had a fox farm. Donie lived with them her first few years in Juneau. Mildred was first assigned to the Interior Department Hospital down on Willoughby Avenue where Alaskan Natives were cared for. It had an outpatient clinic, offices, kitchen and quarters for live-in personnel. There was a forty-bed TB annex.[17]

1926-1928
Sammy taught in Whitehall, Montana.[81] During her tenure she made several trips to Helena in connection with her teaching job.[82] Chet Huntley wrote a piece about her in his book, The Generous Years: "The majority of the teachers in the Whitehall primary and secondary schools boarded and roomed at the Palm Hotel or at a dormitory managed by the school board and located in what had been planned as the living quarters for the employees of the sugar factory. The sugar company had halted its construction and halfway through the project, leaving a tall smokestack, a row of executive houses and the dormitory. Frequently these "homeless"

teachers were guests in our home for one of Mother's heralded dinners. Among these appreciative guests was Marian's teacher, Miss Samuelson. Freshly out of teachers' college in North Dakota, Hedvig Samuelson was a singular girl: decidedly attractive, bright, and finely balanced between gay aggressiveness and reserved shyness. "Sammy" Samuelson was one of the very rare young teachers in that small community who managed the no mean feat of avoiding local gossip. As I recall, it was during the second year of her tenure in the Whitehall school system that Sammy was taken ill with a severe attack of pneumonia. Aunt Cela, who was visiting us at the time, helped nurse her back to health, and she returned to the classroom for the spring months. On her doctor's advice, however, Sammy took a position for the following year in the primary school in Juneau, Alaska. From correspondence with some of the townspeople we then learned that she had contracted a mild case of tuberculosis and was going to spend some time in Phoenix, Arizona. With what shock and dismay, about three years later, we saw Sammy's name and photograph on the front pages, frequently above lurid captions. From all over the nation friends sent the newspaper clippings. Sammy was a victim in the incredible Winnie Ruth Judd case, her dismembered body found in a trunk in the Los Angeles railroad station. A number of newspapers reprinted a bloodstained photograph taken from the trunk, and captioned it: HEDVIG SAMUELSON AND UNIDENTIFIED BOYFRIEND. It was a snapshot of Sammy and me standing on our front porch."[83] (I have never come across this photo.)

Sammy taught with Jessica Williams.[84] Jessica Williams said of her, "When we were at Whitehall, Sammy was almost like a sister to me. I've thought all day of the terrible affair, but can't figure out any reason for it." "Everyone loved her so well. I can't understand why such a girl as Sammy had to be mixed up in a thing like this. She was very attractive and quiet until you knew her quite well."[84] Emil Hoitola stated he met Anne about 5 years before she was killed, in Portland.[85]

1926, September 6

There is a teacher's meeting at 2:00 in preparation for the new school year at Whitehall.[86]

1926, September 7

Sammy starts teaching second grade in Whitehall, Montana. The other new teacher for the grade school is Miss Catherine Hyatt for third grade.[87] The schools in Whitehall have record enrollment. Twenty-five are enrolled in the second grade - Sammy's class.[88] Lunch is

31

served in the home economics department. The lunch room was used as a class room for this year. Teachers supervise during lunch.[86] The dorm of the old sugar factory is ready for residents and Mr. and Mrs. J. L. Houx are the supervisors.[87]

1926, September 9

Several teachers including Sammy move into the sugar factory dormitory (Sugar Hotel). The other teachers living there are Jessica Kremer (Williams), Leona Carney, Ella Bolen, Isabel Brook, Callie Allison, Mildred Bigelow, Alyda Jacobson, Katherine Hyatt, and James Dzur. Thirty-seven teachers or students were living at the dorm.[89]

1926, September 17

Most of the teachers including Sammy were the guests of Mr. and Mrs. S. V. Justus on this Friday night. A tournament of five hundred was played. Mr. James Dzur and Mrs. Hayes sang for 1/2 hour accompanied by Isabel Brook. Prizes were given. - A Shari compact in pink satin and for the man - a utility set. The consolation prizes were a rubber cap for the lady and a rubber cigar for the man. A luncheon of creamed chicken and noodles, potato chips, pickles, cheese sandwiches, orange cake, devil's food and coffee was served.[90]

1926, September 24

Ella Bolen (1st grade teacher and fellow dorm member) receives a telegram in the morning saying that her father suddenly has passed away. She left for Dogden, North Dakota at noon. Sammy substitutes for her 1st grade class and Jennie Houghton takes Sammy's second graders.[91] Sammy is teaching the first grade temporarily for Miss Bolen. The first grade dramatized the story of the three bears and cut out pictures of the furniture belonging to the bears that week.[92]

1926, September 30

The teachers at the dorm gave a surprise party in honor of Mrs. J. L. Houx, Mr. James Dzur, and Miss Jessica Kremer. Games were played and a beautiful lunch was served. Dr. Packard comes to the dorm during the week to do room inspection.[93] Ella Bolen is back at school.[94]

1926, October 1

The first grade class gives a program in Whitehall. The second graders enjoyed the band.[95]

1926, October 2
A party was given at the dormitory for the students by Mrs. Houx in Whitehall. Dancing was the main feature of the evening.[93]

1926, October 5
The children in Sammy's class listen to a record of Hiawatha.[95]

1926, October 7
The second graders are reading Hiawatha's Chickens by Henry Longfellow. They will make a booklet in construction about Indian life.[95] Ella Bolen is in charge of study hour at the dorm this week.[93]

1926, October 12
Dr. Packard was a dinner guest at the dormitory in Whitehall.[96]

1926, October 14
The students at the dorm petition the school board unsuccessfully for permission to attend the Wednesday night shows. The board said they might be able to go to shows if they held some special attraction.[96]

1926, October 15
There is a dormitory dance. Proceeds from the dance go for a billiard table in November.[97]

1926, October 17
The dormitory students and teachers go out to visit Morrison Cave. They are driven out in Mr. Jensen's Reo speed-wagon.[96] They left at 10:00 and returned at 5:30. They spent 2.5 hours in the cave. Howard Woodward was the guide.[98] Access to the cave was not easy in 1926. One must travel by car on undeveloped trails or take the Northern Pacific train to Lime Spur. From the railroad one climbs up the steep mountain for a distance of 1500 feet or comes from the top of the mountain 600 feet from the entrance. In a typical visit a guide takes a party down the side of the mountain after advising everyone to go slow and watch their step. There is an artificial entrance. There is a large crevice or passageway which is six feet wide and extends upward about 150 feet. A stairway is followed to a depth of perhaps 300 feet. It is not long before every one is on all fours, creeping through a small opening into what is known as the "Caskets of the Gods" and sure enough to the left is a square formation consisting of six or eight tiers

33

looking very much as if it were well named. On the uppermost one stalagmites that look very much like unlighted candles adorn the unusual sight. On a little further, the cavern opens up into a large chamber which is 100 feet in diameter and 40 feet high. This is known as the Cathedral room so called because of its many stalagmite combination forming pillars and giving the appearance of a European structure. It also shows the number of years the cave has been in existence due to the fact that it takes many centuries to form one of these stalactites as the saturated solution of lime trickles over them. At present the water just occasionally drops and it evidently must be a slower formation than it was in past years. From the ceiling hang many thousand icicle like formations of varying size and shape. Some of them measure several feet in length and a foot or more in diameter. The color of some of the groups is a sparkling white, while others are of a brown or chocolate color due to the fact that the water has ceased to drip over them. On the floor are a number of pillars or broken stalagmites which leave a statue formation. Close by is the Fountain of Youth. This is where nature has provided a sparkling pool of water which always proved refreshing to the travelers after the climb up and down the mountain. The water trickles over a formation of a wooden pump. It is not difficult for ones' imaginative power to immediately visualize the wooden stand, the handle and the spout from which the water gently flows. Here one can see a variety of formations which would be too numerous to mention. Upon returning to the foot of the first flight of stairs, the sightseers are guided by Mr. Morrison down a winding stair of 300 steps. As one looks down with his flashlight, he wonders where it all leads to and at once he realized the danger and difficult task the explorers must have experienced in getting the timber up the mountain and then putting it in place, piece by piece by means of ropes. All this was to help further the development of one of America's wonders of nature. Further research of the cave brings one through the "Organ Room" which is stalactite in the form of a pipe organ. In some parts, one can tap the projections and they give forth resounding tones. Anyone acquainted with music can easily produce familiar tunes. On many parts of the slanting roofs or sides, the stalactites are formed in narrow bands or ribbons varying in size from one-fourth to one-half inch in thickness ten or more inches vertically, and about three feet in length. If a flashlight is held behind one, the light shines through them showing different colors and density in strips resembling a slice of bacon-hence the name "strips of bacon". These curious formations are also formed into many various fanciful forms as wreaths about pillars, corkscrews, deer antlers, groups of grapes, a handful of popcorn, a waving curtain of fine lace, knotted tassel cords, cascades of flowers, waterfall, wood carvings, and delicate etchings. The cave differs in many respects from other famous places of its kind because others are more or less large openings in the rock, without the picturesque work of art. Rooms of the cave are called, Cathedral, the Bridal Chamber, the Organ Room, Art Gallery, the Music Room, and the Holy of Holies. This constitutes a brief description of the cave that has been explored. The size or depth of the cave has not been fully determined as the exploration is a difficult and dangerous procedure and funds have not been provided by the government to continue any further work. At the present time one can proceed with ease to a depth of one thousand feet and at the various levels geologists believe that many other chambers exist. Some two hundred feet below the lower level, there exists a subterranean flow of water as you can hear it splashing over the rocks, and it sounds very much like the waves of the ocean dashing against the cliffs. The discovery of the cave was made in the early nineties by Donald and George Morrison.[99]

1926, October 21
The boys in Sammy's class have perfect attendance for the week. The students have completed their health booklets and are "trying to keep the rules".[98]

1926, October 25
Sammy goes to a Halloween card party at Mrs. Joe Martindale's and Nellie McFadden's. Ella Bolen got the low score in 500. After cards, the guests were ushered into a room of spooks and goops, where they were presented with favors and fortunes by a ghost. Then they had lunch.[100]

1926, October 29
The dormitory in Whitehall has a Halloween Party. They earned $25 for the dormitory.[101]

1926, November 4
The second graders in Sammy's class had a Halloween Party the previous week. They had a big lunch. They are now studying the Pilgrims in England and Holland.[102]

1926, November 13

A billiard table is purchased for the dorm from Cardwell. The proceeds from the October 15th dance paid for it. Mr. Houx and the boys have started to set it up in the basement which is designated the "great center of amusement".[97]

1926, November 15

School is cancelled in Whitehall because the furnace has gone out in the elementary school.[97]

1926, November 16

The classes have to move to the gym in the high school. It was estimated that it would take several weeks to repair the furnace. The situation in the gym is uncomfortable.[103] School was held for the junior high and the grade school in the assembly hall. It was a confusing situation.[97] Dr. Packard dines at the dorm.[97]

1926, November 17

The junior high moved back to the grade school building in the assembly room where a room furnace was set up. The first six grades were still over at the high school building. Special subjects were curtailed until the furnace could be fixed.[97] Sammy's class is on the west side of the gym for their class. The second graders join the first graders with Ella Bolen for the dancing period.[97] This is Sammy's 23rd Birthday.

1926, November 18

The west side of the gym joined the first grade (on the east side) for music class. The school board recently granted the dorm students two nights out a month. One is for church or choir practice.[97]

1926, November 24

There is an assembly at the school. Sammy sings a vocal solo called "Out of the Dust".[104]

1926, November 25

The second graders were working at writing stories about Pilgrims. They returned to the school. Apparently, the furnace was fixed.[104] The dorm makes a rule that nobody can play pool after 2:30 in the morning.[105]

1926, December 2

The second graders in Sammy's class are studying Christmas stories and poems in language. They are learning Christmas words so they can write their own stories.[106]

1926, December 9

The second graders are practicing with the first graders for the Christmas play.[107] Scarlet fever is going around at the dorm. The snow (or mud) is so bad down by the dorm there is a warning not to drive down there for one is certain to get stuck.[108]

1926, December 16

The teachers from the dorm who are involved in the faculty play "Second Childhood" prepared their dinners in the domestic science kitchen at the school.[109] A Victrola was brought to the dorm. "It can be heard all day and night." All of the dorm people were inoculated (? Scarlet Fever) last week and they all had sore arms.[110]

1926, December 17

There is a performance called "Second Childhood". There is a 35 cent or 50 cent admission. The play was by Zellah Covington and Jules Simonson, the co-author.[111] Sammy played Sylvia Relgea, the daughter of Professor Frederick Relyea who thinks he has discovered the elixir of youth. His young assistant Philip Stanton wants to marry Sylvia, but so does General Henry Burbeck, an elderly man. The professor is going to lose his house and needs to borrow 10K from the General. Philip and the Professor think that the General has drunk a whole bottle of the elixir when a baby is left at the house by a Spanish woman. Sylvia is mad at Philip and decides to marry the General. In the meanwhile another baby is left at the house and Philip and the professor think its Sylvia. Sylvia and the General arrive back at the house ready to be married, but the Professor and Philip think they are ghosts since they are dressed in white. Of course, it all works out in the end.[112]

1926, December 23

A large Christmas tree is delivered for this program. Santa Claus was scheduled to make an appearance with 4 or 5 hundred sacks of sweets and fruit. The boy scouts helped distribute the fruit. The Christmas program started at 8.[113] The 1st and 2nd graders present the play "The

Toy Shop". This program was directed by Ella Bolen, assisted by Sammy.[113] Other parts of the program included tableaus and Christmas carols that were led by the third graders. The 4th, 5th, and 6th grades presented an operetta called "The Fairy Conspiracy". Marian Huntley played the part of Beauty.[113] Sammy leaves with Jessica F. Kremer (later Williams) in the evening for Elk Basin, WY. to spend the holidays with Jessica's relatives.[114] Elk Basin is on the Border of Wyoming and Montana, NE of Cody and on the other side of the Beartooth Pass.

1926, December 25
Santa Claus brings a radio to the dorm. The station they get the best is S-T-A-T-I-C. They get other stations once in a while.[115]

1927, January 2
Sammy returns to Whitehall Sunday morning from a holiday trip from Bozeman with Miss Bigelow. They arrived on the 219.[116] Bozeman may have been on the way back from Elk Basin since it is NW of Elk Basin.

1927, January 6
Dan White is absent from school. Elden Ray moved to California during the break.[115]

1927, January 13
The coming of snow in Whitehall made the second grader's project about Eskimos more realistic. Dan White is still absent from school.[117] A board walk is built by Mr. Houx by the dorm to get from the porch to the road. Now the residents have a way across the mud. Jessica Kremer is called Sherlock Holmes when she locates missing garments, namely hose.[118]

1927, January 15-16
Jessica Kremer, Sammy, Ella Bolen and Leona Carney spent the weekend at the Douglas Ranch.[119]

1927, January 17
Sammy, Jessica, Ella, Leona Carney, Mildred Bigelow, Allda Jacobson, Catherine Hyatt, and Callie Allison were guests this Monday of Mrs. Lot Borden.[119] Sammy knew Mrs. Borden well enough to have corresponded with her when she was in Phoenix. Mrs. Lot

Borden is the hotel proprietress in Whitehall.[82]

1927, January 18
Mrs. Lot Borden has dinner at the dorm. This was also the night that the dorm celebrated the birthday of Fred Noyd. Cake and ice cream was served after the study hour.[119]

1927, January 20
Sometime during the week, Callie Allison was able to mend the broken pool table. The studets appreciated it.[119]

1927, January 27
The dorm is relatively quiet. Sammy is in charge of study hall this week.[120] The second graders are learning words about Lincoln for thei booklets.[117]

1927, January 31
Sammy is forced to leave school on Monday morning and return home because of illness.[117]

1927, February 3
The second graders bring home at least one book per week. They like reading stories at home.[117]

1927, February 9
It is announced that Sammy is ill with pneumonia. There will be a new teacher to take her place.[117] Sammy contracted pneumonia. She is treated by Dr. Packard.[81] Marion Alvina Vrem stated at the time of Sammy's death that, "She first became ill when she was attacked with pneumonia while teaching in Whitehall. The fact that the people of that little town got together and paid her doctor, nurse, hospital and medicine bills are just another example of how much everyone who knew her cared about her."[43]

1927, February 17
There is an epidemic of scarlet fever in Whitehall. However, they decide not to close the schools.[121] Sammy is reported to be improving from a severe attack of pneumonia at the dormitory under the nursing care of Mrs. Vest.[122] (Mrs. Vest is the Aunt Cela, Chet Huntley refers to.)[83] A report says that Cela Vest took care of Sammy during a six-

week attack of pneumonia.[123]

1927, March 3
Sammy is said to be improving from her illness.[120]

1927, March 7
A contract was signed by Sammy to teach in Whitehall Montana for 180 days. This included 180 days of actual teaching, not including holidays or recesses starting about September of 1927 and ending the close of the school year in 1928. She was paid $1150.00 in ten equal installments. The contract states if Sammy is absent or ill she will receive 50% of her salary for up to twenty days. After 20 days, Whitehall was not obligated to pay her.[124] This contract was reportedly found in the large trunk with Anne LeRoi and is currently in the files at the State Archives in Arizona.[125]

1927, March 10
Sammy is still ill, but is said to be improving rapidly. The coming of spring has caused Elwood Leura to bring out his saxophone. He continually plays "Home Sweet Home" at the dorm until others threaten to leave.[120] Here are the words to the song:

Traditional
Written by: John H. Payne
Music By: Henry R. Bishop

'Mid pleasures and palaces
Though we may roam,
Be it ever so humble,
There's no place like home.
A charm from the skies
Seems to hallow us there,
Which seek thro' the world,
Is ne'er met with elsewhere.
Home, home, sweet sweet home,
There's no place like home,
There's no place like home.

I gaze on the moon
As I tread the drear wild,

40

And feel that my mother
Now thinks of her child;
As she looks on that moon
From our own cottage door,
Thro' the woodbine whose fragrance
Shall cheer me no more.
Home, home, sweet sweet home,
There's no place like home,
There's no place like home.

An exile from home,
Splendor dazzles in vain,
Oh, give me my lowly
Thatched cottage again;
The birds singing gaily,
That came at my call:
Give me them and that
Peace of mind, dearer than all.
Home, home, sweet sweet home,
There's no place like home,
There's no place like home.

1927, March 17
The paper states that Sammy is improving daily.[126] The second graders
are happy to hear that Miss Samuelson (Sammy) is up and walking
again. Lenora Conley is now teaching the 2nd grade until Sammy
returns.[117]

1927, March 25
If Sammy suffered pneumonia for six weeks, this is about when she
was better.[123]

1927, April
Captain Lathrop hires George R. Purvis as a contractor to build a 600
seat theater in Fairbanks. The building would have 100 hotel rooms on
the upper floors.[6]

1927, April 23
The play "Second Childhood", which was the faculty play in December
goes to Boulder for a performance. It is not mentioned if Sammy is

well enough to participate. The play is at the Masonic Temple.[127]

1927, May 19
The Whitehall High School burns down.[127]

1927, May 27
32 seniors received their diplomas in the White Hall gymnasium. This was the second highest number in the history of the school.[128] Jessica Kremer gets married in the morning in Billings. She and her new husband – Williams go on a road trip for their honeymoon.[128]

1927, May 27 or 28
Hedvig leaves for her home in White Earth, ND.[128]

1927, Summer
Sammy visited Landa, N.D.[129] Dr. Judd lost his job at Los Charcos and they went out of Mexico to his sister who was a teacher in Santa Monica.[35] Dr. Judd states that Ruth became the "victim of an attack of flu (probably)" and after a lapse of some little time she proved to have become tubercular and to be a "victim of a virulent and rapid form of the damnable thing." Dr. Judd was out of work this summer. Several things had gone wrong and they were very much up against it.[130] Ruth's TB is much worse and Dr. Judd feels that they must return to the states and get Ruth treatment at a Sanitarium.[31] Dr. and Ruth Judd leave Mexico and move to Santa Monica for 6 months.[38] Dr. Judd enters a private sanatorium to kick his narcotics habit. But, he received narcotics regularly from a pharmacist at the Weaver's Drug Store. Ruth noted that every time she went to see him he wanted to meet her at the car line. At first she thought he wanted a walk, but he always went to the back of Weaver's Drug Store and she saw the pharmacist there give him a tiny paper package. After getting back to the sanitarium he changed from shaky listlessness and nausea to vivacious interest.[5] Ruth called the police telling them that this drug store was selling narcotics to patients at the sanitarium, but she refused to help them lay a trap to catch the pharmacist for fear it would involve her husband.[5] Ruth and Dr. Judd run out of money. Ruth starts working at the Broadway Dept. Store. She stated that they were long hard hours going to and fro from the beach. Ruth becomes ill from working very hard. She also caught her husband drinking Upjohn's Cheracol Cough Syrup for the codeine in it.[5] On Sunday, her day off, she would do her weeks laundry and

then go from one drug store to another to persons who did not have a cough as they drank it for the codeine. Some places got angry with her. She worked as an interpreter. She would catch the streetcar and go back out to Santa Monica.[5] She would come back home at night after racing all over the store all day. She worked up in the jewelry marking, where they marked furs and jewelry. The telephone would ring, aisle so and so, department so and so. Away she would run. She ran all day long.[35] After work she would get on the electric train going back to Santa Monica. The cold ocean breeze would strike her. She thought she had just caught a terrible cold. She started coughing terribly and expectorating. She went to a doctor and he said, "You have tuberculosis".[35]

1927, July 22
The deed at the house at 2929 North 2nd Street in Phoenix is transferred from HR Harrison, a widower to the O'Malley Lumber Company, and Arizona Corp.[75]

1927, August 25
The Empress Theater opens with a gala of musical selections by the first Kimball pipe organ in Fairbanks.[6]

1927, September
Sammy teaches during the school year in Whitehall Montana.[124]

1927, September 22
There are 35 students enrolled in the 2nd grade in Sammy's class at Whitehall in Sammy's second year of teaching.[131] She is not mentioned in the Dorm News Notes during the fall. She is only mentioned in reference to the Modern Hotel which is connected to the Palm Hotel run by Mrs. Lot Borden. She probably lived here or at the Palm her second year.

1927, September 27
Sammy is teaching the second graders about Indian life.[132]

1927, October 13
The second graders are making cats, witches, and pumpkins for construction at Whitehall.[133]

1927, October 20

Sammy is teaching the second graders music. They are learning about the lines and spaces. They learned how to make a staff and signature.[133, 134]

1927, November 17

Mrs. Lot Borden gave a dinner party at the Modern Hotel in honor of Sammy's Birthday. She is 24. The table was decorated with yellow chrysanthemums with place cards and nut cups in color to match. Dancing was enjoyed between courses. Sammy received many beautiful gifts. The invited guests were Miss Ella Hansen, Miss Myrick, Mrs. Margaret Hayes, Elvan U. Tuttle, Loell Covert, James Dzur and Clarence O. Anderson.[127]

1927, December 6

Mrs. Lot Borden hosts a party for some young people at the Modern Hotel. The party was in honor of Miss Bernice Blinger of Belgrade who was visiting Miss Martha Campbell. Sammy is listed as a guest as is the Bolen sisters, Edna and Ella.[135]

1927, December 20

Ruth develops hemorrhages from the lungs and starts running a temperature daily of 102 or 103. She went to Barlow's Sanatorium and they told her to go home and rest for 3 months and if she was no better to come back. They told her she was too near death to do anything. She felt that no group of doctors could have been more brutally cold blooded in telling her this.[5] A letter from Munford Smith at the Barlow Sanitarium stated that Ruth was examined on December 20, 1927. She gave a history of being ill from four to six months and that she was raising sputum with tubercle bacilli. She had been spitting up blood and had lost 17 pounds. She was 103 pounds at the time of the examination. He found evidence of tuberculosis with cavitation on fluoroscopic examinationn involving the right upper lobe and involving the left upper lobe. The exam was superficial to determine whether she was a suitable case for the Barlow Sanitarium. She was rejected because in his opinion she required complete bed care and there was no vacancy at that time for a case of this type. He noted in his file, "Reject – May reconsider."[136]

1927, December 23

Anne LeRoi completes her nurses training at Good Samaritan Hospital.[57]

1927, Christmas Time

Winnie returns to work at the Broadway Department Store and worked as the head of the toy department during the Christmas rush for two additional weeks. She was delirious with fever.[5] Bernard Sponberg, president of Sponberg's Department at 1408 Third Street in Santa Monica, stated that Ruth worked at his store at Christmas time. (Says two years ago last Christmas) He stated that she cried a great deal and was very moody. He stated that the tuberculosis had made a nervous wreck of her. He finally notified Dr. Judd of her condition so that she might obtain medical attention. He said he thought she had been placed in a sanitarium in Altadena.[137] Sammy is the guest in Elk Basin at the home of Jessica Kremer – Williams for the winter break.[138]

1927, December 25

Winnie Ruth Judd is at the La Vina Sanatorium near Altadena for lung trouble.[139] Ruth went to the La Vina Sanitarium since Dr. Judd felt that although he couldn't figure out how to pay the bills, he knew that she needed to be properly cared for.[130] On Christmas Day, she was admitted to a TB sanatorium endowed by Doheny. Doheny was the man in the "Teapot Dome Scandal".[35] They collapsed her lung. They wanted to do a thoracoplasty but she only took pneumo-thorax. An x-ray at the time showed a cavity in her right lung and extensive involvement of both lungs. Ruth received pneumothorax treatments twice a week for eighteen months.[140] Dr. Hunt wrote a description of La Vina in the Twenties. Some interesting excerpts include: "Entering the ground from Lincoln Avenue, one passed through a gate, which I learned later, was kept locked at night. The road to the left led to the farm, maintained by Peter Bertin. The road on the right serpentined gently upward past the Century Plant, the olive grove, the workman's cottage, the orange orchard and up to Opportunity Cottage. Across the road from this building was Bridge Cottage constructed across a canyon, and flexible enough to sway in a wind storm, causing the occupants to fear that they would land in the area below. Around the next curve was the recreation hall; across from it was the staff cottage where I would be living for the next two years. At the next curve in the road was the Administration building, the housing office, X-ray room and laboratory. Farther up the hill beyond the lab was the night nurse's cottage in a secluded spot far from daytime noises. At the entrance to the infirmary was a picturesque gate and beyond that were the cottages for ambulatory patients: Sunset, Fleming and Doheny. The dining area and kitchen were across the roadway from the infirmary. Fowler cottage was located in the lower part of the canyon near the infirmary. At first it was used for patients in extremis, for nearby was an exit road to the city, so that other patients would be spared the sight of a hearse. Later, this cottage was used as a school room for the children with early signs of tuberculosis. They received accredited schooling as well as an introduction to bird life as imparted by Miss Gretchen Libby. Among our patients were people from all walks of life, many of them veterans of WWI. The cottages were single board construction (board and bat). When oil was burned for heating, some of the tiny open spaces were filled with soot, which were not already filled with dust. Then when the wind storms came, the accumulation was blown upon everything in the room. This happened so often after fresh linen was provided that we had a saying that Mother Nature always chose a Thursday for a wind storm. Heating was also supplied by solar arrangements on the roof of the infirmary and nearby cottages. This was in 1923 long before the present discussion concerning solar heat. The heaters can be seen in the picture of La Vina taken from Hope Trail. Church services were available on Sunday in the recreation hall. Movies were shown at least once a week. Entertainers came often to present programs. I remember a talented young man who balanced on his head, facing the keyboard and played selections on the piano at the same time. There was no social secretary during my first months at La Vina, and with such a large number of potential and willing actors, I could not resist the pleasure of staging the play of "Dr. Cure-all". This concerned a doctor and his patent medicines, a fat woman who wanted to be thin, a thin woman with the reverse desire, a tall woman, a mother with a shy daughter and a widow looking for a husband. In the second act, the tall woman was indeed very short, for she came on stage moving on her knees. The fat one was too thin, the thin one was too stout and the shy children were too loquacious All were angry at the doctor who managed to escape with the charming widow. The play was a great success and was enjoyed by our large captive audience. My sister who was a graduate nurse had joined the staff at the end of 1923. She had taken special training in surgery. She served not only as nurse and laboratory technician but set up a surgical section for thoracoplasties and minor surgery. At that time the Pasadena Hospital would not admit any patient with tuberculosis, either for medical care or for surgery. It was quite an undertaking. Certain equipment was required; the linen must be sterilized in town and called for and every precaution taken to avoid the slightest slip in technique. Antibiotics were not yet discovered. By March 19th, 1924, we were ready for the first patients. Dr. Sam Mattison was the surgeon, his surgical nurse was Miss Alice Kratka; Dr. John Wilson gave the anesthetic, my sister was roustabout and I had the pleasure of assisting the surgeon. Our first patient was an ideal case for the two stage thoracoplasty. She made an excellent recovery and lived for over 35 years afterward, entering into a full life. At least 24 thoracoplasties were performed and many other major and minor operations, including phrenicotomies, fibrotomies, removal of a mediastinal tumor, cystoscopies, and tonsillectomies. The latter were done under local anesthesia. As I left La Vina in 1926 to set up private practice, I do not have a firsthand account of the fire which totally destroyed the buildings in 1935. According to friends who were there, the brush fire had been contained and it was supposed that all danger was over. But the wind spread embers which caused an engulfing conflagration. The patients took shelter in the orange grove where they huddled in blankets. Harry, the cook who was devoted to the children, loaded his car three times and took them all to safety at his home in Altadena. Someone rescued the bronze plaque of Dr. Stehman from its place over the mantle in the recreation hall. It was a sad visit for my sister and one of the old time nurses when we surveyed the remains of La Vina in October after the fire. The laboratory where my sister had spent so many hours was gone, the centrifuge was bare, the pipes were melted and the delicate flasks which she had handled so carefully were shattered. The infirmary area was a mass of twisted and tortured metal. The recreation hall was marked by the fireplace left standing alone. The sight brought pangs of heartache to all three of us. Those bygone days at La Vina had been very happy ones for us. We made friendships which endured for many years; patients, nurses, and doctors. We owe so much to Dr. Hoit who was the medical director from 1918 to 1929. He had a vision of what could be done if tuberculosis could be discovered early enough to be stopped before damage was done. His endeavor was to make La Vina a haven for early cases. All of the children who came under his care lived to surmount the disease. Not only was Dr. Hoit dedicated to his work, but he was a man to respect and honor. He and his wife befriended us. He taught my sister and me to drive, giving us lessons on that old, narrow, winding road that led up the hill to La Vina. He instructed us in the mysteries of medicine. He helped us to establish the medical practice which my sister and I maintained for over 45 years. He made our time of service at La Vina a labor of lasting value to us and a happy time to remember.[141] A typical schedule at La Vina from a brochure of unknown date included: 7:00 am rising. Temperature, pulse, respiration (by nurse), 7:30-8 Breakfast. 8-8:30 Personal Attention, 8:30-10 Rest hour, absolute. 10:00-11:15 Recreation. 11:15 Dinner. 12:45-3:40 Rest Hour (absolute). 3:00-3:30, Temperature, pulse, respiration (by nurse). 3:30-5:00 Visiting Hours (Daily). 5:20 Supper. 7-8:00 Visiting Hour (Wednesday only). 9:00 lights out. There is an exercise chart, some requiring absolute rest in bed and use of a commode next to the bed, limited bathroom breaks. "All other hours not occupied by prescribed exercise must be spent in BED, resting, dressed in pajamas or other night attire, reading, writing, listening to the radio or amusement requiring a minimum of physical effort."[142]

1927, December 31
Ruth writes a letter from La Vina Sanatorium, La Vina, California to her parents: "Dearest Mamma and Papa, I received your letter from Burton today. Mama dear, I'm so sorry you have broken down. Now absolutely you must rest. Rest is the cure for T.B. Open your windows, have plenty of covers and heat to your feet; drink 1 quart of milk a day and eat eggs and lettuce if you can get it. Lettuce contains vitamins which no other vegetable contains. It is valuable in curing T.B. Eat liver too. It is valuable in curing T.B. The doctors all tell me one may go a long time and never know they had T.B. if they don't overwork. Overwork causes T.B. to work and kill one. Rest is the biggest cure, even above food. You ought to leave Indiana, I think. Do you cough up? Have a sample of sputum examined and if you have broken down with T.B. go to Arizona. A person over 40 should rest. I am happy here in the Sanatorium. I am up in the mountains, real close to the observatory, which are the highest of all in California. I need high altitude you see. I was well in Mexico but broke when I came to sea level. I am taking Pneumo-thorax treatments. They inject a needle in my lung and part of it collapses and rests and heals. My lungs need absolute rest to completely heal. I hate pneumo-thorax. It's a terrible feeling to have part of your lung collapse. It hurts like pleurisy pains and I feel a drip, drip, drip of water or fluid. They give no medicine at this sanatorium. They inject sterile air in my lung. Pretty soon it will

get healthy and fill out my chest cavity as it should. It is very annoying to hear that drip, drip, drip of fluid from my lungs. I do not know whether Doctor Judd approves of pneumo-thorax treatments or not. He believes, as a very great many doctors, in rest and proper food. Some sanatoriums cut part of the rib out and allow the lung to collapse, but I'm glad this place doesn't. I have 15 dollars in my purse yet you've sent me, and I'll keep it one more month. If I don't need it then, I'll return it because you need it, I know. I'll write more later. Please rest, Mamma. We kids need you. Please rest for us. Lovingly, Ruth."[37]

1928, January 5
Somebody is poisoning dogs in Whitehall.[134]

1928, January 12
The second graders are studying Eskimo life. The second graders express relief that they are Americans when they learn about the Eskimo diet.[143]

1928, January 27
The second graders give an assembly program for the school in Whitehall. There is an art exhibit. Two of Sammy's students participate.[144]

1928, January 29
This is Ruth's 23rd Birthday. Dr. Judd brought her a clock. Ruth stated Dr. Judd spent everything he had on her. The first thing he bought her was a clock. He said, "I know what time means to you lying in the sanitarium."[35] She writes to her mother from La Vina Sanatorium: "Dear Mamma, This is my birthday. I've been very happy today. Although I've had some sickness and trouble, I'm glad I am here in this world and am as happy as I am. A bunch of clerks in the store where I was at Santa Monica came to see me today. Wasn't that sweet of them? They came a round trip of 120 miles to see me. They brought me a magazine and a box of candy from another clerk there. They are coming again and so are three other girls. Four girls at the Broadway where I first worked sent me a card and one letter. So, I've oodles of friends every place I've been here. Doctor got me a five-dollar clock for my birthday. He said he knew he didn't have the money to spare but he felt so badly about me here in the hospital having no clock and sick people watch a clock so he got it. Carrie gave me a sweater. It's a

good warm one. Aunt Alice sent me a box of stationery and a lovely box of candy and a bouquet of roses and sweet peas from their own yard. One of the girls here in the hospital, a Catholic also, got me a box of chocolates. So, I've receive three boxes of candy. I've had a lovely birthday. Burton called me up. He comes every Sunday, but he knew I was having so much company today he will wait when he can visit me better. About me, Mamma, I'm not in as bad a condition as you think. This hospital will not tackle cases over 25 years of age. Only children and young people. It is not a home for T. B. It's only a small sanatorium and they pick their cases. This place could be full of T.B.s but they will only take certain types of cases. The doctor here says I'm in a bad condition, but that I will get well. It will be a year before I'll be well, but I'm gaining weight and my blood tests are showing T.B. has quit spreading in my lungs. It's healing now and will be a year before I'm completely healed. People can live with one lung or even one fourth of a lung for years and years. Doctor Hoit here told Burton and Carrie I was a good patient. I was so willing to do as I was told and that I'd get well. The Doctor's name is Hoit. La Vina Calif. So if you worry you might ask him. He is awful busy, but I 'm sure he'd be glad to write my parents. I still have long hair. I comb it myself. I'm with five other girls. I am eating well. It is as warm here as Indiana in May. The girls lie naked in the sun hours every day. It's warmer here, more so than in the valley where Burton is. We have roses, nasturtiums, sweet peas and all kinds of flowers in bloom all winter. Here the grass is green even. I'll not get pneumonia. I can't sleep indoors. I need fresh air to cure my lungs. I dress and go to my meals. I must close; it's bed time. Lovingly, Ruth."[37]

1928, Feb?

Dr. Judd returns to Mexico shortly afterwards.[5] Dr. Judd got a job temporarily under an assumed name, not as a doctor, but as an orderly.[35] Dr. Judd is out of money and felt he needed to return to Mexico and gets a new job. On the day he received the wire that he got the job at Delores, (Says Tayolitita) he came to see Ruth. She had a hemorrhage that night. She was packed in ice. They were also feeding her ice. She said, "Take me with you". He said, "Sweetheart, I can't take you with me. Not in this condition". She said, "If you go back down there alone you will go back on narcotics again. This has nearly cost you your life". He said, "I won't. I will never go back on narcotics again".[35] Ruth remains in Pasadena under Dr. Hoit's care until July.[31] This may have been an offer to be in charge of a mining hospital again in Mexico. Ruth said that he had no narcotics for a year except for the Cheracol he had drunk. Ruth had a large hemorrhage the day before he left. She pleads with him to take her with him. She thought she could keep him from using again. Dr. Judd promises to stay free of narcotics.[5]

1928, January-April

Dr. Judd stated that she stayed there at La Vina for 4 months.[130] She improved rapidly. She gained weight, spirits, and stopped coughing. She received pneumo-thorax treatments.[130] Ruth was under the care of Doctor Henry Hoit at La Vina who gave her pneumothorax treatments which involved injecting air into the lungs. Ruth responds to treatment.[31] Pneumothorax is based on the notion that a lung "put at rest" would be better able to heal. This was the standard treatment for TB between approximately 1915 and World War II. Pneumothorax was a harrowing procedure for the patient. The patient was given morphine and local anesthetics. The procedure involved adding air into the pleural cavity. The procedure could be technically difficult when scar tissue in the lungs and pleurae prevented the needle from entering the pleural space. Several dangerous complications could ensue, including air embolism, leading to breathlessness, seizures, and even sudden death.[145] At La Vina they were allowed up after breakfast. They could be up for a short time; either an hour or half an hour. Then they would have to lie down before lunch. They went to bed immediately after lunch for two hours. At night they had to lie down, and then they could get up for a little while.[35] Ruth thought it was a beautiful view of Los Angeles and Pasadena up there on the mountain. Her husband paid sixty dollars a month for her to be there. They didn't take anybody above the age of 25. They even had a school teacher there, a young school teacher. The doctor gave them lectures on how to take care of themselves.[35] They weren't allowed to have any acid-forming foods. They could only have beans once a month.[35] They had a school there for the children. They had a whole wing at La Vina that was nothing but little children. The teacher took the children on bird walks, to teach them the different birds. Ruth remembers a little girl whose name was Sylvia. Ruth who was in the infirmary heard the little children say, "Sylvia, you've got roses in your cheeks". She replied, "Yes, I know, I always did have and I always will".[35] Dr. Judd goes to Madera without Ruth. There were gold mines there. Ruth states that they were closing. She wrote the letter out to the Continental Railroad Company and the United Fruit Company. They knew the mines were closing, but it was a job temporarily.[35]

1928, February 2
Snow falls in Whitehall. It is great for the game Fox and Geese, which the children like to play.[144]

1928, February 9
The second graders at Whitehall are studying music and the instruments in an orchestra. They are able to recognize the instruments and identify the tones.[146]

1928, February 14
The Whitehall Women's Club held its regular meeting at the Borden Block. The meeting was by way of chiefly a Valentines party and a large number of members attended in old fashioned costumes dating from 1810 to 1920. The first number on the program was a piano and saxophone duet by Jean Thompson and Ray Hixon. It was so well rendered and was so sweet a melody as to be heartily encored. The young people kindly played a second selection. The next thing to occupy the attention of the women was a set of physical welfare questions calculated to set them to thinking as to whether or not each one was giving herself a square deal. Most got very small scores. Following this, roll call was responded to by naming each of her favorite hymns. Mr. Dzur then presented a few of his cast who are giving the operetta next Friday night. Henry McCall sang a solo part, setting forth his ability as a student and scholar. Stanley Brooke Speck and Mabel Lea Foster sang a love duet. Dorothy Manlove, as leading lady, daughter of Ali Baba, also sang very prettily. After the parade of the costumed ladies, Mrs. Ray Miller favored audience with a piano solo. Those in costume and the approximate date of their creations were as follows: Mrs. HH Mills was exquisite in a good co-presentation of a costume of the Colonial times. Mrs. Fred Tebay, in a monstrously large plumed black beaver picture hat and perfectly tailored suit of 1904 was very fetching. Mrs. Dearth in a handsome white silk dress of the style of 1892 with her head done Spanish style was very handsome. Mrs. Martindale in an embroidered dress made with the hobble skirt and peg topped drapes of the early 1900's presented a striking picture. Especially noticed were her beaded theater

cap and quaint necklace. Mrs. Bruner wore a Josie Dress and pantalets, the latter being in style from the late forties till the late fifties. Mrs. Harden had a dress of the majestic style of 1893 and that of 1903 vintage. Both were well suited to Mrs. Harden's petite form. Mrs. Lumpkin who won first prize had a quilted satin skirt of the style of 1810, a shawl of the forties, and a parasol of the sixties and carried a baby dressed in Mrs. Lumpkin's own best baby clothes. Her cap was such as was worn in the theater long ago by ladies of quality. Mrs. Ray Miller had on a very handsome garden party costume of the year 1900. Mrs. Houx was beautifully gotten up in a puffed and draped ashes-of-roses silk dress made in the quaint long-waisted, semi-train style of the late Seventies. Mrs. Watson was gorgeous in a dress of 1903 and a hat of 1913. Mrs. Young rejoiced in a 1905 creation with a huge Merry Widow hat. Mrs. Dan Zink was a very good representation of the Empress Josephine in a quaint Josie's dress of buttercup yellow and a white leghorn Shepherdess hat of that period. Mrs. Root had a dress of her own style of 1916 and the bracelets and purse she brought to Montana when a bride forty years ago. The bracelets are the heavy gold bands with simulated buckles such as were very fashionable in the Seventies and Eighties. Miss Samuelson wore a heavily hand embroidered night gown and night cap of the style of 150 years ago. Mrs. Alex Robert wore a hat of the Merry Widow style and long straight holster of the same date. The hat was fearfully and wonderfully made and resembles a shopping bowl upsides down decorated with a sweeping willow plume. Mrs. Pace loaned this costume. Mrs. Brennan looked strange in a costume of as late date as 1926; fashion surely changes with sweeping strokes. Mrs. John Miller was lovely in a dress of the style of 1920. It was of brown satin mescaline and beautifully beaded to the waist. Mrs. Margaret Hayes came in after school resplendent in a silk coat of the late nineties and a large ostrich feather boa of the same period. Mrs. Packard wore her wedding dress made 15 years ago this spring and it was then the height of the early spring style. Her hat with a long sweeping plume matched the gown. The whole was brown trimmed in canary. Miss Wilkinson wore an embroidered, full organdie skirt full and sweeping with a sleeveless blue, tight fitting bodice. Such a get up was fashionable for parties about 1890. Mrs. Packard read a few notes on etiquette taken from such a manual written ninety years ago. Mrs. Harbison followed with a few extracts from Emily Post's new book on etiquette just off the press. It is needless to say that if the ladies of ninety years ago had heard the article on present day etiquette they would have swooned immediately. There were a number of photos of some lady's present taken in their childhood years. These were numbered and then guessed upon. Mrs. Martindale won this prize. Lunch was served by Mesdames Robert, Reed Selby and Pace. Mrs. Bryan served for Mrs. Pace, who was too ill to be present. Most of the bodies in costume called upon Mrs. Pace after the meeting that she might enjoy the fun. The next meeting of the Woman's Club will be February 29th, with Mrs. Lowry in charge of the program which will be on music.[147]

1928, February 16
This week there is a Valentine's Day party for the second graders at Whitehall. They are working on a health campaign. There are improvements in their hands and fingernails.[148]

1928, February 18
The commercial clubs in western Montana have declared this day, Morrison Cave Membership Button day. The State Highway Commission has officially adopted the Jefferson Canyon route for the "Yellowstone Trail". Morrison's Cave will now be assessable by car for the first time. The inaccessibility of the cave has been the principal obstacle obstructing the opening of the cave by the government. On this day the citizens in that part of the state will be asked to join the association to raise money for the development of the cave. It was thought that the opening of the cave would attract more tourists to the area and would rival Yellowstone and Glacier National Parks. The membership fee being one dollar was evidenced by a Morrison Cave Development Association membership button. Morrison Cave wants to get 200 members.[149]

1928, March 8
The second graders are reading something called, "A Journey to Health Land" in Whitehall.[148]

1928, March 15
Peggy Huntley is listed as one of Sammy's students, not Marian as Chet Huntley had stated. The second graders are making furniture in construction.[148] Peggy Huntley is also listed in the results for the second grade track meet in May.[150]

1928, March 29

The second graders are getting ready for Easter in construction.[143]

1928, April 5

The second graders are working on a health day plan at Whitehall. In their music class, they are pretending that the room is a radio station. They are going to broacast a program.[148]

1928, May 1

Ruth leaves La Vina Sanitarium and goes to Madera at the Dolores Mines to join Dr. Judd.[130] Ruth is able to leave La Vina to join Dr. Judd in Delores. Dr. Leff was a co-worker of Dr. Judd's in Delores at the American Smelting and Refining Company.[151] One of the reasons she was released is that Dr. Judd could continue her pneumothorax treatments in Delores. Dr. Judd is set-up for this.[31] She continues pneumothorax treatments by Dr. Judd in Mexico.[31] Ruth stated when she left La Vina, her parting words to Dr. Hoit were, "The next time we meet, Doctor. I hope it won't be here. I never want to see this place again."[152] She finds when she arrives in Delores that Dr. Judd is using as much as ever. The trip took several days by horse back over mountain roads. Ruth stated that she had to ride with one Mexican guide. They went up Mount Cebadilla. There were log cabins up there to stay overnight in. Ruth slept in the bedroom. The guide spread his pallet across the floor. He slept across her door. There were carbide lights. There was a little table in the cabin. She left her suitcase open overnight and in the morning, it had snowed and had come in between the roof and the logs at the top of the roof. They got up early and went down the mountain. It was an English Limited gold mine. There was a pretty, little home there.[35]

1928, Summer or so

Ruth wanted a cat. She wanted a pet. There were only two American women left at the mine. Dr. Judd said that she could have a cat. The Chinaman had several. So, the doctor asked him if Ruth could have one of his cats. So, Ruth rode on horseback to get the cat. The cat was scared to death when Ruth got on the horse with it. Ruth held on to the cat. The horse was scared of the cat and the cat was scared of the horse. Ruth held on. The horse ran away. She lost her hat under a tree. It tore her hat off. All of her hairpins fell out and her long hair was flowing. She got to the gate and tethered the horse there and held on to the cat. She went up the steps to the house. The cat was still digging its claws into her. She got into the house and put it into the bathroom and shut the door. She took a nap. When her husband came home, he asked if she got the cat. She said yes. He asked where it was. She said, "It is in the bathroom. It ran away. The horse ran away with it. It is in the bathroom." Dr. Judd looks in the bathroom and says, "Well, listen, I told you that you could have a cat. I didn't tell you, you could have four cats." Ruth insisted she got one cat. Dr. Judd stated that there were four in the bathroom. Apparently the cat got so scared she went into labor and had her kittens.[35] One night she went out with a Mexican guide. It got stormy and sleeted. It was dark. They went through a big wood on the side of the mountain. It was so dark, he had to get down and feel the path with his hands. Then they got to the log cabin and stayed. Mrs. Johnson and her husband soon left afterwards to another small mine nearby. Later they were in the Philippines. In WWII they were caught by the Japanese and were kept prisoners in a camp there. Ruth read about them.[35]

1928, May 11
The second graders participate in a track meet at Whitehall.[150]

1928, early June
Sammy leaves Whitehall, Montana in early June [81]

1928, June 1
Junior High School graduation exercises are held in Whitehall.[153]

1928, June 2
Commencement occurs at the Whitehall High School.[153]

1928, June 3
Murdock Ayers, Dave Bryan and Miss Virginia Foster motored to West Yellowstone. Miss Foster planned on being employed there during the park season. The boys returned and reported that many were already in the park through the official opening date was June 15.[154] Sammy leaves Whitehall about June 3rd for Yellowstone as well. She may have motored with them or took the train? Seems like a coincidence. It was said that "Miss Hedvig Samuelson will spend the summer in Yellowstone Park."[155] This does not mean she worked there necessarily. Another source stated Sammy came to Alaska from

Yellowstone Park where she taught school.[52] Sammy works in a curio shop at Yellowstone according to GJ Westerdall, the mother of Inez Westerdall. She said that both her daughter Inez and Sammy were employed there together. She stated that her daughter and Sammy never corresponded although her name appeared in her address book. She claimed that Sammy was probably a girl who just jotted down this type of thing. The address book lists her as Inez Westerdall, 624 West 42nd Street, Los Angeles. Her mother is listed at the same address.[156]

1927, June 28

Dr. Judd writes a letter to Dr. Davis from the Dolores Mines Co., Madera, Chihuahua Mexico. He starts by stating, "By the badly debilitated bowels of Beelzebub, I have put off for months writing to you and now when I have hounded myself into the chair in front of the machine with the determination of doing so, I find that there is not a sheet of paper in the house. Absolutely not one of any kind. So, I have taken these two used sheets and you'll have to do the best you can with them. If I put it off again it may be three months before I get another start. I have no excuse to offer for not writing except one which is perfectly all right to one who knows me well enough to understand my disposition but I suppose you cannot be expected to understand that it is any excuse. In short, I have been having plenty of trouble and I simply cannot write personal letters when I am depressed and sullen and resentful towards the world in general. I do not like to write a letter full of grief, etc., and this is about all I'd have had to write had I written much sooner. Had you been prosperously engaged in work at Matehuala so that I could have figured that I could have borrowed a few hundred dollars, I should have probably written you many months ago. So you can not consider it any lack of regard for you."[130] Dr. Judd says Ruth is doing all right as long as she does not take any "exercise at all violent". He said that on this date, he caught her carrying a pail of tomato plants down a "hell of a mountainside to plant" and that he had to stop her. He stated that if she does all right here with him, she can stay, but if she doesn't, she will have to return to a sanitarium.[130] Eating at Dolores was difficult. Food was at the best monotonous. They were 50 miles from a railroad. Having proper food was forethought and much planning.[130] He hoped he could keep Ruth with him.[130] Dr. Judd stated his permanent address was 873 Seventeenth Street in Santa Monica.[130] He stated, "I am sorry to see that you do not seem to be happy where you are. I am afraid you are like me; not happy anywhere. I think I can describe my condition best by saying that although I am discontented anywhere and everywhere, I am less actively and painfully discontented in Mexico than anywhere else. A US city gets on my nerves within six months and I'd rather just exist here than have all the luxuries of our modern civilization if it meant living in Ft. Worth, Dallas, El Paso, San Antonio, etc."[130] He stated that he and Ruth were at the Dolores Gold Mine, fifty miles west of the town of Madera, which was on the Northwestern RR, the other train line running south of Juarez. It was a small place, but it was the best conditions that they had in Mexico thus far. They had ice, water, lights, fuel, a house but the houses were not very well furnished. 8 out of 10 were Americans there. Ruth was the only American female there. He expected her to be lonesome, he said, but she didn't seem to be. He stated that 'she likes it as well as I do.'"[130] "I think I like a gold mine better than a copper mine. I think the spirit is more generous and they are less penurious. I suppose, tho, that all companies are not like the Asarco. I was told by nearly all old employees that that company was one of the least attractive employers, and I guess it is true. Anyhow, I like this company much better so far. The climate here is about like Dolores S.L.P. There is no smelter here so the air is pure. They mill the ore. The mine is about played out, tho. It may close in a few months tho it may run for years yet. It is uncertain tho.[130]

1928, September 1
Sammy arrives in Juneau with 26 others on the Princess Charlotte at 7:30 on a Saturday night from Vancouver. The Princess Charlotte was a Canadian ship.[157] [158] Sometime while she is in Juneau she meets Game Warden and Mrs. Homer Jewell and Mr. and Mrs. Bob Ellis. They were residents of Anchorage in 1931, but were former residents of Juneau.[159]

1928, September 10
Registration for the new school year is at 9 AM in Juneau. Sammy is listed as the 3rd and 4th grade teacher. The other third grade teacher was Ann Rohwer and fourth grade teacher was Delma Hansen.[160] [161] Sammy is not listed as a new teacher? Typically, teachers that were hired for Alaskan schools were urged to read Dr. Krulish's handbook carefully giving particular attention to the sections on ventilation, quarantine, disinfection, and self-protection. (Handbook published in

1912). The bureau also provided a detailed hygiene curriculum for the students, beginning in the first grade with the importance of cleanliness of hands, opening windows, airing bedding, the dangers of the common drinking cup, and the proper use of handkerchiefs. Over the next few grades, the curriculum enlarged upon these dictums but did not mention such obvious anti-tuberculosis practices as proper disposal of sputum or avoiding close contact with a sick person.[145]

1928, September 11
It's the first regular day of classes in Juneau.[160]

1928, September 12
Thomas Frelinghuysen, his mother Estelle and his sister Estelle sail from South Hampton England on the Olympic. Their address is listed as 104 Library Place, Princeton, NJ. Thomas is 23.[162]

1928, September 18
The SS Olympic arrives in New York with Thomas Frelinghuysen and his mother and sister.[162]

1928, November 17
It is Sammy's Birthday. The new high school is dedicated. There is a dance in the new Gymnasium with music by the high school band.[163]

1928, Thanksgiving
Grant Pearsons, a park ranger at Denali resigns and heads for Seattle to learn to fly planes. He thought that Denali needed plane patrol instead of dog patrol. At Seward, he runs into the new superintendent, Harry J. Liek, who is headed for Denali. He said that he came from Yellowstone and thought that Denali didn't need planes; what Denali needed was tourists.[164]

1928, December 11
Ruth leaves Delores. The doctor is still there. She leaves for El Paso.[37] They left the mine at 11 AM. It clouded up at 6 and got dark and began raining and a little farther up the mountain it began sleeting terribly. For two hours it was so dark that Ruth couldn't even see the mule she was on. They guide had no light and he had to get down on the ground and feel the road with his hands. He had to keep calling to her, "Are you coming all right" in which she would reply, "Yes, I'm coming

OK". They arrived at the log cabin at 9:30, got a hot supper, fed the three mules and went to bed.[37]

1928, December 12
Ruth found a few inches of snow on Cebadilla Mountain. There is snow on the mountain, Mount Cebadilla. Ruth is at the halfway cabin with her guide. It is very slippery going down, but at least this day it's in the light. The horse slipped on icy rocks many times. So, Ruth walked a bunch of the way.[37] She arrives in El Paso, sees doctors and decides to stay in a sanitorium in El Paso for a week's rest.[37]

1928, December 16
Burton visits with Ruth. He was hitchhiking back to Indiana and they arranged to meet. She stated that she came to El Paso to escape the heat and that she had also come to do some shopping in El Paso.[36]

1928, December 18
Ruth was thought to have been at the Hendricks-Laws Sanatorium under the name of Mrs. W. C. Judd. However, they said she was there in 1928, but for two years for the treatment of TB. The pictures of her in the paper did not resemble her but perhaps that was due to her weakened condition.[165] An El Paso man, a former patient states that there is a resemblance.[165] Ruth writes this letter to her parents. "Dear Mamma and Papa, I left Delores December 11, just a week ago this morning. I have been so busy in the last few weeks, I have neglected writing. I met Burton Sunday noon and had a tiny visit with him. He wouldn't stay another day. I didn't coax much, because he was so anxious to get home. I went to the T.B. doctor right after Burton left and they wanted me to come out to the sanatorium for a week's rest so don't get worried. I came because it's a good thing to be under observation for a week, and it is cheaper here than at a hotel. I am feeling OK. I took some pneumo yesterday. Doctor is still at Dolores. He expects to leave there by Xmas. He is going to a place called Estacion Dimas, Sinaloa, with the San Luis Mining Co. It is another place, two days horseback to get there, so I asked the TB doctors here about going home. It's cold riding over those mountains now. Why last Tuesday I left the mine at 11 AM it clouded up at 6 and got dark and began raining and a little farther up the mountain it began sleeting terribly. Cebadilla is where our half way house is, so I had to make it; sleeting, and the wind blowing and dark. For two hours it was so dark I

couldn't even see the mule I was on, much less the pack mule or the guide. Cebadilla Mountains are so high and rocky and the mules have to jump from rock to rock like a rabbit. It was dark and they would slip and get off the path. We had no light, and my guide had to get down and feel the road with his hands. Oh, it was terrible. He kept calling Vienne bien dije me Vienne bien, meaning, "Are you coming all right tell me?" I'd say, "Yes, I am coming ok." This stupid conversation kept up for two solid hours! We arrived at the old log cabin at 9:30, got our hot supper, fed our three mules, and went to bed. The next day the wind was down, but the ground was covered a couple inches with snow. The second day went sliding down the mountain for a couple of hours, but thank goodness it was daylight. My mule slipped on icy rocks and fell three times with me, so I walked a lot of the way. Well, since Doctor's new place is three days, instead of only two from a railroad, one by auto, and two by mule back, I'd rather not go down for three months. So, I asked the doctors about going to Indiana. They say, 'Absolutely, not'. So, Mamma, you'll have to come see me, it seems. Three times I have asked the doctors about going home. It's with one too hot, another too rainy and low altitude with a third, too cold. I must live in a temperate, high dry place or my TB will become active. That's why I broke down in Santa Monica or one reason, low altitude and damp by the ocean. The doctors say two days by horse won't hurt me as badly as a trip to Indiana. They think I can return to Mexico OK, but want me under observation a week so here I am. I hope Burton doesn't take cold on his trip home. I was surely glad to see him. I wanted him to stay longer but he was crazy to get home. I am sending you a box of Xmas cards. I ordered them. Don't know how pretty they are, but thought you'd like to send them for Xmas to different people. I am doing no Xmas shopping. I am going to send you $25.00 in a few days for X-mas. I must close. Lovingly, Ruth".[37]

1928, December 21
School is dismissed in Juneau for Christmas for 11 days. The Christmas Program "Cross Patch Fairies" was cancelled or postponed because of the influenza epidemic which is sweeping Juneau. Each child in the lower grades is checked daily. If any of them has a sore throat, they are sent home immediately.[163]

1928, December 22
A letter is written on stationery with the label "Ferrocarril Sud-Pacifico

De Mexico". This seems like the Southern Pacific Rail Line. I think this may be the same year (year not indicated, but it seems like it could be out of El Paso) Ruth writes this letter: "Dear Mama and Papa. I haven't heard from either of you since I received the Twenty Dollars two weeks ago last Sat. What is the matter mama dear, was it your last penny? Oh, I am so sorry I have used money from you and mama. I hope God spares you to me years yet for I need you oh so much and I do want to pay back something and make things easier for you. I've asked or written Burton twice and read no answer so are you well? Oh, Mama dear how I love you. How I want to talk to you and get your advice on many things. Have you received the two files I have sent back? I've worried that they may have gotten lost in the Xmas rush. Will it be Xmas by the time you get this? I've a package I'll mail tomorrow for you. I'm sorry it will be late. I hope somehow you will have a nice day Xmas dear papa and mama. Dear Papa and Mama will you pray for me? Please. Lovingly, your little girl Ruth."[37]

1928, December 25
The Doctor is expected to leave Dolores about Christmas time.[37]

1928, December 31
The town of Tayoltita existed because of the mine. The company always had a New Year's party and had dances sometime. The New Year's Eve party was an all-night affair.[166]

1929, January 2
School resumes in Juneau.[163]

1929, January 6
Dr. Judd and Ruth leave El Paso.[37]

1929, January 7-?
Ruth and Dr. Judd arrive in Tucson, Arizona on their way to Tayoltita and went down to Nogales Mexico. They caught a train by the Southern Pacific for Mexico. They went along the west coast of Mexico, close to the ocean, through Empalme and Guaymas and Guaymas Bay, down nearly to Mazatlán.[37] Here is some further description of Tayoltita: Ruth came down to Nogales.[35] Then from Nogales she went down by train to Estacion Dimas and then from there it was by mule back, ninety miles up to Tayoltita.[35]

1929, Jan 8-13 or so

At Dimas station, they got off the train and were just ninety-five miles from the mine. They got a car and came forty miles by auto, and the rest by mule back. They crossed the state of Sinaloa by mule back, and the mine was in the state of Durango in the town of Tayoltita. Ruth had no idea about this ahead of time; the trip by mule. They were waiting for them with pack mules. She got on a mule and loaded our luggage on another mule. They had beds, cots, on a mule with that mosquito netting that they hung from trees.[35] At Tayoltita they lived above the hospital. There was a beautiful big patio on it. There was a big bougainvillea vine up there. There was a little stream out back. There was handmade tile there. There were no glass windows. There were just shutters. It never got cold there. There were cows and strawberries. Ruth had milk every day since she was just home from the sanitarium.[35]

1929, Jan before the 20th

Ruth writes from the San Luis Mining Co, Tayoltita Durango, Via Estacion Dimas, Sinaloa, Mexico to her parents. She writes, "Dear Mamma and Papa, Now isn't that some address? Well, I guess you have already received one letter from me here. We had a long trip. We left El Paso the 6th, arrived Tucson, Arizona, the 7th, arrived Nogales, Mexico, (across from Nogales, Arizona), the 7th; left there by way of Southern Pacific for Mexico for here. We went right along the west coast of Mexico, close to the ocean, through Empalme and Guaymas and Guaymas Bay, down nearly to Mazatlan. Daddy can trace it on a map. At Dimas station, we got off the train and were just ninety-five miles from the mine. We got a car and came forty miles by auto, and the rest by mule back. We crossed the State of Sinaloa by mule back, and our mine is in the State of Durango. Tayoltita is the name of the little Mexican town. I doubt your finding it on your map. But, you can find Mazatlan. Trace forty miles north of there, then ninety-five miles due East and mark a dot on your map, and that's me in the front yard at little old Tayoltita. Our trip here by mule back was beautiful. This is my first time to live in the tropics. Can't say how I'll like it. It is beautiful now, but I'm afraid Indiana will be cooler than here in July. The trail is cut, or blasted out of pure rock a great deal of the way along the mountain side above the San Juan River. The river winds along so pretty on one side below and the jungle covered mountain on the other. The trail is narrow and we pass through series of little tunnels. The jungles are full of trees, vines, bird of brilliant colors. There are Birds of Paradise with long, beautiful tails, parrots, canaries and monkeys. Then, there are all kinds of wild, tropical fruits, bananas, and cocoanuts galore, everywhere wild in the jungle. Imagine! Then there are a lot of fruits you never heard of. One, the mango fruit, I sent you one a year or so ago. It has a flat like big seed. Another is chile moya. It is a round, green colored fruit with a cream- colored custard like meat on the inside. Another melon fruit, the papaya, grows like cocoanuts on the palm like this (Drawing). The melons taste just like the sweetest musk melon there ever was. They are almost as big as a watermelon, but taste different, and are the same color as muskmelon. Doctor is a pig when it comes to eating papayas. Then, we have two kinds of cactus bearing fruit and the bread plant, and dates, and cocoanuts, and flowers of hothouse variety. Remember the angel wing begonia Mrs. Hettie Lane sent you at Henning? Well, they grow a couple of feet high all over the mountains here, and ferns. But, to me the most marvelous of all are the orchids. Orchids are a parasite flower. They live on other plants and air, like that lover's knot vine in Indiana. Here, the orchids are found on scrub oak. Anywhere in the United States, one orchid blossom costs just five dollars. It looks very much like a flag lily or a fleur de lis. They are lavender and pink in color The country wide; worth $60 the ...... New York. Well, so much for what all one sees along the trail, but really, I was so thrilled over the scenery that I didn't feel the jolts my old mule gave me! Here's a sketch of our trail and believe me, the trail was narrow with the river below. (DRAWING) This is the lowest altitude in which we've ever lived. It is only 1500 feet here. We've always lived at an altitude above 6000 feet before. Where it was cool at our last place, we were up in the tall pine timber. It is warm here now. Well, you can know it is. Roses are in bloom, plenty of garden, oodles of strawberries ripe now. Doctor is lying right now out on our front porch in a hammock with nothing but his pajamas on. There are seven counting myself, American women here and eighteen American men. I do not like where we live at all. It's above the hospital. Everyone says it's the coolest place here, but I don't like the idea of living upstairs and besides it isn't pretty like my other homes. I have got a big yard full of roses and flowers and orange and mango trees right in my yard. We have our own oranges. It is so hot here in the summer, people live out doors. This is how the houses are built; a little house with screened in porches all around. They sleep, eat, and live out on these porches. Just a dressing room, kitchen, and bath are inside. This is how the manager's house is. They live above the club house (Drawing). So, you can see they live out practically altogether. These porches are screened in and have palms, ferns, and hammocks on them. This is a diagram of my house (Drawing). It is simply rooms. Tell me how to arrange them. There is one very large room, another smaller, but even the smaller can contain two beds, a dresser, wardrobe, and book case. The other room is huge, and so are the screened in porches. The front or porch in front faces the north along the side of the west. This is a diagram of the downstairs or the hospital. (DRAWING). These rooms are not small. The ward contains about ten, maybe only eight beds. There are ten rooms downstairs and only the three, and porches, upstairs. What I want to know is this: First, eight years ago, the doctor here and his wife used room No 1 as kitchen and room no 2 down stairs as their dining room. Six years ago, the doctor and his wife here used room No 2 down stairs as kitchen, but had their meals served up stairs on the porch. The doctor who just left, now was not married so all the furniture except beds and a writing desk and dresser were moved. Now, shall I cook and eat downstairs or both upstairs? I do not want to do as Doctor B did because I have our meals served by courses and it would keep two girls running up and down stairs. Besides I've got to watch the kitchen. Shall I use No 1 as my kitchen and No 2 as my dining room down stairs, or shall I used No 3 upstairs as a kitchen and eat on our porch in front? If I eat on our porch, I'll have to put our beds over on the west side porch and every one coming up stairs will see the beds at once. I wanted that northwest corner as a sitting room, and the northeast corner for beds. If I use No 3 up as a kitchen, the girls will be a nuisance – no privacy. And yet, if I cook and eat down stairs, I'll have to watch the cooking etc. and have to trot up and down stairs and that's very bad for me. Besides I don't like very much to be down stairs where those diseased people are and don't like my food cooked close there either. Oh, shoot! It's all the rot anyhow! I think I'll insist on a new house. Who wants to live above a hospital even if it's on the highest coolest spot in town? I'll bet it gets hot enough to be in Mother Nature's garb in the summer. These natives live in houses made like the Africans- poles stuck in the ground around a thatch roof. Their houses look like this, or this: (DRAWINGS). One can see inside their huts, the poles are so far apart. Their roofs look to me like corn stalks and shucks; haven't really examined them, but a combination of dry palm leaves sticks and leaves stacked up. I've got to take some pictures right away because if it gets too hot, I'm not going to? and I want some pictures. All other pictures I have of Mexico huts are caves or adobe huts, here there are poles, ...? Went to a moving picture last night, hatless and coatless, and under the open sky. The stars were so bright that our picture was dim. Well, our mine is going to get an aeroplane and instead of taking three days to the station, it will only be one half hour. Will you come see me then? They expect to get their plane in three months. I'm sure going to come home if they do then. Believe me, one half hour in an aeroplane beats three days by auto and mule! By the time this letter reaches you, it will be your birthday. Enclosed, is some money to buy yourself a birthday something. I'll send you a check for some more on your wedding anniversary. My, what a long letter! It will cost at least 20 cents to send it. Lovingly, Ruth. PS. Mamma, have you seen a doctor yet? How are you feeling?"[37] The hospital building was maybe a half a mile away from the main house. It was a two story building with a big adobe fence around it with a garden. It was a large garden, probably the largest garden of any house in the area. The doctor was the only doctor in the area, and that was what he was there for; to provide care to all the workers, just the staff. The doctor always had servants as did all of the foreigners. They accepted ridiculously cheap wages, but you had to teach them everything. The hospitall was a two story adobe. The hospital facilities were on the first floor where the doctor had his little pharmacy and waiting room, a place to see patients, a little operating room, and a large open room with cots that served as a ward. It was very primitive. The doctor only performed emergency surgery; anything that could be done elsewhere was sent out to Mazatlán or Guadalajara or Mexico City. People were carried out 4 days on a stretcher. A lot of people went out this way. If you were hospitalized, no meals were provided to you; the family was expected to bring your meals to you. The doctor lived upstairs in the hospital building. It had a porch; one side of the building was just screened in and overlooked the front entrance.[166] She stated when she first got there she had to lie down in bed most of the time. She could take a swim in the afternoon. She would lie in the hammock before dinner. They would go and eat at the main table. There was a Chinaman who was a good cook. She liked his creampuffs. There was green black and white in the dining room. Mrs. Swent made her (or her girl did) a cold tomato soup. She had a pair of parakeets. She paid a little Mexican boy to catch them for her. Her bed was out on the porch and she had the parakeets out there. She had 3-4

birdcages made out of reeds.[35] The mine was called the San Luis
Mining Company. It was based over the mountain between San Dimas
and the Piaxtla River. It is called Bolanos. It was about a three-day
mule back ride from San Dimas. You had to go up; it was a big climb
and then a big descent. The mines were up on the mountainside, but on
the opposite side of the mountain from Tayoltita. Everything had to be
brought in by mule back. Freighting by mule back was a big business.
There were several Mexican ranchers and entrepreneurs who put
together large numbers of mules. They'd have two or three hundred
mules. They were virtually all pack mules. They would bring in the
supplies that way in these big pack trains, running anywhere from a
hundred to two hundred mules at a time. The trails in those days if you
were traveling one way and you met one of these pack trains coming
the other way, it was a disaster. You just had to get off the trail and let
them pass. Sometimes if you were on the high trail, you would have to
go back because the high trail was not very wide. Sometimes there
would be a place you could move over to the side and let them pass
you. But if you saw them coming, it was like passing a car in a one-
way street or something. You looked for a place to go early in the
game. They were running all of the time, so you didn't know when to
expect them. They would come in with all sorts of cargo. They'd
bring in corn, beans, explosives, machine parts, and machinery
sometimes. Machinery was all broken down in pieces, but they brought
them in. They would get to Tayoltita and rest and unload. They picked
up bullion and they would load the bars on one of the mule pack trains.
Not all pack mule trains were trusted with the bullion. In the early days
of the mines (1917 or so) they would send out thirty bars per month
which would take fifteen mules once a month to haul out. Shipment of
bullion was a special occasion. It was stored in the office across from
the 'street' from the house where Langan lived. It was stacked there
because in the rainy season, the mules would not always go across to
the mill. The river could not be forded. The only way to get there was
over a narrow bridge which the mules couldn't go. It was a suspension
bridge. It had just two cables fairly flat, with wooden ties put crosswise
between them for a deck. Even though there were supporting wires
from the upper cables to the lower cables, the bridge swayed terribly.
When Langan was small (born 1916), they had two 12-inch-wide
planks for a walkway 24 inches wide. The cables were about four and a
half to five feet part, so you had plenty of room to fall off either side.
Once his brother did fall through, but he had a sound grip on him and

kept him from falling 30 feet. The bullion was in the safe in the office. The office was a one story building, long, just one story high with a basement. Parallel to it was a house where they lived. The house was two stories high with no basement. Langan and his family lived in the upstairs, and the lower story had a dining room, a large dining room, where his folks and the other people of the staff would eat. Across from the end of the building there was an open space that was cabled, maybe forty feet wide. And then, there was another building that was a kitchen. They usually had a Chinese cook there and he would cook the meals. There was typically a Mexican girl who would act as a waitress and bring the food over on the trays and feed the men. In the later years they ate upstairs when his mother had an electric stove. The company had a vegetable garden there. The garden furnished vegetables to both the staff kitchen and family staffs. There was another building that was a staff house where there just were rooms and a bathroom, a sort of a rooming house where the bachelors lived. There were three other small houses where there were other couples living. All of the buildings were made of adobe, and were plastered and whitewashed. They were all white from the exterior, and the interior, too, was all white. The floors were generally concrete except in the office building where they were wood. In the later years (like 1925) there was a printing press in the basement of the office. The office was an hour and half mule back ride each way. The mill was across the river from the staff house, and was maybe a fifteen-minute walk. A typical day was having breakfast in the dining room and then going to work. Those at the mill would come back for lunch. There were no radios, no phonographs, so people did a lot of reading. Once in a while they would have a little party or get together. The town of Tayoltita was about four thousand people. There were no Caucasians, maybe a few Chinese and Japanese.[166] George Hearst owned the mine at Tayoltita (WR Hearst's father). Ruth stated that she had never met him. She removed this part from her interview with Eleanor Swent however. (from the transcript) It remains in the recorded form.[35]

1929, March 3
The Escobar revolution breaks out in Mexico.[166] It started on March 3.[167] Laveaga was the rebel bandit credited with confiscating Rosalie Evan's hacienda several years previous. She was murdered[5] Don Adrian Laveaga was a very wealthy man in San Dimas. His son was named Miguel Laveaga, who was a general in the Carranza's army.

When the major revolution ended in about 1917 when the new constitution was written, he retired to San Dimas, but he was still a general in the Mexican army. He got a poor reputation from the Rosalie Evans incident. This was part of the Escobar revolution; it was the last of the major armed revolutions. This was part of a nationwide revolution. Communications were terribly disrupted. Telegraph was undependable since telegraph wires were greatly disrupted since some of the wires were cut by rebels. Langan stated that he was intensely excited about the happenings. He remembers when the first gang started to assemble. They assembled behind a stone fence around a corn field above the mill. He could see them from the porch of the house. So, he ran down to the office to tell his dad. He had a similar view from the office and had already seen them. He said, "Well, yes, I've already seen them" and he was very calm. He settled him down. Langan states that the revolution would give people who really didn't have any political objectives just a chance to get together and form armed bands. And they just did banditry in the name of one side or the other. They would march in and say, we're government troops, or we're rebels, and we need supplies and we need this and we need that, and would commandeer money, food, mules, livestock, and things that could be easily carried.[166] According to Langan, Laveaga was not in San Dimas when the revolution broke out. Laveaga was nearer to Tayoltita. So he came into the office and asked permission to use the telephone to send a telegram. So, he told him to go ahead and he used it. Langan's dad heard what he said. He stated the he was ready for duty and he had 201 soldiers ready for action. All he had was one personal attendant. But he was apparently drawing pay for the rest of them. So when he finished the phone call his dad asked him, "Why did you say 201? You don't have that many, why didn't you just say 200?" Laveaga replied, "Oh," he said, "They'd know I was lying then." He laughed. Laveaga was a well-educated man, and spoke well.[196]

1929, March 9
The Alaska Dairy is established near the Mendenhall River in Juneau.[168]

1929, March, late
Laveaga was wandering up around the upper part of the Piaxtla, and was captured by a group of people who said they were rebels, headed by a Colonel Canales. They decided to put Laveaga up as their apparent head. He was really a prisoner, but he didn't dare try to get

69

away because he would have been shot. They could use his good name, what good name he had, his prestige anyway, by making him the head of their gang. Laveaga went along with this. They marched on Tayoltita and came down to thePiaxtla River from the mountains. There were 300-400 of them. They assembled up on the hillside just above the mill. The company had to print its own money to meet payrolls. Normally the company got its cash to meet payrolls from Mazatlán. When asked about this, he stated it was not because they couldn't trust the road. It was that cash just didn't exist. People were hoarding cash and it wasn't being distributed. There was no paper money then; it was all coin, silver coinage. The banks couldn't get it and so then the mines couldn't get it. There was a great hazard of its being stolen anyway. The whole west coast region had no money. The company printed its own money which Mr. Swent and his assistant manager, a fellow named Carlton Cushman, signed each note. They printed the money on the small printing press. All it said on it was San Luis Mining Company will pay to the bearer whatever the amount was written on one inch notes. This money was widely accepted. All local businesses accepted it, so the workers accepted it as well. Eventually it circulated and was accepted as far away as Nogales, some six hundred miles away. They just stopped making it. Mr. Swent decided they would destroy all of the remaining unused paper money that they had signed and put it in the safe when the second group was in the area. They didn't want this falling into the bandit's hands, because it was being accepted. Once they took it there was no way to tell whether it was genuine or whether it had been stolen. So James Swent and his assistant burned all of the money. It was quite a job. They were upset for having to do this after all the work they had put into signing all of the notes. They came drifting in, you know, three or four or five at a time, all one morning long. Langan and the others were watching them from their house with the field glasses, and when they got all assembled, they went down, crossed the river and came into town. They didn't head for the office right away. In fact, the gang of them never came into the little area where they lived. They all stayed downtown in the main parts of the town. But, two of them, good looking well-dressed officers came up. The rest of them had no uniforms. In fact, these didn't have any uniforms either. None of them did. Laveaga was in the lead when they came into town, and we could recognize him through the field glasses because he was wearing the same clothes that he had worn when he came to make that telephone call. Laveaga wasn't the first one to call. Canales and somebody else were the first ones to call. They looked Langan's dad up in the office. Langan didn't recall what he said but they apparently wanted some money and when they left they took a sack of money with them. There was some change left there at that time.[166] Ruth tells it a bit differently. Laveaga and his bandits come back to the mine in Tayoltita.[35] They came to the mines and demanded a big sum of money from Mr. Swent. He said, "No, I won't give you a penny."[35] Or, perhaps, this matches. Later Laveaga came in. The first guys were paving the way for Laveaga. He came in and made more arrangements with Langan's dad. Laveaga pulled a gun on Mr. Swent. His dad had a small derringer, which is just a two bullet little pistol that's about two and a half, three inches long. It could fit in your pocket and not be seen. He always kept it in his pull out top desk drawer. When he was in a tight situation, such as this when somebody might pull a gun on him, he would keep his hand in the drawer of the desk while he was talking across the desk to somebody. He had this little derringer in his hand so he could bring it up very quickly. Laveaga did begin to pull his gun to make his demands more dramatic, I guess. So, Mr. Swent pulled his derringer up before Laveaga could get his gun out, and that stopped it all. There was no more confrontation. He calmed down. But they took some money and then they just took everything they could lay their hands on in town. They didn't take any of the company's mules, and they didn't try to go for the bullion, although the bullion was still in bar form at that time. They stayed for maybe a week. They rounded up everything they could in town, all the livestock. They took such things as chickens and livestock—mules and burros. They ate off the town, of course, while they were there. The mine had an ice machine. One thing Langan had was a note from Colonel Canales asking for another piece of ice, a block of ice.[166] Laveaga stormed in and scared Ruth Judd to death.[35] Ruth claimed there were 300 bandits that came in shooting wildly in the air.[5] They demanded that they wanted to be treated at the hospital. Dr. Judd was very sick. He was off of narcotics. He had an abdominal abscess and in need of an operation. Ruth told them that Dr. Judd was sick.[35] They screamed at her, "Que Le hace!" You take care of them then. What difference does it make?" Ruth ran upstairs and said, "Do you know, the army is in here, and they have some wounded. They want you to take care of them."[35] Dr. Judd put on his bathrobe and he came down. He did his best. He was delirious. They were coming in there. They took every good thing we had in the commissary. They took all of the canned goods. They took all of the woolen blankets. Then they went up the road past the hospital to the open-air theater. The commissary was down the road just a little way from the hospital, farther on down.[35] They camped in the cine (theater). Finally, James Swent went down and made an offer to the Rebels. He said, "I will tell you what we will do. We will give each of your men three pesos a day if they want to stay here and guard the mines from other rebels coming in. If one bunch of you come in and ask for money, then another bunch will come in, then another bunch. We will pay your men if they will stay here during this revolution. We will pay them to guard the mines."[35] Ruth stated that they behaved then after that. They lived in the open air theater. This served as their barracks. They weren't a big group.[35] Ruth stated that the railroads were blown up. Dr. Judd's supply of morphine had been cut off.[5] Langan stated that the relationship with them was fairly cordial. Then they marched back and left town and went back up into the mountains. This was a group that called themselves rebels. This event put Laveaga in a bad light with the government. He later wrote a letter to Mr. Swent asking him to write a letter for him. Langan stated that they gave everybody a pretty good scare since they didn't have a chance to get out of town or anything. They came in very fast. After this the company developed a better scouting system and had people up in the mountains alerted to give regular reports of the whereabouts of any gangs of soldiers or rebels or bandits.[166] A day after the bandits arrived, Ruth and Dr. Judd went down to Mazatlán.[35] Dr. Judd falls ill and has to be hauled out of Mexico over a mountain pass on a stretcher over 50 miles. It was an abscess which required an operation. After the 50 miles, they had to travel 60 more miles over bumpy roads to get to Mazatlán. Dr. Judd was delirious with pain. He states that if Ruth and he would have a baby it would be an idiot because of his drug addiction. He encourages her to have a baby with another healthy younger man.[31] Ruth wanted to have her Mexican assistant physician operate on Dr. Judd. Dr. Judd wanted them to take him to Mazatlán. Ruth was afraid he would obtain narcotics in the city.[5] They had to carry Dr. Judd out on a stretcher. Ruth rode on a mule. They had her and her husband's bed on another mule and some luggage on another one. A runner went ahead and told these farm houses to have food for at least sixteen people. They had to change shifts carrying; their shoulders got sore carrying Dr. Judd on their shoulders. He had gained a lot of weight and was heavy. They carried him in shifts because their shoulders were getting raw. It took four men at a time. So, there were at least 16 men.[35] Ruth said there were 22 Mexicans and carried him 90 miles over a narrow mountain path. She carried blocks of ice on her mule to put on Dr. Judd's head and abdomen.[5] They were crawling through the trenches. There were bloody hats in the bushes, garments in the bushes, bloody things. Ruth felt that she just had to get her husband out. Ruth claims they missed three battles, each by one day. It took 3 days to get to Estacion Dimas.[35] It was 90 miles by mule back to Estacion Dimas.[35] When they got there, they couldn't take the train since it was confiscated for military purposes only. There were soldiers in the boxcars and soldiers on top of the boxcars. Ruth ran around looking for a truck to take her husband to Mazatlán. She claimed she found an old truck and drove from Estacion Dimas down to Mazatlán.[35] Ruth said this was 125 miles in the truck and that it took an additional 13 hours. During this trip Dr. Judd's fever subsided and he grew damp and icy cold. Ruth thought he was dying and knelt by him and told him that she had been happy with him and absolutely true to him, that no other man had even kissed her in the 5 years of marriage and that her only regret was that she did not have a child by him to love. He sat up and said something shocking to Ruth. He said that he would rather I have a child by nearly anyone than by him and he named 3 men. This statement caused Ruth to seek out doctors in the US to see if she could have a test tube baby.[5] She claims they were stopped as they entered the city by bayoneted soldiers. She said they had knives on the end of their guns. They searched them for firearms.[35] It was 4 AM.[5] There had been a battle in Mazatlán the night before.[35] Another account states late afternoon.[5] Calles took the city of Mazatlán. Colonel Villalobos was also involved.[5] The rebels moved out in three little boats into the bay. You could see them from Olas Altas (Avenue) which runs past the Belmar Hotel. She immediately went to the hospital. Dr. Chapman was the doctor there. He was blond and married to a Mexican girl. They had 3 blond children.[35] Dr. Judd was delirious. He had run across the field once. Ruth had to go after him. Ruth was so tired that she just took off her boots and went to bed with her clothes on.[35] Billy Blocker came who was the American consul at Mazatlán. He came to the hospital 24 hours after they had arrived.[5] He received one telegram from Washington and two from Ambassador Morrow. (Anne Lindbergh's father) Ruth's family apparently had been worried about her. The reports stated that Ruth had been lost in the worst revolutionary territory.[5] Apparently, the railroad bridges had been blown up between Mazatlán and the US. So, the only way you could get around was from Mazatlán down to Mexico City, and up another line, through the Eastern part of Mexico. They operated on Ruth's husband who by this time had a very high fever. Ruth thought that he was going to die. They stayed at the hospital for a few days. Then they went to the Belmar Hotel.[35] Ruth stated that Calles was sitting there at the hotel. At least he was around the hotel a lot. She didn't know if he was staying there or not. Lupe Velez's father was also there, Colonel Villalobos.[35] Ruth claims that he was often in the dining room and had the orchestra play tunes and special songs for her.[169] Dr. Judd went back to his addiction.[5] Ruth is responding to treatment and Dr. Judd felt that she would no longer be in danger of TB. She seemed cured. Ruth stated that they stayed in Mazatlán for two months.[169]

1929, April 15
A plane called the Lockheed Vega piloted by Ansel Eckmann touched down in the channel to complete the first non-stop flight between Seattle and Juneau. Navigator on the flight was Robert Ellis, with Jack Halloran as mechanic.[170] They took off from the Renton, Wash. airport early in the morning and arrived in Juneau seven hours and 35 minutes later. It was the first time a Seattle newspaper was read in Juneau the same day it was read in Seattle! Once in Alaska, Bob decided to get married and move north permanently.[171] Joseph Carman Jr., headquartered in Seattle, announced the birth of Alaska-Washington Airways.[172] Sammy must have known Bob Ellis? After her death, the Anchorage paper said that she was well known by Bob Ellis and Homer Jewell, former Juneau residents.[159]

1929, April 16
E. L. Gordon, R. E. Ellis, Ansel C. Eckmann, John Halloran are all listed at the Gastineau Hotel.[173] Of Bob Ellis, the Empire reported, "Navigator Robert Ellis, like his chief, was not prone to talk of his personal air exploits. He said that the trip just ended showed him that no great problems confronted the crew of a plane in successfully navigating the course North or South. He also stated that the proper equipment would, of course, have to be used. This he explained meant planes of a large carrying capacity, reliable power plants and prior study and work involving all the details that are to be encountered, thus knowing how to meet every contingency that may arise. Mr. Ellis

showed the charts used during the northward flight. It was coursed entirely from Seattle to Juneau before the start of the flight. Laid in blue ink lines was the compass course in degrees with the variation and deviation already computed. At 20 minute intervals is a line crossing the flight line showing exactly where the ship should be at the time intervals, flying at a given air speed. These points, Mr. Ellis said were crossed in less than 20 minutes when sailing north. About every 16 minutes we crossed the line due to our faster than calculated air speed. Mr. Ellis, until recently has been teaching air navigation at the Navy school at Sand Point Field Seattle. He also had several years of commercial flight navigation to his credit.[174] It was planned to hold a permanent navigator's berth on one of the ships when the Washington Alaska route entered the Alaskan field commercially.[174] The crew planned to stay a week and then fly to Ketchikan.[174]

1929, April 17
Anscel Eckmann, and Bob Ellis left at 8:45 in the morning for Sitka. It took 45 minutes. They took the following passengers with them: George Rice, Larry Parks, and J. H. Walmer. They made arrangements with the Gastineau Hotel management for people desiring to make flights to complete arrangements there.[175] In the afternoon, they made a second trip leaving at 3 for Sitka taking Wallis George, Harry I Lucas, I Goldstein, and Claire Krough.[175] Mrs. A. J. Dimond, wife of Senator A. J. Dimond of Valdez arrived in Juneau on the Aleutian. She will remain in Juneau until the legislative session is over. She is registered at the Gastineau Hotel.[176]

1929, April 18
Anscel Eckmann, Chief Pilot for AWA spoke before the Juneau Chamber of Commerce at the noon luncheon and said that the coming of air mail service for the Territory depended upon the interest of the people in such a service and their support of that service after it was started.[172] Vern Gorst, president of Gorst Air Transport along with his pilot Clayton Scott, and the mechanic Gordon Graham flew into Juneau in a bright yellow and blue Keyston Loening Air Yacht name the Alaskan. Shortly after their arrival they offered a twenty-minute scenic flight. The first passengers were Governor George Parks, Ben Mullen (grandson of B. M Behrens, a local banker), Harry Lucas who would become the mayor of Juneau and Jack Halloran as the mechanic. He offered airplane rides at $5.00 a trip.[177]

1929, April 19

Nine passengers were taken on round trip flights to Skagway on the seaplane Juneau in the afternoon. Two flights were made and those making the flight were soon enthusiastic air travelers. On the first flight were H. L Faulkner, Fred Sorri and his son, Fred Jr., Joe George and A. Hendrickson. The second flight carried Mr. and Mrs. C. S. Graham, Richard Wohr and Nick Bavard. Joe George kept a time log on the first flight and timed well known landmarks. The Kendler Dairy was passed in 4 minutes after takeoff, Auke Bay was passed in 5 minutes, Tee Harbor in 9 minutes, Sentinel Island in 15 minutes, Vanderbilt Reef in 16 minutes, Berners Bay in 30 minutes and Skagway 47 minutes after takeoff. When it returned, it took off again at 4 for Ketchikan with Eckmann still at the controls, Bob Ellis along as navigator, and Jack Halloran as mechanic, and two passengers, Mrs. C.S. Graham and A. H. Ziegler.[172] Before leaving Eckmann stated that he would return to Juneau on Saturday evening and planned to start on a nonstop flight to Seattle Monday. Data pertaining to the air route will be gathered on the trip south.[178]

1929, April 20

The Moonlight Serenaders (Wilbur Burford, Jack Burford, Bill Vale, Earl Hunter and Alvi Tervinen) took a flight with the Gorst plane, the Alaskan. At 2 o'clock they dropped handbills from the plane advertising the dance that evening.[179]

1929, April 24

Teachers' pensions were considered by and large and at much length by the Senate in the afternoon in studying Senator Dimond's measures on that subject. He asked for an appropriation of $3000 for the system to be established. The measure required teaches to possess an aggregate of 25 years of teaching experience; 15 in Alaskan schools. Voluntary retirement was set at 55 with mandatory retirement at 65. The maximum annual pensions of $800 are to be paid out of a fund derived from a tax of one per cent on teacher's salaries. Teachers' salaries were thought to be $400,000 annually.[180] A committee is formed for the upcoming legislative session. Senate members included Anderson, Frame, and Sundquist. From the house side was Woofter, Fisher and Tarwater. The bill was expected to be passed before adjournment which would be May 2.[181]

1929, April 25

Anthony Dimond's bill creating a Teacher's Pension System and providing for a self-supporting fund to defray expenses passed six to two. The bill is to go on to the house for action. Dimond gave notice that he would make every effort in his power to bring a number of measures back to the floor where they can be considered and to prevent them from being held in committee until it is too late. A house bill to create a territorial boxing commission was also carried out without opposition. Dimond recited that doubt as to the validity of a large number of bills had been raised because they failed to reach the Governor before the Legislature adjourned in 1927. He warned that all indications pointed to such a jam of work at the end of the current session and that it would be physically impossible for the clerical forces of the two houses to get all bills in shape for the Governor.[182]

1929, April 29

Carl Ben Eielson arrived in Juneau from Ketchikan on the Juneau piloted by Anscel Eckmann landing near the rock dump. Hundreds of townspeople lined the waterfront to see him. The Juneau city band headed a parade which escorted Captain Eielson to Main Street along Front up to Seward to Fourth Avenue and to the Legislative Chambers. He then went to the Gastineau Hotel where he stayed while he was in Juneau. He was from North Dakota. Harry Jones, Chief Photographer for Fox – Paramount Moving Picture Company, took several hundred feet of film while flying north.[172] The paper reported that he arrived at 3 and was greeted by the American Legion, Members of the Chamber of Commerce, City Officials, and the Alaska Legislature.[183]

1929, April 30

There is a joint session held in honor of Col. Carl Ben Eielson. He is introduced by Speaker Rothenburg as the man who blazed the trails of the skies of the Territory of Alaska. He was enthusiastically acclaimed by legislators and spectators who filled the balconies as he was escorted to a place on the Speaker's rostrum by Senator R. N. Sundquist and Representative Alfred J. Lomen. Just preceding his presentation by the Speaker, A. J. Dimond read the resolution recently passed by the Legislature praising Col. Eielson's pioneer flights in the Territory and his later feats in aviation. He said, "Flying over Alaskan Mountains, Plains, and Wildernesses and Across Polar wastes, is like viewing a moving picture. The pilot sits in comfort and sees unrolled beneath him the trails, river and wastelands over which other men have passed and viewed lands they have conquered at the cost of untold work and hardships. All I did was to see the country over which the pioneers and explorers have passed. It is one year and one week, he recalled, since he was in Alaska since that time he had spanned the Arctic region from Point Barrow to Spitzbergen, for which he received the Harmon Trophy signalizing the outstanding aviation feat for the last year; visited eight European Countries, spanned the United States, visiting 38 states, covered South America and flew over the Antarctic." Eielson complimented the legislature on its fair-mindedness. He said that no state could show such a record in the construction of 60 airplane landing fields. Eielson said that he expected to be in the territory just now for a week or ten days, returning then to the states. He said that he hoped in a short time to return to Alaska going to Fairbanks where he planned to "unpack his grip and see what's in the bottom of it. Hang up my coat, and remain permanently."[184]

1929, May
In May, the Tayoltita mine got the word that there was a large group of about four hundred Cristeros in the mountains; religious rebels. The Cristero rebellion began after the Mexican government Catholic Church confrontation began in 1926. The name comes from their slogan Cristo Rey which means Christ the King. The Cristeros began by supporting the clergy and raiding and burning government schools, but soon went into other forms of banditry. They carried on through the country until late 1929 when the Catholic priests were temporarily allowed to return to their churches.[166] This particular band was at a point where they could either come down into the Piaxtla canyon to Tayoltita or go down into the Presidio canyon in the mining camps that were over in the next canyon south of them. By this time the cash had disappeared. There were no coins and no cash.[166]

1929, May 3
The gang stayed up in the mountains. But they got close enough in the early days of May that the company ordered all the women and children and all the men but three to leave. Langan Swent's dad, his assistant manager Cushmand, and another man name Lawrence Morel stayed behind in Tayoltita. They were the three top officials there. Everyone else left at midnight. The word came in that the gang was moving towards Tayoltita in the evening. There was a hydroelectric

power plant way up the river. It was an eight hour mule back ride on up the Piaxtla River from Tayoltita. There was a telephone there and they could get telephone reports. But those people were way down in the bottom of the canyon. It was a real box canyon there. The bandits were up on the flatland at the edge of the plateau, some two thousand feet above the plant. Anyway, word came that these people were making a move to come into Tayoltita, so we all left at midnight. They rode down towards the coast. They rode six hours but it was such a large group. There were about twenty people plus twelve pack mules with baggage, and several mules with a few bullion bars. They rode down to a place that normally is about a four hours ride from Tayoltita, but this took six hours to do in the darkness. Two other women and one man had left two days before for Mazatlán to try to catch a ship sailing to San Francisco. There were twenty people in this group including four children, Langan and his brother, Dora Wark, and a girl named Betty Ann Berry. She was the accountant's daughter. There were four American women and 8 American men. They used about thirty-five mules. They went to a substantial place to wait which had adobe buildings. There was a permanent ranch headquarters and people that they knew and were on good terms with. They always tried to stay there when they were riding up and down the trail. The place was called Braziles. Langan thought that this came from the name of a tree. He stated that there is a local tree down there that's called the Brazil and this was an area were Brazil trees grew. Brazils are a hardwood. They stayed down there and slept. The men slept on the ground and the women were able to sleep on cots. Then every few hours, every six or eight hours, they would get messages from Mr. Swent in Tayoltita. They were written messages usually.[166]

1929, Late May
Ruth and Dr. Judd after being in Mazatlán for two months return to Tayoltita.[169] Dr. Judd recovers from his operation in Mazatlán. They leave Mazatlán and go to Agujita in Coahuila. Being in the hospital had curbed his drug habit. He is discharged from the job almost immediately. He is awarded three month's pay but it was very hard to collect. Ruth and he argue about this.[31]

1929, May & June 1929
Labor trouble arose at the mines at Delores. During the rainy season the laborers' homes were knee deep with water, the families were all

sick, dying with cold, pneumonia, etc. Dr. Judd sided with the miners and in his report to the government and labor authorities blamed the existing unsanitary living conditions for the laborers' illnesses. Ruth said James Swent was a brutal and arrogant man and that he was furious. Ruth claimed that to get even with Dr. Judd someone, presumably James Swent, broke into their house, stole part of a trunk with evidence of bottles once containing morphine and he fired Dr. Judd giving him so many hours to leave. Ruth claims the labor authorities stood behind her husband who said the poor were needlessly dying. Ruth claims this manager rolled up in his car to their garage and jumped out with a gun in his hand, and pointed it at the Doctor. Ruth jumped in front of the Doctor. The manager said to him, "I've come to take you for a ride." Ruth dared him to shoot through her. He said if you do not leave within so many hours I'll completely ruin you from ever practicing again and I'll get you out some time where you can't hide behind a woman's skirts. Ruth threatened him by saying, if anything ever happens to the Doctor, I will get you somehow.[5] Langan stated that his father had to fire Dr. Judd. He was ill and he apparently was using some of the hospital drugs and became addicted to them. (He stated that at this time, they took him out on a stretcher.) (?) They sent her out alone. Ruth went out with him in March, but in June she goes out alone?[166] Dr. Judd stated that in May he accepted a job at Aguijita in Coahuila, that his surgery had been a success and he had recovered enough to take a new job. (Had he never come back after Ruth brought him out in March?)[31] Aguijita was a coal mine.[35]

1929, May 6
Finally, a message came saying to keep the mules saddled until 10 o'clock at night. This was the third night and that he would send another message in a few hours or come himself. He came with Cushman and Morel. They got in about 19 pm, but they still were not sure whether the Cristeros had decided to come down to Tayoltita or go down into Ventanas into the Presidio River and raid that camp. In the meantime, word came that they had gone to Ventanas and Tayoltita was spared. Most of them rode back into Tayoltita that same day, May 6. Six of the people had already planned to go out to the States and they continued on down the trail and got out to Mazatlán. They probably got out by ship. Train travel was very unreliable at this time. So, they went back and settled down, but kept things packed for a long time after that. For weeks afterwards they kept things ready to go at a

moment's notice.[166]

1929, May 8

The Juneau arrives from Ketchikan after a one hour and 43 minute flight carrying C. W. Cash of the Northern Commercial Company. A large amount of movie film was also aboard from Harry Jones, Camera Man for Fox Movietone News as well as letters from people in Seattle to friends in Juneau.[172]

1929, May 12

A varied program was given by the students of the Juneau Public Schools at 2:30 at the Elks Club. The Glee Clubs, both Boys' and Girls' High School Orchestras and the grade school orchestra, Little Symphony Orchestra, Boys' Quartette and Girls' Trio took part as well as the students of the Seventh and Eighth grade who put on an operetta called "The Royal Playmate". The operetta is an imaginative little piece and has been carefully rehearsed by those taking part. It is about a little princess, the daughter of King Flores, who is lonely and anxious for a playmate. She opens the door in the garden wall and invites in persons passing by. One of them is a gypsy woman who gives her a ring and allows her to make three wishes. She has a party in the garden and some interesting situations arise before the ending which is a surprise and leaves everyone happy. Some of the numbers included, *Overture, Maritana, Colorado, Songs My Mother Taught Me, To a Wild Rose, Rantasia, Old King Cole, Roll On, Thou Dark and Deep Blue Ocean, Romance, Serenade, Starlight Night, and Joan of Arc.*[185] It was directed by Dorothy Chisholm and Miss Dorothy Fisher.[186]

1929, May 14

Miss Betty Foster, daughter of Representative and Mrs. Frank H Foster of Cordova, marries J. B. Burford at the Burford home on Main Street. They were married by Rev. C. E. Rice. The bride wore a smart white flannel ensemble with a small white felt hat and carried an arm bouquet of white hyacinths and double yellow tulips with ferns. They were unattended and have an informal reception. The couple left in the morning on the Princess Louise for a six weeks motoring trip in California. They planned to live in the Casey-Shattuck Addition after July 1. They had planned to marry later in the summer and the wedding was a surprise. They had a romance which developed during the two months' session of the last Territorial Legislature of which Mr.

Foster was a member. Miss Foster was employed in the House of Representatives. Mr. Burford is the proprietor of the J. B. Burford Company, office suppliers.[187]

1929, May 26
In the evening, the Baccalaureate Exercises (Sermon) took place in the Auditorium of the grade school auditorium in Juneau.[186]

1929, May 27
A boy scout cabin at Eagle River near Juneau was completed over the weekend by a crew of men and scouts. Everything is ready for summer encampment starting next week.[168]

1929, May 29
The Graduation of the High School students occurred at the Juneau grade school auditorium.[186]

1929, May 31
A flying school is established in Juneau. Dr. H. Vance opened the school. The flying instructor is Lyle C. Woods. The first flight was made on this date near the Alaska Dairy.[168]

1929, Late May-June
The revolution in Mexico was finally over somewhere in late May or early June[166]

1929 Legislative Session
Anthony Dimond sponsored an act for the creation of a public school teachers' pension fund. He also co-sponsored another with Senator John W. Dunn designed to revise and codify all laws regarding Alaska's public schools.[188]

1929, Summer
Anne LeRoi worked for two months before going to Alaska for Dr. Roy. C. Baumgarten of Seattle.[189] She nursed in Albany for a time before going to Alaska.[190] This is the year that Karstens built the current dog kennels for the sled dogs at Denali. However, sled dog demos didn't start happening until 1939 by Park staff. The sled dogs were used to patrol the park during the winter.[191] There is a photo of Sammy sitting on top of a double dog kennel. There is a broken down sled sitting on

top.[45] This photo is a bit of a mystery as the sled is either an old wreck or a new construction. The trees are a bit big for Denali at the time but could have been taken near Park headquarters near where the dog kennels were.[192] During the summer, the Alaska Road Commission was doing work in Denali. They set up tent camps along the road as work progressed through the park. They were at mile 6 that summer.[193] There is a picture of the dirt road in Alaska. It seems to be under construction.[45] Jane Bryant, historian at the park, stated, "It could well be the park road, looking east and going downhill into the Savage River drainage. It all looks very familiar. My guess is McKinley Park, near mile 13 or 14."[192] The tourist travel visiting McKinley this summer is reported to be in excess of 700 by July 31 which number is in excess of visitors for any former year for the entire season. At the end of July they estimated their total visits for the season would exceed 1200 and that these tourists would pay out about $36,000 for accommodations.[194] The Alaska Railroad hauled gravel for building a fill for another track at the park.[194] Mr. and Mrs. C. E. Richmond are residents at the park headquarters at a place called Suburban Colony which was two miles west of town.[194] Thirty- eight miles of main road from the railroad towards Mount McKinley was constructed and went into service. The work during this season consisted of maintenance and improvements of the main road from the depot to mile 29, the building of a new road from Teklanika River 400 feet long improvement and maintenance of the road from mile 31 to mile 38, and opening up and preliminary work from mile 38 to mile 43. Road construction was being done by the Alaska Road Commission under cooperative agreement. They built by stage construction opening a one-way passable road to start with and later widening, surfacing and straightening it as traffic demands. The roads were in better condition that summer than before, and there were fewer delays to traffic on account of being mired in the mud. They planned a lodge at the foot of Mt. McKinley. The McKinley Tourist and Transportation Co. is constantly expanding and adding to the equipment and housing facilities to meet the increase in tourist travels. They could accommodate 100 guests at a time in temporary quarters. They didn't make it permanent since they planned to dismantle the camp when the road was completed. They planned to build a hotel afterwards at Copper Mountain. TC Vint, architect, J L Galen, president of the McKinley Tourist and Transportation Co., and the superintendent visited the site of the proposed hotel in August. It was to be built in 1931 at the foot of the Copper Mountain. As soon as this hotel is completed plans contemplate the erection of a hotel at McKinley Park station, which is to be made a division point on the Alaska Railroad to replace the present division station at Curry. This should increase the travel into the park by making a night stopover and thereby giving the tourists the advantage of taking in the park during the long summer evenings without necessitating a stopover of 24 hours, as was the case in 1929.[195] The park telephone system consists of 2 miles of no. 9 copper metallic circuit connecting headquarters with the Alaska Railroad system, giving connection with all points on that line. There are 22 miles of duplex insulated wire between headquarters and the Sanctuary River. This line also served the park transportation company and the Alaska Road Commission. It is a temporary line and mostly lies on the ground. Much trouble has been experienced during the summer months by animals, getting tangled up in the wires and breaking them and also by small rodents chewing the insulation off wires and thus causing the line to become grounded.[195] Patrick Meehan, a well-known old-timer of Anchorage worked on the road that summer. He wrote, "Sheep Tame in McKinley Park". Protection of the game within the boundaries of McKinley National Park is having the effect of making the sheep and caribou and even the foxes very tame, according to old-timer of the Anchorage district, who spent the summer working on the new park highway. The sheep are very tame, the old-timer says – so tame that they get in the way of the trucks on the highway, and there are a lot of them hanging around the camps most of the time, just as might be expected of domestic sheep in the states. At one time Meehan counted as many as 100 of the animals within a stone's throw of the camp where he was stationed in the vicinity of Sable Pass. Some kind of disease, which Meehan likens to the hoof and mouth disease, caused the death of a number of the sheep during the season; seven or eight of the animals having been found dead by the road workers. It was not determined to what extent the disease has invaded the park. A lot of work as done by the road builders during the summer and the new highway is being extended rapidly toward Copper Mountain. The completed portion is in splendid condition and it is the belief of the old-timer that when the road is completed it will add materially to the attraction of the park trip.[196] In the fall the following observations were made, "New Park Station Hotel". "In connection with the developments under way or outlined by the Department of the Interior, the Alaska Railroad is planning the construction of a new hotel at McKinley Park Station, which is now park headquarters as well as a station on the Alaska Railroad. At that time it is expected that travel to the park will be materially increased, since an all-night stop over will be given and tourists will have an excellent opportunity to see the park during the long evenings that prevail under the Arctic summer sun. Pending the installation and completion of these more elaborate facilities, the department has arranged to provide informal accommodations at Savage River, which is 12 miles distant from McKinley Park Station. In all, 38 miles' main road are available from the railroad to mile 38, and preliminary work has been done on five miles more. A number of interesting saddle horse trips is available from the base camp at Savage River to outlying camps. Another interesting way to get a view of the wild area is to fly from Fairbanks along the northern boundaries of the park to the interesting mining camps of the Kantishna district. Many moose can be seen in the beaver lakes and rivers of this district and air views of the north sides of Mount McKinley, Russell, and Foraker are superb."[197] Another report in the fall stated, "The future of McKinley National Park as a tourist attraction is assured by the steady increase in the number of visitors from the states, every season since the opening of the park in 1923 having shown substantial gain. The increase this season was 40 per cent over last year and with improved steamer service during the coming year, there is reason to believe the park business will take a further substantial increase. The park had 912 visitors this year according to Robert E. Sheldon, popular manager of the Mt. McKinley Tourist & Transportation Company, who was an over-night visitor in Anchorage, on his way to Cordova for the winter, and the company is planning to handle considerably more than 1000 guests next summer. This year's business enabled the company to show an operating profit for the first time since the company began business in 1925. Splendid progress was made this year on the park highway; it now being possible for automobiles to go into the park a distance of 50 miles. It is estimated that the highway will be completed in 1931 to the point where the transportation company will erect its Mt McKinley lodge. This site which is in the vicinity of Copper Mountain already has been selected and plans for the hotel are taking form. The details of construction have not been determined but it is the intention to have a substantial structure built partially of stone, perhaps and to provide guests with every convenience of a modern hotel. There will be at least 100 rooms, which will enable it to accommodate at least 200 guests. It is the present plan of the company to increase the capacity of the Savage River Camp and add to the motor equipment so that increasing numbers of visitors can be handled pending the further extension of the highway and the erection of the proposed lodge. The company now has automobiles sufficient to handle 76 persons and in addition, a number of saddle and pack horses are maintained for the numerous side trips. The company has found a splendid range for its stock in the Healy district about 15 miles north of the park. The animals were placed on this range last fall and they came through the unusually severe winter in splendid condition. It will be used again during the coming winter and it is believed the area will provide ample grazing for all time. From a very small start the park business has mounted steadily. When the big reservation was opened to the public in 1923, the Kennedy Company which then held the transportation concession was called upon to handle 12 visitors. The following summer 42 visitors entered the park and in 1925, when the present company took over the Kennedy business, there were 208 visitors. Another substantial gain was shown in 1926 when there were 362 visitors. In 1927 there were 548, in 1928 there were 635, and this season 912. Another four years, Mr. Sheldon believes should bring the season's total close to the 2000 mark."[198] In the summer of 1929 rangers started doing interpretative services. Before this time, it was done only by the park superintendent. The service included illustrated talks at the Savage River tourist camp. A park ranger was generally present at the dog kennels to explain the use of sled dogs in the park.[77]

1929, June 4
Sammy traveled into the interior of Alaska during the summer.[129] Sammy and Dorothy Chisholm sailed from Juneau to Seward on the Yukon. The other passengers for Seward were George Morgan, J. Mewmarker, Leroy Vestal, W.F. Rohrback, W. F. Rosswag, Mrs. F. T. Erstad, Fred Orme, James Orme, J. Janeksela, R. T. L Clark, Mrs. H. J. Thompson, H.J. Thompson, D H. Gillette, and four steerage.[199]

1929, June 7?
Sammy and Dorothy arrive at Seward via the Yukon (The June 8th paper stated it arrived at 1:30 yesterday morning so it could be the 7th)[200]

1929, June 8
The train with the passengers from the Yukon was scheduled to arrive

in Anchorage at 2:30 In the afternoon.[200] Sammy went to Anchorage for a week and took the railroad into the interior with Dorothy Chisholm.[201] Major E. F. McFarland was an arrival in Anchorage this week. He was here for the purpose of making preparations for the opening of a summer station at McKinley Park for the Alaskan Railroad.[202]

1929, June 17
Sammy and Dorothy depart from Anchorage via the Alaska Railroad at 1:45. The Curry, Healy, Nenana, Fairbanks and intermediate points left Anchorage on Mondays and Thursdays.[203] According to a 1927 brochure, a train leaving Anchorage at 1:45 arrives at Curry at 7:00 PM. Accommodations are available at the Curry Hotel. Rates in 1927 were room without bath; single $3.00, double $4.00. Room with a bath; single $4.00, double $5.00 per day. Meals were $1.50 each. The fare from Anchorage to McKinley Park was $14.00 for first class and $1.75 for parlor car fare.[204]

1929, June 18
The train then leaves the next morning at 7:45 leaving for Healy from McKinley Park at 12:05.[204] Sammy arrives at Savage River Camp at Denali Park. She signed the register for the McKinley Tourist & Transportation Company. She is assigned to room 9 – tent 9? She checked in at 1 in the afternoon.[205] The authorized rates for public utilities for the season of 1929 were as follows:
Camps were maintained at Savage River, the head of Savage River, Sable Pass, Polychrome Pass, Toklat River, Copper Mountain, and the head of Clearwater Creek.

Tent occupied by one person per day - $3.00

Tent occupied by two persons per person, per day - $2.00

Note: During periods of heavy travel, at the Savage River base camp, tent houses will not be reserved for exclusive occupancy of one person only. The company reserves the right to allocate these lodgings
Meals: Savage River Base Came   Other

Breakfast $1.50 $2.00

87

| Lunch | $2.00 | $2.00 |
| Dinner | $2.00 | $2.00 |

Weekly rates for all guests:

| | All meals, each | $1.50 |
| | Lodging, per night | $1.00 |

Rates for Children:

Less than 5 years (unless occupying individual bed, in which case one half adult rates will be charged: No Charge

From 5 to 12 years
            One Half Adult Rate

12 years and over
            Full Adult Rate

Transportation from McKinley Park Station, on the Alaska Railroad, to the base camp at Savage River is by automobile. From the base camp, side trips to the other camps and to the outlying parts of the park are made by saddle horse, except as noted below:

McKinley Park station to Savage River camp, by automobile, round trip fare - $7.50

Savage River (base) camp to head of Savage River, by stagecoach or automobile; round trip fare - $7.50

Savage River (base) camp to Inspiration Point on Mount Margaret, round trip fare - $2.50

Savage River camp to Sable Pass camp by automobile, round trip fare – 17.50

All Expense Trips:

Savage River base camp to head of Clearwater by way of Sable Pass, Polychrome Pass, Toklat camp, Highway and Thoroughfare Passes, Copper Mountain Camp to Clearwater Camp, the near Camp to Mount McKinley. A 10-day trip to Sable Pass by automobile, balance of trip by saddle horse. Includes two 1 day layovers at camps if desired. Round Trip fares:

1 person - $425
2 persons, each $325
3 persons, each $280
4 persons, each $260
5 + persons, each $250

On all expense trips the company furnishes
everything which includes help, horses, grub,
bedding tents, and equipment. Each person is
limited to 25 lbs. of duffel.

Other rates:

Saddle horse, per hour	$2.50
Saddle horse, one half day	$5.00
Saddle horse, per day	$10.00
Pack horse, included feed, per day	$8.00
Guide service, per day	$10.00

[206]

1929, Summer
Leo Marks worked at the park this summer. He wrote or told, "as a
bachelor my creed was, see the world before you leave it." His next stop
was Alaska as a guide at Mt. McKinley. He became engaged to Mary, the
hostess at the lodge. She visited Phoenix Arizona, lived with a surgical nurse
who not only killed her friend but dismembered the body and shipped it by
baggage car to her in Los Angeles. Her name and trial were as familiar as
that of the Lizzie Borden case. She was known throughout the country as
Winnie Ruth Judd."[207] Leo Marks appeared in Sammy's Address Book.[208] In
another account from 1981, Leo told the following version, "Prior to 1930 I
was a guide at Mt. McKinley Park and was engaged to a lovely lady from
South Dakota. She worked as a hostess at the lodge. After work we would
mount horses and ride around the park. There were occasions when we
would come upon a threatening grizzly bear and though sometimes quite
frightening, my fiancé had a way of calming the horses and also my nervous
qualms. At the end of the season, I returned to Los Angeles and my fiancé
decided to visit a girlfriend in Phoenix. The friend shared an apartment with
a nurse and the three became acquainted. The nurse was having trouble
with her boyfriend and came to the conclusion that the other two girls were
responsible for this alienation. In a fit of anger Winnie Ruth Judd hit them
both on the head with a hammer (Clara Phillips mistake) and dismembered
the bodies. When a trunk arrived at the Union Station in Los Angeles, traces
of blood were noticed and the police were called. Since the trunk was
addressed to me and some of my love letters were inside with the bodies, I
was immediately picked up by the police for questioning. Of course the
clues lead to Phoenix and the arrest of Winnie Judd. She was declared
insane but managed to escape soon thereafter. She was captured but was

more elusive later when she talked a guard into leaving prison with her. They were both apprehended in Costa Rica (Clara Phillips and Honduras, another confusion). The last I heard she had been released from prison and was living in the San Joaquin Valley under an assumed name."[209] The bridge at the Nenana River at Healy Fork collapsed in the afternoon. They recovered the body of Charles Seaman. They originally thought the bridge would be repaired by June 24 or 25. They found Carl Spach's body on the 22nd and were still looking for Richard Conway.[210] Dorothy Chisholm arrived in Fairbanks as a visitor.[211]

1929, June 15-20?
Langan and his mother left the mine to go to catch a boat out of Mazatlán. Langan was in preparation to start school at the Moses Brown Prep School in Providence. They left in June to beat the rainy season. The rain usually came in late June. The river rises and you can't use the river trail. Otherwise, you have to use the high trail which is a longer trail by several hours of mule back riding. Ruth rode out with Langan, his brother, Mrs. Swent and Mrs. Morel in June. At one point the group was going down, riding through the riverbed where there are lots of boulders and things; the trail is just sort of veering, winding around the boulders and that sort of thing. Just the smaller rocks have been thrown out of the way. Ruth was riding along with her feet out of the stirrups. Langan's mother warned her. She said that she should really have her feet in the stirrups because if the mule stumbled she would be likely to fall off. She said, "Oh, I was raised on the farm and I used to ride bareback. I'll be all right." Well, sure enough, after a little while the mule did stumble and Ruth went right over the head of the mule and fell onto the rocks. Ruth had a whip in her hand. She got up immediately. Of course, when she fell she had let go of the reins. She went to the rear of the mule and just whipped the devil out of that mule, and so it started to run. It ran down the trail and left her on foot. So, Langan had to chase down the mule on his mule. Langan got hold of it and brought it back to her. She immediately took the whip and did the same thing all over again. Again, she hadn't grabbed the reins. She just whipped the mule and it took off down the trail again. So, Langan went down and rounded it up again and brought it back to her. This time, I made sure that she got on it and didn't let it go again. Langan stated that this was all to the incident but it again showed a peculiar reaction; a real temper is what he would call it.[166] Ruth remembers it this way but says she was on a horse then and can't figure out why she

would be on a horse. She stated that when she got to the sandy basin the horse struck the sand, she went over the horse and the horse just stepped over her.[35] Then after a day and a half of riding down the trail they arrived at a ranch called San Juan (a common name) that belonged to a person that we thought a great deal of. It belonged to a man named Poncho Bastidas. Poncho is actually a nickname for Francisco. Poncho Bastidas was a character in his own right. He was a barely literate rancher who had amassed local wealth and was one of the wealthier individuals in this area, on the coastal plain there. San Juan was on the south bank of the Piaxtla River, near a town call San Ignacio in the state of Sinaloa. He had amassed a large number of mules and was one of the principal freight carriers up and down the trail. They had a personal rapport with him. He was one of the men who hauled the Bullion. He was at the ranch at the time, and he was happy to see them. He escorted the party to stay with him in his home. He had just finished building a hot shower. The ladies, Mrs. Swent, Mrs. Morel and Mrs. Judd would be the first ones to use it. They would break it in. This sounded fine to them, a hot shower sounded very good. This sounded good to them. Well, what he had built was out on the patio of the house. He had built a single room, just four walls. On the roof there was a great big barrel, and on the back there were ladders leaned against the building. They would heat the water in buckets over a fire and then men would carry the hot water up in buckets and dump it into the barrel, and there was a pipe running down through the roof and into the room itself with a little valve. You could get in there and turn the value on and then you got a warm shower. The ladies thought this was great. Mrs. Swent was the first one to try it out. She found that there was no door on the open side and no shower curtain. Don Poncho saw her being a little bit hesitant to use it, and he wanted to know what the problem was. She told him that she couldn't be found standing there undressed and having people able to see her. So Don Pablo said, "Oh, don't' worry about that. I'll stand guard. And he drew the two pistols and crossed his arms and stood at the doorway and he said, "Nobody will look." He laughed. He typically had a cartridge belt around his waist with two pistols. She believed him. She went in and had her shower and then Mrs. Morel and Ruth Judd followed and he stood guard for all three of them. That evening they had a big discussion. This ranch was at the end of the mule trail. At this point they could take a truck into Dimas Station where they would catch the train into Mazatlán. So, they were to take the truck very early in the morning because the train came in at 8:00 to the Dimas Station, and they had to leave the ranch at 4 or 5 in the morning in order to make the train. Don Poncho stated that there were still some problems with bandits in the area between the ranch and Dimas, and that they might run into them. He wasn't sure. Mrs. Swent had a lot of silver with her. She had brought along several bags. There was no paper money at this point, the company had stoped using its paper money since the coins had appeared. These were fifty-centavo and one-peso silver pieces. But she had a couple of bags of them and she just didn't know what to do with them. Mrs. Judd had a hundred-peso gold coin, and she was perplexed as to what to do with that. Well, finally, I guess mother stewed and the next morning she started stashing these coins around in her riding boots. She got them so heavy she could hardly move, but that's the way she hid most of them. Mrs. Morel did likewise. When Mrs. Judd showed up to get on the truck, after we got going, my mother asked her what she had decided to do with her hundred-peso gold coin. She said, "Well, if they find it, they're not gentlemen." They did get stopped on the truck, somewhere down the way; it was still dark. Everybody was concerned since everybody thought they were bandits. The guy stopped them and wanted to search the truck. It turned out to be a fellow that was looking for his daughter who had eloped and he thought she might be on board. He had been looking for her. One woman and Langan sat in the front of the truck. The others rode on back. There were benches on the bed of the truck in the back of the cab. It was all quite open. The early trucks were open and it was subtropical weather there. You could talk from the front seat to the people in the rear seats, or rather on the benches.[166] As to where Ruth hid the money there was another hint. In another source she stated that she had gone to the wash room, took off her riding breeches and put the money inside the garment. She knew that Mexican bandits would not ask a woman to take off her riding breeches.[212]

1929, June 20
Evelyn Morel, Ursula Swent, and Langan arrive in Mazatlán from the Delores Mine. Mr. Swent and Langan (probably means Jimmy) joined them in Mazatlán after he pled for De Laveaga's life. They got his life spared Mr. Swent went to Calles and told him that Laveaga was guarding the mines. Laveaga's wife had pleaded for his life, but Calles had refused. This was in Culiacan and then Mr. Swent came down to Mazatlán.[35] They stayed at the Belmar Hotel, which is where everyone stayed in those days. That was THE hotel in town. Langan states that he didn't see much of Ruth after that. His family saw her running

around. They both took a boat out.[166] They had to wait a few days to leave on the boat. The railroad bridges were out (blown up) between Mazatlán and the United States. The only other way out was to go down to Mexico City, and then up the other line, through the Eastern part of Mexico. Ruth stated that Dr. Judd was not with her at this time, that he came out about a month later.[35]

1929, June 21
Sammy arrives in Fairbanks about this date and stay for a week or so.[213] She had been traveling in the interior with Dorothy Chisholm. They parted at Mt. McKinley Park where Sammy stayed for a time and then went to Fairbanks.[201] She panned for gold near Fairbanks in a placer mine.[201]

1929, June 22
Ruth Judd and the Swents (James, Ursula, Langan, and James Jr.) and Evelyn Morel leave Mazatlán aboard the S.S. Venezuela.[214, 215] They came out on a Panama mail boat. Ruth stated they had to go out on little motor boats out to the big ship and had to go up on a rope ladder. The waves would go over it and you had to make that step, up on that ladder before the boats went back out with the wave. If the weather was rough, they would let down a basket for passengers. Once they got up on deck Jimmy's hat blew off into the ocean. He looked so frightened when he saw his hat go.[35] Ruth stated that she was sick for a couple of days ago as Mrs. (Nace?) had been so thrilled over her being pregnant. She was sick on the boat and said that she was pregnant. She hoped for three weeks that it was true. She later wrote to Dr. Judd and stated that she had a miscarriage. She stated that she told Mrs. Johnson and Mrs. Trowbridge she was pregnant when she left there (Tayoltita?) even though she was menstruating the week they left.[12] Noel Wien flies into Fairbanks from Nome. They arrived at 2:30 AM.[216]

1929, June 24
This was the warmest day at McKinley of the season. The temperature reached 84.[195]

1929, June 25
Cap. Lathrop returned to Fairbanks after making a trip to Anchorage. He had intended to go to Suntrana where the coal mine is located but was unable to get across the Nenana River because the bridge was out.

He planned to go on Friday instead if the bridge was repaired.[216]

1929, June 26

Winnie Ruth Judd arrives in Los Angeles after leaving Mazatlán with the Swents. The Swents went on to San Francisco. She stays with Dr. Judd's sister.[214, 215] It was said she was treated again at La Vina Sanitarium in the summer of 1929. One source says she was treated twice at a sanitarium in California. This article says 3 times.[217] Another source states that she entered the La Vina Sanitarium when she got in from Mexico. She thought her lung was in a bad shape because during the revolution she was unable to take treatments and feared that the work of healing might have been interrupted. She had a cavity in the lung the size of an egg. It was examined and they assured her that it was alright.[212] A news article states that Ruth was at La Vina twice, once in 1928, and once in 1929. Miss Dunlap stated she was there for rest only and not for treatment (I guess in 1929).[218] The LA Times stated she was there from June until August.

1929, June 28

Evelyn Morel and James, Ursula, Langan, and James Jr. arrive in San Francisco on the SS Venezuela from Mazatlán.[215] Sammy leaves Fairbanks (perhaps, before the 29th), for McKinley Park where she would accept a position with the Mt. McKinley Tourist & Transportation Compay. She planned to remain at the Park a month or six weeks. She was undecided at the time whether to return to the coast over the railroad or by the Richardson Highway.[213] Sammy visited in Fairbanks and returned and worked at McKinley Park for the rest of the summer and was popular among those who visited the park.[219] The Fairbanks News Miner stated that Sammy was in Fairbanks in the summer of 1929 and although her stay was Short, her sunny good nature brought her many friends. She went from Fairbanks to McKinley Park and worked there all that summer. She was very popular among all who visited the Park.[220] Cap. Lathrop intended to return to the mine at Suntrana on this day if the bridge was back in order. It was part of the Healy River Coal Corporation.[216] Noel Wien flies back to Nome.[216] A brochure from the 1929 season stated that from Savage River Camp an interesting saddle-horse trip can be made over the divide and on to the Sanctuary River, at mile 22. From here the trail leads past Double Mountain, across the Teklanika River and on to Igloo Creek at mile 33.[206] There are photos of Sammy with saddle and pack horses at Igloo Creek. She is feeding a horse in front of one of the tents there. She also took a photo of the row of tents along Igloo Creek. Jane Bryant at Denali Park has a similar photo of the tents in front of Igloo Creek at Denali [221] [45] [192] As for Savage River, the base camp has 50 tents, 10x12 feet in size, to accommodate 100 people. A large tent serves as a dining room and another as a community room for social gatherings, with a matched floor for dancing. Other camps that existed that year were at the head of Savage River, Sable Pass, Polychrome Pass, Toklat River, Copper Mountain, and the head of Clearwater.[206] Passengers are transported from McKinley Park Station to the Savage River Camp by Motor bus.[206] There is a picture of the front hall at Savage River with the bus from the McKinley Tourist and Transportation Company in Sammy's photos. The deer antlers can be seen from the front hall. Maybe somebody is on the bus in an open window. There are tourist cars lining up after the bus.[45] There is a similar picture of the row of cars taken in front of the hall from the opposite direction. [222] From the Savage River camp, the trip to the camp at the head of Savage River may be made either by stage coach or automobile. Sable Pass camp is reached by automobile. The other camps are reached only by saddle horse.[206] There is a photo of the Stage from 1929 among Sammy's photos.[45] Jane Bryant stated that the driver in this photo is Lou Corbley, an MT&TCo. employee and later Chief Ranger at Mt. McKinley National Park." She said there were 4 stage coaches. This is definitely McKinley Park at Savage River.[192] McKinley acquired several stages from Yellowstone. There is another photo at a Tourist Camp up the Savage River (to the South). It may include a picture of Sammy wearing a tie. The slide says 1928, but I believe it is 1929.[223] Tom Walker, photographer and park historian stated that this camp was upstream. Today it is an overnight backpacking trip. The road is barely visible to nonexistent. They took the stages to this place. It is on the site of the Caribou Capture Camp situated by Olaus Murie in the early Twenties.[224] There are also pictures of Sammy downstream in Savage Canyon in 1929. One is where Sammy is in the lead in front of a group of other people on horses. The rocks are jagged. She is wearing her plaid jacket and tie. This is downstream three miles from the bridge.[223] [225] There is another picture of this same group working their way downstream. Sammy is 4-5 people back and is wearing her plaid jacket and tie.[225] There is a possible picture of Sammy on Inspiration Rock with Lena and Johnny Howard.[225] There is a possible picture of Sammy under mosquito netting (definitely her coat). The location may be Sable Pass according to the Bryant presentation.[225] [223] The most humorous photo found during the summer is one of the staff in front of the social hall. Sammy is in a white house dress at the end of the line. The photo is somewhat blurry. It can be found in the SLED photography database online. On closer inspection, it can be seen that the participants in this photo are wearing fake noses and mustaches.[225]

1929, July 19
Dorothy Chisholm arrives at home in Wrangell to spend the rest of her summer vacation with her parents, Mr. and Mrs. L. B. Chisholm.[226]

1929, July 22
Austin Lathrop arrives in Fairbanks from the south.[227] J. B. Burford, owner of the supply business at Juneau, arrived at Fairbanks on the previous Friday by train. This was his first trip to the Interior for over 2 years.[227] C.W. Nickerson was arrested at Brown Alaska Railroad station with an insanity complaint. He had nearly recovered since being in custody of the US Marshall Lynn Smith of Nenana. It is said of Nickerson that he was new to this country and failed to provide himself with mosquito nets and with the pests worse than they have been in years past, he was unable to protect himself and was bothered so much that finally he had a nervous breakdown, which is believed to account for the fact that he was mentally unbalanced for a few days.[227] Miss Fish and Miss Benson of Pasadena spent some time in McKinley Park before coming to Fairbanks. Afterwards, they headed to Dawson on the Yukon.[227] A newspaper article is published about the increase of tourism at McKinley Park. "Park Attracting Many This Year. Business Shows Good Increase, Says Secretary Treasurer of Tourist & Transportation Company. A substantial increase has been noted in the number of visitors to McKinley Park Tourist & Transport- last year, according to John H. Kelly secretary- treasurer of the Mr. McKinley Park Tourist and Transportation Co who returned to Fairbanks late last week after a stay of two weeks in the park. Two large parties are booked for this week. One of 75 will arrive at Nenana on the Steamer Yukon and another of about 45 is now en route to Fairbanks over the Richardson Highway from Chitinia. The Park is the only place in the Interior to get away from mosquitoes, says Mr. Kelly. The camp is at an altitude of 2700 feet, the country is open and with cool nights and breezes the pests simply don't thrive, he declared. Game is exceptionally plentiful in the Park this season, declared Mr. Kelly.

Foxes are seen in abundance and grizzly bears have been seen by nearly every party. One group sighted five bears in one day. Wolves were killed recently near the Savage River Camp."[228]

1929, July 23
Austin Lathrop leaves for Healy after staying in Fairbanks overnight. He accompanied Colonel Ohlson and Colonel Quinlan on the last stage of their northbound jorney yesterday.[227] Near to this time "recently" Dr. And Mrs. H. W. Morsch, residents of New York State, returned to Fairbanks after making a trip to McKinley Park. They will remain in Fairbanks until the next sailing of the steamer Yukon. They came into the interior via the Richardson Highway.[227] Romeo Hoyt visits the Park for a week.[227]

1929, July 30
Mr. Wells, an old timer living at Broad Pass at Mt McKinley Park went out with a bucket and gun to go pick blueberries and failed to return. Hunting parties found no trace of him. They believed he met up with a bear and was killed or badly hurt.[194] Romeo Hoyt came to Fairbanks on the train after spending a week at McKinley Park.[227] Captain Lathop arrived back in Fairbanks from Suntrana. He is listed as president of the Healy River Coal Corporation.[227] Mr. and Mrs. C. E. Richmond are now residents of the suburban colony at Park headquarters two miles west of town.[227] The Alaska Railroad is hauling gravel, building a fill for another track at McKinley Park on the east side of the main line.[227] At this point the tourist travel visiting McKinley that summer was in excess of 700 which was a number in excess of visitors for any former year for the entire season. They thought that the visitors that year might exceed 1200 and thought they would pay out $36,000 for accommodations.[227] Romeo Hoyt returned to Fairbanks after spending a week at McKinley Park.[227]

1929, August 1
Mr. and Mrs. Boone of Seattle leave Fairbanks after visiting for a week. They planned to spend a day at McKinley Park before heading to Seward. He had been in Alaska before and had been on the outside for 19 years.[227]

1929, August 9
Special Agent Paul E. Reynolds of the FBI's El Paso Office was on

assignment in Phoenix, Arizona, at the time of his death. At about 9 p.m. on August 9, 1929, he rented an automobile and departed from his hotel. Three days later, his body was found floating in a canal near Phoenix. An autopsy revealed that death had resulted from a gunshot wound in his heart. A thorough and intensive investigation failed to shed any light on the mystery surrounding his death. He worked as a prohibition agent.[229]

1929, August
Grant Pearson returns to Alaska. He returns to Denali in hopes to get his job as a Ranger back. When he arrived back at Denali, everybody was wearing mosquito netting. It was the worst season for mosquitos in 20 years. Much development had happened that summer. New log buildings were put up, a new water system was laid, and a new guide and lecture service for tourists was installed. There was no work available in August, but Grant worked on the new water system until a position opened up a month later. When he got to McKinley Station he saw Maurice Marino at the door of his roadhouse ready to welcome guests. He said he saw Bobby Sheldon who had three new red buses. Liek was the new superintendent from Yellowstone. Sammy might have known him from the previous summer when she was there.[164] There were 1038 visitors to McKinley Park that summer.[195]

1929, August 17, or so
Sammy comes out of the interior from Fairbanks via the Alaskan highway to Valdez. She spends several days in Valdez before sailing to Juneau.[230]

1929, August 19
The Alameda is scheduled to sail south from Valdez. Sammy leaves Valdez.[231]

1929, August 21
Mrs. J. H. Cann left on the Virginia IV in the evening for Apex El Nido where the mine that Mr. Cann is principal owner is located. Mr. Cann planned to join her in about a week. They planned to remain there a short time before returning to Juneau.[232]

1929, August 22
Sammy arrives back in Juneau from the interior via Valdez on the

Alameda at 10:30 AM. The captain was C. V. Westerlund.[233] It was one of the roughest crossings this ship ever experienced across the Gulf of Alaska. She brings back samples of gold dust from Fairbanks where she panned for gold as evidence of her experience.[201] The Alameda was the ship that the movie, the" Cheechakos" was filmed on.[6]

1929, August 24

Barrett Willoughby leaves Valdez and sails west on the steamship Yukon.[234] She went to Fairbanks this summer to meet aviator Carl Ben Eielsen who she met on a steamer on deck as she was leaving Seattle. She was headed for Ketchikan to work on research for "Spawn of the North".[235] He invited her to fly with him when she was done there. It was not in her plans but took him up on his offer this summer. She went to Fairbanks a few weeks later. Perhaps she was on her way to Fairbanks here.[236]

1929, September 1

Anne LeRoi starts working at the Wrangell Hospital as nurse in charge.[237] Some sources say October 1.[238]

1929, September 3

School started on Tuesday, September 3, 1929 at 9 in Juneau. Sammy is listed as the third and fourth grade teacher. The other third grade teacher was Mildred Abrahamsen and the other fourth grade teacher was Donie Taylor.[239] [161]

1929 September 6

A reception was held for the city teachers by the Juneau Parent Teacher Association at the gym of the high school. The cost for membership was 50 cents. Dancing followed the reception.[240]

1929, September 23

Jack Halloran adopted Baby Jane Doe. Papers were issued by Judge Dudley W. Windes. Halloran found the baby in his car about two weeks previous to the adoption when he and Mrs. Halloran emerged from a local theater late at night. He kept the baby overnight and then took her to police for possible identification.[241] Jack Halloran is pictured in 1932 before his arraignment in court 12/30/32? The adopted daughter in this pictures name is Betty Jane.[242]

1929, October 1

Anne LeRoi starts working as the superintendent at the Wrangell General Hospital.[238] Some sources say September 1.[237] Ruth claims that Anne had trouble with a dentist in Seattle, changed her name and moved to Alaska. Anne worked as a dental technician for a Dr. Brachbogle in Portland.[243] Ruth also said Anne changed her name because she had fights with a woman over a man in Portland.[244] In the 1930 Census she is listed as head of household divorced female, 25 years of age, born in Oregon, father born in Scotland, mother born in Kentucky and listed as the nurse in the hospital. She is living with Sarah Hart, assistant nurse, age 31 single born in North Dakota, parents from Canada. She also lives with Glen Erwing who is 22 and single and is listed as a servant. He was born in the Philippines and so were his parents. He is the cook at the hospital. Enumeration district 1-12, sheet 14B.[245] Sarah Elizabeth Hart's picture was found in the trunk. Miss Hart was a nurse when Anne LeRoi worked in Wrangell as superintendent. Later Sarah went to a hospital at Forks, Washington and was there in 1931.[246] Anne stated that she was divorced and had an adopted son living in Portland.[246]

1929, October 5

Sammy is listed in the 1930 census as living at dwelling number 185 in Juneau district 1-18.[247] This district is bordered on the North by 2nd Street down to the channel – the lower portion of town. There are 1387 people living in this district.[248] Sammy is listed at a hotel with the following persons:

Head- Harold W. McDermott, M 38 single, Hotel Clerk

Frank Huntzman, M, 40, Single, Forester, US Forest Service

Christine Halverson F 29 Single, Proprietor, Halverson's Store

Scott Thomas, M 52 Single, Imposter (?), California Dept. of (?)

Dorothy Israel, 25 or 35, Single, Teacher, Public School

James R. Cann 43 Married, No occupation.[247]

The 1930 census showed that in Juneau Alaska, the ratio of single men to single women was 9 to 1.[249]

This is the Gastineau Hotel. Harold W. McDermott is listed as the proprietor in the Daily Alaska Empire when he leaves for vacation.[176] The Gastineau Hotel was opened on Alaska Day in 1913 as the Cain Hotel. It originally had 3 floors, the 4th floor was added in 1915.[170] James R. Cann is not really unemployed as it seemed. He is actually part owner of the Hotel and his wife and children live elsewhere. His health is not good, he is treated at the Mayo Clinic later in the year, and later sells his interest in the hotel and leaves for the states with his family.[250]

Christine Halverson owns the Halverson Store in Juneau. She makes trips to the states to get new merchandise periodically.[251]

Dorothy Israel taught English in the High School in Juneau.[252]

Mabel Monson who replaced Sammy in the schools in October of 1930 mentioned that when she lived at the Gastineau when she first arrived in Juneau, she had her own room, but shared a bathroom with the other teachers living there. Dorothy and Sammy are the only ones listed in the Census as teachers living there. Mabel lived in a room near the back and paid $35 dollars a month to live there. Her rent included breakfast. Dinners cost 1.50 at local cafes. She went up the hill to the school twice a day. School began at 9 and ended at 3, although she was there from 8-4. She went home for lunch at the hotel. Lunch was provided in her room for herself where simple cooking privileges were allowed which included toast, coffee, soup (on a hot plate) and peanut butter sandwiches. In the evenings she liked to lie in bed at night with her bed pushed up at the window. There, she watched the miners come down from the mine at 11:00 pm with their carbide hats on. The Reliable Transfer Building is there now. The lights reminded her of a parade of fire flies which often lulled her to sleep.[253]

1929, October 26
Barrett Willoughby leaves Fairbanks and heads back to the states. She stated that she and Carl Ben Eielson planned a trip to Point Barrow but winter came early. She said that 14 days later his plane was lost in Siberia.[236]

1929, November 1
Miss Halverson opens her shop at 9 in the morning – Halverson's –

Juneau's own store. Many people were there waiting for it to formally open. The store is located in the Triangle building. The Triangle building is located at the corner of Front and Franklin Streets. This is a clothing store with large fitting rooms, in taupe and rose color scheme with walnut trimmings and yellow parchment shades. Miss Halverson was pleased with the grand opening.[251] She was previously the manager of the ladies' ready-to-wear department at the Goldstein store and resigned to open this store earlier in 1929.[170] Captain Lathrop is listed in the 1930 census (November 1, 1929) as being a 64-year-old white male, single, from Michigan, head of household. He is listed as a coal miner and living in Fairbanks.[254]

1929, November 6
Dorothy Chisholm is the music and art supervisor of the high school and the grade school. On this date she presented the boys glee club for the first time of the season at the PTA meeting. She also accompanied the solos later in the program. Slides of animals were shown by HW Chase who is the president of the Alaska Game Commission.[255]

1929, November 8
Captain Lathrop acquires the *Fairbanks News Miner*. It occupied space in the Empress Theater in Fairbanks. Austin Lathrop makes Fairbanks his official residence during this time period although he had businesses in Anchorage and Cordova also during this time.[6]

1929, November 9
Carl Ben Eielson and his mechanic Earl Borland disappeared in Siberia while finishing a contract to retrieve furs from the icebound schooner NANUK. An air search began immediately.[172]

1929, November 14
Halverson's Store just got a neon sign. It is the fourth of its kind in Juneau. The other buildings in Juneau with neon signs include Nelson Store, Imperial Billiard Hall, and the third at the front of the Coliseum Theatre.[256]

1929, November 27
Harold Philip Bisch sails from Le Havre France with his son Philip who is 6.[257]

1929, December 5
Harold Philip Bisch arrives in New York from France on the SS Ile De France.[257]

1929, December 6
Dorothy Israel directs the play Tommy at the high school. It is the story of Mr. and Mrs. Thurber who sell their land to a golf course to make up for financial losses.[258]

1929, December 16
Broadway Melody, the first Talkie, opens at the Palace Theater. They previously had the *Jazz Singer* in the weeks before, but this was not completely with sound.[259] The Palace Theater was located on the National Bank Building on Franklin Street and first opened in 1916.[170] L.B. Chisholm who is the Municipal Magistrate of Wrangell arrived in Juneau on business on the Queen at 8 in the morning. He is the father of Dorothy Chisholm and is visiting her as well as attending to some business. He is staying at the Gastineau Hotel. He will go back to Wrangell on the Northwestern.[260]

1929, December 17
H. W. McDermott, who is the chief clerk at the Gastineau Hotel left on the Princess Norah to spend the holidays with his parents in Spokane. He planned to return after the New Year.[176]

1929, December 20
"Cross Patch Flowers" is presented at the Elks Club on Friday night. It was directed by Miss Dorothy Chisholm, and Dorothy Israel. Miss Israel directed the speaking parts. The story is of Carol who is a little girl who has been sick and becomes cross. She wishes everybody to be cross. A Cross Patch Fairy takes charge of her and carries her before Santa Claus in his work shop. Everyone then becomes cross there and this causes Santa to go on Strike. Carol realizes her error and then Sunny Smile Fairies take her into their charge and all is happy once again. This performance was by the entire grade school.[261] Sammy is not listed among the staff in the article previewing the performance. Dorothy Chisholm is director and Dorothy Israil was the dramatic coach. It's a huge cast The Wrangell Sentinel reports, "The school operetta: ' Cross Patch Fairies', produced by the Juneau Grade School pupils scored a genuine hit in the performance at the Elks Hall last night. A large and appreciative

audience filled the hall when the High School quartet sang the opening number and the rising curtain on the first act brought applause. The gay colored uniforms of the Toyland Brigade and their well-executed military evolutions called for a big hand, also the setting of Santa Claus' Workshop at the North Pole, with the elves busily engaged in sewing dolls and teddy bears. The last act with the performers in their pajamas was the high spot in the play, judging by the applause. More students took part in the operetta than in any previous production of the Juneau schools. Including the Glee Clubs participating, there were 135 pupils. Miss Dorothy Chisholm, director, is justly proud of her troopers as well as her technical staff. The scenery, props, and costumes were all made locally."[262]

1929, December 22
This is the last day of school before closing for the Winter Break (Monday).[263] Burton McKinnell stated that he had worked in the mailroom at the train station the Christmas before last which would have been 1929.[264]

1929, December 24
Dorothy Chisholm leaves for her home in Wrangell aboard the Alameda.[265] Burton spends Christmas with Ruth and Dr. Judd in El Paso? They went over to Juarez in the evening.[266] Burton mentioned that this was 3 years ago.[266] Is this the period of time they were at Aguajita Coahuila where Dr. Judd was a doctor at a coal mine for a brief time? [35] Is this when Ruth was in the Sanatorium in El Paso? If it was, Dr. Judd came to see her once per month and took her out to Juarez for dinner and to go to the Casino and play roulette.[35] Ruth says Dr. Judd went to El Paso and stayed. She came from Los Angeles to El Paso and intended to go back to LA, but stopped in Phoenix instead.[169] Dr Judd stated that he owned a Ford Sport Coupe in 1929 and part of 1930. Ruth drove this car even though she wasn't a very good driver. He said she drove it 400-500 miles total. He stated that she would have trouble driving in LA because of traffic, but could have driven in Phoenix.[267] Burton said that Ruth told him that she had driven a car in Mexico although he stated that he would hate to drive behind her.[266]

1929, December 26
Miss Dorothy Chisholm arrives on the Alameda to Wrangell to spend the Christmas holidays with her parents, Mr. And Mrs. L. B. Chisholm.[268] The Wrangell General Hospital also played the part of

host at a Christmas dinner. Several members of the school faculty (probably Wrangell?) were dinner guests at the home of Mr. and Mrs. L. B. Chisholm.[269]

1. *Narcotic Illness 'Excuses' Blasted By Coast Doctor*, in *Unknown Newspaper Clippings of Lloyd Andrews*. October 28, 1931.
2. Arizona State Board of Health, *Lillie Lee Judd Death Certificate*, in *Arizona Vital Records*. August 14, 1920: Phoenix.
   http://genealogy.az.gov
3. *Dr. J first Wife Victim of Drug Poisoning*, in *Phoenix Gazette*. October 28, 1931: Phoenix.
4. Lucy, Dan, *Mrs. Judd: Dictated by Dan Lucy*, in *Winnie Ruth Judd Papers, Arizona State Archives*. October 20, 1931: Phoenix.
5. Judd, Winnie Ruth, *Judd Reminiscences*, in *Arizona Historical Society, Southern Arizona Division*. 1941: Tucson, AZ.
6. Tower, Elizabeth A., *Mining, media, movies : Cap Lathrop's keys for Alaska's riches*. 1991, Anchorage, Alaska (6761 Roundtree, Anchorage 99516): E.A. Tower. [v], 110 p.
7. *Testimony of Carrie McKinnell in State Vs Judd*. 1932, Arizona State Archives and Public Records.
8. Judd, Ruth, *Ruth Judd's Life Story in her Own Words*, in *Los Angeles Examiner*. October 28, 1931: Los Angeles.
9. West, Nathaniel, *Legendary 'Trunk Murderess,' Who Once Lived Here, Dead at Age 93*, in *Greenville Advocate*. October 29, 1998: Greenville, IL. 1.
10. *Girl's Abduction Story is Attacked.*, in *Olney Daily Mail*. November 16, 1922.
11. *Frank Leroy Hull, World War I, Draft Registration Card, Sept 1918*, I. Richland County, Editor. 1918.
12. Judd, Winnie Ruth, *Drain Pipe Letter*, L.f.i.B.D.S. Plumbing, Editor. 10/24/1931, 1931, Arizona State Archive RG107: Los Angeles.
13. Judd, Ruth *Do I Dread the Future? There is no Alternative*, in *Los Angeles Examiner*. Ocotber 29, 1931: Los Angeles.
14. *Grand Jury Documents of Richland County Illinois regarding the seduction of Ruth McKinnell by Frank Hull*. 1922, Richland County Courthouse.
15. *Programme: Third Annual Commencement*. June 1, 1922, 1922, White Earth High School: White Earth, ND.

16. Doles, Lucy, *By Lucy Doles*, in *Racine Daily News*. 1931: Racine, Wisconsin. 1, 7.

17. Keaton, Mildred, *No Regrets: Autobiography of an Arctic Nurse*. 1999, Marysville, WA: Pakuk Press.

18. *Girl told of child of fancy*, in *Olney Daily Mail*. November 20, 1922: Olney, IL.

19. *Ruth M'Kinnel Tells Story of Fightful Experience*, in *Olney Daily Mail*. November 18, 1922: Olney, IL.

20. *Testimony of HJ McKinnell*, in *State Vs Judd: Arizona State Archives and Public Records*. 1932: Phoenix, AZ.

21. *Testimony of Dr. Clifford Wright*. Feb 2, 1932, Arizona State Library and Public Records: Phoenix, AZ.

22. *Deposition of Newell Willson?, Toledgo Illinois.*, in *State Vs Judd: Arizona State Archives and Public Records*. 1932: Phoenix, AZ.

23. *Mystery Lies Deep over Girl*, in *Olney Daily Mail*. November 14, 1922.

24. *Weird Story of Abduction Recounted: Mrs. Judd as High School Student at Olney Ill. Believe she was to Become Mother.*, in *Unknown Newspaper Clippings of Lloyd Andrews*. 1931.

25. Unknown author at the Arizona State Hospital, *Ruth Judd: Summary, June 25, 1947*, in *Personal Collection of Jerry Leukowitz*. June 25, 1947: Phoenix. 3.

26. *Court Notes*, in *Olney Daily Mail*. November 21, 1922: Olney, IL.

27. *Take Ruth M'Kinnell over abduction path*, in *Olney Daily Mail*. November 23, 1922: Olney, IL.

28. *Girl points out 2 women, her jailers*, in *Olney Daily Mail*. November 25, 1922: Olney, IL.

29. *Winnie Tells Suicide Idea: Slayer Hurls Charges at J. J. Halloran*, in *Arizona Republic*. January 18, 1933: Phoenix, AZ.

30. Judd, Winnie Ruth, *Killer Shies at Word Murder*, in *San Francisco Examiner*. October 29, 1931: San Francisco. 10.

31. Judd, William C, *My Life with Winnie Ruth Judd - Part 1*, in *Intimate Detective Stories*. March, 1940. 2-7, 52.

32. Peterson, Phyllis, *Anders Severin Samuelson*. August 23, 1998: Carpinteria, CA.

33. State Teachers College (Minot, ND), *Miscellaneous Programs, Schedules, Catalogs, etc.* 1913 1925, Minot, ND: Minot State Teachers College.

34. *Mrs. Judd Formerly Was Telephone Operator*, in *Los Angeles Times*. October 21, 1931: Los Angeles. 9.

35. Swent, Eleanor, *Marian Lane: Mine Doctor's Wife in Mexico.* Western Mining in the Twentieth Century Oral History Services. 1996, Berkeley. 121.
36. McKinnell, Burton Joy, *Brother's Story Vividly tells of Slayer's Girlhood, Wedding,* in *Los Angeles Examiner.* 1931: Los Angeles.
37. McKinnell, Burton Joy, *The Truth about Winnie Ruth Judd by her brother,* in *Winnie Ruth Judd Papers: Clements Library.* 1932: Detroit.
38. *Doctor Wants to Hunt Wife,* in *Los Angeles Times.* October 21, 1931: Los Angeles. 9.
39. *Lively Interest Manifest in All Phases of All Music,* in *Red & Green.* July 1, 1924: Minot, ND.
40. *The Magician: Yearbook of the Minot Normal School.* 1924, Minot, ND.
41. *Letters Give Intimate Picture of Slain Girl,* in *Westhope Standard.* October 29, 1931: Westhope, North Dakota. 1.
42. *Friend Recalls Trunk Murder Victim's Beauty,* in *San Francisco News.* October 23, 1931: San Francisco.
43. *Sammy was good pal, says girl,* in *San Francisco Call Bulletin.* October 22, 1931: San Francisco.
44. *Trunk Victims' Friend is Found,* in *San Francisco News.* October 22, 1931: San Francisco.
45. *Photographs of the Samuelson Family kept by Janet Worel.* 1900-1930: Dayton, MN.
46. *Photographs of the Samuelson Family kept by Dian Darby.* 1900-1930: San Antonio, TX.
47. Hufstetler, Mark, *email with Montana Archetectural Historian Mark Hufstetler regarding photos of Hedvig and friends, I thought was Montana. He knew that they were Minot. Other supporting photos of buildings and the fountain can be found on eBay and on the Web.* 2013.
48. *College Alumna Victim,* in *Red & Green.* Nov 3, 1931: Minot, ND.
49. *The Magician: Yearbook of the Minot Normal School.* 1925, Minot, ND.
50. *Life with Slain Nurse Told by First Husband,* in *Los Angeles Times.* October 23, 1931: Los Angeles. 6.
51. *Former Husband Talks,* in *Daily Alaska Empire.* October 22, 1931: Juneau, AK. 3.
52. *Local Women Slain at Phoenix Arizona,* in *Strollers Weekly & Douglas Island News.* October 23, 1931: Douglas, AK. 1.

53. *First Marriage in 1924*, in *Morning Oregonian*. October 23, 1931: Portland. 2.

54. *Portland Man First Husband*, in *Ketchikan Alaska Chronicle*. October 22, 1931: Ketchikan, AK. 1.

55. *Agnes Leroi Twice Married, Says First Mate's Brother*, in *Los Angeles Evening Express*. October 22, 1931: Los Angeles. 3.

56. *Murdered Woman Native of Oregon: Mrs. Leroi without Enemy, Says Sister, of Aurora*, in *The Morning Oregonian*. October 21, 1931: Portland. 8.

57. *Murdered Woman Traced by Photo: One Victim Believe to Be ex-Portland Nurse*, in *Morning Oregonian*. October 20, 1931: Portland. 1,3.

58. *Inquest Bares Mrs. Judd had Company to L.A.*, in *Los Angeles Evening Express*. October 23, 1931: Los Angeles. 4.

59. *History of Illinois and her people*. 225.

60. *"There's Music in the Air"; All Groups Active*, in *Red & Green*. October 28, 1924: Minot, ND. 1.

61. *Musical organizations of Minot Normal Grow*, in *Red & Green*. January 20, 1925: Minot, ND.

62. Judd, Winnie Ruth, *'Now Facing Reality' Girl Slayer Writes*, in *San Francisco Examiner*. October 30, 1931: San Francisco. 1, 8.

63. Hickernell, FA, *Dr. M. I. Leff*, in *Winnie Ruth Judd Papers, Arizona State Archives*. January 14, 1932: Phoenix.

64. Judd, Winnie Ruth, *Letter from Ruth Judd to Walter Hoffmann; later forwarded to Governor Williams in 1971*. July 26, 1953: Phoenix.

65. Wiles, Otis M, *Friends lift curtain of tragedy*, in *San Francsico Examiner*. October 27, 1931: San Francisco. 3.

66. *Mrs. Judd Took Last Gay Fling at Happiness Before Pair Died*, in *Ketchikan Alaska Chronicle*. October 29, 1931: Ketchikan, AK. 1.

67. *Record house Booked for Mikado*, in *Red & Green*. July 21, 1925: Minot, ND. 1.

68. *"The Mikado" is Revived by College Chorus*, in *Red & Green*. June 23, 1925: Minot, ND.

69. *Students of College Register Decided Hit in Delightful Mikado*, in *Minot Daily News*. July 24, 1925: Minot, ND. 10.

70. *Graduation Exercises Program*. 1925, Minot State University.

71. *Find Sister of Victim Here*, in *Chicago American*. October 20, 1931: Chicago. 6.

72. *Letter Received a Week Ago*, in *Minot Daily News*. 1931: Minot, ND. 2.

73. *1930 Census, Landa Village*, in *1930 Federal Census*. April 23, 1930: Landa Villiage. 1A.

74. *Testimony of William C Judd*, in *State Vs Judd: Arizona State Library and Public Records*. 1932: Phoenix, AZ.

75. *Lot 9, Block 1, La Belle Place, 4/42 Deed Recordings*. Phoenix, Arizona.

76. *Strange Story of Winnie Ruth Judd Closes*, in *Journal Review Weekend*. November 7, 1998: Darlington, IN.

77. Pearson, Grant H, *History of Mount McKinley National Park*, U.S.P. Service, Editor. 1952.

78. *Howard Morten Hagen: World War I Draft Registration Card, August 24, 1918*, N. Bottineau County, Editor. 1918.

79. *Letters of Friendship to Miss Samuelson Bared*, in *Los Angeles Evening Herald*. October 22, 1931: Los Angeles. 11.

80. *Photograph of a dark haired boy. "This is chang M. He was six years old in June. He is the baby.",* in *Winnie Ruth Judd Collection*. Ann Arbor, MI.

81. *Victim Formerly Whitehall Teaher*, in *Great Falls Tribune*. October 20, 1931: Great Fall, MT. 1.

82. *Murdered Girl. Well Know in Whitehall Area*, in *Montana Record Herald*. October 20, 1931: Helena, MT. 1.

83. Huntley, Chet, *The Generous Years*. 1968. 191-192.

84. *Teacher Tells of her Friendship*, in *Montana Standard*. October 21, 1931: Butte, Montana. 2.

85. *Hoitola Call is Explained*, in *Arizona Republic*. April 16, 1933: Phoenix.

86. *Opening of School Tuesday, Sept. 7th*, in *Jefferson Valley News*. September 2, 1926: Whitehall, MT. 1.

87. *Opening of School Tuesday, Sept 7th*, in *Jefferson Vally News*. September 2, 1926: Whitehall, MT. 1.

88. *Whitehall Schools open with Record Enrollment*, in *Jefferson Valley News*. September 9, 1926: Whitehall, MT.

89. *News About Town: Thirty-Seven at Dormitory*, in *Jefferson Valley News*. September 9, 1926: Whitehall, MT. 2.

90. *Local Teachers Entertained at Justus Home*, in *Jefferson Valley News*. September 23, 1926: Whitehall, MT. 1.

91. *Informed of Death of Father in N. Dakota*, in *Jefferson Valley News*. September 16, 1926: Whitehall, MT. 2.

92. Huntley, Marion and Arthur Salvingni, *Whitehall School News*, in *Jefferson Valley News*. September 23, 1926: Whitehall, MT. 5.

93. *Dormitory News Notes*, in *Jefferson Valley News*. October 7, 1926: Whitehall, MT. 4.

94. *Whitehall School News*, in *Jefferson Valley News*. September 30, 1926: Whitehall, MT.

95. Harbison, Cora, *School Notes*, in *Jefferson Valley News*. October 7, 1926: Whitehall, MT. 2.

96. *Dormitory Doings*, in *Jefferson Valley News*. October 14, 1926: Whitehall, MT.

97. *Whitehall School News*, in *Jefferson Valley News*. 1926: Whitehall, MT. 5.

98. *Whitehall School News*, in *Jefferson Valley News*. October 21, 1926: Whitehall, MT. 2.

99. *Morrison Cave Near Three Forks One of Natures Unique Works*, in *Jefferson Valley News*. unknown, 1927?: Whitehall, MT.

100. *News About Town: Entertained At "500" Last Monday Night*, in *Jefferson Valley News*. 1926: Whitehall, MT. 2.

101. *Dormitory News Notes*, in *Jefferson Valley News*. November 4, 1926: Whitehall, MT. 2.

102. *Whitehall School News*, in *Jefferson Vally News*. November 4, 1926: Whitehall, MT. 2.

103. *Furnace In Grade School Causes Trouble*, in *Jefferson Valley News*. November 18, 1926: Whitehall, MT. 1.

104. *Whitehall School News*, in *Jefferson Valley News*. November 25, 1926: Whitehall, MT. 1.

105. *School Notes*, in *Jefferson Valley News*. November 25, 1926: Whitehall, MT. 2.

106. *School Notes*, in *Jefferson Valley News*. December 2, 1926: Whitehall, MT. 5.

107. *School Notes*, in *Jefferson Valley News*. December 9, 1926: Whitehall, MT. 7.

108. *Dormitory News Notes*, in *Jefferson Valley News*. December 9, 1926: Whitehall, MT. 7.

109. *Whitehall School News*, in *Jefferson Valley News*. December 16, 1926: Whitehall, MT. 11.

110. *Dorm Notes*, in *Jefferson Valley News*. December 16, 1926: Whitehall, MT. 11.

111. *Second Childhool*, in *Jefferson Valley News*. December 16, 1926: Whitehall, MT.

112. Covington, Zellah and Jules Simonson, *Second childhood; a farce in three acts*. 1925, New York,: Longmans, Green & co. 2 p. l., 92 p.

113. *Christmas Program at High School December 23*, in *Jefferson Valley News*. December 16, 1926: Whitehall, MT. 2.

114. *News of the Town*, in *Jefferson Valley News*. December 30, 1926: Whitehall, MT. 2.

115. *School News*, in *Jefferson Vally News*. January 6, 1927: Whitehall, MT. 7.

116. *Locals*, in *Jefferson Valley News*. January 6, 1927: Whitehall, MT. 2.

117. *Whitehall School News*, in *Jefferson Valley News*. 1927: Whitehall, MT. 2.

118. *Dormitory News Notes*, in *Jefferson Valley News*. January 13, 1927: Whitehall, MT. 4.

119. *Dormitory News Notes*, in *Jefferson Valley News*. January 20, 1927: Whitehall, MT. 1.

120. *Dormitory News Notes*, in *Jefferson Valley News*. March 10, 1927: Whitehall, MT. 2.

121. *Board Decides not to Close School Because of Epidemic.*, in *Jefferson Vally News*. February 17, 1927: Whitehall, MT. 1.

122. *Do You Know That?*, in *Jefferson Valley News*. February 17, 1927: Whitehall, MT. 2.

123. *Knew Miss Samuelson*, in *Bozeman Daily Chronicle*. October 21, 1931: Bozeman, MT. 1.

124. Schools, Whitehall Public, *Whitehall Public Schools, Teacher's Contract for Hedvig Samuelson*, in *Arizona State Archives*. March 7, 1927: Whitehall, Montana.

125. *Bodies of Two Murdered: Women Hid in Luggage*, in *Los Angeles Times*. October 20, 1931: Los Angeles. 2.

126. in *Jefferson Valley News*. March 17, 1927: Whitehall, MT. 1.

127. in *Jefferson Valley News*. April 14, 1927: Whitehall, MT.

128. *Whitehall News: High School Exercises Held Friday Evening*, in *Anaconda Standard*. May 29, 1927: Anaconda, MT.

129. *Memories of Alaska*, in *Minot Daily News*. October 21, 1931: Minot, ND. 10.

130. Judd, William C, *Letter from Dr. Judd to Dr. Davis from Dolores Mine Co.* . June 28, 1928: Madera, Chihuahua, Mexico.

131. in *Jefferson Valley News*. September 22, 1927: Whitehall, MT. 5.

132. *News notes of the Whitehall Schools*, in *Jefferson Valley News*. September 27, 1927: Whitehall, MT. 1.

133. *News Notes of the Whitehall Schools*, in *Jefferson Valley News*. October 13, 1927: Whitehall, MT.

134. in *Jefferson Valley News*. January 5, 1928: Whitehall, MT.

135.   *Local News Notes*, in *Jefferson Valley News*. December 6, 1927: Whitehall, MT. 2.

136.   Smith, Munford, *Letter from Barlow Sanitarium*. January 16, 1932, Kept at State Vs Judd, Arizona State Library and Public Records: Los Angeles.

137.   *Woman's orgy of tears told*, in *Unknown Newspaper Clippings of Lloyd Andrews*. ?, 1931.

138.   *Whitehall News*, in *Anaconda Standard*. January 1, 1928: Anaconda, MT.

139.   *Letters Tell Life Shadows*, in *Los Angeles Times*. October 22, 1931: Los Angeles. 7.

140.   Catton, Dr. Joseph, *Secret Story of Winnie Ruth Judd*, in *True Crime Detective*. Spring, 1952. 17-30.

141.   Hunt, Irene M MD, *La Vina in the Twenties*, in *Pasadena Historical Society*. ?

142.   La Vina Sanitarium, *For the Patient*, in *Pasadena Historical Society*. ?: Pasadena.

143.   *School News*, in *Jefferson Valley News*. March 29, 1928: Whitehall, MT.

144.   *News Notes of the Whitehall Schools*, in *Jefferson Valley News*. February 2, 1928: Whitehall, MT. Supplement.

145.   Fortuine, Robert, *"Must We All die?" Alaska's Enduring Struggle with Tuberculosis*. 2005, Fairbanks: University of Alaska Press.

146.   *News Notes of the Whitehall Schools*, in *Jefferson Valley News*. February 9, 1928: Whitehall, MT. 2.

147.   Harbison, Mrs. George, *Woman's Clue Members Turn Back the Pages of Time*, in *Jefferson Valley News*. February 16, 1928: Whitehall, MT. 1.

148.   *School News*, in *Jefferson Valley News*. April 5, 1928: Whitehall, MT. 2.

149.   *Morrison Cave Membership Buttons*, in *Jefferson Valley News*. February 16, 1928: Whitehall, MT. 1.

150.   *School News*, in *Jefferson Valley News*. May 10, 1928: Whitehall, MT. 5.

151.   *Mrs. Ruth Judd Characterized as Intelligent*, in *Unknown Newspaper Clippings of Lloyd Andrews*. 1931.

152.   Judd, William C, *My Life with Winnie Ruth Judd - Part 4*, in *Intimate Detective Stories*. June, 1940. 12-15, 45-47.

153.   *Commencement*, in *Jefferson Valley News*. June 7, 1928: Whitehall, MT. 1.

154.   *To West Yellowstone*, in *Jefferson Valley News*. June 7, 1928: Whitehall, MT. 1.

155.   *Teachers Plan Vacations*, in *Jefferson Valley News*. June 7, 1928: Whitehall, MT. 1.

156.   *Mother explains listing of girl's name by victim*, in *Los Angeles Evening Herald*. October 22, 1931: Los Angeles. 11.

157.   *26 Passengers on Charlotte for this Port*, in *Daily Alaska Empire*. September 1, 1928: Juneau, AK. 6.

158.   *Princess Charlotte South Early Today*, in *Daily Alaska Empire*. September 4, 1928: Juneau, AK. 6.

159.   *Murder Victims Are Known Here; Were In Juneau*, in *Anchorage Daily Times*. October 21, 1931: Anchorage, AK. 8.

160.   *School Will Open Here on Next Monday*, in *Daily Alaska Empire*. September 8, 1928: Juneau, AK. 2.

161.   Tillotson, Marjorie, *History of the Schools in the Gastineau Channel Area*. June, 1973: Juneau, Alaska.

162.   *List of US Citizens arriving on the Olympic sailing from Southhampton to New York, September 18, 1928*. 1928.

163.   *High School is Dedicated; Large Crowd*, in *Daily Alaska Empire*. November 17, 1928: Juneau, AK. 8.

164.   Pearson, Grant H, *My Life of High Adventure*. 1962, New York: Ballantine Books.

165.   *Think Ruth Judd was in Sanatorium Here*, in *El Paso Times*. October 30, 1931: El Paso, TX.

166.   Swent, Langan W., et al., *Working for safety and health in underground mines : San Luis and Homestake mining companies, 1946-1988*. Western mining in the twentieth century oral history series. 1995. xix, 1007.

167.   Bodayla, Stephen D., *Financial diplomacy : the United States and Mexico, 1919-1933*. Foreign economic policy of the United States. 1987, New York: Garland. x, 216 p.

168.   Kendler, Mathilde, *Kendlers: The Story of aPioneer Alaska Juneau Dairy*. 1983, Anchorage: Alaska Northwest Publishing Company.

169.   Judd, Ruth, *My Own Story Ruth M Judd: Chapter IV*, in *Rochester Evening Journal*. 1931: Rochester, NY. 1.

170.   DeArmond, RN, *Old Gold: Historical Vignettes of Juneau, Alaska*. 1985, Juneau: Gastineau Channel Historical Society.

171.   Allen, June, *The legendary Bob Ellis, Bush Pilot: A long, full life 1903-1994*, in *SitNews*. August 12, 2004: Ketchikan. http://www.sitnews.net/JuneAllen/BobEllis/062003_bob_ellis.html

172. Ruotsala, Jim, *1929: International Airways - Washington Airways and the Visit of Carl Ben Eielson*, in *Pilots of the Panhandle : Aviation in Southeast Alaska* 1996, Seadrome Press.

173. *At the Hotels*, in *Daily Alaska Empire*. April 16, 1929: Juneau, AK. 2.

174. *Crew of Juneau Tells of Trip; All are Modest*, in *Daily Alaska Empire*. April 16, 1929: Juneau, AK. 1-2.

175. *Juneau Takes Passengers on Sitka Flight*, in *Daily Alaska Empire*. April 17, 1929: Juneau, AK. 2.

176. *Who's Who and Where*, in *Daily Alaska Empire*. December 17, 1929: Juneau, AK. 3.

177. Ruotsala, Jim, *1929: Gorst Air Transport U. S. Naval Survey Flight of 1929 and the Russian Flight*, in *Pilots of the Panhandle : Aviation in Southeast Alaska*. 1996, Seadrome Press.

178. *Alaska Takes Up Air Fans Today, Juneau Leaves*, in *Daily Alaska Empire*. April 20, 1929: Juneau, AK. 2.

179. *Air Advertising Tried Today by The Serenaders*, in *Daily Alaska Empire*. 1929: Juneau, AK. 3.

180. *Pensions for teachers are up in Senate*, in *Daily Alaska Empire*. April 24, 1929: Juneau, AK.

181. *Committee Named to Make Plans for Legislative Ball*, in *Daily Alaska Empire*. April 24, 1929: Juneau.

182. *Senate Passes Pension Bill for Teachers*, in *Daily Alaska Empire*. April 25, 1929: Juneau, AK.

183. *Captain Eielson Arrives here From Seattle: Alaska's Lindy is Greeted by Enthusiastic Crowd this Afternoon*, in *Daily Alaska Empire*. April 29, 1929: Juneau, AK.

184. *Colonol Eielson Greeted by Legislators*, in *Daily Alaska Empire*. April 30, 1929: Juneau, AK. 1.

185. *Sunday Musical tomorrow at the Elk's Hall: Grade and High School Students to take part in last musical*, in *Daily Alaska Empire*. May 11, 1929: Juneau, AK.

186. *School Play Next Sunday*, in *Daily Alaska Empire*. May 7, 1929: Juneau, AK. 3.

187. *J. B. Burford, Miss Foster, are Married*, in *Daily Alaska Empire*. May 15, 1929: Juneau. 5.

188. Mangusso, Mary Childers, *Anthony J. Dimond and the Politics of Integrity*, in *An Alaska Anthology : Interpreting the Past*, S.W. Haycox and M.C. Mangusso, Editors. 1996, University of Washington Press: Seattle. p. 246-266.

189. *Picture in Trunk*, in *Daily Alaska Empire*. October 21, 1931: Juneau, AK. 2.

190. *Ex-Husband Says Victim Romanticist*, in *Phoenix Gazette*. October 23, 1931: Phoenix. 1.

191. *Information Display at the Dog Kennels at Denali National Park*. August 18, 2001: Denali National Park.

192. Bryant, Jane, *Email from Jane Bryant, Photo Archivist at Denali Park*, S. Worel, Editor. December 29, 2006: Denali Park.

193. *Denali: Early Photographs of Our National Parks*. 2000, Whitehorse, Yukon: Wolf Creek Books.

194. *Broad Pass Man Believed Killed*, in *Daily News Miner*. July 31, 1929: Fairbanks, AK.

195. United States. National Park Service., *Annual report of the Director of the National Park Service to the Secretary of the Interior for the fiscal year ended June 30, 1929 and the travel season, 1929*. 1929, Washington: U.S. G.P.O.,.

196. *Sheep Becoming Tame in McKinley Park*, in *Wrangell Sentinel*. October 24, 1929: Wrangell, AK.

197. *McKinley Park Being Made More Accessible to American Tourists*, in *Wrangell Sentinel*. October 31, 1929: Wrangell, AK.

198. *M'Kinley National Park is a Tourist Attraction*, in *Wrangell Sentinel*. October 17, 1929: Wrangell, AK.

199. *Yukon in and out to Westward this A. M. *, in *Daily Alaska Empire*. June 4, 1929: Juneau. 7.

200. *Yukon Arrives from the South; Time to Change*, in *Anchorage Daily Times*. June 8, 1929: Anchorage, AK.

201. *Juneau Teacher Returns from Summer in Interior*, in *Daily Alaska Empire*. August 22, 1929: Juneau, AK. 2.

202. *Personal*, in *Anchorage Daily Times*. June 8, 1929: Anchorage, AK.

203. *Alaska Railroad, Mt McKinley Park Route Schedule*, in *Anchorage Daily Times*. June 10, 1929: Anchorage, AK. 3.

204. *The Alaska Railroad Mt. McKinley Park route* 1927: Department of the Interior, Alaska Railroad.

205. *McKinley Tourist & Transportation Company Guest Register*. 1929: Denali National Park, Alaska.

206. National Park Service, *Circular of General Information Regarding: Mount McKinley National Park, Alaska: Season from June 1 to September 15*. 1929: U.S. Government Printing Office.

207. Marks, Leo, *Leo Marks*, in *Unknown Internet Source*. p. 651.

208. *Scores of Names Found in Book of Miss Samuelson*, in *Los Angeles Herald*. October 22, 1931: Los Angeles. 11.

209. Brown, Bil, *Yesteryears with Leo Marks*, in *Adventurers Club News*. April, 1984: Los Angeles.

210. *Spach's Body is Found in Nenana River on Friday*, in *Daily News Miner*. June 22, 1929: Fairbanks, AK.

211. *Who's Who Around the Town*, in *Fairbanks News Miner*. June 19, 1929: Fairbanks, AK.

212. Judd, Ruth, *Ruth Tells of Mad Hunt for Refuge Here after Killings Known*, in *Los Angeles Examiner*. October 30, 1931: Los Angeles.

213. *Local Jottings*, in *Daily News Miner*. June 29, 1929: Fairbanks, AK. 5.

214. *List of United States Citizens S. S. Venezuela sailing from Mazatlan, Mexico June 22, 1929 arriving at Los Angeles June 26th, 1929*, in *California Passenger and Crew Lists, 1893-1957*. 1929, US Department of Labor: Los Angeles.

215. *List of United States Citizens S. S. Venezuela sailing from Mazatlan, Mexico June 22, 1929 arriving at San Francisco June 28th, 1929*, in *California Passenger and Crew Lists, 1893-1957*. 1929, US Department of Labor.

216. *Personals*, in *Daily News Miner*. June 26, 1929: Fairbanks, AK. 8.

217. *Hunt Still Centers Near Los Angeles*, in *Unknown Newspaper Clippings of Lloyd Andrews*. October 23, 1931.

218. *Sanitarium hunt proves fruitless: wanted Phoenix woman sought in Altadena*, in *Pasadena Star News*. October 23, 1931: Pasadena, CA.

219. *Alaska Women Slain*, in *Fairbanks Daily News Miner*. October 20, 1931: Fairbanks, AK. 1.

220. *Worked In Park*, in *Fairbanks Daily News Minor*. October 20, 1931: Fairbanks, AK. 1.

221. *Photos of Denali Park kept by Historian Jane Bryant of the NPS*. 1920-1935: Denali Park.

222. Norris, Frank B. and United States. National Park Service. Alaska Regional Office., *Crown jewel of the north : an administrative history of Denali National Park and Preserve*. 2006, Anchorage, Alaska: Alaska Regional Office, National Park Service, U.S. Dept. of the Interior.

223. Bryant, Jane, *The Life and Times of Savage Camp: PPT presentation*. 1999: NPS: Denali National Park.

224. *Email from Tom Walker of Denali Alaska*, S. Worel, Editor. 2011: Denali Alaska.

225. *Photos of Denali Park held at UAF*. 1929: Fairbanks, AK.

226. *Local News*, in *Wrangell Sentinal*. July 25, 1929: Wrangell, AK.

227. *Who's Who Around the Town*, in *Daily News Miner*. July 31, 1929: Fairbanks, AK.

228. *Park Attracting Many This Year*, in *Daily News Miner*. July 22, 1929: Fairbanks, AK.

229. *Paul E Reynolds*. Hall of Honor: FBI Agents Killed as the Result of an Adversarial Action [cited 2009 October 15]; Available from: http://www.fbi.gov/libref/hallhonor/reynolds.htm.

230. *Juneau Girls Murdered in Arizona*, in *Valdez Miner*. October 24, 1931: Valdez, AK. 1.

231. *Alaska Steamship Schedule*, in *Valdez Miner*. August 24, 1929: Valdez, AK. 3.

232. *Mrs. J. H. Cann Leaves for Apex El Nido*, in *Daily Alaska Empire*. August 22, 1929: Juneau, AK.

233. *Alameda from West Goes South Today*, in *Daily Alaska Empire*. August 22, 1929: Juneau, AK.

234. *Barrett Willoughby*, in *Valdez Miner*. August 24, 1929, 4.

235. Willoughby, Barrett, *Spawn of the north*. 1932, Boston and New York,: Houghton Mifflin company. 3 p. l., 349 p.

236. Willoughby, Barrett, *Alaskans all*. 1971, Freeport, N.Y.,: Books for Libraries Press. x, 234 p.

237. in *Wrangell Sentinel*. February 13, 1930: Wrangell, AK.

238. *Miss Agnes LeRoi Brutally Murdered*, in *Wrangell Sentinel*. October 23, 1931: Wrangell, AK. 1.

239. *School Opens Next Tuesday Morning at 9*, in *Daily Alaska Empire*. August 30, 1929: Juneau, AK. 8.

240. *Reception to City Teachers*, in *Alaska Daily Empire*. August 23, 1929: Juneau, AK.

241. *Baby adopted by man quizzed on Trunk Murders*, in *Los Angeles Evening Herald*. October 22, 1931: Los Angeles. 13.

242. *Photos Posted on eBay not purchased*. 2010-2014.

243. *Testimony of Jame O'Dell: Coroner's Report in California Inquest, 10-23-31, 9:30*, in *Arizona State Archives*. 1931: Los Angeles.

244. Judd, Winnie Ruth, *Statement of Winnie Ruth Judd taken at the Arizona State Prison 12-19-1932: Interview of JR McFadden Sheriff*, in *Pinal County Records*. December 19, 1932: Florence, Arizona.

245. *1930 Census Wrangell Alaska*, in *1930 Federal Census*. October 1, 1929: Wrangell, Alaska. 14B.

246. *Picture Identified*, in *Daily Alaska Empire*. October 22, 1931: Juneau, AK. 3.

247. *1930 Census, Juneau Town*, in *1930 Federal Census*. October 4, 1929: Juneau, AK. 11A.

248. *First Judicial Division, Alaska*, in *Enumeration Districts of the fifteenth Census*. 1930, 1929: Juneau, AK.

249. in *Wall Street Journal*. January 3, 1931: Washington, DC.

250. *Cann Interest in Hotel Sold To John Biggs*, in *Daily Alaska Empire*. May 16, 1930: Juneau, AK. 8.

251. *Juneau's New Store Opened*, in *Daily Alaska Empire*. Nov 1, 1929: Juneau, AK. 3.

252. *Vacation Days End Next Week for Youngsters*, in *Daily*. August 26, 1930: Juneau, AK. 8.

253. Burford, Mabel, *Mabel Monson Burford*, in *Juneau Stories of Teaching on the Last Frontier*. 1993, Juneau Retired Teachers' Association: Juneau, AK. p. 7-11.

254. *1930 Census, Fairbanks Town*. November 1, 1929. 28A.

255. *Record Crowd PTA Session*, in *Daily Alaska Empire*. November 6, 1931: Juneau, AK. 2.

256. *Halvorsen's Store has Neon Sign Now*, in *Daily Alaskan Empire*. November 14, 1929: Juneau, AK. 5.

257. *SS Ile De France List of United States Citizens, November 27, 1929*. 1929. 109.

258. *Fast Comedy is Presented School Cast*, in *Daily Alaska Empire*. December 7, 1929: Juneau, AK. 3.

259. *Palace Opens with Talkies Next Monday*, in *Daily Alaska Empire*. December 14, 1929: Juneau, AK. 3.

260. *Who's Who and Where*, in *Daily Alaska Empire*. 1929: Juneau, AK. 6.

261. *Operetta To Be Produced by Students*, in *Daily Alaska Empire*. December 14, 1929: Juneau, AK. 3.

262. *Miss Dorothy Chisholm Direct Operetta given by Juneau Public School*, in *Wrangell Sentinel*. December 26, 1929: Wrangell, AK.

263. *Public Schools To Close Next Monday*, in *Daily Alaska Empire*. December 21, 1929: Juneau, AK. 1.

264. McKinnell, Burton Joy, *Brother, for first time, tells own story of meeting slayer*, in *Los Angeles Examiner*. October 27, 1931: Los Angeles.

265. *Alameda Here Enroute South*, in *Daily Alaska Empire*. December 24, 1929: Juneau, AK. 7.

266. *Statement of BJ Mckinnel taken in chief of detectives Jos. F. Taylors Office at 9:20 PM October 20, 1931 in connection of with the murder of Miss Leroy and Miss Samuelson in Phoenix Arizona. Statement*

taken in the presence of chief of dets.Jos F. Taylor..... Questions of Lloyd Andrews, in *Winnie Ruth Judd Collection, Arizona State Archives*. October 20, 1931: Phoenix. Trunk Murderess Phoenix Officers File [Police Report].

267. Bechtel, EJ, *Statement of Mn C Judd taken in Chief of dtectives Joe Taylor's office at 8:10 PM October 20th 1931 in connection with the murder of Miss Leroy and Samuelson at Phoenix Arizona. Statement taken in the presence of the detectives Joe F. Taylor, Issp D. A. Davidson, Phoenix Officers L. Anerws Harry Johnson and J. Brinckerhoff. Notes by E. J. Bectel.*, in *Arizona State Archives and Public Records*. October 20, 1931: Phoenix, Arizona.

268. in *Wrangell Sentinal*. December 26, 1929: Wrangell, AK.

269. *An Enjoyable Christmas*, in *Wrangell Sentinel*. December 26, 1929: Wrangell, AK.

Section 3

1930-1931

1930
The population rises to 48,118 in Phoenix compared to 29,053 in 1920.[1]

1930, January 1
The Alaska-Juneau Gold Mining Company reports that 1929 was the best year recorded. Production was 3.5 million with an operating profit of 1.1 million. A total of 3,840,000 tons of ore was trammed out of the mine.[2]

1930, January 2
School resumes in Juneau.[3]

1930, January 5
Joe Crosson was flying a Waco and Harold Billan was close by in an open cockpit Stearman when they spotted the wreckage of Carl Ben Eielson who crashed on November 9.[4]

1930, January 27
Joe Crosson landed his search plane by the Nanuk and found Carl Ben Eielson's plane. He had crashed by flying into a hillside by a defective altimeter and they were killed instantly. Their bodies were recovered two weeks later.[5]

1930, February 1
Anne LeRoi stops working at the Wrangell General Hospital [6,7] Mrs. S. D. Grant of Wrangell took her place as nurse in charge. They stated Anne was leaving for Juneau.[8]

1930, February 8
Anne LeRoi leaves Wrangell on the Northwestern. (The Northwestern was in Wrangell on that Saturday).[7]

1930, February 9
Anne LeRoi arrives at 8 o'clock on Sunday night aboard the Steamer Northwestern from Wrangell. It was supposed to arrive in the morning but was delayed by snowstorms. The boat contained 11 day's worth of mail and even though it was Sunday night, it was sorted.[9] Ann LeRoi is originally registered at the Alaskan Hotel.[10]

1930, February
Anne LeRoi starts working at St. Ann's Hospital in Juneau.[11] St. Ann's was established in 1886 six years after gold was found in Juneau. It came to serve the miners. It was a Catholic hospital and school. Three Canadian Sisters of St. Ann from Victoria came to establish the hospital in an 18 by 24 foot house which was the former living quarters of the priest, Father Altoff who had first established the Catholic church in Juneau.[12]

1930, February 10
Thomas Scott who lived at the Gastineau Hotel and was a cashier of the Bank of Alaska at Cordova left Juneau with his wife and family and went home on the Northwestern.[13]

1930, February 15
Sammy meets Anne LeRoi in Juneau Alaska.[14] Some sources say they met in the hospital in Wrangell[15, 16] A blizzard starts in Juneau.[2]

1930, February 17
It snowed three feet in Juneau during the past three days. Traffic is limited to delivery trucks and few of them are running. The snowplow kept most streets open except on Starr Hill and in the Seater Tract.[2]

1930, February 20
A roller skating rink opens in Juneau. All skates were in use and some brought their own. 172 skaters attended and there were over 100 spectators.[17]

1930, February 22

The grammar school students gave a program this afternoon to honor Washington. The first 4 grades did the Star Spangled Banner. The third graders did Soldier Boy and Ten Little Soldiers.[18]

1930, March 8

Bob Ellis marries Margaret Roehr.[19]

1930, March 14

Ruth writes the following letter (from where is not determinable but it seems like she was in Mexico): "Dear Mamma, I was just thinking tonight about all the queer things Mexicans eat. When I first came to Mexico, I was so full of surprises. I used to write you what shocking things I heard every day. Well, now I'm so used to things, I guess there is really lots of interesting things I don't tell any more. The Mexicans eat monkeys, parrots, and lizards. An American doctor two miles from here was out one day, and ate at the house where he was. They had soup. It was real good until he noticed a tiny skull in his plate, and to his horror, it looked like an embryo baby. He found it was a monkey! Imagine! Lizards or iguanas have a very white meat and are more tender than chicken. I've never eaten any, although I have their skins made into shoes. In markets, one can buy the Magua worm, sometimes fresh; usually dry. It is a thick, white soft worm, and is found in cactus. They remind me of naked caterpillars. Mexicans eat them. Then too they eat a large, red ant, which they dry. It is sour. They eat burros, too. They also eat cactus; cut the thorns off and eat it. They eat two different cactus fruits; make pulque and tequila broth from it as well as rope and a wadding to stuff pillows. Oh, so many things out of cactus! They make soup out of fish heads. I tasted it once. It's terrible. Down around Mazatlán those Indians eat alligator eggs. The yolk is all. You should see how they eat! I received your letter today. I'll look and see if Dale's letter's still around. I meant to send it. I don't know what to write Sylvia. We've never written. You can write her things I can't. She's near you. Well, I'll write tomorrow. Stay in bed. Lovingly, Ruth"[20]

1930, April 4

Samuel Samuelson (Sammy's Brother) passed the Minnesota State Board Examinations; Medical Boards.[21]

1930, April 23
Captain Lathrop comes through Juneau on the Northwestern. He is headed for Washington DC. He is the Republican National Committeeman from Alaska. He expected to return to Alaska on June 1.[22]

1930, April 25
Bob Ellis brings the Taku to Juneau for the first time. The Taku is a Lockhead Vega almost identical to the Juneau or the Ketchikan. The Taku has red trim on the top of its wings. The Juneau and the Ketchikan had yellow wings and a yellow section on the nose. He came with Frank Hatcher and three passengers, Mrs. Ellis (Bride of the Month), A. B. Hayes, and commissioner WE Winn. Peg Ellis planned to make Juneau her home for the summer. It flew from Seattle to Ketchikan to Juneau. There were no plans at the time, except a rumor that regular Juneau – Seattle service would be offered. Those interested in transport were advised to see Larry Parks on Willoughby Avenue. There was excellent weather for the entire trip.[23]

1930, April 26
Bob Ellis and his wife Peg are staying at the Gastineau Hotel in Juneau.[24] Bob Ellis flies a group to Sitka via the Taku.[23]

1930, Spring?
Ruth says Anne and Sammy are jealous of another teacher, "Tommy" because the boys thought so much of her. So one night they took her with some other boys from Juneau and stripped her clothes and shoes off. It caused quite a stir in Juneau.[25] The other 4th grade teacher was Donie Taylor. (Could this be Tommy?) She taught in Juneau at least from 1926-1931.[26]

1930, May
Ruth and Dr. Judd decide to go to El Paso and Ruth should return to Indiana for a long visit and that when Dr. Judd found another job, he would contact her to come back.[27] Dr. Judd on the stand says that they came out of Mexico at Eagle Pass. He bought Ruth a ticket to go back to Indiana. Dr. Judd went on to El Paso. Shortly afterward Ruth called him in El Paso and told him that she had sold her ticket to Indiana and had purchased one to Mexico City instead. She had only 16 dollars left and it was not enough for her to continue her journey. She told him that she didn't know why she had bought a ticket to go to Mexico

4

City.[28] Ruth stated to one of the alienists that she had a two- year-old named John Robert and he would have been about two during the trial. Because of jealously, her husband had her mother come and take the baby back to Indiana with her. A short time later she said she had heard that the baby was in San Antonio. When asked she said that many people had told her so and that she was receiving messages or hearing voices. Later he said she went to San Antonio to the Robert E. Lee Hotel under an assumed name, Mary Deare. The other names she went by were Mary Deere, either Lola or Lucy Ryder and Marion Loker. She rode around on the street car looking for her baby.[29] An account from one of the psychiatrists states that she said she was at the Robert Lee Hotel in San Antonio since she thought her baby was there. She decided to go to Mexico City to find her mother who had it. She got as far as Eagle Pass and then decided to go back to El Paso. From there she went on to Phoenix.[29] However, Ruth doesn't go to Indiana but plans to go to LA instead and get a job with a woman who worked in a beauty parlor who promised her work. She starts off for LA, but the car breaks down in Phoenix and Ruth decides to stay there and work.[27] When they got to Phoenix, they got a little apartment together for the night. In Ruth's words, she decided to stay in Phoenix, because when she was in LA her tuberculosis became active. Also, the stores were not employing girls at that time. The first thing she did was to visit two hospitals and told them that she wasn't a nurse, but that she had experience helping in a hospital and that she had worked previously in a state hospital. They didn't have anything, but they told her to go to the registries. She also went personally to several doctors around town.[30] She stated that the first two days she worked in a kitchen for her meals.[31] There was nothing, so she went back to the apartment and got a phone call. Two days later, she got a call and said for her to come over to a certain office in the Westward Ho Hotel. Ruth went to the YWCA. There was a postman's wife, that wanted somebody just in the morning and it was only a dollar a morning with carfare. She thought this was enough to live on and it would give her the afternoon to look for a better position. She took this job and the woman's name was Newman. She went and met with the people at the Westward Ho. This is the suite of Mr. Leigh Ford. His secretary talked to her and she said Mr. Ford's wife was ill and that she had tuberculosis and was in the Good Samaritan Hospital. He hired her since they wanted someone who wouldn't "grate on her nerves by being with her constantly", and Ruth looked like a quiet person who would take good care of her. She took the job (see June 24?)[30] The Ford children at this time were in Chicago.[30] Mrs. Ford stated, "You are awfully young, my dear, but I like your looks and so I will engage you."[30] Ruth stated she had this job for 5 months.[30] She met Jack Halloran about this time. Jack was a close friend of the family of this patient.[32] They paid her ninety dollars a month with her room and board.[33] Ruth stated that she had met Mrs. Halloran since she and Mrs. Ford were good friends. She met her before "she went over on the boat" and again when she came back. Jack came over every day. If he wasn't in the house, he was talking to them through the screen porch.[34]

1930, May 11
Bob Ellis has a busy day with the Taku on Sunday, May 11, 1930 in Juneau. Going to the Pacific American Fisheries Plant on Excursion Inlet in the morning, the pilot carried forty passengers aloft on sightseeing trips. For a round trip out of Juneau he had carried, Miss Anne LeRoy, Miss Hedvig Samuelson, Margaret "Peg" Ellis, Larry Parks and AB Cot Hayes. About 2 he returned to the capital city to bring in his round-trippers and gas up.[19] AB Cot Hayes was the manager for the airlines in Juneau.[19] At the PA plant, 41 passengers were taken up for short flights.[35]

1930, May 12
Dorothy Chisholm returns to her position in the Juneau Public Schools. She had been in the hospital at St. Ann's for two weeks.[36]

1930, May 16
James Cann who owned part of the Gastineau Hotel sold his share to John Biggs. James Cann had bad health (had been treated at Mayo) and wanted to renew his mining activities on the Apex-El Nido Group at Lisiansill. So, he and his wife planned to move there.[37]

1930, May 29
School closes for the year at 1 in the afternoon in Juneau. Report cards were given out and students were dismissed.[38]

1930, June 1
Cap. Lathrop expected to return to Alaska about this time from his trip to Washington DC.[22]

1930, June 2

Jack Halloran registers at the Luhrs Hotel in room 9.[39]

1930, June 3

The paper states that Sammy is going to attend the University of Chicago for the summer. Dorothy Israel went to her family in Dayton, Washington. Dalma Hansen went to the University of Washington. Dorothy Chisholm went to Wrangell.[40]

1930, June 6

Jack Halloran registers at the Luhrs Hotel in room 2.[39]

1930, June 13

Sammy leaves Juneau on the Princess Louise for Vancouver at 5:30.[41]

1930, June 24

Ruth applies for work through the YMCA after being rejected at Good Samaritan Hospital.[42] Ruth Judd starts working for the Ford family in Arizona. They had three small children.[43] Mrs. Leigh Ford said Ruth came to her with such a sweet face and such a pleasant personality. She pleaded for the position and told her that she was the mother of a three-month old baby. She stated that her mother in Indiana had the child.[44] They paid her $90 a month and she lived at their house at 28 W. Monroe St. She worked for them for 4-5 months. She left to take another position at the County Physician for $125 per month. The children missed her when she left. They lived next door to Jack Halloran and were very friendly with him. During the time that she lived there she only went out 4-5 times with a doctor from Glendale. Ruth talked about her own baby.[43] He stated that they got her from the YWCA and that she didn't have any money. He stated he lived next door to Jack Halloran and was very friendly with him and thought that he would be a much better witness for the defense than the prosecution. He stated that after the crime he had not seen her since her employment and that he was in New York when the murders happened and read about them in New York papers. He stated that while she stayed at the house he did not think that she left the house in the evening more than four or five times and on those times a doctor from Glendale (Leff) called to take her out for just a short drive. She talked about her own baby during this time and he thought this was the only queer thing he knew about her.[43]

7

1930, July 8

Ruth produces a picture of her 3 month old baby. Dr. Judd is also in the picture. She stated it was quite the coincidence since her baby's birthday was January 29, the same as one of Mrs. Ford's children (and her own). She stated how lonely she was without him. This was actually a child from a family called Dyer. Her duties at the Fords were initially to cook the meals and take care of Mrs. Ford. She did the chores she knew very well. For the housework chores she did not know; she was a hopeless pupil unwilling to learn.[44]

1930 Summer

Sammy attended the Chicago Normal School for 7 weeks.[45]. She called on several faculty members and students at the Minot Normal School [46]

1930 August

Sammy visited her brother Sam in Minneapolis.[47] Dr. Judd enters the hospital at Whipple for treatment and remains there until January 1.[48] Dr. Maudlin who was not yet the county physician made his acquaintance. Dr. Judd had come to his office as he had just returned from Mexico. He came for consultation and advice re his drug addiction. Dr. Maudlin treated him for several weeks. He got him admission at Whipple Barracks Veteran's Bureau where he stayed for several months. Ruth came to call on him several times to inquire concerning his condition.[49] Tom Frelinghuysen wrote to Sammy for the first time from the Princess Louise in August 1930, likely after August 26 when Sammy arrived in Juneau since she was on the Princess Louise. She met him on the boat?[50] – There is some other reference of her meeting somebody on a steamer.

1930, August 26

Sammy arrives in Juneau on the Princess Louise from Vancouver with six other passengers. One of the passengers was V. H. DeBolt who is the school superintendent who arrived to help in preparations for the starting of school.[51]

1930, September 2

School starts in Juneau Alaska. There are 533 registered in the morning hours. There were 43 registered for the third grade and 39 for the fourth grade.[52] The third grade teacher was Donie Taylor, the fourth grade teacher was Dalma Hanson, and Hedvig taught 3rd and 4th grades. Dorothy Israel is the high school English teacher.[53] New automatic electric clocks were installed in the schools and the floors were painted.[53]

1930, September 6
The Glacier Road is completed. People can now drive to the Mendenhall Glacier and Park. There is room for 100 cars to park there on the Spur Road off of the Glacier Highway.[54] There is a picture of Sammy skating in front of the Mendenhall Glacier with a black leather jacket and white hat. It seems to be from the West Glacier side where the skater's cabin was built later on in the Thirties.[55]

1930, September 8
The schools show so much growth that Mildred Abrahamsen is called back to teach even though she resigned last spring. Sammy is now teaching the second-third grade combination. New rooms are being completed at the school to accommodate the influx of students.[56]

1930 September
Sammy is diagnosed with TB, a few weeks after school started. Residents of Juneau raise a fund to send her to Arizona as she was without funds.[57] She is admitted to St. Ann's Hospital in September.[11] Austin Lathrop raised "$1000 – some say $2500 – for Sammy". They pay the expenses of both Anne LeRoi and Sammy to head south.[58] Marion Alvina Vrem stated that her friends in Juneau contributed to a purse of $900 to assist her in moving.[59] Another story states that funds were raised by the board of education and the school teachers in Juneau.[60] Anna Evans, nurse, claimed that the girls told her this.[61] Another account states that Captain A. E. Lathrop, wealthy Alaska theater owner and political leader, had raised a fund of $1000 to aid Miss Hedvig Samuelson.[62] Captain Lathrop wired Sammy from Healey Alaska, "Received your letter today. Deeply grieved over your condition. Hope with rest and good care that you will soon restore your good health and be able to resume your work. Am mailing you check for five hundred, stop, will be glad to hear from you." Signed, A. E. Lathrop.[63] According to Evelyn Nace, the girls shared expenses 50/50 and that Sammy had taken two 500 dollar loans and was living off of those.[64] Tuberculosis deaths and mortality rates in Alaska in 1930 were: White deaths from TB, 11, Native deaths from TB, 224. TB mortality for whites was 37 per 100,000 and 741 for Natives while the US TB Mortality rate was 71 per 100,000.[65] Ruth arranges for Dr.

Judd to be treated at the Veterans' Hospital in Prescott. Dr. Judd leaves El Paso.[27] Ruth had gone to Tucson first. She went to the Veteran's hospital to see if she could get a job. The nurse suggested that she go to Phoenix and go through nurse's training. She stated that her brother would help her. Dr. Judd was staying at the Del Norte Hotel in El Paso. So, she came to Phoenix. She went to the nurse's registry. She went to Good Samaritan Hospital stating that she wasn't a nurse, but could help somebody at home who was leaving the hospital and needed help taking their medicine on time. She also went to St. Joseph's Hospital. Sister Minica was the nurse there then. She stated that she didn't know how to do anything. She and Father Emmett talked it over. Ruth stated that she didn't know a soul in Phoenix. Dr. Leff was standing behind her. She had known him from Mexico. He was practicing in Phoenix.[33] Dr. Leff confirms this. He said "he only saw her a few times during the period which intervened before she came to Phoenix a little over a year ago and only a few days ago after she arrived in Phoenix. I met her in St. Joseph's Hospital. She told me that it would be necessary for her to have some work and I agreed to help her in any way I could. During the next several months I saw her perhaps twice a week and she was quite often a visitor in our home." He said after that he still saw her about once a week.[66] Ruth is living with a family in Phoenix. Dr. Judd is in the Veterans Hospital dealing with his addiction. Ruth is taking care of a man's wife. They have three children (12, 9, 6 years old) who return home to attend school. Ruth adores them.[67] (This must be Mr. And Mrs. Leigh Ford - See December) Ruth meets Jack Halloran at the Ford home. She often sat out on the steps in the evenings with him telling him about the Doctor and Mexico. Occasionally, they would go for a drive or swimming at the County Club, late.[67] They had given her a red "comfort".[25]

1930, October 2
Sammy leaves Juneau AK with Anne LeRoi on the Steamship Admiral Rogers for Seattle. Originally, their destination was Laguna Beach California. Miss Mildred Keaton, Red Cross Nurse employed by the school board, began the physical examination of the public school pupils. She started her examinations in the grade school and will continue them until she has completed both grade and high schools. The examinations are required by territorial law.[68] According to Evelyn Nace of Phoenix, Anne did not want "Sammy to die in the cold-hearted North". Sammy rode in a stretcher the whole way.[64]

1930, October 4

Mabel Monson arrives in Juneau to take Sammy's place in the school system. She is assigned Sammy's second grade class. She arrives on the steamship Yukon from Seattle.[69]

1930, October 7

Ruth Nellie Rinehart, a beautiful Portland nurse, vanishes from the steamer Princess Louise while on route to Portland from Wrangell. She was a friend of Agnes (Anne) Imlah LeRoi. Anne's parents stated that they were all in Wrangell together. (Says two or three friends) Mrs. LeRoi saw Mrs. Rinehart off on the Princess Louise when she left Wrangell to sail south. Anne's family stated she was reluctant to discuss details of it.[70]

1930, October 7-11

Anne and Sammy arrive in Seattle and stay at the Frye Hotel. They both have x-rays taken and Anne LeRoi discovers she shows traces of having TB too.[71] William Mason, Anne's ex-husband is working in Portland and she calls him from a downtown hotel. William Mason goes down to visit them. There was a girl with Anne that he assumed was Miss Samuelson.[72]

1930, October 9

Cap. Lathrop writes to Sammy to say that he received her letters of September 2 and October 5. He states that he had wired her. The letter goes on, "Sammy dear, I was sure shocked when I read your letter. Why did you wait until the last thing before writing me? You might know I would be glad to do anything within the bounds of reason for you, even though I don't know you so very well. But Sammy, you made a good impression on me and that is enough."[50] Somewhere about this time Mrs. C. E. Richmond of McKinley Park writes Sammy a letter on letterhead of the superintendent. It's a six-page letter. The letter confirms the friendly interest of Cap. Lathrop. She wrote, "Captain Lathrop was on the train when we went to Anchorage. We all had dinner together and poor captain was all upset over your illness and talked of nothing else all through dinner." She also wrote, "You are quite a popular girl in Alaska right now, Sammy, but no fooling, if you hadn't been so popular your illness would not have stirred up everybody so honestly, we are all sick about it."[50] Mrs. Richmond also mentions sending Sammy a small check she had received for serving on an election board.[50]

1930 October

Sammy visited Dr. J.M. Odell in Portland Oregon (probably LA, but they first met in Portland).[73] J. H. Cameron, San Francisco publisher met Anne LeRoi and Sammy at the dock in San Francisco. He worked in the Crocker Building. Sammy had written him and asked him to meet them. He met Anne LeRoi for the first time. He thought Anne was a pleasant and intelligent sort of woman. He wished them luck and he never saw them again. His name appeared in Sammy's address book and he stated that he met her in Juneau in 1928 and he went riding with her once or twice. He described her as a nice sort of girl, but shy.[74] They stopped in Los Angeles where specialists told them to go to Phoenix.[11] James Odell examines Anne LeRoi in Los Angeles when she suspects she might have TB as well.[75] Sammy came with her. Anne said that she thought that she had contracted the disease in Alaska or from Sammy.[76] She told James Odell that she was taking Sammy to Phoenix. James Odell worked at 814 Brockman Building in Los Angeles.[76] They visited the brother of William Mason, Anne LeRoi's first husband, Dr. Burgess B. Mason, who was the owner of the hospital at Laguna Beach. Sammy was initially brought there to the hospital for treatment but a specialist referred her to the drier air of Phoenix.[77] Ten days after their arrival, Anne returns to Portland for three months. Sammy collapsed the following day, but refused to remain in a sanitarium and finally Mrs. Evans, a fifty-year-old nurse obtained an apartment in a duplex where Mr. and Mrs. Judd were living. (This last part is definitely wrong; this was much later; this is most likely when Anne went to Portland the following June.) (Perhaps, Sammy collapsed then and then went to Pearl Waggoner's)[60] In a way, it sort of seems that Anna Evans may have come with Anne and Sammy from Laguna Beach to Phoenix. "Mrs. Anna Evans, a nurse, located here tonight by police said she went to Phoenix to nurse both Miss Samuelson and Mrs. LeRoi when they were sent there from Juneau, suffering from tuberculosis."[78]

1930, October 18

Sammy writes in her diary, "Doctor O'Dell came up and we have decided to go to Phoenix, Arizona."[79] Cap. Lathrop wires Sammy while she is at Laguna Beach saying "Your letter received, wired you immediately, was advised you had left for Laguna Beach. Telegram mailed from Juneau. Wire me collect your address and funds necessary. Will wire bank Seattle to forward you money as requested.

Am very sorry for delay, writing you fully".[50]

1930, October 19
Sammy writes in her diary, "Dr. O'Dell drove us to the station. Almost missed our train. Leave at 6 o'clock tonight."[79]

1930, October 20
Sammy writes in her diary, "Woke up in Phoenix this morning. Stayed at the Westward Hotel."[79]

1930, October 21
Sammy is examined by her Phoenix Doctor, Victor Randolph for the first time.[80] Sammy writes in her diary, "Went up to see Dr. Randolph this morning. Loads of tests taken."[79]

1930, October 22
Sammy writes in her diary, "Moved into the cutest little house. Sure we are going to like it."[79] They first lived at 528 W. Portland St. in a duplex in Phoenix.[81]

1930, October 23
Sammy writes in her diary, "A nice hot day".[79]

1930, October 24
Sammy writes in her diary, "Mr. MacIntyre came over".[79]

1930, October 25
Dr. Randolph asked Anne to go on a case about midnight.[79]

1930, October 26
Sammy records in her diary, "Anne came home about 1:30".[79]

1930, October 27
Sammy writes in her diary, "Got a telegram from Captain" (Probably Captain Lathrop).[79] It might be this telegram (or the one put in Sept). Sammy receives another telegram from Austen Lathrop, "Your letter received. Wired you immediately. Was advised you had left for Laguna Beach. Telegram mailed from Juneau. Wire me collect your address and funds necessary. Will wire bank Seattle to forward you money as requested. Am very sorry for delay, Writing you fully."[63]

Another source stated that Cap. Lathrop wired Sammy from Healy to Sammy at 529 West Portland in Phoenix stating "Received your letter today. Am very happy that you feel so encouraged. Have wired Pacific National Bank of Seattle to forward you five hundred dollars. Write often, I want to know how you are progressing".[50]

1930, October 28
Sammy writes in her diary, "Our phonograph finally arrived".[79]

1930, October 29
Sammy wrote in her diary, "Waited for Doctor but he didn't come".[79]

1930, October 30
Sammy wrote in her diary, "Dr. Randolph tried to collapse my right lung, but it wouldn't work."[79] The deed of the house at 2929 North 2nd street was transferred from The O'Malley Lumber Company to O'Malley Investment Company by JG O'Malley President. On the same day it was transferred from the O'Malley Investment Company to the Mitchell Investment Company by JG O'Malley President.[82]

1930, October 31
Sammy wrote in her diary, "Anne went downtown to look for work."[79]

1930, November
Ruth Judd lived at 2201 North Richland according to John Ralston. She lived there until about March of 1931.[83] Ruth works as a live in nurse for Mr. And Mrs. Lee Ford.[84] Little Johanna Ford ran up to Jack one Sunday and told him that Ruthie was leaving. Jack came to the other side of the house, and asked what was wrong and why Ruth was leaving. She stated that she could get a job at the county doctor's office for $125 a month. She was getting 80 dollars a month plus room and board at the Fords. Jack advised her not to leave. Ruth wanted to go since she had to work early morning until late at night. The Fords decided to get another girl and cut her salary. Ruth left shortly afterwards.[85] Ruth weeps going through the baby clothes that Mrs. Ford has. Her children had grown out of them. Mrs. Ford said to take them for her baby. Ruth said she would send them to her baby. Instead later they were found discarded in the garage rolled in a bundle and tossed into a corner. It also became known that Ruth kept a gun with her. It was tossed recklessly among some of her baggage. It was

forwarded to her in Phoenix from Dr. Judd who had been in El Paso. It was just sitting in her room. She was admonished and asked to hide it to keep it away from the children's reach. Something happened between Ruth and another maid in the household, an Indian girl. The maid left without explaining the reason for her hasty departure. Later they learned that Ruth Judd was responsible.[44]

1930, November 1
Sammy wrote in her diary, "Letter from Sister Mary Edwards".[79]

1930, November 4
Sammy wrote in her diary, "Fever 103".[79]

1930, November 5
Sammy wrote in her diary, "Fever 103, Again".[79]

1930, November 6
Sammy wrote in her diary, "Dr. Randolph's Office".[79]

1930, November 7
Sammy wrote in her diary, "Fever".[79]

1930, November 8
Ruth asked Dr. Maudlin about the position at the County Physician Office. Dr. Maudlin met his acquaintance. Dr. Judd had come to his office as he had just returned from Mexico. He came for consultation and advice regarding his drug addiction. Dr. Maudlin treated him for several weeks. He got him admission at Whipple Barracks Veteran's Bureau where he stayed for several months. Ruth came to call on him several times to inquire concerning his condition.[49] Ruth stated that the county medical office needed a girl who could interpret for them. Ruth felt that her peon Spanish was good enough. She got the job. For at least a while Mrs. Ford offered her a small room and her supper each night. She had to be there with the children and see that they got their studies down, and that they get ready in the morning to go to school. She did this for a while when working for the County doctor's office.[33] Ruth worked for Dr. Brown who was the county physician, for 3 weeks about a year before the crime. His nurse had become ill and he called for a relief nurse. Ruth was sent to him. He stated Ruth wanted the job very badly, saying she had a small child in Los Angeles to support.

She went to work for him but she was both erratic and incompetent. Once she started to drop carbolic acid into a baby's eyes instead of boric acid. Dr. Brown went to her home that night and notified her that she was discharged. Ruth cried and became hysterical. There was a man there with her. He stated that he was a big politician here in Phoenix and that he would take care of him for discharging her. The next day Ruth went into the office and wouldn't leave. He had to call a policeman to have her taken out. He saw her several days on the streets and avoided her. One day in a downtown corner, she came up to him and said, "I've got a good notion doctor to shoot your head off with my gun." He remembers very distinctly her saying her gun. Dr. Brown thought that he often noticed how dreamy Ruth's eyes were. He thought it was possible that she was a user of some minor drug.[86] Ruth stated that she worked with a county doctor for a while and had gone over to the jail and helped in cases there, but that those experiences she was sure, played no part in preparing her for her reactions.[87] Dr. Brown stated that she contacted the Board of Supervisors demanding reinstatement. They refused to interfere. When she met him on the corner he had turned away from her, but she grabbed his coat lapels and threatened him by saying, "I should get my gun and blow your head off!"[49] Dr. C. W. Brown discharges Ruth at the clinic and Ruth threatens to "Blow his Head Off". Ruth stated she was the only girl in the county doctor's office. There was no county hospital then. She stated that she worked here until there was a change of politics.[33] Ruth claims that she only worked for him for a few days. She said it was a political job. He said to her, "Ah, listen kid, you are not meant for an office. You are a housewife; that is what you are. You were good enough and so forth, but you don't know politics."[30] She claimed he offered her another position after that.[30] Dr. Percy Brown, the x-ray man at the Grunow clinic, visits Anne and Sammy on Portland Avenue. In the past, he had examined Sammy and had discussed her condition with Anne LeRoi. He talks to Anne and about working for him at the Grunow Clinic. Sammy is quite ill and was in bed.[88] Sammy mails a check to Dr. L. R. Packard of Whitehall Montana.[89] Sammy writes in her diary again, "Fever" [79]

1930, November 9
Sammy writes in her diary again, "Fever"[79]

1930, November 10

Sammy writes in her diary, "Feel better but my 'Temp' is still up".[79]

1930, November 11

This is Armistice Day. Ruth applies for a job at the office of Dr. H McKeown.[30] Dr. McKeown stated that he met her on Armistice Day and that she started working for him a few days later.[90] Sammy receives 3 letters that day. She writes in her diary, "First time my fever has been down for a week."[79]

1930, November 12

Ruth starts working for Dr. McKeown at his downtown office as his secretary and office nurse. She only got 75 dollars a month. She stated she previously was getting 125 dollars a month at the county doctor's office.[30] Dr. McKeown moved to the Grunow Clinic in January when it opened.[30] Dr. McKeown stated that her responsibilities were to take care of all telephone messages, convey them to him, make appointments, and receive patients as they came in. He stated he took the history himself in longhand, wrote it all out. Ruth would attend with him during the physical exam of many patients, especially the women. She also had the duty keeping the charges on the patients. She had a little book in which he entered the daily calls and charges. Ruth copied those into a ledger and kept the accounts each month. She made the statements and he looked them over and sent them out.[90] She also stated to him that she had a child and showed him pictures. He was a little curly haired boy. It was a dark eyed youngster with a hat on as he remembers, a sombrero.[90]

1930, November 13

Sammy writes in her diary, "Dr. Randolph was over."[79]

1930, November 14

Sammy writes in her diary, "Received the books from Tom."[79] Tom Frelinghuysen?

1930, November 17

Sammy writes in her diary, "Birthday again. Package arrived from Anna."[79] The paper thinks this is Anne LeRoi. I bet it's from her sister Anna in Chicago.

17

1930, November 18
Sammy writes in her diary, "Read all day."[79]

1930, November 19
Sammy writes in her diary, "Anne went to work this morning."[79]

1930, November 20
Sammy writes in her diary, "Mother sent a check for my birthday."[79]

1930, November 21
Sammy writes in her diary, "Anne's home again today."[79]

1930, November 23
Sammy writes in her diary, "Anne read the Yellow Mistletoe to me."[79]

1930, November 24
Repeated entry in Sammy's diary, "Package from Anna for my birthday."[79]

1930, November 25
Sammy wrote in her diary, "Lots of mail today."[79]

1930, November 26
Sammy wrote in her diary, "Washed my hair. Package from Alvina."[79] Alvina is listed in her address book as Alvina Admiral Farragut, P.S.S Co. 424 Ellis, San Francisco, Cal.[91]

1930, November 27
Sammy wrote in her diary, "Anne made a lovely 'Thanksgiving Dinner.'"[79]

1930, November 28
Sammy wrote in her diary, "Dr. and Mrs. Mason visited us in the evening."[79] Burgess B Mason was the owner of the hospital at Laguna Beach and the brother of Anne's Ex-husband.[77]

1930, November 29
Sammy wrote in her diary, "Just another Saturday."[79]

1930, November 30
Sammy wrote in her diary, "Anne went for a ride. Such a lovely day."[79]

1930, December
Dr. Percy Brown visits the girls who are living on Portland Street. He went there to discuss the terms and arrangement of Anne coming to work at the clinic. At the time he was introduced to Sammy who was lying in bed fairly sick.[92]

1930, December 1
Sammy wrote in her diary, "One grand day for the first of December."[79]

1930, December 8
Ruth or Dr. Judd pawns her gun for $2.25, a 25 auto 27573 at 236 E Washington Street. Mack Gardner Loan, Inc. Loan and Diamond Brokers. It was signed WC Judd.[93]

1930, December 15
Betty Murray stated that Ruth moved in with her at Monte Vista duplex for three months (until March 1).[94] She said that during this time, Ruth attended night school three nights a week to learn stenography. She washed out her uniforms for the clinic three nights a week. She spent her Sundays cleaning the apartment. Occasionally, she would go out for an automobile ride and this was her only recreation. She stated that when she got the position at the clinic it was with the understanding that she would learn shorthand. She had typing experience but no shorthand. She never had more than three uniforms and every day her work required a clean one. Naturally this meant the evenings away from school she had to spend washing, ironing, and studying. She kept at this all of the time she lived with her until Dr. Judd came back to Phoenix. "Ruth had her little peculiarities. All of us have." I used to say to her, "Ruth, I don't understand you at times" and she would tell me, "Well, Betty, you have too. I don't understand some of the things you do." There were times I thought Ruth was a little flighty. In the midst of a conversation she would suddenly switch to an entirely different subject and she would do little things for no apparent reason. She stated that it is hard for her to understand many of the stories being circulated. Ruth didn't know how to dance. She couldn't. She didn't know how. I never saw her smoke and as far as I know of or ever heard, she neither had the time nor the opportunities to go on the "wild parties" they talk about. One can't imagine the Ruth I knew throwing herself into tantrums of rage. I know there must have been times when she would have been justified in displaying a temper if she had one.

19

She said that Ruth as a woman, too kind, too generous, always flashes before her.[94] Ruth pawns her handgun. She states to the pawnshop owner, "I might as well get rid of this because I wouldn't know what I could ever do with it." She stated that she needed the money to buy gifts for two sick friends. (However, I don't believe that she had met Anne or Sammy yet)[95] Dr. Judd stated that he had given this gun to her in Mexico and she was afraid of it. She would never shoot it. Dr. Judd had bought her a box of cartridges, but she never used it and it became lost. During the fall of 1930 she bought another box of cartridges.[96] Metra Halnan stated that she came over several times to borrow things. One time, Betty was ill and asked her to do her work in the living room. At that time, she did not know anything about shorthand or stenography. One time she came over to borrow a food grinder to make mulched rabbit for the doctor. One time she borrowed clothes pins since she ran out. She never had parties. You could hear her typing at night on the dining room table and she retired early every night. On Sunday or early evening she saw several cars parked there.[97] Cap. Lathrop writes Sammy a cheer up letter on his Healy River Coal Corporation stationary stating that he would like to see her when he made his trip outside, but is afraid that he cannot.[50] Betty Murray said that Ruth owned a gun.[14] Jack phones her at 2201 N Richland frequently, but Ruth says she only went out with him a few times.[67] When Dr. Judd returned the three of them lived together for a while.[84] Mrs. Murray "kicked her out".[98] John Ralston was the landlord.[98] Betty Murray was the historian at Deaconess Hospital.[99] Another source says she was the historian at Good Samaritan Hospital.[84] (Deaconess is the former name of Good Samaritan Hospital).

1930, December 24
Ruth is in Phoenix alone on Christmas Eve. She is worried about her husband's drug addiction. Jack Halloran comes to her apartment for the first time. He had been kind to her in the past, but they had not been close. Jack Halloran stayed at her apartment and they had intimate relations for the first time.[100]

1930, December 25
Ruth helps out at the Ford house with the Christmas dinner. She is fascinated by a toy drum and says how much her baby would like it. She was so interested in it that they gave it to her. She said she would send it to her baby.[101]

1930, Christmas
Burton takes a holiday job at the South Pacific train station in Los Angeles.[102]

1931, January 1
Dr. Judd leaves the hospital at Whipple where he has been since the previous August.[48] He tells Dr. Maudlin that he believes that he is completely cured.[49] Dr. Judd remained at the VA hospital until this January. Not knowing where to go next, he decides to go to Santa Monica where his sister lived and where he could receive regular care. He goes to Phoenix to see Ruth, but she is gloomy and moody. He decides to stay with her for a few weeks before going to his sisters.[27] He could receive free care at the VA hospital in Santa Monica. He stays with Ruth a few weeks (on Brill?) before going on to Santa Monica. Dr. Judd discovered that now, he and Ruth were husband and wife in name only. He stated that Ruth's fever exercised a dominant influence over the sex life of the patient. Ruth's natural youthful appetite for sex was intensified by the fever of her complaint. However, when he was in Phoenix she exhibited none of those former physical passions. Her attitude toward him was more like daughter/father. He sensed something was wrong and her black moods continued.[27]

1931, January 2
The Louis Grunow Clinic in Phoenix opens at Tenth and McDowell.[67] Lester Byron, a Phoenix architect designed the building which cost $250,000 to build. It had the largest medical library in the state as well as its own laboratory, pharmacy and radiology departments. When the clinic opened it had 13 specialists.[103] Since the community did not have a medical school at the time, a medical library was included off of the memorial hall that was open to any medical doctor practicing in the area. All profits for the clinic were put into maintaining and updating the library. The clinic was originally one level with a large patio on the back. This allowed for back entrances. Parking was on the side of the laboratory. (This brochure has a map of the original rooms of the clinic) The patio contained a sunken garden. The grounds had a lawn, trees, flowers, and shrubs. Clinicians were independent, but worked in a collaborative way.[104] Ruth Judd took a job at the clinic. She still lives with the Ford family. In exchange for a bed and an evening meal, Ruth takes care of the Ford children in the evenings, helping them with homework, giving them baths, and getting them to bed.[67] Dr. McKeown arranges for a job for Ruth at the clinic.[84] Dr. McKeown was a chest expert and moved

his offices to the new clinic. At this time, he stated that he would have adjoining offices with the man who did the general examinations. He told Ruth, "I don't know exactly what you are going to do. You are going to take shorthand though. Learn shorthand and learn to take dictation."[30] Ruth is forced to attend business college three nights a week since dictation was necessary for her job at the clinic.[67] On this day, she wanted to see the whole building as she had never been there before.[85] Mrs. Anna Evans, a 50 year old nurse introduces her to Anne LeRoi.[60] She wandered into the X-Ray area and encountered Anne LeRoi. Ruth described her as very beautiful although she didn't take a good picture. Anne said, "I am Anne LeRoi," with a big smile, "and you"? Ruth replied, "I am Ruth Judd," and they talked for a while. Ruth talked about being in Mexico and Anne talked about being in Alaska, from opposite poles, you might say. She also mentioned Sammy on that day and asked if she wanted to meet her. Since the Drs. were always referring cases to X-ray, Ruth often brought patients down there to the care of Anne LeRoi. Ruth described her as always gracious and their work was very close together. Ruth stated that Anne at the time stated that she was supporting Sammy, which was not true.[85] Anne was one of the first employees working there.[84] Ruth Judd meets Anne LeRoi and Sammy.[84] Evelyn Nace meets Anne LeRoi at the Clinic.[105] Soon after Ruth borrows money from Dr. Leff so she can start night school to learn dictation.[30]

1931, January 4
Sammy wrote in her diary:

> God made man frail as a bubble,
> God made love: love made trouble.
> God made wine--was it a sin
> That man took wine to drown trouble in? [14]
> Oliver Herford.[106]

1931, January 6
Sammy wrote in her diary, "Behaviorist. I am what I am. I shall do what I shall do because of the Mendelian laws of heredity and the physical reflexes developed in my childhood. This is wisdom--to love-- to live, to take what fate the gods may give."[14] This last sentence is from the Laurence Hope poem, "The Teak Forest".[107] Another diary article includes more of this poem although, it says that she wrote it in the summer. This is the expanded excerpt. "You are wise. You take

22

what the gods have sent. You ask no questions but rest content. When I am with you, you take my kiss. And perhaps, I value you more for this. For this is wisdom to live, take what fate the gods may give; To ask no questions to make no prayer; To kiss the lips, to caress the hair; Speed passions ebb as you greet its flow. To have to hold and in time-let go!"[108] This is somewhat paraphrased from the actual poem. Her handwriting is not shown for this either. Ruth states that it is actually the front of the diary that said, "I am what I am because of the Mendelian laws of hereditary and habits formed in my childhood. It is as normal for me to love a woman as for some women to love a man" She stated that Sherriff McFadden told her this.[67]

1931, January 7
Sammy wrote in her diary, "Now I am a hedonist. Follower of the doctrine that pleasure is the chief end of man"[109] This sounds like a quote much like the one from the January 6. (? Source)

1931, January 10
Dr. Judd comes to live in Phoenix for the first time. He and Ruth live at the corner of Monte Vista Road and Richland. (2210 North Richland [48] (Is this Betty's Murray's house?) (On his way to CA for a few weeks?) Dr. Judd stated he was in Phoenix for two or three months.[96]

1931, Mid-January
Anne takes Ruth over to the house to meet Sammy. Ruth stated that Sammy was lovely too and that she always took a good picture.[85] Betty Murray stated that when she first met Anne and Sammy she was elated with having formed this friendship. After Dr. Judd had returned and she was still living with her she stated how brilliant Anne was and how sweet Sammy appeared.[94]

1931, January 21
Sammy wrote in her diary, "One day like all the others. How can I fill these pages?"[109]

1931, Early February
Dr. Judd meets Sammy for the first time. He sees her about twice a week.[110] Sammy and Anne LeRoi "were witnesses as to his legal marriage to his wife."[48] I believe Dr. Judd drew disability and used

Sammy and Anne as witnesses. He got 15 dollars for disability.[48] Evelyn Nace claimed that he got a small pension from the government; a very small pension.[111] Dr. Judd liked the girls and shook hands when they met. Sammy's cheeks were red and she looked tubercular. He felt that there was a strong bond of friendship between the girls. Dr. Judd felt it a reminder that here was youth enjoying life while he was aging and ill.[27]

1931, February 3
Radio broadcasting equipment had been received in Juneau for use in Alaska-Washington Airways aircraft. J.B. Burford, Juneau agent for AWA, said the equipment had been tested in the Valentine Building and was successful. Hangars and planes were able to talk to another anytime.[4]

1931, February 9
Sammy wrote in her diary, "They say if you lose a friend you die a little. If that is true, part of me is dead."[112] Howard Hagen's baby is born in February. Sammy gets a letter sometime between Feb and June from Clara Bogstie in Landa saying in part, "Suppose you know Howard H. is married and lives in Atlanta, GA and already has a baby girl. Ralph Hagen is to marry Marguerite Elefson in June. Mrs. Hagen thinks that's fine."[113]

1931, February 10
Dr. and Mrs. Judd came over for dinner. Sammy writes this in her diary.[14] This might have been the night they met before Dr. Judd left for California.

1931, February 11
Anthony Dimond, member of the Alaska senate and of the law firm of Donahoe and Dimond of Valdez Alaska, wrote Sammy a letter.[63] Perhaps somewhere about this time she receives a letter from Dot in Juneau (Dorothy Chisholm, Dorothy Israel?) stating, "I know that you are going to be ok and I still marvel at your good luck in having such a splendid pal".[63]

1931, February 15
Sammy wrote in her diary, "Just think, it's been just a year since I met Anne. It seems that I knew her always".[114]

1931, Late February

One day Ruth is on the phone at the clinic with Jack and Anne walks in dressed in a cute red rain slicker since it had been raining. Ruth told Jack that she was talking to the prettiest girl you have ever seen since Anne was a brunette and looked great in red. Jack said that he would like to meet her since he always liked to meet pretty girls and came over at noon the next day and met her.[85] Ruth introduces Jack Halloran to Anne and Sammy. He then is a constant visitor at their home. She had Anne and Sammy promise not to let Jack know that she and her husband lived next door. Jack visited them 3-4 times per week. Ruth avoided running into Jack.[115] Dr. Judd stated that Sammy didn't drink at all and Ruth and Anne never took but one or two drinks. Jack often brought a bit of liquor over and sat with them for the evening.[32] He would often sit on the side of the bed to cheer them up and maybe lean over and kiss them at the time.[32]

1931, February 26

Sammy wrote in her diary, "Oh, let the solid ground not fail beneath my feet before my life has found what some have found so sweet."[116] – Tennyson[117]

1931, March 1

Ruth rents an apartment from HU Grimm at 1130 East Brill in unit C where she lives for three months.[118] Dr. Judd is living with her then at least a little bit of the time.[27] Ruth moved from 2201 North Richland.[83] Ruth lived with Betty Murray until this time after Dr. Judd had returned.[94] Ruth writes the following letter to her parents, (I believe this must be 1931). "Dear Mama, as soon as Doctor gets his $500 I'm going to send you enough to come out here. If he had had his certificate 15 minutes after the bonus was passed he could have gotten $500 cash. He expects to have it in a couple of weeks, but it may be he will have to present his discharge as it is in Mexico. He may have to wait to get cash for a duplicate. Anyhow, inside of a month we should have $500. I will have to send George $75. He sent me $25 the other day and I want to pay him back. And I want to send you money to come here on. I'm so nervous during the night. I go into nervous chills. I awaken, my heart beating wild and I dream about you so much. I've simply got to see you. I dream of you every night and awaken shaking. Dr. feels my pulse and he says it's too rapid caused by exhaustion. I am going to quit doing my washing from now on. It goes out so as Dr. does the cooking and housework, all I have to do is office and night school. Papa will surly let you come. Then if you like it here and want to stay after Dr. gets a job, Papa can come out. Please come. I'm so nervous. The weather is glorious; grass green and every flower imaginable in bloom. No fires surely, hot glorious weather dry and hot. Dr. is expecting a position in a couple of months anyhow. The 3 of us can live as cheap as 2 so all it will cost is your car fare out. I make enough. I'll get your ticket with my salary and take care of you on my salary. Doctor earns your rent out of his bonus. I will keep up the table on my salary. I think I'm getting $85 a month now or from now on. So, we can get along fine and if Dr. gets a job soon Papa can come out too. If Uncle Winnie could get passes, I'd give him some money. If he could get a pass for one of you, I should send the money for the other fare. I wish you would ask him. Will you come, mama? I can't give up a good job before Doctor gets a position. My job is safe. Both Dr's told me they were going to pay me more money so they like me. I've got to see you. It would do me $50 worth of good to see you. If Papa were the one sick in bed for 3 years it would be he I would want to come out here and get well. Please come, Lovingly, Ruth. It only cost $9.60 round trip ticket now to Los Angeles. Burton is living at Aunt Alice's at Beverly Glen Cottage."[20]

1931, March 13
Kathleen Carlson, one of Sammy's students in Juneau writes her a letter, "Box 751, Juneau Alaska. Dear Miss Samuelson: I just heard the good news four day ago that Mrs. Selby was going to be my teacher. She reminds me so much of you. Yesterday I heard that she was only going to teach until Mrs. Goddard comes. The first thing I did when I came to school in the morning and saw Mrs. Selby, I asked her how you were. I wished so much that you could come back and be my teacher again. When I saw Mrs. Selby it made me think so much of you. When you were in the hospital here I'm awful sorry I didn't come to see you, but I felt so sad to hear you were sick I just couldn't bear to see you lying there. I'm in the sixth grade now. You don't know how glad I am to hear that you were getting better and I hope you will be well soon. I hope I'll have you for a teacher again or see you somewhere again. Best love from Kathleen Carlson."[63]

1931, March 16
Sammy wrote in her diary, "Again we listened to our favorite murder

mystery play over the radio."[116]-Murder on the Bridge.[119] The Sherlock Holmes radio show that aired on this date was called, "Problem of Thor Bridge".[120]

1931, March 22
Sammy wrote a letter to the Bogsties in Landa, North Dakota. "Since I saw you last, that summer so long ago (about 4 years) I've spent most of my time in Alaska. Had some wonderful experiences there, which at least leave me with a lot of memories. You would love the scenery, gorgeous mountains and blue water, with little islands everywhere. Spent one summer way up in the interior... There were plenty of mountain sheep, fox, caribou, grizzly bears, etc. to make it interesting."...."In Juneau, we did a lot of plane riding, friends of mine being connected with the airways. It is the best way to see the country, flying over immense glaciers, lakes, and mountains, gives one the most wonderful thrills. Then we took some wonderful trips by water in and among the islands."........
"During the past summer I came out and went to summer school in Chicago. When I got back to Juneau, I just taught one month, when the doctor discovered that I had tuberculosis. It surely was a blow as I didn't have any suspicions. Very likely I had it since I had pneumonia when I was teaching at Whitehall, Montana. Anyway, they put me right to bed and I've been there ever since. A girl friend of mine in Juneau (Miss LeRoi), quit her job and brought me to Phoenix. By fall I hope to be able to do some kind of light work. I'm 12 pounds heavier so no one will give me any sympathy anymore. The Alaskans were just wonderful to me."
"Anne and I have the cutest little house. Things are beautiful here, but already we feel the heat. The desert is so intriguing and I can hardly wait to get strong again. We plan on going to Mexico or South America someday."[47]

1931, March 26
Anthony Dimond, a member of the Alaska Senate, writes Sammy a letter stating that he called on some other friends of hers – Gertrude and Tom Shelby -- and saw a letter there from her. He wrote, "I was particularly touched by the phrase in your letter to Gertrude in which you wondered if the members of the legislature would miss you. We miss you so greatly that if we had the magic of securing one wish and one only, it would be cheerfully extended in wishing you sound and well and in the city of Juneau. Good night, Sleep Well."[63]

1931, March 28
Austin Lathrop writes Sammy a letter.[63]

1931, April 13
Howard Hagen writes Sammy a letter on stationary from the Sun Life Assurance Co. of Canada from Atlanta, Georgia. The letter reads, "Dear Sammy: Under separate cover I am sending you today your photograph. I had not thought it would have taken so long to get around to it and so I apologize if it has caused you any concern. It is so beautiful here in Georgia now, I wish you could see all the blossoming trees and shrubs. No doubt Phoenix is radiant too and my fervent hope is that you are up and around enjoying it. Please, Sammy, let me know how you're getting on. It's so unkind of you to be so provincial to an old friend because he happens to be married. With best wishes always, I am truly, Howard."[63] It was said that Sammy had written to him of her desire to discontinue their correspondence because of his marriage to another.[113]

1931, mid- April
Mary Lucille Moore meets Agnes Anne LeRoi at the State Board Examination given to nurses at the Arizona Court House. She knew Sammy by sight, but was never formally introduced to her. She considered Anne an acquaintance.[121]

1931, April 15
Anne visits a dentist, John Lentz in Phoenix concerning a cavity in her first molar. This is used to identify her body at the time of her death.[122]

1931, April 21
Ruth reclaims the gun that she had pawned at the pawn shop in December. She was very excited to get it back and paid up the interest that had lapsed. When the pawnshop owner questioned her about her statement about not needing the gun, she replied, "Well, things get different sometimes."[95] The pawn shop ticket is marked Paid, April 21, 1931.[93]

1931, April 23
Ruth saw the new house today?[14] Sammy wrote in her diary, "Ruth saw our new home today."[114]

1931, April 29 or 22
Anne and Hedvig moved to 2929 N. 2nd Street. [81] [116] Sammy wrote in her diary, "We moved into a darling place today, at 2929 North Second Street. It was an event."[114] Dr. Judd stated that less than a month later, the family that occupied the other side of the house moved away. During this time, he and Ruth came over to visit about 1 time per week. While they lived there they had a "negress" come in once a day to do the work.[96]

1931, May 18
Winnie and Dr. Judd move into the other side of the duplex.[123] The Dr. is too ill to do anything, but he looks after Sammy. Ruth doesn't want Jack Halloran to know where she lives.[67] Dr. Judd seemed to remember that Sammy had placed a cot in the vacant lot and used it as an arbor with a palm leaf sun shade. Perhaps it was during this period of time when they both were here.[124] There is a photo at the Arizona State Archives of Sammy in a Janzen bathing suit with a large sombrero on. It is in a desert environment. Could this be next to the vacant lot where she would sun herself?[125] Dr. Judd stated that the girls had a radio and they played cards. They ran back and forth while they all lived in the house. He stated that there were some perfectly good people who brought them gin and so forth, but there was no harm in that. He stated that they were not drinking anything harmful.[96] Dr. Judd stated that he was quite sure that the girls did not use dope of any kind. He stated that one time he remembered Hedvig got the doctor to give her a prescription for a half dozen cold tablet that she wouldn't have done if she were an addict.[96]

1931, May 29
Somebody in Juneau sends Sammy an envelope of photographs.[126] It is addressed to Hedvig at 529 Portland Ave, Phoenix.[89]

1931, May 30
Dr. Judd's aunt in Los Angeles dies and Ruth and Dr. Judd go to the funeral. Ruth returns immediately, but Dr. Judd stays for a week to help out his sister. This is Memorial Day.[67] They went to Los Angeles for Aunt Alice's funeral. Burton saw Ruth there.[127] Carrie stated that Dr. Judd had lost his job in Phoenix. Ruth mentioned that she had fought with Sammy and Anne. Then she went back to Phoenix.[128] Ruth

stated that she arrived in LA on Friday, and departed that Sunday to be back on Monday. She arrived via a "special excursion".[85] She visited a widow and daughter by the name of Lane. They lived on the corner of 17th and Montana in Santa Monica.[96] Burton stated that they built a house in the rear of their bungalow and they rented out the bottom floor of the flat they built. Their names were Mrs. Huelness and her son-in-law Bert. There was another lady there by the name of Nan Coons. They were from the same town when they lived in Illinois when Burton was 10 years old. He once cleaned out the furnace for Mrs. Lane. At the time, they lived three houses above them. He had known Mr. Lane while he was living. He said Mrs. Lane was 50. She was very friendly with Ruth.[127]

1931, May 31
Anne LeRoi stops working at the clinic and plans to leave for Portland for a while.[129] Dr. Judd stated that Sammy went to a private sanitarium and he and Ruth moved into their side of the duplex for no particular reason except that it was better furnished.[96]

Summer 1931
A twenty-six bed annex for the care of tuberculosis patients was constructed in the Juneau Native Hospital which doubled the capacity for patients. The hospital added a laboratory technician to the staff and installed a new x-ray machine.[65] Carol Beery Davis and Ellen Reep travel around Alaska performing music including at McKinley Park. (This may have been 1930 instead. Ellen Reep was the sister of Mary Reep who was in Kake with Mildred Keaton. They stopped to see Cap. Lathrop in Anchorage to ask if they could be put on the schedule at his chain of theaters as an added attraction, but he flatly refused. The girls talked to some friends who had money in his corporations, and asked that Carol and Ellen perform in his theaters or they would withdraw their investment. He then let the women sing, but only in his theater in Anchorage.[130]

1931, June
Dr. McKeown looked at Ruth's x-rays in June and said that they looked tubercular in both lungs. She had no fever, her sputum was negative, and her x-rays were those of healed tuberculosis. She had moisture in her lungs but in view of no clinical symptoms, he did not consider it a case of active TB.[90]

1931, June 1

Ruth arrives home from Los Angeles and calls from the depot. It was 7:30 in the morning. Sammy answered the phone. Ruth said, "What in the world are you answering the phone for, Sammy? You go right back to bed". She replied, "I have to answer the phone, Ruth. Anne is sick." She intended to have her breakfast downtown but instead went over to the girls' house. She found them both with very high fevers. Sammy was burning up with temperature.[85] Anne and Sammy are sick. Anne has the flu with a temp of 102. Ruth said that Anne had pleurisy with effusions.[67] She went out and got breakfast for them and straightened up the house.[85] Sammy had a fever of 101. Ruth made them drink orange juice and ordered soup for them from work. Dr. McKeown visited the girls. Ruth made supper for them and did the dishes. Anne could only drink lemonade.[131] Jack is at the apartment and is massaging Anne's back when Ruth returns from the clinic with Evelyn Nace. She states that the Dr. will be back from LA tomorrow and can take care of the girls. Halloran finds out that she lives next door.[67] Anne wants to go to Portland and asks Jack for $300, but he refuses. Jack told Ruth to get a nurse to take care of the girls. He paid for the nurse. It was Mrs. Evans and he paid her $7 a day. He did not pay her directly. He gave the money to Ruth and Ruth paid her. Jack said, "Ruth, you are doing too much here, taking care of these girls" He asked Evelyn Nace, who was there, also to call up a nurses' directory and get a nurse for them.[85] Dr. Leff of Glendale comes out to help with the girls. Ruth stated that she did this so Anne wouldn't lose her job. He said to Ruth that night, "Ruth, Dr. Judd is one of my best friends, but you're my friend, too. It's a losing battle. Dr. Judd will never be well. If you will leave him, go into training, I'll help you through nurse's training. He said you are breaking down again, I'm afraid with TB."[132] Ruth was running a slight temperature and had a 32 basal metabolism.[132] Ruth replied, "Dr. Leff, I'd rather be happy with Doctor for a few years than live forever without him."[132] She cried a great deal that night.[132] Sometime during this same period Evelyn Nace visits two or three different nights and helped them bathe and take care of the girls. Jack pays Evelyn Nace to take care of the girls.[67] Dr. Judd states that the girls didn't know that Evelyn Nace was paid by Halloran to help them and that he also gave her money to buy them food.[32] Evelyn stated that she called on the girls; just dropped in on them. They were always home. As Sammy was quite ill they never went around much socially or at night.[111] Ruth is living next door and fetches Dr. Judd's

31

medical bag to help Anne take an enema.[133] Dr. Judd is in Pasadena helping his sister for a week and Ruth writes him a letter.[131] The letter says: "My Dear Doctor Billy, I hope that you are lonesome for me tonight. I am very lonesome to see you already. I have been working very hard today, but I am lonesome for you and cannot do any more work. I got off the train and came home on the street car this morning and found Miss LeRoy with a temperature of 102. I made them some orange juice and Dr. McKeown came and said that Anne had the flu and he took me to the office. I sent her out some soup at noon and Dr. Baldwin brought me home tonight, and I have so many histories to do I don't know what to do and I hope that you will be here soon to help me. I got supper for the two sick girls tonight and did the dishes and they are both quite sick. Anne couldn't eat a bite, just drinks lemonades, she craves lemonade. Let's see you have spent today with Carrie and you will want to spend tomorrow with her. Then Wednesday I think you ought to drive over and See Dr. Moore in Pasadena and why don't you also go and see if any of those steamship lines on Los Angeles don't need a doctor? Then, I hope that you will come home not later than Thursday night, will you? I miss you and I can't get along without you. I can't do this work by myself. So, please come by Thursday night or I will be sick myself. You will have to take care of me in a few days. Do you miss seeing me? I do you. I feel like crying tonight. It makes me nervous when you are not here. I have my window open next to the girls so I won't feel so bad. I am not afraid but I miss you so don't stay any longer than Thursday, will you not? I love you even if you are a very naughty boy. You are mine and I worry when you aren't right close to me. I wish that you would write me a nice letter. With lots of love, Ruth."[134]

1931, June 2
In the morning, Evelyn Nace came over and said that she wasn't sure she really ought to engage a nurse because she wasn't sure if Jack meant what he said about paying for it. Ruth stated, "Jack is wealthy and he really meant to take care of the girls." Evelyn Nace decides to call him up and he said, "Absolutely". After that Jack called up Ruth and asked about what was Anne's trouble and Ruth explained that the clinic thought she was having a breakdown from TB because of caring for Sammy. Jack replied, "That is a dirty rotten shame, I want to give her the money to pay the nurse, but I don't want the girls to know it."[85]

1931, June 3
John Barrymore along with Delores Costello and their 14-month old baby spend the day in Ketchikan. They claimed that their baby was a wonderful sailor. They arrived on their yacht Infanta at the Union Oil dock shortly after 1 o'clock. They immediately came up town in a car and were escorted about by Mayor Norman R. Walker. They planned to stay in Ketchikan for a day and then leave for a several week cruise. John had just finished the movie *Svengali* and *the Mad Genius*. John Barrymore thought he needed a vacation before tackling any more serious work and decided to take an Alaskan tour. Delores Costello had just finished *Expensive Women*. The Infanta late this afternoon was brought to the Northland dock. The Barrymores visited Stewart Edward White, and authors and yachtsmen in the afternoon.[135]

1931, June 4
Ruth amends her letter to Dr. Judd from June 1: PS, If San Jose isn't very far, why don't you drive to there and see Lothar Whittman. His address is RFD Saratoga, Calif. San Jose is where the letter was mailed. I am so tired tonight I am going right to bed. Today is Thursday, I didn't get this mailed.[136]

1931, June 5
John Barrymore and Dolores Costello are vacationing on their Yacht in Alaskan waters in search of rest.[137]

1931, June 6
Nurse Anna Evans told police that she was summoned on this day to care for Anne LeRoi and Hedvig Samuelson.[61]

1931, June 7
Anne wants Ruth and Dr. Judd to come over for drinks. Jack is preparing drinks. Ruth refuses, but Jack runs over to their side of the duplex and introduces himself to the Doctor. Ruth didn't want him to know the Doctor (because she previously had an affair with Jack and because she didn't want the Doctor to drink and get back into taking drugs). She claims that after this, Dr. Judd was over there constantly. Dr. Judd stated that he began dropping over to visit him (Halloran). He would come over to chat after visiting with the girls and Ruth and then have a drink or two. He said that Halloran often carried a bottle of liquor with him when he was going to call on people. Dr. Judd stated that he

33

was a generous and big hearted man. He claimed that type was a "good fellow."[32] Often Jack would take Dr. Judd to his house to drink and sing songs late into the night. She said all of them drank with Sammy and Anne. Before Anne went to Portland, she found 16 empty Cheracol bottle out in the alley.[67] Halloran found out she lived next door when the girls were sick. Anne was obligated to go back to Oregon. Ruth says he helped her financially. Halloran confided in her husband and how he helped her and "we were glad".[115] Dr. Judd stated that while Jack offered Agnes Anne money for her trip, she said it was wonderful of him, but she couldn't take the money from him.[32]

1931, June 8
Sam Samuelson, Sammy's brother graduates from Medical school at the U of MN. He finished being an intern and got his medical license.[21] Sammy and Anne serve as witnesses to the lawful marriage of Ruth and Dr. Judd. This was filed at the Veteran's Bureau on this day. This was required so Dr. Judd could get his compensation.[83]

1931, June 11
Ruth has an appointment at the VA to judge her husband mentally incompetent. She fails to keep the appointment because she cannot betray her husband nor does she tell him about her affair with Jack.[67] This appointment was made by Dr. McDonald and Dr. Foster to see Dr. Kingsley to judge Dr. Judd mentally incompetent and would allow Ruth to receive disability compensation.[67] She stated she couldn't tell her husband why she couldn't stand to see him with Halloran because of a book called, "ex-Wife" by Ursula Parrot which she had read with Dr. Judd.[138] She had not been unfaithful at the time, but the Dr. said that the woman in the story got what she deserved and the only reason a woman ever confessed an indiscretion was to boastfully hurt her husband or selfishly relieve her conscience by tormenting him.[67]

1931, June 12
This was Anne LeRoi's birthday. Nora Smith at the clinic states that Ruth suggested taking a collection for a ticket at the clinic so Anne could go home since it was her birthday and she had been ill. Nora Smith thought Ruth was an exceptionally fine girl. She said that she was devoted to her husband, her father, mother and her child (stated on October 24). She was extremely devoted to her work. She was very loyal. She worked very hard for a small salary. She often carried the

doctors' work home and her typewriter and worked. She remarked that she liked her on the job for her pep and attitude. She said that Doctor Baldwin would have a hard time replacing her. She showed her a baby's picture. It was a boy past twenty months; nearly two years. She said the baby was with her parents in Indiana. She once told her that it was so hard for her to be away from her baby. She said she wanted to earn more money so she could have him here. When there were babies in the clinic she said it was so hard. For example, when Mrs. Baldwin came in with her three small children and she wanted her baby so bad she had to leave the room.[139]

1931, June 13
Ruth returns home tired from work to find Dixon, Jack, the Doctor, Anne, and Sammy drinking all afternoon.[67] Halloran and Dixon go to the Country Club to keep an appointment, but intended to return to continue the party.[67] L.E. Dixon was Lucius Earl Dixon of Los Angeles. He is a structural engineer, born on August 23 of 1891. He had blue eyes and brown hair with a medium build.[140] Ruth takes Dr. Judd home and insists that they go to a movie even though she only had 15 cents left until she got paid on the next Monday. So, she suggests that they go downtown and window shop until midnight. Dr. Judd refuses and goes back into the duplex. Later Ruth gets him home and locks the doors and begs him to never drink with Halloran again.[67] Ruth states that this evening she was in the most "terrible turmoil of mind". She was torn between not being able to bear seeing her husband drink with Halloran or hurt him by telling him that she had an appointment with Dr. Kingsley last Thursday to judge him "mentally disabled".[67]

1931, Mid- June
Dr. Sweek calls a day before Anne leaves for Portland. He wanted to talk to Evelyn Nace and he had been drinking. He says that he is coming over. However, Mrs. Sweek shows up instead. Mrs. Sweek quickly answers the phone when Dr. Sweek rings again.[67] Evelyn Nace and Ruth wait outside for Dr. Sweek to arrive and warn him about his wife being over. However, Dr. Guttman arrives to visit with Sammy. Mrs. Sweek came over to Ruth's side of the duplex and offered to drive Evelyn home. Shortly afterwards, Dr. Sweek arrived.[67] Dr. and Ruth Judd move into the side of the duplex Anne and Sammy lived in - Better furniture. [48] Ruth says Sammy had almost $1000 in the bank. Dr. Judd

took her bank book and helped her transfer money from a savings account to a checking account.[84] Dr. Percy Brown and his wife went to the house to say goodbye to Anne. He says that both girls were there then.[92] Anne decides to take a leave of absence from the clinic but has no money to return to Oregon. Ruth visits Dr. Sweek to ask for money on Anne's behalf. Dr. Sweek stated that he thought they were lesbians. Ruth tells him that it wasn't true. Dr. Sweek allows Anne to have 100 dollars from the clinic and said he would pay for it himself if Grunow objected.[67] She receives money from the doctors at the clinic for her trip.[141] Ruth claims that the girls at the clinic raised $60 for Anne's trip. Anne wasted the money and bought a $65 outfit instead and left for Oregon via plane.[67] Nurse Anna Evans states that this is not true that Anne spent the money. Anna stated she was with her when she got the money and when she bought her ticket.[141] Ruth was doing things for the girls via Jack. Jack gave her $20 one time to buy the girls groceries.[85] Anne visits James Odell who she had known for 6-7 years in LA? sometime in June.[75] It was in Portland according to this article.[76] Anne LeRoi visits relatives in Portland arriving by plane.[142] She is under the care of Dr. Ralph Matson for TB and has a minor operation.[143] This doctor was a classmate of Dr. Judd's and she had a phrenectomy. She works for this doctor for two weeks as a roentgenologist while his regular assistant was on vacation. This was to pay for her operation.[67] A phrenectomy is the cutting of the phrenic nerve at the base of the neck, causing paralysis of half the diaphragm and thus greatly diminishing respiratory excursions of that side. The idea is to minimize the expansion of a diseased lung.[65] Anne writes a letter to Ruth while she was gone, about 4 months before the incident. She writes, "Ruthie, darling, I promise never to repeat that episode again. I cannot wait until I can come back to you and to Sammy. I can never thank God enough for giving you to me. You are so sweet."[144] Ruth went around evenings looking for a place for Sammy to go; to a sanitarium that was within reason for her to take treatment. She went around so many evenings that her husband scolded her.[85]

1931, June 16
Anna Evans, started 10 days after (their, I think it means her) arrival. Anne leaves for Portland to be gone three months.[61]

1931, June 17
Anna Evans claims on this day, Sammy collapsed and had to be taken

to a Sanitarium.[61] Sammy moves to live with Pearl Waggoner. (private sanitarium located at 1821 East McDowell Road) Anna and Ruth Judd were frequent visitors. Ruth wrote to her parents in December that she visited Sammy 2-3 times per week and that she had to walk a mile in the hot sun to do so.[20] In another case, she states that it cost her 30 cents every time she went which was a lot for a girl who couldn't afford to buy two or three pairs of hose, but she went to cheer her up.[85] Jack Halloran visited and brought her flowers. One time this summer Jack came with three other men and they stayed in Sammy's room and sang songs. Dr. Goodwin from the clinic visited her in a non-professional capacity on numerous occasions.[145] Ruth says this is Dr. Guttman. He came over just about every evening to visit Sammy. Mrs. Guttman was in Michigan expecting a baby.[67] Sammy is attended by a nurse called Anna Evans, (at home or at Pearl Waggoner's?) She states that the women never had loud parties and were unusually quiet and that they would not shoot or harm anyone. She states that Sammy and Anne were inseparable and that they cared a great deal more about each other than they did in any of the men who visited them.[141] Pearl Waggonner said that Ruth visited two times per week during June, July, and August, and that she usually drove her home.[83]

1931, June 20
The deed at the house at 2929 N 2nd street is transferred from the Mitchell Investment Company to Frank Vance, husband of Estrella Vance by John H. Mitchell, President.[82]

1931, June 27
Anne writes to Ruth Judd from Aurora, OR. (Her married sister lived there) She writes, "Dearest Ruth: How are you coming, honey? I hope you are not working as hard as you did when you had Sammy and me to look after. You've been so sweet to us and such a very good friend, Ruth. Ruth, darling I'll never thank you enough for all the things you've done for me, but Sammy and I will love you always for them. Write me all concerning my baby (Sammy) because I do worry so about her. Love to Dr. Judd and your sweet self, Anne."[146] Additional parts of this letter include, "Ruth darling, I'll never thank you enough for all the things you've done for me, but both Sammy and I will love you always for them."[147] "You've been so sweet to us and such a very good friend, Ruth. You did look tired when I left."[147]

1931, June 30

Winnie Ruth Judd visits Hedvig at the T.B. rest home after work.[123]
The rest home was located at 1821 E. McDowell Rd in Phoenix and
was called, "Miss Wagoner's Sanatorium.[84][81] Winnie Ruth Judd must
have been living in the duplex at this time. Ruth visits Sammy 3-4
times per week.

1931, July

Mrs. Cora Rowe who worked at the clinic testified that in July Ruth
told her one day while they were having lunch that she was very
nervous. She asked her what the matter was. She said, "Oh, I would
like to have my baby with me." And she said, "Why Ruth I didn't
know you had a baby." She replied, "Yes, I have." She asked her
where her child was and Ruth replied that the 18-month old boy was
with her father and mother.[148]

1931, July 1

Anne LeRoi is away in Portland. Hedvig receives a letter from her.[123]
Anne visits with her parents while in Portland in the summer of 1931.[149]
(Anne away in Portland? I bet this is July 1st instead of May 1st as it is
dated) Anne writes a letter to Ruth saying, "Dearest Ruthie, so happy to
have your letters and shall never cease being grateful to God for giving
you to Sammy and me. How is Dr. Judd these hot days? And is Jack
behaving himself? I am so anxious to get back to you all. Visiting here
has been lovely, but I want to get back to my job and my Sammy and
the rest of you all whom I love. Write me here again, Ruthie, and give
everybody a hello. Best ever to you, my dear. From Anne."[146]
Additional excerpts from this letter include, "Doctor ____ is so nice
and far too charming to be wandering around on the loose. How is Dr.
Judd on these hot days?"[147]

1931, July 4

Jack gives a party for sick children out at the country club. One
crippled boy stated that Jack Halloran had a big dinner for us out at the
country club and we had more fun.[85] Ruth stated that Jack was no Don
Juan or Stepper.[85] Austen Lathrop wrote Sammy a letter.[63]

1931, July 5

Sammy attends an auto race with a man. She is photographed with
three of the drivers and a man. (Could this be 1930 instead in

Chicago?) The names of the men are on the photographs and it says, "three drivers" The other guys last name was Anderson (relative from Chicago?)[150] There is an auto race on July 5 in Flagstaff. It is won by a Californian called Herb Balmer.[151] Later determined this was probably Minot in a much earlier year.

1931, July 10 or 11

Ruth Judd meets Betty Lepker while Sammy is hospitalized at Good Samaritan Hospital. Ruth was accompanied by a gentleman friend. She introduced herself as Mrs. Buckley. She was told that Ruth's boyfriend was Jack. They met because Jack knew the man that Betty worked for and they brought him up. Ruth visits three times within the next two weeks, once alone, other times with Jack.[152] (Jack Halloran went by the name of Dr. Buckley when he was drunk)

1931, July 19

Ruth visits Sammy at noon.[109]

1931, July 22

A letter is written to Anne LeRoi from a "Dr. Buckley" addressed to Mrs. LeRoi in care of the Safford Pickle Co, Aurora Ore: Dear A., Now that you are football coach and boxing instructor at the Pickle works you should be in condition to carry on the battle with Buckley. Never felt better, so drink plenty of the brine (mixed with limes, no sugar) and the championship will be decided on your return. One of my favorite dishes, next to pumpkin pie is pickled pigs' feet, so soak yours. That should start an argument. So, glad, A that you are so much improved and knew you were going to be an easy winner, but don't get too frisky for a while. Wouldn't eat so many lunches down town. Stay in the country. You say you are putting on weight. Had a nice visit with Sammie the other evening. She is looking fine and says she is eating like a blacksmith. Change of cooks, I presume. Ouch. No temperature and is quite happy in the surroundings. There are a couple of the male of the species there as patients. Do you suppose that is a contributing factor? Maybe, I don't know. She wouldn't tell me why she went to the hospital but what is the difference as long as she is now OK. You could imagine she would tell me. Dr. Buckley, I understand these things. Eh wot. Mr. Dick was here today and if at all possible will try to bring him out to see Hedvig. Expect to be in Oakland latter part of August so maybe will see you on return. Tell me the color of hat and dress. I'll be seeing you mebbe. Sammy is happy you will be happy and so will I." Signed "Buckley".[153]

1931, July 27
A married man in Juneau Alaska writes Sammy a letter (Pilot Bob Ellis, married to Peg Ellis). "Dear Sammy, we were just sitting her listening to the radio when I had a sudden urge to write. We had a letter from Anne today and she seems so much better but I suppose you know all that. Last week, I had four ambulance trips, people either sick or injured and tomorrow morning I am leaving for Chicago at daybreak for another. I find it so hard to write to a sweet girl like you and not say the things I would like to say especially since my better half is asleep on the sofa behind me reminding me all the time by her snores that I am married. Anyway, I think you know what I mean and if I could just be with you for a little while and hold your hand and kiss you again on that beauty spot behind your ear I am sure you would understand. So many people ask after you and how you are getting along. It's the women that ask, Peg, but every day or so some young man with a calf-like look in his eyes will ask about you and I pass out a few meager details. Love, Bob."[63]

1931, August first week
Dr. Judd sees and visits with Sammy for the last time.[110]

1931, August 5
Sammy writes the following letter to her friend Marion Alvina Vrem who she went to school with in Minot. She writes, "I'm sorry to know you have a cold. Be careful of it. Remember that's all the warning I had and I didn't know enough to heed it. ....Their wives are on the coast, too hot for them here. Papas don't seem to mind the heat somehow. Several of them come over and help me while away the hours; a doctor, lumberman, and a contractor from L.A. building a bank here. It's nice of them because I'm not allowed up, lie out in a swing in the evenings, which doesn't make me very good company when I can't go places or do things. Also have two girl friends that come over, so you see I'm not altogether forsaken. Yes, you sent me "Vagabond's House" and I love it. Are you working now? Much love, Sammy."[59]

1931, August 6
Dr. Judd meets with General Tuthill about a vacancy at the Copper Queen

Hospital at Bisbee.[67]

1931, August 7

Dr. Judd leaves for Bisbee, Arizona to be a doctor and is paid $50 a week. Ruth writes a letter to Burton stating that she is all alone. She will remain working in Phoenix until the Doctor makes enough to take care of her. She didn't want to lose her job and be broke again.[154] Sammy expresses to Ruth that her funds are low and that she would like to move in with her. It cost her $60 a month to remain at Pearl Waggonner's. Ruth lives alone in the duplex for 10 days and is very worried about it.[67] Dr. Judd made the statement to police that he last saw Ruth on the 8th or 9th of August at Phoenix (what about Bisbee?) [96, 155]

1931, August 8

Winnie Ruth Judd asks Sammy to move in with her, back at the duplex since Dr. Judd moved to Bisbee Arizona and she is living alone. Dr. Judd goes to Bisbee to relieve a physician there.[48] Sammy asked her if she could move in with her. Ruth and Dr. Judd were living in the side of the duplex where the girls used to live. They used to live in the other side.[84] [123] Ruth writes a letter to her brother Burton. She writes, "Dear Burton, at last I will write you a few lines. I heard that you had gone to Darlington and didn't stop to see me and I thought of every mean thing I could and told Mama that you were that thing for not coming to see me. She wrote me that you had not come home, that Glen was there, but that you were not. Then, in a couple of days, I got a letter from you. I have been so busy since I came back to Phoenix. Dr and I have scraps every few days. Last night he left for Bisbee. Yesterday, the hospital called me and said that the Crown Queen Copper Co. needed a doctor for a month so he went down there and got the place at $50 a week. If he doesn't get a job by the time that place is over I guess that he will then go to Mexico. We hear that the American doctor at Hermosillo had died and that this was a good place to go into private practice. Doctor wrote to the American Council there and if it is any good, he will try to go there unless he gets a position elsewhere. I will stay here until he makes enough to take care of me. I don't want to give up my job and be broke again. I am all alone. I wish that Mama could come out now. I have a little house and am all alone. Why don't you come over next week? Hike over and visit me. We can talk over how and when we can get Mama out here. Love Ruth."[134] Ruth also writes a letter to Dr. Judd's sister Carrie. She and Dr. Judd are broke and she is looking for solutions to the problem. Doctor Leff loaned them car fare to Bisbee. If Dr. Judd was to get the job it would be about 50 dollars a week and would last a month. Dr. Leff told them that the American doctor in Hermosillo, Senora, Mexico was anxious to sell and William could buy him out. However, they thought he might have died since he had one leg and he had been operated on. Then, they wouldn't have to buy him out. Ruth is angry with somebody named Alice that she wouldn't loan her $15 when she was very desperate and wouldn't ever ask her again. Ruth thought he might go to Hermosillo and try to practice regardless. Ruth states that she could not get a raise in salary for a long time. Ruth wanted to go to Bisbee, but knew that she needed to stay in Phoenix and keep working. Dr. Judd has been waiting for a job since March. Ruth is tired of waiting; she stated that "it is better to be some place than just waiting." She says she is alone and that she is tired.[156] Here is more of the letter, "We were so hard up again that we didn't know what was going to happen to us, really didn't have enough money to write places for a position and buy food. And yesterday the hospital here called me up and said that the Copper Queen Mining Co. in Bisbee had an opening for a doctor about the place. Doctor went and saw him and last night left for Bisbee. Doctor Leff loaned us the money for car fare to Bisbee. The position will last only a month, but that will at $50 a week so we can get along for a month or two. If the manager likes William, maybe he will see he gets a place somewhere else or at least a good recommendation. It is down in the mining country. William has written to quite a number of places for a position and if he doesn't get a position somewhere as soon as this job is through he is thinking or I am thinking of going to Hermosillo, Senora Mexico. Last March Dr. Leff told us that the American doctor there was anxious to sell because he was sick and he wanted to leave there. Well, the other day I met a man who had just been down to Hermosillo and he said that the old one legged doctor there had gone to Mayo Clinic and was operated on and died. So if he has died William wouldn't have to buy him out. William has written to the American Consul at Hermosillo and if it is a good place he may try to go there and go into practice for himself. I will have to stay here for a while for if he goes to Hermosillo he won't have any more than enough for car fare and I will try and send him as much as I can above my board here. Carrie, do you know of any way we could get any money so that he could go into practice and have enough to live on for a couple of months at least until he gets well started? I couldn't send more than 20 dollars a month. I know that you can't loan it as you didn't have the money to go on yourself this summer. I will never write to Alice again. I was down and asked to borrow 15 and she didn't load it to me. And I won't write to her or let William write her or I don't want of anything. She offered one time to do so much anything she ever could, I borrowed one 15 and didn't ask for more until I was in desperate circumstances and she didn't let me have it. Do you know what I can do if William doesn't make a go of it to wait again for a position so he will have a few dollars? He has used all the money we had to live on and no position yet that he has written to, and there are no prospects. So don't you think since he has carfare it is the best thing to ride to Hermaisillo and work hard? Expect that he has to have enough for board for two months. I won't get any raise in salary for a long time. The collections are terrible for doctors here. I wish that I could have gone with William to Bisbee. He doesn't talk and hear about things and then too I want to take care of him. But we can't do it since he must save every penny while he is there and I must hold on to this job if things don't turn out well. I have written to George that William is thinking of going to Hermosillo. George is good to me, but I couldn't ask him when William was sick. You can't do anything. I am not writing for that reason. I am writing you for advice, what to do because you know when I want money or anything else I say so. I am so glad that William has this place now and will have car fare at least to get some place, for I don't think it is wise to just loaf around until a position turns up, do you? He has been waiting for something since March. I am very tired so I guess that I will close. I don't know what William's address is yet. He will have to write me his address before I can write him. I am all alone. I wish that you would drive over and see me. We had the rent paid at the house until the 22nd so I will stay there that long anyhow. I wish you would get Burton to drive you over or you come over and see me. It isn't of how to manage it for William to go to Hermosillo. What do you think can be done? I get so nervous thinking of waiting and it all went waiting for a position and then had to borrow money to get to this place on. So it is better to be someplace instead of just waiting. I am very tired so guess that I will close. I have written you about three letters since I was over there. Did I mail one or two of them? I know that one of them is still here in the drawer. How is little Sue? I like her. She is bright and real genuine, and sweet."[156]

1931, August 9
Miss Spicklemeyer, Ruth's teacher at night school, and Miss Eddington, an RN in the county doctor's office come over and visit Ruth. Both of them expressed an interest in moving into the duplex with Ruth, but she had already promised Sammy. Ruth's rent was $30 a month alone at the duplex.[67]

1931, August 10
Anne LeRoi wrote the following letter to Sammy from 1012 Union Avenue, Portland, Ore. "Sammy Dearest: Haven't written you for a whole week, been so busy working, and when I go home I pile right into bed; sure get tired before the day is over in spite of the fact I have an hour rest each afternoon. Was so happy to have your letter about the house; somehow it just seems to belong to us and I'd hate having to look for another. Think also it would be wise for us to let Ruth stay for a few months; it would help the financial situation a great lot and we could manage for a few months. Would much rather just have you, darling. But we have a lot of problems to work out and it won't hurt us to sacrifice our personal feelings once. Am not sure just when I shall leave. Will finish my work for Dr. Matson the 15th. Had planned on two weeks for Dr. Brochvogal, but some things have happened to delay his vacation, so he may not take it till next month. If not, I shall start south the last week in August and be at the clinic September first, as planned. I'm sorry about not getting my extra two weeks' work because now I'm going to have to borrow money to come down on. My salary from Dr. Matson will just about pay my hospital and doctor bills. So happy you are apparently feeling better, honey. You mustn't spoof me though, because I'll know when I see you. Sammy, please have Ruth get all your chest plates together and send them to me pronto; I'll bring them back when I come. It's very important to me because I'm most anxious for Dr. Watson's opinion. Love and a big kiss to my Baby. Ann."[63]

1931, August 11
Sammy makes the decision to move back to the duplex with Winnie Ruth Judd.[123] Ruth Judd has a cat living there that Sammy refers to in her diary as 'Mister Cat'.[157] Sammy is unable to take care of herself and so they have a "negress" come in once a day to help out and do the house work until Anne LeRoi returned from Portland.[48] Sammy writes the following letter to Anne between August 11 and 14:

"You'll be surprised, pleasantly that I didn't know, however that I could make my first decision since you put me to bed in Juneau September 25, 1930. Sunday I'm moving luggage and self over to 2929 Second Street again. Wouldn't do this, but $80 per month finances were getting to be a big problem. You will see it this way. Dr. Judd is relieving a doctor at Bisbee for a month and Ruth is by herself. She wants me to come over and stay, and I'm going to try it. I don't like it very much, but it will save half. Now, Honey if you don't want to stay over there with three in a house why I'll do whatever you wish when you get here. I realize it's not going to be the same having three, because I'm a jealous little fool, though I do my best to hide it."[158]

1931, August 13
Ruth has a screaming fit and cannot quit screaming. She states that the thoughts she felt were a force greater than herself. Some Italian people from across the alley heard her and came over. Ruth was embarrassed.[67]

1931, August 14
Sammy writes Anne a letter in Portland. "I am so glad you are feeling better and are coming back. It's foolish to be so dependent on someone for happiness, but how can I help it? …. Miss Wagoner has been lovely to me, but she doesn't mean anything to me. It's the same way with Ruth. Now honey, please answer this right away so I will know how you are and when you will get here. Ever Yours, Hedvig"[158]

1931, August 15
Ruth visits Dr. Judd in Bisbee Arizona.[159] Dr. Clifford Wright stated that Ruth got word that her baby John Robert was in Bisbee with Dr. Judd. So, she went down to find him.[29] It was said that Dr. Judd stated to police in LA that when he was with a mining company in Bisbee, Mrs. Judd visited Bisbee. Acquaintances of Dr. Judd recalled that during this residence there, a woman had appeared, made close inquiries about him, and observed his movements for several days.[160]

1931, Middle August
Mrs. Arthur Lepker visits the clinic to see Dr. Sweek. She meets Ruth Judd on the steps and talks with her. Ruth states that she is glad that Sammy's boyfriend L.E. Dixon is in town. She says that Sammy is getting too intimate with Jack and so she is glad Dixon is in town. L.E. Dixon was considering staying in Phoenix. Ruth states that she gets so

mad she could die. She stated that Sammy was trying to take Jack away from her. Jack was in LA. He was coming back for one day and then was leaving for the east for two weeks.[152][161] However, in another account, Ruth stated that L.E. Dixon was interested in Anne.[67]

1931 August 16
Sammy gets positive news about health and x-rays.[162] She is examined by Dr. Randolph who said that her left lung had no activity and that she might be up by Christmas.[81] She left the TB rest home and moved in with Ruth Judd at the duplex where she had lived before with Anne LeRoi at 2929 North Second St. Sammy writes a letter to her parents stating, "I'm leaving the T.B. rest home today, going back to the house Anne and I had. Ruth Judd wants me to stay with her while her husband is away. She moved into our place right after we left in June. Ruth has been supporting her husband, who is an ex-doctor. He has been ill quite a while. Believe it is T. B. She had it, too, but is now working at the clinic. They came here from old Mexico, where he was a doctor in a mining camp. He is taking a doctor's place while he is on vacation, and is now at Bisbee, Arizona."[163] She also writes a letter to her brother saying, "My new X-rays give me a lot of encouragement, so maybe by next spring I'll be out looking for new fields to conquer."[162] A Dr. brought her over since Ruth was in Bisbee.[164] Ruth arrived in Bisbee on the midnight stage.[165] Ruth signed the registry at the Copper Queen Hotel in Bisbee as Lucy Rider.[166] Ruth said she was running a temperature. She was very ill. She registered at the hotel as Lucy Ryder, El Paso, TX at the Hotel and to annoy her husband, she phoned him from a garage across the street telling him that her baby was having convulsions; dying of convulsions. She returned to her room and couldn't stop screaming.[67] Ruth told a doctor that she went to Bisbee and drove around town in a taxi in order to locate her baby. She looked through the keyhole at the hotel to find it. She didn't see it and so dragged a large piece of furniture over in order to look over the transom. She didn't find it so drove to a pit mine to see if it was there; it wasn't.[29] Dr. Judd was living at the Copper Queen Hotel while working there for a month since one doctor was ill and one was on vacation. The garage man reported seeing Ruth and stated she was seeking to investigate thoroughly every action of her husband. He stated that she was looking for second hand information about her husband without Dr. Judd's knowledge. He immediately informed Dr. Judd that his wife was in the city. Dr. Judd thanked him profusely.[165]

Dr. Judd stated that he received a telephone call from his wife. She said she was in the garage and wanted to see him. He suggested she come to his room. She refused. She told him to call on her in room 27 and to give her a few minutes. Dr. Judd checked the register and said it was signed by a Lucy Rider of El Paso. He said the handwriting was his wife's. According to Dr. Judd he went to room 27, Ruth threw herself into his arms and began sobbing hysterically. He drew her to the bed, attempting to quiet her and because the noise could be heard by other guests, he closed the transom. She gave him no explanation, but stated that she didn't know what the matter was with her. Dr. Judd replied after half an hour that "I believe you are right, Ruth. I guess you're crazy". She stated that because of the condition of her dress, she did not register as his wife and would wait until the next day and then communicate with him.[28] Ruth states in the drain pipe letter that she was working so hard and when she got paid she went under an assumed name and called him up. She gave a fictitious address just to hear his voice and see him, and then cried all night for doing it.[167] One article stated that letters between Anne and Ruth indicated an addiction to luminal on the part of Ruth and Anne.[158] Somebody else stated that often people who were addicted to morphine but were trying to quit, look luminal for relief of cravings. However, this only lasts a few hours. Afterwards, the cravings get worse and "patients sometimes become dangerously insane."[168] Dr. Goodman moved Sammy over from Pearl Waggoner's and felt bad about leaving her there alone.[25] Ruth refers to this Doctor as Dr. Guttman. Dr. Guttman liked Sammy quite a bit and called on her often at W. Portland and at Pearl Waggoner's.[67] I believe Anna Evans moved into the opposite side of the duplex to care for Sammy at this time? She stated, "Miss Samuelson refused to stay there (the sanitarium) and finally, I secured an apartment next door to where Dr. and Mrs. Judd were living." Or perhaps, next door?[61]

1931, August 17
Sammy wrote in her diary that it was nice to be home again.[123] Sammy rises at 5 AM thinking Ruth has returned from Bisbee. It is the milkman. He is startled and runs away; although he learns to like Sammy's greetings each morning.[164] Jack brings over Sammy's trunk and puts it into the garage. Two men from the lumber business went out to the house and helped Sammy move her trunk. Jack spends the day visiting Sammy after coming back from Los Angeles.[25] Ruth

reported in a letter to her parents that Sammy was in bed most of the time. Ruth reported doing all of the house work. She said she brought her tray to her in bed as well.[20] Halloran was a frequent visitor when Dr. Judd had his temporary job. Ruth took care of Sammy.[115] Ruth stated she got a car this morning to soothe her nerves and drove to Warren. She stated she finally told Dr. Judd she was there. She stated she was crazy.[167] Ruth phones her husband from the depot in Bisbee to go up to her room in the hotel. Ruth screams so loud that he shut all of the windows and Ruth tells him that, "Oh God Doctor, I don't know what is the matter with me, I must be losing my mind." Dr. Judd wants to tell the people at the hotel that Ruth is his wife. Ruth won't let him stating that she has been doing terrible things. When he asked her what, she replies that she didn't do terrible things; that this was in her mind. She continued to scream and scream. Finally, the Dr. drove her up and down the road between Naco and Bisbee to keep from attracting attention in the hotel. Ruth states that the most insane thoughts in the world possessed her. Dr. Judd was annoyed with her screaming. The Dr. gave her luminal to take. Ruth took Luminal and Veronal each night afterwards for over a month. One article stated that letters between Anne and Ruth indicated an addiction to luminal on the part of Ruth and Anne.[158] Somebody else stated that often people who were addicted to Morphine but were trying to quit, look luminal for relief of cravings. However, this only lasts a few hours. Afterwards, the cravings get worse and "patients sometimes become dangerously insane."[168] Ruth returns to Phoenix from Bisbee on the train at 6 the following afternoon.[28] When she came back (this day?), Halloran was out to see Sammy after he had been on the coast and asked her what the matter was. "You look terrible, you look crazy."[167] Dr. Wright stated that Dr. McKeown who she says is a friend of hers told her she had better go home and rest awhile; that she looked like a crazy person.[29] Dr. McKeown testified that when she returned from Bisbee she looked very tried because she had not slept for 36 hours.[90]

1931, August 20
Letter by Winnie, waiting for Anne to return from Portland and says they can all three get along together.[159] "Dear Anne, I was so glad to get your letter after such a long time. I suppose you know that Sammy and I are together waiting every day for our dear little Anne to return to the fold. Sure I think that we can get along fine, the three of us until I go to the doctor. We talk a lot about our Anne and how she is going to

behave herself when she comes back. Sammy is flirting as per usual. I went to Bisbee on Saturday and Sammy moved over to the house on Sunday night, Doctor brought her over. He hated to leave her, and frankly told me so the next day. Well, at 5am Sammy heard someone come in the back door and she got up and ran out to greet the milk man. He was terribly surprised and started to run. Then Sammy told him she thought it was Ruth. I don't know what to believe. Anyhow, the milk man is as sweet as pie and doesn't run any more, but looks forward to these little morning greetings. You know Anne, I sleep so sound that a truck could run in the house and I would never awaken. Sammy also flirts with the ice man. He stands for hours with my ice box door open and talks, so Sammy says. Jack came back from the coast for a couple days and came out to the house. He brought flowers. He's just as sweet as he can be. Why don't you write Doctor _____? He said rather sadly the other day that you had never written him one line. Doctor _____ and Mrs. _____ do not like him. They are quarreling all the time. Goodbye Anne dear, and I hope that we will all be together soon. Oh, last but not least important. Why don't you go and call on Mrs. _____? She is in Portland, sick. I don't think she loves you or Miss _____ either. At least she raised the devil so over or after that night she came out to tell you good bye that she and her husband separated for a while. Then as soon as they made up she went to Portland. That looked funny. I will bet she gets your past down well before she returns. Better tell her that you are coming back a month later than you intend to and really give her something to think and worry about. Loving, Ruth"[169]

1931, August 22
Had a Spanish woman out to clean, wash and iron Paid her $1.[81]

1931, August 23
Sammy wired Anne LeRoi money.[14] $50 so she could return from Portland. The temperature in Phoenix was 114 degrees and there was a huge dust storm.[81] Sammy said, "Oh, please Ruth, will you get this money to Ann?" At about 10 o'clock Ruth went down to the Western Union and sent Anne fifty dollars which was carfare for her trip back to Phoenix. Sammy burst into tears that night and told Ruth how much she thought of Anne. That she would do anything for Anne; that she was almost broke; that nearly all the money she had received from the people in Alaska was gone; that she would do anything in the world to

get Anne back again.[85]

1931, August 24
Sammy wrote a letter to her sister Anna in Chicago. Part of this letter said, "I hope that everything is all right. Had a dream about you the other night. Dreamt that you gave birth to twins, a boy and a girl. My dream made them look about two months old. A child is something I'll probably never have now. T. B. people haven't any business bringing people into the world. Good thing that has never been my ambition. Now Anne feels very different about it. It's a tragedy in her life."[170] "Anne's lung can't be collapsed either which is a great disappointment to me. She is going to work anyway. She is working now for a doctor in Portland, but will be back here Sept 1. She has only a slight touch of T. B. but will have to take good care of herself."[81] Stated she spent $1200 dollars since she left Juneau the previous October and that it cost her $18 dollars a week currently for "tray service". Somebody named "Captain" in Juneau loaned her money and offered to give her more in a letter if she needed it. She writes about her sister's new baby, "I'm relieved to know it's all over and you are the proud mother of a big strong son. Now, perhaps, you'll be content to leave some of the slackers help populate the world. I'm glad that Robert will be dark. They make such handsome men. Ten pounds seems to be an awful lot for a baby to weigh – no wonder you had such a hard time."[81] She wrote, "Just think that the time I've spent in bed! I could have a baby two months old. Ruth Judd had a baby a couple of years ago. She spent all the time under observation in a tuberculosis sanitarium. She had had T.B. three years when the baby was born. Dr. Judd is in Bisbee Arizona taking another Dr.'s place. I moved over here last Sunday. Just seems like coming home after a vacation. It may not be as good for me over here, but I'm happier. Ruth isn't near as good a cook as Anne, but she's sweet. Works as an office nurse at the clinic."[81] Anne will be back in a few days now. Poor kid, she only made enough money in Portland to pay her hospital and doctor bills, so I wired her $50 dollars last night to come back on. She had a phrenectomy done. Phrenic nerve cut, which helps collapse the lung."[81]

1931, August 29
Dr. Judd's suitcase travelled East on #4, Car 1, space B, Porter 18. Sounds like the suitcase came from LA to Phoenix. (Did Anne LeRoi borrow the suitcase when she went to Portland? Was it at the Duplex?)

The suitcase still had the tag from August on it on Sept 19th.[171]

1931, Late August

Anne LeRoi stopped in Laguna Beach to visit her ex-husband's brother.[172]
This is Dr. B.B. Mason of Laguna Beach. They were still on good terms.
Anne mentioned that she had lived with Sammy for a few years and that
they were taking in a third woman (Ruth Judd) [173] Anne stays with LE Dixon
on the coast at a Hotel?[25] Dixon stated that this wasn't true.[174] Ruth Judd
meets Mrs. Arthur Lepker downtown on Central between Adams and
Monroe. Ruth said that Jack had not returned from the east yet.[161] Ruth
sees a baby in the clinic and decides that it is her baby. It's about 18
months old. She follows the woman home to 361 E Thomas Road. She
made several trips backthere to keep track of the baby. After this, she
didn't know where the baby was.[29]

1931, September 1

Anne LeRoi leaves Portland to come back to Phoenix.[143] Dr. Judd
leaves Bisbee and goes to Mexico for 21 days [48]

1931, September 4

Anne returns from LA with Dixon on the train where she stayed at one
of his apartments.[67] Anne arrived back in the morning[14] looking
healthier than ever. The clinic was doing poor business and they didn't
need Anne back right after she returned and so she didn't work for a while
until October 1.[81] Anne had cut her stay short in Portland and returned
early. She had received word that Ruth was with Jack Halloran perhaps
by a letter from Sammy. She rushed back to Phoenix and once again
humbled Mrs. Judd by taking from her the man whose love she was
trying to win. This was according to Dr. JD Maudlin, the county
physician. He based this upon a statements made to him from a nurse
who was once invited to live with the three women.[86] Ruth wrote to
her parents in December that the clinic wouldn't take Anne back if she
had TB. They were going to examine her and see if she was well
enough to return her job.[20] The Doctors at the clinic voted not to have
Anne back, but Dr. Percy Brown trained Anne and wanted her back. Dr.
Baldwin said that he didn't like Anne, and "didn't want her draped over
his furniture." Anne moves into the side of the duplex where Dr. and
Ruth Judd lived previously and Sammy moves in with her. Ruth lives
in the opposite side. (I thought they all lived together)[84] Ruth said that
Anne returned from Oregon. Sammy had denied herself to help her and

Jack sent her $300. However, Anne returned with a gorgeous wardrobe and very far in debt. They lived together. Ruth was struggling to pay the bills. Anne cooked dinner and Ruth did the dishes. Halloran usually arrived after dinner. Anne always looked fresh in "chiffon and rested". Ruth became jealous of Anne. She said, "Day after day, she lorded it over me, always smiling and fresh and sweet. Well knowing she was hurting me with her taunts." "Anne was used to the world. I truly was not. Halloran was the only man I had gone with since my marriage. I was ashamed of things I had done. I could not openly compete with her." "Many evening Anne would kiss Halloran, caress him in our presence, then after he was gone gloat over not caring a thing for him but merely working him for money." Ruth stated that "this was different with me; secretly Halloran had made love to me at a time when I was most discouraged in life. I had given him everything but truly he had never given me anything. I had never sold my love. It was not what Halloran did but the continual taunts made by Anne which drove me beside myself."[115]

1931 Sept, week 1
Sammy wrote a letter to Ella Bolen, in Minot ND who was a teacher there. She said she could not live any longer.[175] Sammy told her to write often even if she was unable to reply.[163] Lucille Moore states she met Ruth Judd about this time. She does not say how they met.[121]

1931, September 6
Sammy gets dressed this evening and looked cute according to Ruth.[176] Mr. Cat is sick. Ruth states he goes outdoors when he pleases now, and when he sees a dog he runs or hops up on the window-sill by Sammy's bed and hisses at them. Ruth claims he is a dear little cat and loves her and clings to her when he is afraid. She writes this to Dr. Judd on the 7th.[176] There is some sort of fight between Anne LeRoi and Winnie Ruth Judd. This occurs while Anne has not returned to work at the clinic. Anne calls Ruth at the clinic and threatens to put her cat down since it is having fits. Ruth Judd is upset at work regarding this.[177] Ruth later states that "I have heard people believe Anne and Sammy didn't like my cat and that I lost my tempter because they abused it. That is not so. Both of them loved it."[178] Sometime during the summer the cat chewed up a few dolls that Dr. Judd gave to it.[20] Dr. Judd recalls that the cat was half grown, had fits ,and Anne threatened to take it to the humane society, but the cat got better. Ruth was indignant about it.[48]

According to Evelyn Nace, the cat got sick and Anne said that it should be killed. Ruth flew into a rage and called Anne all sorts of names. It was this fight that caused Ruth to move out.[179] Although, I rather think that it was the fact that Dr. Judd was due back that caused her to move. But, then, the opposite side of the duplex was vacant.

1931, September 7
Ruth states in a letter that Sammy, Anne, and she are planning on going to Evelyn Nace's for dinner.[176] Sammy writes in her diary that Ruth and Anne go to Nace's for dinner and leave Sammy at home for health reasons.[109] Evelyn Nace says in her testimony that she invites Ruth, Anne and Sammy over for dinner at her house. Sammy is too ill to go. Things seemed strained between Ruth and Anne. The tension between them seemed to go away as the evening went on. Evelyn's father, sister and family also were there.[133] Evelyn stated that there had been a little misunderstanding between the three girls, but none of them ever had much to say about it. Evelyn stated that she was never as friendly with Mrs. Judd as she was with the other girls. She thought it was because she just wasn't as congenial. She was not the same type as the other girls – not so well educated. Not that that should have made a difference.[111] The Nace family consisted of Alfred and Maggie with children Florence, Evelyn, and Stanley (29, 26, 25 years old in 1931). Alfred was a meat cutter as was Stanley. Florence was a telephone operator and Evelyn a nurse. They lived on North 6th Ave in Phoenix.[180]

1931, September 9
Dr. Judd writes a letter to Ruth from Carrie Judd's house in Santa Monica. He sends the letter to the clinic. He told Ruth that she would be surprised that he is writing from Nogales. He asked if the girls were still together and what they were doing. He said he went to Hermosillo and there was no possibility of work there and it was one of the worst places that he ever saw. He said that the doctor has changed hands twice and was now in the hands of the Mexican Government. He said if she was "in with the two girls it might be better for me to stay awhile." He asked her to let him know what she wished and promised to write a letter in a day or two.[181] Ruth stated that a doctor in Hermosillo had died. His wife wanted to sell his office equipment and his practice to somebody. He wanted to buy this Dr. Burton's practice out. He had gone to Los Angeles to see if his sister could let him have enough money to buy out that practice.[33]

1931, September 10

Anne is examined by Dr. Leff on September 10 or September 11 in Glendale.[182] Sammy writes a letter to her sister Anna, "Anne got back last Friday looking healthier than ever. Feels fine again. The clinic has poor business right now that they don't need her, so she isn't working but is looking for another job. She may do special nursing for a while if nothing turns up. It seems so good to have her back with me again. I'm being bossed and babied again. She has had four proposals of marriage this summer so I should feel quite elated to think she returned to me. We're back at our cute little house. Ruth Judd is staying with us, but somehow it doesn't seem that she belongs here. Don't know how it will work out, but if doctor gets a position she will probably join him. It doesn't bother me, but I don't think Anne likes it. She is determined to get me to gain six more pounds. According to the kind of meals she fixes, I ought to. Although, I am fat enough now. Dr. Randolph examined me a couple of weeks ago. Says my left lung has no activity. That perhaps he will get me up by Christmas. Did I tell you that before? Glad your son is doing nicely. It amused me how Cousin Alice tried to give you pointers. Well, we old maids must have some amusement. Anne is downtown talking to Dr. Randolph getting the low down on me, I suppose. All my independence is gone again. You ought to see her perspire dew drops."[81] Sammy writes in her diary an excerpt from Don Blanding's Driftwood:[108]

> Never a tide goes out to sea
> But carries a bit of the heart of me
> Riding the foam, the gray sea wrack
> Caring no whit if it ne'er comes back.
>
> Drifting over the seven seas
> Driven by trade-wind, storm, and breeze
> Hearing the cry of a sad sea loon
> Floating a while in the blue lagoon.[183]

1931, September 12

Dr. Judd arrives in Mexico. However, this same document also says that he arrives in Los Angeles on this date.[48] Carrie, Dr. Judd's sister stated that Dr. Judd had worked in an Arizona copper mine. Dr. Judd planned to stay with Carrie for just two weeks but got some work in LA and stayed over. During this time, Dr. Judd and Ruth wrote to each other 3-4 times a week. He had planned to return shortly after the tragedy had occurred.[128]

1931, September 15
Listened to Sherlock Holmes. Same diary entry as October 7.[184] Dr. Judd writes to Ruth from Los Angeles. He states concern that he shouldn't say anything much because Ruth is careless about leaving letters lying around for Anne and Sammy to read. He says, "I had supposed you thought so much of those two girls that you would be perfectly happy with them, but if you are not it puts a different face on matters." And "I am not surprised at what you tell me. I do not care to write you freely because you are careless with letters." He expresses concern that Ruth's Clinic will close and that she will be alone.[185] Dr. Leff stated that he last saw Ruth about Mid-September.[182] In another source he stated that he saw her about two weeks before the crime.[66]

1931, September 17
Some type of game of Mr. Duck in Ruth's Pajamas.[14]

1931, September 18
Sammy receives a letter from a Mrs. June Cann who was a society woman of Seattle. It said, "John and Delores Barrymore visited us for 27 days on their yacht, Infanta and it was sure fun to have them, and if we go south this winter they want us to visit them in Beverly Hills. Could you go along with us on our yacht?"[186] Her name is listed in Sammy's diary, as Mrs. J. Cann, The Northcliff Apartments, 308 West, corner Seneca and Boren, Seattle, WA.[58] I believe she is probably married to James Cann who owned part of the Gastineau Hotel when Sammy lived there. An article said, his family lived elsewhere.[37] Another account states that Sammy was invited to make a cruise on the yacht of Delores Costello and John Barrymore.[187] San Francisco Examiner stated that there was an invitation to join a yacht cruise with John Barrymore and Dolores Costello, of the screen.[62] The Los Angeles Evening Herald stated that June wrote this letter on board the "Triton" The Cann family intended to come south for the winter and spend it at the Seattle Yacht club and expressed the hope of seeing Sammy.[63]

1931, September 19

Emil Hoitola writes a letter to Anne. He writes, "Dear Anne: Just finished talking to you less than an hour ago. Gee, it was great to hear your voice again. I miss you so very much dear. I just couldn't go out here and not be thinking of you for everything I see or hear that has beauty or charm reminds me of you. Sure would be nice if you were a bit closer. Dearest, I love you more each day. If that is possible but it seems so and sure enjoyed talking to you. All my love always. Emil. PS. Also sent you a message tonight. I'm sure you received it. Goodnight dear and many kisses."[169]

1931, September 21

About this date, (a few weeks after the 7th) Ruth confesses her infidelity in a letter to Dr. Judd. After she writes this letter, her letters afterwards were very sad and blue. One of the lines in the letter stated, "You know how I wanted a baby. I was lonely and you were so far away. You wouldn't let me have a child. You said I would have to have my baby by some other man-a healthy man. ....Doctor, I can't bring myself to tell you! But I must, even though you'll never be able to forgive me. You'll never love me anymore. Oh, Doctor, I can't live without your love. You will love me in spite of everything, won't you?"[176] Dr. Judd writes to Ruth from California, "I was surprised at your telegram. I took it up to Burton (Winnie's brother) and he decided to start at once. I have no idea what business you have to discuss with him which is important enough to warrant his trip."[188] [134] It is undated, but there is a telegram blank at the State Archives from Burton to Ruth at the Grunow Clinic. It says, "You're blue, advise you to come to Los Angeles. Doc came out today. I have two-part time jobs, am in school, extremely difficult to come now. If absolutely necessary will however. If you need money to come, wire me. Am sending air mail letter to your home. Love Burton"[189]

1931, September 23

Anne writes to her fiancé, Emil Hoitola, "Ruth is leaving us in a few days. Dr. Judd is coming home so she will take an apartment. It really hasn't worked out so well having three of us. We are very fond of her and she is a sweet girl, but there just seems to be a wrong number when one is used to living by oneself and just one other very congenial one."[190] On other occasions, Emil writes to Anne: "Gee, the moon is out so nice and looking down on me here and I'm sure he is peeking down on you way down in Arizona. One thing I do know. I love you, dear. In my dreams I'm always with you, loving you more each day-Emil. Good night dearest. I'll love you always – Emil. Can hardly wait till tomorrow night to talk to you. Love and many kisses – Emil. Glad you and Sammy wrote Sam and sure he appreciates it just seeing you kids planning your trip. Gee, how I'd love to hold you in my arms and give you a nice big kiss. Loving you always-Emil."[64] Ruth's mother writes a letter to Burton, concerned about Ruth. She writes, "Now tell us why Ruth sent for you? All about it. We will write and ask her too. You sent off Glenn's letter so she will know we got into it. Is Dr. Judd at Carries' yet? Or at Ruth's? You see by her letter he was to see you Sunday, the twentieth? What for Burton? Is he trying to give Ruth trouble? Has he left her? Now it is best to tell us all about this affair because Dr. Judd may ask us things and we want to be prepared to know how to answer to avoid trouble." Burton replied in an undated letter that Ruth was simply blue and wanted to see him. She didn't know that he was in school.

1931, September 25
Sammy states in her diary that she has been in bed one year.[14] Ruth gets her period and it lasts for 21 days. Her brother stated that "Ruth had been "unwell" with that periodic sickness common to women. Surely it is not very difficult to imagine the state of nervous and physical exhaustion, and the attendant mental state of anyone who, for such an abnormal length of time as twenty-one days, had been inflicted.[20] Ruth states to Dr. Catton, that she thought that she was pregnant by Jack Halloran. She said, "I wanted a baby by him. And then about twelve days later I had a hemorrhage, probably a miscarriage, and the bleeding kept up until about four days before Sammy and Anne and I quarreled."[100] Ruth also mentioned that the second time she was pregnant (this may be it) that she went to see a doctor to see if she could have the baby and then adopt it as her own without her husband's knowledge.[67] Dr. Judd related that she wanted a baby. She was so lonesome and he was so far away. Dr. Judd told her to have a baby with another man, a healthy man. She said, "After the baby is born I was going to bring him to you. If you liked him, we could keep him. But, if you didn't I wouldn't cry about it. We could have given him away. And now all this has happened and I'm not going to have the baby after all... and you'll never trust me anymore."[191] Homer Quist, the mailman who stated he knew Sammy well and knew Anne

LeRoi stated that there was a small coupe with red wheels standing in front of the duplex almost daily for three weeks. He had only seen Anne LeRoi drive the car although the women did not own any car according to the State of Arizona.[192] Police on October 30 were looking for a black car with red wheels. It was said that Ruth had borrowed the car on Friday night to transport the mattress and other evidence. Some sources point to a woman who disappeared after the murders.[193] Ruth stated that she had never driven a car in Phoenix. She stated she did not drive well enough to trust herself in traffic.[194]

1931, September 27
Sammy writes in her diary, "Dear Lord, I pray. Help me to share somebody's sorrow, somebody's care."[108] On another date (or the same date) she writes something similar: "Wherever, I stray. Dear Lord, I pray. Let me help someone, just for Today."[108]

1931, September 28
Sammy writes to somebody in Juneau and says that she had been in a sanitarium during the summer months; that Miss Leroy has returned from a trip and had gone back to work at the clinic and the two had again taken the same little house they lived in when they first went to Phoenix. She also says, "Ruth Judd, a doctor's wife (he is in California right now) is staying with us. Ruth works at the same clinic too."[11] Sammy writes in her journal a quote from Don Blanding: PHILANDERER [109] [183] Marion Alvina Vrem [59] had mailed her this book since she thanks her for it in a letter saying, "Yes, you sent me Vagabond's House and I love it." This book was NOT given to her by LE Dixon or Jack Halloran since she mentions a lumberman (Halloran) and a contractor from LA building a bank here (Dixon) who help her "while away the hours" in the letter[195]

Philanderer

Love me love, but love me lightly
Weave no silken gauze to tie me.
I acknowledge most contritely
Vows are bonds that in and try me.

If you find a strand enfolds me
Flick a careless finger through it
Break the gossamer that holds me.
But, be sure I see you do it.

And the rest: (not quoted, but appears in one
article)[108]
And then because I think you flout me
I will take the bond you sever
I will wrap it close about me
For awhile, if not forever.

1931, September 29
Harold Bisch, who is one of Dr. Baldwin's patients, was at the clinic and
drove Anne LeRoi home. When they got there Sammy and Ruth were
at the duplex. This is the first time he met Ruth Judd. He took Sammy
and Anne for a ride on north 7th Street. Anne and Sammy remarked
about not having a radio.[196] Bisch said that his radio didn't work since
he lived 10 miles west of Glendale and offered his to them. He brought
the radio with him, but it didn't work in rural districts.[196] He lived 10
miles west of Glendale.[196] Bisch owned a new Cadillac coupe that
had a California license plate and a green Ford Coupe with an Arizona
license plate.[196] Harold Bisch was an undertaker and was interested in
Anne.[67] Ruth said he was a wealthy undertaker.[30] Winnie has not
moved yet, and writes a letter to her husband. She states she is very
busy and will not be able to move until October 3, Saturday night. Dr.
McKeown is going somewhere and she has to do many histories and
his books before he goes. She urges the Doctor to come to her on
Sunday morning the 4th.[131] Harold Bisch was an undertaker in
Springfield who was married to Esther V Antrobus. He belonged to the
Masonic fraternity, the thirty-second degree, and the Shrine, the
Benevolent and Protective Order of Elks, the Knights of Pythias, the
Independent Order of Odd Fellows, and the Improved Order of Red
Men. He was educated in the public schools of Springfield and brought
into his father's business.[197] He was 46 years old in 1931. On his
1918 draft card he was described as medium height, slim build with
blue eyes and dark brown hair. His date of birth was August 14th 1885.[198]

1931, September 30
Harold Bisch drives Ruth Judd home from night school because it is

59

raining.[67] As for Bisch, I believe this is another story about him. Ruth thought that he might have been involved in the crime, but wasn't sure.[25] Ruth called him Lester DePester after the comic strip.[25] She says his name was Bishop. She doesn't know if Jack saw him on Saturday night or not.[25] Ruth thought that he was addicted to Morphine.[25] One time he was at the clinic and picked up a Vanity Fair and he commented about how Ruth would look in evening gowns and stuff. He asked her out.[25] In another source, she says it was Vogue.[30] Ruth claimed after she declined he asked her if she would go to church with him at the Unity.[30] In her talk with McFadden, he asked her to a show and then when she said no, he asked her to go to church over at the Westward Ho.[25] She said no, since she was married.[30] He went to the laboratory and told others the same thing.[25] He told Anne this.[25] He tried to get Anne to come out and take care of his little boy. He wanted her to be the governess and go to France. He asked Ruth the same thing. Bisch's wife was in France. He said that he might give the boy back to his wife and go back to France and take dope the rest of his life.[25] She said he wanted to meet some certain nurses that were real kind and that could take care of his little boy. Ruth found one nurse who wanted to meet him. He said if Ruth didn't get someone he was going to take his boy back to his wife and give it up as a bad job. He would go back to France and smoke dope the rest of his life. Ruth told him that he did not want to ruin his life by starting to take morphine. And he said, "You can get a thrill all the rest of your life by taking dope." Ruth thought that he was a personal addict to that, the use of it or was going to use it. He didn't say that he was addicted at the time.[25] After the crime, Bisch was so frightened he and his colored chauffeur left immediately after the sheriff questioned him. Ruth said he was from Illinois.[67] Bisch did sail from France on November 27, 1929 with his son, Phillip who was 6 at that time, arriving in New York from LeHavre, France.[199] (If Ruth met Bisch on Sept 29, but moved out before the first, this would have to be the day he drove her home?[67] Sammy wrote in her diary of a visit of Dick (Dix?) and Jack. She said she made a fool of herself. "Tried to make me go riding. Anne and I became angry and ran away."[14] This is consistent with what Winnie Ruth Judd wrote in one of her confession articles. She relates that one evening Jack and Mr. D came over. Sammy was tired of being in bed all of the time and tries to get Mr. D to take her for a ride. Mr. D said that Sammy should stay in bed instead until the doctors let her get up and patted her on the head.

Sammy insisted on going for a ride. Anne decides that Dix should take her for a ride in the desert alone and he could take Sammy later when the moon was full. Sammy gets angry and runs out of the house down to the mesquite brush. The men teased her and brought her back to the house.[200] Pearl Wagner (Waggoner) visits the duplex in between 7:30-9:30 with a nurse, Susan Morse. Pearl runs a private sanitarium where Sammy lived while Anne was in Portland.[145] Ruth is packing to move out and does not appear as "tidy" as usual. Ruth was wearing checked pajamas. Sammy was in pajamas and Anne was wearing a dress. They discussed Sammy's condition and examined her recent x-rays. Ruth was moving about packing. Ruth finally came and sat on a chair at the end of Sammy's bed. Apart from talking about Sammy's condition, the girls talked about buying sealskin coats when they go on a trip next June. Anne said that she had met somebody (Bisch?) who was taking a trip north. Sammy and she were planning on enlisting as assistants and going along for three months. It was far enough north to get sealskin to make coats.[201] Harold Bisch was interested in getting Anne to travel with him as a governess for his little boy. He was willing to take Sammy along if there was no other way to get Anne to go with him.[67] These two events probably happened on two different days?

1931, Late September
Dr. Baldwin stated that Ruth told him that she was disappointed in Mrs. LeRoi. She stated that she was not the person that she thought she was. She stated on another occasion that she was shocked when she saw Mrs. LeRoi kiss somebody in the laboratory. Dr. Baldwin told her not to speak about her in that way; that somebody might think that she was jealous of her. She asked who and he named somebody by the name of Robinson. He was not somebody who worked at the clinic. On another occasion he stated that he came into her office and she seemed quite depressed since she was locked out of the laboratory while a patient was having treatment, a patient of Dr. McKeown. She said that she felt very hurt since she was very jealous of her doctors and her work.[202]

1931, Early October
Hedvig is feeling better. She is allowed up to eat meals at the table.[203] Louis Baldwin at the clinic notes that Ruth's efficient work was getting sloppy. She seemed worried about something. He stated that she referred to Anne is slighting terms. Dr. Baldwin told her that Anne

was just jealous and that she should forget about it, but Ruth got worse and worse. Dr. Baldwin thought that Ruth was angry with Anne and that something had happened between them. Dr. Baldwin said that her work was suffering and he was disgusted and considered replacing her.[204] Dr. Baldwin stated that Ruth had stated that she was rather disappointed in Anne, that she wasn't the type of person that she thought she was and that she was going to change her residence to live in some other place. She had told him that she was shocked that she had kissed somebody in the laboratory. Dr. Baldwin told her that she shouldn't speak of Ann this way because people might think that she was jealous of her. Ruth talked about a man by the name of Robinson. When asked who this was, if he was one of the men at the clinic, Dr. Baldwin said no, it was just a name that she mentioned.[202] He also related an occasion when Ruth seemed depressed. He asked her what the trouble was. She said, "Doctor, I feel very hurt. I have been locked out of the X Ray Laboratory where a patient is being given a treatment, a patient of Dr. McKeown's and stated that Anne had been retained in her place. She stated she felt very hurt because she was very jealous of "my doctors and my work".[202]

1931, October 1
A small Chevrolet coupe had been parked out there in the garage at 2929 almost constantly. It had red wheels and a red body. It stopped being there according to the mail carrier about three weeks before October 23rd. Kenneth Grimm stated that this car was there when he moved Ruth.[205] Nurse Anna Evans stopped her care for Sammy and moves to LA when Anne returns.[61] Anne returns to work at the clinic. (? September 29)[129] Ruth moved out of the Duplex to an apartment closer to the clinic.[123] She rents an apartment from HU Grimm at 1130 E Brill. This time she lives in unit F, she previously lived there in unit C.[118] Dr. Judd was expected to return from Bisbee Arizona and she moved to a place on Brill that they both liked. Dr. Judd had been in Mexico since September 12.[48] Ruth stated in another source, that she needed to get away from Anne and her taunts. She stated that she was cruelly made fun of by Anne to Halloran in her presence. So, she finally moved.[115] Kenneth Grimm helps her move over to Brill. They made one trip. He says that Ruth went back into the house to get the gun. She didn't say this to him, but heard her say something to the girls. She indicated that she always kept that gun in the house with her when she was by herself. She came out and got back into the car.

They drove to Seventh Street and she said she forgot something that she left on the couch and so he drove her back. There was a dark haired guy visiting the girls, about 8:30 or 9. He brought Ruth's stuff over and this fellow brought her over to the apartment. It was 8:30 or 9 at night. He didn't see the gun. He did say that she told the girls and that she didn't tell him that she went back in the house after the gun and the pocket book. She did say something about keeping that gun in the house with her when she was by herself.[206] He stated that they had gotten as far as Palm Lane and she asked him to go back. She had gone into the house and stated to Anne and Sammy that she had left her gun and had returned for it.[207] However, Dr. Judd didn't return to Phoenix, but instead went to Santa Monica and Ruth Judd lived alone.[84] However, Jack Halloran spent 10 of 14 nights with Ruth before the murders.[100] Ruth Judd takes her cat, "Mister Cat" with her when she moved, but after that the cat was often at 2929 North Second Street.[157] Ruth occasionally appeared at the duplex and took the cat and walked down the street muttering, according to Evelyn Nace and Lucille Moore.[208] Much of Ruth's stuff was still over at the duplex. She had taken a few small things like underwear with her in a suitcase when she went over to the Brill.[25] It was reported on October 31 that Ruth took her gun with her when she moved.[209] Dr. Judd stated that Ruth wrote to him about this time stating that she couldn't sleep and that she had taken Luminal several nights. He told her that this could be worse than taking morphine and that it would "shatter her nerves". Ruth wrote back that she hadn't taken any more Luminal. [48] Ruth stated that she got paid this evening.[176] Austin Lathrop writes his last letter to Sammy.[63] He sent her a letter inquiring if Sammy needed any more financial aid and that he would be in Seattle on November 1st[210] All of Cap. Lathrop's letters expressed the most friendly interest in her health and welfare, and renewed his offers to send her further funds if she needed them.[63] His last letter was written on stationary from the Republican National Committee.[50]

1931, October 2

Ruth pays Mr. Grimm 10 dollars in the morning. She paid 10 for light and gas and then left 15 in her desk drawer. Somebody stole this money from her desk. She thought at first that one of the doctors had taken the money thinking that it was their own, but they hadn't been in the office while she was out. She was really upset and thought about or exaggerated about having to sell her typewriter to have some money to live on for that month.[176] Ruth receives a letter an hour later from home saying that her Papa had been out chopping wood and a big limb fell on him and broke his ribs, front and back and was in terrible agony. Ruth felt desperate since she hadn't seen her parents for so long.[176] She writes, "Doctor, I don't know what to do. If something doesn't happen soon I will go crazy. I am wild. I haven't seen my parents for so long that I simply can't stand it. And, Doctor, someone is trying to send my parents to the poor farm. I wish you would see about it. I can't stand that. Doctor, can't you do something? I need you so badly. I can't sleep. I want you to get some money from that farm. There is a mortgage for over $600 on the folks' place, so they won't get much more than their carfare out here. Oh, dear, what can I do? So many people have money and there my poor Daddy lays suffering with his chest. Doctor, what shall I do? Please, don't you do anything to worry me or I will just kill myself. I am desperate. I want Papa and Mama, and I want you, too. Please, please, come to me as soon as you can. I am all in. It is because I love you that I haven't given up the struggle before now. Please be good, and if you can save $25, please do it and then come here right away. I love you and I need you so bad. I am breaking so fast. I can't help it. What is best? Should you come here and help me with my far too heavy work at the office so I won't have a complete break? Can't we somehow all live together? Grimm's have a two-bedroom apartment for thirty dollars. I have taken one for twenty-five, but oh, me. I don't know which way to turn. I feel like hitch-hiking, the only way there is to get home. Daddy may die. Please take care of yourself."[176] When Dr. Judd received this letter he wanted to leave for Phoenix right away.[176] There were many "callers".[123] Bill brought Hedvig's books back, Mr. Beil and Mr. Duck (Dick? Dix?).[211] Sammy writes her last letter to her parents. "It was a grand morning, nice and cool. We even used blankets last night. My bedroom is going to be lovely this winter because it faces the east which will give me the lovely morning sunshine. The sun feels good for the first time in months."[212] "Ruth Judd moved, so are alone again and we like it so much better. Three never get along very well."[213] She concludes her letter by writing, "We're looking forward to a happy year in Phoenix. Don't feel badly about my having to stay in bed. Why I have it better than most people that are up. Have a nice home to live in, even a telephone by my bed so I can talk in bed as long as I feel like it without getting tired. My doctor thinks he will let me get up at Christmas, which is a very short time considering the year I have already been in

bed. Don't worry. It would be different if I felt sick, but I don't."[214]
Harold Bisch went to the clinic at about 10:00 in the morning and told
Anne that he had the radio he was going to give them in his car. Anne
told him to go ahead and take it out to the house. Harold Bisch arrives
at the house and finds Sammy home alone. Later, he picks up Anne
LeRoi at the clinic in the evening and drives her home. Sammy, Anne,
and Harold go for a ride in the evening. He stated this was the last time
he saw either of the girls. He owned both a new Cadillac Coupe (with
California License) and a Green Ford Coupe (with Arizona License)[196]
However, Harold Bisch wants more in exchange for the radio than the
girls want to give, so they later hated him. They must have given it
back, but they still have it on October 7, but probably gave it back
before Fred Ryan gave them one on the 15th.[67] Dr. Leff stated to
investigators that he saw Ruth about this day (about two weeks before
the crime.[66]

1931, October 4
Ruth writes the following letter to her husband that was dated June 4,
but I believe it would be October 4: "Dear Doctor. Better wait until
Saturday night to come over. I'm so rushed I can't move until then and I
want to do the moving. I have so many histories to do, statements to get
out and all Dr. McKeown's books to do before he leaves. I simply can't add
one tiny thing to all I have to do this week. And to move, I have so many
things to sort over. I can't do it until the other work is out of my way. I
think I'll move over on the Brill. It's close to the office. There is a phone in
the house. 42955. I will be in the end apartment on Brill. I'm so rushed,
must close. Burton didn't come. Lovingly, Ruth."[134] Ruth had sent
Burton a wire that he considered strange stating that he must come at
once; that she was terribly lonely. Burton decided to go at once, but
then decided it would jeopardize his work at the Jefferson High School.
So he wired her and told her that she was just blue and lonely. He
suggested that she come to Los Angeles.[215] Perhaps this is the day Dr.
Judd received Ruth's letter dated October 2; he planned to leave that
very day for Phoenix. However, a temporary job came up with the
chance to earn some badly needed money. It was to start on October 11
and go until the 20th. He stated that just these 9 days of employment
did fate play another diabolical trick. Nine days! The difference
between a happy reunion and – two lives snuffed out. If that meager
chance at nine days' employment had not turned up just then I would
have joined Ruth when she pleaded for me to come-and this tragic story

would never have been told.[176] It looks like he may have started instead on the 8th according to the police report.[216] Ruth knowing her father had been injured wrote the following letter to a doctor in Darlington. "Dear Dr. Peacock, I've just received a letter from my mother Mrs. H. J. McKinnell, that my father had been hurt and his ribs broken and is suffering quite a lot. I have been planning on having my parents come out here to Phoenix Arizona for the winter. I had a breakdown with tuberculous three years ago and have had to stay in a dry climate like this and have not been able to come home for several years but we had planned on my parents coming out and spending the winter with me here. Will Papa be able to come at all? Or is he in such a condition that I should come home to him? Do you think that his injury to his chest may cause pneumonia and there will be danger of his never getting well? I want to come home at once if he is in danger. So will you please write me frankly and if he needs me, write me collect if I should come home. Papa is very old and I am so afraid of any injury to his chest causing pneumonia. I do not believe that his lungs are very good anyhow. If my father is not in any serious condition to necessitate my coming home, how soon will he be able to be moved here? I can get him a compartment on the train where he will be to himself and be in bed and Mamma can be with him. Will you please be so kind as to write me all about my father's condition? Dr. Peacock, will you please be very kind to my father and send me the bill for all medical attention. Please do everything there is to do for Papa and send me the bills and they will be paid in time at least. My husband has lost a great deal of money in copper mining and I have been in tubercular sanitariums quite a bit in the last three years but can pay you in time and want everything done that can be for Papa and if I should come home to be with him, I can. Thank you for your many kindnesses to my parents. Trusting that Papa is not hurt severely and that I shall receive a letter saying that he can come out to Phoenix very soon. Very sincerely, Mrs. W.C. Judd." Ruth had urged her parents to come to Phoenix several times believing that the change in climate would be beneficial to their health. The retired minister and his wife had discarded the plan as impossible due to the condition of his wife and to a lack of finances.[217]

1931, October 5
Howard Hagen formerly of Landa, North Dakota now married with one child and living in Atlanta writes Sammy a letter. Many of his or

Sammy's letters were published in a San Francisco Newspaper.[28] The San Francisco Examiner states: "Attesting to Miss Samuelson's popularity, there were also letters from an admirer, "Howard" who was Howard Hagen, later married to another woman;[62] See 1926 for one of his letters. The letter on this day read, "Sammy Dear, Am tremendously relieved to learn that you are so much better. Knowing that you were flat on your back with no advice for months and months I worried about you a lot. For goodness sakes take the best care of yourself possible and be up on Christmas. Ann is just eight months old. I am enclosing a snapshot taken when she was 4 months. She was quite cute then to me, as she was just beginning to laugh. Time certainly flies, about six years since we spent the year together in Landa. To spend a year in bed is tough, but the past year of the depression was a good one to spend there if it must be done.[113] He had received a last letter from Sammy about three weeks before October 22. She didn't mention her companions.[219]

1931, October 6
Anne and Sammy listened to Sherlock Holmes radio show.[14] Turned off the lights and were too scared to sleep. Dr. Judd writes Ruth a letter. In it he asked her to "try to exert a little self-control". He wrote, "I will remind you for one thing that you wrote me first that your father was dying fatally injured. Next that you wanted to bring both your parents out here, next that your father was on the verge of pneumonia (which neither you nor anyone else knows to be the case)" The Dr. took "blame for the entire situation during the past year or more." He advised her he was afraid "you are in danger of getting yourself into a serious condition. You want to get hold of yourself." He referred to a mild narcotic she was taking and said, "it will knock your nervous system to a fare thee well if you don't cut it out."[220]

1931, October 7
Anne Leroy writes a letter to somebody in Juneau stating that Sammy was doing better and would be up by Christmas and would be back teaching in Juneau in the next year.[11]

1931, October 8
Dr. Judd was put in charge at the Santa Fe Emergency Hospital while Dr. Benjamin Moss was away. Dr. Judd was there every day in-between October 9th to October 20. He treated several patients according to the records in-between Oct 16 and Oct 17 according to the

slips.[216] During this time Dr. Judd almost thought of leaving for Phoenix immediately. He wrote to Ruth as cheerfully as he could with the promise of joining her soon. He stated he also knew that in Ruth's despair she thought that Dr. Judd had not forgiven her and had no intention of coming to Phoenix. He stated she had written and confessed of her infidelity before the beginning of October.[176]

1931, October 10
Ruth writes her husband a letter, parts of it read, " Dearest Doctor, I start so many letters and then have to do something else and destroy the letter and do not get one mailed. Thank you very much for writing to me whether I write to you or not. I am busy. I don't seem to get things done. When I get home at night I topple down and go to sleep with our cat....We ain't got barrels of money maybe we're all ragged and funny but we'll travel along singing a song side by side (Because we love each other.) Lovingly Ruth"[176] Note that in this intimate detective article, the date looks blotted out. The LAPL website has the whole letter and its dated October 17, the letter she wrote her husband from the clinic.[221] Ruth sobbed with something that kept pounding after her. She took more luminal. She had just gone to sleep, when at about 2AM Halloran drove up in a taxi. He was dead drunk and brought the taxi driver into the house. Ruth ordered him out and begged Halloran to please not come at those hours. He said, alright, he would go to Anne's.[115]

1931, October 11
It is cooler in Phoenix. Anne and Sammy had breakfast by the fire in their living room. Later, Mr. and Mrs. Fitchbew who was the architect for the Grunow Clinic and his wife came over and took them for a ride. They also lived across the street at 2929.[210] Mrs. Fitchbew described Ruth as "the girl who smiled from the teeth out."[222] She knew Anne and Sammy also since they lived nearby.[222] Bessie Humphrey Greene, Astrologer stated about Ruth that during this week starting on this day: "She came under a most terrifying combination of planetary influences which not only attacked her from within herself but in the external world as well, exposing her to the danger of sudden death or calamity, and that during that week she was not at any time responsible for what she did."[223]

1931, October 12

Anne again writes to her fiancé Emil, "Went to Ruth's for luncheon today. She spent seven years in Mexico and prides herself on Spanish dishes. I don't know what it was I ate. It didn't taste so bad but I think it ruined me."[190]

1931, October 14

Gertrude Wilcox cleans the duplex for the last time. She cleaned the duplex one time per week. Sammy was home alone in bed. Her bed was at the right side of the room or along the North wall.[224] A few days before October 16, Anne LeRoi goes into Evelyn Nace's office at the clinic to talk. She asks a hypothetical question about what would she do if she had a very good friend and knew he was going out with someone that had a venereal disease. Evelyn replied that if she knew him very well and there was a reason to believe somebody could be at risk for infection that she would tell him for the sake of humanity.[133] Anne LeRoi meets Dr. Brinckerhoff. She had come over for an eye examination at the eye clinic and Dr. Brinckerhoff came in. Anne said that she was having severe headaches and frontal pains and thought something must be wrong with her eyes. The Dr. examining Anne, Dr. Brinckerhoff and Anne talk and Dr. Brinckerhoff says he is new in town, has no family, and is somewhat lonely. Anne invites him out to the house on Thursday night.[225] She said that he could come out and meet her little girl friend Miss Samuelson.[226] Dr. Brinkerhoff stated that he had met Anne before when his work brought him in contact with her in the X-Ray department.[226] Ann has lunch at Ruth's house and they had chili.[227] At 5 PM, Anne and Ruth were discussing Anne and Sammy moving in with Ruth if she got a place large enough when her parents came out. Mr. Gregory came then and took Ruth to look at the houses and then over to have dinner with his son and wife.[115] Ruth meets with Mr. Gregory, a real estate agent a few hours before dinner according to Burton who is quoting court documents. Ruth was looking for a house for her parents and Anne & Sammy. She had picked out a house at 1200 McDowell Rd. She said, "This room here would be ideal for my two friends." "I know that they would come to live with us," as she said to Mr. Gregory.[20] Mr. Gregory stated that he knew Ruth for the past 3-4 months. His first conversation with her was at the clinic. On this day they were together from 5 to 8 in the evening. They looked at different houses for 3-4 hours. They were at the house she picked out at 7 o'clock which was on the 1200 block of McDowell.[228] Many of these references to Mr. Gregory are placed on October 15, but they fit better here on the 14th. Ruth tells Betty Murray that "it will be best for me never to see them again" meaning Mrs. LeRoi and Miss Samuelson a few days before the crime.[86]   Ruth writes a letter to her husband that he received on the 16th that he described as "bitter, almost reproachful missive".[176] During this day, Ruth writes the following letter to her husband on stationery from the Ingleside Inn: My Dear Doctor, I received your special delivery letter in the long envelop XXXX the other one too. Wish I was over there to take those dinners with you. I did not bring the typewriter home tonight, therefore the pencil. Anne came over to have chili with me today. I've never been out to the house since I moved. I'm too tired to go. Five of the doctors at the clinical and Jack and Mr. Dixon are going to Mr. Wilrow for XXXX deer hunting. They are going to camp there for a week or so. Gee I wish things would straighten up. I'm tired and sleepy and lonesome. Wish we were in Tayoltita now together don't you? I am lonesome tonight so don't know what to write about. The three new doctors in the clinical came and ask me lots of questions of where to get statements printed, what system I use, etc. so I guess I look slightly intelligent. They do talk to me more than any of the other girls I know. Write me often. I love you lots Doctor. Lovingly yours, Ruth. There is another piece of paper attached to this letter, but not part of this letter. It is illegible. Xs here mean it's illegible.[227]

At 9:00 PM Ryan said he met Halloran in front of his hotel in "answer to a telephone call from the latter, with whom he had previously discussed some business." (Hermes? Thompson?) There was a woman in Halloran's car. Ryan was introduced to Anne. They went into the hotel and had a drink in Ryan's room "with the other person". Anne finally said, "Sammy is alone." So, they took Miss LeRoi home in the car. In leaving the hotel they met Hermes. Jack introduced Anne to Hermes as "Miss Stevens". When they got to the house, Sammy was in bed. Jack said to Ryan, "This is the sick girl". Ryan said she looked very ill.[229] Sammy met a man from El Paso. [230] They talked for a while about various things such as the life of the girls in Alaska and their hopes in regaining health. Ryan stated that they appeared to act very affectionately toward each other much as a mother and a daughter might. [229] Ruth cannot sleep again. She went to bed. Anne's thoughts possessed her. She stated her mind was wild. She went to get the gun. She stated that she was running a temperature. She told the neighbors where she was going and went over to Anne's.[115] Miss Marshall stated that Ruth came to her door and said if anyone called for her to tell them that she had gone to visit Lucille.[231] [232] Ruth had told Lucille that she would phone her about 8 to verify that she would have dinner on this Wednesday evening. However, she did not call that evening, but called the following morning instead and explained that the party did not come to her house until 9 on Wednesday evening. So, the plan was to have dinner on Thursday night instead.[233] She waited next door. Ruth's stomach shook inside since she planned to shoot through the window. She started crying so hard. She turned and went home.[115] At about 9:30, a man drove up in a Packard and stopped in front of Ruth's apartment. He knocked at the door and aroused no one. He knocked on Miss Marshall's door. He asked if she knew where Mrs. Judd had gone. She told the gentleman that Mrs. Judd had left word that she could be found at Lucille's. The man said that he did not know anyone by the name of Lucille. He got in his car and drove away.[231] Jack came a bit after 9:00.[232] The man left and then returned about 15 minutes later and asked Miss Marshall if she saw Mrs. Judd when she came back to tell her that he would return. Miss Marshall stated that Ruth returned about 9:30 and she gave her the message.[232] Ruth said Miss Marshall told her that Jack had been there. She went to bed again, took another luminal and cried herself to sleep.[115] Jack and Ryan left about 11:30.[229] According to Ryan, he and Jack left Anne and Sammy's about 11:30 and drove to Ruth's. A young woman came from an open door. When introducing Ryan, Jack referred to the woman as Miss Jones. Ryan said this was Ruth. He said they talked for a few minutes and then went back downtown.[229] Miss Marshall stated that she did not see Ruth, but she heard her in her apartment around 11:00. She was awakened by somebody talking excitedly in Ruth's apartment. She said she could not make out what was said, but came to the conclusion that Ruth was vexed with a gentleman for not having called for her at Lucille's. She said she fell asleep and did not hear a car drive away.[231] According to Ruth, at about midnight, Jack Halloran came again, walked right into the house drunk with Mr. Ryan. Ryan stepped over to Ruth and said something dirty. Ruth stated she felt too dazed to understand and was half asleep. Ryan threw 2$ down the front of her pajama blouse. Ruth flew into a range and Jack calmed her down and apologized. They took Ryan back to the Luhr Hotel. Jack and Ryan started a fight in the lobby. Ruth was sitting in the car in front. Then, Jack took her home and stayed with her that night. Ruth stated that she was very sick that night. She talked a long time to Jack. She told him how she could not sleep and even told him about going over to Anne's that night, but didn't go in but turned around and came back. She told Jack some of her other worries.[115] In 1933, Miss Moore stated she was awakened sometime in the night. It was around 2 am. There were voices at her door. Some man was talking with Ruth. It sounded like she was vexed with him. Miss Marshall turned on the light and found it to be 2 am. Miss Marshall stated that he was trying to persuade her to do something, but she didn't know what it was. Miss Marshall said Ruth sounded like she was put out or something. She said she heard the car drive away.[232]

1931, October 15
Sammy calls up Anne during the day and states that they have friends in town.[225] Sammy writes Ruth a check for $5.[234] Sammy owes Ruth $11 from the deposit on the lights. Anne goes over to Ruth's for lunch and has chili. Ruth states that she hasn't been out to the duplex since she moved and that she is too tired to go there.[227] Herbert Ellis, laboratory technician at the Grunow Clinic claimed he saw Anne and Ruth leave arm and arm about noon. They returned before 2 o'clock and Anne complained to Ellis and others in the hospital of violent pains in her stomach and deathly sickness. Later in Mrs. Judd's apartment it was reported that the authorities found strychnine tablets.[235] Dr. McKeown stated that he gave her a check for her regular pay which was 35 dollars.[236] Jack has a business meeting with Hermes and Ryan at the hotel. Halloran said, "What does a cheap radio cost? I don't want it for myself, but for two girls out here. One is flat on her back, the other has been up awhile. I want it to cheer them up." Hermes explained that they had a small one which had been used and which could be delivered quickly. The question arose as to whether the girls would accept it. Halloran telephoned them, and after some demurring, they accepted. Ryan stated, "We thought we were doing a service to a customer," said Ryan, "as well as a charitable act."[229] They stated that on leaving the hotel, Halloran and Ryan each bought a box of homemade candy from "an old woman" whom they met and took it along with them.[229] Jack calls Winnie at the clinic at 4:00 drunk and Ruth doesn't want to talk to him on the clinic phone. So, she goes and talks with him on another phone. He was singing on the phone, and said he was singing over KTAR which was atop of the Luhrs Building.[25] KTAR joined NBC in 1930 bringing national radio to the Valley.[1] Ruth stated that he and Ryan were drunk. He asked to meet Lucille Moore that night or rather to arrange so he could meet her that night.

Ruth arranged that. Jack stated that he had a bought a new radio for Sammy and Ryan and he were going to take it over to her. Then they would come and get Ruth about 6.[115] Ruth told Ann that she was making heuevos rancheros for supper at her house that night.[25] Anne leaves the clinic shortly after 5 with Dr. Brinckerhoff. Dr. Brinckerhoff drives her home.[225] Dr. Brinkerhoff had only been at the clinic a week.[226] Anne had a small dinner party. Her guest was a new doctor from the clinic who was unmarried, "a tall homely chap, but an interesting talker."[230] Jack goes out to visit Sammy at 4:00 and brings two men with him.[25] Dr. Brinckerhoff states that after he had been there an hour three men came in; Jack, and a gray haired man about 40 and Mr. Ryan. Dr. Brinckerhoff talks to Mr. Ryan of El Paso about baseball and football. Mr. Ryan brought a new radio for Sammy and also a box of candy.[25] Halloran carried the candy into the house.[229] Dr. Brinckerhoff says in his statement that the 3 men were Jack Halloran, Mr. Ryan, and a Mr. Hermes.[237] Ruth said these three men were Fred Ryan of Dunnigan &Ryan Hardware and Mr. Thompson who was a quiet man, a junior of the firm or a buyer for their hardware.[67] Fred Ryan stated that they were out to the house briefly to install a radio set which Halloran had purchased from the firm of the El Paso man. They planned to return to their hotel in Halloran's automobile. Ryan and Hermes stated that Halloran had taken them there shortly after nightfall and had left them there for a short time. Hermes set it up. At the house, they found Miss Samuelson lying on a settee and Mrs. LeRoi was preparing the evening meal. There was a Dr. that they did not know there. Somebody served a drink.[229] Dr. Brinkerhoff was not particularly impressed with them. Dr. Brinkerhoff was impressed by the attractiveness of their home, their friendship and how well they seemed to get along.[25] Jack stated when they dropped by the girls were having dinner.[238] Anne and Sammy were given a radio that had been used for presentations from a man from El Paso whom they met on October 14. "No strings attached" and didn't expect to see him again. It was a Jackson Bell radio valued at 50 dollars and had eight tubes and according to Sammy, "It had the most wonderful tone, I've ever heard."[210] Jack left by himself and was gone about .5 hours and the other men set up the radio in the bedroom. The other men called a taxi while Jack was gone.[225] Ruth said that Mr. Ryan who came out with Jack Halloran and one of Mr. Ryan's buyers while Jack picked up Ruth and Miss Moore [200] Jack arrives at Ruth's after 6:00 and they drive out to pick up Lucille Moore. Ruth introduces her to Jack and they talk about hunting in the White Mountains.[25] Lucille stated that Jack and Ruth came to pick her up at her house at 6:30 and they went to 2929. She asked Ruth who lived there and she gave no reply, but Anne came out she said, "you know who lives here now."[233] Ruth stated that Jack came past her house at 6. They then went over to Lucille Moore's house. He then wanted to go with him over to Anne's and pick up Mr. Ryan and Thompson and have dinner.[115] Ruth wanted to stay back at the house because of this, but Jack insisted that she come because it would save time. He stated that he would park the car in front of the house and not let them know that Ruth and Lucille were waiting inside[115] On the way over Lucille said Ruth made Jack promise her if they went out to the house that they were not to know that she was in the car. Jack stated that he would remember. Lucille and Ruth stayed in the car.[121] Jack stated that they arrived at 7 and stayed for about 20 minutes.[239] Jack went in to get Mr. Ryan.[25] Jack sent the taxi away when he came back.[225] When they went out to get the taxi they had called, Jack was sitting in the automobile with two women. Jack introduced Ruth as "Miss Jones".[229] Ruth didn't want Anne to know she was in the car since she had lied to Anne about having to work that evening and she didn't want Anne to know that she had introduced Jack to Lucille Moore "because he was practically supporting Anne and Sammy. Between Jack Halloran and L. E. Dixon, they were just about supporting them --the hundred dollars that Anne was getting in salary and the books will show that they were living expensive; that it cost them $150.00, $175.00 or $200.00 a month, and the men were helping them, gave them money, helped them financially, and I didn't want to make any trouble with her and the girls."[25] Lucille said Ruth was displeased that Jack brought out the girls and stepped out of the car and around to the front and said a few words to the girls. Lucille stated that Ruth said to Jack, "I asked you not to come out here." While Jack was in the house, Ruth told Lucille that she had had some trouble with the girls living there on account of Jack. She said she loved Jack very much but it would never do her any good, because they were both married.[233] Ruth stated that she had moved away; that the difference with the girls was because of Jack. Ruth stated Anne and Sammy thought Jack was perfectly grand as well.[121] While Jack was in the house she asked Lucille what she thought of Jack. Lucille said he was nice. Ruth replied that he was nicer than that, he is perfectly grand.[121] Ruth didn't want Dr. Brinkerhoff to know she was with Jack, for Dr. Brinkerhoffer at that time had all the respect in the world for her. He had connected with her as a new person in the clinic on where to get different office supplies and he knew Ruth was married.[115] He knew that Ruth was working because her doctor husband was sick.[115] Ryan claimed that Ruth said, "I don't want to see her. I don't want her to know I'm out here. See how I look. Look at my hair." Anne walked towards the car.[229] Lucille said she came to the door of the car, looked in and said Hello. Ruth got out and spoke to them. Lucille did not know what she said.[121] The two women greeted each other by saying Hello. Neither showed any sign of agitation.[229] Ruth stated that Jack went ahead and told Anne and Sammy that they were waiting in the car [115] Anne and Sammy came out to the car and asked them all to stay for dinner. Ruth gets out of the car and Sammy puts her arm around her and kisses her. Ruth talks to Sammy about her troubles with the Dr. being sick and the 15 dollars that was stolen from her desk at work and the tree limb that fell on her father and broke part of his ribs.[25] The party wanted to stay and eat with Anne.[25] Halloran kissed Sammy which started a quarrel between Ruth and Anne and Sammy according to Halloran.[86] Lucille Moore, HJ Brinkerhoff, Fred Thompson and another man witnessed a quarrel starting from that kiss.[86] Ruth wanted them to come to her house. They went to 1130 Brill.[25] Ruth said to Jack that he promised that Anne and Sammy wouldn't know that she was at the house. Jack replied, "Oh, forget it". Nothing more was said about it.[121] Anne cooked dinner at the duplex for Dr. Brinckerhoff as he sat in the living room and talked to Sammy. For dinner they have scalloped potatoes and chops. Ruth Judd was mentioned during dinner in a casual way, but they were very friendly towards her. After the men left, Dr. Brinckerhoff takes Anne for a ride for a few blocks away to get some cigarettes.[225] Sammy is in bed when Anne and Dr. Brinckerhoff come home and she is wearing some type of negligee. She was playing the radio. [225] Sammy is able to get Chicago, Cincinnati, Texas, San Fran, Mexico and Denver on the new radio that evening.[210] Sammy states that this was Dr. Brinckerhoff. He was considering renting the duplex next to them. Sammy states that "if he does we will be either friends or enemies by spring".[210] Dr. Brinckerhoff leaves about 10:30 or 11:00.[225] Sammy wrote in her diary, "Men fight over what? But, I hide myself to the wastelands of the north to try to forget – Rickey"[14] Wrote in her diary, "Biggest Surprise. We were presented with a radio. Dr. B to dinner".[240] Ruth, Miss Moore, and Halloran, Ryan, and Hermes drove to Ruth's apartment.[229] At about 8:30 Miss Marshall stated she returned to her apartment from night school with another girl. She said upon her arrival as she drove in the yard, she saw this same Packard that had been parked in front of Ruth's apartment constantly since Mrs. Judd moved next door to her and that a man was sitting in the car, and that Ruth and two other men went into the apartment leaving the other person sitting in the car. As she and her friend approached the door of her apartment, the man in the car spoke to them saying something in a flirtatious way, and Miss Marshall turned to him and said in an indignant tone, "Did you speak to me?" And the man said, "Well, you don't need to get sore about it." She then entered her apartment and played bridge until about 10:30 and closed the door from her bedroom leading into her living room; that shut out the noise from next door. She said she fell asleep immediately and did not know when the party broke up or as to when the car left.[231] Miss Marshall said a man was seated in the car and Mrs. Judd and two men were standing in the door of her apartment. After she drove into the garage, Ruth and the other two men had closed the door and gone into the apartment, but the other man remained in the car. Miss Marshall stated she and the other girl played cards until about 10. She stated she could hear the occupants of the next apartment singing and laughing and talking. She went to bed about 10 and heard no more of the party and didn't know when it had ended.[232] Ruth had a party with Jack Halloran, Fred Thompson, Phoenix surgical supply salesman, and Fred Ryan who was connected with a hardware company in El Paso.[241] Burton states that a Mr. A attended Ruth's party this night.[20] Lucille Moore stated that on arrival at the Judd apartment, Halloran produced a bottle of whiskey and a bottle of tequila. They mixed some drinks, sang and talked. They had 4 rounds of drinks.[233] Ruth showed the party some picture she had taken in Mexico.[121] The party goes to dinner at the "American Kitchen" and took it back to Ruth's to eat it. Ruth reported that she had to borrow dishes since she didn't have enough for all of them.[20] Ryan said they sent out for food while the women made coffee.[229] Lucille asked to be taken home early in the evening when she found out that Dr. Judd wasn't there. However, she said yes when asked to stay for dinner with them anyway.[121] Halloran and Fred Ryan had been drinking. Fred Ryan states that this was the first meal he had had in 3 days. Jack drove very recklessly because of it. Mr. Ryan got so nervous and upset that he got out of the car. Mr. Thompson took the wheel so they could avoid having an accident.[67] At Ruth's the fellows sang songs. Ruth tells her parents that there was no drinking done and no kissing. Ruth said it was a clean, simple evening and they enjoyed it more than any evening in ages.[242] Hermes said that they sang songs,

had a drink, and made quite a bit of noise, but were not intoxicated.[229]
Lucille stated that during the course of the evening, Ruth kissed Jack
numerous times, in fact every time she passed him or got near him.
Jack did not seem to be the aggressor, but did not resist these advances.
Jack was telling about leaving his pocketbook in a hotel in El Paso, and
the management later called him up and told him they had found his
pocketbook. At the time he pulled the wallet from his pocket, reached
in and pulled out a large roll of bills which he laid over the table.[233]
Jack and Mr. Ryan talked about religion. Ruth told them that
sometimes, although her family was Protestant, that she might find
relief in becoming a Catholic.[115] Jack picked up the bottle of luminal
on Ruth's dresser and said, "Are you or have you gone to taking this
dope?" Ruth stated, "I take it to sleep, I don't know what the matter
with me is, and sometimes I think I am losing my mind." Ruth started
to cry. Ryan sat down on the bed. Ruth again said that sometimes she
thinks if she would become a Catholic her mind might get some rest.
She said, "I wish I could talk my whole soul out to some priest for
relief. I want to be good. I want to do right, but I worry I can't sleep
until it seems I will lose my mind."[115] When the men left one of them
made the sign of the cross and asked a blessing on Ruth. All of the
men were Catholic.[242] [225] They had discussed religion during the
evening.[20] Ruth remarked laughingly that 'Mister Cat', her pet, seemed
to prefer the LeRoi-Samuelson home and that since moving that she
had to keep him locked in. Other than this, the girls were not
mentioned.[238] Hermes stated that the names of Mrs. LeRoi or Hedvig
Samuelson were mentioned.[229] Ruth stated the papers lied about that
night. She said, "No human ever was going through such turmoil of
mind. I am honest. I did want relief to cry my soul out to someone. All
I could think of was a priest for relief. He would perhaps calm
whatever possessed my mind, give me relief, the relief I sought on
drugging myself to unconsciousness with luminal."[115] Frank O Smith
stated that neither Ryan nor Hermes saw Ruth after 11 or 12 this night.
They were with Halloran. Ryan and Hermes were registered at the
Luhrs Hotel[243] The three of them were never at the Adams Hotel
during this week.[243] One source stated that Anne attended this party.
A neighbor said that it lasted well into the following morning and
described it as decidedly hilarious.[244] There were frequent calls to the
drug store for more ginger ale.[244] Hermes stated that about midnight
they left to take the other woman home.[229] Miss Marshall, a neighbor
of Ruth's, says that she and a lady friend were accosted with some

"bright remarks" which were made by an apparently drunk man, who was seated in a large enclosed sedan at 1130 E. Brill, according to Burton, quoting the statement of Miss Marshall on March 2, 1932 made to him and Robert La Due.[20] Miss Moore said that a quarrel followed after the asserted caresses bestowed upon her by Halloran. So, Halloran and the other men offered to take her home. "The men drove me out into the country for about 10 miles and then drove me home." She said that they did not molest her during the drive.[242] She asked them to take her home, but turned and went across the Grand Canal to a service station. Then they came back into Phoenix, dropping Miss Moore at her home about midnight. Miss Moore had the impression that there is considerable affection between Ruth and Jack.[233] They drove to Halloran's house and played the radio for a while and then Ryan and Hermes went back to the hotel.[229] Jack stated that they were at his home for about 10 minutes and then he drove the men to the hotel.[239] Jack stated that when they left her home this was the last time that he saw her during this period of time.[245] Jack said that that he went home afterwards.[239]

1931, October 16
Dr. Judd leaves his sister's house at 823 17th St. and went to 5001 Santa Fe Avenue (the office of Doctor Ross) to work at 7:15 AM. There was an office girl there when he arrived.[48] She was there until noon. Dr. Judd was there until 5:30 and saw 3-12 patients that came in. He went back to Santa Monica at 5:30. He said that he did the same thing on Saturday.[96] Dr. Judd receives a bitter letter from Ruth written on the 14th and decides that he must write to her that evening and let her know for sure that he would come on the 20th.[176] The weather in Phoenix has a low of 50 and a high of 82. It was fair in the evening with very little temperature change.[246] Sammy listens to Montgomery Ward's "Beautiful Thots" on the radio.[210] Sammy wishes to go see Seth Parkers in person in November, but doesn't think it will be possible.[210] Homer Quist, the mailman arrives in the morning. Both Anne and Sammy received an airmail letter and Sammy receives another letter as well. Sammy chatted with the mailman telling him what she planned to do over the next year. She was elated that she had gained the weight that she had lost while being ill the previous May and June and that she was no longer running a temperature. She planned to spend the winter in Phoenix and go back to Alaska in the spring.[247] Anne has lunch at Ruth Judd's house and invites Ruth over for dinner as well as Evelyn

Nace.[200] Anne suggests that the 4 of them play 4 handed bridge because they hadn't had a game for four since the Doctor had been home. Ruth declines stating that she is too far behind with her medical histories.[67] Ruth had gotten her paycheck from Dr. Baldwin for two weeks which was $40. On their way to the house she cashes the check and buys less than $1 of groceries. They eat the leftovers from the dinner before from the American Kitchen.[67] The actual photocopy of the paycheck at the Arizona State Archives was that it was for $35. It was signed by Dr. McKeown.[248] Anne lay down to sleep on the bed while Ruth got lunch.[25] On their way back, she paid Mrs. Grim the land lady $13 of her rent and ordered two pair of hose C.O.D. from the Boston store.[67] Dr. Brinckerhoff sees Anne and Ruth returning to the clinic after lunch and they were chatting in a friendly way.[225] He was at the drug store at 10th and McDowell and he walked back to the clinic with them. She invites Ruth over for dinner. Ruth told her, "Anne, I don't see how I can. I have been going out looking for houses lately, and am way behind on my histories and I don't believe I better go." Anne replied, "Well, if you can't come over for dinner, can't you come over later and play bridge?" And Ruth told her, "Well, I will think about it or I will see about it."[25] Burton stated that he skipped classes both Thursday and Friday afternoons. He said that he was feeling bad. Friday afternoon he reported for work at the Roosevelt school.[127] Sammy wrote a letter to her sister Anna – unsent.[230] In this letter Sammy states, "We are so much happier here by ourselves. Ruth and Anne clashed in many things. We get along so well but it shows that there has to be a lot of tolerance which comes from love. Really, Anna, there are some people in this world that are so kind that they make up for all the selfish ones."[210] Fred Williams states he met Ruth at about 4:00 and she brought him over to meet Sammy. Sammy gets angry and the fight ensues. His story was said to be fantastic.[249] Fred Williams claimed that he had killed using Ruth's gun.[250] Miss Marshall returns to her apartment at 4:30. Ruth is not there.[232] At 5:00 Anne came into Ruth's office dressed to leave. She stated that Ruth had better change her mind and come over. Ruth states that she will be busy typing until 6 anyhow. Anne suggests that she come on over after dinner and play bridge for a while. Dr. Franklin came in then and told Anne it was time to go.[67] Ruth replied, just look at the stack of histories that I have got on my desk to finish." She was typing histories when Anne came in.[25] Nora Smith who worked for Dr. Percy Brown in the X-ray and Pathology laboratory stated that Anne left at 5, the usual time.[251] Dr.

Franklin drove Anne and Evelyn Nace over to the house.[25] Winnie Ruth Judd calls Halloran at his office to see if he was coming over. He wasn't there. So, she called the Luhrs hotel and asked for Mr. Ryan. He was there and stated that Halloran wasn't there yet, but that he expected him in a few minutes. Ruth planned to bundle up her histories and go over to see Anne if Halloran wasn't coming over. She told Ryan to have him call her when he gets in. She waited until 5:30 or a little before 6:00. She went to Wade's grocery store and paid her bill or 15 dollars of it. She talked to Mrs. Wade a bit and apologized for not paying her whole bill but that somebody had stolen 15 dollars from her desk. She promised to try to pay her on her next paycheck. Mrs. Wade told her that was all right.[25] Ruth wondered if Mr. Austin was home since she was in the vicinity.[25] She told Mrs. Wade that she was planning on going out to look at some houses on Saturday night with Anne. Anne was going to try to get Dr. Guttman's car. She borrowed his car often.[25] At 6:30, Ruth went to the grocery store and paid $15 on her bill and ordered two pair of hose from the Boston Store. She had seven dollars left of her check. She returned home to work on her histories.[20] Jack stated that he stayed home on Friday night. His wife was home, his daughter was at a movie, and his son was out and returned about 11. He had planned to go to a game at the stadium with his son but he had another engagement so he stayed home and heard the game on the radio.[239] Winnie Ruth Judd goes to the home of John Ralston at 832 E Monte Vista about 6:00 PM. In court he says she arrives at 5:30.[252] She asks him about the house she is considering buying on East McDowell and his opinion of the price and terms.[67] She asks him to lend her his car on Saturday afternoon because she wants to take the two girls out to the desert for a party. In court he says that she wanted to borrow the car on Saturday to take the girls to visit some friends.[252] He refused saying that his car was not insured and since it was a coupe, they would not all fit. He volunteered to take them out to the desert in two trips. Winnie Ruth says that she asked him if she could use the car to look at the house they were considering buying on Saturday.[67] Winnie Ruth didn't like this option and said that she would get one of the clinic cars. Winnie Ruth said that Anne borrowed Dr. Guttman's car often.[67] John Ralston drove Winnie Ruth back to her apartment. Winnie Ruth Judd invited him in, but he declined. Ralston was Winnie Ruth's old landlord from when she rented an apartment with Mrs. Murray during the winter of 1931.[98] He said as she walked away, she seemed nervous and disappointed that he hadn't loaned her his car.[253] At 6:30 Ruth is at home. She fixes her cat something to eat. She waited for Jack Halloran to come over. [254] Miss Marshall stated she came home from school at 4:30 and from then until about 8:30 when she left she did not hear or see anything of Ruth Judd [231] Dr. Judd left his clinic to return to his sisters at 5:30 reaching there about 6:30.[48] Dr. Judd returns to his sister's house in Santa Monica with a letter he is prepared to write.[176] Evelyn Nace from the Grunow Clinic came over for dinner and stated that she probably was the last one to see the girls alive.[203] Evelyn Nace comes over for dinner. A.M. Ashfort, a patient at the clinic drives her over and she arrives at 5:30.[105] She would have come with Anne, but was delayed 30 minutes. She told her that she would meet her at the house.[111] Dr. Franklin from the clinic drives Anne LeRoi home and stays for about 10 minutes. Sometime during the evening a grocery boy drops off some groceries. Harry Ruppellus, a 17-year-old boy delivered groceries in the afternoon. He says there is a man there who he initially said was Dr. Judd.[255] Later, he stated that this was not Dr. Judd but another man that was there frequently who identified himself.[256] After Evelyn arrived Anne stated that she felt "contaminated" after a day with so many sick people. She bathed and then got dinner. Evelyn stated that she was an excellent cook.[111] Dinner was served about 7:15-7:30.[257] Miss Marshall is at home between 4:30 and 8:30 and does not see Ruth at Brill Street.[232] Sammy got up for dinner and ate at the table. Evelyn said she usually used a tray and ate in bed. They had creamed salmon and canned corn, and some left over pork chops. There was also salad and scalloped potatoes. Evelyn had a highball, but neither Anne nor Sammy drank. Anne wasn't feeling that great and didn't eat any dinner but took an aspirin and tea.[133] Evelyn said that she took ginger ale. She stated that Sammy never drank anything because of her health.[111] Anne and Evelyn sit at the table in the breakfast room for at least an hour after dinner.[133] After about 30 minutes Sammy went into the bedroom and laid down.[111] They talked about school days and nurses training. They did not talk about anybody at the clinic. They did the dishes and put the food in the oven. After dinner the girls played bridge in the bedroom with a small table between the two beds just for thirty-five or forty minutes. Anne talked about her fiancée Hoyt and said "the nearer the time comes the more I feel I don't want to marry him." And then she said, "Sammy just hates me to talk about it." Both Anne and Sammy walked out and stood on the steps when Evelyn's sister arrived to pick her up about 9:30.[133] Another source says 9:45. Sammy was wearing white figured pajamas. Anne was in red pajamas.[111] Evelyn remarked how much better Sammy was looking.[133] Evelyn Nace's sister picks her up. She does not go in, just honks the horn. When they heard the horn they came out, chiding each other about respective scores of a three-handed bridge game. Stanley Nace stated that his sisters came to pick him up at five minutes of 10, telling him that they had come from the duplex. They all went directly home.[258] Anne LeRoi called out to her as she left, "I'll see you in the morning."[259] They had to meet their brother by 10 when he was done with work. There were no phone calls to the house that evening.[105] At about 9:00 Ruth is tired of waiting for Jack to come over. She thinks, "If Jack Halloran thinks he is coming, going to come out here after this time, I am sure going to be gone." She decides to go over to Anne and Sammy's. She misses the Brill street car, and so she walks over to the Indian School car. BJ Jurgemeyer, the railway operator says Ruth Judd got on the McDowell car and went north and got off on Thomas Road at either 9:25 or 10:25.[254] She says she went in the back door.[25] Neighbor Jennie McGrath (2938 North Third Street) heard three shots at 10:30 at night, one, a pause and then two close together.[260] In one account she says she thought nothing of it since somebody was always shooting guns in that neighborhood.[261] Another neighbor Gene Cunningham (2926 N 2nd St) heard three shots about 10:30 at night, two close together and one removed. The longer space was between the first and second shots.[262] Ruth stated that Gene Cunningham was not in bed that night but that he had a party and his house was brilliantly lit when she returned with Halloran.[25] Ruth stated that Gene Cunningham, a lawyer was one of Halloran's playboy friends.[67] Ruth stated that he had a party that night and that the lights were on the entire night.[25] Halloran's lawyer, Frank O. Smith at a later date made the statement that there were two battles; "in the first, Mrs. Judd was the vanquished, in the second, she was the victor".[263] Both girls death certificates states that the cause of death was bullet wound to the head, homicidal.[264, 265] Hermes and Ryan were at the Luhrs hotel lobby until their train left for El Paso at 9:45. A Mr. Martin who is a salesman was with them and he went with them to the train.[243] Ruth stated that Milton Sullivan, night clerk in the Hotel Adams, stated he overheard a conversation between Halloran and Fred Ryan. Sullivan denied having heard any conversation and declared he did not know at what time he had seen Halloran in the hotel or whether it was Friday night, Thursday night, or Saturday night.[266] Ruth claimed that Ryan knew that he was

over at the house Friday night.[25] The clerks saw them and the night
clerk saw them check out, and Mr. Martin who is a salesman was with
them during the evening. He went with them to the train.[243]
Apparently, a few days earlier, Jack said he would come over at 9
o'clock, but he didn't make it until midnight. Lately Ruth thought that
Jack was seeing Anne. She had thought that they were just friends, but
one time when Jack was drunk he had given Ruth other ideas about
Anne. And lately, Anne's attitude had changed.[191] Evelyn was just
leaving and Ruth enters through the back door. Anne and Sammy are
in their pajamas. She tells them she didn't have supper. So she decides
to drink some milk. She stated that she had a small dish of tapioca
pudding in another account.[67] Anne helps her fix the davenport down
in the living room. They closed the windows since it was cool. Ruth
sits down at the end of Sammy's bed wearing pink dotted pajamas with
a ruffle around the neck. Anne sat on her bed. Sammy was lying on
top of her bed. Burton Joy McKinnell describes the fight as, "At this
time, an attack was made on my sister, the nature of which made it
necessary for her to defend her womanhood. I refrain from the exact
nature of the attack."[20] Sammy states that she likes Dr. Franklin's
appearance better than all of the other doctors at the clinic.[67] Ruth
stated that she had just met Dr. Franklin and they were discussing him.[267]
They also discussed the invitation they had received from Dr. Brinkerhoffer
about going horseback riding. They talked about the radio that Bisch had
brought them.[267] One document states that according to Mr. Knuckles of
the Arizona Republic, that the diaries of the girls indicated that Ruth was
attempting to blackmail the girls.[268] Anne asked how Jack met Lucille
Moore. Ruth admitted introducing them. Anne gets angry and asks her
why in the world she would introduce Jack to a girl that had syphilis.
Ruth argues that she could not tell Jack that this girl had syphilis because
of patient confidentiality. Ruth asks her why she would care about that.
She yells at Anne something about knowing about her meeting Jack (?)
in San Francisco and staying at a hotel with him. She also yells at her
about Anne staying with L. E. Dixon on the coast. They start calling each
other names. Anne is still angry about Jack meeting Lucille Moore.
Anne recalls her conversation with Evelyn Nace and informing somebody
if somebody they know has syphilis. Anne yells at Ruth about having
Jack Halloran out at her house just about every night. She threatens to
tell Dr. Judd about her affair with Halloran.[67] Ruth retorts by saying
that all of the doctors in the clinic thought that they were in love with
each other. Ruth threatens to confirm that with the doctors that they

were indeed lesbians instead of defending them. Dr. Sweek and Dr. Baldwin thought they were lesbians. Dr. Sweek said something like "What in the world does she want to sleep with her for. That is love's labor lost." At the time Ruth said that it was not true. On another occasion, Dr. Baldwin advised Ruth not to live with them because of their lifestyle and they would get Ruth into trouble. Ruth didn't believe that they were lesbians, but threatened to tell the people at the clinic that they were. Ruth also threatened to tell the Drs. at the clinic that Anne messed around with the x-ray machine. Apparently, while Anne was in Portland, they trained somebody else to do her work, somebody without the proper training who they could pay less. Anne was angry and come into the clinic just about closing and turned up the dials on the x-ray machine. The voltage would be so high that it would burn somebody. The idea being that the amateur x-ray technician would be fired and she would get her job back. Sammy retreats to the bedroom to get a pen to write to Dr. Judd regarding Ruth's infidelity even though she claimed she had already told him.[191] Ruth yells that Anne went to the coast with an oil salesman when she said she was going to visit her folks.[191] Sammy grabs Ruth's gun. According to one account, Ruth retrieved her gun from a pawn shop shortly before the killings.[269] Ruth was in the kitchen putting the glass of milk into the sink. Sammy enters with the gun and points it at Ruth's heart. According to Ruth, Sammy says, "if you dare say anything like that about Anne."[67] Ruth grabbed for Sammy's hand that held the gun (her left hand). With her other (right) hand, she grabbed the bread knife. At about this time Sammy shot the gun through Ruth's hand. Ruth stabs Sammy twice in the left shoulder with the bread knife and bent the knife. Ruth grabs for the gun with her right hand and twists it. The gun goes off while Sammy still has the gun in her hand and it goes through her left chest and arm.[67] They dropped to the floor and struggle for the gun. Ruth states the gun jammed and one bullet came out through the top of the gun and fell to the floor.[67] Ruth grabs the gun and it is still in Sammy's hand with her finger on the trigger when Sammy gets shot through the chest going through her shoulder. They still fight for the gun. Anne is yelling, "Shoot Sammy Shoot!" Anne gets the ironing board from behind the water heater and is hitting Ruth over the head with it. In another account the blow from the ironing board caused them to fall to the floor and they were standing until then.[67] She kept knocking Ruth down with the ironing board. When Ruth gets the gun she fires at Sammy (doesn't say it's a head wound or that she hit her).[67] There were at least five shots. She does not clearly say anything about getting the gun from Sammy or about the shots in either girl's heads. She did say that she shot Anne just as she hit her with the ironing board and she fell. In another account, she states Anne was going to hit her again with the ironing board and her pajamas slipped from her shoulder. As she bent to pick up her pajamas Ruth shot her. She said, Sammy and she were still fighting for the gun and then she was dead. She doesn't describe shooting Sammy in the hand nor the head. Anne's body fell towards the stove. Sammy's head was toward the breakfast room. No mention of a head wound of Sammy's but states that her chest wound was bleeding profusely.[67] In the hearing against Halloran, she says that in the fight only two shots were fired; in her hand and in Sammy's chest.[270] Ruth states that she was in between both bodies. Ruth got dressed and ran out from that place. Dr, Raney stated that there were two cars at the duplex at 11:00.[20] Ruth stated that her pajamas were bloody. Ruth ran all the way home arriving there about 11:30.[31] Ruth stated she just had a blue dress on and shoes, that's all.[25] McFadden also thought at one time, Ruth had borrowed a coupe from a man who was interested in her that was not Halloran.[271] McFadden speculated that this story was not true; that in fact one of the women was killed while in bed. It took 3 shots to kill Sammy. He said that two shots had entered Sammy's body. Then her slayer decided to finish her off by propping up her body with one hand and fired the gun with the right hand. The bullet passed through Sammy's head embedding in Ruth's left hand.[272] Ruth wrote a letter from the hospital a year later that stated that Dr. Raney and Dr. Stewart were close friends of Halloran's.[273] She went back to Brill Street to get her pocket book (money). BW Jurgemeyer, the railway operator, said Ruth Judd got on the car at 11:25 at Thomas Road and got off at Willetta.[254] Ruth said this was an error and that this was Saturday night she rode back to Brill Street after 11.[274] Jack came to Ruth's apartment very drunk at 11:30.[25] Another account states that Ruth entered a drug store near her house on Brill at 11:45 and calls somebody asking them if she can borrow a car to help an ill friend get some air. She then got in a taxi.[275] Ruth was on her way over to the Ford Hotel to call her husband when he arrived. She used the phone there. They passed each other in the hallway.[25] She had gone home to get her pocketbook. She told Jack what happened and he didn't believe her.[25] Ruth stated that she told him that Anne and Sammy were lying on the floor.[31] Ruth and Halloran drive back to the duplex. Jack parked his car on Pinchot.[67] The car was on the north side of the road.[25] The lights were on at Gene Cunningham's since he had a party that night. Anne was friendly with him and said that he was a friend of Jacks and had been over to the house. They went in the back way going close to the garage. The lights had remained on.[25] She had left the lights on in the kitchen. They arrived back at the house about 11:45. They went in the back door.[25] Jack stated that he did not go to Ruth's apartment, she did not tell him about the crime, and he did not drive her over to the duplex.[239] Miss Marshall stated that she returned to the Brill Street apartment about 12:30 and there was no light inside Mrs. Judd's apartment. There didn't appear to be anybody at home.[232]

1931, October 17
(Note: At the moment of death, the muscles relax completely called flaccidity. The muscles then stiffen into rigor mortis. This occurs within two to six hours after death and affects the whole body. It happens more quickly in a cold environment or when a person has been active right before death. After being rigid for 24-84 hours the body again relaxes.)[276] This was hotly debated and objected to in the court proceedings. Dr. Wagner made the statement that the general rule was the completion of rigor mortis in 6 hours and it's disappearance in 16 hours, but it greatly depended on climate. He stated that this is not manifest for three hours and is complete in six hours in an ordinary case. In the case of Anne LeRoi's body there was no tearing of muscles and tissues which he stated would happen once rigor mortis had set in.[277] On entering the duplex, Jack quickly rushes over to Sammy. He picks her up and puts her on Anne's bed. Ruth states that her chest wound was bleeding profusely again. No word on any head wound or Anne. Ruth states that Jack didn't think Sammy was dead. In her statement with McFadden, Ruth stated that Jack didn't "think that she was shot in the head then." Ruth stated that she didn't know if Sammy was alive or dead but guessed that she was dead.[25] Ruth stated that Jack said, "My God: Sammy!" and he ran over and stooped over her. He felt for Sammy's pulse and examined her chest wound.[31] Ruth stated that there was no blood on the bed. Jack threw the pillows off the bed. The covers had been turned down, pulled down and there was no blood on the covers, no covers were bloody.[25] His hands were bloody. He reached over and pulled down the blind next to the bed with his hand. He went to the kitchen and turned off the light. He came back into the hall and turned on that light. He came back into the

bedroom and felt Sammy's pulse and looked at her chest wound and said he thought he would call a doctor. He dialed the phone several times. Ruth stated that he didn't realize that she had shot Sammy in the head.[31][25] Ruth stated in court that Jack pulled back her pajamas and she saw the chest wound and that this was the only time.[270] Jack's arm and hand was bloody. He reached over and pulled down the blinds. One blind flew back up and nearly tore off the roller when he pulled it down the second time. Jack calls Dr. Charlie Brown. He couldn't get Dr. Brown on the phone so he decides to go get him himself since he didn't think Sammy was dead.[20] He also suggested that Dr. Brown dress Ruth's hand and that "I will attend to the whole thing myself."[25] After he put Sammy on the bed he went out to Anne.[25] In court she says that she walked by Anne's body and he went out into the garage and pulled in a heavy trunk.[31] Sammy's head was not bleeding.[25] Ruth states that while Jack is doing this she took the bullet that was jammed in the gun and put it in the trash can there. She said Jack wanted her to help him straighten things up, but Ruth said she couldn't.[25] Ruth stated that Jack didn't say much but she was talking the whole time.[31] McFadden stated that there was blood spotted that was never mopped in the bedroom. And that the corner of the carpet was cut out. Ruth stated that it was from the blood in the hair and that it splattered off. She stated that some blood probably went through the mattress and leaked onto the rug. McFadden said it was splattered in little pinhead size; not much of it. The carpet had been cut off in the NE section of the bedroom. Ruth states that they have a conversation about him having plenty on Dr. Brown. He told her to go see Judge Gilbert and say that she wanted the position back at the County Physician's Office. Ruth had lost her job there on Election Day.[25] There was some blood splattered on the wall by the bed where the carpet had been cut out, a splattering. Ruth thought it might be from Sammy's hair.[25] Ruth had taken some Veranol and felt dazed. She didn't know whether Halloran brought the trunk in from the garage or if he put Anne's body in it. One account said that he went out to the garage and brought in the trunk before he went to get Dr. Brown. He said that he was going to take Anne out in the trunk. He didn't say anything about Sammy. He left the trunk in the kitchen.[25] Ruth states that he then parked his car in the garage. He stated that he could take the trunk out on his car. Then he could dispose of it.[25] In one account Ruth said that she saw him put Anne's body into the trunk. She said that she saw him do that. Ruth mentions something about a Dr. Leff and then Dr. Leff-- I don't want to bring his name into a case like this because he was such a nice man. What exactly she says is, "He advised me to let Dr. Brown treat my hand for me and never say anything to your husband about this, because he would take care of it himself, and that there would be nothing to it. And then Dr. Leff-- I don't want to bring his name into a case like this because he was such a nice man." McFadden interrupts and says, "Well, then, tell us the conversation that you had there." Ruth continued on regarding Jack. Jack tells her not to call her husband or call the police.[25] In court, she says she saw Jack put Anne in the trunk.[31] Jack dials the phone several times in the dark in the bedroom. Ruth begins to get hysterical and Jack decided to take her home. He mopped up the floor before they left. On the way home he told her not to tell her husband or go to the police; that he would take care of it. He told her to be scared of the state attorney. He said he would take care of this himself. Ruth thought that they left about 12 or 12:30 and were back at her place around 1. He left immediately and did not come in.[25] McFadden asked her what she carried out that night when she slammed the door. Ruth claimed that she carried nothing out, but that she came in between 12 and 1 o'clock.[25] Ruth said that Jack was so drunk that he couldn't drive. He could hardly walk when they first went in.[25] Ruth gets in the car, but Dr. Raney who lived in the neighborhood drives by. Dr. Raney said that he left at 11 and came back at 1.[20] The porch light at Dr. Sults goes on.[67] Miss Marshall, Ruth Judd's neighbor says that she returned to her apartment about 12:30.[231] She stated that Mrs. Judd's apartment was dark and there were all indications that no one was home. She went to bed, and being a little nervous she did not sleep.[231] Miss Marshall made the statement to Rogers that she was not aware that Ruth knew how to drive a car until she saw her drive away early on Friday evening. She said originally that she heard Ruth come and go several times during the night and made no effortt to be quiet about it [253] She heard somebody enter her apartment and heard a car.[267] At 1:30 or 2:00 Miss Marshall said she heard a car drive in and stop in front of Ruth's apartment. She heard someone in the apartment and then a few minutes later she heard the car drive away. She stated that by the sound that the tires made on the gravel and the shifting of gears lead her to believe that it was a large car. She did not hear any more and dropped off to sleep.[231] In 1933, she stated that she went to bed about 1 o'clock. She heard a car drive in and stop in front of Ruth's apartment. She thought she heard things being moved around. [232] Jack drops Ruth off and goes for Dr. Brown.[67] Dr.

Raney stated that he arrived home about 1:00 and sees a car turning around at Pinchot and 2nd with its lights out.[20] A big black sedan arrives at 2929 at 1 AM, the lights in the house were out, but the car lights were shining into the garage.[278] Ruth said she returned there with Jack Halloran.[25] A neighbor near the duplex said she smelled something burning at 1:30 on Saturday.[279] Miss Marshall says that Ruth Judd returns again to her apartment about 1:30-2:00.[231] Milk is delivered about 5 AM by the milkman to the icebox.[157] His name is Wyman Owen and delivered for the Central Avenue Dairy. He stated the bedroom windows faced on the service porch were always open when he called. He heard a sound from the bedroom much like one turning over in bed. He stated that he rattled the milk bottles together to not frighten customers. He stated when he did that the noise inside subsided. There was a 50 cent piece left for payment. He put three quarts of milk in the icebox and left the charge (13 cents).[280] Henri Behoteguy of 2916 N 3rd St. is awakened at a few minutes before 6 am from a commotion at 2929 North Second St. The lights were on. He stated that he heard screams coming from that house for a period of 5 to 7 minutes. Then he stated that he heard two shots about five seconds apart. The first shot was muffled; the second shot was loud. It was a woman screaming. This house is not very close to 2929 North 2nd St.[281] The letter carrier Homer Quist says that it was strange when Sammy did not greet him on Saturday morning since she always did. He left one or two letters and noticed that they were gone on Monday.[247] Miss Marshall stated she did not wake until 8:30 AM and then fell asleep again until 11:00.[231] Dr. Judd stated that he went to work at 7:15 and came back to Santa Monica by street car arriving at 7.[96] Jack calls Ruth the following morning.[25] Ruth calls into the clinic at 9:00 AM and says that she is going to be late.[282] Jack says that he is at his office on Saturday morning until about noon.[239] At about 9:15 Dr. Henry Franklin said he saw Ruth. She drove her car into the driveway and into the parking lot just ahead of him. While he was getting out of his car, she had already gotten out of her car and was approaching the little swinging gate leading into the court. He saw that her right hand was bandaged. When asked about the car, he said it was a two passenger coupe and that it was not new. It was a car that hadn't been polished recently. It was a dull black color. It was a Ford or a Chevrolet.[283] The coupe was not new, probably one or more years old.[205] She walked to the east rear entrance. Her usual entrance was on the west. Dr. Franklin asked her why her hand was bandaged and she said that she had burned it. She had access to Dr. Swenson's office where she went to telephone privately according to Dr. Franklin. He believed that this is where she called from stating that she would be late to work.[205] McFadden stated there was evidence that she had driven a small coupe with red wire wheels to the clinic.[274] Ruth was in a hurry. He said he did not know her well. She had been here since the first and had talked to him in Dr. Baldwin's office. She had told him where he could purchase or have printing done, buy furniture etc. She had come out one day and recommended a certain lady for a position as secretary, a friend of hers. She had been a teacher at class at night school. Her last name was Sticklemeyer.[283] Nora Smith was at the clinic and got the call. Ruth said, "This is Mrs. Judd, Mrs. Smith. Will you please have Emil open my office because I am going to be a little late this morning."[251] Nora lived at 1014 East Palm. She said this call came in shortly after 9. There was nothing in the voice that raised any suspicion. She said she was normally prompt and that this was not an unusual request. She asked one of the girls who was passing through the office to open Ruth's office. Dr. Brown and she were trying to figure out Anne's absence since there were two patients from out of town needing X-ray work. They had been trying to call Mrs. LeRoi and got no response. They didn't know what to think since Sammy, who was an invalid, was always there when Anne was gone.[139] Nora then tried to find Anne since she had not shown up for work.[251] Evelyn Nace says that she dropped off a chart at 9:30 and Ruth wasn't there yet.[133] Ruth doesn't eat at home but after getting to the clinic she thought that she had better. So, she went to the Robinson's Drug Store and ordered some hot chocolate. Ruth calls from the drug store to say that she was going to be a few minutes late. Nora Smith receives another call at 9:45. The voice said, "This is Mrs. LeRoi. Is Dr. Brown in?" Nora was angry and asked her what the idea was of her not coming down here for work since they really needed her. The voice stated that Sammy's brother just arrived and that they were taking him to Tucson.[251] Ruth calls the clinic again and pretends to be Anne LeRoi and says that Sammy's brother is in town and they are taking him to Tucson.[282] Therefore, she would not be in until about 9:45.[282] She told her to wait and tell him that herself since she would not tell Dr. Brown this. She put him on the phone and told him that Anne was on the other end. She knew that it was not Mrs. LeRoi's voice. She hung on the other receiver and listened in because he was sore she wasn't there since they were so busy. She stated to Dr. Brown that that was not Mrs. LeRoi, but that it was Mrs. Judd. Dr. Brown rebuked her on the phone and said, "Well, if you had to change your plans, why didn't you let me know at 8:00 and I could have arranged it." Ruth claimed she would get Mrs. Roe for him. She was the technician who was on vacation. Dr. Brown said they already tried to get Mrs. Roe and that she had left. He told her he was sending Mrs. Brown out to get her. The voice said that she would be there. They laughed when they said to each other that it was Ruth.[139] Ruth was only a few minutes and she came in through the back door so nobody would ask her about her hand. Mr. Lang, a patient was already there waiting when she arrived about 9. She said that she carried a box so they wouldn't see her hand. In this account she said it was about 9. She called this patient Albert Land[25] Harold Bisch stated that he drove his green ford coupe into Phoenix and parked it about 10 at a parking lot at the corner of Monroe and 1st Avenue, and did not remove it until 4:00.[196] Fay Ayres stated that she saw Ruth go out on Friday or Saturday about 10. She said she rushed out the front entrance about this time. She said she had a bandage on her left hand. She said it looked like a towel, a Turkish towel. It was a big clumsy bandage.[284] Nora Smith said that Ruth arrived about 10 and that they questioned her about pretending to be Mrs. LeRoi on the phone. She denied it was her. Nora did not understand why she would lie since she was a good girl. Nora called her out of Dr. Baldwin's office. She seemed pale. She was cross with her. She came out and was taking dictation on her lap. When asked if that was her on the phone, she smiled and said no. And she said "Well, I have a suspicion that Mrs. LeRoi is not coming". Ruth said that she would be there. Nora said, "We need her and I want to know where she is. I think you know. Ruth replied that she didn't know anything about them.[139] Dr. McKeown stated that he examined a boy at 10 and Ruth was not yet present. His patient was CW Timmons from 1009 East Culver [236] Although about this time he said Doctor Brown came into the office and asked Mrs. Judd if she knew where Mrs. LeRoi was. She said,"No, how should I know. I don't live there any more with them." He paid no more attention to it.[236] Dr. Percy Brown stated that he saw Ruth about 9:45 in Dr. Baldwin's office. He said that he was definite about the time since he was anxious for Mrs. LeRoi to return to her work and the patients had been waiting since 9:00. And it was then after 9:30. So, he stated that he was standing around in his anxiety for her to come to work. Ruth said that she didn't know where Anne was. Dr. Brown said he thought she looked like she had been crying since she had injected eyes, thickened nostrils and thickened lips. He said he never spoke to Anne LeRoi about domestic affairs.[92] At about 10:30 he thought that he saw her because he went out and gave a thorough pneumothorax and sat and talked to him.[236] After 10, a man from Wickenburg, Mike Kerkes who worked at the clinic, stated that Ruth's left hand was wrapped up. When he asked her she said she had burned it on the stove.[285] Dr. Baldwin saw Ruth at 10:15 when he came in. He called her into his office to write an important letter. He thinks he was dictating notes. His patient was Mrs. Mitchell. He never noticed a bandage on her hand.[286] Stella Kerkes said that she saw Ruth between 10 and 11, probably about 10:30. She said she looked pale and restless. She stated when she first walked in she was going into the next room and noted a pretty big bandage that looked like a towel had been wrapped on her hand. When she came back, she still had it on and she noticed that it was a bandage. She was writing with her right hand. She didn't have anything to hold her paper and it seemed like she was trying to hide the bandage. It looked like she hated to do it, but there was no one there but Stella and her Dad, so she brought up her left bandaged hand to hold the paper. She types during the half hour they were there just with one hand; just punched with one finger. She kept her other hand down by her side.[287] Mrs. Brown was sent out to get Anne LeRoi. She arrived at the house the first time at 10:30. She knocked on the front door, the curtain was down. There was no response. She said it was like hitting a blank wall; a house without any bell. She decided Miss Samuelson was away or resting and that Anne had gone to work. She found a phone and called Dr. Brown and said that Mrs. LeRoi was probably at the clinic by that time. He told her she was not.[288] Dr. Brinkerhoff stated he saw Ruth at about 11:00 in Dr. Baldwin's office. She was sitting at her desk and when he saw her she was not typing but the typewriter was right before her and he thought that she had been. He stated that there was no bandage on either hand. He asked her if Dr. Baldwin had a tuning fork in his office because he had a patient coming in the afternoon complaining of deafness. Ruth replied that she was certain that he did not have a tuning fork.[289] He stated he was sure neither hand was bandaged.[205] Miss Marshall said that she got out of bed and left the apartment about 11:00 and was gone for about an hour.[231] Mrs. Brown went back to the house at 11:45 to check on Anne LeRoi again to see if she had missed her. She went to the front door and knocked with no results and she went to the little side door, and then she went to a door from the back. She knocked at three doors and one overlooked the bedroom. She went around to the screened porch. She stood there and could see into the bedroom. She knocked again at the door on the south side. She looked and didn't see very much. She saw two beds were covered with rose colored spreads. They were very well made up and it occurred to her how neatly a nurse makes a bed. On one of the beds was a little pink silk brassiere, looked new and unworn. That was on the bed nearest to where she was standing. The bed was against the north wall. There was a little space between the beds, but enough to hold a bedside table and on that table she saw a little bunch of surgeons' gauze, a bandage, something of that nature, that was a little bit tinged with blood. She was not sure it was blood, but she thought to herself that it wasn't very neat to leave those things there, but there were one or two other articles on that table. She did not know what they were.[288] It was said that when they entered the duplex the mattress on Miss Samuelson's side had no mattress. It was said that a blue quilt was folded and pinned so that when covered, it stimulated the appearance and thickness of the mattress on the other bed.[290] Dr. McKeown was done with his patient about 11:30.[236] He said she (Ruth) was in her place, nervous, her hair was disheveled, and her dress was more untidy than usual.[236] Ruth writes a letter to her husband, "Thank you very much for writing me whether I write to you or not. I am busy. I don't seem to get things done. When I get home at night I settle down and go to sleep, if our cat will let me, and then after a short nap I get my supper, do dishes, sometimes a few histories, and then I go to sleep again. I have gained a little, I think, since I left the girls. It's because I rest more. I guess. We eat well enough. Doctor I am lonesome. I will be so glad to have you here. I love you, oh, so tenderly with arms of love. I am usually so tired I can't write how much I love you. Then, after I have rested for a while, I long for you. I will be glad if you are here Tuesday or Wednesday. I need you and have for some time, but we needed money so badly when someone took $15 of my money. It is much cooler her now. Come home soon. It isn't a pretty home, doctor, but again we ain't got barrels of money. Maybe we are all ragged an funny, but we will travel along singing a song, side by side because we love each other."[136] This is abbreviated. The LAPL has a longer more complete version, in her handwriting after she talks about writing to her or not. "Dearest Doctor; I start so many letters and then have to do something else and destroy the letter and simply do not get one mailed. Thank you very much this time for writing to me whether I write to you or not. I am busy I don't seem to get things done when I get home at night I topple down and go to sleep if our cat will let me and there after a short nap. I get my supper, do dishes sometime a few histories and then I got to sleep again. I've gained a little I think since I left the girls. It's because I rest more I guess. We ate well enough. I liked Sue. She is a cute little tike, a very great deal like I use to be at her age. I don't mean I was cute but I loved to talk to people a lot and was friendly like she is and I used to want my own way and never forgot what I was longing to have. Doctor I am lonesome. I'll be so glad to have you here. I love you oh so tenderly with arms of love. I am usually so tired I can't write how much I love you. And after I've rested for a while, I long for you. I'll be glad if you are here Tues or Wed. I need you and have for some time but we needed money so badly and someone took $15 of my money. Everybody is going hunting here. Four of the clinic doctors went. And ever so many people. The deer season is open now. Some of the nurses over at the hospital are going out. (I will be an extra if I go.) They want me to go for the afternoon dove hunting and to eat these out in the desert. It is late now, one, and I haven't had lunch and there is one more patient that I will let off at two. They want to go about 3:30. It will be an outing for me so maybe I will go. I would like to. It is much cooler here now. Come home soon: It isn't a pretty home Doctor but again we ain't got barrels of money, maybe we're all ragged and funny. But will travel along singing a song side by side. (Because I love you. Crossed out.) We love each other. Lovingly, Ruth."[221] Miss Marshall returned to the apartment at noon and remains there for the rest of the day and evening. She did not see any lights or hear any noise coming from the Judd apartment. She did not think anyone was present there.[231] At noon, Ruth had a telephone call for Dr. McKeown. It was a number that she should have known. She said here is a telephone number somebody left. He asked her who it was and if they didn't give their name. She said they did not give their name. He looked at the number and said that she should have known the number since they had been calling her for months. It was one of his old patients.[236] Evelyn Nace said she saw Ruth twice on Saturday, the second time about noon. The first time she said hello to her on her way down to the laboratory. Ruth had asked her if she was very busy. Evelyn said she was. At noon, she had a patient and thought it was a medical case so Evelyn called her and asked her if Dr. Baldwin was still in and could he see her. It was a former patient of Dr. Sweek's.[133] Jack Halloran calls from the lobby at noon. He stated that the body was still at the house and asked her if she had done anything about her hand. Ruth said that she wanted to go to Los Angeles to take care of her hand. Jack said that he thought that this might be a good idea. He stated that he couldn't do anything about that trunk. He says that a young guy named Wilson or Williams would meet her in LA.[25] In one account it's Ruth that talks to him in the lobby. Dr. Sweek and Miss Ayres saw her in the lobby. Jack said that he couldn't do anything about those bodies. He told her that he would meet her over there Saturday night.[25] Jack says this is not true. He stated he left his office at noon, had lunch at home and then went to the Phoenix Country Club for golf in the afternoon.[239] He played golf with the same men nearly every Saturday afternoon.[239] Ruth stated she was at the clinic all day making appointments for patients.[31] Dr. Baldwin stated that Ruth left the clinic around noon or 1, 2:00 at the latest. Dr. McKeown stated that Ruth was still at the clinic at 1:30 when he left. However, she had asked for the afternoon off and he had granted it.[291] Ruth stated on November 2, that she got to the duplex at 2:30 and spent the next 7.5 hours packing the bodies.(Until 10) She said she cut up Sammy's body during this time.[274] Ruth gets off the trolley and walks towards the duplex at 3 in the afternoon.[279] Phoebe Reed, a seventh grade pupil testified before the pardon board that she saw Ruth about 3 PM. Ruth ordered her and some playmates away from a pile of bricks in which they were playing adjacent to and on a vacant lot south of the duplex.[266] Mrs. FH Reed who lives at 2932 North 3rd Street stated that she had known Mrs. Judd for some time by sight from seeing her ride the streetcars. Her daughter, about 10, had become quite friendly with Mrs. Judd in riding back and forth to school. She and her daughter started for her sister's home at 3020 North Third Street which is about one block from where she resides. As she and her daughter approached Pinchot street, she noticed Mrs. Ruth alight from the streetcar at the intersection of 3rd and Pinchot and start to walk west on Pinchot towards 2nd Street. They passed within three feet of Ruth and they spoke to her and she returned the greetings. Ruth was dressed in her uniform which was rather untidy and her hair was stringy and she remarked to herself that Ruth must have had a hard day as she would have been a pretty woman if she had arranged her hair properly. Her daughter remarked that she wondered what was the matter with her as when she spoke, she seemed very cross.[205] In court she says that she did not leave at noon. She stated that she went out about 3 to get some milk and that she didn't leave until closing time.[31] She was supposed to meet Jack there and waited outside.[67] Dr. Gaskins of 355 Catalina stated that he did NOT see a tan Packard around on Saturday night. He said in court that he never had. Although, there was a statement from this date that was written in shorthand that Mrs. Gaskins had told him that she had seen a Packard at the duplex, (didn't say when) Dr. Gaskins stated that he did not know that he was giving a statement at the time about what his wife had said.[291] Jack stated that he left the country club between 5:30 and 6:00 and went home and had dinner. After dinner he went to the office of a business acquaintance where he remained until 9 PM and then went home and entertained visitors until 10. Afterwards, he went to bed.[239] George Lilley stated that he and his wife were at the Halloran home on this evening.[292] Jack was sober on Saturday night.[25] Jack kept driving around the block before he stopped. Ruth said she thought maybe he would kill her. Ruth went into the house. It was about dusk. The trunk was in the living room, back of the door.[25] In court she said he didn't stop from driving around until 8:30. He drove into the alley and she went out to meet him. Jack drove into the garage.[31] She told him that she wanted to go to Los Angeles to get her hand taken care of. Jack said that was best and he said that he thought it was a good idea for her to go to Los Angeles and he wanted her to take the trunk with her. She said that she would not take those to Los Angeles. Jack said that he could not do anything about the trunk. He finally stopped the car and they went into the house and the trunk was in the living room at the back of the door.[25] They went in the back door. The house had been cleaned up and both bodies were in the trunks. She stated that she had not entered the south part of the duplex until Halloran arrived. She had gone in the north part, and had sat on the steps.[31] Jack told her that a man named Wilson or Williams would meet her in Los Angeles. Halloran said that he had to go back to his office and get more money to get a ticket for Ruth to go on to Los Angeles [25] He took out his wallet. He told her to meet him a block from the train station.[31] He told her not to tell her husband. He told her to tell that her hand was wounded on a hunting trip, but Ruth had already told at the clinic that she burned it and that it was a bad accident. He told her that Sammy had been operated on. She avoids questions in 1932 about what Jack Halloran said on Saturday night. Ruth stated that the beds were made up perfectly on Saturday night. They were pulled down on Friday night.[25] She was supposed to arrange to have the trunks picked up and Jack would meet her a block away from the train station. According to Ruth, somebody was in the duplex since the lightning delivery guy tried to go in the back, but somebody turned the knob.[67] At 9:50 in the evening, Ruth calls the Lightning Delivery Company. Richard Schwartz arrives at the duplex at 10:00.[293] Miss Marshall said she went to bed at 10:00 and did not hear Ruth return with the trunks.[231] She said she went to bed about 9:30 or 10 and had not seen Ruth anytime on Saturday. She heard nothing from her apartment on Saturday night.[232] He arrived with helpers Fred Hornberger and Frank Rock[294] The lights are out in the house and Ruth says that they have been disconnected since she is moving. They talk inside by striking matches one at a time. Ruth stated she was planning on leaving that night on the 10:40 train to LA. She accidentally locks herself out and Richard tries to get in the bathroom window. Ruth gets in the back door and turns on the lights. Ruth said it was her sister's house. Richard says the trunk is too heavy to ship. Ruth is confused but decides to take the single trunk to her own apartment at 1130 Brill Street. Richard asked her if the floor was just varnished since the trunk seemed to stick to the floor. Ruth pays him by holding her purse in her left hand and paying him with her right. He claimed that her hand was not bandaged or injured in any way.[293] One article states that a Fred Homberger went there with Richard Schwartz. He claimed that because of the darkness of the house, he thought that somebody else was in the house and Ruth didn't want them to see. He claimed that her hand was not bandaged since he saw her wash her hands and thought it was odd since she did not dry them.[295] Another article states that the men didn't see any man at either apartment.[294] Ruth states that the delivery guy saw the keys on the shelf and gave them to Ruth so she had the keys, but the trunk was locked then. This was when he entered through the bathroom window; he knocked the keys off the shelf and they fell into the toilet. They had to fish them out of the toilet.[25] He would not check them through to its destination stating that it was too much overweight. Ruth said that the trunks contained a number of books and asked Swartz to take it to 1130 Brill Street which he did.[294] The drayman stated that they deposited the trunk in the front room of the Brill Street apartment.[207] Later Swartz said that he must have gotten blood on his hands as later he noticed that they were stained. This article seemed to indicate that both bodies were in the trunk and yet still intact.[294] Ruth stated that she took the gun with her when she left there on Saturday, the first time and that it had blood on it. She was going to wash the gun on Sunday.[25] (Note: Blood from a cadaver clots quickly, but liquifies again within 60-90 minutes when the clotting agents are exhausted.[276]) Dr. Wagner at the trial established when Sammy's body was dismembered within a few hour time frame. He stated that it was more than an hour after her death, but less than eight or nine hours.[296] He also stated that it would be unusual that it could have been severed over eight hours after she died. He had the opinion that he thought the vertebrae was cut with a sharp knife. He said the cuts were irregular, but not jagged.[277] Ruth goes back to the duplex and hosed off the front porch. She took the last street car out there on Saturday night.[25] John Wozniak of 1915 North Central Avenue saw Ruth get off a street car after 10 at night at 3rd and Pinchot. She walked one half blocks west and turned into the alley in the rear of the duplex.[266] A document in the Arizona State Archives states that John (of Polish descent, employed by Archer Sisters) was coming out on the 11:30 PM street car from town. (says October 16 here though) He saw a pretty blond girl on the car. She was holding her hand or arm. She got off at Pinchot Street, and he got out too. He asked her if he might take her any place. She told him to mind his own business, but both proceed to walk west. She turned south down the alley and went into the rear of the Second Street house.[297] Mrs. Reed of 2932 North Third Street stated that she, her husband, and her brother in law smelled something burning in the vicinity of their house late Saturday night and early Sunday morning.[266] She told John Brinkerhoff in October that when she was returning from her sister's residence at 3020 North Street, she noticed a smell as though something was burning in her neighborhood. The odor was very peculiar and she thought at first that she had left her iron on but after arriving home, she found that the iron had not been left on and going outside she noticed that the odor was like burning clothing.[205] Ruth states that the "colored" porter saw Jack hanging around there on Saturday night and that a ticket was purchased, but not used.[67] Blevens, a worker at the station, stated although he couldn't say which night, that he saw Halloran at the station. He said that he saw him, "just previous to the first newspaper accounts of the murder." He thought it was possible Saturday night since it was a busy night when he saw him. Sunday night was not a busy night. In court though, he stated that he could not specify any specific night or date. He claimed that Halloran had not bought a ticket from him. He came in and walked through the lobby. He was by himself. He said it was right after the departure of a westbound train. He didn't know if it was the first or second.[291] Emil Hoitola tries to call Anne LeRoi at the duplex, but there is no answer Saturday night. He called long distance from Twin Falls,

Idaho. He worked for a Milwaukee firm.[298] The time he called was about 8:30.[299] Police state that Ruth had the gun on her table. She picked it up to examine it with the muzzle of the pistol pressing against her left hand. Opening the gun to inspect it for cartridges, it accidentally discharged, a bullet piercing and lodging in her left hand. Neighbors confirm that they heard a shot.[300] Miss Marshall stated she heard no gunshot from Ruth's apartment. She said that there was a very thin partition between the two bathrooms and she could always hear the water in the bathtub.[231]

1931, October 18
The milkman arrives at 5AM and says the milk he left on Saturday morning was 1/2 gone at 2929 North Second Street.[157] Wyman Owen is the milkman on Sunday morning and finds the change he left on Saturday gone (13 cents) as well as less than a half pint of milk. He noted that somebody had left a package of laundry on Saturday that had not been touched.[280] Ruth spends the night at Grimm's house. This is where the trunks were.[25] She stated that she changed the parts at Grimm's house.[25] Ruth doesn't know what to do on Sunday morning. She called Jack's office from Grimm's house. She also called Dr. Leff and Betty Murray.[25] Mrs. Grimm stated that Ruth came to see her at between 8:30 and 9. She wanted to use the phone. She called the little store down there and asked them to send a steak up. That was the only item she requested. Her hand was done up in a large cloth. She didn't consider it a bandage because of the way it stood out.[301] She told them that she had burned her hand. A bullet is found in the bedroom at Brill Street, the lead part. Ruth said she thought she had thrown one of those away at the duplex. However, she thought that this might have fallen out of the trunk. The gun had jammed and there was one of those caught in the top of the revolver. Jack had asked her to help pick up and she put the bullet into the garbage can.[25] Jack stated that he played golf on Sunday morning with the business acquaintance whose office he had visited the night before.[239] When asked by McFadden she stated she had no idea how the bullet at the Brill Street address got there unless it fell out of the trunk. She said she thought she threw that bullet in the trash when she was over at 2929 when Jack was putting Sammy in the trunk.[25] Winnie Ruth Judd is home at 10:00 and asks her neighbor Miss Marshall to open a can of salmon for her cat.[231] (Ruth states that she did this after the gun went off in her sink to see if anybody had heard it. The cat was crying and she fed it right away.

Miss Marshall said nothing.)[25] Miss Marshall stated that she heard no gunshot from Ruth's apartment. She stated that Ruth had come to her door at 10:00 and asked her to open a can of salmon as she had burned her hand, and wanted to feed her cat. She stated that one of Ruth's hands was bandaged, but she did not pay attention to which one. Ruth did not sit down but kept walking up and down in her living room until the can was opened and she seemed very excited.[231] The cat is not located at either place after the crime investigation starts.[208] L. C. Baumgartner delivers groceries to Ruth Judd. He puts them on the table by the door. Ruth talks about the dog in his car. He does not notice a bandage.[302] In the afternoon, Ruth again appears at Miss Marshall's door and asks to borrow a pencil stating that she had considerable writing to do. Miss Marshall heard a typewriter running in Mrs. Judd's apartment that afternoon, and later, Ruth returned the pencil. Miss Marshall remarked that she was a very fast typist. Ruth said that she wrote her letters in long hand. She said that she did not see any more of Ruth any time that evening or any time since then.[231] Ruth went over to Grimm's again about 2 to use the phone. She said she was going to take three days off and go to California. So she called and told one of the doctors to say she was going to California. She said she burned her hand and was going to take a trip to California and come back by Wednesday or Thursday. She made several calls, but phoned two doctors and asked them for money.[301] Ruth calls Dr. Leff in the forenoon to ask for a loan. He didn't have any money at the time, but promised to borrow some if Ruth needed it. She said that she burned her hand badly. Dr. Leff saw Ruth about once per week. He stated that in his observations he did not believe she used dope of any kind. He thought Ruth was normal in sexual matters, but wasn't too sure about Sammy. He stated that "Miss Samuelson might have been somewhat abnormal as far as sex matters are concerned."[66] What exactly he said to investigators was, "Mrs. Judd called me on the telephone and I recognized her voice. She told me that she had burned her hand badly and could not work and it would be necessary for her to go to California and she needed some money, but did not state any particular amount. It just so happened that I had no money and told her if it was very urgent that I would go out and borrow the money for her. She said it was not that important and thanked me for my consideration."[66] Jack Halloran stated he went to a movie in the afternoon with his wife and afterwards went to dinner at a downtown restaurant with his son and two daughters in the evening.[239] Josephine

Hadland said Ruth came to see her at 1:30 or 2. She waited over an hour for John Ralston. Her hand was bandaged. Ruth smoked. She wanted to borrow 10 dollars from Metra. She said she would pay it back on Thursday. The bandage was loosely done as if she had a bandage or something underneath and then a good sized towel, and then tucked the four corners in. Metra gave her a safety pin and she wanted to pin it and she said no, she could do it herself and she suggested maybe she should soak her hand in warm water and put some Unguentine on it and that might be better. She said that was why it was so bandaged since it was saturated with this medical stuff. She said she would just as soon leave it like it was.[303] Metra, her sister also said it was 1:30 and she was waiting for John Ralston. In describing her hand, she had a handkerchief for the outside bandage and a bar pin. When asked if she could put Unguentine on it, she declined and said in medical terms what she already put on it. She said she didn't want the air to get at it. She gave her an Elgin watch for security for the loan. Eddie drove her back to the clinic. He drove a new Ford.[97] Winnie Ruth visits the Hadland home at 824 E Monte Vista about 3 pm. She was waiting to see John Ralston, her former landlord at 832 E. Monte Vista and stayed for about an hour. John Ralston did not come home. She talked about burning her hand and wanting to get to the coast to see her husband. Josephine Hadland tried to talk Ruth into getting her hand dressed, but she declined. They had the impression she was concealing a gun in her hand under the bandage later on. Josephine was the one who knew Ruth, but her sister Metra who didn't know Ruth loaned her $10. Ruth said she would pay it back in the middle of the week since rent was due. She gave them her Elgin wrist watch, and a slim bar pin about 1.5 inches long. She asked for a ride back to her apartment and she seemed relaxed and natural. (From who - Shimfessel, brother?) [25] Metra said that Eddie drove her back to the clinic. He had a new Ford. They went out on Pierce Street to pick up another girl and he let them out at the clinic.[97] At 3 o'clock Ruth puts the gun with blood on it into a basin of water. The gun went off in the water while she was washing it. She said that there was a nick of black lead flattened out in the bowl and some went down the pipe in the basin. She took that piece of lead and dropped it into the toilet. She transfers parts of Sammy's body from the big trunk to the other trunk and case by lifting up the pieces with a Turkish towel and letting them fall into the other cases. Something messy in a towel fell out. This was left out of the trunks once they were packed. This was placed in the black bag with the two pairs of dotted pajamas. She put the piece of Sammy first into the smaller steamer trunk and then put the suitcase on top of that and lowered Sammy's torso in. Ruth said this was about 3 o'clock as well.[25] Sammy's torso was wraped in a sheet and blanket.[277] Ruth made no great preparation for her departure. While the apartment was in perfect order, many of her clothes were still hanging in the closet and a good supply of food was in the ice box. There were several mystery thrillers in her apartment. Among them were "The Insidious Dr. Fu-Manchu", "The Golden Scorpion" and "Evolution".[304-306] Evolution was left open at this poem, "Then light and swift through the jungle trees, fronded palms. We swing in our airy flights, or breathed in the palms of the fronded balms. In the hush of the moonless nights. And oh! What beautiful years were these, when our hearts clung each to each; when life was filled and our senses thrilled. In the first faint dawn of speech."[244] Ed Shimfessel stated that he drove Ruth to the clinic and she went in the side entrance. She went in for 7 or 8 minutes. She phoned a girl to relieve her in the office while she was gone.[307] At 4. Ruth called on a Miss Spickelmier and arrived in a new coupe driven by a thin man with prominent teeth. (Mr. Shimfessel – Ed?). She stated that the couple had no license.[153] Miss Spickelmier stated that Mrs. Judd phoned her and asked if she would work for her for three days. She said she would come by and pick her up and take her to the clinic so she could show her the office routine. Miss Spickelmier stated that she knew a William Shimfessel who attended business college where she taught and when she asked him about it, he said that William was his cousin.[153] Ed drove over to 754 Pierce from the clinic to pick up a girl who was waiting outside. Ruth introduced her to Ed as Spicklemier. While they drove back to the clinic Ruth gave her instructions.[307] Since she asked Viola Spickelmier to work for her for only 3 days, it seemed that Winnie Ruth Judd intended to return by Wednesday. Ruth said she was going to visit her sick husband. Ruth was wearing a crumpled uniform and her hair was disarranged. She thought she had never seen her this untidy. She had a rather large bruise (hard to read). After they went out, Ruth asked her to come across the street with her while she cashed a check for expense money on her trip. Viola told her that she needed to hurry home to meet some friends, but Ruth insisted that she come along saying that she was so dirty she hated to go into the drug store alone. So, she went with her. She indorsed and cashed a check receiving in payment two bills. She said she did not notice their denominations. Viola said, "I do not believe I said goodbye then, for I saw someone I knew and stopped to talk. My last impression of her is that she was walking east down the street from the drug store."[153] Jack Robinson from the drug store at the corner of 10th and McDowell states he saw Mrs. Judd on Sunday between 5:15 and 5:45. She had come into and asked to have a check cashed. She was with a young lady who she was breaking in to take her place for a week while she went to the coast. It was a check from Metra Halnan. He held the paper since her left hand was bandaged. He said that it was silly that she burned her hand before vacation and Ruth laughed and agreed that it was silly as hell. She was in the drug store about 7 or 8 minutes. She was wearing a white uniform with very little under it and was quite excited over the fact her uniform blew open when she came in the door. She said to the girl who was with her that if there was anything else she wanted to know about the office to call her before train time.[308] He stated that that it was too bad for her to take a trip with an injured hand. Ruth said, "It isn't much. I burned my hand." Robinson said he often waited on the three women and remarked frequently the devotion of both Mrs. Judd and Miss LeRoi towards Sammy. They bought her ice cream, malted milks and dainty sandwiches and gifts of perfumes and candy. When she was in the store Sunday, she was perfectly calm. She gave not the slightest indication of nervousness or irregularity. He said he thought her heart was beating at a normal rate.[309] Dr. Baldwin said Ruth stopped in the office about an hour before she left for LA and her hand was bandaged and she wouldn't let him dress the wound.[204] It was her left hand that was bandaged and Dr. Baldwin thought that she was hiding something. Dr. Baldwin stated that during the previous two weeks, he was sort of disgusted with her work, and was considering replacing her. She apparently had something on her mind that was causing her work to suffer.[242] Dr. Baldwin stated that he did not see the bandage on Saturday, but saw it on Sunday afternoon. She did not do any writing on Sunday. He told her that he was peeved and he said she was very curt with him.[286] Ed Shimfissel, who had never met Ruth before, drove her home about 6 and picked up a "Miss S." on the way back to the Hadland home.[99] Mrs. HU Grimm urges Ruth to store the trunks in her house. She said, "I told her it was foolish to cart those trunks to Los Angeles when I had plenty of room in my house and she could store them there without charge as long as she wanted to." Ruth declines and says, "Oh, you might get tired of having them around after a while."[310] Sometime during the day she sent Burton a telegram to have him meet her at the train station. Burton never received the telegram; the police intercepted it.[215] At 5:30 HU Grimm, Ruth's landlord takes Ruth and 2 trunks, a suitcase, and a hatbox to the train station.[118] Miss Marshall heard Mr. Grimm talking to Ruth about 5:45 on the same evening with reference to the taking of the trunks to the station. She heard Ruth Judd say to Mr. Grimm that the trunks were very heavy, and thought that he had better get someone to help him load them on the truck. Mr. Grimm stated that he had handled trunks before and could manage very well himself.[231] HU Grimm said he took the trunk from the back room, about 15 feet from where the Lightning Delivery company had deposited it the night before.[207] Kenneth Grimm thought it was her right hand that was bandaged. Beverly Scallings said it was between 4:30 and 5:00.[311] Jack stated that he returned home from the restaurant from dinner about 7 or 8 and remained there.[239] The baggage man at the train station, Avis Butchee says Ruth came about 4:30 and he weighed in the trunks and collected the money from Ruth. He did not say anything about her hands. Ruth gave her address as 201 Pinchot St. (This is the address for the other side of the Duplex). The trunks were put on the train at 7:55. He thought they might be leaking medicine.[312] He stated that Ruth had signed the baggage claim check as BJ McKinnell.[313] The baggage tags were dated October 18th, 1931 and signed BJ McKinnell of 201 Pinchot. A passenger value at $100.[314] Beverly Scallings also saw this and thought it was medicine.[311] When Ruth arrived in LA she spent two hours there looking for the guy that Halloran said she should meet there. The man's name was Williams, or Wilson and was supposed to meet her at ten fifteen or ten something. Ruth indicates that this fellow came up to the jail.[25] ? "And not to tell my husband, and I don't know which one it was that spoke about an accident on the hunting trip, but I had already said I burnt it at the clinic, but I said it was a bad accident." Jack stated that Sammy had been operated on, but that she was dead. He stated that he would get a ticket for her. He was supposed to meet her a block from the depot. She said she was sure that Jack bought the ticket, but the only other person who could have was Ryan. Ruth stated that Ryan was drunk on Friday night as well.[25] Ruth gets rid of two messy towels from the trunk. They were the pajamas that Anne wore and the pair that she was wearing that night. They were in the black bag and she threw them out of the train window. They were both the same pajamas with the dots on them. With the pajamas she threw out a few other towels. The conductor talked to Ruth quite a bit on the train ride.[25] The black bag was empty when the police recovered the hat box with the surgeon's bag in it.[171] Ruth admitted she wrapped the small portion of the severed intestine in a towel at the Brill Street house, placed it in a small bag, took it with her on the train and she threw the towel and contents out of the train window.[207] (Instruments from the bag?) Ruth claimed he kept bothering her. Ruth claimed that there wasn't anything wrapped in the towels. She threw two towels and the pajamas out the window. She said nobody noticed. There were some Mexican people on the train who got on at Yuma and had a very cute baby.[25] Dr. Judd stated that the black bag was not his. He said that he remembered seeing it in the garage. He believed that it belonged to one of the girls. He thought that he had seen it in the garage with perfume and stuff in it. He stated that he had many medical instruments in Phoenix and they were about the size of the black bag.[155]

1931, October 19

Burton arose at 6AM in LA, happy to be alive. He whistled while he dressed, dashed down to the kitchen to eat breakfast and went off to the University of California for his Maritime law class at 8.[102] He stated that he fried two eggs. He dropped off his roommate Jerry Moore at USC.[315] He was studying diplomacy at USC.[78] Ruth arrives in Los Angeles at 7:40 AM on the "Golden State#3".[316] She sent a telegram to Burton in Beverly Glen at 8:03. It simply read, "Please meet me at Depot this morning. Ruth."[317] Burton stated that he did not receive the telegram.[127] Burton had no class at 9:00 so went to the YMCA to study.[102] He sat under a palm tree and was studying French.[315] Stella Conley, the restroom attendant, stated that Ruth came in with a porter and put her suitcase behind the door. She held the hatbox. At 9:30 they called for the Southern Pacific 10:00 train and she asked her if she was taking that train. Ruth replied that she was waiting. Later she asked what was wrong with her hand. Ruth replied that she got it burned. Then she asked if it was ok if she left the suitcase behind the door. Stella suggested that she check them. She stated that she didn't have the money to check them and that she had sent her brother a message and if he was at the University, he couldn't come since they wouldn't deliver a message to him. Ruth leaves the restroom about 10:00.[318] After Ruth arrives in LA, she contacts her brother Burton about 11 o'clock by finding him at school.[127] She went to the registrar's office to check on his schedule. She went to his 9:00 French class and he was not there. He had changed his schedule to have an hour off. Miss Jallade told her that he was registered for the class. When he arrived at French class at 10, he was told by Miss Jallade, "There is a lady looking for you."[315] He was walking up the steps of Old College on the way to foreign law at 11.[102] Burton stated that she hunted him up at the University of Southern California Monday morning. She seemed very nervous and excited. He said, "I could tell that there was something on her mind. He was a bit worried about that.[319] She looked worn, weary, and wan. She was glad to see him. She was calm and collected. She was wearing a black loose fitting hat and a black and white dress.[315] She said, "Hello Burton, Come on down," taking him by the arm and taking him down the steps. "No, I have classes. Come with me," he said. She declined, she said, "Burton, I must talk to you." He noticed the clean bandage on her hand and asked her what was wrong. She didn't say and he said he had to get to class. She said, "Burton I want you to get a couple of trunks for me." Burton replied, "OK, I will get them after class." She grabbed his arm and insisted, "No, Burton, I want you to go get them right now." He thought this was funny and asked her why the hurry. Burton skipped class and they went behind Old College to his car.[102] Burton stated that when Ruth says, right away, she means right away. He stated that she had been in a tense state of mind for some time, because of "worries". He stated that the worries were working beyond her strength, and the desire to get her folks out to the West.[127] They passed a couple of students on their way to class and they teased him about being late, but they went on. On their way to the station, he asked Ruth how they would affix the trunks to the car since the back was sloping. She said rope. They stopped at two places for rope and they didn't have any. Finally, they found some clothesline at a wallpaper store and Burton paid 40 cents for the line. They drove on in silence. Finally, Burton asked her what they would do with the trunks once they picked them up. Ruth hesitated. Then she said, "Dump them into the ocean." Burton thought that she was joking. Ruth suggested using the boat Burton used to take out. It was the school launch kept at the California Yacht Club. He asked her what was in the trunks. She refused to say.[315] Burton asked her what was in the trunks, but she did not answer. Burton stated that he accepted this logic and did not press the question. He felt that she was right and that he should not know.[127] Burton told the police that Ruth knew he was once a skipper on a yacht here.[171] They presented the checks and then waited for a very long time for the trunks. Anderson came out and said that there was something wrong with the trunks. Ruth said she didn't know what he meant.[315] Ruth and Burton arrives about 11:30 to pick up the trunks. Burton stopped to buy rope on the way.[127] Burton said clothesline.[102] Burton asked her what they were going to do with the trunks once they claimed them. Ruth hesitated and said, "Do with them? We'll dump them in the ocean."[102] "The ocean?" asked Burton. "Yes, the Ocean. We'll drive them down to the oceanfront and get them out in that boat you used to go out on and when we are far enough out, we'll throw them into the water."[102] Burton asks about the contents, but Ruth doesn't tell him. Burton drives around the back to pick up the trunks in the delivery area.[102] Burton was tying the rope on the car when Ruth tried to claim the bags.[127] She took two checks out of her purse or bag. Mr. Anderson or Andrews came out and said, "there is something wrong with these trunks; come on back and take a look at them."[127] Burton was dressed in typical collegiate attire; red turtle necked sweater and baggy corduroys. Ruth produced two claim checks from her purse. The clerk took the stubs and went away, returning to the window a moment later and said, "I'm sorry, Madame," he said, "but we have been given orders that before we surrender those trunks we must ask you to open them in the presence of an inspector." The clerk said Burton seemed unconcerned, but that Ruth appeared pale and agitated.[176] Burton went back and looked at them. He didn't have any words. He saw a lot of flies. He was 12 or 14 feet from the trunks.[127] Arthur Anderson, the baggage guy in Los Angeles, notices that the two trunks checked to Ruth Judd smelled rather foul. He orders the trunks to be held since he suspected they contained contraband venison.[320] After the trunks had been unloaded, the trunks were waiting to be claimed. Arthur Anderson nudged the larger trunk with his shoulder and smelled it and confirmed that it contained venison and told the others to not let those trunks go out of there until the owner opens them for inspection.[176] Anderson asked Ruth if she smelled the odor. She said no. He asked her to step closer. She did and said she could smell something and made a joke that it definitely was not booze and laughed. She said, "You can bet it's not a broken bottle of booze." Anderson laughed. They asked her to open the trunks. She said that she didn't have the keys. She asked Burton for change to use the phone. Anderson said she should use the phone in the office. Ruth fumbled with the phonebook and for the first time was terribly nervous. Burton saw Anderson head upstairs. He suggested that they go for the keys in person. Ruth agreed. Anderson and some other men came down and stood next to the trunks. Ruth was in control and went and told them she was going for the keys. Burton thought that it was the end.[315] They asked Ruth to open the trunk, but she said that she didn't have the keys. Burton said that there were a lot of flies. They were at the station for about 20 minutes. Ruth did not say what was in the trunks.[127] Burton said it reminded him of the story of Solomon and the two bouquets of flowers, one real and one fake.[315] Ruth and Burton left the station and the clerk alerted the nearby railroad detective, who followed the pair into the street. As they drove away, the plainclothes detective jotted down the license number. They later tracked that number to Beverly Glen where Burton lived.[176] They didn't speak and Burton sped off in the car. When he was a bit away he turned to her and talked to her.[315] Burton asked if it was a man or a woman, but Ruth didn't answer. She said she refused to answer questions about it.[127] Burton gave her 5 dollars and said, that her leaving was the best, and said, "I wish you all the luck in the world, kid." Ruth left the car at 7th and Broadway.[127] He said he may be mistaken in that street, that it might have been 7th and Main or 6th and Broadway.[127] Ruth said these things to Burton, "The less you know about those trunks the better". When she got out of the car, she said, "Burton, I was justified in what I did, always remember that."[176] Burton stated that she was nervous and almost hysterical. She asked him to help her throw her two trunks into the ocean. Burton finally said that he would, but he didn't know what was in the trunks. He stated when she left she was almost crying and said she had to have some money. He gave her $5, all he had.[319] Burton told her that he was not interested in hearing her justification, but wanted to know her next steps. He was not angry and never thought that he would see her again. When she got out of the car, she dropped something off of her arm like a scarf or something to wear. A kind lady stooped and picked it up and poked her to give it back to her.[315] Burton stated she walked north on Broadway.[171] Burton stated that he went down a block or two and turned over again and went back to the University.[127] He arrived back there at 1 and stayed until 1:30.[171] Burton stated that people had said that he approached them for money in the afternoon and "about this, I have nothing to say."[315] One source stated that Winnie Ruth Judd kept a prearranged appointment with a man in Los Angeles, a man believed to have had knowledge of the grim butchery of Mrs. Agnes A LeRoi and Hedvig Samuelson according to information given to Sheriff McFadden. He drove through the night from Phoenix to meet her but was late. According to McFadden, he stated that in addition to Halloran, Ruth had one other close male friend. (He owned a small coupe, which he stated she used during the slayings. Her romance with him was surreptitious because of Halloran's interest in her.)[271] Police believe that new holes were dug in the ground that afternoon out at Burton's house in Beverly Glen. They discovered a deep concrete pit in the yard behind the little house and on the premise that there were numerous freshly dug holes in the ground, each deep enough to have become a grave.[321] Burton gave the following explanation on October 28, "Ruth came up to see the place and praised me for working on the garden as I have done." (When she was there for the funeral in May) "I dug a deep hole, concreted it for an old fashioned well and dug ditches for a circulating fountain. She even wanted to help me plant flowers. It is ridiculous to believe that this garden was planned to dispose of those bodies as has been suggested. She went back to Phoenix."[215] Burton did his janitorial work at Roosevelt High School at 2.[127] His duties were to clean the auto shop, sinks and sweep the wood shop out. He left there about 4 o'clock or a little earlier.[127] Mr. Smith (Swift?) the head janitor confirmed this. He did his regular work consisting of cleaning the auto shop and sinks and sweeping the carpenter or wood shop out, meaning the sawdust from the wood trimmings. Typically, he would be there until 4 or so, but got out a bit early. Some of the boys there were mischievous and the instructors sent them out to do some janitorial work.[127] Police said he stayed at the University for about 2.5 hours.[171] Some students were disciplined and had picked up a little bit. He went to the law school to look up some cases, but couldn't concentrate. He was studying some Maritime law cases that were assigned by his professor. He ate at the Coola Shanta about 6 or 6:30. He called Dr. Judd at Carrie's, but he wasn't there. This was about 6 o'clock or 6:30 after he ate.[127] The LA times stated that a witness at the bus stop in front of the Beverly Glen store saw Burton driving his car up into the Glen about 6 o'clock with a woman in the car. The witness was Jack Etler, a gardener, 55 years old. They seemed to be in a hurry. Burton approached another student Monday night regarding borrowing money. He stated that his sister had become involved in a "terrible tragedy". This indicated according to Lloyd Andrews that he knew where his sister was.[322] They did not believe that Burton having a car would just let his sister out and wish her God speed.[127] Torres and Davidson received a call from SPS saying that they had a trunk down there from which an odor of decayed flesh was coming and they were asked to make an investigation. One of the trunks was bearing an excess baggage check 663165 and the other had 406749.[171] The coroner's office was called at 5:30 PM by Detective Ryan.[323] The bodies were received at the coroner's office at 6:20. The undertakers were associated with Peck & Chase. Both bodies were embalmed. They were listed as died on October 16. They did not say why they thought this. Both were listed as "shot by unknown person, unjustifiable." The probable cause of homicide was listed as unknown. The bodies were brought in by Y. D. Evers.[323] Ruth left her brother late afternoon. She walked for several blocks. She did not have a specific plan except that she planned to get in touch with her husband. She tried to find Carrie's phone number in the phone book, but she was not listed. She dialed Information and requested the number. There was a delay on the other end of the line and Ruth got frightened and hung up. She thought they might be tracing the call and notifying the police. Later, the police did place a watch on his calls at his sisters and the information exchange was also supposed to report any queries of Carrie's phone number. She walked several more blocks and called Information again. There was a delay again and Ruth stated she was in a dreadful hurry. The operator replied that she could not give her the number unless she provided her name and address. Ruth dropped the receiver without hanging it up and rushed away. She crossed Broadway and stood in the doorway of the department store and watched the telephone. A few minutes later a police department car rushed up and several plainclothesmen jumped out and ran into the store. So, she knew the police were now after her. She entered the department store thinking that she would be safer in there. She disappears into the crowded aisles. She wandered around the store. She found herself in the drapery department and then a hiding place suggested itself. Against the walls were huge frames over which curtains and drapes were hung in display. She slipped unnoticed behind the heavy folds that reached down to the floor. She stayed there until the store closed.[250] Later, Frank Ryan arrives and investigates the trunks. In the large trunk he finds the body of Anne LeRoi along with an old quilt on top, a bent bread knife with a green handle, 2 purses, a piece of rug about 3 feet long, photographs, letters in a bundle, canceled checks to a Dr. Packer in Whitehall Montana.[171] The piece of the rug cut from the bedroom rug was said to have been "heavily stained with blood" and the opinion given was the woman who laid on this bed was bleeding profusely since the mattress was disposed of and the piece of the rug was cut out.[290] Another account stated the piece of rug was cut out with a knife. This piece of rug had been burned in a stove evidently to hide bloodstains.[259] An early report stated that the rug had been burned in the fireplace.[324] [325] There were several spots of blood on the rug and there were two blood rings found near the door at 2929.[325] One of the letters was signed Thomas Frelinghuysen of Elberson, NJ. He addressed Sammy as "sweetheart"[187]. The family estate was in Oakhurst in Elberon near Newark.[326] Thomas probably attended Princeton University as the Frelinghuysen brothers attended Princeton.[326] TJ Matthews described Frelinghuysen as he knew him in 1934 as a "proud, reckless, arrogant young bachelor with more money than was good for him, and not quite enough, artistic talent. He couldn't be bothered to go to art school but taught himself to draw and model in clay. The subjects that most attracted him were unusual: a dead horse, a Doberman pinscher shitting. He was also a self-taught portrait painter, and some of his portraits I liked. He also tried his hand at writing, though I don't think he ever published anything. Julie was much impressed by a play he had written, and got him to show it to me. I thought it had some good things in it, but could see many others that needed amending, and made the mistake of pointing them out to him. He did not take my criticism kindly, and I never saw any more of his writing."[327] There were also letters of cheer from a member of the Alaska Senate, Anthony J. Diamond (Dimond), also a prominent lawyer.[62] Evelyn Nace, however, stated that there were no letters from men found to Sammy and while, "though Agnes LeRoi had a sweetheart, Sammy was her hobby."[64] One of the purses contained a thermometer, 2 shells, .25 caliber, one exploded, one not exploded. The other purse had one empty 25 caliber bullet and a penny. The smaller trunk contained Sammy's torso wrapped in a blanket with a pink border, and her legs (below the knees) were wrapped in women's underclothing. Sammy is wearing a slip. There is personal belongings in the trunk which were assumed were turned over to the district attorney, but were first delivered to Coroner Nance.[328] The police report said that there were 3 .25 caliber shells and one bullet seeming to have passed through something. One bullet seemed to be missing. There were 40 rounds of 25 caliber bullets in the trunk. Of Anne LeRoi's body, "One Bullet hole in head. One .25 automatic bullet recovered from the body". Of Hedvig the police report said, the old tan suitcase contained the lower female torso (waist to knees) clothed in pink pajamas and wrapped in a sheet and blanket. The intestines and bladder were missing.[171] Of the hatbox, it was said to contain an empty black surgeon's bag, surgical dressing, and an old kit of surgeon's instruments (a single hair two inches long, having the appearance of being hennaed was found in the kit. Several scalpels showed evidence of recent rust), one .25 colt automatic pistol (stained with rust and blood), several pieces of women's wearing apparel, 40 round Winchester.25 automatic cartridges and misc. cosmetics. The surgeon's black bag was said to be empty, but had the odor of a decaying cadaver.[171] A newspaper article stated that the disfiguration of Mrs. LeRoi's head, which led police to believe at first that she had been clubbed was due to decomposition.[89] Wagner who did the autopsy on Anne LeRoi stated that a bullet was extracted from Anne LeRoi's head.[329] He said the bullet entered the left side. Its course was from left to right, backward and downward. The bullet was beneath the scalp. There was a powder smudge. He stated that he thought the gun was held against the head.[277] At trial he said the bullet entered her left temple and lodged beneath the scalp on the right side of the head.[330] On Anne's body there were severe bruises on the head and upper portions of the body.[89] A ballistics expert, Mr. Moxley was supposed to testify that this bullet did indeed come from the gun in the hatbox and what range it had been fired at.[329] The coroner's report was read at the coroner's inquest. It read, "Office of County Coroner. I performed an autopsy on Agnes Alexander LeRoi Smith, October 20, 1931, at the Los Angeles County Coroner's Mortuary and found the body considerably decomposed and distended with postmortem gas. The eyeballs protruded and tongue, lips and other parts enormously swollen and putrid. There was no evidence of contusions or injuries on the body, except a gunshot wound and such superficial abrasions as could be made in handling the body. The gunshot wound was located in the head. The bullet entered the left side, 1.5 inches above and backward diagonally from the outer angle of the left eye. This wound was considerably lacerated and powder smudged. The course of the bullet was through the lower portions of both hemispheres of the brain in a direction from left to right, somewhat backward and downward to the lower posterior angle of the right parietal bone, which was penetrated and I found the bullet just beneath the scalp at this point. I opened the body and found the same degree of decomposition of the internal organs as was shown in the superficial part and so far as could be determined there was no grossly visible disease. The cause of death was bullet wound of the head. Signed AF Wagner, Los Angeles County autopsy surgeon."[331] He testified that bullets came from the same gun. Lewkowitz pointed out however that the markings on one of the shells varied from the others He called this fact to the attention of the jury during the trial.[277] Dr. Brinkerhoff stated that Anne LeRoi had been shot on the left side of the head. One hole.[332] Other items in the trunk included Sammy's diploma from the Minot Normal School and a teacher's contract for Whitehall Montana.[333] There was a picture of Sarah Elizabeth Hart of Wrangell taken on September 19, 1919 in the trunk.[334] Another source states this photograph was taken September 10, 1929 in Seattle at the Hartsock studio in Seattle.[16] There was a picture of Marion Alvina Vrem which was unidentified at the time, but the picture later appeared in the Oregon Journal. C.E. Chatfield, druggist said that Marion's brother had entered the store and identified the picture of his sister Marion who was a friend from Minot.[335] A copy of the Rubaiyat and a book called Rainbow Weather by Margaret Hargray was in the trunk along with three teachers' portfolios, a stack of Christmas Cards, and a list of student names.[126] Dr. Judd stated that he read in the paper that there were women's underthings, hosiery, dresses, newspapers, towels, toilet articles, and Christmas cards and personal letters in the trunks.[176] A pair of ice skates was also in the trunk.[25] In the hatbox, Ray Pinker stated that there was a surgical dress, a blue dress, surgeon's tools and a .25 caliber automatic pistol. There were blood stains on the gun.[277] Eloise Stafford, Anne LeRoi's sister in Aurora Oregon receives her last letter from Anne. She said that she expected to travel to Phoenix to spend Christmas with them.[143] Jack Halloran hears about the crime on Monday night from a physician acquaintance who telephoned him.[239] In Phoenix, Photographer, E.D. Newcomer receives a call from Los Angeles regarding two addresses in Phoenix. The first house was occupied but the second at 2929 was empty. Newcomer arrived before the police. Newcomer entered the duplex, collected a DIARY, and all of the photographs he could find. He answered the telephone and ran across the street to trace the call. He returned to the duplex and waited for the Phoenix police to arrive.[336] Another source states that while the newspaper men and a doctor were at the house, a telephone call came in for Miss Samuelson from Boise, Idaho. The doctor answered the phone and told the party to hold the wire and that he would call Miss Samuelson. Instead he rushed to another telephone and asked to have the call traced and the operator informed him the call was from Los Angeles and not Boise. When he returned to the telephone, the party in Los Angeles had hung up.[337] Another source stated that he copped Samuelson's diary from the table between the two beds in the bedroom.[338] Emil Hoitola, Anne's Fiancé tries to call the duplex again on Monday and it is answered by a man who stated that Anne LeRoi was out. Emil believed it was one of the officers.[298] Emil said this was at 10 at night on Monday when it was answered by a newspaperman. He started calling at 8:30 that night from the Rogerson Hotel in Twin Falls, ID. He finally got an answer at 10. He said the man inquired as to the name of the caller and appeared to be "stalling" stating that Mrs. LeRoi was out. He had believed him to be a detective.[299] He had been trying to reach Anne at Phoenix since Saturday night.[294] McCord Harrison and George Larrison of the Phoenix police arrive at the house about 10:00 in the evening. The lights are out and the doors are locked. The empty side of the duplex is unlocked. They opened the window to get in by prying loose a screen. There were 2 newspaper men there. They were inside with them, but they did not see them touch anything. One did touch some remains in the fireplace, however. There were some papers on the table. Orville Bechtol arrived at 10 to take fingerprints. No blood was seen except for in the bedroom. A corner of the rug on the floor from the bed room was cut out.[339] George Larrison stated that his partner M. S. Freasier entered the house first. The front door was locked. He wasn't sure about the back. He noted two beds, one was completely made up but the other had quilts folded on it, but there was no mattress. He said that there were no marks or abrasions on the walls. He recalled seeing no ironing board. He saw no blood.[291] It was said when they first entered that a blue quilt was folded on the bed without the mattress in such a way that when covered it simulated the appearance and thickness of the mattress on the other bed.[290] Ruth stated that she had carried the mattress to a clump of bushes about twenty feet away on the south side of the bungalow. She had seen a man approach on the sidewalk. He was whistling. She had intended on burning it, but changed her mind. So, she thrust the mattress into the foliage and hurried back into the house.[194] Bechtel stated that back door was unlocked. He said that Larrison and Freasier were there when he arrived and that Harrison and Moore arrived later. He said there were some people in the yard, just two or three people. Ruth stated that she knew that there was some blood on the molding in the breakfast room. Ruth asked McFadden if there was any blood on the bathroom floor. McFadden stated that there was right up against the tub. [25] D. Kelly Turner claims he was the first one there arriving within 5 minutes after the police. He was a reporter at the time for the Gazette and later became a federal judge.[340] Dozens of letters were found in the Samuelson-LeRoi duplex indicating that the girls had many men friends who wrote to them in affectionate terms.[298] Treasure hunters and spectators start visiting the house.[341] There were scores of letters found in the apartment and numerous photographs of men of all ages. Two albums, one belonging to Mrs. LeRoi and the other to Miss Samuelson were being scrutinized by investigators.[63] The house was in order and neat. On the library table in the living room were several books including, "Grand Hotel", "Education of a Princess", "Cakes and Ale", "Beau Sabreur", "The Care of Tuberculosis", and "The Rubaiyat." Detective, Love and Adventure magazines were heaped in the garage along with a story about a woman who was murdered and hidden in a desk.[342] Other books mentioned to be in the duplex included, "Number Seven", a book with a skull on its black and red cover, "The King's Minion", "Chances", "Shepherds in Sackcloth" among others. [230] There were two sayings on the wall, one with a poem on it called, "Say Damn" that was hung above Sammy's bed and another with a verse from the "House by the Side of the Road" by Sam Walter Foss[230] Interestingly, the Arizona State Archives has "The House by the Side of the Road" typed out on a piece of paper in their files on the case, but no explanation is given [343] A whisky bottle almost empty was found in the duplex. The fingerprints turned out to be Anne LeRoi's[344] A pair of mud caked slippers were found under the sink.[345]

Say Damn

It does you no good to grow bitter
When Luck up and hands you a slam
Lie Down and you lose as a quitter.
So, just grit your teeth and say damn.[230]

The police visit Beverly Glenn looking for Burton since they had traced his car. Nobody was home there, but they searched the premises and found names and addresses of friends and relatives.[176] Police believe that Ruth had the opportunity to connect again with Burton in the evening.[219] Dr. Judd returns to his sisters after work in a great mood. His sister exclaims, "You're looking better than I've seen you in years," as he entered through the door. Carrie says, "Dinner will be ready in a little while. You've just got time to wash up and listen to the news broadcast."[176] Dr. Judd twisted the dial to his favorite radio station and heard the following conclusion, "And the police are searching for a young man in collegiate clothes and a pale-looking young woman with light hair. Detectives say this is one of the most baffling cases they have encountered in years. You have just heard the highlights of the day's news. For further details, see your local newspaper.[176] Dr. Judd wondered what the baffling crime could be, but was too busy to give it much thought. Then he heard a newsboy shout, "Extra, Read all about the trunk murders! Extra!" He bought one of the papers out of curiosity. He returned to the house and under the screaming black headlines began to read the details of the crime.[176] In the evening, Burton goes to the home of Carrie to see Dr. Judd about 8:30 or 9. He stops to see his friend Bill to borrow some money. He was short. Santa Monica was about 35 miles away.[127] The police report states that Burton was there when they arrived at the house. They had gone to 5001 Santa Fe Ave and found it closed at 9:30. It was the office of Benjamin Moss, Industrial Injury Service. They then went to the house.[171] Dr. Judd stated he arrived about 9:30. Dr. Judd made the statement to police that he last saw Ruth on the 8th or 9th of August. (what about Bisbee?)[155] Dr. Judd stated that Burton arrived and that the sound of the doorbell made him panic. Burton appeared worried and nervous. Dr. Judd invited him in. Carrie and Dr. Judd were making fudge. Dr. Judd was cracking nuts. Burton thought that perhaps, "the boys" would have been there and taken away Dr. Judd. Ruth had said that she was going to call Dr. Judd and tell him everything, but she hadn't contacted him. Burton had a newspaper with him. They had put out an Extra. He thought that it was the Examiner. They sat in the little room in the garage and talked about it.[127] Dr. Judd said that Burton stated he wanted to speak to him alone and took him into the library and said that he had awful news to tell. Burton was confused and incoherent.[96] According to Dr. Judd, their conversation went like this, when did you last hear from Ruth? Dr. Judd claimed that he just got a letter and was going to answer it today. Burton asked if he had seen her. Dr. Judd said no. Burton said that she was in terrible trouble. He related the train station story.[176] They went over the story that had been in the Extra he had brought with him. It was the first that Dr. Judd had heard about it.[127] They went in to have dinner. During the soup, the doorbell rang and it was the police. Burton told the police that he was 25.[127] He knew that he would not finish his soup.[127][176] The police report stated that they found Burton, Dr. Judd, and Carrie at the kitchen table eating.[171] Burton told police he had come to see Dr. Judd regarding Ruth's recent letters to see if he knew what was wrong with her. He said that her letters had been incoherent lately. He stated he believed that she had an insane temper but wouldn't say that she was crazy.[346] Burton told police that Ruth had come to him at school about 11 and said he had a job for him to do.[171] Carrie stated that Burton arrived about 9:30 and he seemed distracted as if something had shaken him. He appeared worried. She said that her brother and Burton went into another room. The doorbell rang and there were two men on the porch who asked for Mrs. Judd. They talked to Dr. Judd. Dr. Judd stated that he had to go into town. He said, "Carrie, there's hell to pay and I don't know whether I ought to tell you". He told her however, that two women had been found in a trunk and that Ruth was in a jam.[128] Dr. Judd said Burton told him that Ruth wanted to toss the trunks into the ocean.[96] He stated that Winnie didn't drink, she didn't take dope. She was an adoring wife.[128] The police took Burton and Dr. Judd into custody that night.[128] When Clark and Bergeron arrived at the house, they questioned Burton about the battered roadster parked outside. Then they talked to Dr. Judd and asked him where his wife was. Dr. Judd replied that he had thought she was in Phoenix. He pulled out the letter that he had received from her on the previous evening hoping to prove that Ruth was still in Phoenix. The pair replied that he would have to go to the central station with Burton to be questioned. They said, "Your wife, Winnie Ruth Judd is wanted for questioning in the murders of Anne LeRoi and Hedvig Samuelson." Dr. Judd said he felt like he would collapse. They rushed both of them downtown with the sirens screaming.[176] The police report confirms that Dr. Judd gave them the letter that he had received that day and told them she was in Phoenix.[171] At Joe Taylor's office one of the questions he asked Dr. Judd was why they lived apart. They finished with Dr. Judd and took him to another room and began to question Burton. Dr. Judd's impulse was to go and look for Ruth himself. Dr. Judd thought his part was done, but Joe Taylor asked Dr. Judd to go to the morgue and identify the victims. They knew who they were, but wanted a person who knew them personally to identify them. Dr. Judd identified the bodies of Anne and Sammy at the LA county morgue. The smaller trunk was his army trunk.[347] Dr. Judd said there were many things in the trunks that he recognized; things Ruth had worn, a card he had sent to Sammy on her birthday (?), and an Indian rug that had been woven for their bedroom for their first home in Mexico.[347] Dr. Judd was visibly shaken even though he was long accustomed to standing in the presence of death as he emerged from the death room at the morgue. He said the crime was beyond his belief and he could not conceive that his wife had committed the murders. "I knew both these girls when they were alive; active and apparently without a care. They were gay and happy when I last saw them. It was a great shock to me to look at them lying there dead and disfigured. I hope my wife is never found alive. It is my belief that she will be taken from the ocean. She is frail and delicate; she could never stand the ordeal of a trial. If she were found alive it would prolong the agony."[348] It was stated by the United Press that Miss Nace and Mrs. Sweek, wife of the clinic surgeon, rushed into the murder cottage less than two minutes after the police arrived and immediately began searching for any notes the women may have left. Later Brinkerhoff was surprised when told this.[349] Mrs. Sweek and Evelyn Nace search for Sammy's diary at the duplex after the tragedy. The diary mentions various men callers; among them Dr. Sweek. Dr. Sweek supposedly liked Evelyn Nace. Anne supposedly like Dr. Sweek.[67] The diary was entitled "Milestones". Evelyn Nace and Mrs. Sweek were looking for "notes" that the women may have left. Supposedly Mrs. and Dr. Sweek intended to separate.[351] Evelyn Nace stated that Monday night after the reporters called her, they started questioning her. Mrs. Sweek called her and said she would like to go over. She said, "Maybe you can be of some value to the officers. The officers are there and newspaper reporters. Maybe you can be of some value to them, to give them some information. She asked if she made a statement or asked the reporters if they found any notes or letters. She said, "No, I didn't because I had no reason why I should because my acquaintance with the girls had been such that there was no reason why I should have asked." Evelyn said that this was between 10 and 10:30 on Monday night. She said that the Arizona Republic had called her, a reporter. They had at first when the press reports came in called the nurse's directory to find out if there were any nurses missing. When they asked for Mrs. LeRoi they asked the directory if they knew whether she had been working on Saturday or Monday. Since the person at the nurse's directory did not know, she referred them to Evelyn Nace since she might know.[133] Ruth hides out in the Broadway Department Store during this night. She waited until the store closed and customers and clerks left for the day. When the place became deserted she prowled around the store. She took a pencil and a tablet of writing paper. She wrote Dr. Judd a 16-page letter, begging him to help her and putting down the details of the last week's events. She planned to mail it when the store opened

the next day and she would be free to go out on the street again.[250] She
did not sign the letter [352] The first part is to Dr. Moore and it states
that she is being sought by the police and can't get any message to
her husband at 823 17th St. in Santa Monica.[167] Police believe that she
wrote this letter during the four days she hid out in Los Angeles. She
disposed of it when she was able to contact her husband (So, Friday,
not Monday).[353]

1931, October 20
After midnight at 12:15 A.M., they question Dr. Judd formally for the
first time and he gives a formal statement. At one point they show him
the gun and he stated that that was it, but that it was not rusty the last
time he saw it. Of the medical instruments he said they were his. He
stated that he got those in 1906. He didn't say where those were, but
said that the last time he saw those was in Phoenix. He stated that he
had a lot of medical instruments there. He was asked if the instruments
had cotton on them like these. He said that he thought he had all of
them wrapped to protect the edges. They asked him if they had been
used. He stated that he couldn't tell because they were clean now. He
stated the instruments he had in Phoenix "were in the house". He said
he had a whole bag full of them.[155] John L Brinkerhoff, chief
investigator, went to the duplex for the first time and found ample
evidence of a crime.[354] Frank Vance enters the duplex and sees that
one of the two mattresses was missing.[291] Mrs. Vance noted that a
piece was cut out of the rug in the bedroom. She stated that she found
two distinct tracks from the garage to the back door that were 21 inches
apart leading from the Southwest corner of the garage. The trunk
tracks continued through the service porch, the kitchen, a small hallway
and into the living room. The trunk had been dragged, not carried.[355]
Ruth returns to her hiding place behind the curtains at the Broadway
Department Store when the store opened. She waited until she heard
customers walking around on the same floor. Then she slipped out,
downstairs to the main floor and out into the sunshine. She had a new
plan on this day; she decided to disguise herself. She went into the
drug store and she bought a package of black dye. She returned to the
store and into one of the women's rest rooms. She mixed the dye in a
washbowl and plunged her head into it. She took off her dress and
dipped it too into the dye. She dried her hair by dabbing it with heavy
paper towels. The dress was more of a problem. She tried to dry it by
wringing it out and then swished it back and forth in the air. She tore

up the letter she had written to her husband and flushed it down the toilet.[250] She made the mistake of tearing it up and then wadding it together instead of scattering it in the toilet. The pieces would not have been recovered if she had scattered instead of wadded them together since it clogged the toilet. Also, if she had written it in pen instead of pencil, it would not have been recovered and been legible.[352] Her dress was still wet when she put it back on as it clung to her undergarments, and her hair was still wet but she made it to the door and out to the street without interruption. She planned to head to Pasadena. She walks to the La Vina Sanitarium which was secluded among quiet trees almost 20 miles away. She planned to hunt out an unused bungalow on the grounds and rest there until her hand healed.[250] Ruth stated she wrote her husband two letters during her hideout at the sanitarium. She said she put one in her purse and destroyed the other in the lavatory at La Vina.[194] Police doubt this story that she walked up there. Ruth entered into one of the apartments in one of the dormitories and there stole a dress and coat belonging to a patient (Mrs. Aida Zuniga). She later identified the coat and dress as hers. It was not a vacant bungalow as stated by Ruth. It was more like a dormitory. The place where it was evident someone had stopped is the south end of the main kitchen and dining room building which crests one of the highest hills in the estate. On the hilltop are three building; the kitchen, the dining room structure and two long dormitories. The only room on that end of the building was the x-ray room which had a door onto the rather narrow central hallway which divides those half dozen small rooms. In each of these rooms is a bed with two mattresses and a rather heavy mattress cover. To get to this south end of the main building after dark would be easy for anyone as there are no guards. By walking up the roadway from the administration building anybody would get to the foot of a flight of steps that lead up the hillside to the dining room structure. After the dinner dishes are done, there is no one in the entire dining room building at night. There were six empty rooms there. They said it was likely she left her room at night, walked north to the dining room and went into the kitchen where in an ice box, she found bottles of milk. There were frequently fifty bottles of milk on hand. One or two missing would not be noticed. In one of the small bedrooms it was evident there had been an unknown occupant. The mattresses were mussed. The mattress cover evidently had been used to cover someone on the bed. Pieces of paper containing crumbs were in the dresser drawers, and on the shelf in the closet were more paper napkins containing date stones. Ruth had stated she on one afternoon had walked the short distance to the south to the dormitory, where Mrs. Zuniga was and stole her coat and dress. People thought that she would have been seen by a dozen patients, but they thought perhaps she made the trip during the rest period of the afternoon and all patients would have been in bed resting. Dr. Hodges stated that when the reporters were up at La Vina looking for Ruth, they did not look at the south end near the dining room.[356] Dr. Judd stated that through this day, he was paralyzed with cracking nerves. He was determined to find Ruth. He felt that she would be dead too. At times he wished that she were dead so she would be spared of all of the trouble. Dr. Judd went downtown to the corner where she had left from Burton's car. He wandered aimlessly through the streets. All he could hear is the newspaper boys selling papers. Everywhere he looked he saw Ruth on the front pages of the newspapers beneath great black headlines. His pictures were in a lot of the papers as well and people began to recognize him with curious stares. People started following him and he thought that Joe Taylor was having him followed, but instead they were amateur detectives trying to find the "velvet tigress". After wandering around aimlessly for a while, one of the newspaper men suggested that instead of looking for Ruth that it might be better for him to have Ruth look for him instead. When he asked him how to do this, he suggested for him to get a lawyer and then he would print his name in the paper to get in touch with him. He suggested telling her that he would do anything to help her and it would be better for her to come out of hiding herself than be found. And that she would be found since she was in all of the papers. When Dr. Judd said that he had no money for a lawyer, the reporter said to leave it up to him. The reporter enlisted the services of a law firm called Cantillon and Russill. Cantillon was on the threshold of becoming the pacific coast's most brilliant criminal attorneys. Louis P. Russill was formerly a judge. They provided support to Dr. Judd during the next few days.[347] The Rev. Knox Ford of Stanley, North Dakota brings the news of Sammy's death to her parents in White Earth, North Dakota.[357] The people of Juneau Alaska are upset about the murder, as "news of the tragedy appalled both child and adult, especially as regarded Miss Samuelson who was so favorably and widely known."[334] Police discover newly dug holes out at Burton's house at Beverly Glenn. His roommate Gerald Moore stated that it was probable that Mrs. Judd had actually visited the shack Monday after police had discovered the two murdered bodies at the railroad station.

A bag of four sandwiches and half a lemon pie bought at a café nearby had been barely touched like it had been left in haste. His roommate Moore said that neither one of them was in the habit of bringing home food from cafes. It was not his.[321] A.F. Wagner performs an autopsy on Sammy's body in Los Angeles. He states that her body was severed through the abdomen horizontally passing through the third and fourth vertebrae. There was a 10 inch cut in the right groin area about 2 inches deep. The legs were severed at the knee joints. There was a gunshot wound to the head which was the cause of death. The bullet entered the right side above the ear. The bullet came out the left side of the head .5 inches above the ear. There was a powder smudge near the entrance wound. There was a small wound at the left side of the neck. Another bullet wound near her left chest exited near her left shoulder. This wound was superficial. Another bullet wound was found on her right hand which grazed the ring finger and penetrated the middle finger on the palm side.[358] In court Dr. Wagner stated that there was a gunshot wound in the head, the entrance wound lacerated and the margin powder smudged. There was a superficial wound on the left side of the neck, a bullet wound in the left chest, ranging upward, penetrating only superficial tissues, a lacerating wound on the right finger of the left hand, and a penetrating wound on the right hand. Death was from the head wound and that it was fired at and he stated it was "close to the head".[277] In court he also made it sound like there were two bullets (I had always thought 3). He testified to a second bullet hole in the chest of the girl and illustrated the path of the shot as passing between the third and fourth fingers of her right hand.[330] The coroner's report and testimony of the autopsy surgeon stated that Sammy had not been operated upon. She was not pregnant, the womb being of normal size and in place. None of the organs were missing except a small portion of the lower intestine.[207] Her body is pieced back together and sent to Peck and Chase Mortuary in Los Angeles.[359] Peck and Chase Mortuary was listed on the death certificates.[264, 265] A newspaper article states that except for the bullet holes and the dissection of Sammy's body, there were no other signs of physical violence.[360] Burton McKinnell and Dr. Judd are held and questioned by the Los Angeles Police and Lloyd Andrews. Burton states in his interview "the point is that; will it be over when the questioning is over?" They record a statement at 9:20 on the 20th. According to Burton, they had been questioning him for twenty-four hours and stated he had a tired feeling. They didn't seem to believe that he was giving all of the information.[127] Burton claimed that Ruth was justified in whatever she did. He stated Ruth hadn't said she murdered anyone. He stated, "I know in my heart that she felt she was justified in whatever she did do. If Ruth killed those women, she must have gone crazy for some reason."[319] Arthur Bergerson announced that McKinnell told him that Mrs. Judd had confessed to the double slayings.[346] Dr. Judd is questioned at 8:10 PM.[48] He states that Ruth will be dead when they find her. When asked about her mental condition he stated, "I don't want to talk about that; there are some things that are too close to me to discuss". He stated that they never had an argument. He stated that Ruth was not well, but had TB and he watched her constantly.[361] He breaks down and wept while the police were questioning him.[78] A small Persian cat which may have been the object of the quarrel which resulted in the double trunk murder here was found today playing in the yard within a few feet of the windows behind which the two women are believed to have been slain. A bowl of milk and a plate of beefsteak had been thoughtfully provided for the pet.[362] In Phoenix, William J. Burns, internationally known detective, conferred with the Chief of Police, George O Brisbois on the case.[363] Some of his conclusions were: The cat incident was the spark needed to light the explosion even though the discovery of the fight seems unimportant; there were no signs of a struggle at either residence. He stated that, "I have seen persons under stress of violent emotion, commit the seemingly impossible." He also stated, "this crime just carries out my theory that there is no intelligent crime; no intelligent criminal – all this trouble of shipping the bodies when they could so easily have been disposed of in the vast desert lying about this city."[337] Ruth walked the whole way to La Vina Sanitarium. She was too afraid to get on a bus or a streetcar. She saw cops several times on the way. She hid in doorways or behind palm trees. At nightfall, she arrived up the mountain at La Vina. She found a deserted bungalow. She paused only long enough to bolt the screen door before dropping on the bed in exhaustion.[250] Ruth's story was substantiated when Mrs. Aida Zuniga, an employee of La Vina identified the dress and coat Winnie Ruth Judd was wearing when she was arrested. The coat and dress had been stolen from her room.[356] A .25 caliber automatic shell was found in the Brill street apartment where Ruth lived in the evening. Police state that the gun had been lying on the table before she packed it to bring it to LA.[300] Dr. Judd, when questioned about the Colt .25 automatic (no 27573), stated that he didn't remember it being rusty. He said that she had a box of

123

cartridges. He said a year before he had removed the clip and pretended it was lost just for fun and to tease her.[155] Anna Evans, the nurse who introduced Winnie Ruth Judd to Anne LeRoi is now living in LA at 1400 West Fifty-Eighth Street and was interviewed by Police. She claimed that Ruth and Sammy were unnaturally attached to each other.[61]

1931, October 21
The police report stated that the McMarr's stores investigator told police a woman fitting the description got on a street car at Melrose and Larchmont at 10:30 AM. She had a letter that she wanted mailed. She gave it to a lady on the other side of the car to mail. It was the number 3 car at the end of the line.[171] Birds awaken Ruth the next day at La Vina and she discovers that she is terribly hungry. She had not made plans for food. She also realized that her hand was not going to heal until the bullet was removed. She realized she was in a worse position than if she had stayed behind the curtain in the store. She wept. She was extremely sore from the 20 mile walk the previous day. She wondered how long it would take her to die from starvation. Birds chirped outside her window all day and she lay there in a stupor.[250] The toilet overflows at the Broadway department store where Ruth had wadded up the letter. The plumber found one piece of paper floating in the toilet on which he spied the name "Judd". He turned the water off and from the trap of the toilet a number of torn pieces were recovered. They were able to retrieve all of the eight sheets of the letter since it was written on both sides with the lines closely written. One piece was missing less than one inch in diameter.[352] On Wednesday Dr. Hodges, Medical Administrator, was working in the X-ray room. He went to the lavatory room in the wing and found the door locked. He thought the janitor or a nurse was using the room. He stated that the bathroom was locked from the inside and he could not get in. As that area was not in general use he decided to speak to the janitor about the door being locked but it slipped his mind. He believed Ruth was in there at the time.[364] Dr. Judd in the presence of Lloyd J Andrews, Harry Johnson, Coroner Frank Nance, and Dr. Wagner viewed the bodies of Anne LeRoi Smith and Miss Hedvig Samuelson at 10:45 AM. He said of Sammy that it looked very much like her and that the profile and the contour of her head were almost identical. However, she looked different without a makeup such as rouge and lipstick. He stated that her outstanding features were her extra heavy lips. He thought the

body was Hedvig. The coroner brought out a "can" containing portions of a human body. Dr. Judd stated that he could make no identification whatever. He recalled Miss LeRoy having black hair but that the face and head were so distorted it was impossible for him to state or attempt to identify the body. Coroner Nance asked if he remembered her hands and if they were well kept, also her feet and her general build. He stated that Miss Le Roy had small hands, well- kept, and her fingernails highly polished; that she had small feet and her legs were shapely. She was flat breasted and was neat and trim at all times. He stated that the papers referred to her as being of a mannish type which was not true. He said she was erect and of an athletic type. He said she had brown eyes.[171] Dr. Judd was then shown the large trunk, the articles therein and identified the following as belonging to himself and his wife, to Miss Samuelson and Mrs. LeRoi Smith. He identified the larger trunk as belonging to Mrs. LeRoi Smith, and having been stored in the garage in the rear of 2929 North Second Street. He identified a quilt that was found in the larger trunk, as belonging to his wife. He last saw it at her apartment. A manicure set found in the large trunk, also a red stone ring with a white gold mounting he failed to identify. The ring was found in a fingernail compact.[17] The piece that was cut from the rug at 2929 North Second Street was found covered with blood in the large trunk, and identified by Dr. Judd as a piece of the rug that was found on the bedroom floor at 2929 North Second Street. Dr. Judd recognized the suit case that had carried the lower portion of the torso as one of his own, and was last seen by him in his wife's possession. He had taken that suitcase to the war with him in France. He also identified the small steamer trunk as his own, and was in the possession of his wife at Phoenix. He further identified a green bath mat, covered with blood that was in the bathroom at 2929 North Second Street, as the property of Miss Samuelson and Mrs. LeRoi. He identified one half of a baby blanket that was used by Mrs. Judd in Phoenix to wrap her kitten in, which was found in the suit case, the other half which he also identified was found in the large trunk. [205] Burton admits for the first time that Ruth might not be found alive. "I am afraid she has killed herself. What else was there for her to do?"[348] The police disclose a letter written by Burton to his parents in Darlington Indiana. In it he states, "She has told me nothing unless she is caught by the law or gives herself up and is brought to trial. That will be soon enough to learn the facts. I want you, Mom to go through what back letters you have of Ruth's which would be evidence to show her insanity. Many of her letters are incoherent and contradictory. The girl is mentally off balance I am sure. She is innocent in the eyes of the Higher Court, I am sure."[365] Police say that they believed McKinnell was attempting to have published a letter which would cause her to give herself up and at the same time suggest that she plead insanity. McKinnell also wanted her to know that he hadn't talked.[366] A letter arrives for Sammy from her mother Marie. It is sent back to White Earth, North Dakota.[247] Ruth goes out in the evening looking in other bungalows for food and finds none. She realizes that she will have to go another day without food [250] Jack Halloran was brought into the case for the first time. His car had been identified as being outside 1130 Brill street several nights last week. Police would not say whether they had questioned Halloran, but said that alleged fact of his presence at the home of Mrs. Judd was filed with other evidence to be considered for whatever it was worth as the case developed. Halloran himself declined either to deny or affirm that he was in the habit of visiting Mrs. Judd when questioned by newspapermen, although he did not deny that he knew her. "I'm on the spot and I won't talk," Halloran said. "Everybody would misconstrue anything I might say. I won't tell you a thing, and that's final." Later, asked if he knew whether Mrs. Judd had given any indication last week of antagonism towards Mrs. LeRoi and Miss Samuelson, Halloran first refused to say, but changed his mind and answered, "Well, no, nothing that I know of indicated anything like that."[160]

1931, October last week
Burton Joy McKinnell reports that he was held against his will in LA by LA gangsters for several days. They said his sister was "up for a rap". Purposively, a Superior Court judge of LA was involved with these gangsters. This judge was not married. LA Superior Court judge said that "Your sister's case will not be tried in the courts. We are going to try her in the newspapers"[20] Burton makes the statement that he is sure that he could get a message to Ruth if he wanted to. He said that she would reply to his message if he sent one. He indicated that there may be a message waiting for him now. He also approached WI Gilbert and Leonard Wilson to retain them. He said that he didn't have the funds, but that they would get worldwide publicity if they took the case. They said that they were looking for fees, not headlines. Lloyd Andrews ordered that Burton and Dr. Judd be released.[367] Mrs. Blanche Huntley and Cela Vest formerly of Whitehall stated that

Sammy was a "sweet and ladylike girl". They were impressed with her fine character. This was Chet Huntley's mother. It was Aunt Cela who nursed Sammy when she had pneumonia for six weeks in 1927.[368]

1931, October 22

Ruth remains in hiding at La Vina. In the early mornings, she found some quarts of milk she took from neighboring doorsteps. She remains there for 4 days[250] A newspaper reports a rumor that she had sought refuge at La Vina. Staff stated that she had not been there since the summer of 1929 when she last was a patient there. Newspaper men descended on the sanitarium but didn't find Ruth.[369] A person there said, "If she should come here, we will certainly notify the police but she hadn't been here."[370] Moise of the LA examiner suggested that Ruth might be at La Vina since she had been a patient there. He suggested to the other reporters that they go out there and look around. Tom Treanor and Geoffrey Homes drove out to find her. They were able to drive through the gate and go to the superintendent's office. The superintendent was annoyed. They did not look around since the superintendent stated that she wasn't there. Police and other reporters had already been there[371] In the afternoon a horde of newspaper men from Los Angeles were tipped off to a rumor that Ruth was in hiding at La Vina. A Miss Dunlap, who was now head nurse remembered Ruth and stated that she was a very sweet natured person, but high strung and nervous. She said she only met her on occasion. She said Ruth was there for rest only. The reporters returned to LA empty handed.[372] Residents and former students of Whitehall, MT were shocked to hear of the brutal slaying.[373] Treasure hunters took everything not nailed done at the house including two of the numbers on the house at 2929. Spectators glance in the windows. A blanket dress and two hats thrown over a chair resemble a person sitting inside the duplex. Two French dolls, one wearing a red dress and one wearing a black dress are in the duplex. One doll was on Anne LeRoi's bed. The other doll was by the front door where the police entered.[341] A different article says there are two French dolls; one on Anne LeRoi's bed, the other on a small table. The one on the table is wearing a pink dress.[230] Lloyd Andrews arrives in LA with Sammy's diary to aid in the investigation of the case.[374] He stated that he thought Ruth was in contact with her brother. He said, "I am not satisfied with Burton McKinnell's story. I am not through with him."[369] His assistants and members of the Phoenix Police Department were Dave Montgomery, Dan Lucey, and EC

(Eddie) Moore.[325] Police discredit the theory that an unusual love between the girls had resulted in jealously leading to the double slaying.[86] Dr. Gaskins, a neighbor of Ruth Judd stated to the press that, "I got a telephone call from a man who told me if I didn't 'shut up' I would get what was coming to me. You know too much," he said and then slammed the receiver on the hook. He stated that, "What I know of these woman is at the service of the police and has been related in full detail to Investigator F. A. Hickersnell. From my experience in handling victims of narcotic addiction, I believe all three women were users of drugs. Miss LeRoi and Miss Samuelson were more deeply attached to one another than is consistent except on the assumption of psychopathy. Mrs. Judd might be diagnosed as maniacal depressive. These women stretched their nerves to the snapping point with their avid thrill seeking and turned to soothing or sedative medicines for relief."[375] Lucille Moore also received a call from a man stating, "You've talked too much!" The call was traced to somebody in Phoenix, but was not traced to an exact source. Lucille Moore left her home at 317 Taylor Street and went and stayed with some friends on the outskirts of Phoenix. The police questioned her with the county attorney. "She has revealed a new angle on the case which we can't divulge at this time," Hickerrell said. "It may prove important." She gave the names of Halloran and Ryan. Halloran made the following statement to the Examiner. He stated that he knew the three girls and talked about the party. He did not reveal the names of the men he was with. He said, "I am waiting to give them a chance to call me so we can give out a statement together. I think this is only fair insomuch as it was I who took them to the party." He told of the radio, "The whole thing was very innocent. Miss Samuelsson had one-foot in the grave from tuberculosis and we were trying to cheer her up and make her a little happy." He admitted kissing both victims on various occasions, but it had not bothered Ruth. He also said, "Both girls were well. They were trying to regain their health here. I tried to be nice to them. As a matter of fact, on Thursday night I had planned on taking my son with me to visit Mrs. Judd and the two girls. Now I wish I had." McFadden made the statement that he was going to ask the Lightning Delivery Company about a large sedan that followed them to the Brill street apartment at a distance. McFadden brought up the narcotic theory. "Without the shadow of a doubt the narcotic angle is plainly visible in this case. It isn't the first case we've had here where men and woman had have paid with their lives for knowing too much about the traffic in narcotics." McFadden discussed the case of Paul Reynolds and Paul Denaer whose bodies on different occasions were found floating in the Arizona Canal on the outskirts of the city. He said Reynolds was in Phoenix to try to break up the narcotics ring. "On the eve of returning to Washington with his confidential information he was slain. Since that date two other Department of Justice agents have been here attempting to solve the murder. Their assignment is to remain here until the case is solved. Three years before that it was Denaer who had learned much about the distribution of narcotics through this central point. He was murdered and his body tossed into the canal. The murder has never been solved. In the same manner Mrs. LeRoi and Miss Samuelson learned too much about the narcotic situation, Sheriff McFadden believes, and Mrs. Judd for some unknown reason was selected as the tool to carry out the death sentence of the two women. In some manner, Mrs. Judd become so involved in the grim secrets of the narcotic ring that she was forced to take orders-orders to kill." "I am convinced that the murder was bungled-that it was not carried out according to orders. When we find Mrs. Judd, I believe if she isn't afraid to talk we will learn the mysterious hold that someone had upon her. I am convinced that a man aided her in the sordid mess I believe the dissection of the Samuelson woman was a task that couldn't have been done by Mrs. Judd alone."[219] Marion Vrem made a statement in San Francisco. She did not know of Sammy's death when the Ruth Alexander docked in San Francisco. It had sailed from Seattle on Saturday. She stated, "It is something no one would believe. This is a terrible shock." She covered her eyes sorrowfully when she learned for the first time today of the brutal murder of her friend.[376] Marion Alvina Vrem made a statement in San Francisco before the Alexander sailed for Los Angeles. She was a telephone operator on the boat. She said, "Sammy was a wonderful pal. She was the best kind of a friend and a happy normal girl who was loved by all her friends." "We were classmates together at the Teacher's college at Minot, North Dakota. After graduation we corresponded regularly." "Sammy practically put herself through school at Minot and later in a post-graduate course at the University of Chicago. She was always strong and athletic, one of the best ice skaters at Minot and a splendid horsewoman. She first became ill when she was attacked with pneumonia while teaching in Whitehall, Montana. The fact that the people of that little town got together and paid her doctor, nurse, hospital and medicine bills is just another example of how much everyone who knew her cared about her. When she was able to get up, she took the doctor's advice for a change of climate and seems she went to Juneau Alaska where she taught school for two years. She was apparently in good health there until a cold she caught developed into a complete breakdown and medical examination revealed tuberculosis. She was ordered to bed immediately and it was imperative that she come south again. Her friends in Juneau contributed to a purse of $900 to assist her in moving. That was in September, 1930. Miss LeRoi, whom I have never met, was a fast friend Sammy made in Alaska. Sammy always spoke of her as Anne. She wrote me that Anne gave up her position as a nurse in Juneau in order to accompany her on her voyage south. They sailed down on the steamer Dorothy Alexander and Sammy was taken off the boat here on a stretcher. She wanted to stay at Laguna Beach, but there seemed not to be room for her there at the time, and she and Anne decided on Phoenix. She never mentioned the Judds by name in her correspondence with me."[59] Marion was a telephone operator aboard the liner Ruth Alexander.[377] Thomas Frelinghuysen makes a statement in Elberon, New Jersey regarding his relationship with Sammy. He stated that his acquaintance with her was of a casual nature. A letter was found among Sammy's effects.[378] A funny article appears in the SF News Call stating that numerology could have predicted the Disaster. Edith Bristol stated that the name Ruth Judd without the name Winnie would be a clam poised level nature. With the name Winnie, the individual is erratic, unbalanced, unrestrained and liable to deeds of violence. She stated that never in her life had she worked out such an astounding combination of names. Hedwig Samuelson indicates 11 emotional characteristics and only 5 balanced or self-controlled figures. Agnes LeRoi has 9 emotional figures and only 1 balanced number. "What else but tragedy, bloodshed and crime can possible results when characters of such nature meet other individuals of the same traits." She stated that they are marked by a remarkable preponderance of 5s. It is the 5 that does the mischief, she said, five with sufficient balance figures makes a good combination for 5 is the figure of force strength accomplishment. But when you have so many 5s without balance, then you find deeds of violence. The year 1931 she concluded reduces to the figure 5. "That's why so many crimes have been committed this year."[379] Sammy's address book is found in Phoenix. It's a small leather bound book and the name Hedvig Samuelson was on the front cover. Police planned to work though the names and addresses in the book. Names included:

Mrs. C. P Anderson 2836 North Albany Avenue, Chicago,IL
Arnold 530 South Third Street, Box 813, University of Minnesota
Mr. Stugic Ataka Sumiycshi Mura Nar. Kobe Japan
Mrs. Loren Pitman, Belgrade, Montana
Greta Burns 521 Eighth Helena, Mont. Telephone 1495-R
V. Bourgette. Agg grocery, Three Point, Seattle, Wash
E. C. Bolen, 702 Third Street Northwest Minot, ND
Mrs. J. Cann, Northcliff apartments, 309 southwest corner Seneca and
    Boren Seattle Wash
L Carney, 1219 Eighth, Helena Mont Tel. 1035-J.
Donne Cummins, 1912 East Cherry, Seattle, Manitou, Bainbridge
    Island, Wash
J. H. Cameron, 300 Crocker Bldg. San Francisco
J. H. Clausen 528 Republic Bldg, Seattle
Mr. and Mrs. Druiff, Chelsea Hotel, 924 Wilson Ave, Chicago
E. C. Elkema, box 2 Cheyenne Wyo, 2301 Prairie Avenue, Chicago,
    Cim and Company
Selma Gillette, 1027 S. Street, Greeley, Colo.
Carroll W. Griffith Jr. 2700 Harrison Street, Wilmington Del.
Mildred Guptil, Sumne, Wash
Francis B. Gornick, Corwin Springs, Mont.
Hagen, Care Sun Life Assurance Co. 1235 Leeder Bldg, Atlanta
GAMarilyn Holmes, Fair Hotel, Great Falls, MT
Mrs. A. C. D. Henman, Yellowstone Park, Wyo P.O. Box 135.
Frances Grace Huson, Marray hospital, Butte, Mont.
Carlton Kane, 248 Lara Avenue, Youngstown, Ohio
Alma L. N. W. Clinic
G. Levang, 3123 North Linder Avenue, Chicago, Il
Mrs. Marie W. Lind, 7 East Gotthe Street, Chicago, IL
John G. Lund, 807 Leary Building, Seattle, Main 7489.
Julian Mandster, 703 Bittersweet Place E. Lakeview 9088Chicago IL
Mrs. K. A. Menaglia 1608 Benedum Frees building, Pittsburg, PA
William E. Miller, 753 East Seventy ninth street, Stewart 6120 Room
    224, Chicago, IL
John J. Mulkern, 332 South Michigan Avenues, 1101 McCormick
    Building, Harrison 4034, Chicago, IL
Stanley McPherrin, 1666 Hoffman, Long Beach, Cal.
Mrs. R. Mitchell, East Olive Bozeman, Mont

Marianne Maxwell, 228 South Normandie, Los Angeles, WA 1508

Dan Masilotte, 101 Second Avenue, S. Main 1149, Seattle, WA

Leo Marks, 5206 Amaroon (Cimarron St. – according to voter
registration) Street, Los Angeles

Neilson, 1148 National Avenue, Richard 5172 W. Milwaukee.

M. M. O'Brien 3820 West Twelfth, Bayview 5686, Vancouver, BC

Dr. F. R. Packard, Whitehall, MT

Peach Ruie, Rock Glenn, Mason City, Iowa

Mrs. A Renwick, Apt 19, Davidson Hotel, Seilda, Colo

Cecil Shup, 524 East Central Avenue, Minot, N. D.

Mr. S. Samuelson 2724 West Forty third, Minneapolis, Minn, 2115
Franklin Street.(Unreadable), Haie, 144 Clay Street, San Francisco, CA

C. E. Richmond, A Marion Vrem. SS Company. Ruth Alexander, San
Francisco

Mrs. Gillespie, Bellingham, Wash.

Denary, assn. national dir of parks 422 Simcoe Street, Victoria, B. C.

CS. Smythe, Juneau, Alaska

Herbert Seyainy, 4850 Wrightwood Avenue, Chicago Ill

Mrs. G. D. Twitchell 320 Addison Street, Wellington 3145 Chicago,
IL

Mrs. G. Tobler, Servilla Court, Belacynwyd. Pa.

Alvina Admiral Farragut P. S. S. Co 424 Ellis, San Francisco, CA

Jimmy Ellis, Lankarshim Hotel, Los Angeles, Cal.

Kenneth .E. Whittembre, 512 28th. Wash Avenue North, Great Falls,
Mont.

Inez Westerdall, 624 West Forty second street Los Angeles, Cal AX
4542.

Dorothy Simonson 2220 North Laporte Street, Berkshire 4792,
Chicago, IL.

Bill Maag, 4714 Byron 3429 Chicago, IL.

Pearl Wagoner 1821 East McDowell, Phoenix, AZ

J. L. Stafford, Aurora Oregon

Lisianski Apex Elmido Mining Co. P. O. 281 Juneau, AK.[91]

A car circles the block of 2929 twice and then pulled into the driveway
about 3 AM. It was a large 7 passenger sedan. The guard flipped on
the porch light and the car immediately backed out and drove away.
They had the car traced, but didn't find it. It was thought that this was
a car of an accomplice returning to the scene of the crime.[322] Dr. Judd
announces that he had retained Judge Louis P Russill and Richard H.

Cantillon to care for Ruth Judd's interests. He urged his wife to give herself up and to communicate with him or with the attorneys. He also issued this statement in part, "That after years of association with my wife, I have found her to be kind, affectionate and perfectly loyal and faithful. I know that she has not a violent temper. If she has committed the crime with which she is now charged it seems that without a doubt it was done in a period of irresponsibility or in an irrational state or condition." He instructed Ruth to come to the subway terminal building or to call Mutual 7235 or Cleveland 61720. Jack Halloran was questioned regarding his association with Ruth and the two victims.[219]

1931, October 23
The Los Angeles Examiner offers $1000 reward for information leading to the arrest of Ruth Judd.[219] Another report said two Los Angeles newspapers offered rewards totaling $2500 for exclusive information leading to the arrest of Ruth Judd.[325] Ruth had her hand dressed at the Sanitarium. While she was being examined she came near capture by two Los Angeles policemen who had walked into the place and questioned her, but she managed to escape.[380] Friday morning one of the bookkeepers, Miss Marieitte remembered meeting a woman answering her description. Miss Mariette was returning to La Vina about 7:45 AM after a brief absence on vacation and says she is quite certain that Mrs. Judd is the woman she met as she neared the institution. Thinking it was one of the nurses that she knew, she glanced up expecting to speak, but the woman kept her head constantly turned in the opposite direction.[356] Ruth stated that she had attempted to dye the black dress she arrived in LA with all black, but she botched the job so this was the reason she stole the dress. She had her black dress in a piece of paper she had found. She took this with her.[194] Before dawn, Ruth leaves the LaVina Sanitarium and decides to walk back to town. The pain in her hand and her hunger drove her out of her hiding place. She walked down the mountain side road towards the Pasadena car line that took her back to the Broadway downtown area.[250] Louis Geuerer, a truck driver for the sanitarium early Friday morning gave a lift to a woman that answered the description of Mrs. Judd who wanted to get downtown in a hurry. He stated that the woman stood in the middle of the road and as he came along and waved so persistently that he stopped and took her in. He carried her to his destination, Lake Avenue and Washington Street in Pasadena, but what became of her after that he does not know, as he drove away. He

said that the woman remained absolutely silent as they drove along, not answering a number of question he asked her and kept one hand concealed beneath her coat.[356] Ruth telephones Dr. Moore at the Pasadena Sanitarium about 8:30 AM. He had just arrived at his office (Barlow Sanitarium in South Pasadena, I believe). She identified herself and then told him in brief the story that was printed in the Times. At the time she wanted him to find Dr. Judd for her and also to give her some treatment for her hand. She wished to come to his office. Dr. Moore advised her to go to the nearest police station and give herself up. Before she hung up, she promised to call him back. The next he heard she had surrendered.[364] When she was in Pasadena, she disposed of the black dress she had tried to dye. She went in a yard behind a store. Smoke was coming out of the chimney so she assumed it was an incinerator. She dumped her dress there. She was wearing the stolen green dress.[194] She got back there three hours after she left. She enters a lunch fountain in a drug store where she tried to swallow a few mouthfuls of food. She was startled by her own image in the mirror behind the counter. It was her hair more than her haggard features. She had dyed it black only a few days before but it had already almost returned to its natural color. It was not meant to be used on hair she realized. She saw a newspaper with her picture on it, saying that she was wanted for murder. She thought about leaving, but she was compelled to read it. She read that she had been dubbed the Velvet Tigress; that an offer for $1000 dollars was made regarding her whereabouts. Then she read the appeal of her husband to give herself up. The phone number of Richard H. Cantillon was provided as a contact. She didn't know what to do anymore, so walked directly to a telephone booth and called Cantillion.[250] The Los Angeles Times offered $1500 for her capture and the Los Angeles Examiner offered $1000 for information leading to her arrest. McFadden talks to Governor Hunt about offering a reward of $500.[322] On the day she surrenders or the day before, she phoned Dr. Moore and Dr. Bishop and talked for a long time. Both of these men begged her to tell them where she was. They said, "Ruth you are a very sick girl, please tell us where you are so we can come and get you and bring you here to the Sanatorium and do something for you."[132] She stated that she mailed a letter to her husband in their care at the Bishop's Sanatorium in South Pasadena. She stated that Judge Russill intercepted that letter, opened it, a federal offense. She said her husband then fired Russill for publishing a story that she never wrote or even saw. Russill was mad and later sold the letter to Lloyd Andrews and Judge Rodgers of the prosecution.[132] Ruth stated she wrote two letters at the sanitarium, she kept one in her purse and the other she destroyed at La Vina. The third she stated she wrote on Friday morning at the Broadway Department store. She did not intend to give herself up at the time. She wrote a little on each floor in the lavatory. Then she would go up a floor and write some more. She stated that it was impossible to collect herself so she finally tossed the letter she was working on in the lavatory at the Broadway Department Store and held on to the other one in her purse.[194] An inquest is held in LA.[323] James O'Dell identifies Anne LeRoi's body. He stated that her right ear and the right side of her face was sort of a peculiar face.[76] James O'Dell signs the death certificate of Anne LeRoi. It was also signed by autopsy surgeon AL Wagner and Frank Nance.[265] Dr. Judd also testified at the inquest. Cantillon and Russill went with him to protect his rights. Dr. Judd also gave a positive ID on the two women.[250] He signs Hedvig's death certificate and lists his address as 823 17th Street, Santa Monica. AL Wagner was the autopsy surgeon and the certificate was also signed by Frank Nance[264] He expected more questions, but this is all they asked.[250] John Brinkerhoff was the only Arizona witness. He stated that he first went to the duplex on the morning of Tuesday October 20. When asked if he found evidence of crime he replied, "Ample evidence".[354] County Attorney Lloyd Andrews stated that he believed that Burton was not telling the truth and that he "was not through with him yet".[354] Burton made the statement that he was displeased about missing classes at USC. He said, "This is playing the mischief with my college work." He kept running his hand through his red hair. "I am afraid Ruth is dead, but if she isn't I hope she keeps going. She's kept out of the way so far and she's clever. During the rest of the witnesses in the inquest, a note was passed into his hand by Mr. Cantillon. He told him to be unconcerned when he read the note. It said, "Ruth has called me. Keep a straight face and don't tip off the reporters. I've arranged for her to call again after we get away from here. Whatever you do, keep still until this hearing is over." He was able to maintain his excitement for the rest of the inquest and then they left with Dr. Judd in between the two lawyers. They got in Judge Russill's car. Ruth was to call again at 1 o'clock and that Dr. Judd would be there. Dr. Judd was afraid the wire in the office would be tapped, so they used a phone in another law office, a friend of Mr. Cantillon. He then was afraid that the police might follow them. At 1 she called and spoke in Spanish and she stated she was in downtown Los Angeles. They tell her to meet Dr. Judd in the lobby of the Biltmore Theater in half an hour.[347] They took the call in the office of Attorney Patrick Cooney. This was because Mr. Cantillon was very popular with the press and a number of reporters were in the outer office drinking his gin at the time. Geoffry and Tom were among them. Cantillon stepped out and gave the reporters the slip.[371] Ruth was said to have telephoned several times during the day. She disapproved of each suggested meeting place, however, until Mr. Cantillion mentioned a funeral parlor operated by an old friend of his.[381] The doctor argued with her for fifteen minutes and finally she said alright, she was fed up with hiding out and would meet him in the lobby of the Biltmore Theatre.[371] They met her at 3:30.[382] The arrangement was for a David Malloy, an employee, to pick her up in an automobile at Alvarez and Moore.[380] Ruth rushed to Dr. Judd, whimpered and fervently kissed him at the Biltmore Theater Lobby where they met her. There were people around, but they did not recognize her. She walked firmly into the garage. She collapsed in the back of the car. They told her to sit up. She pulled herself together and then fell on the floor sobbing that why should people think that she is a criminal.[382] Ruth said, "I'm a little nervous" as she entered his automobile.[381] They cross the street where the car is in a garage. They speed around the corner into Live Street, and up the hill toward First Street. The county jail was on First Street and Dr. Judd had the feeling they might be going to the jail. They turned on Court Street and went left. They swung into a driveway. They entered into the rear of a building. Ruth stated that it was an awful place. She stated that she could feel something like death in there. They were both terrified to find that they were in a mortuary. Ruth gave a small scream. Russill had selected this place as someplace they would unlikely to be disturbed. He stated it was a lawyer's privilege to discuss a case, even murder, before surrendering his client to the police. Dr. Judd was concerned about Ruth's hand. A woman came into the room; a member of the staff. Dr. Judd requested a warm bowl of water. They soaked off the blood caked handkerchief from her hand. He noted that between the first and second knuckle joints a bullet was imbedded in her hand. Dr. Judd stated that the hand was badly swollen and inflamed. It would have been dangerous to attempt to probe without sterilized instruments. All he could do was wash it with antiseptic and apply a moist compress. He stated that she would need to go to a hospital right away. He said she would be lucky if blood poisoning hadn't already set in. Russill agreed, but said that she would have to be aroused for a few minutes of questioning before they would call Central. Dr. Judd was aghast that they would go to the police. Russill stated that they would do her more harm than good by hiding her, not to mention the hospitalization. Ruth arose and stated, "Don't let the police get me!" Judge Russill tried to reason with her unsuccessfully. Then he tried to reason with Dr. Judd. Dr. Judd said, "Ruth Dear, tell us who shot you." "Sammy shot me", she said weakly "Doctor, I fought so hard but they hurt me so…". Russill then asked her who shot Anne and Sammy. She replied, "I fought so hard…" Over and over she moaned the refrain. She was incoherent. They had pieced together that there was an ironing board and that there had been a fight. Ruth stated that her side hurt so badly. Dr. Judd examined her and noted bruises caused by blows but no other bullet wounds. They asked her again about what happened but Ruth was incoherent and talked about many different things. The only certain rationality was about the wound in her hand. Finally, they tried a new line of questioning and asked her where she went after Sammy shot her. Ruth stated a bunch of unrelated sentences. She stated that she "went behind the curtains in the store". She stated she had had some "milk in the kitchen"[347] They gave her eggnog and some other stimulants and advised her to turn herself in.[380] They couldn't make it out. Dr. Judd stated that she was in no condition to give an account of the last week. Judge Russill finally stated that they must notify the police. Then Ruth was very coherent and screamed, "Not the police! I am going to run away and hide!" They restrained her. Dr. Judd knew that she needed to surrender.[347] According to another story, Cantillon returned to his office and let the others know where Mrs. Judd was. They went over to Alvarez and Moore at Court and Olive. According to them she told her full story then. According to this reporter, she stated she had made the friendship of a millionaire lumberman. He was a splendid fellow, a good scout and a true friend to her. Jack seemed to like Anne when Ruth introduced them. Jack was interested in Anne and kind to Ruth. Anne began to resent it. Anne was cool to her after she took her own apartment. On the evening of the crime, Ruth said she slept on the davenport. They were getting breakfast on the next day when Anne started to upbraid her for introducing other women to Jack. Anne threatened to tell him things about other girls that Ruth had introduced to him. Ruth told her if she did that, she would tell him about her. Sammy came out with a gun Ruth had left behind. Sammy pulled the trigger of the gun, Ruth threw up her arms and the bullet struck her in the hand. She threw her whole weight against Sammy and grabbed the gun. She fell behind the breakfast nook table. Ruth got over her and shot twice. Anne was screaming at her and ran at her with the ironing board. Ruth pointed the gun at her and fired one shot. She said she cut up Sammy with a meat saw. Ruth kept this story the whole time she was in Los Angeles. They wanted to buy the story for the Express, but another newspaper had more money and was able to buy it.[371] At 5 PM Joe Taylor walked in followed by Treanor. A formal surrender took place shortly afterwards.[382] The arrest slip stated that Ruth was 125 pounds. She was wearing a black and white dress and a black hat. [171] According to another account, the police burst into the room. The officers had a scuffle with Dr. Judd and Burton McKinnell when they tried to serve the warrant. Malloy was declared to be hiding the suspect. He was struck on the nose by one of the officers and he retreated. The warrant was served.[380] She is rushed to Georgia Street Receiving Hospital.[347] The first picture that is taken of Ruth is one that was analyzed by a criminologist in New York. Dr. Judd states that this photo was taken right after her arrest, yet before the bullet was removed so she was in great pain and exhausted. He said, "her features are twisted and with pain and fear and hysteria.[250] He stated that from the features of her face that, "she was a person emotionally cold, a nature which must see itself as the leading one in all groups, the kind which is unhappy when someone else supersedes it in achievement. Her lips revealed love for fine things, her furrowed brow denoted cynicism, the eyebrows tended to violence and jealousy, and the corner lines of her mouth portrayed an unhappy dissatisfied nature."[250] Ruth is driven to the hospital in a cop car accompanied by Dr. Judd, Detective Frank Ryan, and David Davidson for care of the gunshot wound. The accident is listed to have occurred at: Court and Olive. She is admitted at 6:55 PM.[383] They wanted to administer anti-tetanus antitoxin but it was kept on hand at the hospital. There was a delay while a messenger was dispatched to obtain the preparation. During this wait, Ruth redressed into her green silk frock, and combed out her hair with precise strokes and sat willingly for more pictures. Here her apparent composure was in striking contrast to her husband. He sat beside her, his hands resting limply in his lap, his bald head drooping; his eyes fixed in a lackluster stare at the floor.[384] The operation took 35 minutes. Her left hand was swollen and discolored from the bullet wound. Nurses noted the bruises on her body. She bore bruises on the upper one third of her right arm over the triceps and inner biceps muscles; on the lower third of her left arm, on the left hip and thigh, on her right hip and right thigh, on the inner side of her right knee and inner upper one third of her right leg and the back of the upper third of her right leg. There were also bruises around the base of her neck and on her back, the nurses reported. The bruises were never explained. The nurses also reported that Mrs. Judd's body was stained with what appeared to be black dye over the front of her torso and her underwear was stained with the same sort of dye. Abrasions on her wounded hand were also stained with the black dye.[385] Her princess slip had red blotched color faded mostly on the back panel. In this scenario she stated that she had accidently scorched another green dress she was wearing so she attempted to dye it black. She was at all times very calm and self-possessed.[384] They found black dye stains on the upper part of her body. Ruth told Ryan that she went into a drug store two days ago and purchased a brand of quick dye, went into a woman's rest room downtown and there dyed her brown dress green. The officer asserts she said she dyed the garment in a basin, swung it around her head until it partly dyed and emerged wearing a green dress. Further questioning of this story was pursued.[382] There were abrasions on her right finger as well and her right arm was badly bruised. The dye stains were on the upper part of her body [382] Ruth claimed that "my husband located me and carried me in his arms and turned me over to the police."[386] At the hospital Doctor J. Edwin Kirkpatrick, a specialist in bone disease and fractures, attended to Ruth. They removed a .25 caliber bullet from her hand which was imbedded in her knuckle of the forefinger. Infection had set in and it was necessary to administer an anesthetic. Ruth continued to speak incoherently and said things like; "I fought so hard, Sammy shot me. I fought..." Alongside the operating table, Chief Taylor stood and listened to her. Chief Taylor was a kindly and soft-spoken man but was also a shrewd officer. She said nothing that incriminated her but talked of curtains, and stores. Dr. Judd watched Joe Taylor out of the corner of his eye. Ruth agreed to eat something once she regained consciousness.[250] Then they let her sleep. Joe Taylor agreed to defer questioning for when she was stronger. She slept for a few hours, when the hospital officials announced that Ruth had awakened and could answer questions. Chief Taylor and other officers started for her room with a stenographer to take shorthand notes of every word. Dr. Judd expected that he wouldn't be allowed to go with, but Joe Taylor encouraged him to come stating that she would probably feel more like telling her story if he was present. Ruth said nothing and talked about everything except the crime. Joe Taylor and his men were stern and pleading by turn. They tried to trip her up on the most innocuous statements. They even enlisted the help of Dr. Judd in questioning her. Ruth never wavered. She prattled about everything except the subject at hand. Outright questions were ignored as completely as if they never had been asked or answered with replies utterly irrelevant and incomprehensible.[250] They finally ask her where she had been during the last 5 days. They expected her not to answer but she answered clearly: "The first night I hid in a Broadway department store." Dr. Judd said, "For a moment we were all too surprised to say anything. She had answered as calmly and rationally as if none of the other bizarre dialogue ever had been uttered." Ruth clearly then told where she had been since Burton dropped her off earlier in the week.[250] The last question they asked her was where she had mailed the letter she had written. She replied that she had not mailed it but disposed of it in the lady's room at the Broadway Department Store.[250] Joe Taylor and the others left and made arrangements for Ruth to be transferred from the Georgia Receiving Hospital which was for emergencies only to a hospital cot in the county jail. There she would wait arraignment and for it to be decided whether the state of California would agree to her extradition to Arizona. Dr. Judd thought they made arrangements to check out the plumbing in the lady's room at the Broadway Department Store where portions of the letter were recovered and they pieced together the smeared water soaked fragments. Dr. Judd thought it was only the damning parts that they retrieved. Dr. Judd was not allowed to accompany Ruth to the county jail, but he had a small opportunity to see her after that.[250] They went to dinner at a restaurant at Eighth and Hill Streets. Ruth had vegetable soup and nibbled at a piece of meat and ate a few bites of dessert. It was on their way to Chief Taylor's office at City Hall. Chief Taylor threw the lawyers and Dr. Judd out. Russill and Cantillion told her of her rights and not to talk. Taylor told them to leave. They said he'd have to order them out. The order was made. They left to mingle with the reporters outside the door. Dr. Judd lingered outside, got into action right away and wrote her a note. The note said, "I hereby demand that my lawyers be admitted." They rapped vigorously as Chief Taylor made no response. They poked the note under the door. It just lay on the floor.[382] Joe Taylor stated that Ruth said that she started the fatal argument when she made an uncomplimentary remark about Mrs. LeRoi while visiting the girls on Friday night. Joe Taylor said that Ruth stated, "I killed them after Miss Samuelson shot me in the hand during the quarrel. I scuffled with Miss Samuelson and the gun dropped to the floor. Mrs. LeRoi hit me on the head with an ironing board. I fell to the floor. I picked up Miss Samuelson's gun. Then I shot them both."[381] Russill sold the story under her name which Ruth claims, "I never wrote, saw or heard or read".[386] One source states that she sold her story to the Los Angeles paper for $3000, then she varied it a bit and sold it to the Los Angeles Examiner for $5000 plus attorney's fees plus court costs.[268] According to Ruth's testimony in 1933, a nurse brought her a statement to sign. She refused. Then, she returned and said her husband said it was ok. She refused. Then she had her husband came and stood by the door but they wouldn't let him talk to her. She signed the statement. This was supposedly the statement that appeared with the LA Times article.[387] A bottle of ether and small drug tablets were recovered from the duplex where Sammy and Anne LeRoi lived.[388] Dr. Judd slept well for the first time that week since he thought that the truth would come out and Ruth would not stand accused of the crime. He was relieved that she had destroyed the letter.[250] Frank Vance puts a placard outside of the duplex at 2929 admitting people for 10 cents. On the first day, he admits 102 persons. He hired a Mr. Bond to bring people through. He wanted to make up for lost rent. The house rented for $25 a month.[389] Corinne Babcock makes a statement regarding her friendship with Sammy. She is the ex- daughter-in-law of Assistant District Attorney, G. A Rodgers of Los Angeles. She resides at the Lombard Hotel. She knew Sammy when she taught at Landa, N.D. and at the Minot Normal School.[390]

1931, October 24
Ruth didn't sleep well even though she had a sedative. Reporters were permitted to go to her cell when she awakened. She declined to discuss her case. When asked where she was staying while hiding, she replied, "Here and there around town." Dr. Judd stated that she had stayed in an unoccupied house near the city since Monday.[381] The duplex is not open for visitors.[291] Dr. Judd wakes the next day to his wife's handwritten letter in the paper, which was enlarged to an enormous proportion, but he knew it was her writing. The first thing he read was Anne was going to blackmail me and I fired at her twice. I hate her yet."[250] The drain pipe letter is recovered from the drain of the Broadway

Department Store. There are two parts of the letter, one written to Dr. Moore and the other to Dr. Judd.[167] The letter was found by a scrub woman. It was floating in the water of a toilet, although unsuccessful effort had been made to flush it down the drain. She noted the name Judd on the paper and notified the police. In the letter she says she killed both women to avoid exposure, but maintains that she killed in self-defense. Police believed that the letter had been dropped there by Mrs. Judd. Due to the fact that the document was found floating in the water without having clogged the drain leads to the belief that Mrs. Judd could have disposed of it in that manner.[391] The bodies of Anne LeRoi and Sammy arrive back in Phoenix for more investigation.[392] At this time the bodies were in two caskets (not cremated).[393] They are returned in two California redwood boxes off of the Golden State Limited shortly after 7 o'clock. A crowd of about 100 people gathered along with two hearses from the A. L Moore and Sons Mortuary. Several railroad detectives mingled among the crowd. Four men entered the baggage car and carried each casket onto an express company truck. Afterwards, an express man brought the trunks, suitcases, and hatbox into the room. He placed them on the spot where the two trunks stood last Sunday night before shipment to LA. For convenience, the little trunk and suitcase was put into the larger trunk. Clothes inside the larger trunk were bloodstained.[394] They are brought to Moore and Sons mortuary in Phoenix.[359] Brinckerhoff instructed the AL Moore and Son Mortuary to allow no one to view the bodies and to hold them for further instructions.[394] The bodies are identified by Dr. Maudlin and Victor Randolph. Dr. Maudlin stated that Anne LeRoi was shot through the head with the bullet entering slightly above the ear and came out the opposite side, slightly backward and downward.[395] He said, "This is the bullet that entered the left side, as best as I could tell from the state of the body, of her head, slightly above the angle of the ear and went horizontally through the brain and came out the other side slightly backward and downward from the place of entrance.[395] A newspaper stated that he found the bullet beneath the scalp. In his opinion the bullet was held up against the head. There was a dark smudge; it appeared to be unconsumed gun powder.[277] Dr. Maudlin said at the first court proceeding on November 11 that, "Both bullets ranged down, decidedly so in the case of Miss Samuelson. The wound through Miss Samuelson's chest also was downward", he said. When asked by Schneck if there was a knife wound in the neck, he replied "no".[313] Dr. Randolph, who was

Sammy's doctor, confirmed that the body was hers. He noticed an abnormal pigmentation she had on her face, which often is present with those who have tuberculosis.[396] HJ McKinnell writes a letter to Ruth at the Los Angeles County Jail. He says, "My dear daughter. You have many friends, even the law is your friend and not your enemy. Above all Jesus was accused of being the friend of sinners. He did not deny it because he knew it was the truth. He is the judge of the Supreme Court and He is your friend. You mother and I will come to you as early as we can and will do anything that we can do lawfully for you. Frame all answers to questions with full consideration of the judgement day of Jesus Christ, where all must meet."[397] It is said that Ruth Judd gave out her story from a hospital bed at the county jail hospital. Dr. Judd said, "I instructed my wife to deny giving out any interview to the Times. I believe that if she will just continue to refuse to talk to the newspaper reporters she will affect a quicker recovery from her present serious physical condition." He does claim that story printed that morning was just as she first told it to himself and her counsel. It was printed that morning with his authorization. He said, "I checked the article and found it to be correct. My wife also checked the facts related in the article over with me and we are agreed that her position in the entire affair has been correctly stated." Andrews stated that the reason she said she slew them on Saturday morning was to show that she was on friendly terms with the girls having had spent the night.[398] Regarding his agreement with the Times, a newspaper article appeared later detailing this. Bill Henry stated that "once the jail doors had clanged on Winnie there was obviously only one source of news—her husband, Dr. William C. Judd." "The Times boys grabbed the Doc out of the clutches of the Hearst opposition and gave him enough money to make some plans for her defense. Doc agreed to get his wife's own true, signed confession, exclusively for the Times. The old Doc did his stuff. Winnie in her own handwriting provided a statement which read, "This is to certify that the articles appearing in the Los Angeles Times are correct and authorized by me – Winnie Ruth Judd." "Private War—unless you know newspaper folk, particularly the go getter city editors and police reporters you can't imagine what a commotion it all stirred up in the journalistic world. Nobody could get in to talk to Winnie except the Doc. We had him. Word came down from the Sultan of San Simeon that the boys down the street had better get him away from the Times if they wanted to be considered the Times newspapermen. The Times gang formed a bodyguard for Doc. They

whisked him to a different hotel each night. They fed him in secrecy."
"In Demand, when reporters took Doc Judd up to the jail to see Winnie
to get new installments of her confession, they surrounded him with
loving care while the Hearst minions danced around outside the
bodyguard waving hatches of folding money and saying, "Hey Doc you
can have this if you'll come with us." When the Doc stuck with the
Times gang the next move came in the form of a legal emissary of
some sort who had a warrant for the Doc's arrest, charging something
or other. They thought that the charge was inspired from down the
street although this was never proved. "The Times boys, after herding
the Doc around for those three or four hectic days took such a liking to
him that they hatched up a little plot. Why, they though should all that
money offered by the frantic opposition down the street be allowed to
go to waste. Once the Judd confession was run in the Times, they were
all through with the Doc and his presence was depriving them of sleep
and the normal thing was just to let him go. But, the impish instincts of
their kind, they thought it would be much more fun to make the fellows
down the street pay for something they could have had for nothing. So
they framed it all up, took Doc down to the jail and told him what to
do. When the Hearst boys showed up waving these big bills again, The
Times gang appeared to put up an awful struggle to hold Doc back.
Finally, he broke away from them took the Hearst money, it was
something like $5000 and financed Winnie's defense and the Times
boys did their best to register frustration dismay and other suitable
emotions until the Hearst minions had dragged their prize away in
triumph. Our crowd were weak from laughing for days."[399] Ruth
Judd's parents make statements to the Darlington Herald. Mother's
Statement: "To Whom It May Concern – Thank God my darling girl is
found. May God help her in every way she needs His help. We all
need His help in everything. God is a God of Justice and mercy and
love and helps all who come to him in faith and asks for pardon. May
we all believe in him in all things. If ye forgive not men for their
trespasses neither will the heavenly Father forgive you your trespasses.
We have the knowledge of many who have been praying for us and
ours for which we are thankful to both God and them. May we all be
brought closer to him and know there is a God of the universe. May we
all remember this and not forget him. Everybody pray, everybody
pray. The World will be made better if everybody will pray. Sin will
cease to be and peace will reign wherever mankind is found O God
may it begin this hour. Will everybody pray, pray, pray and help to

bring it to pass. Oh! My darling, precious Ruthie, you know mother
has always loved you with a perfect love ever ready to forgive you, no
matter what you did and our blessed Savior is more willing to forgive
and give good gifts to them that ask Him, than parents are to give good
gifts to their children. If we ask an egg, he will not give a scorpion. O
believer in that dear Lamb that was slain and shed His blood to wash
away all the stains of sin. Through they be as scarlet, they shall be as
white as snow. Praise God though they be red as crimson they shall be
as wool. O what a wonderful Savior is Jesus our Lord to leave heaven
to come down here to the world lost in sin and suffer as He did to
redeem us back to God and reconcile us to Him whom we had so
shamefully offended and grieved. He bore our sins on the rugged cross
of Calvary, O Ruthie dear, precious child, believe and receive him this
moment into thy heart. I love you unto death, but His Death can save
you by believing he is the One who is ready and willing to call upon
Him. O God, bring the whole world to repentance and salvation. Carrie
McKinnell." Father's Statement: "To any and All Concerned; This
night that marks the close of an awful week of our dear child's time of
being a fugitive from justice to the beginning of the dawn of day when
once again in a radical sense, the law becomes her friend instead of her
enemy, shall ever to us be observed like Israel's of old, one of the
beginning of Gold's mercies in answer to prayer. HJ McKinnell."
Also on this day townspeople begin to raise funds for the McKinnell's
to go to Arizona. They were practically penniless with the exception of
the mortgage to their home. Those wishing to contribute were urged
to leave money at the office of the Darlington Herald or at the office of
the Journal and Review.[400] Apparently all the money the retired Free
Methodist minister and his wife have is invested in the home at the end
of the street. HJ said, "We will get to Ruth somehow, some way. We
have no money other than is in the house and we owe $600 on it. We
hope to get to Ruth before the beginning of her trial." Both newspapers
started funds for them to finance their trip. Sitting in an old automobile
seat which had been made into a porch swing Rev. McKinnell mused
over the past when his daughter was a lively, vivacious girl. He said in
recent years however, her letters had told of her being overworked and
being too exhausted to write of any length. He said he was writing to
Ruth through the police and giving her encouragement. He said if he
had been her age he would have disappeared too and following the
fight and what happened. He said it would have been better for her to
have surrendered immediately but "youth does not always think things

out clearly." They wanted her to feel that the law was her friend. He said that lack of money had forced Ruth to work beyond her strength and endurance in recent years. He said Dr. Judd was seriously ill while living in Phoenix and had been confined to a sanitarium for five months. He said Ruth had to work hard through that period and she became very nervous and her letters home were short. She was too tried o write much at a time."[401]

1931, October 25
Arnold, Sam, and Hilda arrive in White Earth to take Anders and Marie to Minneapolis.[402] More than 2000 people tour the duplex where the murders took place by paying 10 cents for admission.[403] It was revealed that 1500 visitors had toured the duplex for 10 cents a head. This Sunday, cars were lined up for blocks waiting to get into the duplex. The owners were afraid that the duplex would be vacant for a long period of time. So, they decided to capitalize on the morbid curiosity of the onlookers.[404] Dr. Judd remained with his wife during the morning and came from her bedside weeping. He stated, "I believe that her mind is wandering," when he left the hall of justice. Ruth told him that she was glad that he had been able to spend the night with her. She seemed to be convinced that he had been with her for hours. He feared that she may not recover. Sheriff McFadden made the statement that he had known Ruth while she was in Phoenix. His wife was treated by a physician and he tried to talk to her considerably. He considered himself a friend of hers.[364] Officials confirm Ruth's stay at La Vina. Mrs. Aida Zuniga, a patient claimed she was the owner of the green dress and the fur collared coat that Ruth had surrendered in. She had not missed it. Two nurses, Parsons and Harris, talked about the crime outside the window on a bench where Ruth stayed. She related this story in her version to the Times. A large ice box from which Mrs. Judd in her story told of taking milk, was in a kitchen at the opposite end of the building where Mrs. Judd slept. The bed she had slept in had no covers, but a light spread had been slept on. A dresser drawer had rolls of tissue paper spotted with blood which seemed to be used as a bandage. There was some matted blond hair. A number of paper napkins had date pits and some grape seeds in a paper sack were also discovered.[364]

1931, October 26
Staff of two different newspapers in LA fought outside the hospital

room of Ruth. One morning paper sought to purchase Ruth's own story despite the fact that a competing paper already had contracted for the story. Jailer Ed White kept the combatants apart. Ruth saw neither of the parties.[405] Ruth hints that she might be pregnant and states that they would never hang a mother. But she also stated that it was neither the time nor the place for such an intimate and personal question. She stated that she had always wanted a child and stated, "I hope". Lloyd Andrews declared that she would have a thorough medical examination as soon as they arrive in Phoenix.[406] Sometime this week, Ruth's husband fires Judge Russill. He wrote vengeance and threatened me with a letter he had intercepted which Ruth had mailed her husband. He sold me for a few pieces of silver which another attorney Leukowitz slid in and received [386] The representative of the syndicate of newspapers including the Chicago Herald and Examiner (Hearst) contacted HJ McKinnell twice on this day offering $8500 (or perhaps it says $500) for an autobiography of Ruth, a running sketch of her childhood and girlhood. He refused to do it unless they would agree that everything he presented was first read by the senior attorney of Ruth's defense. He stated, "I told them that no amount of money, not fifty thousand, not a hundred thousand dollars, no sum that could be named would induce us to consider writing one scratch unless the defense attorney had first examined it and approved it; in fact every word of it must pass through his hands to theirs."[397] They argued that this would greatly help Ruth's defense. He said the defense attorney would be the final say in that. He said, "If the defense attorney ordered such a course, we would consider it." They told him that he would hear from the senior defense attorney on this point.[397] The El Paso Times (says out of Los Angeles UP), stated that a wealthy Phoenix man has marshalled $20000 for Ruth's defense. This was according to Milan Medigovich who was formerly of her defense. He said he had received his information from a Phoenix attorney who asked him to confirm it. The Phoenix lawyer said he had been informed that $20000 had been deposited in a Los Angeles bank to Mrs. Judd's account, but that he did not know the name of the man supposed to have offered the fortune.[407, 408] It was said that Russill had abandoned the original self-defense and would seek to obtain her acquittal on an insanity plea.[408] Ruth made her first court appearance at the Hall of Justice at her arraignment. When the case was called, Attorney Louis Russill arose and announced himself as the attorney. Immediately Milan Medigovich was on his feet. He said, "I wish to enter Attorney Richard

Cantillon and myself as counsel for Mrs. Judd." So the judge asked who was representing her. There was a hesitation and Ruth and Dr. Judd whispered to each other. Finally, Ruth said, "My husband says that it is Mr. Russill." In view of this Medigovich told the court, "Mr. Cantillon and I will withdraw from the case." After the arraignment, Cantillon explained that ever since the three lawyers had been associated with the case there had been constant friction between himself and Medigovich on the one side and Russill on the other.[409] This was the day Richard Cantillon and Milan Medigovich withdrew from the case. Cantillion explained that he and Medigovich had been unable to agree with Russill "on matters of policy regarding our client."[407] Dr. Judd was arrested on a complaint charging him with practicing medicine without a license. He had no license to practice medicine in California.[407] Ruth announces that the mattress would be found in the weeds south of the Duplex. That area had been searched before, but it was checked again and got no results.[410] There were two sofa pillows found in the weeds across the street from the duplex. These were being subjected to chemical test to determine whether dark stains upon them were blood. The pillows were grimy, appearing to have been ground in the dirt before being discarded.[410] Dr. Judd stated that Ruth admitted to him that she burned the mattress on a vacant lot near the Second Street house, and that he had searched the premises and had been unable to find any place on the grounds that might indicate that a mattress had been burned.[207] Chemical tests were made on the sofa pillow (singular) that was found in the weeds of a vacant lot. Authorities said superficial examination did not indicate the pillow to be blood stained.[245] Meanwhile sheriff's investigators let it be known that they found two miles north of the house, the mattress they are now holding. It was a bloodstained mattress, together with two bed sheets, also stained. Deputies were holding the mattress under lock and key, and which investigators asserted were found on the outskirts of Phoenix and partly identified as having come from the duplex. It was considered one of the most important pieces of evidence. Tracks of an automobile was found near the mattress.[410] Jack Halloran makes a statement regarding his involvement in the news stories. He said, "I have not seen nor in any way communicated with or heard from Mrs. Ruth Judd since we left her at her home" on Thursday night. "I have told my story to the proper officials. I have told everything I know. I stand on my statements made heretofore to constituted authorities. The grievousness of my deeds consists of no greater a fault than having been indiscreet. That this indiscretion has become related to so important a matter is the only reason it has become magnified. The three young women were always on the most friendly terms to the best of my knowledge and belief. At no time did I ever see anything of the contrary. So far as I know, too, they all three, were honorable women."[245] Evelyn Nace, accompanied by her uncle Harry Nace, a prominent theatrical man, and her attorney was the first of the material witnesses to be called in for examination. She arrived shortly before 10 o'clock.[349] Bobbie Sheldon returned to McKinley Park on the train from Fairbanks where he had been staying since October 22. Likewise, Cap. Lathrop and his secretary Miss Miriam Dickey left Fairbanks that morning to Suntrana after staying in Fairbanks for 10 days.[411]

1931, October 27

L. E. Dixon of Los Angeles makes a statement to the LA Times. He is said to be a wealthy contractor and president of the L. E. Dixon Company. He says that the friendship with the women was casual and knows nothing about the murder. He stated that he has met both Mrs. LeRoi and Miss Samuelson and that he has seen them only a few times. He said that he had not seen them in about a month prior to their death. L. E. Dixon was currently building a bank building in Phoenix. He had built several other buildings in Phoenix and was a close business associate of JJ Halloran.[412] A mattress and bedding is found tightly rolled and tightly tied about 15 miles outside of Phoenix in a pile of cactus. Tire marks were nearby. Investigators planned to use the tracks to try to identify if this was the missing mattress from the duplex. This doesn't seem to have ever been followed up on or is lost to history.[295] Lon Jordan announced the finding of this mattress. He stated it was two thirds of the whole mattress. It was cotton stuffed and covered with flowered blue cloth. This mattress was found in the desert two miles north of the Arizona Canal, some 50 yards off Nineteenth Avenue many miles from 2929. It appeared to have been thrown from a car and was tightly tied[290]. Anders Samuelson wires Phoenix to have Sammy's body returned to Minneapolis for burial.[295] In LA, William C. Judd appears before Municipal Judge Harold Landreth and asked for additional time to plead on the charge of practicing medicine without a license. He was released on $500 dollars bail. He said, "Technically, I have violated the law. I'll pay any penalty inflicted."[413] Apparently, Dr. Judd was a licensed physician and surgeon in 4 states, but apparently not in California. He had been engaged by the Dr. J. B. Moss Industrial Hospital to operate the establishment during a short absence of Dr. Moss. The complaint gave names of 11 men that were treated by Dr. Judd.[412] Among Mrs. LeRoi's affects was found an "unprintable threat" thought to be written by WRJ. It was hurriedly scribbled across the top of a budget sheet kept by Anne LeRoi. The note was found tucked away, carefully folded beneath a maze of correspondence from her mother and her fiancé Emil. It was thought to be from August and was planned to be used against WRJ in view of premeditation for the crime.[414] The townspeople in Darlington Indiana raised $12 in churches for Ruth's parents so they could travel to Phoenix. In a half dozen stores in the business section were subscription lists on which citizens pledged their humble contributions. The WCTU church workers canvassed the town asking for contributions of clothing for the aged pair. Shut in by illness for three years, Mrs. McKinnell didn't have any clothing. HJ planned to mortgage their home, but their equity had a value of less than $200 and the house was mortgaged for $600.[415] There were plans for a baseball game and benefit moving picture show for the next week to raise funds. HJ was described as having "much of Lincoln" in the man who has spent half of his life serving small town churches. He is gaunt and weathered and has a childlike naiveté and a rustic courtliness that has won him the warm regard of his fellow townsmen. HJ made the statement, "I fear that my daughter may spend the rest of her days behind prison walls. I do not know whether she will be spared her life. But, I do hope to win her soul back to God." He also said, "Three times in Ruth's life she has shown certain symptoms of insanity." We checked with his wife, but did not clarify this statement.[415] HJ McKinnell writes a letter to his son Burton McKinnell stating that William Randolph Hearst offered him $8500 (or just $500) for a biography of Ruth.[397] He told him that if he heard from the head of the defense counsel he would do it, but he didn't even know their names. So, he asked Burton for that. He stated that they were getting ready to start to come to be beside Ruth. He said, "Unless we get a better offer we will come on the Santa Fe RR via Chicago and Amarillo." He thought the fare would be $5.90 to Chicago and then to either Phoenix or Los Angeles $40. The total for both of them would be $90.60. They wanted to get to the place of trial a couple of days before the time of the trial, so that the defense attorney could have time to question them. He said they were character witnesses.[397] Burton's story (1st installment) appeared in the Los Angeles Examiner. Some interesting quotes included, "When a person does thinking like that, they have a reason to do it. Some have reasons that are logical. Some have reasons that are based on illogical reasoning. But there is always a reason. If the reason is illogical it is too bad, all around, but if the reason is logical and I know my sister's reason was- though I don't know what it is, to this day, then my heart is not heavy." "Behind every overt act there lies a motivating cause. It is an axiom of every school of psychology. There is a motivating cause that will come to light when the real facts in this case are threshed out in open court bit by bit by the people of Arizona. I am sure they will prove my sister not guilty." There was more than one part planned for this article set by Burton.[315]

1931, October 28

A single .25 caliber bullet shell was found at the Brill Street apartment in the corner of the bedroom, in the southwest corner.[355] Fred Williams, transient chemist appears before Ruth and is asked, "Do you know this woman?" Williams confessed that he had aided Ruth, but most considered the story fantastic. They held him for further questioning. Ruth called him back to her door and told him, "I want to tell you again not to talk and if you do, tell your story at the trial".[416] Ruth pretended to know him.[250] Williams asserts, according to Inspector Davidson, that he met Mrs. Judd in front of the city hall in Phoenix about 4 pm on the day on which Phoenix authorities say the murders were committed, shortly after he had arrived by stage from El Paso, Tex. Mrs. Judd, he said took him to Miss Samuelson's apartment and there introduced him to Miss Samuelson and Mrs. LeRoi as an old friend from Old Mexico. Miss Samuelson, he says resented his presence in the apartment and ordered him out. This started an argument between Miss Samuelson and Mrs. Judd, he declares, which reached a climax when the former obtained a pistol and threatened to shoot Mrs. Judd. A scuffle happened, Williams continues, in which Mrs. Judd wrestled the weapon from Miss Samuelson and shot her. Mrs. LeRoi then interfered, he asserts, and he knocked her down. "Williams", Davidson asserted, "is either psychopathic, a seeker for notoriety or has been planted to disrupt the prosecution's case against Mrs. Judd. His story is full of holes and doesn't hold water "[249] Later in the day, while detectives were still checking on the Fred William's story, Joseph Filkas strolled into Ruth's cell and chatted with her on casual subjects. Presently he remarked that the Williams episode had been quite a joke. Ruth replies, "Yes, we certainly fooled the police for a while didn't we? I wonder what put it in the boy's head to tell such a story," she smiled.[250] When they had asked Williams about his residence in El Paso he was evasive. Williams was wearing a USC belt buckle. Police believed that he was a friend of Burton McKinnell who also was a student there. Police decided to hold Williams as a material witness to determine whether some "ulterior motive" prompted his story, which differed from facts in the case.[417] Another story circulates in the Hearst papers. "It concerns a nationwide dope ring, with headquarters at Phoenix and casts Hedvig Samuelson, one of the murder victims in the role of an undercover agent for the United States Customs Service set on the trail of the dope smugglers. Miss Samuelson was slain, according to the tale, because she knew too much and Agnes Anne LeRoi was put out of the way because her friendship for Miss Samuelson and her knowledge of her affairs." This story was claimed to be among the half dozen true stories of the crime which has been whispered about the homicide division of the police department in city hall, in newspaper rooms and within the Hall of Justice. The story is discredited, but has many details. "This story, which has most general circulation, was brought to Los Angeles by a man who came here at his own expense to see County Attorney Lloyd J. Andrews, of Phoenix to lay his information before that law enforcement officer, who promptly discredited the entire tale as being fanciful. The story dates back some 18 months ago when a government agent named Reynolds was killed in Phoenix and his body thrown into an irrigation canal. Dope runners were said to have had a hand in his sudden death, but so far, nothing has been accomplished in clearing up the mystery it is asserted. Then so the story goes. Hedvig Samuelson, one of the victims of the recent murders, was living in Juneau, Alaska where she posed as a school teacher. In actuality, the tale goes; she was an undercover agent for the United States Customs Service. She was at once transferred to Phoenix. (missing a section) Suddenly Mrs. Judd moved in close to the two women and using her knowledge as a nurse and her ability to mix, soon won the confidence of the women. Mrs. Judd had lived in Mexico where it was asserted Dr. Judd her husband had used narcotics. In the meantime, an agent living in the Wilshire district was cutting in on the Phoenix business by getting his own dope from Mexico, it is asserted. Then all of the cunning and ugliness of the dope crowd was crowded into a diabolical scheme to rid the industry of two undesirables at one time. Mrs. Judd, it is said, did not do any actual shooting but she is said to have been present when it was done.

Her bullet wound is said to have come from holding Miss Samuelson while a bullet was fired into the struggling woman's body. Miss Samuelson was to have been killed alone and her body shipped to Los Angeles by train where the body was to have been taken to the apartment of the Los Angeles dope peddler; the police were to be informed and the victim left to explain his plight as best he could. When both women were killed, the plans were somewhat upset, and both bodies were then shipped to Los Angeles where a gray automobile was to have met them. A week ago Monday morning when the bodies arrived in Los Angeles, Mrs. Judd stepped from the train but instead of being met by a representative, so the story states, she was cautioned by a signal to be careful. For through some strange circumstance, a police car drove up and remained parked behind the automobile bearing a Nevada license plate. The driver became panic stricken believing the crime had been detected and at the first opportunity fled from the scene, leaving Mrs. Judd alone at the station.[418] The state medical board was trying to check on Dr. Judd's record as a doctor. Dr. Charles B. Pinkham, secretary of the California Board, stated that he could not find Dr. Judd's name in the Medical Associations directory of doctors licensed to practice in the United States.[419] Dr. Judd stated that this was a technicality. He had been licensed to practice medicine in several states, including California. However, since the last time he worked in the state they changed their policy. He had neglected to report that he had resumed practicing medicine within the state.[250] Burton was arrested and was hauled into court for a traffic offense.[250] Dr. Benjamin Blank who had done several examinations of Mrs. Judd, made a statement that Mrs. Judd is sane beyond the slightest question. He said that she was sane, is not a narcotic addict and does not have an active case of tuberculosis.[420] Sheriff McFadden goes to Sacramento to see the Governor with the extradition papers. Governor James Rolph, Junior was ill in the hospital so that Sheriff McFadden had to take the papers to the Chief Executive's bedside. McFadden told the governor, "When we get her back to Arizona we'll hang her, in my opinion. We have only men juries in our state, but we don't stand for vamping. It won't be the first time we hanged a woman."[250] An article appears regarding a diary of Anne LeRoi (see note about this as a hoax on the 29th). The diary mentioned the names of prominent Phoenix business men and which may contain a clue to the real motive for the double trunk murders, was sought by authorities today. The diary vanished mysteriously after the bodies of Mrs. LeRoi and Hedvig

Samuelson were found in LA. It was said that two days after the finding of the bodies, men mentioned in the diary received telephone calls offering them pages from the diary for a money consideration. "The voice of the salesman was that of a man, but authorities have no clue to his identity. They pointed out, however, that two motives may have inspired him, one if he was an accomplice to raise money to flee from Phoenix, the other that he may not have been connected with the crime but discovered the diary at the LeRoi-Samuelson apartment and picked it up with the hope of extorting money from the persons mentioned as the price of keeping their names secret."[258] Ruth's story appears in the Los Angeles Examiner. It features a full page in her handwriting saying, "My own story in my own words by Ruth M Judd. Here it is, my own story in my own words. I don't know what is ahead of me. It may be a long trail, it may be prison, and it may be death. A week ago the name of Ruth Judd meant nothing except to the people who knew me. Now I think everybody knows of me. All sorts of things are being said about me. All sorts of people are guessing, judging, condemning. I want to tell the truth that nobody else can possibly know. And this is it. This is my story, not hearsay or second handed, just my life as I see it now. My life, my childhood, girlhood and mature years – my loves and dreams have been my own. Now that I am before the world, charged with terrible crimes and painted as a tigress and as a woman apart from the rest, my story must be told.[421] Burton was not able to get up to the jail to see Ruth. He advised her to "change her attorneys" by letter. Schenck was employed by Dr. Judd. On this day many tried to come to see Ruth. Judge Russill brought up Bert Wheeler and Robert Woolsey, movie comedians to have a peep at her.[422]

1931, October 29
Dr. Judd's defense on the charge of practicing medicine without a license was delayed until November 27th.[423] Four men's neckties were found at 2929. GA Rogers was trying to trace the ownership of the neckties to determine if they belonged to the owner of the black sedan. The detectives were suspicious of the neckties since they were not discovered in a dozen previous searches of the house.[424] A witness tells of a telephone call. The witness had seen Ruth enter a drug store near her home on East Brill about 11:45. There she dialed a number and when she had a connection said, "I want to borrow your car for a little while. A friend of mine is terribly ill and I must drive her around

for some air." Ruth hurried out and caught a taxi. They also reported that there was a pair of gloves which were found hanging on a clothes line at the duplex. They were white kid gloves. They had been freshly washed but still bore traces of blood on them. They had misplaced them but investigators were diligently looking for them.[275] A bridge score sheet was found on the ledge of the bedroom. The players were labeled We and They[425]. Investigators examine a stack of mystery story magazines from a book rack from the duplex. In a book called, Mystery of Salvic House, they find a piece of paper being used as a bookmark with Sammy's handwriting on it. It said, "Someday someone is going to get you, and then you won't be so fresh." The investigators conclude that this quote was simply jotted down as a quote from a book or from a radio show.[184] Another source states that this was on a budget sheet kept by Mrs. LeRoi. It was not in Mrs. LeRoi's handwriting, but appeared to have been written by Ruth.[258] Apparently, Sammy left behind a radio log with some quotes from murder mystery plays, some of the other quotes were "I'll Get you for That" and Now your Doom is Sealed."[426] The plumbing is examined at 2929 in hopes of finding evidence of Hedvig's missing intestines. They examined the line to the cesspool. The house at Brill street was served by the city sewer system so that was not possible.[425] Mr. Henry F. Fliendner of the plumbing company of Fliendner and Company located at 915 North Seventh Street opened the traps of the bath tub, toilet and basin in the bathroom and the cesspool located in the yard at 2929 North Second Street to determine whether there was any blood or if any parts of missing entrails from Miss Samuelson could be found. The examination of the traps in the bathroom showed nothing but water and a little dirt. The cesspool was dry; having drained itself into the ground and just a particle of hair and a little piece of cloth was found.[205] A hoax emerges regarding a diary of Anne LeRoi. Cash offers were made for the diary. The article says that there was indeed a diary by Hedvig Samuelson. Investigators knew nothing about a diary of Anne LeRoi. The reporters made it up.[427] The diary was the Phoenix reporter's idea of a joke to play on Los Angeles newspaper men who came to try to uncover all of the details of the crime.[428] The article confirms that a diary of Hedvig Samuelson was found in the duplex where the murder occurred.[428] The Los Angeles Evening Express picks up on the story of Anne LeRoi's Diary. The diary contained reactions of the women to Radclyffe Hall's sensational "Well of Loneliness", full of quotations from the sensational and forbidden book, the "Well of Loneliness". The diary was replete with word pictures of her own emotions and said also to reveal names of social and business leaders which had been suppressed according to investigators because of its damaging contents. Bitterness, jealousy, rivalry and hatred were said to be the theme of Mrs. LeRoi's Diary. Officials admitted the diary existed but sought to give the impression that it might not be used as evidence in the trial. The diary was divided into two parts, one containing intimate details of the party lives of the slain girls. This section of the diary is said to be in the hands of an attorney who is guarding its contents in the interests of wealthy men clients whose names may be drawn into the baffling all woman triangle. The weird contents of the diary were discussed everywhere on this day. Deputy County Attorney Harry Johnson confirmed the existence of the diary. He was asked if he had the diary or had seen it. "I have not been able to obtain the diary," Johnson said. Questioned as to why the diary could not be produced through an official demand Johnson replied, "I have been instructed by County Attorney Lloyd Andrews by telephone not to give out anything to the press." "Why was this order issued?", Johnson was asked. "I can't discuss that". A prominent resident of Phoenix said he had seen the diary shortly after it was found in Mrs. LeRoi's rooms. A representative of a local organization, this resident said, had taken the diary to an office and it was locked up in a safe. This was a day following the discovery of the bodies in two trunks at Los Angeles. Revelation of the contents of the diary it was admitted would wreck several prominent homes and efforts were being made to keep names in the diary from being drawn into the court records although the names were generally mentioned in street talk. The efforts to keep secret the names were reflected in LosAngeles dispatches which told of an attempt by Mrs. Judd's brother, Burton McKinnell, to employ a noted Arizona lawyer to defend his sister.[429] The book (the diary) contained a lifetime of reactions to pathological emotions; bitterness against abnormal emotions, rivalry for one another's affections. Jealousy and brooding quarrels all were indicated in the revelations contained in the diary. The other section was devoted to Mrs. LeRoi's asserted brooding introspection on conditions as they existed in the intimate lives of herself, Mrs. Judd, and Miss Samuelson.[430] Tourists are no longer allowed to enter the duplex where the murders took place by order of the county attorney's office. Property guard F.M. Bond and Special Deputy Sheriff William guard the house from spectators. They live in the side where Dr. and Ruth Judd once lived. F. M. Bond writes a poem about the two women while he guards the house [403]

A Wonderful Friendship

In a beautiful sunlit cottage
With furnishings tasty and neat
There dwelt two loving companions
Whose devotion to each other was sweet.

They share in each other's sorrows
Seemed first and always in mind
And if Days at times they were cloudy
A true friend at home each would find.

Then one night they were quietly sleeping
In two soft downy beds, side-by-side
When Lo! There came stealthy creeping
A serpent with them to abide.

When the snake was coiled and ready
It struck with venomous blows.
Two loving souls then soon departed
From this earth with its sorrows and woes.

Two loving hearts are now silent
And soon flowers will bloom on new graves
The waters of life will flow onward
Often forcing up troublesome waves.

May their friendship so pure and holy,
God with them to their home up above
And through all eternity grow in greatness
Fulfilling the great mission of love.

To those of you that feel lonely
And are wondering if friends are true.
Please read this true story of friendship;
It may be an inspiration to you.[403]

Ruth is in custody of Sheriff J. R. McFadden and Jail Matron J. Lou Jordan. She left the hall of Justice at 9:40. They expected to arrive in Phoenix at 10 AM the next day. Dr. Judd and Paul Schenck were with Ruth in the hospital at the county jail. At 9:00, Schenck and Dr. Judd left Ruth. McFadden went up and got Ruth. When he emerged from the building, he held her firmly by her arm. Ruth said nothing, just signed out. She was taken to an automobile below. She was in a car with McFadden, Mrs. Jordan and Gene Biscailuz. In another car were county attorney Lloyd J. Andrews and Frank Dewar, deputy sheriff. A third car had Dr. Judd and the Examiners' Reporters.[431] Gene Biscailuz was not impressed with this situation. He wrote: "The under-sheriff was back again at his piled up desk, but before he had caught up with his correspondence, a murder occurred. A trunk shipped to the city from Arizona, was opened at the railroad station. It held the dismembered bodies of two women who had vanished in Phoenix. The murder had been carelessly planned, and Winnie Ruth Judd, its perpetrator, had been lax enough to follow the trunk to Los Angeles, where she was taken up by the police. It was a gory and spectacular case. Mrs. Judd, small and engaging, met fully the photogenic demands of her fame, and the newspaper did all they could with the materials at hand. No skill could frame a drama of it, however; there was no surprise, no shifting of scenes and lights. It was a mere butchery job, and an "out of town" case. The end had come too fast; the lady had been too easily caught. The Clara Phillips case had made the public taste more cautious, more exacting for color, for wonders, for romance, possibly with swamps and alligators, and suspense drawn out to the breaking point. The officer from Arizona arrived to take custody of his prisoner and invited Traeger and Gene to ride back to Phoenix with them. Law officers have their own code of etiquette. The Sheriff could not go; Biscailuz went, and Frank Dewar with him, also Tom Treanor of the Los Angeles Times, who was to report events on the journey. A carful of photographers followed. A major performance was somehow expected of Gene. It was illogical, but belief is not always based on logic or reasons. It was as if one might expect an actor who had been triumphant in a smash hit to repeat his success in an inferior play and an obscure role. Biscailuz went ruefully, for he had had to leave much work undone. The trip was eventless. The photographers toiled with faith, and the undersheriff posed with never a twitch of an eyelid. But, Mrs. Judd was no Clara, and the journey no flight from Honduras. It was merely jog trot routine. A columnist on the Los Angeles Times was to write of it with unleashed humor, comparing it with the earlier affair."[432] Afterwards Biscailuz stated that Ruth displayed a keen mind but at times chattered profusely about inconsequential matters. She talked simply and plainly like a child telling her toys and on the whole was easy to please. She seemed completely bewildered about the trunk murders and cried a little at times when her thoughts turned to the gruesome killings."[124] Geoffrey Homes of the Los Angeles Evening Express tells a more eventful tale as they travelled back to Phoenix. Moise thought it was a good idea for him and Tom Treanor to go along. He said that they took shadowy, little used roads. They described the trip as amazing. They found themselves at Lake Elsinore which is out of the way. They were lost it seemed. Tom stepped forward and suggested a short cut. He said he knew a way that would save hours of driving. Tom led the caravan. The road got worse and worse. At two in the morning they approached a settlement. Everybody was dubious. Tom reassured them that he knew this country like a book. He asked if anybody was hungry. Ruth stated that she wanted some coffee. Tom went behind one of the buildings. Then things began to happen. Lights went on. Men came running. Stoves were lit. Food was produced. They were at Warner Hot Springs and management was more than glad to see them. They weren't on the right road. Geoffrey had it out with Tom in the car. He confessed. He said it was a short cut of sorts. His father had lived and owned Warner Hot Springs. He had wanted to be able to give it publicity for the resort. They lost the caravan at dawn and they never caught up with it. They missed the return of Winnie Ruth Judd to the scene of the crime. They got a flat at El Centro road. He didn't have his jack with him. He used rocks to get the tire changed. Out of El Centro they ran out of gas and had to push the car two miles. When they got to Phoenix, it was all over.[371] Paul Schenk. Herman Lewkowitz, and Zaversack were employed by Winnie Ruth Judd [433] Jack Halloran stated that he had never seen Mrs. Judd display any signs of insanity and that she always seemed in complete control of herself.[244] It was published in the Examiner, Ruth's second part of her story. Part of what she wrote was, "I want to deny as soon as possible, that there ever was anything but friendship between me and Jack J. J. Halloran. If there is any proof needed for that, there are just dozens and dozens of girls that I have introduced him to. This Lucille Moore I introduced him to was going on a hunting trip in the White Mountains. I introduced them so that they could know each other. If I were jealous or in love with the man, do you think I would have done that? But when I say this I do not mean that my husband is not always in my mind. Our romance was the big thing in my life—a thrilling love affair."[87]

1931, October 30

Anders and Marie Samuelson (Hedvig's Parents) move from White Earth to Minneapolis[402] McFadden brings Ruth back to Arizona at night. McFadden rode with Ruth and two armed guards in one car while Dr. Judd followed in another. A group of Los Angeles reporters covering the story furnished the cars. It was quiet as they moved across the California desert, but as soon as they crossed the state line, a fleet of motorcycle officers and high speed patrol cars came and formed to escort them for the rest of the drive. They were accompanied according to Dr. Judd with shrieking sirens, honking horns, forty fives, sawed off shotguns and machine guns.[250] When they arrived at the jail, the police literally had to fight a path through the dense throngs to permit Ruth to walk into the building.[250] It was beginning to be the resort season in Phoenix, but even so because of this, all of the hotels and rooming houses were overflowing.[250] Picture postcards of Ruth and her victims were hawked on the streets.[250] Ruth was kept at the top of the courthouse in "a room".[250] She refused to tell anybody her story including her lawyers who had to prepare her defense without any information.[250] Dr. Judd was not allowed to see her.[250] A newspaper states that there is no evidence that would indicate any one of the three principals were a drug addict or were in any way connected with the so called powerful Phoenix drug ring which murdered two men; one a government narcotic squad secret service agent two years ago. "Evidence that not one of the three women ever used a narcotic became an almost established fact. However, Ruth's use of a sleep inducing sedative, which caused her doctor husband considerable concern in fear of the habit forming qualities was admitted by Rogers." Examination of the plumbing at the Samuelson apartment came as the results of persistent rumors that the results of an illegal operation figures in the background of the murders. The name of a prominent Phoenix surgeon and an equally prominent "fourth" woman had been injected into the foreground of the investigations. It was also thought that a doctor and another woman may be implicated. The cesspool at the duplex was examined to find the missing parts of Miss Samuelson. Substance found in it was turned over to the county physician.[193] Blood spots were found in the duplex. In the place where in the rug was cut away in the bedroom a spattering of blood marred the floor. Near the front door were two round spots of blood. It was thought that this is where the men removing the trunk had rested it. Detective Weage found on the screened porch at the rear of the house a garment from which a lower section had been sheared and on which were two distinct blood stains.[261] Paul Schenk took over the defense of Ruth Judd [434]

1931, October 31
Frank Vance of Rural Route 1 of Mesa visited the police station and asked for protection of the house at 2929. He rented the house to the 2 girls. He said the curiosity seekers were destroying valuable furniture and furnishings.[261] It is reported that while Winnie Ruth Judd was receiving the attention of thousands, the girls were locked in a room alone at a funeral home that was 5 blocks away. The article said that none but the curious had inquired about them. No friends came to pay them an affectionate glance. There were no flowers in the room. Burial and funeral arrangements hang in abeyance under orders of County Attorney Lloyd Andres of Maricopa County until an inquest. The date of the inquest has not been set, but it was expected the following week. The room where the girls were would not have gained entrance. It was locked to everyone under the county attorney's orders. The disposition of Mrs. LeRoi's body rests only upon the time when an Arizona coroner's jury shall repeat the conclusions of the California coroner's jury that passed upon the case before the two were returned here. Instructions have been received from a funeral parlor in Portland that the body be cremated it was learned today and her ashes sent to Portland where her parents live. So, far though, now two weeks since the night of the quarrel that ended in the killings, no plans have been made for the burial of Miss Samuelson. No word has been received from her parents or from any of her friends [435] A ring was added to the Coroner's register for Anne LeRoi. It was called a woman's ring with a red stone.[323]

1931, November 1
Sammy stated in her unsent letter to her sister Anna that Captain Lathrop would be in Seattle on November 1. He sent her a letter inquiring if Sammy needed any more financial aid.[210] Ruth spends a quiet Sunday in isolation in the Maricopa County jail. Late in the afternoon Herman Lewkowitz was admitted to her cell and conferred

with her for some time. Lewkowitz asked McFadden if he could interview Mrs. Judd alone but the request was denied. McFadden said, "I'm sorry, but you cannot see her alone. We are watching her very carefully; therefore, you will have to talk to her with Mrs. Jordan, the jail matron, nearby." When asked about this, McFadden replied, "If you knew what I know, you would understand." Later he added, "Anything might happen." Dr. Judd had time on his hands. He spent the day familiarizing himself again with the scenes he once knew when he was a resident of Phoenix.[434] He stated that he was not convinced that she had told him the whole story. He stated the he thought perhaps the mattress was not an error. He thought it may have been found by investigators or prowlers. He stated that the bush where it was supposed to be found was the location at one time used as an arbor under which Sammy had placed a cot and a palm leaf sun shade. The arbor was born away by investigators and every bush in the lot had the appearance of having been beaten and thoroughly searched. He noted the house was closed. He also wanted to visit the Brill Street apartment.[124]

1931, November 2
The authorities in Phoenix decided that the inquest held in Los Angeles by Coroner Nance was sufficient. The bodies of Anne LeRoi and Hedvig Samuelson's were immediately released to their families. They planned to cremate them and send their ashes home.[345] Dr. Maudlin gives Ruth a thorough examination and determines that she is in good physical condition.[345] Irrigation canals in the back country were dragged in hope of finding the mattresses.[345] They were talking about bringing Ruth back to the house to reenact the crime [345] B. O. Smith visits the duplex to look for blood evidence. He finds a fingerprint on the shade that he believes is blood and is a left thumb. It was too smudged to identify.[436] Ruth again tells the story to Sheriff McFadden, Lewkowitz and Zaversack. The sheriff announced after she finished that he expected to "blast her story sky high". He indicated that someone else knew of her crime before she left Phoenix. He claimed that a professional man loaned her a car with which she accomplished the last few errands after the murder. Ruth's story remained pretty much the same saying the crime happened on Saturday morning and that she had spent Friday night on the davenport. She had come back Saturday afternoon (at 2:30) and severed Sammy's body which took forever (until almost 10). She said her first impulse was to set fire to the house and burn the bodies and all evidence of the crime.

She had thought about going to the police but realized it was her own gun. She took a bath after the crime. They questioned her for 10 hours.[274]

1931, November 3
Sam, Sammy's brother from Minneapolis writes a letter to Hedvig's Doctor, Victor Randolph inquiring about her personal effects.[437]

1931, November 4
Ruth's lawyers requested the county attorney and sheriff for permission to inspect and examine the premises with a view to the preparation of her defense. They were refused. They immediately filed in the superior court of Maricopa County a petition entitled, "In the Matter of the State of Arizona against Winnie Ruth Judd" requesting that the court issue an order authorizing any and all of the attorneys for the accused to view the premises in question at all reasonable times and hours.[433] All attorneys and Sheriff McFadden were then allowed full access to 2929 N 2nd Street and to 1130 Brill unit F.[433]

1931, November 7
Sammy's body arrives in Minneapolis from Phoenix in the afternoon. Ashes?[345] Another article says that Mrs. Agnes LeRoi's body was cremated and the ashes shipped to the Portland Ore. home of her parents, Mr. and Mrs. Alex A. Imlah. Miss Hedwig Samuelson's body was shipped to Minneapolis MN where her brother Dr. Samuel Samuelson resides.[438] Their bodies left Phoenix early in the morning as inconspicuously and as unnoticed as the arrival here of the two woman in life more than a year ago as health seekers. Only a mortician's assistant accompanied the bodies today to the railroad station [438] Hedwig was buried that evening at Crystal Lake Cemetery in Minneapolis[439] The service was attended by Mr. and Mrs. A. Samuelson, and her two brothers.[440] A letter was received from Dr. Randolph and he replies and says he spoke to the county attorney and that somebody would get back to him regarding Hedvig's belongings. Says he will follow up when he knows more.[437] The prosecution on this day appealed from the superior court decision that allowed defense counsel to inspect the murder scene. A writ of appeal was filed in the Supreme Court and it was made returnable Monday morning at the preliminary hearing.[438]

1931, November 8
Lewkowitz obtains permission (without interference) from the court to visit both the duplex and the Brill Street apartment. Lewkowitz and Zaversack tour both houses with Sheriff McFadden.[441]

1931, November 13
Dr. Harry Goss visits the duplex to collect blood samples.[442] The spots in the bedroom were blood, as were one of the spots from the kitchen and the dining room. Other samples taken were not blood.[339] Goss stated that only spots from the bedroom floor and baseboard in the bedroom and one spot in the kitchen gave positive tests as being blood. In the bedroom the spots were colored dark brown. They were relatively profuse but the individual spots were not thick. He removed them with a sharp knife. The bed was not above the spots. The blood on the baseboard had the appearance of having been spurted. They had a pear shape. On the floor they were more circular. Lewkowitz asked him at trial if he had seen the handprints on the south wall of the hallway. Goss said no. He also asked him about a large spot as big as a penny and had a hair on it leaving from the hallway to the kitchen. He did not see that.[355]

1931, November 16
Ruth Judd is arraigned and plead not guilty to the two first degree murder complaints.[443] H.J. Mckinnell objected to the early trial date, but Howard Speakman declined to change it. He indicated that he would consider a plea by the defense attorney that six weeks would be required to prepare a case.[443]

1931, November 17
A man visited Sheriff McFadden but refused to give his name. The man told him to tell Mrs. Judd he would pay her $10000 if she would write the words for a song he had composed. McFadden said that he didn't know whether Mrs. Judd (who is quite a writer) would accept the offer. McFadden said, "Mrs. Judd has written her reminiscences for publication in a number of newspapers following her surrender in Los Angeles last month."[443] He also states that the general tenor of the correspondence to the county officials is in protest against any attempt to send Mrs. Judd to the gallows. A good many quotations from the Bible are said to be in the letters, but the contents have not been made public. Some of the letters contain newspaper clippings about the case

and not a few have religious pamphlets as enclosures.[443]

1931, November 21
Dr. Edward Huntington Williams, an LA psychiatrist met with Ruth in the jail at the request of Paul Schenk.[444]

1931, November 25
Dr. Edward Huntington Williams met with Ruth again and spoke with her at length. He thought that Ruth did not know the difference between right and wrong. He stated, "She has what we would consider a bad heredity".[444] She had several relatives who are insane and particularly those that had Dementia Praecox. He believed that the thyroid gland was a recognized cause of insanity, believed in the heredity angle. The other glands that were involved were the ovaries and the testicles.[444]

1931, November 27
Dr. Judd's delay on the case of practicing medicine without a license in California was postponed until this date.[423] It was then postponed until December 24 since Dr. Judd claimed he could not leave his wife at this time.[445] Dr. Catton examined Ruth on the 27th and the 28th.

1931, Fall
Sometime before she is awaiting trial, Ruth states that Judge Russill approached her attorneys with the proposition that if she would not mention Halloran's name while on the witness stand he had evidence that the girls were in love with each other to use the defense that the girls made a sex attack on her and he forged some pictures which took Anne and Sammy's faces and put them on the bodies of other persons in indecent positions. Ruth refused tell such a lie. She stated that this was why she was unable to take the witness stand.[386]

1931, December 18
Ruth apparently doesn't know where the cat is. She writes a letter to her brother to find it.[20] She writes the following letter to Burton from a Phoenix jail: "Dear Burton, I am so glad that you came to see me. I am sorry that I cannot see Bob. Maybe they will let him come up Tuesday. Burton honey, do take Papa and Mamma out to the orange groves, and also to see the desert. You see, honey, I used to live in the wilds of Mexico, up in the mountains, overlooking desert land. I have

ridden ninety miles a stretch on mule back over land like Arizona
desert land. I loved it. If you can, or if mamma is able to stand the trip,
I wish they would go to Prescott. They have wanted to move there for
years and years, ever since they knew I had tuberculosis. Be a good
boy, honey. Go to church with the folks. Try and cheer them up. They
are heart-broken. Poor mamma has been sick for so long. She has
been in bed ever since she heard I had tuberculosis, early. She
worships me almost and is just killed over me being here in this thing.
Be so good to Doctor, too, Burton. He is so precious. He is broken-
hearted too. I am the only thing in the world he loves. Take mamma
and papa out to see Grimm's at 1130 E McDowell. They were my land
lord and are good Christian people. Take them out to see Mrs. Wade at
9th St. and Monte Vista. I bought all my groceries there. FIND MY
KITTY, Burton. I loved my kitty. Last summer he used to get so
warm he would stick his little paws in water to cool off. Doctor
brought some dolls for the kitty and he played all day with them, until
he chewed them up. Why didn't Mamma come today? Is she sick?
Why didn't you tell me today? I want to see my Mamma. Is it far to
walk here? If she isn't sick, every time you come, bring her.
Everybody says I look just like Mamma. Do you stay with Doctor?
You looked handsome today, Burton. Tell Daddy everybody likes him
here. He's such a kind old Daddy. I love you all. Here are all kinds of
loving kisses to Mamma, Papa, Burton and Doctor. RUTH."[20]

1931, December 19
HJ Mckinnell writes the following letter home to the Darlington
Herald, "I have learned all that I know by personal visits to the jail, the
poorhouse, one of the churches, a city mission, a few miles' trip among
the mountains and over the desert sands and also from what the
newspapers tell me. Arizona's scenic attractions, infinite in number
and kind, range from nature's own masterpieces to the handiwork of
primitive and modern man, and the splendid network of highways is a
delight to tourists bringing extremely varied scenery closer together.
The courthouse and jail is a combination and is a majestic six story
building, surrounded by stately palm trees and beautiful flowers. There
are on average about one hundred prisoners. The Maricopa County
Hospital for the Poor, is composed of several large buildings with wide
verandas. The superintendent and the employees are courteous and
kind. There are religious services held by the various churches each
Sabbath. There are at present one hundred and eight inmates. There

are several city missions, some of which give food and clothing with religious services, and some give religious services only. The mountains in Phoenix are like the mountains around Jerusalem. Old Camelback appears about one fourth mile away, but I am told it is about eight miles away. Four Peaks and Squaw Peak are still farther away. The people here are like people elsewhere. Some of them tell us that Phoenix is a grand place while others think it should be simply left for the Indians, Mexicans and coyotes. I am finding out by experience that the high cost of living at Phoenix Arizona is at least four times as high as Darlington, Indiana."[446]

1931, December 17-24
Dr. George Stephens meets with Ruth Judd for the first time. He testifies at the trial that he probably met with her 20-25 times. He was gone over New Years. He stated that he began by talking to Ruth Judd in a conversational way. He didn't want to excite her. He wanted to get her confidence and friendship as nearly as possible and have her be friendly with him. He didn't ask her any questions that might seem to be impertinent or anything of that sort. On the second day Ruth said, "You haven't seen my baby; have you Doctor?" He said no and asked her if she had a child. She said yes and asked him to help her get that child. She claimed that a lady or a woman at 364 East Thomas Road had the child last year and that she watched this particular house. She said that they were holding the child and keeping it from her. She said that she planned on taking the child away with her because they did not have a right to it. Dr. Stephens thought this was fanciful and that she had previously been described as a psychopathic personality. He explained that it is a cross between dementia, idiocy and true psychosis or insanity. He asked where the child was now. She said she didn't know since the people left 364 East Thomas and went to Iron Spring and took the child with them this past summer, and since they came back they had taken the child away and it was now on Portland or Moreland Street. She forgot which. A day or two later she asked him if he wanted to see a picture of the baby. He said yes. This was just before he was leaving. She told him to wait and she would get it. He followed her into the cell room. She took down a picture that was pinned up under the mattress on the mattress over her. She slept on the first tier and somebody slept, I suppose above her. Dr. Stephens asked if he could take it. She said yes, and asked that he bring it back the next day. It was a matter of pleasing her. She also had two other

pictures which were victims of the tragedy and he thought it was a rather queer place to have this picture gallery. He brought the picture back the next day. He told her that he would see what he could do about finding the child. He decided later that it was not just something to tell him but that she really had a delusion regarding a child. He said that this was part of insanity. He said there were other delusions. She told him other things, like mistreatment by the county officials in the jail that he thought were paranoid delusions on her part. His diagnosis was Dementia Praecox. At first he thought that it was psychosis with a psychopathic personality, that is a psychosis or insanity based or superimposed upon a psychopathic individual, or psychopathic personality. When asked if he thought it was dementia praecox with a paranoic strain he replied that yet there are other trends and other things that go to make up dementia praecox, schizophrenia. He said they called it schizophrenia. When they asked him about schizophrenia he said, well, that is just another term for another term that you don't probably understand. And that is dementia praecox. Dementia praecox is a definite disease or insanity which has an insidious oncoming along about the time of adolescence; usually between the ages of fifteen and twenty-five, has definite characteristics which fix it as that type of disease. There are a number of types of insanity or psychosis, and psychosis and insanity is the same thing. On further explanation he stated that it further means an egocentric existence, living within one's self, or rather, I don't know exactly how I could express it to the jury. When asked about schizoid. He stated it meant split personality. He stated that he was strictly on the practical side of the insanity problem rather than the theoretical. He didn't want to discuss definitions or scientific terms. He said that he had decided on a definite diagnosis of dementia praecox. He didn't say definitely paranoia dementia praecox. He thought that it was a mixed type and he hadn't definitely decided. He stated that deterioration had been happening with Ruth since infancy to the present time and that particularly deterioration that had come about in the last two years. He mentioned that there was a number of factors regarding Ruth including emotional instability, and emotional inadequacy. He said that when her mother was on the stand in January she was absolutely indifferent and apathetic. She folded her handkerchief; he counted and estimated that she folded the handkerchief 1640 times per day. He said something like 10 times per minute, or four times a minute, or seven times another minute. He said that you find this type of stereotyped movements in psychiatry. She paid no attention to her mother who was on the stand. The same day, she flew into a rage because she imagined that the sheriff was speaking to somebody and he thought that he was speaking about her. She was hard to calm down. He sat down and tried to calm her and talked with her and mentioned something that was, that struck her fancy and she immediately burst out into laughter and enjoyed it very much. Right after the recess, he claimed that it was not normal for somebody's emotions to jump from blazing anger to mirth. He said this emotional disturbance was part of dementia praecox. He claimed that she had no connected train of thought. That she jumped from one subject to another. While you are trying to keep her on one thing, she will begin speaking about something that happened back in Mexico or somewhere else and just talk insistently along that line. He thought there was reason to think that Ruth had some sort of focal infection. He took her temperature religiously day after day and there was a slight rise. It was about 100 or 100.2. He thought the elevation of temperature might be important. He mentioned that outburst regarding Dr. Catton and said that it was more than once. She mentioned on a number of occasions not liking Dr. Catton who told everything to people; that he had told things about her in pool halls. This was one of her favorite expressions. He stated that he didn't think he frequented pool halls. He thought that this was a paranoid idea. He thought that the mythical child was a particular delusion that stood out. He talked about heredity. In her history he found that one of the grandparents was insane and that a first cousin was insane and had dementia praecox. He talked about the great grandmother in Scotland that went insane when her husband was murdered. He claimed that this trait was handed down. He said that many dementia praecox cases developed TB, that patients are conducive to tuberculosis. He claimed that one of the reasons for this is that these people did not take care of their person. He claimed of Halloran that one time she had an outburst when discussing him and another time she spoke very highly of him. On cross examination he stated that she had a mixed type of dementia praecox for now. He might change his mind if he had a month or two to study her. He claimed her symptoms were indifference, emotional instability or inadequacy, stereotyped movements and gestures, lack of interest or apathy. He made a reference that in some cases people became slovenly and in some cases like tramps that go about the country, shiftless, ne'er do wells, lack of concentration, judgement, lack of reasoning, a tendency to go into a fit of anger or show emotion in other ways, like silliness or laughter when it isn't called for. He stated that he noticed certain symptoms that made him suspicious of dementia praecox on his examinations but wasn't sure that she wasn't trying to put something over on him. However, what he observed in court confirmed to him that they were actually symptoms of a definite psychosis. He stated that he tried to get her to stop twisting the handkerchief one time. She would not hesitate a minute from going through that, no matter what they were discussing. He stated that as a psychopathic personality, he thought she was queer and thought she was eccentric. He stated that he had gone out to 364 Thomas Road to see about the baby. He stated that there was such a house and that it was in such a position that one could watch it. As a definition of delusion he stated that it was "a false conclusion, a false conception, something that cannot be reasoned out in one's mind. It is not in harmony with normal thinking." He stated as an example that she slays two of her best friends but that a day or two before she demonstrated friendship by trying to get a house where they could all live together because she was friends with them. He claimed that she always spoke of them as friends. He claimed that what she had done seemed impossible to him but that he had seen the insane spurred by insanity do superhuman things. He stated that he thought she killed her friends. He stated that it had been proven that she had done that. He stated that another incident was that there was an insane patient that was brought to the jail with a similar name to Lucy or Lola Rider. She claimed that that patient was brought in by the sheriff as a frame up on her and as a punishment to her and put there to annoy her. She claimed that the woman was not insane, she could see it. This woman was implying that she was Ruth Judd herself, very insane. He argued and reasoned with her but she couldn't see it. She believed all the time that this woman was brought up there to act crazy and annoy her. He asked her why she signed Lucy Rider when she went to Bisbee and she replied that she did that because she was looking for a baby and she didn't want Dr. Judd to know that she was there. The object of that visit was a search for a baby that belonged to her. He stated that before he had thought she was a pathological liar which was a part of a psychopathic personality but he saw in court that she really did believe that she had a baby.[447]

1931, Christmas
Ruth wrote this letter on Christmas to her husband. "My Dear Doctor, I

have been thinking of how happy we have been together. Remember the first morning you ever talked to me in the dining room at the Hospital? You got to coming every morning. Then those stolen moments when we slipped into the dining room and had iced watermelon. My tongue would stick to the roof of my mouth, I was so excited. Remember our first date? I was to speak a piece at a missionary meeting that night. We had dinner together at the Blub. How funny - I can see how I looked that night. I had every new thing I owned on. And what a combination! Black satin dress, tan shoes, lavender hat, right from the country! How proud, how happy I was at the club. I felt like a millionaire. Remember the Worcestershire and ice water? Then, I left Evansville. I bet you can't remember what we had in a hurry to eat just before train time. I do. We had scrambled brains on toast. Oh, do you remember the lavaliere I lost and had to buy a new one? How I cried and cried. Remember how I cried when it rained in the evening. I wanted to go home? Then after I got those precious letters of yours. I used to walk two miles at noon to see if only there might be a letter from you. Then Christmas – then January you came to see me. How thrilled I was! You were at the Smart Hotel. Remember our dinner there? That was the first time I had ever been inside a hotel or eaten in one. We had lamb. You said it was no good. The rug on the floor was red. Do you remember the ice cream parlor? I always wanted to go get hot fudge sundaes. You sent me nice things, nice stationery, good pencils, parker pen books. Then in April you came again. We were going to get married. Remember how I slid all over the sidewalk on the ice? Our wedding was sweet. Then our trip on the Pullman, the first one I had ever been on. To New Orleans! Our lovely room, the first one I had ever had in a hotel. Remember the clock in the tower out from our room? Then on to San Antonio and down into Mexico. Remember how scared I was of the first Mexican I saw in Houston, all done up in blankets and Sombrero? Remember the casino in Laredo? You drank two glasses of beer. I was afraid you would get drunk. Oh, then one morning on the train about 5AM, the music, the reception for a general at the station in Sawatelle. How scary! Bon fires, women, children, men in blankets and sombreros, a band shouting and chatter in a foreign language, a faint glow of dawn across the mountains. The first mountains I had ever seen – Mexico, my honeymoon! Doctor, love, everything beautiful – happy. Then, Vanegas, those poor people, blind crippled. I gave them all your change. I learned a few words in Spanish there; cinco, quiero. I learned those two and all that was from our guide. Then Matehuala, the Henderson. They called you Doctor Williams. Mrs. Henderson kissed me. We had tea with lemon and mint leaves. I had on that lavender hat and the new grey coat you had bought me. Then our ride in the car up in the mountain with Casiano. I snuggled to you in the back seat and said, "I am so happy, Doctor Williams; we are going to our home up in the mountains." The Reyers welcomed us there on the rough mountain side. Doctor Wilkinson scared me. We arrived on Don Antonio's Saints Day. He had wine and women that night didn't he? All the Americans had to drop in and salute; such chatter! I couldn't understand a word. They all knew I was a bride. They all kissed me on both cheeks. Then our little home! They tinted it all in colors I wanted. Everything brand new. I caressed every shiny pan and kettle. I loved everything. It was new and complete. How amused the criadas were at my reading from the Spanish book everything. Then, alas, one day, I lost my book in the market before I completed buying groceries. You had to wire for a new book in Mexico City. Then we got Bruno. Remember how we let his brother in one night, THINKING it was Bruno and as he was eating a piece of cheese Bruno let out big objections and here he was outside! He ran his brother all over the place. Then little Hop, our bunny. He ate your felt slippers and I hated him so much. He looked ragged. He never knew he was a rabbit. He was afraid of other rabbits. He hid from the other rabbits and would come tearing to us when we called Hop. I loved living at Dolores, our hikes together, our car rides together. Remember the morning you went to the dentist? I made Chile Con Carne for dinner; you didn't come. Bruno and I sat on the stone wall eating oranges and looking over the valley. Bruno ate most of my orange. So finally we walked clear to Matehuala, seven miles, and a bunch of burros came along and you passed me. I called and called to you and Manuel heard me. I was so tired and dusty, and Bruno got in a fight with a goat and was butted into some cactus. He was full of cactus and we were both ready to cry when you passed us there on that dusty road. Bruno was only a pup, poor little fellow and he was so tired. Remember our first Christmas in Mexico? The moxo and Vilador fixed it up. It was so pretty. You had so many packages for me. All done up so pretty. I made you handkerchiefs, pajamas you never could wear, and a shirt. You ate up all the fruit cake before Christmas. So did I and we made more. Bruno was so careful of the tree. Do you remember the light fixtures you made me? I painted the bulbs. You got a wire and fastened each one on a big wire, then you got a battery down at the garage and I had a real lighted up tree. Wasn't it fun? We were so happy there. It's too bad we left, but the promise of more money, etc. I loved both Dolores we lived in and Tayoltita. Doctor, I want to go home. I am tried here all the time. I am so tired I can't even read. All I do is write and write to my darling precious Doctor. Papa and Mamma were here today. Poor Mamma's knees give out. She can hardly walk. When I don't cry about you being lonesome, I cry about Mamma and Papa. I wish I could be home to take care of you. I would put Mamma to bed and I would make you some Limeade and then get you to rub my back. My pleurisy hurts me all the time. I love you. Both handkerchiefs are for my Darling Billy for Christmas. Lovingly, Ruth."[20]

1931, December

Ruth writes a letter to her parents describing where she lived and who she knew in Phoenix to show that she had lived according to her upbringing. She stated that she went to the Free Methodist just once. When she was with the Colomons, she went with them and Doctor Barlows to the Mormon Church. She stated she did not smoke, had never gone to a dance in Phoenix, and did not chase around. She stated that she had gone to only 4 movies since she had been in Phoenix. She stated that they were all based on books that she had read (Ex-wife?). She stated that the Doctor had been so good to her. He had never given her a cross word. She stated that they had never quarreled in all the eight years they were married. She stated that in all her jobs, she had good positions and in all but one got promotions and raises in salary. She stated that no one in jail was bad to her. They are strict because the papers stated that she was getting treated too nice.[20]

1.   Johnson, G. Wesley, *Phoenix in the Twentieth Century: Essays in Community History*. 1993, Norman, Oklahoma: University of Oklahoma Press.

2.   Kendler, Mathilde, *Kendlers: The Story of a Pioneer Alaska Juneau Dairy*. 1983, Anchorage: Alaska Northwest Publishing Company.

3.   *Public Schools To Close Next Monday*, in *Daily Alaska Empire*. December 21, 1929: Juneau, AK. 1.

4.   Ruotsala, Jim, *1929: International Airways - Washington Airways and the Visit of Carl Ben Eielson*, in *Pilots of the Panhandle : Aviation in Southeast Alaska* 1996, Seadrome Press.

5. Herron, Edward Albert, *Wings over Alaska, the story of Carl Ben Eielson, born: July 10, 1897.* 1959, New York,: J. Messner. 192 p.
6. *Miss Agnes LeRoi Brutally Murdered,* in *Wrangell Sentinel.* October 23, 1931: Wrangell, AK. 1.
7. in *Wrangell Sentinel.* February 13, 1930: Wrangell, AK.
8. *Hospital Notes,* in *Wrangel Sentinel.* January 30, 1930: Wrangell, AK.
9. *Northwestern in from South,* in *Daily Alaska Empire.* February 10, 1930: Juneau, AK. 7.
10. *At the Hotels,* in *Daily Alaska Empire.* February 10, 1930: Juneau, AK. 4.
11. *Juneau Women Found Slain in Los Angeles,* in *Daily Alaska Empire.* October 20, 1931: Juneau, AK. 1,8.
12. Muänoz, Rie and Alaska Nurses' Association., *Nursing in the north, 1867-1967.* 1967, [Juneau?]: Published under the auspices of the Alaska Nurses' Association. 50 p.
13. *Whos' Who and Where,* in *Daily Alaska Empire.* 1930: Juneau, AK. 3.
14. *Trunk Slayer Has Killed Self, Police Believe,* in *Chicago Daily Tribune.* October 22, 1931: Chicago, IL.
15. *Picture in Trunk,* in *Daily Alaska Empire.* October 21, 1931: Juneau, AK. 2.
16. *Woman Suspected of Murdering 2 Alaskan Women,* in *Petersberg Press.* October 23, 1931: Petersberg, AK.
17. *Roller Rink Opened Here,* in *Daily Alaska Empire.* February 21, 1930: Juneau, AK. 2.
18. *Programs Given By Grammar School To Honor Washington,* in *Daily Alaska Empire.* February 24, 1930: Juneau, AK. 6.
19. Stevens, Robert W., *Alaskan aviation history.* 1990, Des Moines, Wash.: Polynyas Press. v.
20. McKinnell, Burton Joy, *The Truth about Winnie Ruth Judd by her brother,* in *Winnie Ruth Judd Papers: Clements Library.* 1932: Detroit.
21. Peterson, Phyllis, *Anders Severin Samuelson.* August 23, 1998: Carpinteria, CA.
22. *Capt. Lathrop on Way to Washington,* in *Daily Alaska Empire.* April 24, 1930: Juneau, AK.
23. *Taku Arrives Yesterday on Maiden Flight,* in *Daily Alaska Empire.* April 26, 1930: Juneau, AK. 2.
24. *At the Hotels,* in *Daily Alaska Empire.* April 26, 1930: Juneau, AK.

25. Judd, Winnie Ruth, *Statement of Winnie Ruth Judd taken at the Arizona State Prison 12-19-1932: Interview of JR McFadden Sheriff*, in *Pinal County Records*. December 19, 1932: Florence, Arizona.

26. Tillotson, Marjorie, *History of the Schools in the Gastineau Channel Area*. June, 1973: Juneau, Alaska.

27. Judd, William C, *My Life with Winnie Ruth Judd - Part 1*, in *Intimate Detective Stories*. March, 1940. 2-7, 52.

28. *Alienist Heard in Judd Case*, in *Unknown newspaper clippings of Lloyd Andrews*. Feburary 2?, 1932.

29. *Testimony of Dr. Clifford Wright*. Feb 2, 1932, Arizona State library and Public Records: Phoenix, AZ.

30. Judd, Winnie Ruth, *Ruth Judd Describes Incidents Leading to Meeting With Girls She Killed*, in *San Francisco Examiner*. October 31, 1931: San Francisco. 5.

31. *Winnie Tells Suicide Idea: Slayer Hurls Charges at J. J. Halloran*, in *Arizona Republic*. January 18, 1933: Phoenix, AZ.

32. *Friendship of rich man for 3 women is tragedy is told*, in *Los Angeles Herald Express*. October 23, 1931: Los Angeles. 11.

33. Swent, Eleanor, *Marian Lane: Mine Doctor's Wife in Mexico*. Western Mining in the Twentieth Century Oral History Services. 1996, Berkeley. 121.

34. Judd, Ruth, *Ruth Tells Penniless Arrival at Arizona City in Story of Life*, in *Los Angeles Examiner*. October 31, 1931: Los Angeles.

35. *Seaplane has busy Sunday*, in *Daily Alaska Empire*. May 12, 1930: Juneau, AK.

36. *Miss Chisholm Recovered*, in *Daily Alaska Empire*. May 12, 1930: Juneau, AK.

37. *Cann Interest in Hotel Sold To John Biggs*, in *Daily Alaska Empire*. May 16, 1930: Juneau, AK. 8.

38. *Juneau Schools Close Yesterday Until Next Fall*, in *Daily Alaska Empire*. May 30, 1930: Juneau, AK. 8.

39. *Luhrs Hotel Registry*. 1930, at Arizona State Archives RG107: Phoenix.

40. *School Staff Scatters for Three Months*, in *Daily Alaska Empire*. June 3, 1930: Juneau, AK. 8.

41. *Princess Louise in Juneau Today*, in *Daily Alaska Empire*. June 13, 1930: Juneau, AK. 7.

42. Wiles, Otis M, *Friends lift curtain of tragedy*, in *San Francsico Examiner*. October 27, 1931: San Francisco. 3.

43. Hickernell, FA, *Leigh Ford, 28 W. Monroe St*, in *Winnie Ruth Judd Papers, Arizona State Archives*. January 14, 1932: Phoenix.

44. Wiles, Otis M, *Slayer Often Seen Weeping for her Baby*, in *San Francisco Examiner*. October 29, 1931: San Francisco. 10.

45. *Sister of Trunk Murder Victim Bares Quarrel: Friction with Suspect Told in Letter*, in *Chicago Daily Tribune*. October 21, 1931: Chicago. ?

46. *College Alumna Victim*, in *Red & Green*. Nov 3, 1931: Minot, ND.

47. *Memories of Alaska*, in *Minot Daily News*. October 21, 1931: Minot, ND. 10.

48. *Statement of WM. C. Judd taken in Chief Of Detectives Joe Taylor's Office*, in *Arizona State Archives*. October 20, 1931: Los Angeles.

49. Thiers, Stanley, *Phoenix employer reveals murderess suspect's hysterical rage when discharged*, in *Los Angeles Times*. October 22, 1931: Los Angeles.

50. *Letters Bare Rich Friends Sent Sammy Money*, in *San Francisco Call Bulletin*. October 22, 1931: San Francisco. 3.

51. *Six passengers on Louise for Juneau*, in *Daily Alaska Empire*. August 26, 1930: Juneau, AK. 7.

52. *Public schools show increase in enrollment*, in *Daily Alaska Empire*. September 2, 1930: Juneau, AK. 3.

53. *Vacation Days End Next Week for Youngsters*, in *Daily*. August 26, 1930: Juneau, AK. 8.

54. *Glacier Road is Completed*, in *Dail Alaska Empire*. September 6, 1930: Juneau, AK. 8.

55. *Photographs of the Samuelson Family kept by Janet Worel*. 1900-1930: Dayton, MN.

56. *Local Schools Show Increase in Enrollment*, in *Daily Alaska Empire*. September 8, 1930: Juneau, AK. 2.

57. *"Sunshine" to Juneau*, in *Minot Daily News*. October 22, 1931: Minot, ND. 2.

58. *Trunk Murder Jealousy is Revealed*, in *Chicago American*. October 23, 1931: Chicago. 34.

59. *Sammy was good pal, says girl*, in *San Francisco Call Bulletin*. October 22, 1931: San Francisco.

60. *Trunk Killing Jealousy Told*, in *Detroit News*. October 21, 1931: Detroit. 1,36.

61. *Rivalship as murder cause suggested by friend in L. A.*, in *Illustrated Daily News*. October 21, 1931: Los Angeles.

62.   *Samuelson Girl's Bid to Barrymore Cruise Found*, in *San Francisco Examiner*. October 23, 1931: San Francisco. 8.

63.   *Letters of Friendship to Miss Samuelson Bared*, in *Los Angeles Evening Herald*. October 22, 1931: Los Angeles. 11.

64.   *Damon-Pythias Affection of Victims Told: Mrs. Le Roi and Hedvig Samuleson Devoted to Each Other Since Their Meeting in Alaska*, in *San Francisco Examiner*. October 31, 1931: San Francisco. 5.

65.   Fortuine, Robert, *"Must We All die?" Alaska's Enduring Struggle with Tuberculosis*. 2005, Fairbanks: University of Alaska Press.

66.   Hickernell, FA, *Dr. M. I. Leff*, in *Winnie Ruth Judd Papers, Arizona State Archives*. January 14, 1932: Phoenix.

67.   Judd, Winnie Ruth, *Judd Reminiscences*, in *Arizona Historical Society, Southern Arizona Division*. 1941: Tucson, AZ.

68.   *Ailing Teacher Leaves Here for California*, in *Daily Alaska Empire*. October 2, 1930: Juneau, AK. 8.

69.   *unknown*, in *Daily Alaska Empire*. October 4, 1930: Juneau, AK. ?

70.   *Link Mystery Disappearance to Murders: Portland Nurse who Vanished year ago was friend of Phoenix Victims*, in *San Francisco Call Bulletin*. October 21, 1931: San Francisco. 1.

71.   *Two Former Alaska Girls Victim of Brutal Murder Dismembered Bodies Found*, in *Alaska Weekly*. October 23, 1931: Seattle. 1.

72.   *Ex-Husband Says Victim Romanticist*, in *Phoenix Gazette*. October 23, 1931: Phoenix. 1.

73.   *Police Claim M'Kinnell not telling facts*, in *Daily Alaska Empire*. October 23, 1931: Juneau, AK. 1,8.

74.   *S.F. Man Tells of Meeting "Trunk Victim"*, in *San Francisco Call Bulletin*. October 22, 1931: San Francisco, CA.

75.   *Testimony of Jame O'Dell: Coroner's Report in California Inquest, 10-23-31, 9:30*, in *Arizona State Archives*. 1931: Los Angeles.

76.   *Inquest Bares Mrs. Judd had Company to L.A.*, in *Los Angeles Evening Express*. October 23, 1931: Los Angeles. 4.

77.   *Fate Brought Victims to Phoenix*, in *Bibee Daily Review*. October 22, 1931: Bisbee. 1.

78.   *Brother's Story Aids in Search*, in *El Paso TImes*. October 21, 1931: El Paso, TX.

79.   *Diary Notations*, in *Los Angeles Herald Express*. October 23, 1931: Los Angeles. 11.

80.   *Testimony of Victor Randolph: 1-25-32, afternoon session*, in *State vs. Judd*. 1932: Phoenix.

81.   *Tell Chicago Kin of Health Fight of Three Women*, in? 1931.

82. *Lot 9, Block 1, La Belle Place, 4/42 Deed Recordings.* Phoenix, Arizona.

83. Lucy, Dan, *Mrs. Judd: Dictated by Dan Lucy*, in *Winnie Ruth Judd Papers, Arizona State Archives.* October 20, 1931: Phoenix.

84. Judd, Winnie Ruth, *Empty Threat Tragedy's Cause, Says Mrs. Judd*, in *Los Angeles Times.* 1931: Los Angeles. 1,4.

85. Judd, Ruth, *'Try to think only of our happy momments together' says Mrs. Judd. I Can't Think of Them as Dead, Ruth Writes*, in *San Francisco Examiner.* November 1, 1931: San Francisco. 21.

86. *Trunk Murder Quiz Reveals Jealousy Inflamed by Kiss*, in *San Francisco Examiner.* October 22, 1931: San Francisco. 1,4.

87. Judd, Ruth *Do I Dread the Future? There is no Alternative*, in *Los Angeles Examiner.* Ocotber 29, 1931: Los Angeles.

88. *Statement of Dr. Percy Brown: Statements made in Judd Case 10-24-31*, in *State vs. Judd.* 1931: Phoenix.

89. Carey, James, *Blood Soaking Through Trunk Bares Murder*, in *Arizona State Democrat.* October 20, 1931. ?

90. *Testimony of Dr. Hilton J McKeown*, in *State Vs Judd.* . 1932: Phoenix, AZ.

91. *Scores of Names Found in Book of Miss Samuelson*, in *Los Angeles Herald.* October 22, 1931: Los Angeles. 11.

92. *Statement by Dr. Percy Brown*, in *State Vs Judd: Arizona State Archives and Public Records.* October 24, 1931: Phoenix, Arizona.

93. Judd, Winnie Ruth, *Pawn Shop Notice Ticket 6339.* December 8, 1930, 236 E Washington Street, Phoenix, AZ: Gardner Loan and Diamond Brokers.

94. Murray, Betty, *Ex-Roomate Says 'Tigeress' 'Flighty'*, in *Los Angeles Evening Express.* October 30, 1931: Los Angeles. 16.

95. *Pawnshop Gun Hints Mrs. Judd Had Death Plot*, in *Los Angeles Evening Express.* October 24, 1931: Los Angeles. 2.

96. Bechtel, EJ, *Statement of Mn C Judd taken in Chief of dtectives Joe Taylor's office at 8:10 PM October 20th 1931 in connection with the murder of Miss Leroy and Samuelson at Phoenix Arizona. Statement taken in the presence of the detectives Joe F. Taylor, Issp D. A. Davidson, Phoenix Officers L. Anerws Harry Johnson and J. Brinckerhoff. Notes by E. J. Bectel.*, in *Arizona State Archives and Public Records.* October 20, 1931: Phoenix, Arizona.

97. *Statement by Metra Halnan*, in *State Vs Judd: Arizona State Library and Public Records.* October 24, 1931: Phoenix, AZ.

98. *John Ralston - 832 E. Monte Vista*, in *State vs. Judd*. 10-21, 1931: Phoenix.

99. *Mrs Metra Halnan, who loaned $10 by check, Sunday Miss Josephine Hadland, her sister Ed Shimfessel, and Ted Harris - American Express*, in *State vs. Judd*. 10-21, 1931: Phoenix.

100. Catton, Dr. Joseph, *Secret Story of Winnie Ruth Judd*, in *True Crime Detective*. Spring, 1952. 17-30.

101. Wiles, Otis M, *Mythical Baby Aids Ruth in Getting First Job*, in *Los Angeles Examiner*. October 28, 1931: Los Angeles.

102. McKinnell, Burton Joy, *Brother Tells Dramatic Story of Calling for Fateful Trunks*, in *San Francisco Examiner*. October 27, 1931: San Francisco. 4.

103. Snyder, Jodie, *A Medical Marvel Historic, Stately Grunow Endures Long Recovery*, in *Phoenix Gazette*. October 3, 1993: Phoenix. G3.

104. Lois Grunow Memorial Clinic, *The Lois Grunow Memorial Clinic (title from cover)*. 1931: Phoenix, Arizona.

105. *Reporters Transcript 11-9-31 A.M.: Testimony of Evelyn Nace*, in *State vs Judd*. 11-9, 1931: Phoenix.

106. Herford, Oliver, *Overheard in a garden, et cœtera*. 1900, New York: C. Scribner's sons. 104.

107. Hope, Laurence, *The garden of Kama, and other love lyrics from India*. [New] ed. 1914, London: W. Heinemann. vii, 173, [1].

108. *Dream World of Victim Bared*, in *Los Angeles Evening Express*. October 24, 1931: Los Angeles. 5.

109. *Diary of Murder Victim Reveal Hedonistic Lure*, in *Daily Alaska Empire*. October 31, 1931: Juneau, AK. 1, 4.

110. *Testimony of WC Judd: Coroner's Report in California Inquest, 10-23-31, 9:30*, in *Arizona State Archives*. 1931: Los Angeles.

111. Nace, Evelyn, *Nurse tells last party*, in *San Francisco Call Bulletin*. October 21, 1931: San Francisco.

112. *Diary of Murder Victim Bares Loss of Friend*, in *Wisconsin News*. October 22, 1931: Milwaukee, WI. 2.

113. *Intimate picture given of Sammy by Letters*, in *San Franciso Call Bulltetin*. October 23, 1931: San Francisco. 1,12.

114. *It's Wisdom to Love, Live, Wrote Trunk Death Victim*, in *Los Angeles Evening Express*. October 21, 1931: Los Angeles. 5.

115. Judd, Winnie Ruth, *Confession Letter of Winnie Ruth Judd: Letter to HG Richardson.*, in *Winnie Ruth Judd, Arizona Historical Society*. April 6, 8, 1933: Tuscon,.

116.   *Trunk Victim Leaves Weird Diary*, in *Chicago American*. October 21, 1931: Chicago. 3.

117.   Tennyson, Alfred, *Maud, and other poems*. 1870, London: Strahan and co. [6], 170.

118.   *Reporters Transcript 11-9-31 A.M.: Testimony of H.U. Grimm*, in *State vs Judd*. 11-9, 1931: Phoenix.

119.   *2nd page of Newspaper Story, unknown title, next to "Mrs. Judd Gets Safety Promise"*, in *Arizona Daily Star*. October 29, 1931: Tucson. 16.

120.   Haendiges, Jerry. *Jerry Haendiges Vintage Radio Logs: Sherlock Holmes*. [Web site] 2001 [cited 2002 3/18/2002]; Available from: http://otrsite.com/logs/logs1041.htm.

121.   *Direct Examination of Mary Lucille Moore*, in *State vs Judd*. 1932, Arizona State Archives: Phoenix, Arizona.

122.   *Reporters Transcript 11-9-31 A.M.: Testimony of John Lentz*, in *State vs Judd*. 11-9, 1931: Phoenix.

123.   *Diary Entries Revealed*, in *San Francisco Chronicle*. October 22, 1931: San Franscisco.

124.   Thiers, Stanley, *Judd Aids Officials: Doctor to Check Wife's Story*, in *Los Angeles Times*. November 1, 1931.

125.   *Photos of the Arizona State Archives and Public Record*. 1931-.

126.   *Incidents in Case in LA are related*, in *Daily Alaska Empire*. October 24, 1931: Juneau, AK. 8.

127.   *Statement of BJ Mckinnel taken in chief of detectives jos. F. Taylors Office at 9:20 PM October 20, 1931 in connection of with the murder of Miss Leroy and Miss Samuelson in Phoenix Arizona. Statement taken in the presence of chief of dets.Jos F. Taylor..... Questions of Lloyd Andrews*, in *Winnie Ruth Judd Collection, Arizona State Archives*. October 20, 1931: Phoenix. Trunk Murderess Phoenix Officers File [Police Report].

128.   *Mrs. Judd Held as Model Wife: Suspect Never Used Liquor or Deope, Avers Spinster*, in *Unknown Newspaper Clipping of Lloyd Andrews*. 1931.

129.   *Testimony of Nora Smith: Opening Statements, 1-21-32*, in *State vs. Judd*. 1932: Phoenix.

130.   Davis, Carol Beery, *Northwind Rhapsody*. 1983, Juneau: Miner Publishing Company.

131.   *Winnie Judd's Letters to Mate Tell of Longing Desires*, in *Chicago American*. October 20, 1931: Chicago. 6.

132.   Judd, Winnie Ruth, *Letter from Ruth Judd to Walter Hoffmann; later forwarded to Governor Williams in 1971.* July 26, 1953: Phoenix.

133.   *Statement of Evelyn Nace,* in *Statements taken in Judd Case, 10-24-31.* 1-24-31, 1931: Phoenix. 80-101.

134.   *Wife's Letters to Doctor Hint at 'Trouble'; Notes Scanned for Clew to Murder Motive,* in *Los Angeles Evening Express.* October 20, 1931: Los Angeles. 3.

135.   *Barrymores Spending Day in Ketchikan,* in *Ketchikan Alaska Chronicle.* June 3, 1931: Ketchikan, AK.

136.   *Letters Tell of Love and Loneliness,* in *San Francisco Examiner.* October 21, 1931: San Francisco. 5.

137.   *Barrymores on Vacation,* in *Kingston Daily Freeman.* June 5, 1931: Kingston, NY. 1.

138.   Parrott, Ursula, *Ex-wife.* 1929, New York.: J. Cape & H. Smith. 4 p.

139.   *Statement of Mrs. Ernest Smith (Nora),* in *State Vs Judd: Arizona State Archives and Public Records.* October 24, 1931: Phoenix, Arizona.

140.   *Lucius Earl Dixon, WWI Draft Card, May 29, 1917.* 1917, Los Angeles.

141.   *Trunk Victims Even-Tempered,* in *Los Angeles Times.* October 27, 1931: Los Angeles. 8.

142.   *Parents Stunned by Crime,* in *Los Angeles Times.* October 21, 1931: Los Angeles. 9.

143.   *Murdered Woman Native of Oregon: Mrs. Leroi without Enemy, Says Sister, of Aurora,* in *The Morning Oregonian.* October 21, 1931: Portland. 8.

144.   *Letter Bares Girl's Quarrel,* in *Los Angeles Evening Express.* October 22, 1931: Los Angeles. 1.

145.   *Lawyers notes on Pearl Waggoner,* in *State vs. Judd.* 1932?: Phoenix. un-numbered.

146.   *Private Lives of Trunk-Murder Principals Checked: Sheriff Points to Other Drug Traffic Killings,* in *Los Angeles Times.* October 23, 1931: Los Angeles. 6.

147.   *Sammy and I both Love You, Mrs. Judd Assured,* in *Los Angeles Examiner.* October 23, 1931: Los Angeles.

148.   *Testimony of Cora Rowe,* in *State Vs Judd: Arizona State Library and Public Records.* 1932: Phoenix, AZ.

149.   *Man in Judd Case Partied and is Sorry,* in *Daily Alaska Empire.* October 31, 1931: Juneau, AK. 8.

150.   *Hedvig Samuelson with Some Friends*. 1931, Los Angeles Public Library Photo Archive: Los Angeles.
       http://jpg3.lapl.org/pics03/00021195.jpg

151.   *Californian Wins Flagstaff Race*, in *Phoenix Gazette*. 7-6, 1931: Phoenix. 7.

152.   *Statement of Mrs. Arthur Lepker before Harry Johnson*. November 3, 1931, Phoenix, County Attorney's Office: Phoenix.

153.   *Denial by rich man after admission of Rum Party Incident*, in *Los Angeles Herald*. October 22, 1931: Los Angeles. 13.

154.   Judd, Winnie Ruth, *Alone Now, Says Woman's Note*, in *Los Angeles Evening Express*. October 20, 1931: Los Angeles. 3.

155.   Bechtel, *Statement of William C Judd taken in Central Homocide Detail Los Angeles Police Departent at 12:15 AM October 20th, 1931 in connection to the Trunk Murders.*, in *Arizona State Archives*, L.A.P.D. Central Homicide Detail, Editor. 1931, Arizon: Phoenix.

156.   Judd, Winnie Ruth, *Letter to Carrie Judd*, C. Judd, Editor. August 8, 1931: Phoenix, Az.

157.   *Ruth Judd's 'Mister Cat' Adds Puzzle*, in *Arizona Republic*. October 22, 1931: Phoenix.

158.   *Letters Bare Mrs. Judd Drug Bond to Victim*, in *Los Angeles Evening Express*. October 22, 1931: Los Angeles. 4.

159.   *Strong Bond of Friendship Shown in Ruth's Letter*, in *Chicago Herald & Examiner*. October 22, 1931: Chicago.

160.   *Jealousy motive of trunk murders, say authorities.*, in *Tucson Daily Citizen*. October 21, 1931: Tucson, AZ.

161.   *Testimony of Mrs. Arthur Lepker*, in *State Vs. Judd, 1-26-32 (Morning Session)*. 1-26, 1932: Phoenix. 651-653.

162.   *Slain Girl's Letters Fail to Solve Mystery*, in *Chicago Daily Tribune*. October 21, 1931: Chicago.

163.   *Minot State Teachers College Graduate Murdered in Arizona*, in *Ward County Independent*. October 22, 1931: Minot, ND. 2.

164.   *Murder Sequel to Gay Revels*, in *Los Angeles Times*. October 21, 1931: Los Angeles. 9.

165.   *Mrs. Judd Followed Her Husband Here: Garage Employee is sure woman here in August.*, in *Bisbee Daily Review*. October 22, 1931: Bisbee. 1.

166.   *Copper Queen Hotel Registry - Bisbee Arizona*, in *State Vs. Judd*. 8-16-31, 1931: Phoenix.

167.   Judd, Winnie Ruth, *Drain Pipe Letter*, L.f.i.B.D.S. Plumbing, Editor. 10/24/1931, 1931, Arizona State Archive RG107: Los Angeles.

168. *Victim's Friend Hints at Motive: Pasadena Man Thinks Slain Pair Denied Suspect Drugs*, in *Los Angeles Evening Express*. October 23, 1931: Los Angeles. 5.

169. *Hates and Intrigues Revealed by Letter*, in *Los Angeles Examiner*. October 21, 1931: Los Angeles.

170. *Sister Bares Letters of Dead Girl*, in *Chicago American*. October 21, 1931: Chicago. 3, 18.

171. Davidson, DA and HL Barlow, *Los Angeles Police Department Report: Officers Report Regarding Homicide Investigation.*, in *Winnie Ruth Judd Collection. Arizona State Archives*. October 19, 1931: Phoenix.

172. *Mrs. Le Roi Wed Twice: Facts of Her Life Bared*, in? 1931.

173. *Agnes Leroi Twice Married, Says First Mate's Brother*, in *Los Angeles Evening Express*. October 22, 1931: Los Angeles. 3.

174. *Mrs. Judd's 'Playboy" Charge Stirs L. A. Contractor's Ire*, in *Los Angeles Evening Express*. October 27, 1931: Los Angeles. 5.

175. *Letter Received a Week Ago*, in *Minot Daily News*. 1931: Minot, ND. 2.

176. Judd, William C, *My Life with Winnie Ruth Judd - Part 2*, in *Intimate Detective Stories*. April, 1940. 14-17, 42.

177. *Statement of HJ McKeon: Statements Reported January 7th.*, in *State Vs. Judd*. 1932: Phoenix.

178. *Mrs. Judd Says Friends She Killed Loved Her Pet Cat*, in *Los Angeles Evening Express*. October 28, 1931: Los Angeles. 4.

179. *Sleuths Claim Killer had Aid*, in *Los Angeles Evening Express*. October 21, 1931: Los Angeles. 3.

180. Bethaucourt, Mary, *1930 Census Phoenix City*. 1930: Phoenix, Arizona. 8B.

181. Judd, William C, *Letter to Winnie Ruth Judd*, W.R. Judd, Editor. September 9, 1931: Santa Monica, CA.

182. *Mrs. Ruth Judd Characterized as Intelligent*, in *Unknown Newspaper Clippings of Lloyd Andrews*. 1931.

183. Blanding, Don, *Vagabond's house*. 1928, New York,: Dodd Mead & company. 114 incl. front.,.

184. *Judd Story Hit by Fresh Data*, in *Los Angeles Times*. October 29, 1931: Los Angeles. 2.

185. *Formerly Teacher in Whitehall, Montana*, in *Great Falls Tribune*. October 20, 1931: Great Falls, Montana. 1.

186. *Victim Invited to Visit Stars*, in *Los Angeles Evening Express*. October 22, 1931: Los Angeles. 3.

187. *Mrs. Judd Now Thot to be in Hiding*, in *Coshocton Tribune*. October 22, 1931: Coshocton, Ohio. 14.

188. *Heart Pangs Revealed In Mrs. Judd's Letters Telling of Loneliness*, in *San Francisco Chronicle*. October 22, 1931: San Francisco.

189. McKinnell, Burton Joy, *Western Union Telegram to Winnie Ruth Judd*, in *Arizona State Archives and Public Records*. 1931: Los Angeles.

190. *Trunk Slaying Motive Sought*, in *Arizona Daily Star*. October 21, 1931: Tucson. 9.

191. Judd, William C, *My Life with Winnie Ruth Judd - Part 5*, in *Intimate Detective Stories*. July, 1940. 16-18, 44-45.

192. *Victim's Friend Tells of Red-Wheeled Coupe*, in *San Francisco Examiner*. OCtober 30, 1931: San Francisco. 9.

193. *Crowd Awaits Tiger woman at Phoenix*, in *Los Angeles Evening Express*. October 30, 1931: Phoenix. 16.

194. *Mrs. Judd replies to attacks on her story*, in *Los Angeles TImes*. October 27, 1931: Los Angeles.

195. *Last Letter?*, in *J. Worel Misc Newspaper Clippings*. 1931.

196. *Statement of Harold Philips Bisch for John L Brinchkerhoff*, in *State vs Judd*. 1931: Phoenix. 1-2.

197. *History of Illinois and her people*. 225.

198. *Harold Phillip Bisch: WWI draft card, Sept 12, 1918*, S. City, Editor. 1918.

199. *SS Ile De France List of United States Citizens, November 27, 1929*. 1929. 109.

200. *Ruth Tells of Events Before Killings*, in *Chicago American*. November 3, 1931: Chicago. 16.

201. *Testimony of Pearl D. Wagner (Waggoner?)*, in *State Vs. Judd, 2-2-32 (All Day)*. 2-2, 1932: Phoenix. 1181-1183.

202. *Testimony of Louis Baldwin*. 1932, State Vs Judd: Arizona State Library and Public Records: Phoenix.

203. Nace, Evelyn, *Letter from Eveyln Nace to Miss Nelson of Milwaukee*. April 19, 1933.

204. *Halloran Says Mrs. Judd Gay*, in *Los Angeles Evening Express*. October 22, 1931: Los Angeles. 6.

205. Brinkerhoff, John, *Investigations and Interviews by John Brinkerhoff*. October, 1931, Arizona State Archives and Public Records: Phoenix, AZ.

206. Hinkernell, FA, *Statement of Kenneth Grimm, Given before Mr. FA Hinkernell, Special Investigator, and L. L. Billar, Court Reporter.* November 7, 1931: Phoenix.

207. *Text of Board Decision*, in *Arizona Republic.* March 31, 1933: Phoenix, Arizona.

208. *Mrs. Judd's Cat Believed Slain*, in *Los Angeles Evening Express.* October 22, 1931: Los Angeles. 5.

209. *Tragedy Cottage*, in *Unknown newspaper clippings of Lloyd Andrews.* October 31, 1931.

210. Samuelson, Hedvig, *Correspondence of Hedvig Samuelson to Anna Samuelson.* October 16, 1931, RG107, Box 2, Arizona State Archives, folder labeled Judd Correspondence.

211. *Diary of Trunk Murder Victim Shows Friendship for Suspected Slayer and Bares a Poetic, Romantic Yearning*, in *Los Angeles Evening Express.* October 22, 1931: Los Angeles. 3.

212. *? Section called, "Refers to Chum" contains last letter to parents*, in *J. Worel, Misc newspaper clippings.* 1931.

213. *Letters Reveal Doctor's Wife Storm Center*, in *San Francisco Chronicle.* October 21, 1931: San Franscisco.

214. *Stricken Parents Mourn For Girl Slain in West; Paster Tells Sad Story*, in *Minot Daily News.* October 21, 1931: Minot, ND. 10.

215. McKinnell, Burton Joy, *Brother's Story Vividly tells of Slayer's Girlhood, Wedding*, in *Los Angeles Examiner.* 1931: Los Angeles.

216. Davidson, DA, *Los Angeles Police Department, Dead Bodies Found in Trunks*, in *Winnie Ruth Judd Collection, Arizona State Archives.* 10-19, 1931: Phoenix,.

217. *Letter from Ruth Judd Shows Deep Feeling For Her Father*, in *Darlington Herald.* October 24, 1931: Darlington, Indiana.

218. *Letters Give Intimate Picture of Slain Girl*, in *Westhope Standard.* October 29, 1931: Westhope, North Dakota. 1.

219. *Girl Turnk Witness Gets Death Threat!*, in *Los Angeles Examiner.* October 23, 1931: Los Angeles, CA.

220. *All Clues In Manhunt for Suspect Fail*, in *Tucson Daily Citizen.* October 21, 1931: Tucson, AZ.

221. Judd, Winnie Ruth, *Letter to Dr. Judd: From LAPL Photo Archives.* October 17, 1931: Phoenix, AZ.

222. Miner, Mary, *Tell-Tale Eyes Described in Murders*, in *Los Angeles Herald.* October 22, 1931: Los Angeles.

223.   Greene, Bessie Humphrey, *Letter from Bessie Humphrey Greene, Astrologer to Mr. Herman Lewkowitz*. February 10, 1932: Perkins, CA.

224.   *Testimony of Gertrude Wilcox: 1-25-32, afternoon session*, in *State vs. Judd*. 1932: Phoenix.

225.   *Dr. Brinckerhoff, Grunow Clinic*, in *State vs. Judd*. 10-21, 1931: Phoenix.

226.   Brinkerhoff, Dr. D.E., *Meeting girls told by man*, in *San Francisco Call Bulletin*. October 21, 1931: San Francisco.

227.   Judd, Winnie Ruth, *Letter to WC Judd*, in *State vs. Judd*. 10-14, 1931: Phoenix.

228.   *Testimony of Mr. Gregory*, in *State Vs Judd: Arizona State Archives and Public Record*. 1932: Phoenix, AZ.

229.   *Tell About Judd Case*, in *El Paso Times*. October 25, 1931: El Paso, TX.

230.   *Murder Mystery Stories Had Thrilled Two Victims of Phoenix Trunk Slayings*, in *Minot Daily News*. October 26, 1931: Minot, ND. 3.

231.   *Statement of Miss Marshall taken by John L. Brinckerhoff*, in *State vs Judd*. 1931: Phoenix.

232.   Jennings, Renz, *Statement of Miss Maude Marshall* in *State Vs Judd 3:27*. January 7, 1933, 1933.

233.   *Miss Lucille Moore - 317 East Taylor Street*, in *State Vs Judd*. 10/21/1931, 1931, Arizona State Archives: Phoenix, Arizona.

234.   *Mystery of Dual Murder Deepens: Evidence Hints at Aid in Moving Bodies*, in *The Morning Oregonian*. October 21, 1931: Portland. 1.

235.   *Claim Ruth Tried to Poison Friend Day Preceding Murder*, in *Olney Daily Mail*. November 4, 1931: Oleney, IL.

236.   *Statement of Dr. HJ McKeown*, in *State Vs Judd: Arizona State Archives and Public Records*. October 24, 1931: Phoenix, AZ.

237.   *Statement of Dr. Brinckerhoff: Statements made in Judd Case 10-24-31*, in *State vs. Judd*. 1931: Phoenix.

238.   *Mrs. Judd Gay on Eve of Murder, Says Party Guest*, in *San Francisco News*. October 22, 1931: San Francisco. 5.

239.   *Halloran Firm in Denials*, in *Arizona Republic*. March 22, 1933: Phoenix, Arizona.

240.   *Letters Tell Life Shadows*, in *Los Angeles Times*. October 22, 1931: Los Angeles. 7.

241.   *Illegal Operation on One is Cause*, in *Great Falls Tribune*. October 23, 1931: Great Fall, MT. 1.

242. *Halloran says Mrs. Judd Gay: Declares Suspectged Slayer Bore No Ill Will to Pair*, in *Los Angeles Evening Express*. October 22, 1931: Los Angeles. 6.

243. Smith, Frank O, *Letter from Attorney Frank O Smith to the board of pardons & paroles*. March 28, 1933: Phoenix.

244. *Mrs. Judd Took Last Gay Fling at Happiness Before Pair Died*, in *Ketchikan Alaska Chronicle*. October 29, 1931: Ketchikan, AK. 1.

245. *Phoenix Officials Claim "Clear-Cut Case"*, in *Tucson Daily Citizen*. October 26, 1931: Tucson, AZ.

246. *Weather*, in *Arizona Republic*. October 16, 1931: Phoenix.

247. *Slain Samuelsen Girl Planned Return to Alaska Next Spring*, in *Arizona Republic*. October 22, 1931: Phoenix. 4.

248. McKeown, *Photocopy of Ruth's Paycheck*, in *Arizona State Archives and Public Records*. October 15, 1931: Phoenix, Arizona.

249. *Story of Williams*, in *Los Angeles Times*. October 29, 1931: Los Angeles. 2.

250. Judd, William C, *My Life with Winnie Ruth Judd - Part 4*, in *Intimate Detective Stories*. June, 1940. 12-15, 45-47.

251. *Testimony of Nora Smith*, in *Arizona State Archives, State Vs Judd*. 1932: Phoenix.

252. *Testimony of John Ralston: 1-25-32, afternoon session*, in *State vs. Judd*. 1932: Phoenix.

253. *Phoenix witnesses assert Mrs. Judd's "wounded hand" varied on day after killing*, in *Los Angeles Times*. October 24, 1931: Los Angeles.

254. *Testimony of BW Jurgemeyer: Opening Statements 1-21-32*, in *State vs. Judd*. 1-21-32, 1932: Phoenix.

255. *Woman Trunk Murder Suspect Eludes Police: Boy Says He Saw Doctor at Scene of Brutal Crime*, in *Vancouver Province*. October 20, 1931: Vancouver. 1.

256. *Police Seek in Vain for Murderess*, in *Vancouver Province*. October 21, 1931: Vancouver. 24.

257. *Testimony of Evelyn Nace: Opening Statements 1-21-32*, in *State vs. Judd*. 1-21-32, 1932: Phoenix.

258. *Open hunt for Missing Diary of Mrs. LeRoi*, in *Los Angeles Evening Herald*. October 28, 1931: Los Angeles.

259. *Last Seen Here on Friday*, in *Unknown Newspaper Clippings of Lloyd Andrews*. October 19, 1931.

260. *Testimony of Jennie McGrath: Opening Statements, 1-21-32*, in *State Vs. Judd*. 1-21, 1932: Phoenix. 46-48.

261. *Ruth Judd Charged as Slayer*, in *Unknown Newspaper Clippings of Lloyd Andrews*. 1931.

262. *Testimony of Gene Cunnigham: Opening Statements, 1-21-32*, in *State Vs. Judd*. 1-21, 1932: Phoenix. 62-64.

263. *Halloran Complaint Dismissed. New Judd Story Hinted by Lumbermans Council*, in *Arizona Republic*. January 26, 1933: Phoenix.

264. State of Arizona and State of California Department of Public Health, *Hedvig Samuelson Death Certificate*, in *Arizona Vital Records*. October 16, 1931: Phoenix. http://genealogy.az.gov

265. State of Arizona and State of California Department of Public Health, *Agnes Alexandria Leroi Smith Death Certificate*, in *Arizona Vital Records*. October 16, 1931: Phoenix, Arizona. http://genealogy.az.gov

266. *Sheriff aids Judd Appeal for Clemency*, in *Arizona Republic*. March 21, 1933: Phoenix, Arizona.

267. *Winnie Ruth Judd Denounces Halloran Across Court Table*, in *Arizona Republic*. January 19, 1933: Phoenix, Arizona.

268. Unknown author at the Arizona State Hospital, *Ruth Judd: Summary, June 25, 1947*, in *Personal Collection of Jerry Leukowitz*. June 25, 1947: Phoenix. 3.

269. *Judd Extradition Papers Approved*, in *Daily Missoulian*. October 28, 1931: Missoula, MT. 2.

270. *Ruth Judd breaks down in court describing death fight story*, in *Phoenix Gazette*. January 18, 1933: Phoenix, Arizona.

271. Birdwell, Russell J, *Secret Wooer Hinted Trunk Murder Aide*, in *San Francisco Examiner*. October 24, 1931: San Francisco. 2.

272. *New Version is Advanced: McFadden Says Mrs. Judd Wounded by Spent Bullet*, in *Unknown Newspaper Clipping of L. Andrews*. 1931.

273. Judd, Winnie Ruth, *Letter from Winnie Ruth Judd intended for Mr. Richardson of Florence Az - not mailed. Given to George W. Stephens instead*, in *Winnie Ruth Judd Papers*. October 26, 1932: Ann Arbor, MI.

274. Rochlen, AM, *Official Ends Quiz; sure killer had accomplice; car hunted*, in *Unknown newspaper clippings of Lloyd Andrews*. November 2, 1931.

275. Birdwell, Russell J, *Mysterious Auto Hunted in Phoenix*, in *Los Angeles Examiner*. October 30, 1931: Los Angeles.

276. Iserson, Kenneth V., *Death to dust : what happens to dead bodies?* 1994, Tucson, AZ: Galen Press. xx, 709 p.

277. *Heads of Slain Women Powder-Burned*, in *Phoenix Gazette*. January 23, 1932: Phoenix, AZ.
278. *Mrs. Judd Gets Safety Promise*, in *Arizona Daily Star*. October 29, 1931: Tucson. 16.
279. *Statement of Mrs. FH Reed of 2932 N 3rd taken by John Brinckerhoff*, in *State vs. Judd*. 1931: Phoenix.
280. *LeRoi Home Occupied Saturday Says Deliveryman for Dairy.*, in *Unknown newspaper clippings of Lloyd Andrews*. 1931.
281. *Testimony of Henri Behoteguy*, in *State Vs. Judd, 1-26-32 (Morning Session)*. 1-26, 1932: Phoenix. 670-671.
282. *Statement of Nora Smith: Statements Reported January 7th.*, in *State vs Judd*. 1-7, 1931: Phoenix.
283. *Statement of Dr. Henry Franklin*, in *State Vs Judd: Arizona State Archives and Public Records*. 1931: Phoenix, AZ. October 24.
284. *Statement of Fay Ayres*, in *State Vs Judd: Arizona State Archives and Public Records*. October 24, 1931: Phoenix, AZ.
285. *Statement by Mike Kerkes*, in *State Vs Judd: Arizona State Archives and Public Records*. October 24, 1931: Phoenix, Arizona.
286. *Statement by Dr LB Baldwin*, in *State Vs Judd: Arizona State Archives and Public Record*. October 24, 1931: Phoenix, AZ.
287. *Statement by Stella Kerkes*, in *State Vs Judd: Arizona State Archives and Public Records*. October 24, 1931: Phoenix, AZ.
288. *Statement made by Mrs. Percy Brown*, in *State Vs Judd: Arizona State Archives and Public Records*. October 21, 1931: Phoenix, AZ.
289. *Statement by DR. Brinkerhoff*, in *State Vs Judd: Arizona State Archives and Public Records*. October 24, 1931: Phoenix, AZ.
290. *Mattress Believed Link in Slayings is Located on Desert*, in *Unknown Newspaper Clipping of Lloyd Andrews*. Unknown, 1931.
291. *Halloran Hearing Near End*, in *Arizona Republic*. January 21, 1933: Phoenix, Arizona.
292. *Dr. Judd Fights for Wife's Life*, in *Arizona Republic*. March 23, 1933: Phoenix, Arizona.
293. *Reporters Transcript 11-9-31 A.M.: Testimony of Richard Schwartz*, in *State vs Judd*. 11-9, 1931: Phoenix.
294. *Truck Driver Tells Hauling Heavy Trunk*, in *Los Angeles Evening Herald*. October 21, 1931: Los Angeles. 13.
295. *New Clew Found on Desert Hits Judd Defense: Missing Bedding is Linked to Phoenix Death House*, in *Los Angeles Evening Express*. October 27, 1931: Los Angeles. 3.

296. *Testimony of Surgeon deals blow to possible plea of self-defense*, in *Unknown Newspaper Clippings of Lloyd Andrews*. ?, 1932.

297. *Statement in Arizona State Archives and Public Records - no title, no date*, in *Arizona State Archives and Public Records*. Phoenix, AZ.

298. *Murder Suspects' Haste to leave Phoenix Told*, in *San Francisco Examiner*. October 21, 1931: San Francisco. 4.

299. *Hoitola Call is Explained*, in *Arizona Republic*. April 16, 1933: Phoenix.

300. Birdwell, Russell J, *Wound in Hand Held Accident*, in *San Francisco Examiner*. October 25, 1931: San Francisco. 3.

301. *Statement of Mrs. HU Grimm*, in *State Vs Judd: Arizona State Archives and Public Records*. October 24, 1931: Phoenix, AZ.

302. *The State of Arizona against Winnie Ruth Judd: Statement of L. C. Bumgardner*, in *Winnie Ruth Judd Papers, Arizona State Archives*. October 26, 1931: Phoenix.

303. *Statement of Josephine Hadland* in *State Vs Judd: Arizona State Archives and Public Records*. October 24, 1931: Phoenix, AZ.

304. Smith, Langdon and Laurens Maynard, *Evolution : a fantasy*. 1915, Boston: J. W. Luce. ix, 60 p.

305. Rohmer, Sax, *The insidious Dr. Fu-Manchu : being a somewhat detailed account of the amazing adventures of Nayland Smith in his trailing of the sinister Chinaman*. 1920, New York: A.L. Burt. 383, [10] p.

306. Rohmer, Sax, *The golden scorpion*. 1920, New York,. 1 v.

307. *Statement by Ed Shimfessel*, in *State Vs Judd: Arizona State Archives and Public Records*. October 24, 1931: Phoenix, AZ.

308. *Statement By Jack Robinson*, in *State Vs Judd: Arizona State Archives and Public Records*. October 24, 1931: Phoenix, AZ.

309. Labowich, Edward, *Doctor Calls Ruth and Victims Avid Thrill Seekers*, in *Unknown Clippings of Lloyd Andrews*. October 22?, 1931.

310. *Refusal of Free Trunk Storage Told*, in *San Francisco Examiner*. October 24, 1931: San Francisco. 2.

311. *Reporters Transcript 11-9-31 A.M.: Testimony of Beverly Scallings*, in *State vs Judd*. 1932: Phoenix.

312. *Reporters Transcript 11-9-31 A.M.: Testimony of Avis Butchee*, in *State vs Judd*. 11-9, 1931: Phoenix.

313. *Mrs. Judd in Court: Justice orders Murder Trial*, in *Los Angeles TImes*. November 10, 1931: Los Angeles.

314. Judd, Winnie Ruth, *Baggage Tags*. October 18th, 1931, Arizona State Archives and Public Records: Phoenix, Arizona.

315. McKinnell, Burton Joy, *Brother, for first time, tells own story of meeting slayer*, in *Los Angeles Examiner*. October 27, 1931: Los Angeles.

316. Davidson, DA and P Stevens, *Los Angeles Police Department Officers Report Concerning Bodies Found in Trunk DR#607337*, in *Winnie Ruth Judd Papers, Arizona State Archives*. October 19, 1931: Phoenix.

317. Judd, Winnie Ruth, *Western Union Telegram of Winnie Ruth Judd to Burton McKinnell*, in *Arizona State Archives and Public Records*. October 19, 1931: Phoenix, Arizona.

318. *Testimony of Stella Conley*, in *State Vs Judd*. 1932: Phoenix.

319. *Youth denies he knew what was in trunks*, in *San Francisco Examiner*. October 21, 1931: San Francisco. 5.

320. *Reporters Transcript 11-9-31 A.M.: Testimony of Arthur Anderson*, in *State vs Judd*. November 9, 1931: Phoenix.

321. *Woman Planned to Bury Bodies, Officers Believe*, in *San Francisco Examiner*. October 22, 1931: San Francisco. 4.

322. *Suspected Slayer Said to be Rady to Give Up*, in *Unknown Newspaper Clippings of Lloyd Andrews*. October 23, 1931.

323. *Los Angeles County Coroner's Register for Anne LeRoi and Hedvig Samuelson*. October 23, 1931: Los Angeles.

324. *Close Guard Maintained at Border*, in *Los Angeles Examiner*. October 21, 1931: Los Angeles.

325. Arline, *Untitled draft for Arizona Republic? (from the collection of Patrick Millikin)*. 1946.

326. Frelinghuysen, Kinney, *Suzy Frelinghuysen*. 1997, New York: Salander-O'Reilly Galleries.

327. Matthews, T. S., *Jacks or better : a narrative*. 1st ed. 1977, New York: Harper & Row. vii, 354 p.

328. *Reporters Transcript 11-9-31 A.M.: Testimony of Frank Ryan*, in *State vs Judd*. 11-9, 1931: Phoenix. 140.

329. *Dr. Wagner, Surgeon, Los Angeles*, in *Winnie Ruth Judd Collection, Arizona State Archives*. 1931: Phoenix.

330. *Judd shots said near*, in *Los Angeles Times*. January 24, 1932: Los Angeles.

331. Wagner, AF, *Autopsy Report of Agnes Alexander LeRoi Smith (as quoted in the Coroner's inquest)*, in *Arizona State Archives and Public Records*. October 20, 1931: Phoenix, Arizona.

332. *Testimoney, John L Brinkerhoff*, in *Winnie Ruth Judd Papers, Arizona State Archives*. January 28, 1932: Phoenix. 485-489.

333. *Bodies of Two Murdered: Women Hid in Luggage*, in *Los Angeles Times*. October 20, 1931: Los Angeles. 2.

334. *Whereabouts of Mrs. Judd Now Mystery*, in *Daily Alaska Empire*. October 21, 1931: Juneau, AK. 2.

335. *Brother Identifies picture of girl in murder trunk*, in *Los Angeles Evening Herald*. 1931: Los Angeles.

336. Johnson, Burke, *He was There: Arizona Republic Presents and Exhibit of Photographs 1928-1968 by E. D. Newcomer*, in *Arizona Historical Foundation*. 1971: Phoenix. 5.

337. *W.J. Burns Reveals Theory in Murders*, in *Los Angeles Evening Herald*. October 21, 1931: Los Angeles.

338. Cook, James E, *Radio's Mental Exercises Lost Upon TV Era*, in *Arizona Republic*. April 1, 1990: Phoenix. E2.

339. *John L. Brinckerhoff: Monday January 25, 1932 Morning Session*, in *State vs. Judd*. 1-25, 1932: Phoenix.

340. Hogue, Ruthann, *D. Kelly Turner, Judge with ties to the valley*, in *Arizona Republic*. August 18, 1996: Phoenix. B6.

341. *French Dolls hold Secrets in Slayings*, in *Phoenix Gazette*. October 23, 1931: Phoenix. 1.

342. Miner, Mary, *Stunned Phoenix Gathers on Street Corners: Eye Character of 'Girl with Iron Claw'*, in *Chicago American*. October 21, 1931: Chicago. 4.

343. Foss, Sam Walter, *The House by the Side of the Road*, in *State Vs. Judd, Arizona State Archives*. Phoenix.

344. *Bare Attempt By Ruth Judd to Poison Ann*, in *Los Angeles Evening Express*. November 2, 1931: Los Angeles. 4.

345. *Arizona Drops Inquest into Trunk Killings*, in *San Francisco Examiner*. November 2, 1931: San Francisco. 10.

346. *Bodies found in Two Trunks at S. P. Station*, in *Unknown Newspaper Clippings of Lloyd Andrews*. October 20, 1931.

347. Judd, William C, *My Life with Winnie Ruth Judd - Part 3*, in *Intimate Detective Stories*. May, 1940.

348. Driscoll, Marjorie, *Suicide Fear Spurs Search*, in *San Francisco Examiner*. October 22, 1931: San Francisco. 4.

349. *Say Witness 'Knows More'*, in *Los Angeles Record*. October 26, 1931: Los Angeles. 1.

350. *Kiss Party Denial Adds More Mystery to Trunk Murder*, in *San Francisco Call Bulletin*. October 22, 1931: San Francisco. 4.

351. *Judd Killing Brands Many*, in *Los Angeles Evening Express*. October 26, 1931: Los Angeles. 6.

352.   Sellers, James Clark, *Science and advancements in the examination of questioned documents.* American Journal of Police Science, 1932. 3(2): p. 110-123.

353.   *Written Trunk Murder Confession Discovered,* in *Los Angeles Times.* October 25, 1931.

354.   *'I Will Not Aid Police, Brother's Defiant Response,* in *San Francisco Examiner.* October 24, 1931: San Francisco. 3.

355.   *New evidence points to Ruth Judd being shot in hand at own apartment,* in *Phoenix Gazette.* January 25, 1932: Phoenix, AZ.

356.   *Judd La Vina stays said to check: woman's story sustained by investigation,* in *Pasadena Star News.* October 26, 1931: Pasadena, CA.

357.   *T.B. Sufferer and Nurse Brutally Slain in Arizona by Woman Companion; Motive Remains Mystery,* in *Tioga Gazette.* October 22, 1931: Tioga, ND.

358.   Wagner, AF, *Autopsy Report regarding Hedvig Samuelson.* 10-20, 1931, Office of the County Coroner of Los Angeles: Los Angeles.

359.   *Reporters Transcript 11-9-31 A.M.: Testimony of John Brinckerhoff, County Investigator,* in *State vs Judd.* 11-9, 1931: Phoenix.

360.   *Report shows pair shot, not clubbed,* in *Los Angeles Evening Herald.* October 21, 1931: Los Angeles. 13.

361.   *Doctor Shies At Question on Wife's Sanity,* in *San Francisco Examiner.* October 21, 1931: San Francisco. 5.

362.   *Fight over Pet Cat Revealed in Phoenix Inquiry,* in *San Francisco Examiner.* October 21, 1931: San Francisco. 4.

363.   *Burns Helps in Death Quiz,* in *San Francisco Examiner.* October 20, 1931: San Francisco. 4.

364.   *Verified, flouted, Mrs. Judd's story stirs storm,* in *Los Angeles Times.* October 26, 1931: Los Angeles.

365.   *'Key' Letter of Crime Written,* in *Illustrated Daily News.* October 21, 1931: Los Angeles.

366.   *Brother Writes for "Insanity Proofs",* in *El Paso Times.* October 21, 1931: El Paso, TX.

367.   *Judd Chums Watched,* in *Los Angeles Times.* October 22, 1931: Los Angeles.

368.   *Knew Miss Samuelson,* in *Bozeman Daily Chronicle.* October 21, 1931: Bozeman, MT. 1.

369.   *Hunt Still Centers Near Los Angeles,* in *Unknown Newspaper Clippings of Lloyd Andrews.* October 23, 1931.

370. *Brother irked over missing USC Classes*, in *Los Angeles Examiner*. October 23, 1931: Los Angeles.

371. Rice, Craig, *Los Angeles murders*. 1947, New York,: Duell, Sloan. 4 1., 3-249p.

372. *Sanitarium hunt proves fruitless: wanted Phoenix woman souhgt in Altadena*, in *Pasadena Star News*. October 23, 1931: Pasadena, CA.

373. *Hedvig Samuelson, a Former Whitehall Teacher, Murdered*, in *Jefferson Valley News*. October 22, 1931: Whitehall, MT. 1.

374. *Slayer Still Free Despite Wide Dragnet*, in *Grand Forks Herald*. October 22, 1931: Grand Forks, ND. 1.

375. *Doctor Friend of Women Threatened*, in *Los Angeles Evening Herald*. October 22, 1931: Los Angeles.

376. *Crime Shocks Girl's Friend*, in *San Francisco Call Bulletin*. October 21, 1931: San Francisco.

377. *Trunk Victims' Friend is Found*, in *San Francisco News*. October 22, 1931: San Francisco.

378. *Acquantance 'Casual' writer of letter says*, in *Los Angeles Examiner*. October 23, 1931: Los Angeles.

379. Bristol, Edith, *Numerologist says trunk names told disaster*, in *San Francisco News Call*. October 22, 1931: San Francisco.

380. *Admits Phoenix Killings*, in *El Paso Times*. October 24, 1931: El Paso, TX.

381. *Shows bullet wound at dramatic surrender: extradition fight already started*, in *Pasadena Star News*. October 25, 1931: Pasadena, CA.

382. *Mrs. Judd Gives Self Up: Admits she killed pair*, in *Los Angeles Times*. October 24, 1931: Los Angeles.

383. *Hospital Record of Ruth Judd*, in *LAPL Photograph Database: Herald Examiner Collection*. 1931: Los Angeles, CA. http://jpg3.lapl.org/pics03/00021196.jpg

384. *Had to fight slayer cries*, in *Los Angeles Times*. October 24, 1931: Los Angeles.

385. *Tigress Body Covered with Bruises*, in *Unknown Newspaper Clippings of Lloyd Andrews*. Oct, 1931.

386. Judd, Winnie Ruth, *Letter of Winnie Ruth Judd written at the state hospital some 20 years after she arrived there. This may be the letter she wrote to Governor Pyle on January 25, 1953?*, in *Collection of Jerry Lewkowitz*. January 25, 1951?: Phoenix, Arizona. 1-12, 13, 21-22, incomplete.

387. *Winnie Judd fights to balk impeachment of whole testimony*, in *Arizona Republic*. Janaury 22, 1933: Phoenix, AZ.

388. *Murder Clews Hint Narcotics may be Motive*, in *Los Angeles Evening Express*. October 23, 1931: Los Angeles. 3.

389. *Admission 10 cents!*, in *San Francisco Examiner*. October 24, 1931: San Francisco.

390. *Friend Recalls Trunk Murder Victim's Beauty*, in *San Francisco News*. October 23, 1931: San Francisco.

391. Carey, James, *Letter Thrown Away by Mrs. Judd gives details of Atrocities*, in *Arizona State Democrat*. October 25, 1931: Phoenix, Arizona.

392. *Self-Defense Plea Hit*, in *Sunday Oregonian*. October 25, 1931: Portland. 2.

393. *In City of Dual Killing*, in *Unknown newspaper clippings of Lloyd Andrews*. October 25, 1931.

394. *Return Bodies of Victims to City of Death: Remains of two Murdered Women Sent From Los Angeles*, in *Unknown Newspaper Clippings of Lloyd Andrews*. 1931.

395. *Reporters Transcript 11-9-31 A.M.: Testimony of Dr. Mauldin, County Physician, Maricopa County*, in *State vs Judd*. 11-9, 1931: Phoenix.

396. *Reporters Transcript 11-9-31 A.M.: Testimony of Dr. Victor Randolph*, in *State vs Judd*. 11-9, 1931: Phoenix.

397. McKinnell, HJ, *Letter from HJ Mckinnell to Burton McKinnell*. October 27, 1931: Darlington, IN.

398. *Dual Slaying was Planned says Andrews*, in *Unknown newspaper clippings of Lloyd Andrews*. October 25, 1931.

399. Henry, Bill, *By the Way with Bill Henry*, in *Los Angeles TImes* December 14, 1939: Los Angeles.

400. *Ruth Judd's Parents in Statements to Their Daughter and the Public*, in *Darlington Herald*. October 24, 1931: Darlington, IN.

401. *Quarrel is Blamed for Double Slaying*, in *Darlington Herald*. October 24, 1931: Darlington, IN.

402. *Slayer Surrenders to Police; Confesses Killing of 2 Girls: Hedvig Samuelson Funeral Will be Held in Minneapolis*, in *Tioga Gazette*. October 29, 1931: Tioga, ND. 1.

403. *Guard Writes Poem on Trunk Murder Tragedy*, in *Phoenix Gazette*. October 29, 1931: Phoenix.

404. *1500 Pay Fee at Death Scene*, in *Los Angeles Evening Express*. October 26, 1931: Los Angeles. 1.

405. Carey, James, *Newspaper Men Fight for Mrs. Judd's Story*, in *Arizona State Democrat*. October 27, 1931. 1.

406. Carey, James, *Slayer Suspect Ready to Leave for Phoenix Wednesday with Party*, in *Arizona State Democrat*. October 27, 1931. 1.

407. *Wealthy Man Provides $20000 for Defense*, in *El Paso Times*. October 27, 1931: El Paso, TX.

408. *Insanity Defense Planned; $20,000 Fund Arrives*, in *Unknown Newspaper Clippings of Lloyd Andrews*. October 26, 1931.

409. *Defense Attorneys Row at Arraignment; 2 Quit*, in *Unknown newspaper clippings of Lloyd Andrews*. October 27?, 1931.

410. *Extradition of Mrs. Judd is Approved*, in *Tucson Daily Citizen*. October 27, 1931: Tucson, AZ.

411. *Personals*, in *Daily News Miner*. October 26, 1931: Fairbanks, AK.

412. *Court Ordeal Tires Mrs. Judd*, in *Los Angeles Times*. October 27, 1931: Los Angeles. 8.

413. Carey, James, *New Legal Battle Begins as Sheriff Gets Papers To Extradite Suspect*, in *Arizona State Democrat*. October 27, 1931. ?

414. Birdwell, Russell J, *Sinister Threat Puts New Aspect on Case*, in *San Francisco Examiner*. October 28, 1931: San Francisco. 9.

415. *Darling, Ind. to Aid M'Kinnells*, in *Olney Daily Mail*. October 27, 1931: Olney, IL.

416. *Narcotic Illness 'Excuses' Blasted By Coast Doctor*, in *Unknown Newspaper Clippings of Lloyd Andrews*. October 28, 1931.

417. *'El Pasoan's' Story Doubted: 'Local Chemist' who injected self in Judd Case is Evasive*, in *El Paso TImes*. October 29, 1931: El Paso, TX.

418. *Strange Dope Theory in Killings*, in *Los Angeles Evening Herald*. October 28, 1931: Los Angeles.

419. *Checks record*, in *Los Angeles Times*. October 29, 1931: Los Angeles. 2.

420. *Narcotic, Illness 'Excuses' blasted by coast doctor*, in *Unknown newspaper clippings of Lloyd Andrews*. October 28, 1931.

421. Judd, Ruth, *Ruth Judd's Life Story in her Own Words*, in *Los Angeles Examiner*. October 28, 1931: Los Angeles.

422. *New Lawyer hired for Prisoner*, in *Los Angeles Examiner*. 1931: Los Angeles.

423. *Killer's Spouse wins delay on license hearing*, in *San Francisco Examiner*. October 30, 1931: San Francisco. 9.

424. *Men's Neckties Found in House*, in *Los Angeles Evening Express*. October 29, 1931: Los Angeles. 3.

425. *Return Trip to be made by Airplane says Sheriff*, in *Phoenix Gazette*. October 29, 1931: Phoenix.

426. *'Threat Letters' in Slayings Found to Be Radio Notes: Mysterious Writing in Samuelson Girl's Home Revealed Copied from Ether Waves*, in *Los Angeles Evening Express*. October 27, 1931: Los Angeles. 6.

427. *Making Joke Out of Murder Gets Reporters in Trouble*, in *Arizona Daily Star*. October 30, 1931: Tuscon. 1.

428. *Admit Faking Woman's Diary*, in *Los Angeles Evening Express*. October 30, 1931: Los Angeles. 8.

429. Bishop, W. M, *Slain LeRoi Girl's Diary to Expose Playboys*, in *Los Angeles Evening Express*. October 29, 1931: Los Angeles. 1.

430. *Rivalry of Trio Shown in Diary: 'Little Book' Kept by Agnes Leroi is Found.*, in *Los Angeles Evening Express*. October 29, 1931: Los Angeles. 3.

431. *Ruth Judd Starts Car Trip Back to Phoenix for Trial on Trunk Slaying Charges*, in *San Franscisco Examiner*. October 30, 1931: San Francisco. 1.

432. Bynum, Lindley, Eugene W. Biscailuz, and Idwal Jones, *Biscailuz, sheriff of the new West*. 1950, New York,: Morrow. 208 p.

433. *State ex rel. Andrews, County Attorney, Et al. V. Superior Court of Maricopa County et al.*, in *Pacific Reporter, .* 1931, Supreme Court of Arizona. 192.

434. *Winnie Ruth Judd is kept in virtual isolation over Sunday*, in *Unknown newspaper clippings of Lloyd Andrews*. November 2?, 1931.

435. *Victims alone as slayer in limelight*, in *Los Angeles Evening Express*. October 31, 1931: Los Angeles. 6.

436. *Ruth Judd Story is Challenged by Halloran Counsel*, in *Arizona Republic*. January 20, 1933: Phoenix, Arizona.

437. Randolph, Victor MD, *Letter from Victor Randolph to Samuel Samuelson*. November 7, 1931.

438. *Two Trunk Victims' bodies sent home*, in *Los Angeles Evening Express*. November 7, 1931: Los Angeles. 4.

439. *Trunk Murder Victim Buried In Mill City*, in *Williston Herald*. November 12, 1931: Williston, ND.

440. *Mrs. LeRoi's Body Will Be Sent North*, in *Arizona Republic*. November 9, 1931: Phoenix.

441. *Accompanied by Sheriff He Visits Scene of Alleged Murders*, in *Unknown Newspaper Clippings of Lloyd Andrews*. November 9, 1931.

442. *Notes of John L Brinckerhoff*, in *State vs. Judd*. November 13, 1931: Phoenix. 1.

443. *Offers Trunk Killer $1000 for Song*, in *Los Angeles Evening Express*. November 17, 1931: Los Angeles. A5.

444. *Testimony of Edward Huntington Williams*, in *Arizona State Archives State vs Judd*. 1932: Phoenix.

445. *Dr. Judd Granted Delay in Trial*, in *San Antonio Light*. November 28, 1931: San Antonio. 1.

446. *M'Kinnell Tells of Arizona*, in *Darlington Herald*. December 19, 1931: Darlington, IN.

447. *Testimony of Dr. George Stephens*, in *State Vs Judd: Arizona State Archives and Public Records*. 1932: Phoenix, AZ.

Section 4

1932-1939

1932, January 7

Dr. Catton is allowed to visit Ruth Judd for the second time. Ruth Judd's attorney Mr. Lewkowitz took Dr. Bower and him to the jail. Ruth was informed through the wicket in the jail door that some doctors had come to see her and she immediately yelled in a loud voice, "I don't want any doctors, I won't talk to any of them, this is terrible." Lewkowitz stepped forward and told Ruth Judd that she should cut out her talking and that she was to be examined. She would allow Mr. Lewkowitz to say but a word or two and then became exited, gesticulated and yelled, "I don't want to be examined, I won't be examined; they are just treating me terrible. I will talk to no doctors. This Dr. Catton went right from his examination to a cheap pool hall and told all of those terrible people in the pool hall there that I didn't have any baby and he knows I have a baby and I will not have these pool hall bums coming up here and making fun of me. I am the laughing stock of everybody with this doctor going to these cheap pool halls." Dr. Catton stepped up to the wicket and talked quietly to Ruth and told her that he did not visit pool halls and that he had not gone to any pool hall following his examination of her and that he had discussed her case with nobody and that he had written up a report of her examination and furnished it to the District Attorney and nobody else. She stated, "Yes, I knew it was the District Attorney that did that." Dr. Catton said, "Now, as a matter of fact, the District Attorney would do no such thing and you must know that that is the case." She said, "I know that fellow Andrews, I know him, and I know all about him and he went to those pool halls and talked about me." Dr. Catton stated that he did not think Andrews had read his report yet. Ruth stated that he did not know that man Andrews. Lewkowitz talked with Ruth Judd and calmed her down a bit and he instructed her to allow herself to be examined by both of the doctors. He introduced Dr.

1

Bowers. After 10 minutes elapsed, they were informed that Ruth Judd had insisted on completing her morning bath and getting dressed, during which time she said, "I know doctors; they always keep people waiting so now they can wait for me." The jail matron stated that she and the occupants of Ruth Judd's cell room had cooperated and calmed her down. When she came out she said that she didn't want to talk. She did not want to be examined. She also said, "They are not going to do any spinal puncture on me; I am not going to have any needles put in me; they are not going to hurt me." Dr. Catton said he was going to do none of these things. Ruth desired her husband there with her and her attorney and stated that she had some doubt as to whether Mr. Lewkowitz had in fact told her to be examined. After more assurance she went voluntarily to the Identification Room and examinations proceeded. These are some things she said: She said she had proof that Jack Halloran was having relations with other women. She said that he had relations with many other women. When asked specifically whether the conversation in question if she had proof that showed that he had relations or other such contacts with either one of the girls who had been killed, she said, "I don't think that he ever had relations with either one of them." Here is another excerpt, "I asked her why she wrote the article for the paper and she informed me that she had not written it. I told her that she had previously told me that she had written the article, but that in some places she had been misquoted and she said, 'I did not write that article.' I asked her if it were true that she had received about $5000.00 for writing that article and she answered 'Yes'. I asked her if she had any other source of finances to help her in her trial and she closed her lips tightly and appeared to be thinking deeply and turned away and said, 'I will not answer that.' I asked her specifically if Jack Halloran or any other person was putting up money and she said she would not answer that. She did not report writing any newspaper articles except those in the Los Angeles Examiner. And, 'concerning babies', Mrs. Judd now makes the definite and frank statement without any reservation that she had a baby boy two years of age, of whom Dr. Judd is the father and which baby is now in Mexico and which baby looks more like Dr. Judd of the Mayo's than does it resemble her husband Dr. Judd." An interesting statement he made is, "There seems to be a central role in all of this behavior, namely, that her actions are all self-serving." Regarding hallucinations, he reported that on one occasion there were a lot of men out on the roof of the jail scratching and making noises and trying to annoy her and

2

that sometimes they called her name. Asked if she knew now whether there were such individuals on the roof, she stated that the other girls in the cell heard them too. He stated that he made no examination of her abdomen without clothing, nor of the genitals or rectum. He did not observe striate that may be related to having a child. She stated that she thought it was possible to love two men. When asked if she was polyandrous she got angry and stated that "there was nothing between those girls and me." She was told that this did not apply to homosexual relations. In talking about wanting children she told them repeatedly she had received Dr. Judd's seminal fluid on her hand and had placed it in her parts, but that she had not been successful. Dr. Catton stated that Dr. Judd did not want to have a baby and always withdrew before the culmination of the act. In her intimacies with Jack Halloran, the act was always complete without any contraceptive methods. She stated that neither Anne nor Sammy stepped out. Later she stated that Sammy never stepped out, but that Anne had some days in Los Angeles with one Mr. Dixon. There was a copy of a stenographic report of questions and answers involving statements made by various persons at the Grunow Clinic, but it is not at the Arizona State Archives as far as I could tell [1] Dr. Bowers gave testimony to this as well.[2] He stated she was slim and undernourished. The skin of the neck and face were pale and there were some discolorations about the fingers of her left hand and forefinger and thumb and there was some diminution in the size of the web between the forefinger and thumb of the hand. He said she made statements about people on the roof. She said, "They are scratching around up there. I hear them calling my name. They talk about me in the pool rooms because Dr. Catton went to those places and told them about me. I am very angry about that."[2] She stated that Halloran was true to her, but he was in no position to come to the jail to help her. She stated that she had sexual relations with her husband when he was well and had orgasms. She wished she had become pregnant. She stated that she was wild about children. She was anxious to have a baby by Mr. Halloran. She had had sexual relations with him for a number of months and that sexual relations with him were satisfactory. She wanted to become pregnant. She said she loved her husband in a maternalistic way since he had been sick. She said she felt different about Halloran, a romantic feeling rather than a feeling a mother might have for her child or for her husband. She was sorry for her husband to know about her sexual relations because this information might hurt him, and she was sorry for that. She remarked that she wished her

3

husband was there, and asked if he were out of town. She stated she had a baby and that her baby was about two years old, that it was taken away from her by her mother when it was four months old and that her mother chased all her pets away and her cats and her dogs. When asked where the baby was now she was evasive for a long time and then said, "Why talk about that?" She said that Dr. Judd was the father of the baby. She stated that she thought she was going to have a baby by Mr. Halloran, but she missed her period so many times and it was so irregular she could not tell if she was pregnant or not. She thought that she was pregnant for a while since she was in jail, but then admitted she was not. She said she wished she were pregnant. She said she would like to have a baby. When asked what kind of defense she was going to give, she replied that it would depend on what kind of break she could get. She stated that she might tell everything. She would have to wait and see. She said Halloran would be arrested if he came to see her. She said she was not jealous and that he may have loved other people too. She said he may have loved other girls but that he gave himself mostly to her. Of adultery she stated she didn't care to talk about it and if one were really in love with a person, that adultery was not so wrong as it might seem.[2] Of homosexuality of Anne and Sammy she said, "Sammy and Anne may have had those kind of relations. They seemed to have loved one another more than usual, but I won't say they did have, I won't talk about them like that. I could not quite understand them. I can tell you this, that I have never had any experiences like that. Why talk about that?"[2] He concluded that there was no clouding of her consciousness. Her conversation was coherent and relevant to the point, when she desired it to be so. There was no motor impairment of speech. She had no real hallucinations or delusions. He said that she was pretending to have auditory hallucinations. She was evasive in her answers and molded her remarks to suit the circumstances. There was no evidence of any impairment of her perceptions. Her memory so far as he could discern was good for remote and recent events. Her general fund of information seemed to be in harmony with her educational advents and experiences. She was alert and keen to notice what affect her answers had upon the examiner. He stated she was not insane when he examined her. No history or evidence was given to indicate that she was insane at the time of the commission of the criminal act with which she is being charged. She is laboring under great strain but bearing up very well under a most trying and difficult situation. He said that she was underweight and had tuberculosis.

There was no evidence of any organic disease of the brain or spinal cord or their coverings. He stated she knows the nature and quality of her acts and the difference between right and wrong generally and with regard to special acts also.[2]

1932, Judd Trial Period

Dr. Catton relates this story regarding the trial later in his book in his chapter that is called, "Psychiatrists, too, are human". The psychiatrist is human, and one of his attributes is to be either male or female. As I walked from the courthouse to the Westward Ho Hotel one day during the Ruth Judd trial, I met a young and attractive woman. She looked at me and smiled. I tipped my hat, and as she stopped I said, "I don't know you, do I?" Her answer was "Not yet". I continued on my way. That evening at about ten-thirty I was returning from a motion picture show and I came upon the same woman as she was leaving the hotel. She smiled, bowed, acted as though each of us should stop. I doffed my hat stiffly, said nothing, and went on. In the hotel lobby I was accosted by two Los Angeles policemen who were witnesses in the case. One said, "Come over here, doc. We want to talk with you. We were up in our room, and we couldn't help overhear some loud talking in the room next to us. There were two middle-aged people there-a man and a woman-and suddenly we heard them giving hell to some younger woman. Her name was Madge. It seems she was supposed to contact you this afternoon after court and use every means to get you out of town. She didn't do her job and now somebody is not going to pay these people five hundred dollars. Well, the play now is that she's to get into your room tonight. No harm, mind you, but you'll be discovered, and they'll give you the choice of going home or facing some nice newspaper publicity." We arranged for a change of quarters. The hotel management was informed of the transaction and notified the three parties to leave the hotel. They did [3] Dr. Judd calls Jack Halloran during the trial. Jack suggested that he meet him in his office. Dr. Judd changes his mind since detectives might be following him and the visit might be misunderstood. [4]

1932, January 14

J Clark Sellers wrote a letter to Lloyd Andrews regarding the Drain Pipe Letter. He stated that he looked at Ruth's ability to concentrate over a period of time, failure to let down near the end of a long sentence, her sequence of ideas, her memory, her grammatical construction, her punctuation, spelling, alignment of writing, her clarity of conception, her maturity in her writing, her reaction of the crime, and her nerve, muscular, and brain coordination in the line quality. He stated, "I think there is so much in the physical and mental makeup of these letters which clearly shows the vigor and cunningness of her mind, that such evidence of sanity far outweighs her occasional statement that at times she thinks she is crazy. In other words, the indications of her mental, physical, and nervous makeup, as shown in what she does, show more truly what her mental ability is than does her conscious attempts in proclaiming she is crazy." He thought the pages in the letter to Dr. Judd were not numbered in their proper sequence. He stated that writing is a reflex of mental and psychical reactions, and is usually so unconscious to the writer that he does not realize the telltale evidence contained therein. He said, "I am taking the liberty of writing you these things, not knowing whether you have exhausted this angle of the investigationn or not. I consider it is a part of my business to make any suggestions my experience and judgement indicate should be made." He created the large photographs of the letters found at the Arizona State Archives. He stated that there can be no reasonable doubt that Ruth wrote both of the torn letters.[5] Dr. Leff makes his statement to FA Hickernell. In part he says, "In my observations of Mrs. Judd I always have thought of her as being a perfectly normal self-effacing woman. She was a woman who was unusually devoted to her husband and would do almost anything to help any of her friends who were in trouble. I cannot believe that she committed the crime and would like nothing better than to help her if I could but I have not seen any way to do this."[6]

1932, January 20
JA Gillie of the Crime Study Bureau of Zayante, CA writes a letter to Herman Lewkowitz in Phoenix encouraging him to exhume the body of Agnes LeRoi. He suggested that they should have an examination by a competent phrenologist and then compare it to Ruth Judd. He (She) stated that he should convince the judge and jury that Agnes was the "Tigress" and "Killer" and Ruth the victim of unfortunate circumstances. He continued, "Ruth Judd is not insane, but she is the unfortunate victim of abnormal FEAR AND TERROR under such circumstances as being threatened with death and that fear and terror would give her the superhuman ability to make a desperate fight and kill to save her life. The same terror would enable her to do the other unbelievable things in

connection with this sad affair."[7]

1932, January 22

Much of the forensic and physical evidence is presented at the trial. Dr. Wagner and Mr. Moxley testify. The trunk was brought in. It was locked but had the blood stained piece of rug inside as well as the bedding. When they showed the bullets from the trunk, Ruth flinched and then rocked more vigorously. Ruth seemed to concentrate on the crowds in the courroomm once things settled down. The morbidly curious seem to interest her equally as much as she seems to interest them. She glanced about. She seemed to miss no one. She did not allow her eyes to rest on the group of men who were behind her. These were reporters. She glanced over and beyond them when she studied her audience to the rear of the courtroom. She seemed to be focusing on people who were trickling through the courtroom's doorways. At one point she pulled at her right shoulder as to fix a slipped shoulder strap or a wrinkled collar. Her leg never stopped swinging back and forth. She does not react to the trial; she just watches the door. A statement was made that Ruth said that she wanted to tell her story of the dual killings and the subsequent butchering of one victim.[8] Indications that Jack Halloran may not be called as a witness in the trial, appeared today. Halloran was named by Mrs. Judd as the big brother to herself and the two friends she killed. He was told by Andrews to hold himself in readiness to take the stand. He was a member of the crowd of prosecution witnesses but his name was not called and he failed to raise his right hand and take the oath. They said this was an oversight. Andrews made it known that Halloran had voluntarily offered his service to Arizona in any way that might be desired. Andrews said that he didn't know that he would find it necessary to use Halloran's testimony to bolster his case of circumstantial evidence against Mrs. Judd. "Halloran came to me several days ago and voluntarily offered to aid in solving the case. Only the trend of the case will decide Halloran's appearance on the stand. He will be used then if needed."[9]

1932, January 23

AR Gatter of the San Francisco Tourist Bureau writes to George W. Stephens and states, "Dear 'Old Doc', You and Jack are sort of getting into the Amies Class when it comes to publicity. The attached is from last night's Evening News and from your attitude, I could almost imagine you were sort of propositioning Ruth; that is if I didn't know you better. I do hope Jack doesn't get any further in the mud than he is."[10] Halloran attended the trial every day and expected to be called. He was never called because it was thought that his testimony was not material. Frank O Smith stated that he personally went to Lloyd Andrews and asked him if Halloran could go before the Grand Jury. Lloyd Andrews said no.[11]

1932, January 24
Dr. Clifford Wright talks and examines Ruth Judd in the jail for 3.5 hours on this Sunday in preparation for his testimony for February 2. His driver helped take measurements of her. He was not able to do metabolism tests which he wished to do. He told her that she believed her mother had her baby. He stated that the measurements of a woman should be equal from a certain bone to the floor as to the top of her head. Ruth was much longer on the bottom half being 35.5 and the upper half 29.5. He said she had a long narrow hand which was cold, mottled and sweaty which indicated an ovarian disturbance. She had little or no breast development. She is more or less juvenile in her reactions. Her whole condition is that of eunuchoidism or under activity of the ovaries. He stated that her physical condition was very poor at this time, with her weight being only 105. He stated that she should weigh 137 or 138. He stated that she talked in random. She was subject to rambling. He had trouble keeping her on any given subject. He talked about her delusions about Dr. Catton going down to the pool halls and talking about her. He also said that she thought people were laughing at her at the clinic. She stated many people came to the jail to tell her this. She stated that Lloyd Andrews and Jack Halloran play golf together and they put up a job to have her blamed. She stated that Jack Halloran would kill her on the street if he could. She seemed to think that there is a man on the roof of the jail. They come over nearly every night and call her by name. Sometimes they had a flashlight. At first she thought that they were friends, but now, she thought they were there to kill her. Dr. Wright went out of the cell and talked to a jailer and he stated that this could not be possible. He stated that she acted on these delusions. She turned the bed to the opposite direction and hung up clothes to protect her from the view of the men that were on the roof. She also stated that the people over at the Ford Hotel across from the jail have told Mr. McFadden that they see men on the roof. She feels that the people in the jail are against her

and want to see her hanged. She told him some story about having a fight with someone and felt very strongly of throwing boiling hot water in the face of somebody that was bothering her. She refused some ham brought in by the night sheriff and offered it to some of the girls. She then said it was probably all right since none of the girls got sick. She squatted down in her chair once because she was afraid that they were going to shoot her through the court window. She stated that McFadden wants to shoot her. She didn't have a reaction to the most gruesome testimony in court he later observed. He stated she yawned when they were showing the cut out piece of rug. She twisted her handkerchief and tossed her head from side to side. He stated that he couldn't imagine anybody sitting quietly and calmly in the rest room of the Broadway Department store and writing the Drain Pipe Letter. He stated that she told him that she had no feeling whatever about the two girls who were killed. She said that she was sorry that they were sick and now she had no feeling about them at all. She walked up to the trunk at the station and recognized it and saw the policemen around it. She said that she had no feeling about it. These were the reasons that he felt she was insane.[12]

1932, February 1
Ruth claimed to be too ill to appear in court at 8:30. She refused to get out of bed. The sheriff promised she would be taken into court in a wheel chair wearing handcuffs if she didn't walk there without further argument. She obeyed immediately. Dr. Judd and Dr. Stephens testify on this day.[13]

1932, February 5
Dr. Catton received a threat during a court holiday. He received a note stating, Dr. Joe Catton – Beware. The threat came at midnight. The authorities thought that it was a hoax [14]

1932, February 6
Dr. Catton insists that Dr. Judd be searched before entering the courtroom since he had received a threat at midnight the night before and had fear of his life. Sheriff McFadden found no weapons on Dr. Judd. He was denied a request for two guards by Sheriff McFadden. After his testimony, he left the courtroom and sought seclusion.[14] Dr. Catton is on the stand. Here is what he says about it in his book. "Then came early February, 1932, and I was on the witness stand in the Winnie Ruth Judd case. There was a lull in the proceedings. I was

studying the jurors, the twelve men who were to hear my medical story of the defendant. They were God-fearing men, men of the earth; many had had no schooling; some had seldom, or never, visited large cities, or attended the theater. These were the persons to whom I must relate a psychological analysis in which I believed, and unless I made them believe it with me, my opinion had not a shred of worth. One of the medical witnesses who was appearing for Mrs. Judd and testifying that she was insane must have had a job even more difficult than mine. He was addressing a group of men, a typical jury, concerning whom he had already written in a published work: 'The pitiful inefficiency of the jury trial becomes obvious. When it is a question of determining officially whether or not a man is afflicted with insanity, the decision is placed at the discretion of utter ignoramuses.' I have never thought of juries as ignoramuses. I have thought of them as an average sampling of the society in which they live, I have believed them to share with that society similar thought feeling behavior patterns, and, therefore, to be the "court" which should determine what that society wants to do with the defendant at the bar. Statements of the law by the court, facts by fact witnesses, and opinions by expert witnesses are placed before them. They reach a decision. Often the medical witness does not approve of the jury's judgment; even the public whom the jury represents may be displeased with the verdict. The jury, however, has heard all the evidence, and the public has been less well informed. With all the criticism that may be leveled at the jury system, or any other human institution, it is my opinion that we have no substitute to offer at the present moment which would do any better job. Even psychiatrists are subject to the same human frailties which, in the last analysis, become the only remaining arguments against juries. Well, there was the Judd jury, and I awaited the first question of counsel. I was not like the drowning man whose life is supposed to parade before his mind in the moments preceding death. Nor had I smoked some marijuana and passed into a one hour's dream that lasted a hundred years. But my mind traveled fast. I thought, "This is my first case for the state of Arizona. I would like to be called again I want the judge and the district attorney to like me and my work. Ruth Judd's counsel is a noted criminal lawyer. Often an attorney whom I oppose today seeks my advice tomorrow. The courtroom is jammed...yes, it titillates the vanity of a witness when his point goes home and the audience is moved to break the decorum of the courtroom. Ruth Judd is guilty...she is sane... but she is attractive... she is a woman; she has

10

had bad breaks, and tuberculosis, and ...One of my best friends, a physician, tells me to use good English, no slang... my profession wants dignity in the medical man on the stand... But I made my decision. "To hell with all these considerations. I have only one job here. I have formed an opinion about the mental condition of Ruth Judd, and I must testify in such a manner as shall move the jury to accept my opinion." And so with no prescription except that I state a scientific opinion, honestly arrive at, in words the jury would understand, and in a manner which would move them towards its acceptance, I proceeded. This has been my policy since. If behaving in accordance with this attitude is advocacy, then I plead guilty to such."[3]

1932, February 8
Ruth is declared guilty and sentenced to hang. On the way to the death cell Mr. Leukowitz told her to say nothing. A Mr. AB England, political financier who backed many Arizona politicians in their campaigns, took a stenographer and went along with the sheriff. He pictured the gallows to her and told her that the Sheriff knew Halloran and was guilty of this and that and if I didn't tell them she would be hung. [15] Then he said, "I'm campaign manager for K Jerry Peterson. If you will only give me certain statements, things I didn't know because I had gone through such a terrific battle and scarce nothing registered. My mind was paralyzed or blocked; there are things I did not know which happened after the tragedy." [15] He stated that he could wrap K. Berry around his little finger and would get her freedom.[15]

1932, February 10
Astrologer Bessie Humphrey Greene writes her first letter to Herman Leukowitz and Paul Schenk in Phoenix regarding her reading of Winnie Ruth Judd. She states, "It is the more difficult for me to approach you on this subject in as much as I realize fully that you probably have no knowledge of the accuracy of astrological work and that you quite likely regard it as fraudulent. I am not asking you to believe. I am only asking you for the sake of your client to give serious consideration to what I shall tell you." ... "Since the verdict I have gone more thoroughly into the mathematical calculations in her chart and I find that you did need it. I only hope I am not too late to help you and that you will accept my advice in the spirit in which it is offered. Due to the fact that I am making a study of the horoscopes of legal offenders with the hope of locating through statistical records the

positions which threaten the individual with this kind of trouble, I made an intensive study of the chart of Mrs. Judd. In these cases, the most difficult part of the work is to obtain an authentic birth record and in her case I was able to do this. It has been a most interesting and informative chart, for it clearly indicates that all of this might have been prevented had she been given the necessary warning. It further indicates that, although she has withheld circumstances connecting with events which preceded the tragedy, she is capable of action of its kind in an effort to shield others. Her chart substantiates every claim made by the defense. It leaves no doubt of her emotional and mental instability. It indicates that she is unquestionably subject to periods of insanity of a hereditary nature. That this may really become permanent insanity, is further indicated by the chart. It reveals the fact that during the year which preceded the tragedy her mentality was under a strain which seriously undermined it and that during the two months which preceded the tragedy she was subject to a fear of an unknown quantity which was well calculated to drive her literally insane. It shows that on October 11, 1931 she came under a most terrifying combination of planetary influences which not only attacked her from within herself but in the external world as well, exposing her to the danger of sudden death or calamity and that during that week she was not at any time responsible for what she did. On October 16 events precipitated themselves over which she had at that time no manner of control and which she did not foresee or anticipate. She was caught in their maelstrom as a man may be caught in a cyclone. And her chart indicates that under circumstances of that kind her wits and judgement forsake her completely so that she would be totally irresponsible and erratic."[16] "She reminds me of a little untrained child placed at the wheel of a powerful automobile and set going at a fast pace down a crowded highway. The chart indicates that she is mentally and emotionally incapable of premeditating, planning and carrying through any such an event. She is much too fearful and too sympathetic, at heart very kindly; and she does not plan things; she acts under impulse and without due forethought and consideration."[16] "If astrology were at the present time the recognized science which it will be in the future I would have volunteered my services to the defense in this particular case despite my dislike of notoriety. I could have proven all the claims of the defense astrologically. Her horoscope at no time and in no manner has held out hope of complete acquittal. But due to the fact that powerful beneficent influences are still operating throughout the maximum of threatening positions, I confidently expect either life imprisonment or commitment for insanity. I was stunned with the verdict." "There is no fate except that which lies within. It is the individual's response to conditions which he meets which determines his fate, although events over which one has no control do present themselves."[16] She concludes by saying, "My position in the matter is purely scientific and is based upon a desire to be of service in a matter which I regard as one of mercy as well as justice."[16]

1932, February 12-15
The winter Olympics are in Lake Placid, New York. Tom Frelinghuysen attends the games and is very impressed by the ski jumpers. "He himself had never been on skies in his life. He thought and brooded, and at last made up his mind that he would try the Olympic ski jump when no one was around. That night a night of brilliant moon, he got a pair of skis, went to the silent, deserted ski jump, climbed it, fastened his skis, and started down the precipitous run. As he got to the takeoff he tried to lean forward as he had seen the champion ski jumpers do. Though he might have been killed he landed in more or less good order, he fell and slid for some distance and was badly bruised, but broke no bones. He never made a ski jump again."[17]

1932, Late February
Ruth claims that she is in the dark in her death cell for two weeks due to a charge in the lighting system. She claimed the only light came down from the gallows. She claimed the prison doctor himself was insane and later committed suicide in a private mental institution. He tortured her with gruesome stories, told her how Eva Dugan had been beheaded there and her head flew 20 feet in the air. She claimed if she didn't tell him about Halloran whom he knew was guilty and that Ruth was protecting him, he would climb the 13 steps and throw a lever and make a horrible clanking noise. Ruth stated she'd cry and cry and pray to God to help her clear up some things that either she could not remember or that she did not know. She claimed, "There is a curtain. I remember some things vaguely but many other things before my God, I do not know. This I know, that I am no criminal."[15]

1932, March 3
Bessie Humphrey Greene writes a follow-up letter to Herman Lewkowitz regarding the astrological reading of Winnie Ruth Judd.

She stated that this was taking her longer than expected. She stated the average number of minor directions in charts for 12 months is 35. She stated in the case of Ruth that there were 75 for three months which make it over 300 for a whole year. She stated it was hard to not say more than he could use because of this. She stated, "The influence upon the earth of the various planets is one of vibration and energy and that we may use this energy much in the same way a sailor uses the winds to sail a boat, perhaps you will find it easier to understand me. 'One ship sails east and the other west by the selfsame winds that Blow.' You never can go against the planetary indications. But you can co-operate with them, take advantage of them, follow a non-resistant and inactive course when they are against you and wait for the wind to turn your way. I believe that in the solution and prevention of crime astrology will, when it is recognized, be a very material aid. And that it will go a long way toward apprehending and curtailing the activities of the professional criminal and toward discipline and training the emotional unfortunate who does not belong in the criminal class and who could be salvaged and made a useful citizen."[18] "In reference to a direction in Mrs. Judd's chart which is delineated on page 9 paragraph 5 and page 10 paragraph 1 and 2 the parallel of Uranus to Jupiter which became effective on February 23, I would say that this influence might indicate only the interest of an astrologer if left to work itself out unaided. But that it is again possible that you could take advantage of it to use it further than this."[18] She goes on for another page indicating her credentials and offering her services to them freely and gladly. "I wonder if you realize that a great many highly intelligent and influential people today are interested in the science of astrology; that many of them are guided entirely by it; that such persons will accept the evidence of the stars in preference to any circumstantial evidence possible to produce in a court of law. There may be such a person on your pardon board or high up in politics or the government of the State of Arizona. If you could find such a one perhaps I could help very materially to win for Mrs. Judd a powerful friend. I am sure that I could convince anyone who knew anything at all about a horoscope that Mrs. Judd never premeditated this murder and that very possibly she did not even commit it. Moreover, that she is not a normal person mentally."[18] She gives herself a reference of Lewellyn George of 8921 National Boulevard, Los Angeles, a retired astrologer and the publisher of the most widely circulated astrological magazine in the world; also, the author of many recognized books on this subject."[18]

14

1932, March 21

Jerry McLain writes an article for the Arizona Republic and requests his byline not be used. There was an opportunity giving to Winnie Ruth Judd to tell all concerning the trunk murders and the "best she would do was to accuse the two women of being sexual perverts". There was a 30-minute jail cell interview to which two Phoenix newspapermen were admitted. She hinted time and time again that she had an accomplice in the double killing. She referred to him as "he" but refused consistently to utter his name. So, they took her back to the death cell at the Arizona State Prison, and left Maricopa county officials still puzzled as to whether or not she could have without aid, slain two women, dismembered one of the bodies and shipped all in trunks to Los Angeles. Mrs. Judd was returned to Phoenix for a hearing on her financial status, a hearing demanded by Andrews after she had filed an affidavit of inability to pay costs on a Supreme Court appeal. Andrews wanted to know how much she received from coast newspapers and national publications for "life stories". They also wanted to learn if there was any financial backing provided by wealthy friends interested in her case. Ruth said, "I am here to talk." She was screaming at Andrews. "You are trying to protect a political friend of yours, and you're trying to protect him and trying to hang me." Judge Speakman thundered an order that she be taken immediately to jail. She was dragged from the court by 6 people after ineffectual efforts to silence her. They met her in her jail an hour later with Andrews and two newspaper men. Two shorthand reporters were ready to take her statement. Ruth talked. She began a bitter denunciation of Arizona law. Her anger flamed and her voice rose to a shriek. She stormed from one end of the cell to another, gesticulating wildly, talking incoherently much of the time. She pleaded, raved and threatened, but she guarded any statement that might have shed light on an accomplice in the twin killings. "Dr. Catton said I was a sexual pervert." She said. "Well, I am not. But Anne and Sammy were. Do you hear? They were. But they can't practice their perversions on me anymore. They can't do that to me anymore. They can't do that to me anymore. I said, "My God, you can't do that to me anymore." "You paid $12000 to bring California witnesses over here to lie about me." She shrieked at Andrews, "You just want to see me hanged, and see my head flip up in the air, like Eva Dugan's." Andrews reminded her that she had requested to make a statement concerning the crimes. "When I talk I'll talk at my second trial, or else in the courtroom before people. I will talk in the courtroom. I am not in the courtroom now." Andrews pleaded with her to tell the facts in the case. Ruth replied, "What do you want them for? You want them to go out here and try to hang somebody else." To the next question that she identify "somebody else", she replied, "No, I will not. You know, and I know that you know!" "You said the shooting occurred at 10:30 PM." Andrews said, "That is when it was." "It is? Well, you will find out something different when I get my new trial. Hedvig Samuelson!! I was never jealous of her in my life. I worked all day, and went home at night and nursed her and took care of her, and fed her and cleaned the house. I was her friend. My God, you leave me alone. You can't do that to me anymore. You can't do that anymore. My God, you leave me alone. You can't do that to me anymore. You can't do that anymore. Sammy shot me.... You're trying to keep me from a new trial because I have no money. I've been a political football—that's all. It's a little bit of notoriety to hang a woman. They don't do that in most civilized states." Judge Speakman said, "My God have mercy on your soul." Ruth said, "I haven't got a soul.... 'He' killed that. You know good and well that I never cut up a body. And I couldn't drag that big heavy trunk weighting more than 400 pounds through that house. You said the shooting occurred at 10:30. Well, I was at the home in my own home until 11:30 and a man came over to my house and picked me up in a car...." They asked her if the county attorney was trying to protect somebody. "Yes." But she evaded the question as to who and went rambling off on her stereotyped statement. She paced the cell floor, her eyes flashing hate or anger, nervously wrapping and unwrapping a large white handkerchieff around her left hand, the hand which had been wounded by a gunshot when she surrendered in Los Angeles last October. That wound had been her basis for the self-defense plea that Miss Samuelson first shot her and she killed to protect herself. She turned to Andrews and exclaimed, "He wants the glory of hanging another woman. He thinks if I'm hanged he'll get to be governor of this state." She added the denunciation that if she were hanged and went to hell, she'd hope he never became governor. They asked her if there was anything that she was willing to do to help the county attorney. "My God no!" she screamed. "I will do anything to help myself. I'm not helping him." "My heart goes out to you .. All of you...May God have mercy on your souls." She once more swung into the tantrum "My God, leave me alone. You leave me alone. You won't do that to me anymore."[19]

1932, April 15

The deed of the house at 2929 N 2nd Street is transferred from Frank and Estella Vance h/w back to the O'Malley Investment Company.[20]

1932, July 14

Burton McKinnell was hauled into traffic court and charged with blocking traffic and selling merchandise from a parked vehicle following his effort to sell from his car parked near Third street and Broadway. He was selling, "The Truth about Winnie Ruth Judd". McKinnell refused to sign the traffic tag tendered to him and was taken to the police station and to court to answer the charges. He pleaded not guilty and was released without bail pending jury trial next Thursday. He was told to halt selling the booklets until after the trial.[21]

1932, July 22

A jury decides that Burton McKinnell is guilty of obstructing traffic while selling his pamphlet at 3rd and Broadway. The jury found McKinnell not guilty of driving without an operator's license and of parking a car with a for sale sign on it on a public street. The police officer stated that he had not seen McKinnell drive and saw no for sale sign. He insisted on conducting his own case, but was forced by Judge Clarke to accept deputy City Public Defender Hamilton as an adviser after he had insisted on debating the merits of his sister's trial with the prospective jurors for more than an hour. After he was convicted, Hamilton made a motion for a new trial which was to be argued on Monday morning.[22]

1932, July 27

Burton is reported to be selling his pamphlet in Phoenix now instead of Los Angeles.[23]

1932, August

Dr. Judd states that this is when Ruth sawed through the bars of her prison cell in Florence. (See 1933, March) Dr. Judd stated she had been caught as she had squeezed through the bars. She would not have been able to get over the main wall. The warden kept this a secret [24]

1932, August 16

Joe Mayer, assistant State Criminologist was robbed. The thief only took a set of pictures of the bodies of Anne and Sammy. He also took

17

$1 in small change, but took nothing else. The pictures had been prepared for use during the trial but never were entered in evidence.[25]

1932, September 30
Burton and Nina Hamm appeared at the marriage license bureau where they filed a notice of intention to wed. The ceremony was going to be in a month. Her address was given as 1331 East Willetta Street in Phoenix. She was a student attending the Tempe Normal School. They appeared in LA it seems from this article. He is listed as still living in Beverly Glen.[26]

1932, October 26
Ruth writes a letter to a Mr. Richardson of Florence AZ. It was never mailed but given to George W. Stephens instead. Stephens was the superintendent of the State Hospital in Phoenix. She pleads for aspirin in this letter. It is a crazy letter and she defends herself vehemently about not being an addict of any kind. She talks about taking aspirin for rheumatism of the shoulder. She states that somebody is saying that she is an addict. She says that she takes nothing. Although she offers this statement, "Dr. Stewart is friendly towards Dr. Raney and his is Halloran's close friend. If Dr. Stewart would keep out of my care and not be for or against me, I would be nice to him, but he is against me." This is a letter pleading for aspirin [27]

1932, October?
Ruth writes a letter to Dr. Judd which is never sent. Another crazy letter. She states that other women in her position would be allowed to see their baby. She stated that the baby's name was John Robert and he was staying on West Moreland. Ruth is on death row in Florence. Here is a quote from the letter, "I am sure if two women had attacked his wife and she were in a similar position you would not torment her, . . You would let her see her baby." And "I hope God strikes me dead if I ever did what that gazette says." And "John Robert is out on West Moreland and I will see him if I die?"[28] There is a picture of Winnie Ruth Judd in a Michigan newspaper. It states in Ruth Judd's handwriting on the back: This is Chang M. He was six years old in June. He is the baby.[29]

1932, October 31
Dr. Judd finally appears in court in LA for practicing medicine without

a license. He was found not guilty. His argument was that he told nobody that he was a physician while he was at the clinic. He stated that he prescribed for no one and took no money from any patient. He was paid 6 dollars a day to handle the clinic during Moss's absence.[30]

1932, December 7

Ruth writes a letter to her husband which is never sent and intercepted by the Warden who gives it to George Stephens MD. She states that she is very hungry. She cannot eat. She states, "I am sick, I am tired, and I will take them by my own hand someday." Ruth states that she doubts the existence of God.[31]

1932, December 12

Warden William Delbridge left his office about 4. The Gazette had told him of the Supreme Court decision. He decided not to tell Ruth Judd until he was officially notified. Shortly after re-entering the penitentiary at Florence Ruth staged several of her antics. One of which was placing string about the death cell cautioning prison authorities to stay away from them because they were charged with electricity. Delbridge had said of her several months before that Ruth had become a model prisoner but had developed a nervous condition. She doesn't cause any trouble although at times she gets into a wrangle with other inmates when they talk about her.[32]

1932, December 13

The State Supreme court, in an opinion ruled that Ruth Judd must pay with her life for the murder of Agnes Ann LeRoi. The ruling came when the high court affirmed the judgement of the Maricopa County Superior Court which found her guilty of murder. Her death date was set for Feb 17, 1933. She was left with two options; one being a sanity hearing before a Pinal County jury. The warden is the only person authorized to initiate a hearing. Or she may resort to an appeal for clemency to the state board of pardons and parole. Since she didn't take the stand in her defense, the drain pipe letter was the primary evidence. In this she states she shot Sammy in self-defense but out rightly killed Anne LeRoi.[33] Ruth is brought the news at Florence. Ruth's mother spent the night with her in the cell and was with her the entire day. Mr. Richardson met with her and told her that there were a number of things that they expected to do to save her. When given the news, she was perfectly normal and then shouted, "I'm no murderer. I fought for my life when she came at me with the gun. Mother, I am a good woman. I have never associated with bad, low or degenerate people. I never cut up those bodies. I could not have done it." When retelling the killings, she said that Sammy came through the door of the kitchen with a gun in her hand. Although, the difference here was that she stabbed her in the back instead of in the neck or chest.[34]

1932, December 16
Dr. Judd is kicked out from the US Veterans Hospital at Fort Whipple because he failed to heed the advice of his physicians. Dr. Judd who had previously been denied a furlough, went to Florence to confer with his wife.[35] Jack Halloran received a letter from a Los Angeles attorney who said he recently had been in Phoenix but had not called on him. It outlined plans for gaining clemency for Ruth. It said in part, "I feel if I should come to Phoenix again you would be willing to aid..." Jack Halloran did not answer the letter.[4]

1932, December 28
Ruth tells her story before the Maricopa County grand jury. She told her story from 10:30-12:05 and was to return to tell the second half of her story at 1 o'clock. Over lunch she poses for a picture for the Gazette even though she said bashfully that she would rather not. Ruth stated that she was surprised that she was subpoenaed to testify. She was laughing and chatting before her appearance. Outside in the hall her voice would at times be raised to strident tones. Individual words were not intelligible. There were times when she sounded almost hysterical. She was excited at the lunch break, said that she was not even half through and that she was invited to talk as long she felt like it.[36]

1932, December 30
Ruth writes a very sane letter to George Stephens. Even the handwriting looks different. She thanks him for his x-mas card and the kindness he has shown to her.[37] Since Dr. Stephens ran the insanity campaign as far as the letters go, it makes you wonder if Ruth wrote those unsent crazy letters as evidence of her insanity so she could save her own life. Jack Halloran goes to the office of Frank O Smith and hires him to be his attorney or at least has his first discussion with him.[11] It is recommended that Ruth's sentence be commuted to life imprisonment by the state board of pardons and paroles. This was

because of the self-defense story she had told the Grand Jury. It was said that her testimony had a discrepancy as to the location of the bullet wounds in the bodies of the victims. It is understood that her version of the slayings did not correspond with the locations of the wounds. It was Andrews last day on the job as county attorney. He declared that her latest story would have to fit in with six other versions related to him indirectly and with the record in the case before he would accept it as truth. He stated although his term was done, he would keep the Judd case in mind. Andrews stated that he did not know whether this was a true story or an attempt to ward off the inevitable. Lloyd Andrews was with the grand jury during the whole proceeding.[38]

1932, December 31
Probate is submitted in Hennepin County regarding Sammy's estate. It was submitted on behalf of Marie. Sam was the special administrator of her estate."The petition of Marie Samuelson of said county respectfully shows that Hedvig Samuelson who was a resident of said county died on or about the 1st day of Oct 1931 leaving goods, chattels, and effects with said Hennepin County the probate value whereof does not exceed the sum of 300 dollars consisting of the following; "Cash which was not sufficient to pay the funeral expenses which have been advanced by your petitioner, the mother of said deceased."[39]

1933, January 1
Ruth was optimistic in her cell that she would receive a commutation of sentence because of the self-defense story she told in front of the Grand Jury late December. She had a quiet day in her cell at the state prison. She felt good that she told her story and welcomed her mother and father with a pleasant smile and a warm hello as they paid their regular visit. Mrs. McKinnell has been permitted to see her daughter without restriction and has been spending each night with her since the Supreme Court denied Mrs. Judd a new trial. Ruth had become quite bitter and contended she had not been given a fair deal. She was quite happy that she was informed that the grand jury had interceded for her and the state board of pardons and paroles to commute her sentence. They all declared that the New Year has started very happily for them and they expect better things.[40]

1933, January 3
Renz Jennings on his first day on the job got a continuance in order to

21

study the indictment for Ruth Judd.[41]

1933, January 4
Louis P Russill Attorney at Law at suite 420 Subway Terminal Building, 417 South Hill Street in Los Angeles writes a letter to Lin B. Orme. He asked whether or not a petition has been filed with the board on behalf of Winnie Ruth Judd. He stated, "Being Mrs. Judd's first attorney in this unfortunate matter (in fact I personally apprehended her and subsequently turned her over to the authorities), I am in possession of certain evidence which I feel should be presented to your board, and if I am notified in time and am permitted I shall attend the hearing and present these matters to the board for its consideration." "Inasmuch as I have no official connection with this case, or with any of the attorneys acting for or on behalf of Mrs. Judd, I respectfully request that this communication be treated confidentially. I have not communicated directly or indirectly with Mrs. Judd, or any member of the Judd family, since she has been in Arizona, and they are entirely unaware of what I contemplate doing in this matter. I particularly desire no newspaper publicity in connection with this matter so would appreciate it if you would treat this communication with the utmost secrecy and advise me in the premises.[42] Jack Halloran declares that Mrs. Judd's statements to the grand jury contained no basis in truth. Frank O Smith made it clear that they did not want to delay the case so Renz Jennings would have time to review the case. In the grand jury case, the jury petitioned the state board of pardons and paroles to grant Mrs. Judd an immediate commutation of sentence to life imprisonment. They declared Mrs. Judd had convinced them that she killed Agnes Anne LeRoi in self-defense. However, if that was true, then Halloran would not have been indicted. Before the board could do this they would have to file an application for commutation.[40] Jack Halloran and Frank O Smith were scheduled to appear before Judge Speakman at 9:30 for a hearing on a motion to quash the indictment. One of the problems was that the grand jury was petitioning the pardon board for the self-defense plea given by Ruth Judd, but contradictorily the indictment of Halloran as an accessory.[41] Judge Speakman denied motions to set aside and quash the indictment of Jack Halloran.[43] In the evening Lloyd Andrews stated that whole Ruth story to the grand jury was untrue. "I don't believe her story and I wouldn't consider going before the pardon board on her behalf." "Mrs. Judd has told too many stories –five or six in all and there are discrepancies in each of them. There are too many

things which would have to be explained before I could believe any of her stories. He claimed that she first sold her true story to the Los Angeles Examiner for $5000. He claimed she consistently had sought to commercialize this atrocious crime. He claimed that every story that he has heard is different. He reviewed the grand jury story." He claimed that "I tried to get Mrs. Judd to tell me what actually happened when I first saw her in the office of Chief of Detective Joe Taylor in Los Angeles. She refused to talk at the time at the advice of counsel. He again tried to get the real story from her when she was brought from the county jail to his office for a conference on her return to Phoenix. Her answer was the same. He again gave her the opportunity after her conviction. He claimed that the wounds in the women's head must be reconciled and also the blood spots on the window shade next to the bed and underneath the bed must be explained. Although, the fact that Mrs. Judd's own gun was used in the slaying, the shell found at the Brill Street apartment needs some explanation. He said he emphatically did not believe her story.[44]

1933, January 5
Frank O Smith makes a second argument about quashing the indictment by the Grand Jury.[43] He succeeded in filing with the court the affidavit against each grand juror and particularly against G. A. White, the foreman. Smith argued that the indictment is not direct and was not certain as to the offense charged and was not direct and certain as to the particular circumstance of the offense charged. There were no facts or circumstances constituting any offense in the indictment. No alleged criminal acts or omissions. The indictment left them questioning what the charges were.[45]

1933, January 6
The indictment was tossed out of Superior Court regarding Jack Halloran. It was defectivee in that it failed to state facts constituting a public offense on the part of Halloran. He did not quash the charge. The current indictment could not be amended. The new indictment must have some specifics about how Halloran was an accomplice. He made him post $3000 bail and have the indictment resubmitted the next day.[46]

1933, January 7
The hearing for Jack Halloran was set to start on the following

Wednesday. The new indictment that was filed charges Halloran as an accessory to the crime of murder in that he aided and assisted Winnie Ruth Judd in disposing of and concealing the body of Agnes Anne LeRoi and for aiding assisting and advising her to escape from Maricopa County Arizona to California. Halloran waived service of a warrant of arrest and reading of the complaint. He was released on the $3000 cash bond he furnished on December 30th.

1933, January 9
Frank O Smith fought for a copy of Ruth's testimony that she gave in front of the grand jury. He claimed he was entitled to the evidence.[47]

1933, January 10
Ruth was scheduled to begin her testimony on this date. However, it was thought that the trial might be continued because of the illness of Justice McKee who had been ill at his home for two days. Howard Speakman denied a motion of defense counsel for a transcript of Mrs. Judd's testimony before the grand jury.[48]

1933, January 11
McFadden stated that he would go to Florence and return Mrs. Judd to Phoenix. There was a rumor that he would question Ruth in the county jail here before to learn what she plans to testify.[48]

1933, January 13
Justice McKee who was to preside over the Halloran proceeding has pneumonia. He would not be out of bed for a week. The hearing was scheduled to start on Monday with another justice... Clarence E. Ice and Marlin T. Phelps were mentioned as substitutes. Frank O Smith did not want to delay this hearing any further.[49]

1933, January 14
A petition to the board of pardons and paroles was filed in order for Ruth to tell her whole true story. The points were that her counsel at her superior court trial based their defense on insanity, that she was promised by Paul Schenck of Los Angeles then a member of her counsel that she would be able to testify on her own behalf, that she would have testified if she had been permitted to do so and given her self-defense story, that she had been in mental turmoil during her trial and did not understand the legal proceeding, and that she trusted her

counsel. It also said that in the year before her trial she was intermittently mentally not normal by reason of the insanity of her ancestors both direct and collateral, and with the excitement of the quarrel, and of the shooting, and the consequential acts, she was in no condition mentally then to accept the advice of her counsel. The petition was signed by Mrs. Judd, W.C. Judd, and five attorneys, OV Willson, Erwin H. Karz, and Jacob Morgan, Arthur Berge of Los Angeles, and Howard G Richardson of Florence.[50] It was thought that the Halloran trial would delay her execution currently set for February 17 since her pardon board hearing would not be set until after the Halloran hearing was over since her testimony would be necessary. "Her testimony it is believed may have some bearing on the action of the pardon board in her application." Halloran's hearing was transferred to Judge Niles court. Lin B. Orme, parole board chairman, stated that "a hearing will be granted, the time and place to be fixed later."[51]

1933, January 16
Marie Samuelson is awarded the 300 dollars from Sammy's probate.[39] Frank O Smith is awarded access to a transcript of Ruth's testimony before the grand jury from December 1932. The transcript could be used to impeach any of Ruth's testimony if she deviated from it. Ruth's testimony stated that it was self-defense posed a problem since if she shot in self-defense Halloran would not have been said to be an accessory of the crime. It was thought that the charges against Halloran were not very specific in Ruth's testimony to the grand jury.[52]

1933, January 17
Winnie Ruth Judd makes her first statements in court. Her temper was frequently raging beyond control, yet at times cringing as though she feared the attorney who plied her with questions. Many of her statements were stricken from the record by the court. She testified for three hours. The court room was packed. When she entered the courtroom before Halloran in the morning he passed near her chair. She stared fixedly at him for a moment, then glanced away and did not look at him again until she took the stand. Halloran did not show any sign of knowledge of her presence in the room until she was sent to the stand. Then he watched her closely. He smiled when she became vehement. The Republic made the statement that she seemed to forget everything it seemed, but only that she was in court to accuse Jack

Halloran. She charged Halloran packed the bodies in the trunk, told her that Miss Samuelson had been operated upon, advised her to say nothing of the slayings, and sent her to Los Angeles. She stated that Halloran disposed of a mattress missing from one of the beds in the cottage. They asked her how she knew about the mattress. Ruth screamed, "Well, he's done some trick about that mattress... You're trying to trick me now.... I'm telling you God's truth...I'm telling you what I intend to write when I commit suicide." After this, she refused to answer yes or no to questions about the mattress. She was calm when she took the stand, but became more hysterical as the afternoon wore on. At one point she said, "I'm not here for the purpose of clearing Jack Halloran. He had an opportunity to clear me at my trial, but he didn't." Halloran was said to laugh at this statement. Once she accused the lumberman of attempting to signal answers to her. She said, "I don't want him to talk to me. He's talked to me too much already. He told me not to tell anyone what had happened, not even my husband." She complained that he was too much of a coward to tell everything. "When he came into this room, I wanted to scream at him, the longer this case goes on, the bigger coward he is." One main difference of the story she told on this day is that she stated the crime happened before midnight on Friday instead of Saturday morning. She stated at one point that Jack was shaking his head at her and that she didn't want him to talk to her. Deputy County Attorney David Lathan jumped up and stated that the defendant and the witness be not permitted to communicate in any manner. Judge Niles made the statement that he did not see Mr. Halloran make any signs or endeavor to communicate with Ruth. In the afternoon she was asked about her childhood and early marriage. When asked about Mexico, she said she had left Mexico, two or three times to enter sanitariums. She stated that she broke down with TB and that she had been told that she had goiter. Smith asked her if she also had glandular trouble. She replied that she had a gland in her brain that was growing and then objected to his questioning.[53] McFadden also testified on this day. He admitted that he had brought the ironing board to the court house and locked it up in the "booze room." When he went to look for it, he admitted that he could not find it. He stated that any of 21 deputies had access to the vault. He stated that he had never ironed, but that the ironing board was about three feet long and that it had folding legs on it. He said that he did not know if blood appeared on it. He said that Ruth had talked about the ironing board shortly before she was arrested. He stated that the ironing board had not been marked as a Judd exhibit and in the past the room had been cleaned out before. He stated that he did not have an inventory as to what the storage room contained. He said most everything you would look for was in that room except for the ironing board. He said he did not keep the inventory. McFadden said he was too busy to keep the inventory for the booze vault. Frank O Smith said he needed the ironing board as evidence.[53]

1933, January 18
Winnie Ruth Judd breaks down on the witness stand during cross examination. She ended by sobbing hysterically and had to be led from the courtroom while she was shouting accusations across the defense counsel table at Halloran. She said things such as "He don't care that Anne is dead...or that I'm going to die. He just sits and laughs about it." Halloran was said to be smiling at her. "He is responsible for the death of three girls in this state. Anne and Sammy are dead... and I have only four more weeks to live." "I hope you've suffered everything that I've suffered and I hope you suffer as my mother, and Anne's mother and Sammy's mother have suffered." "You want to set Jack Halloran free and hang me for something that Jack Halloran did' when I shot in self-defense and he..." "I know that Sammy is dead and Anne is dead, and I'm going to be dead..." Miss Marshall was also on the stand. She told of having seen Halloran visit Mrs. Judd at her Brill Street apartment previous to the night of the murder and testified she saw him arrive in a tan Packard automobile. She declared that she and a friend took the license number of the automobile and later turned it over to the sheriff. She said she heard an automobile drive up in front of Mrs. Judd's apartment shortly after 12:30 during the night of the slaying and heard someone enter the apartment. She admitted that she didn't remember having recognized any voices nor could she identify the car by the sounds of it.[54] There were so many people present in the courtroom that they removed some of the seats in order to provide more standing space and increase the capacity of the room. When Ruth had her outburst during the cross examination, court was halted for 2 hours. Matrons of the jail calmed her before her return to the witness stand. They tried to remove McFadden from the courtroom, but ended up moving him to the side where he would not be in the eyesight of Ruth Judd. The defense had charged that he was coaching her during her testimony. In the afternoon, there was an argument about whether she appeared voluntarily before the grand jury. Smith argued that she

27

had voluntarily done this while Jennings held she had been subpoenaed and that it was by law and not voluntary. The ironing board made its appearance. Ruth, when asked if it was the ironing board that was used, stated only that it was a similar ironing board. Ruth stated that she saw Mr. Ralston Thursday and asked to borrow a car to show Anne some houses. She said she couldn't drive, but Anne could. She denied taking them out to the desert for a picnic. She said that Anne's bed was on the north side of the bedroom and Sammy's was on the south. There was a telephone between the beds and a dresser. There was a stool that Sammy had made herself. Ruth tells about the argument. She screams, "I begged to take the witness stand and tell everything in my defense – I prayed that Jack Halloran would take the stand and tell everything."[54] For some reason, Smith asked her who her first attorneys were in California. With that she screamed at him and stood up, "I don't have to tell you and that is on advice of counsel." When asked the names, she said, "You can find out yourself. I am saying right here and now that not one of them can take this stand." When the court admonished her, he said that he would ask her a leading question, "Was not Mr. Verge one of them?" Judge Niles ruled that the last part of the statement be stricken. When asked about Leukowitz and Zaversack she said they were her attorneys. When asked whether she fired them and hired others she stated that was true. When asked if she had told them this story, she said, "What I told them is none of your business." She stated that she had expected to testify at her own trial after the testimony of Jack Halloran. When asked if she sold her story to newspapers she said, "I'll not tell you what I said to my attorneys or what they said to me. Four weeks when I am hung, you may find out." Smith told the court that a book apparently published by Judd's brother was being circulated among spectators in the court room containing that statement and the same statement had been published in newspapers as part of her appeal to the board of pardons and paroles for commutation. Smith asked her if her account of the slayings had been told to Arthur Verge, Los Angeles, a member of her counsel. When asked if she sold stories to the Herald, she said she did not. She said she wrote letters to her husband and she "didn't personally sell" or "didn't personally write" any stories. When asked if somebody else had written them she said, she couldn't say what somebody else did. When asked to say yes or no to the questions of whether "Did you have someone write the story for you" she replied she couldn't do that; she would have to explain instead. She said she received no money for a story. She said she did not know if anybody else received any money for any story. After she stated that she had been subpoenaed. She stated a volley of abuse at Halloran. He for the first time during the hearing became angered and started to arise from counsel table. He was restrained by his attorneys and the court quieted her and ordered her remarks be stricken. It was difficult to quiet the audience. When she and Smith argue about what voluntary means and whether she wanted to testify or not, he says to her, "You seem to be suspicious of what I'm trying to do." She replied, "I am."[54] Some notes from the Phoenix Gazette: She said after the struggle that two shots were fired. She stated she never saw the chest wound in Sammy. She said the only time she saw it was when Jack pulled her pajamas back. She stated that when she came over Anne had asked her why she hadn't come earlier and she stated it was because she was waiting for Jack to come over.[55]

1933, January 19
Ruth again is on the witness stand in the Halloran trial. She refused to tell of the packing of the bodies; she refused to reveal the contents of a letter written to her husband. Frank O Smith stated that she was not a voluntary witness and that she was unable to comprehend the oath willingly and is concealing the facts. She is repeatedly committing perjury. He also said that she was physically and mentally diseased to the extent that she was incompetent to testify. The courtroom was packed and the crowd overflowed into the hallway. Frank O Smith made the surprise move of attempting to stricken her entire testimony saying that she was incompetent. He said Mrs. Judd was the only one accusing Halloran to date. At one point Ruth said to Smith, "Now listen, the other day you tried to stop me when I tried to tell you what Halloran did to Sammy, and now I don't have to tell." She also said at one point, "May I then ask for my constitutional rights to say nothing about another case that may be incriminating to myself." As for the letter to her husband she stated that it was privileged communication between a man and wife. Another witness was on the stand, B. O. Smith, fingerprint expert. Smith said he told of visiting the duplex on about November 2 to look for fingerprints and to take pictures of the bed room. He said he found a bloody print of a left thumb on a window shade in the apartment. He said it was smudged. He had a picture of the bedroom. He could not produce the window shade with the fingerprint on it. Dr. Judd was too ill to be present in court.[56] Ruth was

on the stand again in the afternoon after several consultations by her attorneys. She was asked about the operation. She said, "I just know that an operation was performed. Mr. Halloran told me Sammy was operated upon Saturday night." Frank O Smith turned towards questions about the gun. He walked up to the stand calmly tossing the gun from one hand to the other. He asked her if she recognized it. She nodded her head and drew back in her chair, turning away from the gun, refusing to look directly at the weapon. Frank O Smith asked her to lay her handkerchief on the railing. She said that when she had the gun it was in her right hand since her left hand had been shot. He asked her to take it in her right hand. Ruth said, "I don't want to," and drew away. "I don't know why you want me to do this," she said. Smith asked how far away the gun was when it was fired and went into Sammy's head. Ruth replied that they were on the floor grappling for the gun. "We were clinching. We were rolling on the floor. We were fighting for the gun." Frank Smith claimed she had memorized this answer. When pressed, she said, "We were in each other's arms, it was that close." She said it was closer than 3 feet since they both were in the doorway. She said Sammy was "trying to get the gun, and that she was trying to keep the gun." She checked herself after she said this. She then shot at Smith, "I am not on trial here now." Ruth said that there were more than 3 shots, she knew this much. She claimed that her husband had left the gun for her. She claimed that it was in the dresser drawer. When asked how she knew this she claimed that it was there when she left. As for Anne she said, "As I started to get up. She hit me again with the ironing board. I was in a half rising position, she had the ironing board raised in her hands. I started to rise. I fired at her as she hit me with the ironing board and we both fell at the same time. I fired in the left side of her head." She said she didn't know how close she was to Anne. She said she thought that she was closer to Ann than two feet. When asked if it were closer than a foot she said she didn't remember. She said Anne was swinging the ironing board from side to side and that it was not in front of her. She said she was dazed and did not know how long she was lying there. She said she might have fainted but she didn't think she was unconscious. In the afternoon Smith tried to strike her testimony from not being competent. He made the point that she was not of sane mind when she went back to the duplex 24 hours later when she had no agreement about what time Halloran had agreed to meet her. He said her testimony was memorized and that getting her away from it left her lost. Smith talks about her testimony that if Halloran was meeting her to help her get away wouldn't he have brought money with him. And he pointed out if they were going to meet at the train station, wouldn't he have found her afterwards when he didn't meet her there. He pointed out that she could have sent a messenger, telephone or through friends sent a message to him. He points out that she did not communicate to them. He also pointed out that why would two accomplices would meet at the murder scene 24 hours later and not specify a time. He claimed that she had a disordered mind. He said that some of her testimony was "absolutely false." He threatened to have her competency reviewed by saying, "Experts say without a doubt that here is a case of dementia praecox; a woman with fanciful illusions and it is utterly impossible for a person with such a mind to appear on the witness stand and testify competently." He said her competency was in question; not her sanity. He pointed out that when she didn't have her handkerchief, she started on her dress. Judge Niles made the statement, "I think I shall get a supply of handkerchiefs and keep them on my desk. I don't like to have her run out. It makes me nervous when she starts on her dress." He smiled. Niles stated that this was not a sanity hearing and that he would not waste time on that at this time. Court resumes. Ruth is on the stand again at 2:20. They discuss the idea that Halloran was supposed to meet her one block from the train station on Saturday night. She was to take a taxi and walk to where his car was parked. She tried this on Sunday night. Smith asked her about the main streets of Phoenix. She kept saying that she didn't know. "I am very confused at this time. If given time to figure out, I could tell you better. If there were not perhaps a thousand people watching me, perhaps I could tell you." Smith suggested a smaller audience. "I am very tired. I have been on the stand two or three days. I am under a nervous strain. The reason I can't answer is that I am confused. I can tell you why I am confused; because he is trying to prove me insane. I am trying to do the best I can. I've got stage fright, I guess. If he wants to ask other questions now, I can come back to this later." Smith started something new. He asked her if she tried to meet him Saturday night. She said no. She said she expected to meet Halloran Sunday night since "I waited for him all night and day at my apartment." Then she asked, "Are you or Mr. Halloran cross examining me?" Then she turned to Judge Niles and said, "He is irritating me terribly." Judge Niles said that Halloran had the right to prompt his attorney. She said she expected Halloran to come to her house since he was in the habit of coming to her house. She reported that when she was back at Brill Street that she was waiting for him to come and kept going out on the porch in anticipation of seeing him drive up and even once walked to the street to see if he had parked in front of the apartment court. When asked if he had a reason for coming, she said, "There certainly was a reason for him coming, a terrible reason for him coming." Smith changed his tact and asked her about having keys to the duplex. She vigorously denied having had any keys to the apartment. She talks about Sunday afternoon and borrowing money. She said she had a high fever. She refused to talk about the repacking of the bodies since it related to a case that she had not been tried for yet. Renz Jennings backed her up. She was asked about the letter she wrote her husband the day after. She refused to answer. As she left the stand she said, "I've been accused of publishing letters I wrote to my husband. Well, I did not."[56]

1933, January 20
Fifteen witnesses testifyed in the Halloran trial this day. The state rested. Halloran's counsel moved for dismissal for formal evidence in support of a motion to have all of Mrs. Judd's testimony was stricken from the record as incompetent. This motion would have automatically ended the case if it were granted. B. O. Smith was on the stand again. He was shown the curtain shade which he had testified to. He had taken a picture of it two weeks after the slayings. Smith asked him to identify the blind. He said he believed it was the same blind since there was "Yet some slight blood marks on it that I saw when I took the picture." Smith asked him if it were blood. He replied that it has indications of being blood. He said he was sure that it was bloody in November. He asked him if it was torn then (as it was then). He stated it was not torn. He asked him if Winnie Ruth Judd could have made the prints. He said yes. He asked if a man or a woman made the prints. He said that he could not tell. When asked if the spots could be from a spurting wound he replied that he was sure that they were made by fingers. He also said the spots could have been made by something besides fingers. He also said the smudges could have been made at different times. Smith moved to strike all of the testimony of the expert from the case because of the ambiguity of the fingerprint. The point being that the prints could have been made by anybody. Niles said that it agreed with Ruth's testimony. The shade was admitted into evidence. Ruth went on the stand again. Smith asked her if what she said in this hearing could be

held against her at a future date. There was a huge objection by Jacob Morgan her personal counsel. The day before he had been excluded from the court room. He shouted at Smith, "She has been badgered here for three days, not only without advice of her counsel, but also of her husband. She has been a legal prisoner. I understand the record does not show she was apprised of her rights. They've delved into everything here and pretty nearly tore the very clothing off of her." He accused Smith of calling Mrs. Judd's attorney at Florence and having him bring her parents here not only for the purpose of intimidating the witness, but also to intimidate her counsel." "This man is doing nothing more than jeopardizing this woman's rights. She is entitled to her rights as long as there is life in her body. I'm a man of peace primarily but I resent this man antagonizing me unnecessarily and I'll come back stronger every time." Smith said he had nothing to do with bringing her parents here. Ruth left the stand. Frank Vance, owner of the duplex was called to the stand. He stated that the mattress was missing when he entered the house, the Tuesday after the slayings. Vance identified the ironing board as the one at the duplex. He said that there were no marks of blood on the ironing board. He answered, "No Sir" to the question of Smith in that regard. He stated to Jennings that he had the ironing board ever since the Judd trial. So they must have given it back. Sheriff McFadden was on the stand. He claimed he had checked a license number given to him by a woman at the Brill street apartment. It was registered to the Halloran-Bennett Lumber Company. It was a tan Packard. When asked by Smith about the window shade he shouted at him that he thought there were bloody fingerprints on the shade. When asked if it were large or small he only replied that they were smeared. He said that he did not think that the smears were made by anything other than fingers. Smith attempted again to call Ruth incompetent and strike her testimony. Ruth smiled broadly and appeared to be enjoying the exchange. They asked her if she understands the solemnity and binding order of an oath. She replied yes. She said, "I have answered every question as conscientiously and truthfully as I could." Smith tried to question Ruth on a number of items, but all questions were met with objections. Smith made a statement that nobody had told her what the punishment could be for her for perjury. Ruth only smiled. Gertrude Wilcox, housekeeper for the girls took the stand. She was asked if she ever saw the two mattresses. She said she had seen them the last time she was at the house which was Thursday evening. She said the beds were made

33

up but she saw the mattresses when she swept under them. Fred
Homberger who had been with when the trunks were picked up at 10
for the 10:40 train stated that they did not take the trunks to the train,
but to Brill street. George Larisson policeman took the stand. He
stated that he had entered the duplex on the Monday after the crime.
The front door was locked. He wasn't sure about the back door, but his
partner got in somehow. He stated that there were two beds. One was
completely made up. The other bed had quilts folded on it. There was
no mattress. He saw no blood. He saw no ironing board.[57] Violet
Grimm testified next. All she said was that Ruth made phone calls on
Sunday and said she was going to Los Angeles to get Dr. Judd. HU
Grimm also testified. He said he and his son had taken Ruth to the
station and left her there before train time. She paid him $1.50 and
borrowed back $1 since the baggage fees were more than she expected.
Dr. Baldwin also testified. He reviewed the time she was at the clinic
on Saturday. He said she was there until 12 and he thought she left by
12 or 1 o'clock, possible 2:00. He said she did not return that day. Mrs.
Maude Wade, the grocer was called. They decided her testimony was
irrelevant. Miss Halanan was called. She confirmed that Ruth had
visited and borrowed $10. Ruth left her a wristwatch and a bar pin as
security. She had wanted to talk to John Ralston and had waited for
him for a while. Dr. McKeown testified about Saturday at the clinic.
He said he saw her on the forenoon. He did not know when she left
work. She was still there at 1:30 when he left. He mentioned that he
had granted her request for the afternoon off. They argued over the
next witness Blevins who worked at Union Station. He stated he had
seen Halloran at the station, "just previous to the first newspaper
accounts of the murder." When pressed he stated he could not specify
a date or day of the week. He said it was a busy day and that Saturday
had been busy. Sunday night had not been busy. Jennings and Smith
have a fight in court. Jennings was yelling at him when Smith said he
was moving things along as fast as possible. Jennings yelled, "We'll be
good friends when we get out of court, but we're going to fight now."
Blevins did say that Jack did not buy a ticket from him. He had walked
through the lobby alone. It was before a West bound train, but he
didn't know if it was the early or late one. He said that he was positive
that it was Halloran. Dr. Gaskins said that he had never seen a tan
Packard over at the house. There was a statement from October 20 in
which he said his wife had seen a Packard over there. He didn't say
when. He stated that he saw nothing of interest. He was the last

witness.[57]

1933, January 21

Winnie Ruth Judd is on the stand once again to prevent impeachment of her testimony. She denied that she had written of authorized newspaper trunk slaying stories which were read into the record by defense counsel to impeach her testimony. She admitted in court that she alone rearranged the bodies of her two friends two days after the killings in her own home, distributing portions of Hedvig Samuelson's body among other pieces of luggage. She said it was untrue a previous statement published in the paper a week after the slayings in which she herself placed the bodies in a trunk with no help of any kind from anyone. She talked about the stories appearing in the LA Times on October 25, 26, 27th. She "jerkily" acknowledged truth of portions of the story as they were read to her. Frank O Smith quoted part of the story, "Sunday morning when I lifted Sammy from the trunk I tried to place her in my own little metal locking trunk." He asked her if it was true. She did not answer. She said she needed to know the rest of it before she could give an answer. Judge Niles asked her if she could answer that. She said, "I know whether it is true or not. – Yes, she answered when the judge admonished her. "No." She said, "I didn't lift Sammy – I lifted a part... a portion." Her voice was near to a whisper. Smith asked, "And you lifted other portions and changed them?" "Yes" she said. Ruth was excused after that. At some point they review the story from the Times. She said that she didn't write that at all. She said the part where she went to the theater was untrue. She reads the article silently. She was reading the part of the story about having the fight over breakfast, she said, "Anyhow the fight was on the night of October 16." "It says here, she shouted a moment later, I dragged Sammy's body to the bathroom. Well, I did not. And it says I dragged Anne to the bedroom and lifted her body to the bed. I did not. Then it says I went and dragged Sammy to the bedroom and put her on the bed. As far as lifting her it was an utter impossibility and I did not say that, and I did not do it." "I didn't move either of those bodies. Mr. Halloran moved both of them." She continued to scan the document. When she came to the part point where it said Sunday morning when I lifted Sammy from the trunk I tried to place her in my own little metal locker trunk, but that was too small. So I dragged her to the bathroom and in the bathtub and I severed her body with a butcher knife. The upper part I put in the locker trunk. It was not too

35

small for that. Then I divided the lower part, removing the legs at the knees and put them in the little locker trunk. The rest I placed in my suitcase. It says here, began the blond reading from the article that I dragged her to the bathroom and in the bathroom, well, that's untrue. She claimed that she had told her husband a few things about the case, but no detail at all. The defense claimed that this story in the Times was "made before she received various theories from other persons." Regarding the story in the Times, Ruth claimed that she was delirious and she didn't recall if she ever made the statement of certification and the accompanying signature. She claimed that there were about 50 versions of the crime and that this was the first time she had heard this one. Smith argued with her about her signature and if she told her husband the story. She would not answer. The article had the following certificate, "This is to certify that the articles appearing in the Los Angeles Times are correct and authorized by me Winnie Ruth Judd." Smith claimed the Times had the original certificate. The story also said, this is my own story-the whole truth of the double tragedy which ended the lives of Agnes Anne LeRoi and Hedvig Samuelson in Phoenix on Friday Oct 16, 1931. I have given it to my husband William C. Judd to dispose of as he sees fit and in order that the world may know the exact facts of the whole terrible affair. Other parts say, "It has been charged that I had an accomplice either before during or after the actual tragedy. This is not true." "I alone shot and killed both the women who were once my friends. I did it in self-defense to save my own life and for no other reason. I alone disposed of the bodies in a manner which I shall describe in more detail later. I had no help of any kind from anyone." She said she could not say if she signed the certificate since she was delirious at the time. Smith attempted to get her to give a handwriting sample. Ruth said she was under a sedative the whole time she was in LA. She would not say if she had signed that. She said, "There is a lot to explain- it might be- I can say this much- It looks similar to my handwriting." "I was delirious in Los Angeles. I have no idea what I said." She said for him to ask the hospital about when she was delirious. She said the certificate was not in her language and she did not make the statement. When pressed she said, "I never made such a statement to anyone under oath." Later after being admonished by the court she made the statement, "It was privileged testimony to my husband. I deny making them to the Los Angeles Times – yes. Part of them yes, and part of them no." She finally admitted that it looked like her signature. She argued that others could have made up the story. Jennings questioned her after lunch. She said that she did tell her husband some of the things that were in the article. Some were true, some were not true. Things that she claimed were not true were the time of the fight; Saturday morning instead of Friday night. She said it was not true that she had any involvement in the operation of Sammy. She said they quizzed her about that and she said they should talk to Jack Halloran. The reason she lied she said was that she would have rather died than let her husband know about Halloran. She said the part about her taking the mattress to the south of the house is untrue. She said Jack Halloran took the mattress. As for dismembering the body she said she didn't move either body. The article said that Sunday morning she took Sammy from the trunk and tried to place her in her own little metal locker trunk. It was too small so she dragged her to the bathroom and in the bathtub and with a butcher knife removed the legs at the knees after severing the body in half. She said that she had told some of those things to her husband. Referring to the certificate she said that a hospital matron brought her a slip of paper, said it had been brought to the hospital by a reporter and that she was to copy and sign it. She said she refused. The nurse brought it back and said that her husband had said it was alright. Her husband came to the door and she signed the statement as Ruth M. Judd.[58]

1933, January 22
Ruth was returned to Florence. Smith and Jennings prepared the case. Judge Niles wanted to hear about whether a person could be an accessary to a crime when the crime had already been committed previously. Also, if it were self-defense, was there any crime to be an accessory to.[59]

1933, January 24
The hearing for Jack Halloran was set to resume. However, it was thought that Winnie Ruth Judd might do an about face in regards to her testimony to prove that she committed a crime (not self-defense) so Jack could be named an accessory. Jennings was set with the task that to prove, "She was all wrong" and "committed murder in the killings." This hearing was to stand on its own apart from Judd's trial a year earlier.[60] Judge Niles made the statement late afternoon that Renz Jennings had until 9 o'clock the following morning to produce authority to hold Halloran. Judge Niles stated that "not a single case

was cited in which the facts even remotely approach the matters before us." Smith included in the argument that it would have been easier if the hearing had been private without all the public there so they could have gotten to the heart of the truth much faster. He stated that he thought the truth had not yet been told.[61]

1933, January 25
The complaint regarding Halloran is dismissed. Frank O Smith stated that in the near future, "a true disclosure of circumstances" of the case would arise.[62] However, an article states that there were two battles. "In the first, "Mrs. Judd was the vanquished, in the second, she was the victor." Frank O Smith, the lawyer of Jack Halloran said this.[63] He refused to answer other questions about this.[64] It was thought that there was a theory now that there was a fight as detailed by Ruth Friday night, but that the actual slaying did not occur until later. Halloran stated that he was, "pleased with the result. I have had continuous faith and confidence that the truth would prevail and it has."[62] He continued, "I have no bitterness whatsoever against the witness Winnie Ruth Judd or against any official of this county or any person whomsoever. When this charge was presented through the indictment by the grand jury I was amazed. And I have suffered greatly. I am sorry to say that my family also has been compelled to undergo great suffering during this period of nearly a month that this matter has been before the courts. But I have had continuous faith and confidence that the truth would prevail and it has. That has been a source of sustaining strength to me and to those who knew me though the past month. It has been a source of great comfort to me that my wife, my mother, my children, my brother, all of my family and even my friends have had the utmost confidence in me throughout. No one doubted about what result would vindicate me."[64] Halloran posted $3000 bond.[62] Renz Jennings made the following statement, "Before I took office the grand jury presented an indictment against Jack Halloran. The superior court before which this indictment was presented held it insufficient and directed me as county attorney to file information before a justice of the peace. I complied with that order. In presenting the matter to the magistrate I felt it my duty as county attorney to present to the court the testimony of Winnie Ruth Judd and all other facts and circumstances coming to my attention, or which I was able to discover. The court held that all this testimony was insufficient to bind the defendant to answer in the superior court. The court has ruled and I have nothing further to say."[64]

1933, February 2

According to an Affidavit by W Robert LaDue, a Mr. A. N. Smith of Tempe, Arizona stopped at the place where he was living in Chandler and asked him if he would come to his home in Tempe the following morning at 10, to talk over the Judd case with him and his son. He appeared at his home the next morning, but he missed him since he was detained in Chandler. The same day, he met Mr. Smith and his son in Phoenix, and returned that evening with the Smiths to their home. After dinner, they discussed the Judd case until about 11:30 PM. He discussed the case with the Smiths and stated the facts as Mrs. Judd stated them to be at the Halloran preliminary. He stayed at the Smith's overnight. During breakfast with them just before leaving for Phoenix, the elder Mr. Smith asked him whom it was "that now has and has always had the controlling power in regards to the Judd case." He replied that he did not know definitely that anyone or more individuals ever did have or now have any such alleged controlling power. He said, "You know that Halloran has been legally exonerated in Judge Niles," thru his influential friends can control the forthcoming Judd decision of the Pardons Board. He interrupted by stating that he was not convinced of his statement regarding Halloran's friends being able to determine the decision of the Board of Pardons and Paroles and that he would have to be convinced of the same before he could agree with him. He drove to Phoenix. The Elder Mr. Smith told him that if he could get a written statement from Mrs. Judd wherein she would exonerate Jack Halloran of the part he had in the tragedy, and publish the said statement in the press, Jack's powerful and influential friend, business, and otherwise would see to it that the Pardons Board would commute Mrs. Judd's death sentence. He promised the elder Mr. Smith that he would talk it over with Mrs. Judd's brother that same morning, but was convinced in his mind that Mrs. Judd would never perjure her testimony before Judge Niles' court. Mr. AN Smith said that he would be glad to have a conference with Mr. McKinnell regarding the proposition. He left the Smiths at the corner of Washington and Central and met Burton. Burton and LaDue were going to the professional building to OV Willson's office. As they were going, Mr. AN Smith tapped on the plate glass window of the Santa Fe Travel Bureau and motioned to them to come inside. They entered and talked to Mr. Smith regarding the above proposition to him. He asked Mr. Smith to get definite, tangible evidence from "those influential friends" showing to him that Mr. Smith was truly authorized as their representative. At 2 or 3 they again met Mr. Smith in the lobby of the Adams Hotel. He attempted to persuade them that he was truly authorized as the representative of the "powerful and influential friends of Jack Halloran". He told him that he was not satisfactorily convinced, and definitely refused his offer. At this point, Mr. Smith became inflamed, got up out of his seat, and started talking unnecessarily loud. LaDue and Burton left.[65]

1933, February 20
Ruth writes a letter to Mr. Renz Jennings. She says that she has been propositioned by representatives of Jack Halloran. He wanted her to tell a lie about Anne and Sammy. He promised her a commutation of sentence. She is sorry that she called her what she did during the quarrel. She states that 3 men have her life in their hands. She said before she could tell such a lie that she would write to Anne and Sammy's parents first. She said that she would rather end her life rather than being bullied into doing what Halloran wanted. The intent of the letter is to be tried on Sammy's crime. She would not be convicted, she believes.[66] She stated that unless she tells that lie, her life will be taken. She stated that she was sorry that she called them what she did during the fight. She stated that Halloran is about the lowest being possible to wish to circulate "such filth" on the girls. She stated that the girls cared enough for him to quarrel and fight even to death over his going out with another woman who might hurt him. She stated that "It isn't as though someone had killed a bitter enemy. Both girls were my friends. They were beautiful girls; the quarrel was sudden and the fight and no one in this whole world can feel as bad as I do over it, with on top of it every other kind of sorrow and worry." She stated that she is afraid of Halloran's and his friend's political power against her. She stated that she was "here" because she listened to him once. She wouldn't listen to him again, but that she is afraid of him. The letter was postmarked February 21.[66]

1933, February 27
Edward Huntington Williams MD of 910 Pacific Mutual Building writes a letter to George Stephens, "I am greatly interested to know that the Halloran people sought your advice in the case. It seemed to be perfectly obvious to everyone now that Ruth is insane, good and plenty and I don't believe they will ever hang her." "I suppose the best they will do, and about the best thing they could do, will be to commute her

sentence to life imprisonment. If so, after a while, she will get so crazy in the prison that they will finally transfer her to the state hospital."[67]

1933, Early March
Ruth convinces her mother that she has a razor blade in her mouth and intends to swallow it. This was not true. This was the testimony six weeks later by Warden Shute.[68]

1933, March 1
Ruth writes a letter to Mr. L. S. Todd of Tipton, Indiana. She thanks him for the articles that he wrote and also for the petitions he gathered. She states that she has few friends in Arizona that she is among strangers. She states that all twenty-two of the grand jurors are doing all they can for her. She states that several members of the senate and representatives have been down to see her and they are doing all they can for her. She states that the Phoenix papers are bitter against her and refuse to print anything written by friends of mine. She stated that Halloran has propositioned her that if she would tell a story he made up in the case, in order to exonerate him of the part he did in the case, he will use all his power and influence either way. She states that she refuses to let him bully her any more in this case even though he is blocking every move she makes towards a commutation of sentence. So, she is asking the state to try her on the Samuelson case since she is charged with John Doe and Richard Roe. She stated that she didn't get to take the witness stand on the LeRoi case. She stated that her lawyers tricked her into not geting to take the stand, first they told her that Jack Halloran was going to take the stand for the state and that when they cross examined him, they would tear him to pieces and that she did not need to worry. Halloran was never called and his name was never on the list.[69] She states she is worried over Halloran's threats to her. She stated she was convicted on the drain pipe letter in which she said that they had quarreled and that Anne said that she was going to kill me. She closes by stating that if they commute her sentence she will do her very best. She will try to prove herself worthy of all that he is doing for her.[69]

1933, March 3
Ruth writes another letter to Renz Jennings, county attorney trying to get them to try her for Sammy's death. She says that Halloran has propositioned her and threatened her. He wants her to tell a lie about

41

Anne and Sammy to help clear his name. She says that Halloran will sway his influence against her if she doesn't. She talks about writing a letter to the families to get them worked up over the lies and they will sue him. She states that Mr. Frank Smith is going around telling people that the two girls bit her and the bruises on her body were bite marks.[70] Ruth stated that no man, woman, child, or animal has ever bitten her. She also stated that she could certainly prove that Jack Halloran was with her after midnight at the girls' house on Friday night. She stated she wanted to tell why she felt sure Jack Halloran had Sammy operated on. She wanted to put a stop to those lies Mr. Frank Smith is telling everyone. She wanted the girl's families to get so worked up over the lies that they would sue Halloran. Ruth stated that she would be glad to testify even if it cost her, her own life.[66]

1933, March 10 or so
Ruth tries to saw through a bar in her prison cell. The saw was believed given to her by her brother Burton. She claimed when asked that she wanted to be ready if she had an opportunity to escape. The warden on duty saw her sawing at the bars. No warrant for Burton's arrest had been issued.[71] She had sawed through one bar. It was said even if she could escape her cell, she would be surrounded by concrete and masonry and a very high steel picketed spiked fence around the women's ward.[72] Ruth stated that her reason for tampering with the window was that she "wanted to let somebody else in."[68] In one source, she had two small saws and had sawed through 2 bars before anybody noticed. Carrie McKinnell pleaded for her not to be put away in a dungeon. Her hands were "raw and bleeding."[73]

1933, March 13
HA Anspach writes a letter to the Arizona Board of Pardons. He is the paster at the Grace Lutheran Church at Third Street at Moreland. He stated that he had been asked to sign a petition to commute Ruth Judd's sentence. He states that he cannot do so and so is writing this letter. He stated that the law should take its course. He believed that there was a fair trial and that Mrs. Judd was not at all interested in justice but in saving her own neck. He stated that he interviewed five men who have been or are officially connected with the case. From them I gather that there was no self-defense involved, and that therefore her attorneys did not defend on that ground. He stated that some members of the jury agreed to the death penalty to get her to talk. He suggested that they

give her a 50-80-year sentence provided she come clean with what you believe to be the real truth. He stated that if it develops that there was unusually great provocation, such as, for instance an attack upon her by the two women (who are thought by some to have been perverts of the sadist type), that a pardon could be given after a few years. But if she doesn't tell the truth, the death penalty should stand.[74]

1933, March 14
Ruth was wearing a blue and white gingham dress with some pansies pinned on them. She greeted her husband and parents in the lobby of the administration building. They were not allowed in the proceedings. In the room she sat across from board members, Lin B. Orme, Arthur La Prade, and attorney HE Hendrix. She was represented by EH Karz, and HG Richardson. The warden Walker was there and Gene Shute of the prison. She was with her matron and a half dozen newspapermen represented the public. Ruth's appearance before the Pardon Board begins at 2:25 and ends at 5:20. Several recesses were granted at times when Ruth seemed to border on hysterics. She retold the story much as she had during the Halloran hearing including that Jack had aided her in disposing of the bodies and advised her to conceal the crime. Other details included that she had never assisted in any kind of surgical operation. She talked about how she met Anne and Sammy (details not found in the Arizona Rpublic unfortunately). She broke down and sobbed and stated that she loved her husband and she loved him still. She stated that she had not been permitted to testify at her trial. She said that at the time she was told that the jury was fixed and that one man would hang up the jury and that she would not be convicted. She flipped charges at the board that she was being "influenced" to tell an untrue story on the promise if she exonerated others that her sentence would be commuted and if she didn't she would be hanged. She re-enacted the fight including showing how she was on the floor on her knees.[75]

1933, March 15
Charges were made to the Arizona Board of Pardons and Paroles that the Superior Court jury which convicted Winnie Ruth Judd made a "deal to impose capital punishment only for the purpose of making her talk." The session that occurred on this evening was a secret sitting and newspapermen and Mrs. Judd's attorney were excluded. Mrs. Judd was not present when her attorneys made the accusation to the board. The

board decided that it should hear the testimony of four witnesses. There was one juror in particular that felt that he arranged the deal and asserted that this juror had informed the others that he could influence the board of pardons and paroles to commute the death sentence. Several of the jurors had stated that they would not have returned the death verdict if she had talked. After argument, the board declined to hear the jurors. La Prade stated, "Take those jurors to the superior court and let them confess their sins and let the superior court prosecute." Willson abandoned his attempt to have the jurors called and allowed their names to be stricken from the list Ruth had told the board in secret essentially the same story she told at the Halloran hearing. Details were not related. Ruth asked the board for a trial to be tried for the death of Hedvig Samuelson. She claimed that during her trial, her lawyers wanted the insanity defense. She said, "I did not want it and I did not like some of the things they said about me." She said she would be sent to the state hospital for two or three years and then would be paroled to her husband. In recounting parts of her trial and story she said several things including that she couldn't budge the trunk when it was at the duplex. She denied that she had severed the body of Miss Samuelson. She denied that there was a surgical operation. She admitted moving portions of Hedvig from the large trunk to smaller trunks since the large trunk weighed too much to be checked as baggage.[76]

1933, March 16
Thomas Frelinghuysen, now 28 (a friend of Sammy's) sails on a two-week cruise out of New York with no other family members aboard the SS Quiniouas. His address is listed as 19 E 59th Street in New York. He is listed as single. [77]

1933, March 17
Witnesses (at least 6) were said to be scheduled to appear before the Arizona Board of Pardons and Paroles. People who were subpoenaed included Maude Marshall, A. D. Leyhe, attorney, Nora Smith, Lloyd Andrews, Betty Murray, and Dr. HJ McKeown. Willson also stated that he might submit the names of one or more other witnesses stating, "I'm on the track of some new evidence." They argued whether Judge Niles testimony should be allowed.[78]

1933, March 19

A telegram arrives for La Prade from the LA Times. RW Trueblood stated that, "The confession of Mrs. Judd Published in Times of October 25-27 was given to us by her husband acting as her authorized agent and was certified by Mrs. Judd in her own handwriting as correct and authorized by her. Stop. Our reporters had a number of confirmatory interviews with her subsequently but these were not in form of statements directly dictated by her.[79]

1933, March 20

Twelve witnesses appeared in front of the pardon board. In the evening, counsel for Ruth conferred with her at the state prison regarding whether Louis P Russill would be permitted to relate to the board her first confession. Russill told the board on this day that Mrs. Judd gave the statement to him and a shorthand reporter in the presence of her husband Dr. WC Judd in Los Angeles before she surrendered to the police. Ruth had acquired new council before her trial so her first statement had never been used. Willson, Karz and Richardson were unsuccessful in determining what Russill had to tell. Russill had appeared at the hearing as a surprise witness of his own volition. Russill spent much of the morning scolding newspapermen for their activities in Los Angeles prior to and after Mrs. Judd's arrest, declined to discuss his testimony with Mrs. Judd's present counsel, and refused to accompany them to Florence for a conference in the evening with the convicted woman. Russill stated that he offered to present his evidence only after Ruth had agreed to such action in a written statement. The board said that they would hear him in the morning. Ruth's attorneys met with her to try to find out what she had told Russill in Los Angeles. La Prade had told Russill that "We don't want any half disclosures; either all of it or none of it. I want to know what Ruth Judd told you that is incriminating as well as what she told you that exonerates her." People who were examined on this day included Dr. McKeown, Nora Smith, Attorney Russill, Phoebe Reed, Mrs. F. H. Reed, Betty Murray, John Wozniak, Lloyd Andrews, AD Leyhe, Milton O Sullivan, Kenneth Grimm, Renz Jennings, and Sheriff McFadden. McFadden said for the first time that the missing organs of Sammy "fell out" when she was transferring the body and that she had wrapped them in towels and tossed them out a window on the train. Ruth didn't know where she tossed them out. He tried to find them. McFadden also told of finding considerable evidence of blood in the breakfast room and

45

kitchen of the duplex. McFadden stated that Ruth had first told him of the self-defense story on the second day after she was returned to Phoenix. McFadden stated that Ruth did not know Sammy had been dissected until she transferred her body. She didn't know the whereabouts of the missing mattress. She did not know that the piece of the rug had been cut out. Phoebe Reed declared she saw Ruth at 3 PM on Saturday afternoon near the duplex. She told her playmates and her to move away from a pile of bricks on which they were playing or in the vacant lot across from the duplex. Her mother RH Reed stated that she and her husband and brother in law smelled something burning late Saturday and into Sunday morning. John Wozniak of 2915 Central Ave stated that he saw Ruth step off a street car after 10 and walk one half blocks west and turn into the alley in the rear of the duplex. Lloyd Andrews stated that the bullet wounds in the heads and the powder burns around the wounds did not fit Ruth's story. Leyhe stated that he had heard Ruth ask Lewkowitz when she would be able to tell her story and he said for her not to worry that she would have that chance. Betty Murray stated that several times Ruth stated that she couldn't stand the sight of blood and that she didn't like to cut up chickens. Dr. McKeown revealed that there was "something wrong" with the X-ray machine at the Grunow clinic prior to the slaying. Nora Smith stated that both women were friendly, that she could not prove that the double slaying was not premeditated, but that she thought Ruth deserved another chance. Ruth had claimed Milton Sullivan the night clerk at the Hotel Adams stated he overheard a conversation between Halloran and Fred Ryan. Sullivan stated he was very surprised to be called as a witness and that he did not know at what time he had seen Halloran in the hotel or whether it was Friday night, Thursday night or Saturday night. Sheriff McFadden stated that Sullivan had told him that Halloran and Ryan and another man were in the Hotel at 10 PM and that they left about 10:20 PM returning soon seemingly very excited. Sullivan asked what the matter was, but they gave him no reply. Kenneth Grimm told of aiding Ruth to move from the duplex to the Brill street apartment in August (?) He stated that after returning her to the duplex she said she had forgotten something. He heard her say, "I went off and forgot my gun. I always keep it with me when I'm alone. So, I came back for it." Note: in August she moved from Brill to the duplex, not from the duplex to Brill. Renz Jennings stated that he was not able to get the right statements from Halloran or Andrew Blevins, railway station employee without asking leading statements.[80] W. Robert LaDue signed an affidavit regarding his interaction with AN Smith regarding Jack Halloran being in control of the pardon board outcome. That if Ruth would exonerate Jack in the press, he would see to it that the Pardon Board would change her sentence from death to life.[65]

1933, March 22
Jack Halloran appears before the board of pardons and paroles as a witness and for the first time publically denied that he ever had any knowledge of the slaying by Ruth Judd. He was summoned by the board at the insistence of Mrs. Judd who accused him as an accessory to the crime. Arthur La Prade questioned him. In other news from that day, Ruth refused to allow three of her former attorneys' facts in regard to the case to what she had revealed to them (Russill). Attorney La Prade made it known that Ruth during their secret session at the state penitentiary last week said that she had shot and killed Mrs. LeRoi in bed and then wounded Miss Samuelson as she emerged from the bathroom, then killed her in a struggle in the kitchen. He also said it was his theory that she dismembered the body of Miss Samuelson. La Prade said that she at one time told such a story to one of her attorneys as a substitute for another story which he checked with the physical facts in the case and told her that he "didn't believe it was true." Louis R. Russill was excused from the hearing with his story untold. He declined to testify after Mrs. Judd refused to waive the right of confidential relationship existing between an attorney and his client. Willson explained to the board about why Russill should not testify to tell "her first story". He said that he might not remember exactly what she had told him. Ruth also penned a statement declining to permit any testimony she made to Lewkowitz and Zaversack who were also called as witnesses. The board denied again the idea that there was a deal between members of the jury which convicted her in "order to make her talk" Mrs. Lon Jordan, matron for Mrs. Judd, was called by the Judd attorneys. She declared that Ruth had never told her that she was alone in the aftermath of the slayings. Halloran was subpoenaed by the board. He testified that he had seen Ruth Judd on October 15 and that this was the last time that he saw her until the trial in 1932. Halloran said, "I have been subpoenaed here, and I am not a voluntary witness in answering that subpoena – but I am not a hostile witness. Under no conditions can it be understood that my appearance here indicates any bitterness in my mind toward anyone. I was subpoenaed at the trial (Mrs. Judd's trial for murder) and I attended the trial every day, but I

was never called. My name has been blazoned through the land, in an untruthful manner – whether vindictively or not. I am not judging. I am here to tell the truth, to answer truthfully all questions involving my alleged appearance at either of the houses mentioned or of having seen or talked with Mrs. Judd after Thursday night, October 15, 1931." La Prade asked him if he had gone to Brill street at any time on October 16. He answered, "I did not." Did you see Mrs. Judd there about 11 or 12 o'clock? "I did not," Halloran said. La Prade asked him if Ruth had told him that she had killed Mrs. LeRoi and Miss Samuelson. He said, "I never saw Mrs. Judd after Thursday night, and I was not the last to see her at that time. She was escorted to her door by another man as I sat in the car outside." La Prade asked if he had gone with her to Second Street. He said he had not. La Prade asked him if he saw any bodies there. He answerred, "I did not." He said that he knew Mrs. LeRoi and Miss Samuelson. LaPrade asked him if he had cut up a body. Halloran answered, "I certainly did not." LaPrade asked if he arranged to have it done. He said, "I did not." Halloran continued to say that prior to Ruth's return from Los Angeles to stand trial he had received a phone call from a Phoenix attorney who asked if he "knew anyone connected with the case" stating he had received a call from Los Angeles and "presumed it was a case of money." Halloran told him that "if that was the situation, I was not interested." Halloran said that he received a secondd call from a Los Angeles attorney who did not, however, inquire about the slayings, but merely asked regarding the whereabouts of another man. He did not ask anything about Ruth Judd and did not talk about money. Halloran stated that he had received a third call a month or two ago from "A man named Barber" apparently in Santa Monica who "had some story about knowing the McKinnell's and Burton." He said, "I just figured it was another one of those mysterious calls or letters I had been receiving and paid no attention to it." Halloran stated that he had never had any conversations with HJ McKinnell. He said that he had talked with Burton. He said that Burton McKinnell had telephoned him; said he was "interested in saving his sister's life" and asked to see Halloran "away from his office." Halloran told him that when Burton told him that he wanted to talk to him he told him, "Fine, come to my office." Burton said that he would phone him the next day and see if he changed his mind. He said again that Burton could come to his office or that he was willing to see him in Burton's lawyer's office." Burton did not ask him to aid or assist his sister. There was no talk about money. Halloran said that Dr. Judd also called him during the trial. He said that he wanted to see the lumberman. Halloran said that he would be in his office in 15 minutes if he wanted to come. Dr. Judd phoned again and Halloran said, "He phoned again in about 30 minutes, said he had decided not to come, that detectives might be following him and his visit might be misunderstood. I said probably he was right." Halloran stated that he had not received any letters from Ruth Judd, Dr. Judd, Burton, or Carrie. When asked if any of Ruth's attorneys had ever written to him he replied in the affirmative. He said on December 16 of 1932, a Los Angeles attorney said he recently had been in Phoenix but had not called on him. It outlined plans for gaining clemency for Ruth Judd and said in part, "I feel if I should come to Phoenix again you would be willing to aid…" When asked if he replied to it. Halloran said, "I did not." Halloran stated that he was at home Friday night in the early part of the evening. On Thursday he said he went to the Second Street house in company with two other men, arriving there about 7 and remained for about 20 minutes and then went to Ruth's apartment on Brill Street. They talked and had something to eat and then took a ride for about 20 minutes. He returned to her home with another woman who had been at the Judd apartment and immediately after he took Ruth to her home. Then he said he stopped at his own home for about 10 minutes and then took the other men to their hotel. After that he said he went home and remained there. He said the guy who made the statement about him being excited at the Adams hotel on Friday night to be untrue; that he had not left his house on Friday night. He stated that his wife was at home. His daughter was home, and his son was out and returned about 11 pm. Halloran stated that he had planned on going to a football game with his son at the stadium, but he had another engagement so he stayed home and listened to the game on the radio. He said that he didn't call Ruth on Saturday morning. He did not communicate with her on Saturday night. As for Saturday morning he said, "I was at my office." Halloran stated that he left the office about noon, had lunch at home, and went to the Phoenix Country Club for golf in the afternoon. He named the men he played golf with. He said it was his habit to play golf on Saturday afternoon. When asked if those men remember if he played golf with them that day he stated he had not asked them. He said he left the club between 5:30 and 6, had dinner at home, and went to the office of a business acquaintance, where he remained until 9 PM and then went home again and entertained visitors until 10 PM. He said after that he went to bed. On

Sunday he stated he played golf with his business acquaintances whom he had visited the night before, went to a show with his wife in the afternoon, and to dinner at a downtown restaurant with his son and two daughters in the evening, returning home between 7 and 8 to remain there. He said he first learned of the tragedy when a physician acquaintance called him by telephone on Monday night. He said he was shocked to learn of the tragedy. La Prade asked him if he knew why Ruth was telling the story she did. He replied, "I cannot. It's a mystery to me why after a year and a half my name has been brought into this case in this way. If I had been connected with the case, Mrs. Judd certainly would have brought the charges originally." Willson tried to get into the relationship he had with Ruth and the girls. Halloran told him that what happened before the tragedy was not relevant at this hearing. He demanded that Willson, "stick to the issue" and to not delve into something that does not involve him. Willson asked why he had not attempted to clear his name. Halloran said, "I saw no necessity to rushing into print. I made one statement. Your question is not properly put and has no bearing on the issue at hand. I have sat calmly by and suffered, knowing that the truth would come out. I am making no refusal to answer any question directly bearing on charges against me."[4]

1933, March 22
Dr. Judd appeared before the pardon board on Ruth's behalf. He related Ruth's story and stated reasons why he deemed that there were flaws in her story. He said of Jack Halloran, "I know Jack Halloran, and it is very difficult for me to believe that Jack had anything to do with that. But, I am absolutely unable to believe that she was alone in that.... Of course, I have no knowledge of that except what she told me." Other people appearing were Lloyd Andrews, Jack Halloran, Milton O Sullivan, Sheriff McFadden, George E Lilley, Maude Wade, Dave Fulbright, Maude Marshall, HG Richardson, and Burton McKinnell. Mrs. Maude Wade stated that Ruth had never bought a chicken that wasn't already cut up and prepared since she couldn't kill one or cut one up. Dr. Judd told the board that his wife concealed the story for more than three weeks from him. Now, he believes he knew the real story. He believed that she was not alone in the attempted disposal of the bodies. Her second story to him, (what she has told the board) that he never was able to forget or to disbelieve. He said this was because of the amount of detail; that nobody would be able to

make up those sorts of things since there were so many improbable little things in it. He said her first story in LA shortly after her arrest; that she alone killed the women and had not help from anyone in disposing of the bodies he declared was utterly unreasonable and improbable.... "I wouldn't want to say it was impossible, but it is unreasonable beyond belief." "There is no use denying she has contradicted herself time after time. I don't know when she will do it again. That was the chief reason she did not testify at her trial. We couldn't trust her for 24 hours. The thing that struck me first as strange was the emphasis she placed on being alone. Without being asked a question, repeatedly and emphatically she volunteered, 'I was alone.' She first told him a new story in the county jail here about three weeks after she was returned from Los Angeles. She was sobbing and crying in my arms. She seemed to attach no importance to the deaths of the girls themselves. Uppermost then in her mind appeared to be her confession that she had been deceiving her husband." When they questioned him about the bodies he said, "She shrugged her shoulders and said, 'Why you know I didn't do that. I couldn't cut up a chicken.'" She told her lawyers later that she had told her husband this in private. Dr. Judd stated she changed her story almost every day. "We never knew for 24 hours what she would say. That was the chief reason she didn't testify at her trial." Dr. Judd said, "Once she let me write out a story for her to sign, but she wouldn't sign it." Dr. Judd talked about her movements around LA after coming in with the trunks. He talks about her going to the Broadway Department store, the one place she might be known. He said, "She met a buyer she once knew in the elevator. He didn't recognize her, but it frightened her. She knew she couldn't stay long in that store, so then where does she go? To the sanitarium where she had once been a patient, another of the few places she might have been recognized. Where does she go the next day to do her telephoning? Back to the Broadway Department Store. It is interesting to show her state of mind during that period of stress and her complete lack of planning." Regarding the dismemberment of Sammy, he said, "Knowing myself something of the difficulty of disarticulating a spinal column, I told her I thought it almost impossible for her to have done it." Dr. Judd related in detail various methods which he said his wife had told him she used to cut up Miss Samuelson's body in a bathtub. Each time he objected to her on the ground of impossibility. Ruth would think a few minutes and make up a new method. He said, "My reason for relating to you all these gruesome details, is to show you that girl had no understanding of how that thing could be done. At the same time, she was insisting she did it. That was why we couldn't believe her story from one day to the next." He continued, "To this day she shows lack of knowledge of the condition of those bodies. Part of it I don't understand at all. The other day I talked with her at the prison and she told me how Sammy's body was dressed – the pajama jacket on the upper part, the pajama trousers on the lower part. The evidence of officers in Los Angeles showed the body was nude. She doesn't know yet. I am absolutely unable to believe she was alone in that, but of course I have no more knowledge of it than you men have." He talked about the bullet course using a desk telephone. He said it was impossible that Anne was in bed since the bullet was ranged backward and downward since her head would have had to have been at the foot of the bed. He stated the story of shooting Anne in a crouching position on the floor will explain the course of the bullet and "nothing else will explain it." He said in the end, "Almost nothing is impossible." I would say it was probably impossible for a woman in her condition with the use of one hand. I think it utterly unreasonable and improbable. Unreasonable beyond belief." He stated that she had not had any experience in surgical operations. "I tried many times when I was in Mexico to get her to help me with dressings, but she never could do it." HJ asked Dr. Judd if he believed that Ruth Judd was a woman of sound reasoning. Dr. Judd said, "No. I do not." Lloyd Andrews stated that she had told at least 5 stories that were all different. He stated that there was no evidence except for hearsay. Sheriff McFadden collaborated with Andrews that corroborative evidence was necessary before action. George Lilly testified that he and his wife visited the Halloran home on the night following the slayings; the night Ruth insisted that she met him at the duplex. Maude Marshall stated that she heard a car in the apartment court about midnight and heard voices in Mrs. Judd's apartment, but did not recognize them. On Sunday, Ruth came to her apartment with her hand bandaged and asked her to open a can of salmon for her.[81]

1933, March 23
A telegram is received from RW Trueblood of the LA Times. He stated that Dr. Judd testified that Times story was dictated by him to your Mrs. Hotchkiss; that Hotchkiss wrote the story on the typewriter as Dr. Judd dictated, Hotchkiss using her own judgement as to literary form and phraseology. Stop. Wire me collect any explanation that you

can give on this subject matter.[82] Another telegram arrives on this date
stating Dr. Judd's story was dictated to Kenneth O'Hara, rewrite man at
LA times, with Carton Williams and Albert Nathan reporters present.
Stop. O'Hara writing directly on typewriter stop phraseology and
literary form chosen by O'Hara but the facts contained in the story
were given by Judd. Stop. Judd also read all proofs before story was
printed and corroborated by checking with his wife in county jail. Stop.
She signed the proofs signifying them to be correct.[82] The pardon
board hearing ends. The surprise was that they asked Dr. Judd to return
the following day for a conference on March 24. Dr. Judd also testified
on this day. Three witnesses were heard on this day, Dr. Judd, Frank O
Smith, and HJ McKinnell. Dr. Judd chain smoked while testifying and
he seemed quite nervous. The inquiry was to determine whether Mrs.
LeRoi could have been shot in bed and also what may have happened
to the missing mattress, the sale of stories regarding the double slaying,
and a detailed account about what Ruth told him regarding the
dismembering of Sammy's body. He repeated his faith in the self-
defense story and stated that her dismembering the corpse was
impossible. HJ McKinnell pleads mercy for his daughter and said, "I
do not wish to appear as courting personal sympathy. My wife and I
are not entitled to any more consideration than the parents of Anne
LeRoi and Hedvig Samuelson. I may bring no new evidence for many
angles in this case are fictitious. Who mutilated a human body and
who shipped certain bodies is not in legitimate consideration for the
state never charged Ruth with doing either. There are but three things
to weigh: Did Ruth Judd kill Anne LeRoi, which is confessed; was it
with malice aforethought or was it in a fight, and if in a fight, may it be
a defensive fight; and if punishment be deserved what should that
punishment be? Granted that I am supposed to be prejudiced on my
child's side, while I do not want her considered as a paragon of
perfection, yet in view of the judgement at which I must shortly appear,
in considering her life from the dawn of responsibility to the present
hour, I brand the assaults on her chastity and veracity a false...." He
choked back tears. Willson closed and talked about her sanity. He was
pessimistic over the probability a jury of laymen would find her insane.
He said she had already been before a jury. He said if she were
imprisoned for the rest of her life, she would grow worse and worse
and finally the warden would call a lunacy commission and she would
be placed in an asylum. HG Richardson of Florence begged the board
to consider itself the court of last resort. He thought there was no way

that they would be going to the US Supreme Court.[83]

1933, March 28
Frank O Smith writes a letter to the Arizona Board of Pardons and
Paroles detailing that whereabouts of Jack Halloran during October of
1931.[11] Smith claims that he has made a thorough investigation into
the matter with independent investigators, and every statement made by
Mr. Halloran was verified and he believed correct. He stated that Ryan
and Hermes live in El Paso but that they would come to Phoenix if
needed.[11] He ends the letter by saying, "I appreciate the length of time
which the members of the Board have given to the consideration of this
matter and the great patience they have displayed. This letter is written
with the sole point in mind that in view of the fact that Mr. Halloran
has been a citizen here for many years, has raised a family here and
built up a business enterprise he very greatly desires, and I concur with
him in the desire and his friends are also desirous that the Board be
completely satisfied with reference to his whereabouts during the
periods that have been brought into question in this case. We do not
want any matter left in doubt on this subject."[11]

1933, March 30
The Arizona Board of Pardons and Paroles gave their last word. They
denied commutation of the death sentence for Ruth Judd. The hanging
date for Ruth Judd was moved to April 21 so it would not fall on Good
Friday.[84] Ruth has a secret meeting with the Board of Pardons and
Paroles during March. Lin Orme stated later that she claimed that if
her sentence was not commuted; she would impregnate herself since
they would not kill her if she was going to be a mother.[85] Kirk
McKinnell tells a corroborated story about this, "When she was within
about 48 hours of being executed, my dad supposedly went out into the
"alley", found a "bum", and persuaded him to deposit his sperm sample
into a "cup", which Burton then smuggled into Ruth's cell, where the
idea was to get a stay of execution, on the grounds that she was
pregnant. I don't know if you or any of the books ever heard this story.
It is my personal guess, that there was no bum, and Ruth probably
knew that there was no bum, and that she did use the sample, probably
from my Dad, to impregnate herself."[86] She sobs and wails that the
pardon board has turned her down. She is not sleeping. The pardon
board releases a 2500-word decision. The pardon board also revealed
that Dr. Judd had given them some important new evidence during a

private conference. Part of the report said, "Dr. Judd appeared before the board and among other things he said Mrs. Judd told him she dismembered the body of Miss Samuelson in a bathtub. He related in detail the manner in which the dismemberment was accomplished as told by Ruth. Dr. Judd stated she stuck to this story for several weeks, and then denied dismembering the body, both to him and to her lawyers. He further said the matter was considered at great length by him and her attorneys to present a self-defense plea, but that the reason they were afraid to do so was that Mrs. Judd under cross examination might admit she killed Miss LeRoi on the bed, and dismembered Miss Samuelson's body in the bathtub as related to him previously. A thorough, thoughtful consideration of all the testimony and Mrs. Judd's own statement to the board together with a careful review of all the facts and circumstances attendant on the tragedy compels the board to believe that Mrs. Judd shot Miss LeRoi through the temple while she was in bed, the muzzle of the gun being held at or near the surface of the skin. And that Miss LeRoi was not killed in self-defense. The Supreme Court of the state held that she had a fair and impartial trial." There was reason to believe that the board made a last minute change in its decision. The board stated that they had visited with Orme, Hendrix, and Laprade making a two-hour visit to the murder apartment. Returning they tore up their original statement and rewrote it entirely. None of them commented on this. It was believed that until the end, one of them had held out on Mrs. Judd's behalf.[73]

1933, March 31
Warden AG Walker announced that Ruth had tried to saw through a cell bar with a hacksaw believed delivered to her by her brother Burton.[71] Apparently, she had two small saws in her cell and she had sawed through two bars before anybody noticed.[73] The Arizona Republic publishes the full text of the Board's decision. Selected quotes include: "She explained the presence of the gun at the house of the deceased by saying that she had previously lived with the deceased women and had left the gun there. In this behalf the board learned through a creditable witness who had assisted Mrs. Judd in moving from the Second Street apartment to the Brill Street Apartment on October 1, 1931, that Mrs. Judd during the removal trip, having gone from the North Second Street Apartment as far as Palm Lane asked him to return with her to get 'something that she had left.' He did return with Mrs. Judd; that Mrs. Judd went into the house and stated to Mrs.

LeRoi and Miss Samuelson that she had left her gun and returned for it. The board is thoroughly satisfied from the testimony of two creditable witnesses that Ruth Judd was at the Second Street house for a considerable length of time on Saturday afternoon, October 17th." "The defendant would not make this statement directly to the county attorney in the presence of a court reporter, or at all, nor would she sign a written statement setting out the above alleged facts, through repeatedly requested so to do by both the sheriff and the county attorney. So far as the board is able to learn she never related the foregoing self-defense story and the alleged connection of Mr. Halloran with the disposal of the bodies to any one in authority, other than the sheriff and matron at the county jail, until December 1932. Then she related the story to the sheriff and the warden of the state prison, in the presence of a shorthand reporter. Within a short time thereafter she again related the story to the Maricopa County grand jury." "The drayman testified that he delivered the exceedingly heavy trunk to the Brill Street apartment and placed the same in the front room. When MR. Grimm and his son, at the request of Ruth Judd, was called to take the trunk to the railroad station Sunday afternoon, they found the trunk in the rear room, approximately 15 feet from the place where it had been left by the Lightning Delivery drayman." "The coroner's report, together with that of the autopsy surgeon, shows that none of the vital organs of the body of Miss Samuelson had been operated upon. She was not pregnant, the womb being of normal size and in place. None of the organs were missing except a small portion of the lower intestine. Mrs. Judd now admits that she wrapped this small portion of the severed intestine in a towel at the Brill Street house, placed it in a small bag, took it with her on the train, and that during the trip to Los Angeles she threw the towel and contents out the train window." "Dr. Judd also testified that Mrs. Judd admitted to him that she burned the mattress on a vacant lot near the Second Street house, and that he had searched the premises and had been unable to find any place on the ground that might indicate that a mattress had been burned." "Dr. Judd appeared before the board and, among other things, testified that Mrs. Judd, shortly after her return by the officers from Los Angeles, told him that she dismembered the body of Miss Samuelson in the bathtub at the Second Street house. He related in detail the manner in which the dismemberment was accomplished, as told to him by Ruth Judd. He stated that she stuck to this story for some two or three weeks, and that he related it to her lawyers, Messrs, Lewkowitz and Zaversac; that these lawyers then asked her about this story; that she reproached Dr. Judd for having told the lawyers saying, "I told you this in confidence. It was for your ears alone." Dr. Judd testified that shortly thereafter she denied both to him and the lawyers, that she had dismembered the body at the Second Street house or anywhere else." "Mrs. Judd voluntarily admitted to the board that at one time she had told one of her lawyers that she had killed Mrs. LeRoi in bed; that when the shot was fired Miss Samuelson was in the bathroom; that Miss Samuelson opened the bathroom door and that she fired the first shot into the body of Miss Samuelson at or near the bathroom door; and that Miss Samuelson retreated to the kitchen where she received the second shot. The muzzle of the gun being held on or near the surface of the skin."[87]

1933, April 1

AG Walker increases the guard around Ruth's cell since she had repeatedly threatened to commit suicide. He made this decision after he announced that Ruth Judd had been caught trying to saw her way through one of the bars in her cell. He put out a search for Burton J McKinnell who allegedly brought her the tools. Burton was thought to be in California at this time.[88] Burton stated that he would return if there was a warrant out for his arrest. There was not any warrant.[72] They searched her cell and found no vials or knives in which she could take her own life.[88] Ruth was extremely cheerful on this day and this puzzled the guards. She calmly went into counsel with her attorneys regarding their decision of the night before that she had shot Anne LeRoi while she slept in bed and killed Hedvig Samuelson in a deadly pursuit around the house silencing the second woman's outcry.[72]

1933, April 2

The warden AG Walkerstated that "there's not a question in my mind that she will kill herself if the opportunity arises, rather than hang." He brought 2 more women guards from Phoenix to help Ella Heath in the rigid day and night watch over Ruth.[89]

1933, April 3

The Warden gave the Governor an anonymous letter threatening to bomb the state capital building unless Mrs. Judd was released to her mother. Otherwise, explosives would be used powerful enough to kill all Phoenix residents and shake the buildings worse than the recent Pacific Coast Earthquakes. The letter was signed, the Gangster from Germany.[84]

1933, April 4

Burton is arrested and put into jail. It is not for assistance in giving his sister a hacksaw to escape from prison. Police had taken him into custody for that, but released him since there was no warrant out for his arrest. Burton denied that he had given his sister a saw. Later a motor patrol officer arrested Burton on a charge for failing to adjust glaring headlights and he was unable to pay the $10 bail for his release.[90] Officials received a letter from an anonymous author carrying a threat to bomb the capital if Ruth were not released to her mother. The writer called himself the Gangster from Germany, who claimed to have a bomb powerful enough to kill all Phoenix residents and shake the building worse than the recent Pacific coast earthquake. The letter read, "Release this woman by the name of Winnie Ruth Judd for her old mother's sake and if they are going to hang her or if she died, then the whole capitol or the whole prison will be destroyed by a very powerful bomb enough to kill all the people and also shake up whole buildings all over town worse than an earthquake. I have already destroyed the judge's home several months ago in Los Angeles. Do what you please with her. If you turned her loose at free will, your capitol and the prison will be safe. If not, I have four men to destroy which I paid them lots of money to do. This is the last warning to you. So watch out and free her to her mother. I used a German powerful bomb."[91] At the bottom of the ruled tablet paper were the words, <u>BeWare</u> which were underlined. The governor's office stated that numerous threatening letters had been received. This was the only letter that stated she should be released to her mother.[91] The Board was considering an application that Ruth be reprieved until June 2nd. The reasons being: 1. Time to file in superior court, 2. Plans for an application to the US Supreme Court for a writ of habeas corpus or a writ of certiorari. 3. Time for Warden A. G. Walker to recommend a sanity hearing [91] Dr. Judd arrived in Los Angeles and severely censured the Arizona Board of Pardons and Paroles saying that they had grossly distorted the testimony given by himself and Ruth. He claimed that he had no such statement before the parole board that stated that Ruth had admitted shooting Anne LeRoi as she lay in bed and had admitted cutting up the bodies of both Mrs. LeRoi and Hedvig Samuelson. OV Willson and Edwin Karz, went to LA with Dr. Judd.[92]

1933, April 5

Burton was being held by the police in connection with an asserted attempt at escape by his sister. McKinnell denied his sister's statement that he furnished saws with which she tried to hack away the bars of her cell. He declared she had been frightened into implicating him. AG Walker stated that McKinnell was not wanted in Arizona and so they released him.[92]

1933, April 6
The Board of Pardons of Paroles met to reconsider its ruling or grant a reprieve of 42 days to allow for possible appeal to the US Supreme Court. The board quickly issued a twenty-eight-word statement of refusal to do so. Winnie became hysterical when Richardson brought her the news. He said, "We feel that Mrs. Judd has suffered a living death already, and that if the Board of Pardons and paroles could see fit to grant her a new lease on life, even if it erred, it would be erring on the side of mercy, and in the face of great doubt.[84] HG Richardson stated that she took the news the previous day with remarkable calm under the circumstances.[93] HG Richardson stated that after he had visited her in the women's ward "She accepted it quite calmly, though under the circumstances but of course, she is upset. She feels strongly that at several points along the way, during and since her trial, fairness and justice have not prevailed. She has not lost hope, however, that she still may live.[93] He stated that Ruth in conference with him cited five instances in which law had not dealt squarely with her. 1. The allegation that the trial jury which found her guilty and fixed the death penalty was influenced by a juror who was alleged before being placed in the box to have made prejudiced remarks against her. 2. The refusal of her defending counsel in the trial to allow her to take the witness stand and tell a story of self-defense. 3. The allegations that the jury once having found her guilty as influenced by several of its members in making a deal to name the death penalty in order to make her talk. 4. The board of pardons and paroles has declined to go into the matters of the prejudice on the part of the jurors or to investigate the alleged deal involving the death penalty. 5. Testimony of the two surprise witnesses before the board of pardons and paroles that they saw Mrs. Judd Saturday afternoon at the apartment where Mrs. LeRoi and Mrs. Samuelson were killed that was false although cited by the board as one of its reasons for disbelieving Mrs. Judd's own story. He stated Ruth could prove that she was at her place of employment until evening.[93] Ruth starts a letter to, HG Richardson at 7 PM. She states that it is the first and only confession of the case of the homicide of Agnes Anne

LeRoi and Hedvig Samuelson. In this letter she tells a different story of the crimes. She states that she waited on the porch all night with the intention of shooting Anne. Sammy kept using the bathroom and in the morning she went in and shot Anne in bed. Sammy confronts her afterwards and takes the gun from her and then the rest of the struggle was similar to what she told before.[94] They were still considering an appeal to the US Supreme Court. The board did approve a reprieve of one week from April 14 which was Good Friday to the 21st.[93] Fifteen years after the crime, it was reported that Ruth "stalked" into the residence and fired shots that killed both women. [95]

1933, April 7
Winnie's attorneys immediately filed in Maricopa County Superior Court a motion for a new trial, contending that the jury had no intention that the defendant should suffer the death penalty.[84] They claimed that the jury had no intentionn that the defendant should suffer the death penalty. Three jurors had signed affidavits. The one by Landrisen stated, "I was the last Judd juror who changed my verdict from life imprisonment to the death penalty. I was so worried over having changed, I didn't sleep that night. Never would I have changed as I did, had it not have been for Dan Kleinman who insisted that we would vote the extreme penalty." "Then he argued such a verdict would make Mrs. Judd talk, including the accomplice or accomplices. Dan said he had a good political friend on the board of pardons and paroles and that he would get the sentence commuted if Mrs. Judd would talk." He stated that he would not have voted for the death penalty otherwise. Gray gave a similar affidavit.[93] Winnie breaks with fits of nervousness and hysteria. The warden stated that he was surprised that this hadn't happened before since she had an "iron nerve".[84] Warden AG Walker said the young woman's nerve which enabled her to receive the news of the Arizona board of pardons and paroles refusal of a commutation without flinching apparently has begun to break. "She is becoming subject to fits of nervousness and hysteria, he said, as the probable day of her doom approaches hour by hour." Prison authorities generally have been amazed that the break has not been apparent sooner. "She has an iron nerve, said E. H Shute, assistant warden. "I never saw anything like it. She is not holding up so well now. But it is surprising she has not let down sooner."[96] Warden Walker said he had not yet made up his mind whether he would request a sanity hearing and pending such decision, he was not in a position to say in what light he

regards her mental condition.[96]

1933, April 8

Thomas Frelinghuysen arrives back in New York aboard the
Quirigua.[77] Dr. Berends of the Arizona State Hospital visits Ruth to
observe her mental condition.[97] Ruth continues her confession letter to
HG Richardson at 3 in the afternoon. She continues by describing
Thursday having finished discussing Wednesday on April 6th. She
finishes the letter on this date.[94]

1933, April 9

Ruth tries to swallow a double sided safety razor blade in a suicide attempt.
The result was a furious battle with the guards. When the matron watching
her relaxed for a moment, she popped the razor blade into her mouth. The
matron screamed for help. The guard responded and they proceeded to
choke her until she ceased to resist when the razor blade dropped from
her mouth after several minutes. She kicked, she repeatedly yelled, "I
want to kill myself. I won't be hung!" It took the combined effort of
two matrons and the guard in order to gain control. They took her from
the women's ward to a special cell.[98] The defense subpoenaed the
original jurors from the trial. MT White, ED Landrigan, Ed Gray, DH
Peterson, AJ McFee, FJ Lassen, Stewart V Thompson, William Lester,
Oscar A Jones, TT Kunze, Dan H Kleinman, H Hilker and the alternate
JL Standage. They were seeking the evidence of a purported deal
between the jurors by which the death penalty allegedly was imposed
only to make Ruth Judd talk.[99]

1933, April 11

Death watch was placed over Ruth Judd. She was allowed to stay on
the woman's ward instead of moving her to death row because of her
mental condition.[84] [100] Judge Howard Speakman declined to entertain
the new trial motion or to hear any affidavits or evidence of a purported
jury deal for the imposition of the death penalty to make her talk. At
Florence, Ruth rapidly is breaking under the strain of approaching
death stated the Warden to the press. Her fits of extreme nervousness
and hysteria have increased during the past couple of days. The warden
stated that he hadn't decided whether he would ask for a sanity hearing
for her. Arizona law stated that a formal request of the warden was
required accompanied by the expression of a belief a condemned
person has become insane while in prison. All of the former jury was

dismissed without testifying. The court declined to permit the filing or reading of the affidavits. The Reverend McKinnell and his wife accepted this calmly. They seemed prepared for it. Renz Jennings was present but did not say anything. Judge Speakman claimed that he had no jurisdiction in this case even though he had sympathy for Ruth Judd. Back at the state prison attendants of Ruth Judd described her as extremely nervous and frequently subject to attacks of hysteria as she heard the news. Although, she seemed calm at times talking to visitors about her plight, she had made frequent threats of suicide. The Warden claimed that this was not possible since she was allowed to have nothing with her which she might harm herself. He stated that in a day or two she will be moved from the women's ward to the death cell.[101] Dr. Berends visited Ruth Judd in the morning to observe her mental condition for the warden.[97]

1933, April 12
The petition placed before the high tribunal was denied, closing off the Arizona Supreme Court as a means for Winnie Ruth Judd to escape the gallows.[84] A sanity hearing for Ruth Judd was requested by the warden in the morning. This announcement was followed by two visits to the prison by Dr. E. D Berends, a physician in charge of the women's department at the Arizona State Hospital. He made no official mention of his observations. The warden said that what he stated the night before was "not so good". He stated that he would not tell her until the following day.[97] The Mertz (?) League of Mercy petitioned on the behalf of Ruth Judd. They had fought for the commutation of Ruth Snyder and Judd Gray.[102] AG Walker filed petition 1438 saying that there is good reason to believe that Winnie Ruth Judd under sentence of death has become insane since she was delivered to the Arizona State Prison for execution.[103] Response was the same day and so the insanity trail was to start the 14th of April at 9:30.

1933, April 13
Winnie cowers in her cell, hysterical and incoherent. In the evening, the Warden issued fifty small white black-bordered invitations to Winnie's execution. The invitations read, "You are invited to be present at the state prison, Florence, April 21, to witness the execution of Winnie Ruth Judd.[84] On the news that she was getting a sanity hearing Ruth showed no interest. She continued fondling her prison mascot, a coal black cat.[100]

1933, April 14

The matron Mrs. Devore said that before the hearing started Ruth was singing English and Spanish songs to her.[68] A hearing is set for determining Ruth's mental condition.[84] It is scheduled to start at 9:30.[100] It is decided that Ruth will not be placed on the witness stand by the defense during her sanity trial. They claimed she was not a competent witness so they decided not to call her. Dr. Catton and Dr. Bowers were in route from California. The defense stated that "they were tickled to death" and "would welcome them with open arms."[104] Renz Jennings stated that he would not be able to attend the hearing. Ruth continues to cower in her cell. The cat and her kittens no longer stirred her.[104] She sat in court with her eyes downcast, frowning nervously or, with her chin in her hands, elbows on her knees her body working gently backward and forward, throughout the day. Twenty talesmen were chosen, 12 of who would decide if she was sane.[105] Dr. Catton and Paul Bowers arrived in Florence. Dr. Catton said, "We are here, not as persecutors, but to express our views in accordance with justice. The Arizona law under which this hearing is being held provides substantially that if Mrs. Judd has appreciation of her circumstances and the mental capacity to comprehend the fate awaiting her, she must stand. We no more than the great state of Arizona desire to be charged with the responsibility of hanging any one whose mentally is so diseased that she goes to the execution chamber unknowingly."[106] He also said he would be glad to testify on behalf of Mrs. Judd if his observantions convinced him that the woman was mentally incompetent. They had had a chance to observe her in a 20-minute interview and during the 3 hours of court that day. Dr. Bowers expressed the view that Mrs. Judd's physical condition had improved materially since he last saw her. She was in better flesh and had a generally improved physical appearance. Dr. Catton said she appeared paler and of course the bleaching of her hair has given her a vastly changed appearance at the same time adding to her pallor. In court Ruth appeared bored. She twisted the handkerchief about her hand less frequently than in previous court appearance and frequently bent forward to rest her head on her hands. She talked but seldom and then only with the matrons attending her. She tried to follow one of them out of the court room when she got up but she was pulled back into her chair by another matron. Before the afternoon session at 2:15, Dr. Stephans spoke a few words to her and shook her hand. Her reply was "I've been taunted and tormented and that's the truth," was her only reply.[106] Later she said, "I've been tormented enough and I'm tired of it."[106] As a flash lamp was exploded by a photographer when she reentered the room with her matrons after a short midafternoon recess, Winnie turned her head from the camera. She made no comment though while earlier in the day she had upbraided newspapermen as they attempted to photograph her.[106]

1933, April 15
Ruth's insanity trial continues. The judge was Pinal Superior Court Judge E. L. Green. W. C. Truman, conducted the prosecution to uphold sanity, O. V. Willson continued to head the defense which now included Phoenix lawyerr Edwin Karz and from Florence H G Richardson, McFarland, and his partner Tom Fulbright. Winnie Ruth Judd continued to suffer from nervous breakdowns and continued to threaten to commit suicide during this time.[107] According to Fulbright none of the lawyers received compensation. A prominent lawyer wanting publicity nosed his way into the trial and Fulbright stated that he basically had to physically minimize his role.[108] Two prominent alienists testified against her. Joseph Catton and Paul Bowers had just recently testified in the Massey Case in Honolulu.[108] Local psychiatrists defended her, Dr. Huffman of Florence, and Dr. Pinkerton of Coolidge. Also, Dr. Stephens of the Arizona state hospital defended her.[108] Fulbright stated that she had the same blank look and stare day after day.[108] He stated that this never changed but only one time when Halloran was mentioned. At this she stood up and yelled, "That damn Jack Halloran, I would like to take his head and break it against the ceiling and spatter his brains like a dish of oatmeal."[108] Dr. James R. Moore becomes the superintendent of the Arizona State Hospital.[109] After 1.5 days of court observation Dr. Paul Bowers and Joseph Catton found nothing to alter their previously formed opinions that Winnie Ruth Judd is legally insane. They said, "Something may develop to cause us to change our view between now and the time we take the witness stand, but so far no such developments have appeared."[68] Dr. Catton expressed the view that Mrs. Judd partially feigned the morning and afternoon periods of hysteria in which she laughed and cried in turn, with an occasional clapping of her hands. "One under sentence of death must necessarily be of such a highly strung nervous state that hysteria at first feigned could readily become actual," he said.[68] CR Bowers said he did not consider Mrs. Judd a normal woman but added that under the legal interpretation of insanity, he could not at this time

put her under that classification. It had not been decided if the alienists would get to see Ruth Judd without the presence of her lawyers or husband. Ruth occupied the attention of matrons with mild attacks of apparent hysteria and threatened to throw herself from the courtroom window. There would be no execution stay. If they didn't finish the trial, Ruth would be hung. The jurors didn't seem to notice Ruth's nervousness. When Ruth stated to her husband by leaning over (he was seated in front of her) that he should get out of the way so she would throw herself out of the window, the jury was not in the courtroom. Dr. Judd and two matrons had quieted her. Also, she had hissed that "they are all gangsters" shortly after the jury had been empaneled. Later in apparent hysteria she chuckled and sobbed softly by turns but the eyes of the jury were fixed on witnesses.[68] Warden Walker testified that he believed that Ruth did not understand all the facts of the crime in which she was convicted. He stated that he believed she had been insane all of the time she had been in his charge since January. He stated he waited to say this until he was sure and had spoken to CR Berends a second time. He didn't want to have the responsibility of her hanging on him. Four matron witnesses and Warden Shute agreed with him. Shute stated that she is absolutely indifferent. I have gone so far as to ask her if she realized a noose was around her neck. She shrugged her shoulders and laughed and moved onto another conversation. He also related her gathering stones in the yard of the women's ward. These she laid in rows across the floor of her room. Also, once she hid herself under her bed and pulled the blankets down around the sides so the matron in charge was frightened and thought she had escaped. At another time about 6 weeks ago, she had convinced her mother that she had a razor blade in her mouth and intended to swallow it. This was not true.[68] When Mrs. Heath got up to testify, Ruth started to leave her chair, but they stopped her. Dr. Judd came and sat next to her in the vacant seat. She said, "They're all gangsters and degenerates – all of them."[110] She turned to her husband and he responded by shaking his head. She turned to the matron next to her and whispered something about Judge Green who was presiding.[110] Of the matrons' testimony, Mrs. Heath said, "I feel she is very much off."[68] She declared that Ruth appeared convinced that she was being persecuted, but not to punish her, but in a spirit of revenge by someone.[68] Mrs. Heath talked about Ruth's lack of interest in personal appearance and of her childish and playful habits. She would climb into and sit in the window of her cell for hours like a monkey in a cage.[110] When she mentioned that the condemned woman for several weeks had not attended to her hair, the spectators all looked at the stringy blond hair of Ruth.[110] They all stated that she sleeps sound and eats well, often ravenously. Mrs. Rossitor said Mrs. Judd "sings a lot and climbs in the window. One minute she laughs and the next she cries. She takes her slipper off and beats herself on the back of the neck with it."[68] Mrs. Devore said that Ruth sang English and Spanish songs to her.[68] Ruth had planned for the future in that she had planned flights to Alaska and Latin America. She had not prepared for death.[68] Ruth sat motionless much of the day during the trial, staring blankly. Her mother sat tight lipped and listened and her aged father placed his hand over his eyes and dropped his head. Occasionally Ruth would screw her mouth into grotesque shapes and her face would twitch convulsively. She rocked back and forth in the straight backed chair.[110]

1933, April 16
This was Easter Sunday. Ruth did not ask to attend chapel. She could not even if she wished. The death watch doesn't allow it. A year before she kneeled by her chair (in prison) and prayed for her parents, but not for herself.[111]

1933, April 17
McFarland evokes the image of the thief on the cross asking for the forgiveness of Jesus. Mac stated, "That is what we are asking for Ruth Judd. If she is to be executed, it would be at a time that she is sane and able to ask forgiveness." It was stated that his speech won the case for Ruth Judd's insanity.[107] Ruth has a sudden outburst in court stating, "You bullies! You cowards! You gangsters! Quit torturing me! Quit taunting me!"[112] Two matrons tried to silence her. They placed their hands over her mouth but she bit them and screamed on. Judge Green called for the warden. Warden Walker hurried to her side. He lifted her from her chair and took her bodily from the court room. Her foot dragged on the floor; nearly her whole weight was suspended on the Warden's arm. She kept screaming, "Let me alone, let me alone, quit torturing me!"[112] She beat her free arm in the air and continued to scream after the warden and the matron placed her on the court house lawn and attempted again to quiet her. The noise she made was so loud that it could be heard in the court room. Ruth was lying on the lawn and beating her heels on the grass yelling, "They keep torturing me! They keep taunting me! The bullies! The cowards! The cowards!"[112]

The warden was told to take the insane person out of the hearing of the jury. They took her for a 30-minute ride over a quiet country road in the warden's automobile. She was back in court at first smiling, then somber, but quiet, then on hands studying the floor.[112] In court they tried to get a reprieve until the middle of May to allow time for this hearing to be concluded. Dr. Judd was on the stand that morning. He declared his wife to be suffering from dementia praecox. "God himself", he told the jury "could not cause that woman to act insane – all she h as to do is act natural."[112] He described her mental characteristics as "entirely inconsistent".[112] "At one moment she is in a state of exultation," he said, "in another moment she is quiet – from intense depression she rises to the most supreme exhilaration."[112] They postponed the examination by Dr. Catton and Bowers because of her outburst that morning. Dr. Berends in testimony stated he found Mrs. Judd to be suffering from a disturbed emotional state. He agreed with Dr. Judd regarding Dementia Praecox. "She is lacking in judgement. Lacking in reason and insight and apparently suffering from delusion. She is unable to take care of herself and is a menace to herself and others. She is unable to concentrate and lacks attention. Her speech is abnormal, irrelevant and delivered under great pressure," he said.[112] He said that he did not think that she was malingering.[112] Mrs. Carrie McKinnell gave testimony that there was a strain of insanity in their family, "a taint, that had been visited on myself and even more on my daughter."[112] Carrie sparred with both counsel and the court when they tried to limit her testimony. "He knows she's insane," she said to Reed, "but he wants to hang her."[112] She said of Willson, "And he's a pill too".[112] She told the jury, "There is insanity on both sides of my family. I have always felt that insanity fell on me to some extent and on Ruth even more. I want you to know that girl is insane and has been more or less insane all her life."[112]

1933, April 18

George Stephens who had testified during her trial told the jury that she was suffering from Dementia Praecox and she was deteriorating. He stated that she had a persecution complex. He said he had a letter in his pocket which she wrote to her husband. That letter shows a paranoid trend regarding the prison warden, her mother, her father, and her attorneys. She speaks of "John Robert" and says she is going to see him when she dies. John Robert, he explained was her name for a child who never existed.[84] A reprieve is granted to Ruth to move her execution date to April 28 to allow time for the hearing to finish. The defense was trying for May 13 to allow for an appeal to the Supreme Court.[113] Dr. Paul Bowers testified that Ruth was sane. He said, "She is suffering from a state of great fear and is thoroughly frightened. But, wouldn't you be frightened if death were as near for you as it is for her? Her actions in the court room yesterday afternoon were an emotional outburst, not uncommon for a woman. Many women whose minds are not mentally unbalanced have such outbursts over trivial matters, but it only goes to show that she is under a highly nervous strain," he said.[114] When asked by reporters about Ruth's blank stare during the court proceedings, he said, "Look here," and copied her blank stare for several minutes.[114] Of her ability as an actress he said, "She has great histrionic ability."[114] He pointed out that during recesses Ruth would speak freely and smile at Dr. George Stephans.[114] Dr. Catton and Bowers were granted time to interview Ruth in the prison that morning without her attorneys or husband but she resisted this by refusing to answer their questions and talking of inconsequential things. She played with the kittens in her cell.[114] An argument about the financing of Ruth's defense broke out in court. Rumors had been circulating that William Randolph Hearst's chain was financing the defense case. The argument between the attorneys lasted several minutes and was heated until Judge Green quieted them down. Dr. Harry Pinkerton testified that Ruth suffered from Dementia Praecox. He claimed he was not receiving any compensation for his testimony. He was asked whether he knew the fact that the defense was being financed by the Hearst Newspapers. The defense objected and a heated argument ensued. Dr. Pinkerton replied that this was the first time he had heard of this compensation. He stated that he expected to receive no compensation for his testimony.[115]

1933, April 19
Ruth had to be removed for the second time during the hearing by the warden. Lin Orme of the board of pardons and paroles was speaking.[116] He stated that Mrs. Judd, during a secret session about commutation last month, had said that she would attempt to impregnate herself if the board ignored her plea for a life sentence. She said that she wanted to save her life and she wanted them to commute her."[85] Ruth was sitting abstractedly hunched up in her chair with her chin cupped in her hands. Suddenly she tensed up and, like a spring, flung herself into furious action as Orme described a hearing which had been

granted Mrs. Judd before the board denied her appeal for clemency. "You told me," she cried raising her right arm and striking a dramatic posture toward the pardon board chairmen, "That if I would not exonerate Jack Halloran you would kill me!"[116] She said, "I said, 'Please don't kill me because I am going to have a baby and that you want to kill my baby. You said if I exonerate Jack Halloran you would not kill me. That is all I said."[85] "Where is Jack Halloran? Mash his brains over the ceiling like a dish of oatmeal," she said.[85] The outburst was so sudden that the court room momentarily remained stunned. Mrs. Judd held her pose, singling out the witness on the stand, but the jury was watching her. Ruth turned to the spectators with her eyes blazing. She demanded, "Where is Jack Halloran? Where is he? Bring him here!"[116] She looked around frantically for Jack Halloran who was not there. Several people held her down in her chair. The warden led her down the aisle and the spectators fell back, making a lane for the procession. Mrs. Judd swung her free arm over the heads of the nearest in the audience who ducked hastily. She cried, "They are not going to kill me! They are not going to kill my babies!" They walked her around the court house briefly and returned her to the court room chair and she subsided into an apparent abstraction.[116] Orme testified that Mrs. Judd had begged the board of pardons and paroles not to allow her to hang and had informed the board members that if she was to have a child they could not hang her. Other witnesses also referred to one of or more non-existent children and that she called four kittens her babies. Wallace Gordor stated that he believed that she was fully aware and fully conversant with all of the facts of her case during the Halloran indictment in January. He did not know about her current mental state. The chairman of the board of pardons and paroles said he believed Mrs. Judd realized she was in prison and sentenced to death when she appeared before the board. "She said if we would commute her sentence she would try to be good. That she would try to make reparation for the mistake she had made. She begged us not to allow her to be executed."[116] He said that she was nervous at the hearing, but he though her reaction was more or less normal under the circumstances. She stated several times that she was going to be hanged on Good Friday. Hendrix declared that "at all times she seemed very much informed as to the position which seemed to be hers in the situation. She continually said, 'You won't hang me will you?'"[116] He claimed at the time that he had no thought of an abnormal or subnormal intelligence. Her appearance was good. Her diction was good, her sentence structure good. He asked Hendrix if he had not seen her in hysteria wailing and crying. Hendrix said that he had, but "I have seen high school girls act worse."[116] When asked if he thought she was sane that day he replied that he thought that she comprehended her surroundings on Saturday. He and Orme were sitting in the rear of the room while the jury was out. He said that he would like to see Mrs. Judd face to face again. She looked around and turned her eyes away and called them four names.[116] A threat to avenge a Winnie Ruth Judd death was circulating through the prison. It said, "We all know Ruth Judd is insane, just as we all know she is broke. So does anyone else who is sane. We are all wise as to who is behind the whole deal and whose money is paying those fancy doctors and other witnesses against her, and we have all made up our minds that if Ruth hangs those responsible will follow her to hell in short order. There are 700 of us here, and we will all be free someday. There won't be any rioting here – we all respect Warden Walker and Cap Shute too much to make things tough for them – but don't forget someday, someway, the guilty ones will have to pay. After she had gone through the trap and is pronounced dead, the state will hire a preacher to preach her into heaven; if she is good enough to be preached into heaven, she is good enough to live on this earth of ours."[117]

1933, April 20
A meeting of the sympathizers for Ruth Judd met at 3:00 at the Free Methodist Church at Fifth and Adams Street. The address would be, "Should Ruth Judd hang". The Rev WC Reynolds, pastor of the church presided. John E Ford, evangelist spoke and several state senators and representatives were guests.[118] In court, Paul Bowers declared Ruth is neurotic, depressed, "scared to death almost" but is "malingering-feigning the aspects of insanity."[119] Dr. Joseph Catton tempered his opinion that she is legally sane with an expression of regret that the legal definition of insanity as propounded by the court bound him to the factual statements which have found their way into the record rather than allowing him to express what might be his personal wish in regard to a statement of Ruth Judd's condition. He stated that she was suffering from "neurosis of the condemned" consisting in of consciously simulated symptoms and in part of mechanics beyond the control of Mrs. Judd which relatively promptly would be ameliorated should the death penalty be commuted.[119] Both Bowers and Catton said she is not suffering from dementia praecox and declared she is

sane under the court's definition. - that she comprehends her situation, understands the facts of the crime for which sentence was imposed, realized her impending fate and is able to intelligently inform her counsel or the court of any evidence which might tend to establish execution of sentence as unjust and unlawful. Dr. HB Steward, physician at the prison, never thought she was insane. He claimed she was nervous and showed emotional reactions such as any person would if under the sentence of death. He said, "I have always believed that Mrs. Judd is a very emotional person."[119] Dr. Uttzinger of Ray assistant county physician stated that her insanity was feigned because of the general normal condition of her mind on some subjects. "She seems clearer mentally to me than a person would who knew nothing of the impending fate – I took under the consideration the fact she answers some question and totally ignores others which are of utmost importance.[119] Dr. Bowers summarized his analysis by stating that there was no evince of any insanity or any delusions, no hallucinations, no illusions, no evidence of any behaviors belonging to the category of insanity. "I saw none of the behavior that goes with dementia praecox. I saw behavior that goes with the deliberation; behavior that goes with a self-serving attitude of mind; I reached the conclusion she didn't because she deliberately did not talk."[119] He stated that she was disagreeable to her parents and treated them miserably. He was not impressed by that. He stated that when a person has a particular purpose in mind, they carry out that purpose and what greater purpose than to save one's life?[119] He continued, "I considered her family history and I felt it possibly is a bit tainted, but knowing many sane individuals have insane relatives and knowing I had examined such patients of tainted heredity, it did not count for much. I feel this lady is in a nervous condition. I feel she is under a great strain. She is depressed, seeking rescue from a terrible situation."[119] Dr. Catton also discounted the hereditary taint of insanity in her ancestry stating, "Family history helps explain insanity in an individual," he told the jury, "but it does not help you to say an individual is insane. I know Mrs. Judd does not talk in certain instances, but whether or not she is able to talk on those occasions, frankly, I do not know. I am not so smart I cannot be fooled. I believe about 60 percent that this woman has a definite prison psychosis or insanity. I believe with the other 40 percent the picture she presents may be fraudulent. According to the legal definition, she is sane. I am driven in spite of the fact this woman is mentally ill and sick, to stand on the fact in this record that she does know what is going on. I believe it is a fact that, as long as society at this moment unfortunately is arrayed against Mrs. Judd, her ideas of persecution are in a way sound, not under the circumstances a true delusion as at all. It is my opinion that her present mental condition had its birth in feigning and simulation. Beyond a doubt she is suffering from a condition I would term neurosis of the condemned. It is my belief that neurosis is made up in part of simulated symptoms and in part consists of mechanics beyond Mrs. Judd's control. It is my opinion beyond any doubt this subject is not suffering from dementia praecox in any of its forms. Mrs. Judd never has been the type of personality from which an insanity of that type might spring. Certain of Mrs. Judd's symptoms, if believed truly present, must be considered psychotic or insane. Such psychosis as is present it is my opinion will disappear if commutation be granted within a period of weeks or months at most. Mrs. Judd's nervous reserve has been much reduced until she has come to show all sorts of signs and symptoms of nervous irritability and fatigue."[119]

1933, April 21
Delays happened on this day during the hearing. First there were missing state witnesses. Reed was given the morning to try to find them. Other delays happened in the afternoon. They argued about the instructions for the Jury. Ruth sat in her chair waiting for news of her fate. At 4 an official announced that the hearing would be delayed until the following day. Mrs. Judd was taken back to her cell. The jury would only be able to render two opinions; either that Ruth was sane or insane according to the court's definition. They were to consider her sane when she entered prison. It was just the last 15 months to be considered. This was the 4th hanging day that Ruth lived to see.[120]

1933, April 22
Winnie Ruth Judd is declared insane.[84] The jury deliberated one hour and 57 minutes, asking for instructions once and taking five ballots. The first ballot resulted in a note of 10 to 2 for insanity, but two of the jurors withdrew before signing the verdict. They were only required to have 6.[121] The courtroom was silent. Then it erupted with applause. There was no yelling or shouting. In a minute the court was quiet again.[122] Ruth Judd was not present. She was coming up from the car. She could not hear the word of the clerk, but a second later she did hear the clapping of hands that must have conveyed the knowledge that

victory was hers. Three minutes later she entered the court room on the arm of her aged father who was also absent when the verdict was read. She got to her chair. They thanked the jury for their service.[122] Fulbright recalls watching her face as the jury read the verdict. He concluded that if the verdict was sane and she was not insane, there would be a look of hopelessness and despair. If the verdict was insanity, she would have a look of relief. Her expression however, never changed. She kept twisting the handkerchief in her hands and stared blankly. Fulbright thought that she was insane as decided by the court.[108] Dr. Judd,face flushed with emotion, sat down next to Ruth and placed an arm about her shoulders. He said to her, "You will not be hanged, everything is all right. Do you hear? You are going to the hospital."[121] She stared blankly showing no comprehension. Dr. Stephens went to congratulate Ruth. He extended his hand in a friendly grasp; she recognized him and took his hand. Her features were lighted by a faint smile and a nod of appreciation. Dr. Stephen said, "I'd like one of your kittens."[122] Ruth said, "I'll give you one of them, too, even though I only have three left. I'll give you Tom, but you can't have Angel."[122] OV Willson was visibly affected. He seemed on the verge of slumping to the floor as colleagues rushed to his side.[122] Fulbright also stated, "In terms of coin of the realm, it was nil, but we were all compensated. Lawyers on both sides profited from an experience which does not come to many in a lifetime. And the publicity did none of us any harm."[108] Charlie Reed said of Dr. Catton when the trial was over that he insisted in sleeping in a different place each night. Then, he would lock the door and crawl under the bed. Also, Dr. Judd offered Fulbright's daughter Nancy two of Ruth's cats that she was allowed to keep in her cell at the time, Midnight and Egypt. They declined since they already had a dog. They all ate at the American Café after the trial each night.[108] Matrons wept at their inability to evoke any indication from Mrs. Judd. Mrs. Judd finally said, "Lin Orme can't have any of my kittens."[121] Mrs. McKinnell expressed her gratitude to the jury. "I'm thankful those men brought in a verdict of insanity. Ruth needs rest and treatment."[121] She went to their home in Florence where they had been staying. She stated that she had not had a fair trial and should have been tried for the death of Hedvig Samuelson in which she would argue self-defense.[121] The Republic stated that she did not flicker an eyelash and did not show any understanding of the jury's verdict which set the courtroom into a tumult. Her features were blank and her eyes uncomprehending as she walked for the last time from the Pinal County Courthouse. The Warden smiled and sought a way for her through the crowd. Women sought to grasp her hand; to pat her on the shoulder. She paid no attention to them. She was pale and icily aloof. She did not return caresses showered on her by her aged parents. She went back to her cell in the women's ward, sat down on the cot, and made ready to allow the matrons to prepare her for bed. She said nothing.[121]

1933, April 24
Ruth waits to be transferred to the State Hospital. Her visitors are limited to her family, prison officials and newspapermen. She conversed intelligently and was keenly interested in activities around her. The wrapping of the handkerchief around her hand was abandoned. When Warden Walker mentioned it, she looked down at her hand, smiled sheepishly and rapped the handkerchief several times more. She did not do that again for the rest of the day. She seemed to have lost the blank stare that she had for most of the hearing. She slept rather soundly the night before. She slept until 9 in the morning. She had her hair marceled that morning done by one of the matrons. She wore a simple blue gingham dress and black pumps. She spent most of the day playing on a patch of grass with her black cat Egypt and her 4 kittens. She decided to give one of the kittens to George Stephens and to Ed. W. Powers, Phoenix court reporter, to Judge El Green and one of her matrons. She was visited by WC Judd and her father. Many other visitors were turned away. The rope which was to hang Ruth was still being stretched by the weight.[123, 124] Lucille Hamm and Burton McKinnell have a son. He lives less than 3 hours. The address listed on the death certificate is 1331 E Willetta, Phoenix. It is listed as baby boy McKinnell and the cause of death is listed as "premature"[125] He is buried at Greenwood Memory Lawn at 2300 West Van Buren St, Phoenix, section 60 north of the Encanto, Mausoleum. There is no marker.[126]

1933, April 25
Mrs. McKinnell visits her daughter at the State Prison shortly before she was taken to Phoenix. The mother left the cell when Ruth became enraged and threatened to kill herself during a discussion of family affairs according to Mrs. Heath, the matron. The papers for Ruth's transfer was signed by Judge E. L. Green at 11:30. Ruth is transferred to the State Hospital from Florence around mid-day . The trip took 95

minutes. At intervals she talked about being in Mexico, of the lots of rocks along the highway, and of the awful pains in her head. She paid no attention to the conversation regarding the scenery between the warden's daughter and the matron. On occasion she sat silently her elbows resting on her knees and her chin cupped in her hands and worried because her cats didn't appear to fare so well on the automobile ride. "They are so sick," she replied occasionally. Much of the trip over, she sat curled up on the corner of the rear seat of the sedan with her head in the matron's lap. A party of 5 persons transferred her including AG Walker. She is sentenced to stay at the state prison until normalcy returned and then be returned to prison where a new date would be set for execution. They stopped at the rear entrance to the women's ward where there were newspaper photographers. She shouted at them, "I never saw such a bunch of morbids" while she was ushered inside. She also said, "Look at them. They've made a shell out of me and they're not going to take any pictures of a corpse. They can't taunt me anymore. They can't take any more pictures of me." Mrs. Heath quieted her. Her black cat Egypt and two of her kittens were brought with her in a box. The matron agreed to let her keep the cats for a while in order that she would remain quiet. The other of the four kittens was given Sunday afternoon to Mrs. Laura Lossiter, one of the matrons. Her new quarters were much more pleasant than the tiny dark cell at the state prison. She is confined to a small room and under observation. They stated she would get plenty of air, light and sunshine. She would be regarded as just another prisoner. Her only visitors would be her husband and her parents.[127]

1933, April 28

Ernest "Mac" McFarland goes to visit Winnie Ruth Judd for the first time. She said to him what a great speech he had made. Winnie was all dressed up in her cell at Florence that day. Mac said, "How would you know? You're crazy". Ruth laughs at this comment. Mac was convinced though that in talking with her that she really did have a streak of insanity. He talked to her about the night of the trunk murders and questioned her about somebody at the party that night. Her answers helped convince him that she "had a streak" of insanity. He had heard testimony that Ruth stated that she had a family. Mac didn't know if this was true or not at the trial. However, a business man in Florence once told him that while he was at the Grunow Clinic in

Phoenix while Ruth worked there, she had told him about her 4 beautiful children.[128] Ruth is sent to the State Hospital in Phoenix. Ruth stated the first few years she was there most everyone was very kind to her; particularly the doctors. She claimed she would do nothing to break her trust with them and she didn't.[15] Dr. Moore was superintendent the first four years she was there. Mrs. Gowdy, Mrs. Bernard, and Mrs. Jennie Young all graduate nurses were charges on the hospital. They were wonderful women according to Ruth.[15] Ruth stated that during the depression, they would get the best nurses for attendant's salaries. There were a few who at times were unkind to patients; used wet towels or ducked patients. She wrote to her husband about that. He advised her to mind her own business as long as no one did those things to her and not tell any doctor even if a doctor asked her.[15] A report in 1969 by Rex Whitney at the State Hospital stated that, "During the months following her admission, she had many delusions of persecution and many times voiced the thought that agents of a Mr. H------- were persecuting her and trying to keep her in the hospital so that she would die of tuberculosis. During the first years of her hospitalization, it was the opinion of the physicians of this hospital who were in contact with her that she had been psychotic since her admission, although none of them were in a position to state her condition at the time of the murders."[129]

1933, May 24
Dr. Judd is admitted to the military home at Sawtelle. His disabilities are listed as Diabetes Mellitus, old injury of right leg (illegible) of muscle of right calf.[130]

1933, June
Dolores Costello (and John Barrymore) anchor the Yacht, the Infanta in the Gastineau channel. Many of the folks around Juneau were invited aboard. One woman gave birth to a daughter while they were in Juneau and they named her Dolores Costello. Dolores delivered to her a small layette as a namesake.[131]

1933, July
Judge La Prade and Dr. Hendrix of the pardon board visited Ruth Judd at the hospital and said, "We came to tell you we are your friends. Today we commuted a man Janvetechel here six years under the death sentence. We are deporting him to Syria and as soon as public

sentiment dies down we are going to do something likewise for you."[15]

1933, November 18

Dr. Judd was arrested in West Los Angeles for a charge of drunkenness. He failed to make $20 bond and was put in the city jail. He was arrested by radio officers Krog and Romer at Federal and Kiowa Avenues in West Los Angeles. At the time he gave his name as William A Brown.[132]

1933, November 22

Dr. Judd pled not guilty for drunkenness and requested a jury trial. He was returned to his cell.[132]

1933, November 24

Dr. Judd still was unable to post 20 dollars' bail and was still in jail. He was released without bail pending his trial which was to be the 29th. This would give Dr. Judd time to subpoena witnesses.[133]

1934

The NTA office in New York connected with a number of prominent Alaskans. They sold Christmas seals in Alaska. The list included Governor John Troy as chairman, together with several well-known Alaskan physicians, the territorial commissioner of health, officials from the Alaska Native Service, and other businessmen from around the territory.[134]

1934, January

Tom Frelinghuysen (Sammy's friend) was in love with Julie, TJ Matthew's wife in 1934, and she had a breakdown. Matthews took her to Jamaica to recover for a month. Matthews thought later that was because Julie was considering leaving him for Frelinghuysen that added much to her mental anguish. Matthews did not know the details or extent of their affair, but it gradually diminished and Julie stayed with Matthews.[17]

1934, Spring

Arnold Samuelson, Sammy's brother, hitchhikes to Key West in hopes of meeting Hemingway and getting some advice about his writing.[135]

1935, February

Dr. Judd is interviewed by the press stating that he hopes to come back from a protracted illness. He was allowed to review medical charts at the National Military Home in West Los Angeles. He stated that he corresponded often with his wife. He stated she continued to brood over the slaying of her two friends and still suffers the delusion she has an arch enemy. He stated that one day he hoped to go back to Mexico and resume his practice. He stated he liked it down there.[136]

1935, May 15

The deed at the house at 2929 N 2nd Street is transferred from the O'Malley Investment Company, JG O'Malley President to Alice V Orndorff.[20]

1935, Spring

Arnold Samuelson has stayed with Hemingway for a year. Close to the time he departed, Hemingway tells him, "Most writers keep on writing about their childhood until they're forty. They spend their youths concealing their love affairs and their old age revealing them. The best stuff you've got is from your farm life in North Dakota and your sister's murder. That's something nobody else can write and nobody can ever take it away from you, but you don't want to use it for a long time. Save your best stuff until you've learned how to handle it, because you can't write the same thing twice unless you rewrite it. Wait until you've learned how to become detached. In order to write tragedy, you've got to be absolutely detached, no matter how much it hurts you. Tragedy is the peak of the art and that's the hardest thing there is to do. You never lose a story by not writing it."[135]

1936, June 25

Anne LeRoi's ring with the red stone was sold at a Coroner Sale in LA for 20 cents.[137]

1937, January 15

Dr. B. M. Berger becomes the superintendent at the Arizona State Hospital.[109]

1937

Ruth states that during 1937-1939, the staff at the state hospital changes. Dr. Berger was now superintendent. They were good kind capable people donating much of their last month's salary to campaign deficit. Mr. A Kelly announced they would pay a certain percent or he had 400 more people to take their place. Mrs. Gallaahue was the superintendent of nurses under Dr. Berger. Ruth stated that she was kind. She insisted that patients be treated very kindly. Dr. Saxe was one of the staff doctors then. Mrs. Bankston, the superintendent's secretary, had her over to her apartment for lunch one Sunday afternoon. Dr. Saxe didn't like it. So Mrs. Bankston said that she would not get permission to have her over again. Instead, Mrs. Gallahue would take her for walks and over to her apartment instead so as to not anger Dr. Saxe.[15]

1937, November 20
Collier's publishes a story about Mildred Keaton who was in Juneau as a nurse in the school and at St. Ann's when Anne and Sammy were in Juneau. She is presently stationed in Barrow. The magazine describes her as an angel in furs; the most beloved women in Alaska. She was born in Kentucky and was said to enjoy her tobacco strong, her bourbon neat and liked four-legged animals. She was the youngest of 11, behind 10 boys. She was said to be a tomboy. She was of Irish decent with dark hair and a quick temper.[138]

1938, July 25
Ruth took an overdose of Luminal. She responded to treatment which included a gastric lavage.[129] Ruth stated that she was working 12-14 hours a day straight doing hair and she started taking thyroid pills a patient, Mildred Snowden, had left hoping it would make her skin transparent and beautiful like hers. She said it made her highly nervous with the other strain she was under. So, she took an overdose of sleeping tablets.[15] She stated that she was foolish because previously at the time of the tragedy her thyroid was a +32 under a basal metabolism so she couldn't take iodides because of her tuberculosis. She stated that "many women are foolish when they want to look pretty and take thyroid".[15] The other reason she overdosed was Dr. O'Connor began making remarks about Mrs. Owen taking me for drives out to see my parents. He called her my lady love. I cried and cried and told her not to come near me anymore. There was no truth in it. I told her I would just concentrate on all the kind things she had done for me. Then she wrote an order I was not to go to any more ball games. Dr. O'Connor wrote Miss Sheehan, an attendant, who was to take another patient and

Mrs. Owen told the attendant not to. Two pages were written full of orders. Dr. O'Connor finally wrote, "Ruth is to go and no nurse is to contridict my orders." I didn't want to go, but was made to go. Dr. O'Connor and Mrs. Owen each went in their cars and sat glaring at each other. I got so upset. Both were equally kind to me."[15]

1938, December
Thomas Frelinghuysen (Sammy's friend) debuts his work of 10 years at the Marie Sterner Galleries until December 3rd in New York in a one-man exhibit. It was said to have been his work for the past 10 years (1928). It consisted of 30 figures and animal studies in bronze, marble, terra cotta, aluminum, and limestone. The sculptor's love particularly for dogs and horses are evident as his work exhibits; both their actions and moods. His portraits typically have colored mouths and range from a very green bronze Sally to a poised Alene in marble, with extraneous details smoothed over. There are several nudes in this exhibition, showing a variety in technique. Nude number 1, is a plump oriental figure and 'torso with head' is a stylized and lively rendering of a thoroughly modern miss.[139] Another one of the sculptures in this exhibit is called, aluminum torso. There is a picture of this sculpture in this article.[140]

1938, December 4-5
Governor Stanford phoned Mrs. Owen at the State Hospital and told her she could take Ruth home for the evening to have dinner with her parents. It was no secret and Ruth stated she could have told anyone. Ruth told the attendants. 10 minutes later Dr. O'Connor came over and demanded to know what Ruth meant by sneaking off the grounds without his permission. Ruth stated she hadn't known until the previous 10 minutes when the Governor called. Mrs. O'Connor started crying that she wanted to wave Ruth's hair. She said, "Pay no attention to Dad, Ruth, He's drinking." Then she told Ruth that Mr. Hoffman of the Pardon Board had phoned Dr. O'Connor asking him to give him a sworn statement that her mental condition had not improved since she had been committed. She said; don't let anyone know you've given me this statement, but there is a trick in Mrs. Judd's case and that the Board is not going to do what they expect.[15] Later that afternoon, Mrs. Heath Matron from the prison came to see Ruth with Rev. Hagar. Ruth told them about the governor's phone call and how angry it made Dr. O'Connor. They told her to have Mrs. Owen phone the Governor and

thank him but not to go or do anything to make Dr. O'Connor angry. When Ruth told this to Mrs. Owen, she said, "You have to go now Ruth. Someone made an anonymous phone call that you are to be kidnapped tonight and the highway dept. has been instructed to circle your parents' home."[15]

1938, December 6
Dr. O'Connor became superintendent. Dr. Berger had left. Dr. O'Connor was superintendent for about 3 weeks.[15] Some politicians had come out and asked Ruth how well she liked Dr. O'Connor. Ruth said she liked him. "Why? They asked. Ruth stated that she had been very ill last summer and no one could have been kinder. They asked her how she would like to see him become superintendent. Ruth said, "For his wife and children's sake of whom I am most fond, I would like to see him receive the appointment.[141] Ruth stated that Governor Stanford phoned Mrs. Owen and told her she could take her home for the evening to have dinner with her parents. It wasn't a secret. Dr. O Connor came over demanding to know what I meant by sneaking off the ground without his knowledge. She answered that she was not sneaking around since the governor had called about 10 minutes previous. Mrs. O' Connor started crying she wanted to wave Ruth's hair. She said, "Pay no attention to Dad, Ruth, he's drinking. Then she told Ruth that Mr. Hoffman of the Pardon Board had phoned Dr. O Conner asking him to give him a sworn statement about her mental condition, say that it had not improved since she had been committed. Mrs. O'Conner said he said don't let anyone know you've given me this statement, but there is a trick in Mrs. Judd's case and that Board is not going to do what they expect.[15] Mrs. O'Connor was going to the Phoenix school of Beauty Culture. Ruth stated that she had been doing the patient's hair for 5 years but she brought her books to study and her instructor came out and taught her many useful things in doing hair. Soon the attendants started paying Ruth 25 cents to do their hair. Ruth stated she used that money to buy supplies.[15]

1938, December 23
Ruth received a box of chocolates from Mr. CV Hill, a politician. Mrs. O'Connor phoned her, the same day she was giving Ruth a permanent that evening. Ruth tried to refuse. She stated that she only had $5 for Christmas. Ruth stated she was too tired from doing patient's hair in preparation for the dance. She insisted on coming and brought Dr.

81

O'Connor with her. As soon as she got her head blocked, CV Hill and another politician came down from Prescott. He said that he came down to take Ruth to the dance. Dr. O'Connor glared at him. She stated then that she realized that her case was in politics. She didn't know how much since she discussed it with no one.[15] Ruth stated that CV Hill, politician started coming to see her. He was allowed to take her for walks on the grounds. He told her, "Ruth if you will return to the Prison at Florence and get WL Barnum for your attorney you will be free in 13 months."[15]

1939, January 2
Dr. Louis J. Saxe becomes Superintendent of the Arizona State Hospital. Dr. Saxe and Dr. O'Connor came to see Ruth together. Ruth stated that she like both of them. She said, "I am glad to see you" She meant nothing more than it was pleasant to say hello. She stated that Dr. O'Connor looked very hurt.[15]

1939, January 13
Dr. O'Connor phoned an attendant to bring Ruth over to their apartment and later to take her to the cottage to do an attendant's finger nails. Ruth stayed quite a while at Dr. O'Connor's since they had company from Clarksdale. Ruth was late getting to the cottage so only painted the attendant's nails and she and her date took her to the auditorium in time for the show.[15]

1939, January 15
Dr. Saxe called Ruth over to his office a day or two after going over to the cottage and said "Mrs. Judd, many people do not like your prejudice of course. They would frame me out there over you if they could do so. I understand you were over at the cottage the other evening and two men were present. Some of these attendants are utterly unscrupulous and without morals so I'm asking you not to go to the cottage anymore." Ruth replied, "Well, Dr. Saxe had I been able to go where I was supposed to neither man would have been there. Her date didn't even come in; they took me over to the auditorium to the show. It hadn't started yet. But it is more important to me not to be talked about than you. It is my life, my freedom. It's only your job. I want out of here someday. The Haleys, friends of my father are here from South Africa where they have had a mission school for 35 years. They would like to take me back with them if I can go."[15] Ruth stated

that Dr. Saxe read her a kind letter he had just written to the legislators talking about the two children in the institution given special care; one little boy Mrs. Judd gives a true mothers love and care to. Another, a little girl cared for by Mrs. Harval, a patient.[15]

1939

Rose Mofford works at the Arizona State Hospital for a month. She stated that Ruth was doing the patient's hair at that time. She stated that she was quiet and was very good to other patients, especially the children and others who were facing hardship.[142] She stated she knew Ruth rather well.[142] Ruth stated she first met her when she visited a family member who also was a patient at the hospital.[143] [On tape, edited out on the transcript].

1939, January

Ruth Judd ordered these materials for the use at the State Hospital Beauty Salon: 1 pound of Henna, 10 dyes per pound of Henna @ $1 each, 1 large bottle of sparkle shine (rinse) - 4 Gallons. One pint is used for each rinse, making the total, 32 rinses @ 10 cents a rinse. ½ pound of bobby pins, sufficient for 20 finger waves @ $.50 each. 3 pounds of shampoo soap; (6 gallons of shampoo solution), approximately .5 pint of shampoo solution used in one shampoo, making the total of 96 shampoos $.50 per shampoo. The total cost of supplies in January was $3.00. A licensed shop would have made $71.20 with these materials, including the cost of knowledge, rent, utilities, personal, property and income taxation; also license fees and salaries.[144]

1939, February

Ruth Judd ordered this material for use at the State Hospital Beauty Salon: 1 box of Louise Norris' Eyebrow and Eyelash dye, 15 dyes to the box, $1.00 for each dye; 10 bottles of Revlon Nail Polish in assorted shades, 10 manicures to the bottle, making the total of 100 manicures @ $.50 cents each; 21 ounces of Marrow oil, 10 Marrow Oil Shampoos @ $.75 each; 1 pound of Henna, 10 dyes to a pound of Henna @1.00 each; 1 dozen emery boards, sufficient for 15 manicures. Used alternatively on any amount of beauty work: 2 hair nets. Total cost of supplies in February was $7.00. Total returns that a beauty parlor would make with these goods, $82.00 after taxation, rent utilities, personal property, license fees and salaries.[144]

1939, March

Ruth Judd ordered the following materials for the beauty parlor at the state hospital: 1 bottle of Hollywood Blonde Bleach, regulation size, sufficient for 10 bleaches, $2.00/each; 1-pint bottle of peroxide, sufficient for 10 bleaches (Used with the Hollywood Blonde Bleach); 1 bottle of cuticle lotion, sufficient for 10 manicures, used in conjunction with nail polish etc.; 1 pound of shampoo soap (2 gallons of shampoo solution), approximately .5 pint of shampoo solution used in one shampoo, making the total of 32 shampoos @.50 a shampoo. Total supplies for March $3.00. A licensed shop would have made $36.00 from these materials minus knowledge, rent, utilities, personal, property, taxes, and license fees and salaries [144] Ruth stated that in March of 1939, all of a sudden she was attacked with headlines in every paper in the US for operating a beauty parlor without a license. She stated she took the 25 cents each attendant paid her to buy supplies to do the patients hair. Mrs. O'Conner had been phoning me to get 6 or 8 patients with straight long hair shampooed so she could bring some students from the Phoenix school of Beauty Culture out to practice marcels since they only get to practice on wigs at the school. She felt it made the patients happy and never thought it was wrong.[15]

1939, April

Dr. Louis J. Saxe, superintendent of the hospital, puts an end to the "beauty culturist" business Ruth has going at the state hospital. He stated that the Arizona State Board of Beauty Culturist Examiners charged her with "unfair competition" because of her low prices[84]. Ruth described this situation as "All of a sudden twelve years ago in 1939, I was attacked over doing the patients hair without a license. Governor Jones stated to the press when my political enemies stoop in order to get at me, pick on a patient out there they are getting mighty low. It is my opinion Mrs. Judd has been persecuted too much. I plead with Mr. Hoffman, then chairman of the Board, to please do something for me." I was being torn to pieces between two political factions. He answered, "Mrs. Judd, you must realize the Pardon Board is between those same two political factions in doing something for you. Is that Justice?" [15] Ruth stated that she took 25 cents each from attendants which paid for supplies to do the patients' hair. Mrs. O' Connor had been phoning Ruth to get 6 or 8 patients with straight long hair shampooed so she could bring some students from the Phoenix school of Beauty Culture out to practice marcels on. They only had wigs to practice on. Ruth thought it made the patients happy getting their hair done. Mrs. Nora Shapley and Pearl had been for the defeated candidate Mr. Osborne for Governor. Governor Jones ousted them from the State Board of Cosmetologists because they were the ones who "made the attack" against Ruth. Two years later when Osborn was elected as governor, Ruth claimed that these two women were put back on the board.[15]

1939, May 10

Pearl Ware and Nora B. Shapely of the Board of Beauty Culturist Examiners write a letter addressed to Governor Jones indicating the exact amount of materials Ruth Judd had used at the State Hospital. The letter contains a list of materials from a local supply house for the months of January, February, and March of 1939. The letter's intent was to clarify the exact profit that Ruth Judd had taken from beauty shop owners and operators.[144]

1939, June

Governor Robert T. Jones held a conference with three members of the Board of Beauty Culturist Examiners with eleven beauty shop operators outside. Governor Jones refused to hear them. Governor Jones stated that he believed Mrs. Judd was being persecuted in the matter.[84] Ruth overdosed a few days later and was in a coma for two days.[84] Ruth started a laundry business instead, washing uniforms from hospital attendants for ten cents each.[84] Governor Jones asked Ruth not to do any more hair.[15] Shortly later Richard Harless, prosecuting attorney and Tom Hannon, politician came in with Mattie, Dr. O'Connor's sister and tried to get her to do her hair in their presence. Ruth refused.[15] Apparently Mattie O'Connor had been posing as a PWA or WPA model and Ruth had done her hair previously (with a cluster of curls on top). She wanted Ruth to fix the curls as they had been previously since they were going to finish her pose. She had been to a beauty parlor and her hair was still wet. Ruth said, "Oh, Mattie, I can't fix your curls; you can dry your hair though".[15] Dick Harless demanded to know if Ruth had bleached Mattie's hair. Ruth said she had, but that she had put coffee on it to cause it to break off.[15]

1939, June 30

Dr. O'Connor and Dr. Bendheim came to see Ruth. Dr. O'Connor said "Good Bye, I've got it". He had a letter in his hand and continued, "I intend to make Dr. Saxe eat every word of it"[15]

1939, July 3
Ruth phoned Mrs. O'Connor about some money she owed her for 3 boxes of cosmetics she had sold. She stated that she didn't think they were leaving and would come over to tell her about it if her Dad would let her. She and Dr. O'Connor came over and told her about it. Dr. Patterson was not going to review Dr. Scholp's temporary license so no emergency would exist and that Bill Peterson politician, Jack Sparks, State purchasing agent and Lynn Lockhart, the governor's campaign manager was going to get the governor when he came back from seeing President Roosevelt in NY to force Dr. Saxe to keep Dr. O'Connor. As they were telling Ruth this, a group of "bullies", Mr. Raymond, supervisor and a man or two from the power house appeared. Ruth was very frightened. Dr. Scholp came in and they leaped on Dr. O'Connor, knocking him down and took his keys and seized Ruth and locked her in her room. Ruth stated that this was the first time she had ever been locked in her room. They stated that they had come to kidnap her. Ruth was so frightened she started to scream out the window for Lon Jordon, the sheriff to come and to arrest everyone on a kidnap frame up. Men guards were placed over Ruth, one outside her room by the door and one outside her window. She was drugged with hyoscine until she found it hard to tell the real from the unreal. Ruth stated she was frightened to death.[15]

1939, October
Ruth had earned about $30 from her laundry business.[84] She sent Dr. Judd $20 to come visit her. He was now residing in a government hospital in Sawtelle, California. He had not visited her since she entered the hospital. Her only communication with him was frequent lengthy letters which he answered.[84] She bought a new dress of purple rayon, a new pair of shoes, and some soft drinks for the Sunday Dr. Judd was to arrive. He never came.[84] Ruth talked about leaving the hospital for California, or South Africa or Mexico.[84]

1939, October 24
Ruth escapes from the hospital. She did not attend a dance arranged by the therapy department. She artfully transformed an assortment of boxes, bath towels, cosmetic containers and bottles into a dummy resembling herself asleep in bed.[84] At midnight, she arrived at her

parent's house on 1328 East Moreland Street. Her mother urged her to stay and return to the hospital in the morning. She writes a letter to Governor Jones which she asked her mother to deliver and walked out the door.[84] The letter said, my husband coaxed me to surrender to the police. I did and look what happens. Dr. Saxe tortures me. Even Hitler would not torture his prisoners when they surrender. I was not overcome, so I had to surrender. Only a coward would torture one helpless. I am helpless because I trusted fairness. I do not get it. Dr. Saxe says I have no privileges. I did have until he came here. He took them away. For 18 months I had yard parole, could sit on the yard alone or with my family. I never abused a privilege or broke a trust. Dr. Saxe took my privileges away because he hates me. I am persecuted by the Catholics. ... him, $20 to come on. But, he can only stay one day. $20 just to see him two or three hours, and now they have ordered that I have to visit him in Mrs. Lassiter's presence, my bitter enemy. I will not. Tonight I am running away. I hate everyone who has forced me to do it. May God punish them. I want to be a good patient. I like you. I hope you may be governor again. You have been kind to me and I do not want to do anything ever to hurt you. I am desperate to see my father. I am going to see him tonight, then somehow see my husband and I will surrender to you on condition you promise me Dr. Saxe will be forced to leave me alone. I will not run away. I do not want my freedom illegal.[84]

1939, October 25

Ruth is found missing at 10:45 on the next day. She typically slept late, but they became worried that she might have overdosed on sleeping pills. In San Francisco, Dr. Catton said he believed Ruth would try to resume a normal life in a distant city as a secretary or nurse. He said he thought she was clever enough to evade the police. He also suggested that she might go to Mexico because she loved it. Dr. Judd issued a plea for his wife to "Surrender to the nearest officers of the law, wherever you are, for only disaster awaits you if you attempt to remain in hiding or to continue your flight."[84] Dr. Judd also said he believed his wife's escape was not a plot hatched over a long period of time, but that "she acted on the spur on the moment, as insane persons often do."[84]

1939, October 26

Police believed that Winnie Ruth Judd had made her way to the coast based on a cryptic message made by Dr. Judd. He had made a statement to the Times for her surrender. However, Burton McKinnell who was living in Hyatville MD at the time said, "Only one major blunder has been made. If everything goes well the next 20 hours there will be no need for court action. I have all the trail briefs and they are available to OV Willson. The last part of the message indicating that a contact is near was kept secret at the request of Dr. Judd. Burton made the statement from DC. She will give herself up automatically if they only will let her carry out her plans. He also predicted that if she were captured she would be returned to the hospital and possible be found sane, which would then place her in jeopardy of being hanged. The governor Jones said that he had conducted an investigation into the escape and found no evidence of inside aid to Mrs. Judd. He was told that Mrs. Judd had grown increasingly nervous and irritable since her privileges were curbed several months ago. He said she developed a persecution complex. Carrie Judd stated that she thought Ruth went to Mexico. She expressed hope that she would give herself up soon for her own safety and for the sake of those who love her. Carrie had been at home for several weeks recovering from a recent heart attack. Some people at Long Beach said they thought they saw her. Sheriff Biscailuz stated that Ruth was seen near Vista Wednesday night with a man and woman headed toward Los Angeles. This woman was very intoxicated. Dr. Judd pointed out that Ruth never drank except on one or two occasions with medical compunction. Dr. Judd had been out to visit his sister and was assisting in locating Ruth.[145]

1939, October 27
Ruth is thought to be hitchhiking her way up the California Coast. They believed she had stopped in an auto court at 1821 San Fernando Road. The woman walked into the office at 8 saying she had no automobile but wanted to rent a small cabin for a dollar which was all she could afford. She signed the book. In the morning she arose early and left a half hour after sunrise walking northward along San Fernando Road. She was carrying a long coat with a dark lining over her arm. She was wearing a brown blouse, a black skirt, new tan, low heeled shoes and a small hat. He checked the register and there it was signed, "Mr. and Mrs. R. C. Judd." The new shoes indicated an ID since she had left a new pair of shoes in the alley in back of her parent's house. They took prints from the cabin and compared her handwriting. One man stated that he saw Mrs. Judd with a male companion at Baker California and she was later seen with him in Montrose. Another report stated that

Mrs. Judd was headed for Honolulu.[146]

1939, October 28

Dr. Judd was brought to Phoenix where he went to a hotel in hopes of attracting Ruth there. The McKinnell's visited him on Saturday, but by Sunday night, Dr. Judd's whereabouts were unknown.[84]

1939, October 30

A minister in Tempe sees Ruth in his yard Sunday night. They take her inside and talk to her for 3 hours. They urged her to return to the hospital and prayed with her. He dropped her off near the hospital and reported it to the Sheriff's office. Before dropping her off, he pleaded with her to return to the hospital. She threatened to cut her throat with a razor. Ruth got out of the car at Roosevelt Street just north of the hospital grounds about 2 AM[84] The LA times stated that she threatened the couple with the razor blade and made them drive out of Phoenix. When she found they were driving back towards the hospital, she demanded to get out. Then, she fled into the orange grove.[147] Ruth wandered back to the hospital. They took her to Dr. Saxe's office where she announced, "Well, here I am!" When Dr. Saxe pressed her for details, he stated that she became more and more hysterical and she was given sedatives. She was shoeless; stockings torn off, her feet and legs were bruised and were dirty. Her ankle was sprained and she had fashioned a brace for it from her girdle.[84] A hospital report stated that she returned by herself. [129] The LA Times stated that after a search, it was found that Mrs. Judd's small overnight bag was hidden in an incubator near the chicken house. In the bag were two pairs of shoes, cans of soup, some grapes, bread, a broken mirror, a road map, a can of spaghetti and a sweater.[147] She stated that most of the six days she hid in a cornfield across the road from a cemetery that adjoined the hospital. This field is about a mile and a half from the main building. She was barefoot and disheveled. When questioning her she stated, "You are trying to get information from me, but you are not giving me any information." She was weak and nervous. They put her to bed and she was reported to be sleeping fitfully.[147] A contrary statement emerged that she had gone to the vacant half of a duplex near Seventh and Brill. They found footprints in the dust and the letters WRJ carved on the window sill. Ruth was found with a razor.[147]

1939, October 31

It was reported that Ruth might see a reduction in her privileges at the hospital. Louis J. Saxe stated that she would not be permitted to roam the grounds as freely as formerly. He also stated that she will be denied the privilege for the time being of operating a beauty parlor at the hospital. Previously, he said a new beauty parlor was being installed and she would be permitted to work for inmates if she would surrender. They were also going to watch all visitors more closely. He had a list of 50 visitors to check with on her last escape. On Sunday when she was at Mr. Ankerbergs she told them that she had plans to flee to Mexico. The minister said that Mrs. Judd told him she was unable to complete plans because of inability to contact a prominent Phoenix businessman who she said promised to help her if she ever escaped. At first she pleaded with Ankerberg to hide her and later sought his aid to rent an apartment in Phoenix. She made the following claims according to the pastor. 1. She said she hid in an orange grove and in a vacant house with only green oranges to eat while law officers were all around her hiding place. 2. She charged that she had been enduring a life of horror at the hospital and could stand it no longer. 3. While lurking in the orange grove she wrote a letter to her husband seeking to arrange a rendezvous. She then walked into town and mailed the letter. Dr. Saxe would declare her sane and order her returned to the jail. 5. She threatened to kill herself before agreeing to return to the hospital but a moment later in a reversal of mood said she wanted to see her husband and have him obtain certain guarantees from officials of the institution before returning there. They said that when she came her eyes were blackened by long periods of crying. Her dress was dirty and her features were worn and haggard. Mrs. Ankerberg was standing in the front bedroom of the partially finished parsonage when she looked out a window and saw a figure standing a few feet from the front porch peering through a door. She refused food, but she drank some milk. She said that she did not want to stay in Tempe, but if she could get an apartment in Phoenix she could live on cheese and crackers and sardines for a long time without leaving. She said that she would be quiet. She said she feared a sanity hearing. Dr. Saxe stated that they were not considering a hearing. Dr. Judd did receive Ruth's letter. It was written on one side of a piece of paper. It revealed how frantic she was to find freedom; physical freedom. Portions read, "I'm lying out here in the moonlight in the desert, but there are mountains all around. I can't get out. I do want to see you. I have a new razor and will cut my head off with it if they try to take me back. It is so cold and I have a sprained ankle. Dr. Judd said the rest of it was incoherent and jumbled. Dr. Judd was not intending to share the letter, but if it were to help Dr. Saxe, he complied.[148]

1939, November 1
Dr. Saxe said that a key to her ward door had been found on her person after her return. This key was said to be lost for months. Dr. Saxe took away most of Ruth's privileges including visiting her parents or going out on hospital grounds. She was kept inside her box like wire screen cubicle for the next four weeks.[84] Reverend Albert Hager of Pekin, Ill wrote an affidavit regarding Ruth Judd. He stated that his main fear was that she would be sent to the gallows since she was convicted twice. He said Mrs. Judd believes that she is sane. He was a friend of her Father's. HJ was currently in critical condition. He had been bedridden for 18 months. He had been in Phoenix previously. He said that Ruth confided her plans to escape because of her fear that Dr. Saxe would discover her to be a sane woman and reopen the doors to the gallows. Dr. Saxe admitted that hospital attendants had found a key on Ruth. She had told the pastor that was stolen several years previous. Dr. Judd stated that he had been approached by a national magazine with an offer to buy the rights to the story of his life with Winnie Ruth Judd. He said he has not made up his mind about the proposition. After her return for the first two weeks, Fel Fox, assistant secretary to the Governor RT Jones, said she was kept in one room under guard to calm her down. Then she was taken back to her old ward to soothe her. The WPA was building a higher fence around the asylum but they hadn't finished it yet. They had started 5 months ago.[149] There is a picture of this built fence at Kent State in the Borrowitz Crime Collection.[150]

1939, December 3
Ruth flees from the state hospital again. She walks through the same locked door she had before.[84] Ruth spent an hour at a pastor's house between 8:30 and 9:30 on Sunday night. She gained entry by cutting a screen, taking a coat, sweater, two oranges, crackers, and milk. She left two notes, one for taking the items from the pastor, regretting her theft, and one to Governor Jones expressing dissatisfaction with conditions and treatment at the hospital, stating, "Its either this or suicide."[84] They called in the bloodhounds from Florence to find her. She was

wearing a wine colored dress and brown shoes. She had no coat. She was thought to have a paper wrapped bundle of personal effects. She first visited her parents as her first stop. She was seen at 6:30 and then thirty minutes later she was gone. They said she had been sitting on the edge of her bed looking nervous. Dr. Ankerburg of Tempe who Ruth had threatened with a razor blade hurried to the sheriff's office and asked for protection. Dr. Saxe was home ill when she escaped, but came into the office to start the search for her.[151]

1939, December 4
A hospital report stated that she escaped by way of an unlocked door.[129] HJ McKinnell and Carrie stated that they thought she would commit suicide rather than return to the hospital. Rev Paul Ankerberg also thought she would kill herself. The officials were more afraid that she might die from exposure. They stated that when she returned before, she was left in a frail condition. They thought this time that she was in the vicinity of Phoenix. Bloodhounds were able to track her from the woman's dormitory at the hospital to a nearby cemetery about a half mile before losing the trail. She burglarized the Phoenix parsonage of a minister Robert A, Warren. Mrs. Judd entered the parsonage while Mr. Warren was conducting services in a nearby church. She took one of Mrs. Warren's coats, some oranges and crackers. She left a note apologizing for her act. The blood hounds picked up Ruth's scent at the Warren residence; the dogs followed it half a block down into an alley and then lost the scent near a fish market. Dr. Judd was waiting by the phone in Santa Monica awaiting outcome of the chase. He had no reason to believe she was in Los Angeles. He said he got a letter a few days ago from Carrie McKinnell. He quoted the letter as saying Ruth had been unhappy because she claimed that she had been kept in a strait jacket for two or three days after her return from her earlier escape.[152]

1939, December 6
Dr. Judd arrives in Phoenix. He claimed he would deliver the note to the governor and serve as "bait" for his wife's capture[84].

1939, December 12
Governor Jones indicates that there will be a shakeup at the State Hospital. It is not just because of Ruth Judd's escape. He indicated that there would be a shakeup of personnel but would still back Dr.

Saxe as superintendent. He stated, "Just keep your eyes open and you'll see some smoke on the street in a few days." Further criticism was laid on the governor because of the 4th escape of Brino Hanks. He was a maniacal rapist. He had escaped 4 times and was recaptured in El Paso. Ruth had been gone for a while. Sheriff Lon Jordan stated that he felt Ruth had died from exposure or had committed suicide with a razor blade that she had stolen from the asylum.[153]

1939, December 15
Ruth is seen in Yuma. The police followed her down a street and into a drugstore where she mde a phone call. They asked her to get in the car. She stated she was a hitchhiker named Marian Burke. She got in the car and was taken to the Yuma County Sheriff. She had a razor blade knotted into her hair with chewing gum. Ruth said she kept it there for suicidal use, "If I felt I had to do it."[84] She stated she had walked 24 of the 198 miles to Yuma.[84] Ruth talked to reporters and gave them a twelve-page statement addressed to the Arizona Legislature. In it she named the person Mrs. Judd said had dismembered Sammy's body and another person she said had arranged for the operation. She elaborated to other reporters at Gila Bend, Buckeye and the remainder of the trip.[84] Note, Interesting that this document at the Arizona Historical Society starts on page 13 and the first 12 pages are missing. It is not longhand, however. They thought this was written in 1941 however.[141] Ruth states she went down the railroad track in the dead of winter 175 miles in her stocking feet without food for 12 days except for a box of crackers and some milk that she swiped.[141] She states that Mrs. Eldred said that all of the patients except Ruth were to be transferred to the new hospital the following day. Ruth asked her where she was going. She replied, "They are going to chop your head off and I hope I see them do it." Ruth stated she ran like wild as fast as she could to Yuma where they caught her phoning her husband.[141]

1939, December 16
Ruth is returned to the State hospital. Following an examination, razor blades were found in her hair, slippers, vagina, and rectum. In addition, the key to her former ward was also found in her rectum.[129] Ruth said she was kept in solitary confinement after this without clothes, chair, comb or even a magazine to look at for a year. They treated her like a dog.[141] She stated that they shot her full of hyoscine and kept her in

wet sheet packs and pulled her hair. When she was bound up they taunted her about letters I'd written my husband which her lawyers sold to them.[141]

1939, December 19
Someone gave Ruth a little red stocking of candy like was given to all of the other patients. She was sitting on the cement floor eating her candy since she had no chair. She stated she was starving since she lost 35 pounds when she walked to Yuma. She stated she had walked 175 miles, drinking out of irrigation ditches. An attendant came in and slapped her face and snatched her sack of candy.[15]

1.	Catton, Dr. Joseph, *Observations of Ruth Judd of January 7, 1932*, in *In State Vs Judd, Arizona State Archives*. 1932: Phoenix, Az.
2.	*Testimony of Paul E Bowers*, in *State Vs Judd*. 1932: Phoenix, AZ.
3.	Catton, Joseph, *Behind the scenes of murder*. "First edition". ed. 1940, New York: W.W. Norton & company, inc. 355 p.
4.	*Halloran Firm in Denials*, in *Arizona Republic*. March 22, 1933: Phoenix, Arizona.
5.	Sellers, James Clark, *Letter from J Clark Sellers to Lloyd Andrews*. January 14, 1932, Kept at Arizona State Archives and Public Records.
6.	Hickernell, FA, *Dr. M. I. Leff*, in *Winnie Ruth Judd Papers, Arizona State Archives*. January 14, 1932: Phoenix.
7.	Gillie, J. A, *Letter from J. A Gillie to Harman Lewkowitz entitled a grusome secret*. January 20, 1932: Zayante, CA.
8.	*Heads of Slain Women Powder-Burned*, in *Phoenix Gazette*. January 23, 1932: Phoenix, AZ.
9.	*Judd shots said near*, in *Los Angeles Times*. January 24, 1932: Los Angeles.
10.	Gatter, AR, *Letter from AR Gatter of the San Franscisco Tourist Bureau to George W. Stephens.*, in *Winnie Ruth Judd Papers*. 1-23, 1932: Ann Arbor, MI.
11.	Smith, Frank O, *Letter from Attorney Frank O Smith to the board of pardons & paroles*. March 28, 1933: Phoenix.
12.	*Testimony of Dr. Clifford Wright*. Feb 2, 1932, Arizona State library and Public Records: Phoenix, AZ.
13.	*Alienist Heard in Judd Case*, in *Unknown newspaper clippings of Lloyd Andrews*. Feburary 2?, 1932.

14. *Alienist Fears for Life at Trial*, in *Ellensburg Daily Record*. February 6, 1932: Ellensburg, WA.

15. Judd, Winnie Ruth, *Letter of Winnie Ruth Judd written at the state hospital some 20 years after she arrived there. This may be the letter she wrote to Governor Pyle on January 25, 1953?*, in *Collection of Jerry Lewkowitz*. January 25, 1951?: Phoenix, Arizona. 1-12, 13, 21-22, incomplete.

16. Greene, Bessie Humphrey, *Letter from Bessie Humphrey Greene, Astrologer to Mr. Herman Lewkowitz*. February 10, 1932: Perkins, CA.

17. Matthews, T. S., *Jacks or better : a narrative*. 1st ed. 1977, New York: Harper & Row. vii, 354 p.

18. Greene, Bessie Humphrey, *Letter from Bessie Humphrey Greene to Herman Lewkowitz* March 3, 1932: Perkins, CA.

19. McLain, Jerry, *Exclusive - Article for the Arizona Republic _Unpublished*, in *Arizona State Archives and Public Records*. March 21, 1932: Phoenix.

20. *Lot 9, Block 1, La Belle Place, 4/42 Deed Recordings*. Phoenix, Arizona.

21. *Brother of Mrs. Judd fights pamphlet case*, in *Los Angeles TImes*. July 15, 1932: Los Angeles.

22. *Brother of Ruth Judd convicted*, in *Los Angeles Times*. July 23, 1932: Los Angeles.

23. *Ruth Judd's Brother Selling in Phoenix*, in *Los Angeles Times*. July 28, 1932: Los Angeles.

24. Judd, William C, *My Life with Winnie Ruth Judd - Part 1*, in *Intimate Detective Stories*. March, 1940. 2-7, 52.

25. *Murder Photos Taken by Thief*, in *Los Angeles Times*. August 17, 1932: Los Angeles.

26. *Winnie Ruth Judd's Brother Will Wed*, in *Los Angeles Times*. October 1, 1932: Los Angeles.

27. Judd, Winnie Ruth, *Letter from Winnie Ruth Judd intended for Mr. Richardson of Florence Az - not mailed. Given to George W. Stephens instead*, in *Winnie Ruth Judd Papers*. October 26, 1932: Ann Arbor, MI.

28. Judd, Winnie Ruth, *Letter to Dr. Judd from Winnie Ruth Judd from Florence - not sent*, in *Winnie Ruth Judd papers*. unknown probably October 1932, 1932?: Ann Arbor, MI.

29. *Photograph of a dark haired boy. "This is chang M. He was six years old in June. He is the baby.",* in *Winnie Ruth Judd Collection.* Ann Arbor, MI.

30. *Dr. Judd Exonerated by Verdict,* in *Los Angeles Times.* November 1, 1932: Los Angeles.

31. Judd, Winnie Ruth, *Letter to Dr. Judd from Ruth, never sent, the wardon gives it to Dr. Stephens.,* in *Winnie Ruth Judd Papers.* December 7, 1932: Ann Arbor, MI.

32. *Ruth Ignorant of Court Rule,* in *Unknown clippings of Lloyd Andrews.* December 12, 1932.

33. *Must Hang: Tigress ordered to gallows Feb 17 by Supreme Court,* in *Unknown newspaper clippings of Lloyd Andrews.* December 13, 1932.

34. *I will never hang, asserts Ruth Judd,* in *Unknown newspaper clippings of Lloyd Andrews.* December 17, 1932.

35. *Hospital Ousts Judd From Roll,* in *Unknown Clippings of Lloyd Andrews.* December 16, 1932.

36. *High-Pitched Voice of Convicted Slayer Heard in Corridors,* in *Unknown Newspaper Clippings of Lloyd Andrews.* December 28, 1932.

37. Judd, Winnie Ruth, *Letter from Winnie Ruth to Dr. Stephens,* in *Winnie Ruth Judd Papers.* 12-30, 1932: Ann Arbor MI.

38. *Leniency asked for Ruth Judd,* in *Arizona Republic.* December 31, 1932: Phoenix, AZ.

39. *Probate of Hedvig Samuelson.* January 16, 1933, Hennepin County District Court: Minneapolis, MN.

40. *Winnie Judd awaits pardon board action,* in *Arizona Republic.* January 2, 1933: Phoenix, Arizona.

41. *Grand Jury's Indictments are Attacked,* in *Arizona Republic.* January 4, 1933: Phoenix Republic.

42. Russill, Louis P, *Letter of Louis P Russill Attorney at law to Lin B. Orme, chairman of Arizona State Board of Pardons and Paroles.* January 4, 1933: Los Angeles.

43. *Court Denies J. J. Halloran Defense Move,* in *Arizona Republic.* January 5, 1933: Phoenix, Arizona.

44. *Andrews says Judd Jury Story Untrue,* in *Arizona Republic.* January 5, 1933: Phoenix, Arizona.

45. *Jury Charged with Bias by J. J. Halloran,* in *Arizona Republic.* January 6, 1933: Phoenix, Arizona.

46. *New Halloran Charge Will be Filed Today*, in *Arizona Republic*. January 7, 1933: Phoenix, Arizona.
47. *Halloran's Counsel Seeks Transcript of Ruth Judd Statement*, in *Arizona Republic*. January 10, 1933: Phoenix, Arizona.
48. *Trunk slayer to appear on stand today*, in *Arizona Republic*. January 11, 1933 Phoenix, Arizona.
49. *Halloran Case Delay Unlikely*, in *Arizona Republic*. January 14, 1933: Phoenix, Arizona.
50. *Ruth Judd Petitions Board to Hear Story*, in *Arizona Republic*. January 14, 1933: Phoenix, Arizona.
51. *Halloran Tiral Seen as Delaying Hanging of Winnie Ruth Judd*, in *Arizona Republic*. January 15, 1933: Phoenix, Arizona.
52. *Transcript of Judd Story Given Counsel For Jack Halloran*, in *Arizona Republic*. January 17, 1933: Phoenix, Arizona.
53. *Winnie Tells Suicide Idea: Slayer Hurls Charges at J. J. Halloran*, in *Arizona Republic*. January 18, 1933: Phoenix, AZ.
54. *Winnie Ruth Judd Denounces Halloran Across Court Table*, in *Arizona Republic*. January 19, 1933: Phoenix, Arizona.
55. *Ruth Judd breaks down in court describing death fight story*, in *Phoenix Gazette*. January 18, 1933: Phoenix, Arizona.
56. *Ruth Judd Story is Challenged by Halloran Counsel*, in *Arizona Republic*. January 20, 1933: Phoenix, Arizona.
57. *Halloran Hearing Near End*, in *Arizona Republic*. January 21, 1933: Phoenix, Arizona.
58. *Winnie Judd fights to balk impeachment of whole testimony*, in *Arizona Republic*. Janaury 22, 1933: Phoenix, AZ.
59. *Decision Near in Hearing of Halloran Case*, in *Arizona Republic*. January 23, 1933: Phoenix, AZ.
60. *J. J. Halloran Hearing Will Resume Today*, in *Arizona Republic*. January 24, 1933: Phoenix, Arizona.
61. *Halloran to be released unless case is pefected*, in *Arizona Republic*. January 25, 1933: Phoenix, Arizona.
62. *Halloran freed of accusation in Judd Case*, in *Phoenix Gazette*. January 25, 1933: Phoenix, Arizona.
63. *Halloran Complaint Dismissed. New Judd Story Hinted by Lumbermans Council*, in *Arizona Republic*. January 26, 1933: Phoenix.
64. *Halloran Complaint Dismissed*, in *Arizona Republic*. January 26, 1933: Phoenix, Arizona.

65. LaDue, W Robert, *Affidavit of W Robert LaDue*, in *Arizona State Archives and Public Records*. March 20, 1933: Phoenix.

66. Judd, Ruth, *Letter to Mr. Renz Jennings, Court House, Phoenix*, in *Winnie Ruth Judd Collection, Arizona State Archives*. Feb 20, 1933: Phoenix.

67. *Letter from George W. Stephens from Edward Huntington Williams MD at the 910 Pacific Mutual Building*, in *Winnie Ruth Judd Papers*. 2-27, 1933: Ann Arbor, MI.

68. *Catton Calls Winnie Sane: Alienists Adhere to Trial View*, in *Arizona Republic*. April 16, 1933: Phoenix.

69. Judd, Winnie Ruth, *Letter from Ruth Judd written to Mr. L. S. Todd, Tipton Indiana*. March 1, 1933: Florence, Az.

70. Judd, Ruth, *Letter to Mr. Renz Jennings, County Attorney*, in *Winnie Ruth Judd Collection, Arizona State Archives*. March 3, 1933: Phoenix.

71. *Catch Ruth Judd Sawing Cell Bar*, in *Spokane Daily Chronicle*. March 31, 1933: Spokane, WA. 13.

72. *Cheerfulness of Woman Surprises*, in *Spartanburg Herald*. April 1, 1933: Spartanburg, SC. 2.

73. *Mrs Judd Fails in Plot to Saw Way to Freedom*, in *Deseret News*. March 31, 1933: Salt Lake City, UT.

74. Anspach, HA, *Letter from HA Anspach to the Arizona Board of Pardons*, A.B.o. Pardons, Editor. March 13, 1933: Phoenix.

75. *Board hears Judd Appeal*, in *Arizona Republic*. March 14, 1933.

76. *Judd Jury 'Plot' is charged*, in *Arizona Republic*. March 15, 1933.

77. *List of United States Citizens on the SS Quirigua Arriving April 8, 1933 to New York*. 1933.

78. *Pardon Board to Hear Six Judd Witnesses*, in *Arizona Republic*. March 17, 1933.

79. *Western Union Telegram to La Prade from the LA Times.*, in *Arizona STate Archives and Public Records*. March 19, 1933: Phoenix.

80. *Sheriff aids Judd Appeal for Clemency*, in *Arizona Republic*. March 21, 1933: Phoenix, Arizona.

81. *Dr. Judd Fights for Wife's Life*, in *Arizona Republic*. March 23, 1933: Phoenix, Arizona.

82. *Western Union Telegrams from the LA Times*, in *Arizona State Archives and Public Records*. March 23, 1933: Phoenix, Arizona.

83. *Pardon Board Hearing In Judd Case Ends With Father's Appeal*, in *Arizona Republic*. March 24, 1933: Phoenix, Arizona.

84.   Dobkins, J.D. and R. J. Hendricks, *Winnie Ruth Judd: The Trunk Murders*. 1973, New York: Grosset & Dunlap.

85.   *Ruth Judd Becomes Hysterical During Testimony of Lin Orme*, in *Arizona Republic*. April 20, 1933: Phoenix.

86.   Mckinnell, Kirk, *Email titled: Rewriting missing Email*. September 8, 2000: Ava, MO.

87.   *Text of Board Decision*, in *Arizona Republic*. March 31, 1933: Phoenix, Arizona.

88.   *Suicide Watch Put Over Winnie Judd*, in *Pittsburgh PRess*. April 1, 1933: Pittsburgh, PA.

89.   *Four Women on guard to Thwart Ruth Judd Suicide*, in *Milwaukee Sentinal*. April 2, 1933: Milwaukee, WI. 2.

90.   *Doomed Woman's Brother in Jail*, in *Deseret News*. April 5, 1933: Salt Lake City, UT. 1.

91.   *Further Judd Delay Asked*, in *Arizona Republic*. April 4, 1933: Phoenix, AZ.

92.   *Judd Censures Pardon Board*, in *Arizona Republic*. April 5, 1933: Phoenix.

93.   *Court Gets New Judd Request*, in *Arizona Republic*. April 7, 1933: Phoenix.

94.   Judd, Winnie Ruth, *Confession Letter of Winnie Ruth Judd: Letter to HG Richardson.*, in *Winnie Ruth Judd, Arizona Historical Society*. April 6, 8, 1933: Tuscon,.

95.   Arline, *Untitled draft for Arizona Republic? (from the collection of Patrick Millikin)*. 1946.

96.   *Winnie Judd Losing Poise*, in *Arizona Republic*. April 8, 1933: Phoenix.

97.   *Warden Will File Request*, in *Arizona Republic*. April 12, 1933: Phoenix.

98.   *Guards Balk Ruth Judd's Suicide Try*, in *Milwaukee Sentinal*. April 9, 1933: Milwaukee, WI. 1.

99.   *Defense Calls Judd Jurors*, in *Arizona Republic*. April 9, 1933: Phoenix.

100.   *Ruth Judd Hearing Scheduled*, in *Arizona Republic*. April 13, 1933: Phoenix.

101.   *Court Denies Retrial Plea of Ruth Judd*, in *Arizona Republic*. April 11, 1933: Phoenix.

102.   *League Asks Ruth Judd Aid*, in *Arizona Republic*. April 13, 1933: Phoenix.

103. *Petition 1438*, in *State Vs Judd: Arizona State Archives and Public Records*. April 12, 1933: Phoenix, AZ.

104. *Ruth Judd Is Denied Stand*, in *Arizona Republic*. April 14, 1933: Phoenix.

105. *Ruth Begins Last Battle*, in *Arizona Republic*. April 15, 1933: Phoenix.

106. *Californians May Aid Ruth*, in *Arizona Republic*. April 14, 1933: Phoenix.

107. McMillan, James E. and Sharlot Hall Museum (Prescott Ariz.). Press., *Ernest W. McFarland : Majority Leader of the United States Senate, Governor and Chief Justice of the State of Arizona : a biography*. 2004, Prescott, Ariz.: Sharlot Hall Museum Press. xxii, 618 p.

108. Fulbright, Tom, *Cow-country counselor*. [1st ed. 1968, New York,: Exposition Press. 196 p.

109. Arizona. State Hospital Phoenix. [from old catalog], *Milestones; a history of seventy-five years of progress at the Arizona State Hospital, Phoenix, Arizona, 1887-1962*. 1962, [Phoenix,. 150 p.

110. *Winnie Alters Court Manner*, in *Arizona Republic*. April 16, 1933: Phoenix.

111. *Winnie Judd May Get Stay of Few Days*, in *Arizona Republic*. April 17, 1933: Phoenix.

112. *Hysteria Displayed by Slayer*, in *Arizona Republic*. April 18, 1933: Phoenix.

113. *Judd Jury Lockup: Hearing Recesses in Uproar*, in *Arizona Republic*. April 19, 1933: Phoenix.

114. *Winnie Sane Says Bowers*, in *Arizona Republic*. April 19, 1933: Phoenix.

115. *Financing of Judd Case Stirs Argument*, in *Arizona Republic*. April 19, 1933: Phoenix.

116. *Ruth Furiously Assails Orme; State Opens Insanity Attack*, in *Arizona Republic*. April 20, 1933: Phoenix.

117. *Threat Made in Judd Case*, in *Arizona Republic*. April 20, 1933: Phoenix.

118. *Judd Friends Meeting Today*, in *Arizona Republic*. April 20, 1933: Phoenix.

119. *Judd Hearing Nears End: Defendant Sane Say Alienists*, in *Arizona Republic*. April 21, 1933: Phoenix.

120. *Judd Hearing is Continued today: Final Arguments and Jury Decision are Expected Before Night*, in *Arizona Republic*. April 22, 1933: Phoenix.

SECTION FOUR 1932-1939

121. *Ruth Judd Escapes Noose: Trunk Slayer Found Insane*, in *Arizona Republic*. April 23, 1933: Phoenix.

122. *Drama, Joy Mingled in Judd Verdict*, in *Arizona Republic*. April 23, 1933: Phoenix.

123. *Winnie Judd Leaves Today for Hospital*, in *Arizona Republic*. April 24, 1933: Phoenix.

124. Suttliff, Curt, et al., *Trunk Murderess Winnie Judd Held in Eastbay*, in *Oakland Tribune*. June 28, 1969.

125. Arizona State Board of Health, *Baby Boy McKinnell Death Certificate*, in *Arizona VItal Records*. April 24, 1933: Phoenix. http://genealogy.az.gov/

126. Greenwood Memorial Lawn, *Section 60- Forest Lawn*, in *Greenwood Memorial Cemetery Records,*. 1933: Phoenix. 1.

127. *Asylum Doors Close Behind Winnie Judd*, in *Arizona Republic*. April 25, 1933: Phoenix.

128. McFarland, Ernest William, *Mac : the autobiography of Ernest W. McFarland*. 1979, [s.l.]: McFarland. ix, 342 p.

129. Whitney, Rex E., *Memo to Willis H Bower Director regarding Winnie Ruth Judd. from Rex E Whitney, Assistant to the director*, in *Pineal County Historical Museum*. August 15, 1969: Florence, AZ.

130. US National Homes for Disabled Volunteer Soldiers, *William Craig Judd Admission Record*. 1933. www.ancestry.com

131. Keaton, Mildred, *No Regrets: Autobiography of an Arctic Nurse*. 1999, Marysville, WA: Pakuk Press.

132. *Dr. Judd Asks Jury Trial in Drunk Case*, in *Los Angeles Times*. November 22, 1933: Los Angeles.

133. *Unable to make bail, court releases Dr. Judd*, in *Los Angeles Times*. November 25, 1933: Los Angeles.

134. Fortuine, Robert, *"Must We All die?" Alaska's Enduring Struggle with Tuberculosis*. 2005, Fairbanks: University of Alaska Press.

135. Samuelson, Arnold, *With Hemingway : a year in Key West and Cuba*. 1985, New York: Holt, Rinehart and Winston.

136. *Trunk slayer's husband battles to come back*, in *Los Angeles Times*. February 7, 1935: Los Angeles.

137. *Los Angeles County Coroner's Register for Anne LeRoi and Hedvig Samuelson*. October 23, 1931: Los Angeles.

138. Courtney, WB, *Angel in Furs*. Collier's, 1937: p. 67.

139. *Exhibition, Marie Sterner galleries*. Art Digest, 1938. 13: p. 20.

140. *Aluminum torso at the Marie Sterner Gallories*. Parnassus, 1938. 10: p. 35.

141.   Judd, Winnie Ruth, *Judd Reminiscences*, in *Arizona Historical Society, Southern Arizona Division*. 1941: Tucson, AZ.

142.   Mofford, Rose, *Phone call from Rose Mofford*. November 16, 2007.

143.   Swent, Eleanor, *Marian Lane: Mine Doctor's Wife in Mexico*. Western Mining in the Twentieth Century Oral History Services. 1996, Berkeley. 121.

144.   Ware, Pearl, *Letter from the Arizona State Board of Beauty Culturist Examiners to Governor Jones*, G.R.T. Jones, Editor. May 10, 1939, RG1 Box 12 Folder 9 Arizona State Archives, Phoenix, Arizona: Phoenix.

145.   *Escaped Trunk Murderess Believed Hiding on Coast*, in *Los Angeles Times*. October 27, 1939.

146.   *Ruth Judd's Trail Found in Los Angeles*, in *Los Angeles Times*. October 28, 1939: Los Angeles.

147.   *Ruth Judd walks into asylum and surrenders to guards*, in *Los Angeles Times*. October 31, 1939: Los Angeles.

148.   *Ruth Judd faces restriction of privileges in Arizona Asylum*, in *Los Angeles Times*. October 31, 1939: Los Angeles.

149.   *Preacher declares Ruth Judd escape due to fear of gallows*, in *Los Angeles Times*. November 2, 1939: Los Angeles.

150.   *Winnie Ruth Judd Photos collected by Kent State as part of the Borrowitz Crime Collection*. Kent, Ohio.

151.   *Ruth Judd disappears again from hospital*, in *Los Angeles TImes* December 4, 1939: Los Angeles.

152.   *Flight may bring death to Ruth Judd*, in *Los Angeles Times*. December 5, 1939: Los Angeles.

153.   *Shakeup Looms After Escapes*, in *Telegraph Herald*. December 12, 1939: Dubuque, IA. 1.

Section 5

1940-1949

1940

Ruth was making suicidal threats and attempts, and she still had numerous ideas of persecution and considerable paranoid behavior. At this time, she had also lost some weight, and she had a positive sputum for M. Tub. She was treated for this condition.[1]

1940, January

Dr. Judd came to visit Ruth in the hospital as soon as they would let him. Ruth stated that even though she had clothes of her own, they attired her in the worst old stained gown they could find. It had a tear in the shoulder. Ruth told him about Governor Jones who said she got him into more trouble than he had even been in during his life. Dr. Judd replied that she hadn't done anything so terrible. However, he said "You must stop fighting Dr. Saxe. The thing I am about to do is because I love you." Ruth asked, "You are not going to kill anyone over me are you?" He said, "Not as long as there is anything I can do for you. You are the only thing in this world I give a damn about. Stop fighting Dr. Saxe and I will be over in 3 months again." Ruth stated that she couldn't stop fighting since she was filled with such fears.[2] Ruth stated that she was in solitary confinement for the whole year of 1940 and that she was not allowed pencil or paper.[2]

1940, March

Dr. Judd publishes a six-part story of his life with Ruth Judd in Intimate Detective Stories.[3] Ruth was told about this.[2] Renz Jennings came to visit Ruth. An attendant stayed in the room all of the time. Mr. Jennings picked up a missionary magazine on her bed and with a pencil pointed to letters under pictures saying who is this and who is that and spelled "I'll bring you a saw." He never came back until after the election.[2] Ruth stated that Renz Jennings came to see her several times

I

about a book he was writing. He wanted her consent about parts of it. He told her, "If you will let the Labor Union get behind you we will get you out of here like we did Mooney." Ruth said, "No, I don't want any publicity", as the Pardon Board had promised her as soon as public sentiment died down they would do something for her.[2]

1940, November 5

Governor Jones of Arizona is not re-elected. Ruth expected the worst with the new administration, but was pleased that Dr. Metzger kept his word, taking the hospital out of politics. She felt she and the other patients had much better treatment under this administration than the former.[4] Ruth states that about this time Dr. Judd was very ill with diabetes and severe heart trouble and was at the veteran's hospital.[4] Ruth claimed that the Republican candidate Jerry Lee said if he was elected he would do something for her but for her to understand that he was keeping all the same personnel at the hospital.[2]

1940, December 23

Burton announced that he planned to reopen the case against his sister. He was currently a federal employee in Los Angeles. He hoped to hire an attorney. He stated, "I have buried myself in the law library at night for the last six months to find an absolutely valid court procedure and at last it has been found," he said.[5]

1940, December 31

Sheriff McFadden let Ruth's husband come and have dinner with her. Ruth stated that she had been in solitary confinement for nine months. Ruth wanted to wear an evening gown that the doctor said she looked beautiful in. McFadden trailed it out of the box through the court house corridors. A few days later, Mr. Osborn had an article making up six stories regarding why Sheriff McFadden was delivering an evening dress to Ruth Judd on New Year's Eve. It was written by Osborn's wife. It contained a statement such as "perhaps he can tell us their whereabouts as they watch the old year out and the new one in." Ruth claimed these articles were written to ridicule her.[2]

1941, January 1

Hedvig's father Anders dies at the age of 80. He was up 5 days before and his mind was sharp. His last address was 2940 Vincent Ave. N in Minneapolis.[6]

1941, January 4

Anders Samuelson was buried at Crystal Lake Cemetery.[6]

1941, January

Dr. Judd wrote to Ruth and asked her if she had stopped fighting with Dr. Saxe. He stated that he would have done what he promised to do. As it is, she was simply going to have to cooperate and perhaps someday a superintendent will come who thought enough of her to do something for her.[2] Ruth told Dr. Seth Howes this and he told her that he liked her very much.[2] Ruth stated that when Dr. Saxe left he came to see her and she said that she was sorry for I heard he wanted to give insulin and Metrazol shock to try and cure patients and relieve their mental suffering.[2]

1941, January 6

Dr. Jeremiah Metzger became the superintendent of the state hospital.[7] At this time, Dr. Hurianck, was ward doctor. Dr. Metzger had Ruth's door opened day and night.[2] Ruth was crocheting a lot during this time. She said she crocheted several tablecloths and Dr. Metzger stated he wanted one. He saw that she had made some wonderful doll clothes and asked that her doors be left open.[8] Dr. Hurianck told all of the patients to not speak to Ruth and to have nothing to do with her. She grabbed patients by the back and dragged them to their rooms and locked them up for talking to her. She told them that Ruth had killed 2 people. Ruth later retorted that lots of patients had killed somebody or tried to kill somebody and that she knew this because she had typed medical records for a while.[2] Ruth stated that she confronted Dr. Hurianck in front of some of her friends about this. A couple of days later Dr. Hurianck left. She came in to taunt her or threaten her or "however one interprets it." She stated that she was leaving, but that she wanted her to know that she would still be in Phoenix.[2] Dr. Schuster and Dr. Doyne also left. Ruth claimed they followed Dr. Hurianck.[2]

1941, April 1 (week)

Winnie Ruth Judd cuts the screen outside her cell in preparation to escape.[9]

1941, April 8

Dr. Metzger reports to the Governor an attempt by Ruth to leave the

State Hospital. He stated that in the previous week she planned to escape. As a precautionary measure, he placed a watchman outside of the hospital building, and nothing happened. Ruth called the superintendent and asked him if he would be embarrassed by her escape. She was told that it would be embarrassing and would result in drastic measures in connection with her confinement. So, she told them of her escape plans. They verified them. Ruth was moved to another room in the hospital and on this date, she was quiet and satisfied. He stated that a patient leaving the state hospital was not an unusual experience and it must be remembered that this is not a penal institution. "Patients have a large scope of privileges and very frequently just wander and walk away. We have had eight or ten so-called escapes of this nature in the past three months; all have been returned excepting two." He stated that Ruth was not successful because of her manifest frankness and fairness in the situation.[10]

1941, May 15
Sammy's body is moved to a new site at Crystal Lake Cemetery in Minneapolis. [6] She is now next to her father Anders.[6] The space is for a full length casket and not cremains.[11]

1941, June 1
O. L Bendheim becomes the superintendent of the Arizona State Hospital.[7]

1941, July 1
Ruth asks the Arizona Board of Pardons and Paroles to reconsider her case. The committee of nine asked the Arizona Board to hold a public hearing to determine if the death penalty hanging over Mrs. Judd was an obstacle to her treatment for dementia praecox and to take appropriate action.[12]

1941, October
Thomas Frelinghuysen is reviewed in Art Digest. He is exhibiting his sculptures of animals at the O'Toole Galleries on 57th street in New York. He is said to be the operator of a "large gentleman's farm in northern New Jersey and is interested in prize stock, his favorite subject." He sees beauty in bulls, awkward young colts and virile boars that he recreates in brass. There is a strange line to this article, "Nor will the animals divulge that they are all of them self-portraits of the artist in some of his domestic incarnations runs the rather startling

4

catalogue preface, 'indeed vestiges of recent roles still cling to Frelinghuysen who occasionally seeks the seclusion of some bosky dell in which to chew his quid, and frequently froths at the mouth remembering the bitter moments of his boredom.'" Frelinghuysen also was said to have written a racy monograph called "what Tomcats Dream About" and "Songs of a Swineherd". After all, he said, "I was a tomcat once myself".[13] Winnie Ruth Judd enters some of her crocheted doll clothes at the Arizona State Fair and she wins first place.[8]

1941, December 8
Carrie McKinnell was admitted to the Arizona State Hospital as a voluntary patient.[1, 14]

1942, July 16
Reverend Harvey J McKinnell passed away at 12:15 AM. He is listed as living at 1328 East Moreland as a retired minister. The cause of death was fractured hip of several years, old age, and emaciation-(Alzheimer's?) He is at the funeral home of AL Moore and Sons and is buried at Greenwood Cemetery in Phoenix. Carrie is listed as his wife and her maiden name was "Joy" (Burton's middle name) It was stated he lived in Arizona for 8 years (since 1934?)[15] He is actually buried in Inglewood Cemetery in Los Angeles.[16]

1942, August 4
O.L. Bendheim writes a letter to Jeremiah Metzger at the State Hospital. It seems that he is happy in his new position as he states, "It was bad enough here, but the working conditions, associates, and the general atmosphere of this group here is so splendid that I dare not complain. It is too good to last very long, but every week spent here is an unexpected blessing, because so many from here are leaving for unknown destinations every week." He says this about Ruth Judd, "I had a big laugh about your remark re Mrs. B and Ruth Judd. I would have given a lot to see her face when you pulled that one. The board meeting must have been quite up to tradition – or better if that is possible! Some people here by the way, know Dr. Howes and I've heard a good deal about him. Hope he'll work out alright. Dr. Schwartz, the poor fellow must have had a lot of trouble with these females on and off the board but I gather that he stood up under the ordeal." There is further talk about leaves of absence in regard to

service in times of war. Some of the stationary this letter is written on is from the Red Cross.[17]

1942, September 11
Dr. BL Shuster writes a letter to Dr. Metzger. Some of the highlights include: "There have been quite a number of resignations recently. Mrs. Dailey, Mrs. Richardson and a number of attendants resigned because of their inability to get along with the salary offered and better opportunities for a higher salary. Upon the recommendation of Mrs. Bowling (maybe the Mrs. B from August 4th?), I discharged Mrs. Kathryn Miller. Mrs. Bowling stated in her letter to me the following. "On numerous occasions Mrs. Miller has received orders concerning patients in restraints and work to be done on the afternoon shift; such as pedicures, manicures and various other duties outlined by the charge attendant on the yard. She does what she wishes to do, leaving the undesirable things undone. She is very uncooperative and an agitator. I have repeatedly talked to her about her slovenly personal appearance; there has been no change to date." "I have had no news from Dr. Howes, but we have received quite a number of his belongings. I expect him here, as stated in his original letter, on or about the 15th. I do hope that he will be here in time for the Board meeting. Dr. Goodwin was re-examined at Luke Field and is expecting to be called shortly. His former rank is Lieutenant Colonel. We have no other physician to take his place at the present time. I have written to the different agencies. Dr. Goodwin has been a good, faithful worker and we are sorry to lose him." [18]

1942, September 14
Seth F. H. Howes becomes the superintendent of the Arizona State Hospital.[7]

1944, January 16
Ruth writes a letter to HG Richardson. She writes: "Dear Mr. Richardson: This hospital is supposed to be out of politics. I hope it is. I still hold to a confidence in Dr. Metzger. My husband told me 14 years ago I could always be frank and honest with doctors. I have always been with these doctors. Several months after I came here, I cannot remember how many for I do not know when I came; the Pardon Board La Prade and Hendricks came to see me. They said, "We came to tell you we are your friends!!" I said, "Oh, no you are not my

friends; as far as you are concerned, I'm dead." They said, "We are your friends and want you to know we came out here today and commuted a man by the name of Janovitch here 6 years under the death sentence and he is going to Syria and as soon as public sentiment dies down we are going to do likewise the same for you. Several years later, Dr. Sastuc, to whom as well as Dr. Curtis and Moore I had always been honest, said as soon as you have been here 5 years we doctors' are all going together and do something for you. A group of politicians blocked it. I kept on trying to do my best in this Hospital – never being allowed the privileges granted others even. Here under the same circumstances suddenly Nora Shapley and Bill Peterson politically attack Dr. Saxe and Governor Jones over my doing hair and because of that I was so unjustly punished and also fear over that Dr. O Connor kidnap frame up caused me to ran away and tried to get to my husband. But as you know before my God I did not do it for any political reason to hurt Governor Jones. I told some of Jones's campaigners if they had spent as much time campaigning for him as they did coming out here upsetting me their man might not have been defeated – All I had in solitary confinement was a ball of thread and needle and made him a table cloth after he was defeated to show that I did not run away to hurt him. Recently I have found out the Matron here Mrs. Boerin (?) is a close friend of Nora Shapely and Bill Peterson. Nora Shapely paid patients here to pass bills for Bill Peterson and Governor Osborn. Mrs. Bowling takes these patients over to Nora Shapley's – Mrs. Bowling herself campaigned for Dick Harkes – Dick Harless, Tom Hannon and Mattie O'Connor came in on the wad without a permit, 2 months' after governor Jones stopped my doing hair and tried to get me to do Mattie's hair. Mrs. Greson, an attendant who tried to frame Dr. Saxe by offering to be Bill Peterson and Joe Conway's star witness if they preferred murder charges against Dr. Saxe for letting Dr. Schopp give insulin to a patient who expired, let them in. I did not do the hair and notified Dr. Saxe of the whole thing. He punished me by locking me up more for telling him. Four years ago Mrs. Bowling asked me to work in the diet kitchen. Mrs. Hess, an attendant, objected and threw me out saying if you are still insane you cannot work in my kitchen where you can poison anyone. There was no poison and I had no thought of any such thing. Mrs. Bowling cried and cried and said she would protect me with her own life or give up her job. Five days after, Mrs. Martin blew her child's brains out after it sneaked off to a show. She was working in the diet kitchen. Helen Rice who killed her husband, works there. Addie...." Letter abruptly ends.[19]

1944, May 27
A patient at the state hospital, Matthew (Melvin?) Matheson, escaped by cutting the screen of the porch on Ward I. He went to his mother's in Phoenix. His brother returned him reluctantly to the hospital but insisted that his brother had been mistreated.[20]

1944, May 30
Melvin's brothers come to see Seth Howes and insist that their brother be released. They are extremely belligerent.[20]

1944, June 2
The brothers of Melvin Matheson visit Reverend Hoffman of the Board of Pardons and Paroles and request that their brother be released.[20]

1944, June 9
Three men drive into the Ward I and threaten the attendant with a gun. They were masked and escaped with Melvin Matheson. The men had a key and went through the west end and through the kitchen. It was determined to be the two brothers and a former attendant. They held the staff at gunpoint while telling the patient to dress. They went out the same way and locked the door behind them. They drove out of the gate in an old car. The former attendant was thought to be Harry L Dodd. They were soon picked up and put into custody.[20]

1944, October 16
Jeremiah Metzger becomes superintendent of the Arizona State Hospital.[7]

1944, November 29
Seth Howes writes a letter to Jeremiah Metzger. There are several interesting things to note. He had left the State Hospital. He had heard no news except for some clippings that somebody had sent him anonymously. He is concerned about the labor crowd and hopes that they will lay off. He is currently pleased with the Governor's stand in this, but had been discouraged in the past and wish he would have done this since the beginning. "I was sorry to hear that Berus and Matheson had escaped. I hope that they have been caught by now. When I first came to Phoenix, Berus had all sorts of privileges – I believe with Dr.

Carr's (illegible). He carried keys, dispensed drugs, handled the property of patients, made out ward reports and many other things. I did not become aware of the situation for quite a while. I saw him around and thought he was an attendant. Mrs. McCarthy was not the only one he let into the ward. He let (illegible) in a number of times. When I finally found out who he was, I took his privileges away from him, but I received very little cooperation from the nurse or physicians or anyone else and it was a constant struggle to keep him in line. You will find pretty complete account of the situation in the records of Berus, Mrs. Bowling, and Miss Sapez (who was the worst offender). They took (illegible) terribly when he was sent to Ward I. I often wondered what it was he had that made him such a lady killer. Whatever it was, it was not apparent on the surface. Things seem very quiet and peaceful here after Phoenix, though I do manage to keep busy. I am trying to get myself back into the habit of treating patients individually. We have had an awful time finding a place to live. W Orday has allowed us to use one of her houses in (illegible) but it is too far away from my work and makes it inconvenient. At least we have a nice place in Reading, north of Boston, and now we are trying to find things with which to furnish it. We hope to be settled by Christmas.... I hope that you will write to me once in a while. I enjoy hearing from you. The family sends best regards. My regard to the other members of the board and to all of my friends in Phoenix. Sincerely, Seth Howes. PS: CR William A. Bryan recently died. I received a letter from a member of the Board of Trustees asking me if I wanted to apply for the place but I declined. I am going to try to keep away from state hospitals.[21]

1945, February
Ruth is bedridden and remains this way until at least late October.[22] A report from 1946 states that because of her TB she was confined to her bed from February 1945 to February 1946.[23]

1945, April 25
Dr. Metzger who is listed as the superintendent writes a letter to the Reverend Dr. Walter Hoffman who is listed as being the chairman of the Arizona State Board of Pardons and Paroles regarding Ruth Judd. The letter says, Sir: The welfare, care and cure of those citizens of Arizona who are so unfortunate as to be declared insane are the primary responsibility of the superintendent of the Arizona State Hospital. This responsibility is

the same for all, including the criminally insane. Therefore, I wish to submit for your consideration the following facts: First: Keeping in mind the close relationship of mental disease to psychology, it must be evident that the psychological disturbance caused in anyone under sentence of death and the resulting emotional reaction of fear would inhibit or prevent the benefit to be derived from shock treatment for dementia praecox, or other treatment which might be instituted, and I therefor respectfully request that the sentence of Ruth Judd, a patient at the Arizona State Hospital for the past twelve years and under sentence of death, be commuted to life imprisonment.Second: Such action would undoubtedly result in making Ruth Judd a better patient, a better worker, and improve her morale. The recorded diagnosis in this case is dementia praecox which is especially amenable to electric shock treatment With these two phases of confinement at the Hospital, the State Board of Pardons and Paroles can materially assist me in my responsibility by a commutation. Many citizens of Arizona no doubt feel that a commutation from a penalty of death to life imprisonment is never called for. That may be true for the criminal but for the criminally insane that opinion cannot be defended. A given patient may have a recurrence between the time that the patient is pronounced cured and the time of execution, or the hospital staff might make a mistake in pronouncing a cure. I believe that every member of your board is conversant with the difficult question of cure in mental disease. It is a debatable question; the Hospital staff frequently pronounces a cure and in a great many cases the patients are returned to the Hospital. Cure is a greatly involved matter. I trust I am not presuming when I say that the interpretation of the law furnished me is that when an insane convict is cured it is mandatory that the patient be returned to the Arizona State Penitentiary to complete his sentence.Incidentally, it can make no possible difference to me whether Ruth Judd be confined to the Hospital or the Penitentiary under sentence of life imprisonment but it does make a difference to me and is a grave matter of importance to the institution that she receives the maximum benefit from treatment as a patient. Furthermore, it will also make a difference to me and to the institution if the conduct of a patient can be made better. Living continually under the death sentence is not conducive to either cure or improvement. If there is any other information which I can furnish from the Patient-Hospital standpoint, I shall be glad to write you further or appear before the Board. Yours respectfully, Jeremiah Metzger, MD Superintendent.[24]

1945, May 1

Charles E Clark becomes the superintendent of the Arizona State Hospital.[7]

1945, October 19

Dr. Judd is admitted to a hospital suffering from a lingering disease.[22]

1945, October 23

Dr. Judd dies at the National Military Home in West Los Angeles (Sawtelle). The exact cause of his death was not disclosed. He was 62.[25]

1945, October 24

Ruth is told about the death of her husband and asked about her wishes for the funeral arrangements. She said that her brother Burton of Los Angeles was in charge of the funeral plans. She was somewhat upset by the news of her husband's death, but took it all right in a general way – as stated by superintendent Charles E Clark. Ruth had been bedridden since February 1945.[22] Dr. Judd is buried at the Golden Gate National Cemetery Section K Site 3151-B.[26] Ruth stated that somebody told her" "just follow your husband's plans. He loves you, has stood by you and he always will. Doctor Judd died without my knowing his plans."[2] Dr. Judd was cremated.[8]

1945, December22

The story of *Why the Chimes Rang* was read by Ruth Judd at the State Hospital for the Christmas program. It was the pageant produced under the direction of Miss Z. Hall, Occupational Therapist. The story was by Raymond MacDonald Alden. The program was given in pantomime in the auditorium. The auditorium was beautifully decorated in order to reproduce the "most beautiful and costly church in the whole world". The big and beautiful stained window was painted by the patients.[27] A picture of this auditorium can be found in the Borowitz Crime Collection at Kent State.[28]

1946

Ruth becomes rather disturbed. The doctors attribute this to the recent death of her husband.[1] Dr. Catton was working on a novel and a new book regarding sex. I see no record if either was ever published.[29] One report in October stated that she spent her time sewing doll clothes and doing nice needle work. They reported she held her weight well

11

and was still particular about her appearance.[23]

1946, February
Ruth is recovering from being in bed from TB for a year. After this she is able to be up for the larger part of the day.[23]

1946, April 3
Burton McKinnell filed a petition in Superior Court seeking approval as his sister's legal guardian to care for her real and personal property in California. A hearing was set for June 6.[30]

1946, October
Ruth is housed across the hall from her mother. They are said to see much of each other.. Dr. Clark, the superintendent, described Ruth as being a model inmate except on a few occasions when she has the delusion that somebody is persecuting her. Dr. Clark stated that except for a few religious and personal friends, Ruth was allowed no visitors. He stated that she has not been outside the woman's ward since he became superintendent.[23]

1947, January 22
Dr. Metzger becomes superintendent of the Arizona State Hospital.[7]

1947, March 21
Dr. John A Larson becomes the superintendent of the Arizona State Hospital.[7]

1947, May 9
Mr. May stated that he was out somewhere around this date. Ruth was threatening to leave the state hospital. He told her, "Ruth don't ever try that. You won't even get downtown! If you come to our house, I will turn you in." She replied, "Wouldn't you let me in?" He said, "Just long enough to call the police."[31]

1947, May 10
The staff at the state hospital asked if Ruth would like to see her mother. (She is on ward C and then over to B) Dr. Larson said, "I will gladly take you over". Ruth stated that Dr. Larson wouldn't be superintendent long and that she was leaving his office to think of how to get back to her mother. Dr. Larson stated that he wanted three

guards with her when she visited her mother.[31]

1947, May 11

Dr. Larson stated that the second door was left open by negligence. The carpenter was changing that lock that day and Ruth knew it.[31] At 11:00 AM, Dr. Larson couldn't find Dr. Musgrave whom Ruth resented. Dr. Larson took a driver and a social worker and went over there. He sent the worker up to get Ruth. Ruth sent word that she didn't want to see her mother but that "She would soon even up".[31] Ruth claimed she would get Dr. Larson fired unless he brought her back to live at the hospital near her mother. She spoke of many things and Dr. Larson thought she was slightly delusional. At 9:00 she had full freedom of the ward. By 10:30, a patient walked by her room and reported her missing.[31] Ruth escapes for the third time.[12] She escaped from the second floor. She was believed to have used a key which opened two doors, one on the second floor, which allowed her to descend a stairway, and another on the ground level. A gate on the north side of the hospital grounds was found open. She was last seen about 9 o'clock.[32] This was Sunday, Mother's Day. John Larson was quoted in the press as saying she left about 9:30 by opening a defective lock probably with a small nail file.[14]

1947, May 12

The people at the state hospital go through Ruth's things and confiscate things like sewing and crochet needles. Dr. Larson told the sheriff that there were two places to cover, her brother in Los Angeles and her guardian. He asked Dr. Musgrave what the chances of the guardian covering her and she said none at all.[31] Ruth is recaptured near the Biltmore Hotel in Phoenix. She was found in an orange grove on a tip that a woman was sleeping there. She had with her a flour sack filled with clothing and food. She was wearing a blue cotton dress and scuffed brown shoes. She had no hat or stockings. Ruth complained that Superintendent Dr. John A Larson took her mother away. Dr. Larson had moved her from the infirmary quarters to ward quarters and a cell like room. Ruth's mother was a patient in the infirmary at the hospital. She complained that her new quarters kept her from her mother and left her with nothing else to do except "sit and brood." Ruth also stated about Dr. Larson that "you told me I had to tell the truth about my case, but I am in a daze about a great deal of my tragedy."[32] She surrendered quietly but berated John Larson with tears

13

about him transferring her from the infirmary to a cell like room. "Yesterday was mother's day", she said, "I asked to see her but he told me that I could see her for only five minutes and then under three guards."[14] When they asked her where she planned to go she said, "I don't know, I was simply going off someplace to draw some sort of plan to help my mother"[14]

1947, May 13
A report of the state hospital stated that there was some evidence that at times Ruth physically abused her mother.[1] Dr. Larson of the Arizona State Hospital stated that Ruth is behind double locks worked by two keys, each entrusted to a different attendant. He said it was a lie that he would not allow Ruth to visit her mother on Mother's day. He stated that she had insisted on visiting her alone and he didn't want to take the chance of letting her. He offered to go with her in the company of a supervisor but she refused demanding that she should be allowed to go alone. Dr. Larson claimed that the real reason that she was moved from the infirmary was because Ruth had recently beaten her mother and given her a black eye. He said this was verifiable in the records. Carrie McKinnell, her mother had already had several heart attacks and he was afraid she would die if it were to happen again. He also stated that this was not the first time Ruth had beaten her mother. He stated, "She is too dangerous for the infirmary ward. She is one of the most dangerous women I have ever worked with and I have worked with a lot of them. She has been too petted and pampered and the minute I clamped down on her, she had tantrums. In fact, she told me that the actual reason she skipped was to try to force me to return her to the infirmary."[33]

1947, third week
Mrs. Harvey, Mrs. Barry, Mr. and Mrs. May, Mrs. Hahnenkratt, and Mr. and Mrs. Hamm meet with Dr. Larson at the State Hospital in Dr. Larson's office. Most of this is about Ruth's location in the state hospital (not in the infirmary) and that she is not allowed to visit her mother unattended. They were not interested in letting out to the press, but were friends of Ruth and wanted the best for her. Apparently, they had been denied a visit several weeks before because of "some brawl" during a dance and they eliminated visits for a while across the institution. Apparently, they took away her sewing and crocheting and Mrs. Barry thought that was an important activity to help Ruth soothe

her mind. They felt that Ruth needed something to keep her busy and that she needed to be with her mother.[31] Mr. Hamm, asked why Dr. Larson stated that Ruth was the worst character you had ever met? It was in the paper. Dr. Larson stated that he didn't say that. Mrs. Hahnenkratt stated that she had promised Ruth's father that he would always visit her. She claimed that she was happy when she was busy. Dr. Larson stated, "We forget one thing, she was committed not as an ordinary patient. She was committed very strictly by the court as criminally insane. She was merely given into our custody until such time as her mental condition would be changed and then sent back. So, we have some responsibility to the state." "If she keeps eloping, I have to fix it so that she can't. But primary to me, she is a patient and I want to give her all activity commensurate with her cooperation. I had put her up with maximum freedom except she couldn't go out by herself. I think one of you ladies had let her out to play records with patients. Somebody called up. Because of the elopement and the obligation I owe to the court that doesn't mean that I will put her as the papers said in solitary confinement. This woman is here, a criminally insane patient; alright, I don't interfere until something comes up which she violates. I gave her complete run of the ward which she violated, and now I have her restricted to the room. You people came here with questions, you forget how ill she is, delusional screaming, etc. so I will restrict her, but the judge in going through her stuff, giving her temporary restraint, and because of trends of behavior her crocheting materials are not allowed her. I told her this morning she could have books".[31] He had just sent somebody up to see Ruth to see if she wanted a special book. He continued, "So for practical purposes I am with you 100% but the activities have to be restricted. Now the next possibility involves two divisions. You have to consider her past, the mother and the hospital as a whole. It was nice as long as we could keep Ruth with her mother. Her mother is a voluntary patient and I may be wrong, but the brother told me that the mother was put in primarily – it had been stated that her mother had been placed here to keep Ruth occupied. Her brother promised to come take his mother away, but has not done so."[31] Somebody replied that the mother was off and they had to put her here. Dr. Larson continues, "If they are definitely off they are not able to commit themselves. When we are considering her (Ruth) return to the hospital, that comes in. We could say it is just for the mother. But, that isn't the question. We have much sicker people than Ruth Judd. Every minute we keep her on the

15

hospital ward deprives somebody else of a room. We had a 'hot appendix' we couldn't get her in. We have no place to put them. All new patients automatically go in there. This is a problem of the community." "The problem as to whether she and her mother are good for each other can be debated. It is one question and the reason I don't like to bring it up is because it is controversial as far as you are concerned. The reason I brought up that question, I myself investigated. A visitor allegedly told somebody that you could not believe Dr. Musgrave as she is too biased. It happened that she did not have anything to do with it. I went over, and after the behavior of Ruth toward her mother, I drew my own inferences. You don't have any responsibility in this case. If her mother had died the day of the attack and the coroner had seen the eyes, I alone would have been responsible."[31] Mr. Harvey stated that he saw it the day it happened. "I made a firsthand investigation. She had the black eyes. Things were such at that time that no attendants would have given it to her. What I am trying to put over, I am not trying to take any one episode, there is one thing on the basis of that information that is enough and if it went out it would cause a tremendous outcry. The pressure now is enough until this thing subsides. You can visit as much as you want but one of the staff is going to be there until we know everybody."[31] "Ruth was once seen slapping her mother by a physician."[31] "Now because of this one incident, I am not describing that one incident, I would have to take her away from the hospital. There are other things. Ruth has tantrums. I have seen her in tantrums. We can't give other patients enough protection. Now there are other things; the privileges, the garden, the taking care of the children. Because of her instability she killed two people. I have that problem. She made the statement I put her there and told her she was going to stay until she told about the crime. I have never asked about the crime. I never mentioned the crime. If she gets better she leaves us, because of certain things I know about her. The incident of finding razor blades; she accused me that there was some former prosecutor whom she said I had brought down and I am in cahoots with him to resurrect the old case. She told this and there it was, a nice sob story. I said, 'Ruth, I can't have you in the hospital west as long as I am superintendent". And she said, "You will not be superintendent long." He said that Ruth had not been in solitary confinement. He said, "Every hospital has cubicles for use if the patient doesn't cooperate." "We should take more care of her security than the average patient. That hasn't been done in the past. Proof is that she escaped three times. To illustrate, if we are going to cooperate I am going to put my cards on the table. If you are going to buck me when I say she isn't going to the hospital and I have a good reason, then you might force me to release something to the papers that isn't going to help anyone. I am telling you frankly whether I release this depends on the group visiting. After listening to you we are not going to give it out. I don't want to argue for a minute that she struck her mother; I am not talking about her mother at all. If you want to go along with me I will go all the way but if I want to screen the next visitors, I have to screen everyone. My plan is to give her all the activities possible. Bring in sewing if you want. My plan is to screen everyone until I know you and see which one of you upsets her. If you want to go along, alright, because she isn't going back to the hospital. Now, I can give her some leeway. This one item means I would have to keep her locked up all of the time. I believe that she is sick or I couldn't keep her here. My past experience shows there is always someone who gossips falsely, but if you talk and it isn't given out it will come back distorted to me. And if you can't take my word, regardless of her mother; I have a specific incident and it wouldn't help Ruth any. It would turn more heat on me and block me in giving her more freedom. She can see her mother but under supervision. We happen to know that she struck her mother. You say no. She came in because she killed two people. She has demonstrated that she can't control herself and live up to the terms of her freedom. She said I tried to degrade her and was going to lock her up for life until she told me the crime. I said, 'Ruth, as far as I am concerned, I can't have you in the hospital'.[31] They asked if she was worse than she had been the last 10-15 years. Dr. Larson stated that her diagnosis was dementia praecox which was the same as schizophrenia. He said, "Dementia praecox predisposes a progression becoming worse. We have been fighting that for years with electric shock and insulin. When we know it is schizophrenia we know there may be a remission but we know the prognosis is poor. We don't guess, we know she will have another attack, assuming that is the diagnosis. She is fixated against Dr. Musgrave, she is fixated against me. Pressure on me is being transferred to her so I have to put pressure on her. She definitely thinks I am against her, dating from the first time I ever saw her. If she isn't delusional and insane, she doesn't belong here. She has the best behavior with you people, you don't cross her. I crossed her. I said, 'I don't care what it is, submit it to me and I will submit it to the board.

17

That fact that I submit it is in your favor.' Then she said I was trying to get something on her. You know why I had to send her in and have her examined yesterday? The reason I had someone with me today; I want to be consistent. There is one thing I held back, if you are going to buck me." None of them said that they were here for that purpose. Dr. Larson stated that he was debating whether he should release some information. The public would wonder what the hospital is doing having a woman where she could do that thing. So, he said to the group that it would depend on them that day. "If I don't have your confidence it is too bad." When asked what is was that he would release, he replied, "I have been two timed. I can't afford to take chances. Some visitors in the past have connived with her and assisted her in cutting and grating, but she changed her mind and did not go out. If it leaked out in the wrong way, first, it would show she should have never been in the hospital ward and second, it would show almost diagnostically her mental condition." "She is as dangerous as anyone I have ever seen and I once wrote a paper in New York on some 1700 homicides. As to say which is the most dangerous, that is academic. So if you ask me if she is the most dangerous I would have to debate. I am trying to show that diagnosis, paranoid schizophrenia, because of underlying delusions and explosiveness. You say she is competent and she doesn't belong here. To show you what I mean by most dangerous, and I am not backing up, I had charge of the writs of letting people in and out and one prominent psychiatrist was told to go along with us, to agree that the paranoid schizophrenic is dangerous and should not be turned out. Well, certainly none of us ever disagreed on that. So actually that type is most dangerous of any, theoretically, and otherwise. To me, it is academic to answer your questions. Probably she has not been like this; some call it storms. She becomes delusional and right away she misinterprets because I would not parole her. I have no jurisdiction."[31] "All I am trying to show is that she has already had the maximum explosion. She has constantly shown tantrums. Here she shows them constantly over anything. You could say the doctor is prejudiced. The business of the mother is just one of the facts. We always try to do all we can until we have to tighten up. I have to be in a position to defend her if she should be in the hospital."[31] Dr. Larson stated that in the past somebody was set to take her out. Dr. Larson stated that he didn't know who it was. He said that some person made an impression and made a key. He stated that he was fixing it now to one attendant having the key. So, he could pinpoint the

18

problem. He stated that he was short of attendants and was having personnel problems. He stated that he was never going to see Ruth alone ever; "The way Ruth lied yesterday and laughed about it." He stated that he was supposed to be a doctor, but because he had worked with the police in the past, he had that against him. He continues, "I am working with Ruth as a mental patient but in the eyes of the public she is being held here for the Court". Now I know this, she went out Sunday just to "get me"; that I didn't do enough. I want her out of circulation. I said, 'If she is ever going to be suicidal this will be the night' and one half hour later the door was open This was with the night supervisor. I have both physical factor and the personnel problem. The difference is in prison it is discipline, here it is protective treatment. It is treatment more than discipline. "Knowing that she has emotional storms, I am not going to let her roam around. This was a spite thing. She said, "Doctor, you know we women like to be mastered". It would have been a very lurid headline if this thing had come out."[31] They asked if she was well enough for visitors. Dr. Larson said now that she was more restricted than in the past; they would work out what were too many visits. For now, since Ruth liked to read, he suggested they bring in books that they didn't have in the hospital library. When they asked if she would ever be well he said, "That is a good question. Statistically, the chances are very much against it. Actually this thing comes up." Statistically she is not going to get well. Even if there were no legal hold on this woman, I would never turn her out in the community. If she apparently got better she would have the original weakness where she would not have the supervision. I am convinced that she is going downhill. [31] Dr. Larson suggested that the best time to visit was in-between 2 to 4. He stated that the stuff she told the papers was totally fabricated. The group said that they had come because they did not understand why she couldn't see her mother. He replied, "Now you should understand."[31]

1947, June 25
Somebody at the State Hospital writes a summary of Ruth Judd. It's almost like a history, except that it relies on reporters and others for information. It is from the state hospital though since it concludes: "After several months of postponement, patient was found insane and committed to this institution."[34]

19

1947, September 22

John Larson writes a letter to Adolf Meyer who he addresses as Chief. He writes that he is having trouble with political snipers friendly to the former superintendent. (Clark or Metzger) He stated that the former superintendent was discharged following the death of a patient from alleged beatings of which two employees were currently serving sentences in the penitentiary. He states that they may attack him because he did not have his diploma. He had just had to discharge the brother in law of a doctor and said he was gradually cleaning up "an awful mess." He talks about why he did not take his examinations since he graduated about 1919 and it wasn't required. He stated that the Statutes of the APA Council ask for it for superintendents, although they make exceptions. He stated that "they (political enemies of the Governor) may attack me." He stated that probably nothing could be done. He closes by saying as soon as he gets over the throes of the annual report he will type out the material.[35]

1949, April

Ruth claims that Dr. Larson's attitude changed towards her before he left. He said, "If you only knew what I'm trying to do for you, you wouldn't be so smart." She said he brought many politicians up on the ward and said very kind things about her to them such as Mrs. Judd does all these patient's hair. I can always tell a ward B patient, they are the nicest looking patients in the institution because Mrs. Judd has obtained all these nice dresses for them from donations and she keeps their hair dressed. She doesn't work union hours but often 12-14 hours a day. She claims before he left he called her to his office and said, "If you will notice I'm the only doctor here who has stuck his neck out to get your sentence commuted so we can do something for you. If I stay I shall continue to try and get something done for you."[2]

1949, April 14

Dr. Bruce D. Hart becomes superintendent of the Arizona State Hospital.[7] Ruth said he let her bring her mother over for her to care for.[2] Shortly after Dr. Hart became superintendent, Renz Jennings came over with Dr. Hart to speak with Ruth. This was the only time she had talked to Dr. Hart. He told her guardian that he wants Ruth to trust him and he won't upset her unlike the previous administrations. Renz Jennings said, "I have some plans I want to work on to get Mrs. Judd out of here". Ruth replied, "I lost all hopes when my husband died." Renz Jennings stated that he was still her friend. Ruth stated that she did not know what his plans were. She just knew he was the only person living who knew what took place in Judge Niles private chambers when she was taken off the stand at Halloran's preliminary hearing where Judge Niles ruled "Mrs. Judd's Testimony is most persuasive. The state of Arizona has definitely proved that Mrs. Judd acted in self-defense, there was no crime committed."[2]

1. Whitney, Rex E., *Memo to Willis H Bower Director regarding Winnie Ruth Judd. from Rex E Whitney, Assistant to the director*, in *Pineal County Historical Museum*. August 15, 1969: Florence, AZ.

2. Judd, Winnie Ruth, *Letter of Winnie Ruth Judd written at the state hospital some 20 years after she arrived there. This may be the letter she wrote to Governor Pyle on January 25, 1953?*, in *Collection of Jerry Lewkowitz*. January 25, 1951?: Phoenix, Arizona. 1-12, 13, 21-22, incomplete.

3. Judd, William C, *My Life with Winnie Ruth Judd - Part 1*, in *Intimate Detective Stories*. March, 1940. 2-7, 52.

4. Judd, Winnie Ruth, *Judd Reminiscences*, in *Arizona Historical Society, Southern Arizona Division*. 1941: Tucson, AZ.

5. *Ruth Judd's brother plans to reopen case*, in *Los Angeles Times*. December 24, 1940: Los Angeles.

6. Peterson, Phyllis, *Anders Severin Samuelson*. August 23, 1998: Carpinteria, CA.

7. Arizona. State Hospital Phoenix. [from old catalog], *Milestones; a history of seventy-five years of progress at the Arizona State Hospital, Phoenix, Arizona, 1887-1962*. 1962, [Phoenix,. 150 p.

8. Swent, Eleanor, *Marian Lane: Mine Doctor's Wife in Mexico*. Western Mining in the Twentieth Century Oral History Services. 1996, Berkeley. 121.

9. *Slayer almost escapes again*, in *Pittsburgh Post Gazette*. 1941: Pittsburgh. 1.

10. Metzger, Jeremiah, *Report of Metger, superintendant of the Arizona State Hospital to the Governor*. April 8, 1941: Phoenix,.

11. *Consultation with Al Blau mortician of Gearty Delmore Mortuary*. 2013: Robbinsdale, MN.

12. Dobkins, J.D. and R. J. Hendricks, *Winnie Ruth Judd: The Trunk Murders*. 1973, New York: Grosset & Dunlap.

13.	Boswell, H, *Animals at James St L. O'Toole galleries*. Art Digest, 1941. 16: p. 19, 30.

14.	*Free Twelve Hours, Winnie Ruth Judd Recaptured*, in *Milwaukee Sentinal*. May 13, 1947: Milwaukee.

15.	Arizona State Department of Health, *Harvey J. Mckinnell Death Certificate*, in *Arizona Vital Records*. July 16, 1942: Phoenix. http://genealogy.az.gov/

16.	Inglewood Park Cemetery, *Inglewood Park Cemetery Database,*. 2007. http://www.inglewoodparkcemetery.com/search_db.html

17.	Bendheim, Otto L, *Letter of Otto L Bendheim to Jeremiah Metzger from Beaumont General Hospital*. August 4, 1942: El Paso, TX.

18.	Schuster, BL, *Letter to Jeremiah Metzger from BL Schuster MC*. September 11, 1942: Phoenix, AZ.

19.	Judd, Winnie Ruth, *Letter from Ruth Judd to Mr. Richardson*. 1944: Phoenix.

20.	Howes, Seth, *Notes regarding Melvin Matheson*. June 9, 1944, Arizona State Hospital: Phoenix.

21.	Howes, Seth, *Letter to Jeremiah Metzger from Seth Howes from Glenside Hospital*. November 29, 1944: Jessica Plain, MA.

22.	*Dr. W. C. Judd, Husband of Slayer Dies*, in *Tucson Daily Citizen*. October 24, 1945: Tucson.

23.	Arline, *Untitled draft for Arizona Republic? (from the collection of Patrick Millikin)*. 1946.

24.	Metzger, Jeremiah, *Letter from Jeremiah Metzger to Reverend Dr. Walter Hoffman, Arizona State Board of Pardons and Paroles*. April 25, 1945: Phoenix, AZ.

25.	*Judd, Slayers Husband Dead*, in *Reno Evening Gazette*. October 24, 1945: Reno.

26.	Veteran's Administration, *Nationwide Gravesite Locator*. 10/23/2007, 2007, Veteran's Administration. http://gravelocator.cem.va.gov

27.	*Christmas Play*, in *Sun Valley News*. Dec, 1945.

28.	*Winnie Ruth Judd Photos collected by Kent State as part of the Borrowitz Crime Collection*. Kent, Ohio.

29.	Atherton, Gertrude Franklin Horn, *My San Francisco, a wayward biography*. 1946, Indianapolis, New York,: The Bobbs-Merrill company. 334 p.

30.	*Los Angeles Briefs*, in *Los Angeles Times*. April 3, 1946: Los Angeles.

31.	Arizona State Hospital, *Interview in Dr. Larson's office. Those present include Mrs. Harvey, Mrs. Barry, Mr. and Mrs. May, Mrs.*

Hahenenkratt, and Mr and Mrs. Hamm, in *Collection of Jerry Leukowitz*. May?, 1947: Phoenix.

32.   *Winnie Ruth Judd Flees, Recaptured*, in *Tucson Daily Citizen*. May 12, 1947: Tucson.

33.   *Double Locks Hold Winnie*, in *Tucson Daily Citizen*. May 13, 1947: Tucson.

34.   Unknown author at the Arizona State Hospital, *Ruth Judd: Summary, June 25, 1947*, in *Personal Collection of Jerry Leukowitz*. June 25, 1947: Phoenix. 3.

35.   Larson, John A, *Letter of John Larson to Adolf Meyer*. September 22, 1947, Alan Mason Chesney Medical Archives: Johns Hopkins: Phoenix, Arizona.

Section 6

1950-1959

1950, November 2
Arthur B Madden became superintendent of the Arizona State Hospital.[1]

1951
Sometime in about 1951, Ruth writes a letter summarizing her time in the state hospital and describes how she has been treated as a "political football" and treated unfairly while serving her time at the state hospital.[2]

1951, November1
MW Conway becomes the superintendent of the Arizona State Hospital.[1]

1952, January 20
Ruth had a visit from William Beeman who was a San Francisco Engineer.[3]

1952, February 2
Ruth escaped by pulling a screen out and making a rope out of soft restraints. She stated that there were five attendants and one nurse who were hired by the current administration who helped her in the escape.[4] She claimed in a letter to her niece that five attendants and an RN used their hypnotic influence to frighten her into escaping. They took advantage of her predicament and they hid her in a god awful hole where she was kept captive by them until they let her back. She stated that she had two keys. One was to a house on Broadway. The other was to the front door. She stated Dr. Conway's patient helper gave it to her, but that she had never tried it on any door.[5] Her escape was between 8:25 and 8:35 while other inmates were watching a TV show. Ruth had gone back to her room on the third floor. She made a rope cut of restraining harnesses, attached it to a bed spring, removed screws

1

from the wired window and apparently slide down the rope to the ground. She was believed to have gone over the high wire fence. Two women driving a black 1948 Hudson Sedan with California license plates were reported to have picked her up at the west gate of the hospital on 24th street north of Van Buren. A woman fitting the description of Ruth Judd was seen at Carl's Café at 7th Street and Van Buren a bit after 9. She called attention to herself by complaining that cigarettes from the vending machines cost 25 cents. They were surprised that anyone would find this price new. The café was only a block away from the apartment of Mrs. Ellen Evans, former attendant at the state hospital. Ruth had broken into her apartment during her last escape. She was wearing a brown coat, brown shoes and brown stockings.[3]

1952, February 7
Ruth returns to the State Hospital looking battered and scratched. A car had apparently dropped her off at MW Conway's house just outside the asylum. She said, "Well, I'm back." Dr. Conway stated that he almost did not recognize her. He said that she had her hair line lifted by plucking the front part of her head. Her hair was dyed a darker color. He had made the mistake of saying at first that she appeared to have had a face-lifting procedure. Her eyebrows had been plucked. It was about midnight that she returned. Nobody got a good look at the car that brought her back. There were many reports that she would give herself up if she could talk to the grand jury.[6] When she returned, the key was found in her hair and a razor blade divided lengthwise under her tongue.[7]

1952, February 13
The grand jury voted unanimously to the commutation of Mrs. Judd's death penalty sentence to life imprisonment.[8]

1952, March 20
Ruth writes a letter to her brother Burton. Apparently she expected Burton to get her an attorney and never heard back from him. She states that Conway wants her out of there. She said he had twice tried to send her to prison. Ruth states she won't run away right now; she has too much hope that something will be done for her. She states she came back to get her freedom legally. She states that she will not be present at the Pardon Board Meeting. She wants Burton to come immediately

to represent her before the pardon board. She stated that all of the stories put in the paper were put in on purpose to hurt her with the Grand Jury. She stated that she had no man friend to knock old man wood in the head. There was no car waiting for her. She had no underground for the underworld queen with a hypnotic personality to help. She stated that she led a more sheltered life than any of the doctor's wives. She had never slummed, had never been to a bowling alley, a skating rink, a public dance parlor, a bar, a carnival, or a circus. She stated in her last escape that ½ of the staff knew where she was. She stated that there were kind nurses and a lot of them were crying when they feared she was going to prison. They felt sorry for her. She claims that she has been offered $20000 for a story of her case. She said she didn't want money; she just wanted to be out of the hospital some time. She stated that Hoffman, chairman of the pardon board, said there was a trick in her case.[9]

1952, May 10
Ruth Judd's sentence is commuted from Death to Life in Prison by Governor Pyle. The Grand Jury recommended it and he approved it.

1952, July 20
Carrie McKinnell is very sick with a fever of 102 and is delirious of dehydration. She could not perspire. According to Ruth she was kept in a room of a temp of 104 to 112 for a week before they gave her glucose twice.[5]

1952, August 24
Ruth writes her niece Carolyn the following letter: My dear Niece: I have been wondering if you found work this school vacation and if so, what? Are you a Soph. at U of Calif LA now? Are you majoring in Math or what? Things have been very unhappy here since Joel left and I have no one to protect me. Dr. Wolfe, Mrs. Loofboro and Mrs. McLaughlin started picking at me every few days over the most trivial innocent things until I tremble like a clock spring. God himself couldn't have tried harder to XXXX; as soon as Joel went back to Indiana they started on me. Loofboro picked at me terribly before I ran away. Two doctors here told me mama was going to die, that she had a cancer and let me believe it for 3 months. Now Dr. Conway says there is no indication she has a cancer! Worrying about my commutation and then believing that was more than I could stand. Mama was sick

3

July 20, temp 102 and so delirious from dehydration she couldn't perspire and her lungs were congested. I begged the doctors to give her saline or glucose intravenously or transfer her to the hospital where they have facilities to give forced fluid. They refused and let mama lie there in a room un-cooled at 104° to 112° for 1 week before they tube fed her which I have never seen done on any one her age. Then she was given glucose twice. It is downright cruel to strike at me through my mother. Mama has been too good all her life; caring for the sick in the church and any of our relatives. If I had a family close by they could look after such things but I have to fight for mama and I- Don't let Burton kid you into thinking Dr. Conway is trying to do something for me. Dr. Judd said someday my sentence would be commuted and a superintendent would think enough of me to do something for me. But, Dr. Conway said something to cause the paper to say I was queen of the underground with a hypnotic personality and Jack Murphy stated over TV that Dr. Conway said I was queen of the underworld with a hypnotic personality. Five attendants and one RN used their hypnotic influence to frighten me into escaping. They took advantage of my predicament and they hid me in a god awful hole where I was kept captive by them until they brought me back. When my sentence was commuted, I wrote Dr. Conway I was sorry I had caused him unfavorable criticism and I realized he had made enemies by not sending me to Florence and I would not escape or do anything to cause him any more criticism. I would show him how good a patient I could be. Immediately after Joel left, Dr. Wolfe Loofbora and McLaughlin started picking at me. I've cried until I can hardly see with my glasses even anymore and I tremble like a clock spring. Dr. Conway gives me no encouragement what so ever. He says things like this when I ask him to sew or crochet that I might commit suicide when I say I won't. He said, no you won't until you have exhausted all other avenues. Then he says, why there are attendants here who would spring you out of here tomorrow. If that Mrs. Holmes hadn't resigned, I'd have made her resign – then he said once I was known to be a kind man but I come from a long line of cops. I can be mean also. The other day he threw a tear gas bomb in a feeble minded girls face and excused himself by saying we have criminals here from prison. Why blame them for his tactics? No patients from the prison threw the bomb and that poor girl wasn't from the prison. He was just mad at criticism and wanted to throw his rage on someone so he threw it at patients who were sick and hard boiled prison officials realized they didn't belong in prison but needed medical care. Dr. Conway hates me. I said nothing against him or this institution to the Grand Jury or press but the papers quoted him as saying I was an underground and underworld queen that the same rough characters connected with me, hit Mr. Wood in the head. When he was off his beam from diabetes and couldn't tell a straight story of how he fell on his head and that he thwarted another escape. I had keys – I had 2 keys but one was the front door key to a house on Broadway there. Attendants gave me the front door key to – the other key. Dr. Conway's patient helper gave it to me and I never tried it in any door in this place. Everything is being done to hurt me, to upset me. I can go to the OT 5 afternoons a week and 1 needle is given to me. I return it. Then he ordered I'm to be searched head to foot when I return. Burton promised me when Mama came out here he would never let her die in this place. In April when he was here he said I'll be back in 60 days. It is 120 days. Now he writes me if this place was a good enough place for her to live in why in the hell isn't it a good enough place to die in. Poor mama. She'd never let Burton or I die in here. She'd fight for us. Care for us herself. I've written the Pardon Board that I can lead a useful life. But Dr. Conway says if he had been superintendent here I wouldn't have been doing hair. I've done thousands of heads in 20 years and legislators have told me I was doing good work. I want to be paroled out of here to go to the Ryckmans at Asuncion Paraguay – I speak Spanish and I love children. The children are segregated from the old lepers. I could do those children's hair, teach them to weave, knit, sew, embroider, crochet, etc. and lead a useful life. Soon, here I will be completely destroyed mentally and physically. I got a letter from Hoffmann and he says he will be out after Sept 15; that he is just out of the Hospital and can't drive yet until after Sept 15. Some friends are going to see him about my going to South America and Mr. Barry said he'd take one off with his "All State Insurance" to take me. I'll take mama with me. We could go by plane instead of ship- Well, I must close. Write me about your schoolwork and what you've done all summer. Love, Ruth. Kiss little Kirk for me. The letter was addressed to Carolyn McKinnell 10520 Selkirk, LA Calif.[5]

1952, September

Mr. Hoffman came to see Ruth and told her that she would have to go back to Florence before anything more could be done for her.[10]

5

1952, November 27

Ruth escapes the state hospital on Thanksgiving night. She left in between 6:30 and 7:00 PM. She cut across vacant lots to the corner of 19th and Portland. She hid in some palm trees there because of school kids playing on their bicycles on the corner. At 8:30, two police cars parked at 19th and Portland were talking about her. She stayed there until midnight and was "frozen". When all house lights were dark, she cut across lot 15th or 16th and Belview. She hid there for a while. Then she went to 13th and Brill, from there to 13th and McDowell to hide for a while. She went to the alley to "your house" – her guardian at 2AM.[11] Ruth had escaped to the house of her guardian, Mrs. Fay L Harvey at 2342 N 11th Street. She was out of town. [12]

1952, November 28

She slept on the couch. There were two phone calls on Friday.[11]

1952, November 29

There were no phone calls on Saturday until 1:30 when the phone started ringing constantly until the police found her.[11] Police stated that a light that was turned off was turned back on. They searched the living room, bathroom, kitchen and service porch. Then Geiger slid back the closet door, and spotted what appeared to be a large pile of clothing. Ruth was under it. Ruth was dressed in a house coat. When Lt. Vic Soule and Detective Everett Geiger dug into the clothing pile she moaned, "Why don't you leave me alone. I'm so tired of being locked up. It has been long enough. They say I'm dangerous. I am not." In the bedroom there was the green dress, sweater, and white shoes she was wearing when she escaped. The officers turned their backs while she changed from the housecoat back into her clothes before taking her in. She said she was going to get a job in town and lead a normal life. She wanted to mix with people. She said she was lonely for other people. She refused to pose for newspaper photos at police headquarters, saying that her well-kept auburn hair was a mess. She asked for a comb but they took her picture anyway.[12]

1952, December 1

At least 5 staff members of the state hospital in Phoenix are implicated in the sixth escape of Ruth Judd. M. W. Conway stated that she also had help on the outside. She was captured the Saturday night previous. Police found her crouched in an empty house under a pile of dirty clothes. She had cut through a window screen and escaped from the hospital. It was stated that Governor Pyle would probably order an investigation of the conditions at the hospital.[13] Ruth told Dr. Conway that no one helped her. She cut the window herself. He said that she was lying; that he knew that she didn't do it.[11] She was told unless somebody told him who did it, she wouldn't get a sanity hearing.[11] She stated that Mrs. Matz (Now Mrs. Bratton) that her husband never helped her escape. Mrs. Clark told her husband offered to help her escape and she tried to place the blame on Mr. Bratton. Ruth stated that they wanted to fire both Mrs. Matz who was good to her mother and her new husband Bratton.[11] In a letter to Governor Pyle in December she stated that the window had been cut for 2 months to enable her to escape. She held off and refused to go until 3 weeks after the election so she wouldn't infuriatee any politicians.[4] She stated that in this escape there were men who were recent employees (and not employees of the last administration) who helped her in her exit this time.[4] Ruth stated that, "Mrs. Clark reported hearing Mr. Clark offer to help me escape. She reported Bratton and Clark were trying to get me to escape and hide in Bratton's new trailer which he asked and was refused permission to park outside the back gate. A few days later she married Clark who she only went with for 10 days. Then Bratton married Mrs. Matz and neither man was interested in me, but because Mrs. Clark reported Clark a few days before she knew she would marry him since those men were under suspicion. I never went near them or anyone but straight to your house getting there at 2AM frozen."[11]Dr. Conway said that the hospital was not strong enough to hold Mrs. Judd, "You can't hold that type of woman in a paper sack."[8]

1952, December 8
Dr. Conway writes a letter to Governor Pyle. "My dear Governor: You may be interested in the enclosed letter from the sister of Agnes Anne LeRoi, one of the victims of the Judd Murder Incident. I would like to have this correspondence for the files after your perusal of it. Kindest Personal Regards, M. W. Conway, M.D. Governor Pyle received this letter on December 10 and returned the letter to M. W. Conway.[14]

1952, December 15
Governor Pyle announced that a special ward built to hold the criminally insane is the answer to the periodics at the Arizona State

Hospital. He stated that future breaks can be expected until a facility of that type is provided. Besides Ruth, a Peter Saunders, 17-year-old murderer escaped the previous Thursday night.[15]

1952, December 21
Ruth writes a letter to Governor Pyle.[16] Jerry Lewkowitz had a copy of this letter. She is asking for a sanity hearing. She states that there is nothing wrong with her. She says, she is just a boarder there. She says that MW Conway mistreats her. She states that every night every 15 minutes between 8 pm and midnight a light is shined in her eyes and held there to awaken her and keep her awake. She stated that if she turned her head from either side, she is grabbed by the hair and her night clothes are torn. She stated that for one year, she had been forced to walk on cold cement floors barefoot. She was denied even a roll of toilet paper when she had a cold.[4]

1953, January 25
Ruth writes another letter to Governor Pyle.[16]

1953, January 27
MW Conway writes a letter to Governor Pyle regarding Ruth Judd. He sends a letter written by Ruth Judd. He stated, "Some of her letters are withheld after censoring because they needlessly involve us in a lot of correspondence and difficulties. They are all very similar in tenor, and I have red-penciled a section of her letter to you which expresses very definitely some of her paranoid trends. Most of her letters are very lengthy and full of repetition which taxes one's patience to finish them. They are all self-centered in character; and exaggerations and deliberate falsehoods are expressed many times in most of her compositions."[17]

1953, February 7
MW Conway writes another letter to the governor with a copy of notes that Ruth tried to smuggle out uncensored by secreting them in her guardian's dress front on her last visit. The original was penciled on the fly pages of books that were given her to read, and the source of her pencil is yet to be discovered. "This unfortunate girl has been a very desperate character since the legislature convened, and the reason is pretty well outlined in the content of her note. We are doing our best to hold her through all of the humane facilities we possess, but there are advance rumors at this time, as there were before, that there is another

attempt at delivery impending, but this is only rumor thus far. We are, on the strength of the rumor, building a wire box outside her window in an effort to keep people away. She is under the personal supervision of a special attendant on each 8-hour shift around the clock, and they are doing a very good job on supervising her every move. This copy may help acquaint you with the present desperate attitude of the girl. This care will be very greatly simplified if the legislature provides us with a security building in the near future."[17] Some excerpts from the notes included: "The back gate is open all day for workmen and cars and trucks on building. Phone Burton and Joel; they've got to come. I do not think there is any night watch – one could check before they come to my window. It wasn't Joel or Burton or pay someone $300 or $400 to bring me a gun with a cord tied to it and preferably between 9:30 and 11:30 PM. I will cut a small hole hurriedly in window, get cord and then through window big enough to admit gun. I only want it to frighten attendants into giving up keys. I should have one shot in gun to shoot down hall if they think it isn't loaded. I only want to frighten them to open outside door and I'll take their keys and lock them in a room and will hurt no one—If driving up alley parking the night before to watch one does see a night watch other than car which I always watched and timed – then someone will have to bring me the gun during the day time. With so many strange men, workmen and even their wives and kids out back, no one will notice anyone coming to my window if they only stay a moment. I can hold gun by cord until I can cut window big enough to admit it. I prefer going at night because I'll have to go same shift I get the gun. Meyer works in the next building. She could slip over easily and give me gun through window but she was afraid to even give me a saw—The gate isn't open nights or on Sat or Sun—5 days a week from 8 to 5 PM and it is safe for anyone to come to my window preferably 9AM to 12 because I go to the patio sometimes in afternoon."[11] "Please tell Burton and Joel if they don't come I'm going to hit this bitch who pulled my hair and slapped me in the head and I'll take her keys and try to escape. Those politicians are stringing you along until Legislature is over to send me to Florence for the rest of my life. I'm escaping from here. I'll hurt no one with a gun, but either I'll get hurt or hurt that bitch who pulled my hair, overpowering her to get her keys. When I escape I'll go to FM Church Annex."[11] "Go see VJ Hash and see if he will get me Writ of Habeas Corpus. He got several patients out of here that the hospital doctors fought to keep here. You're being strung along until after Legislature is over and then I'm sunk. I've got to escape now. Tell Burton he has to come or I'll bust this woman's head in who pulled my hair and I'll escape again. Send him $25.00. I've stood all I can. If God or man won't help me I'll fight for my life."[11] "I think the Business Manager is going to ask the house appropriations committee for money for 3 special men guards outside my window because he is trying to force me to tell him who cut the window before then, and twice lately he has come and examined barb at window. So you've got to get someone to bring me a gun this next week, preferably 8:30 to 11:30 at night but they can easily come during the day for there are 30-50 workmen milling around all day and the gate is wide open all the time trucks and cars and people coming and going. It is 18 inches or 12 inches from bars to window so gun must have cord attached and I can hold it by cord until I get opening large enough for gun to enter. One will have to have some kind of pliers to hold gun to reach window, the bars are too small for an arm or wrist to go through. This has to be done if you have to pay someone $400-$500 to do it. Maybe Burton will for $400 – He won't for love. Isn't $500 better than prison the rest of my life and that's what it will be, waiting until legislature is over to get me a sanity hearing. For God sakes help me or I'll have to do something desperate and if I do, it will be knock that bitch who pulled my hair unconscious, steal her keys and try to escape. If I have a gun, I'll only frighten them into handing me the keys. Otherwise, in a tussle trying to get keys I'll hurt someone or get hurt, and I'll hurt no one, only frighten them with the gun. Please phone Burton and Joel to come this week or I'll break that bitch in the head who pulled my hair and escape. I can't live here terrorized any longer."[11] "Tie a cord well around gun then to a piece of steel until I can cut hole big enough to admit gun. It will take me some time to cut 8 or 10 wires so I can cut them easier at night than day time. I've got to do it. Please don't keep putting me off until the legislature is over and all hopes gone but spending the rest of my life in prison. I want you to send Burton $25. Tell him I am escaping and want him to come and bring Mama over to see me. He can wheel her over in a wheel chair. When I escape I'll go to FM church annex for a few days. Phone Joel. I want some copies of story printed with introduction of why I am escaping – Conway's refusal to give me a sanity hearing and mistreating me. Please do something – to keep Mrs. Johnson from pulling my hair, terrorizing me."[11]

1953, March 3

Governor Pyle returns Ruth's letters to Dr. Conway for his files.[18] He writes a letter that same day to Ruth that stated her letters have reached him, promptly and in good order. Her letters were dated December 21 and January 25. He stated that the business of his office has delayed acknowledgment of their receipt.[16]

1953, March 14

Elizabeth Harvey, Guardian of Winnie Ruth Judd files a petition. The fourth point stated, "That the said Winnie Ruth Judd is now being held and detained in the custody of Manius W. Conway, director of the Arizona State Hospital at Phoenix, Arizona, that she should no longer be held and detained as aforesaid by reason that the said Winnie Ruth Judd is not insane, and other statutes of Arizona governing the commitment of detention of person to and in the State Hospital for the Insane. Wherefore, your petitioner pray that a hearing be had under section 42-137 ACA 1939 so that the said Winnie Ruth Judd may be brought before this honorable court to have the question of her mental illness and her confinement and detention tested in accordance with said statute.[19] This was dismissed since it did not have a cause of action.

1953, March 16

Dr. Wolfe told Ruth that she had to go back to Florence.[20] While she was talking to Dr. Wolfe, the phone rang. Dr. Wick said to Dr. Wolfe, "The Attorney General is here." [20] Dr. Wolfe told Ruth that she would have to go back to Florence.[10]

1953, March 19

Petition by Elizabeth Harvey was denied since it did not list a cause of action. It was dismissed by TJ Mahoney county attorney.[19]

1953, March 20

The grounds for dismissal of the petition of Elizabeth Harvey was based on the grounds for an improper venue. Mahoney also stated that the court lacks jurisdiction over the person and subject matter involved in the action.[19]

1953, March 27

Letter from the superior court to TJ Marks states to let the record show

11

that the motion to dismiss by respondent, state of Arizona, is granted to the entitled action. Signed by Morter Murry.[21]

1953, April 7
Winnie Ruth Judd writes to Marian A. Childs of the Woman's Humane Club asking that she come to visit her at the state hospital.[22] She phoned the superintendent Dr. Conway concerning permission to visit with Ruth. She got permission to visit for a short time.[22]

1953, April 14
Marian A. Childs of the Woman's Humane Club visits Ruth at the Arizona State Hospital. Her father had been a minister with the Reverend McKinnell. She knew both him and her mother. She visited Ruth for 30 minutes in the presence of an attendant since Ruth was in solitary confinement. Ruth claimed that she had been suffering certain physical restrictions during her solitary confinement that caused her health to be impaired. Ruth stated that she had been "spirited out of the institution" to the rear of a pool hall (Opposite to Kay's cocktail lounge in Phoenix) where she was kept for 5 days while certain "interested parties" discussed the sale of her "Life Story"[22] She verified this afterwards with Ruth Judd's attorney. Ruth also told her that recently Mrs. Judd was served a cup of tea in her room. The nurse later removed the cup and saucer but left the spoon on the table. Later a nurse found the spoon on the table and accused Mrs. Judd of having concealed weapons. Ruth stated that she was strapped down by her waist and wrists for 30 hours. She stated that the straps were so tight that it buckled the mattress.[22] Marian thought that her being taken away to the pool hall was a crime in itself.[22]

1953, April 21
Marian A. Childs of the Woman's Humane Club writes a letter to Governor Pyle regarding the conditions at the State Hospital and the treatment of Ruth Judd. [22]

1953, April 25
Dr. MW Conway writes to Governor Pyle regarding the complaints Ruth Judd made about her recent treatment at the State Hospital. "This is in answer to a communication from Miss Bateman dated April 24th inquiring about certain phases of the Judd Case. In Mrs. Judd's conversation, as well as her correspondence, she reveals to anyone who

will listen or accept her letters a stereotyped expose of her past. And most of the material about which she writes or talks concerns her own psychosis. This is in perfect harmony with a paranoid psychosis. All of whom are litigious and self-centered. She exaggerates and often calls upon her imagination in what she represents to be facts; and we have in her file many, many letters characterized by repetitions of abuses with definite paranoid coloring. I hesitated to give permission to Rev. Childs to visit with her because I could anticipate the effect of Ruth's presentation of her many complaints and her lurid story. The event to which the Reverend refers was Mrs. Judd's second escape in February 1952 in which she was absent for some five days and came back voluntarily. The patient gave me some account of her experiences which she has related to the Rev. But the only names she revealed of past or present employees who were involved in her escape were three who were no longer here. She did reveal the location of the pool hall which she orientated through a sign on a road house on South Central which is still open for business. I relayed this information to Deputy Sheriff Barnes shortly after the return of the patients on one of his visits during his follow-up of the escape. To date Mrs. Judd has never revealed but has stolidly refused to implicate anyone still on the state payroll. It is Mrs. Judd's' present idea that she will have far more consideration at her pending insanity hearing if she can create a sensation and get a little additional publicity and sympathy at this time, and she bends every effort toward this end. Indicative of her mental condition is her obstinacy in cooperating with her attorney who desires her hair gray when she comes to trial instead of tinted an auburn hue. Numbers of times she has been skeptical of her attorney's genuine interest in her case, and it is highly probable that because she is through her litigation she will accuse him of double-crossing her as she has her attorney during her original hearing. Her good memory and more than average intelligence serves her well in her attempts to convince the average lay person of her "sound mental condition." She has recently made some very dire threats as to what she will do unless she is successful at her approaching trial. The complaint about being put into restraint was in reference to a recent incident and was the only occasion in which restraint thus far has been used during my regime, although records show that, contrary to her story, she was in restraint numbers of times some years ago. This recent restraint was authorized by me personally after she had used a spoon handle to unscrew a door plate on her room door. She was kept in long enough for repairs to be made and somewhat as a disciplinary measure to which she is amenable. I'm sure that Rev. Childs has only shown the usual reaction of one who is unfamiliar with such a mental case and problem individual as Mrs. Judd, and is motivated by the highest ideals. I had no opportunity to discuss these matters with her; but regardless of my attempts in the past to convince some of Mrs. Judd's Indiana relatives, I made but little headway because of their utter lack of knowledge of the paranoid type of individual. She is capable of presenting her material, like many other true paranoids, in a most convincing manner. Sincerely, M. W. Conway, M.D."[17]

1953, April 28
Dr. Conway told Ruth he had tried to send her to Florence and found out that he couldn't, that someone had more power than he did but he would not tell her who, except that it was not Governor Pyle. She said that he intimated that she was awaiting trial. [20]

1953, April 29
Dr. Conway told Ruth that he tried to send her back to Florence but found out that he couldn't since someone has more power than he has. Ruth asked if it was the Governor. He said no and refused to tell her anymore. She couldn't understand who. She thought that it wasn't the pardon board.[10]

1953, June 7
Ruth writes a letter to Mrs. Richardson, the wife of HG Richardson. She writes, "Dear Mrs. Richardson: Yesterday I told my attorney Mr. Harold Whitney about some legal papers of mine which Mr. Richardson was keeping for me in a safety deposit box in the bank which he told me he had instructed you to turn over to me in case of death. You will probably be hearing from Mr. Whitney in the next day or two instructing you to mail all legal papers of mine to his office. Since talking to him, I believe it would be better for some member of my family to come to you personally with a note from me authorizing them to get all of my legal papers to avoid any possibility of their being lost in transit unless the papers are in a safety deposit box in a Phoenix bank. Will you kindly advise me when I can send for these papers? My guardian has several transcripts, affidavits – my attorney, others, and I would like to get everything together – not scattered around and destroy such as is not necessary to keep and put everything else

altogether. Thanking you – Most sincerely, Ruth Judd."[23] This part
possibly goes with this letter, "I am waiting trial; don't you see how
absolutely necessary it is I have all legal documents on my case
together – I want everything Mrs. Richardson had of mine in a safety
deposit box. He told me you knew of everything and in case of death
he had instructed you to see that I got them. I would have liked to look
over everything myself first before or in my present attorney's
presence. If you would have come out – gone over things saving what I
need and destroying anything else. Would you give me your address
on the coast – so that my brother or my attorney Mr. C Watson on the
coast could come talk to you. It is so important to have everything
ready if my sanity hearing comes up this month. Most Sincerely, Ruth
Judd. PS: Visiting hours are 1-4 daily except Monday and Friday – and
11-12 (crossed out) daily except Mon & Fri."[24]

1953, June 21
Ruth writes a letter to Mrs. Richardson, wife of HG Richardson. She
writes, "My Dear Mrs. Richardson: I was very happy to receive such a
prompt reply. I was afraid when I mailed my other letter you might
have moved from Coolidge. It has been several years since I have
heard any news of you. Since Judge Richardson's death I read a very
interesting piece in the paper about what a wonderful hero your son
was in this World War II; what an outstanding act of bravery in the
Navy. I know how proud of him you must be. As I know you are also
of your adorable twin granddaughters. Last fall when it was a
Republican land slide in the elections I thought if only Judge
Richardson were alive he undoubtable would be our attorney general
for he was the strongest Republican Barrister in the State. I think of a
number of the women at Florence who were kind to me and my parents
and wondered how some of them are. Several of them came to see me
here a number of years ago. Mrs. Bohree, Mrs. Kathryn Lavries and I
think of Kelner Claypool. Mrs. Richardson if you are coming to
Phoenix in the near future, I prefer than you come see me and bring all
legal papers Judge Richardson has in a safety deposit box to me direct
instead of taking them to my attorney. I want to sort them over and see
what all there is, destroy what I no longer need and put the rest in my
attorney or my guardian's hands. A number of years ago some of the
superintendents of this hospital told me my case was in politics and Mr.
Hoffman, chairman of the Board of Pardons and Paroles told me the
Pardon Board was between two political factions in doing anything for

15

me. Dr. Metzger, Chairman of this hospital Board of Control for 10 years, Dr. Larsen Superintendent and Dr. Simley fought for 4 hours before the Pardon Board trying to get my sentence commuted and Dr. Metzger told me that Jack Halloran and his country club bunch were the ones who kept me in here year after year, not mean enough to want any harm to happen to me, but kept right here and that I had had nothing but dirty tricks played on me in my case. Then I told Dr. Metzger that Sheriff Lon Jordon said if I'd run away from here, go to Mexico, I could stay a good long time for they'd never bring me back for half the politicians in the state would be tickled to death if I'd get away and stay away. Dr. Metzger said "Well that's true, I've always said why in the Hell don't you go to Mexico." I told him I've lived in Mexico, one has to carry their passport at all times and when one goes there to live over 10 days or 3 months and establishes a residence they have to register with the President (or mayor) of the municipal and an American woman is too conspicuous in a Latin American country alone. Well, I've no idea who these so called politicians are. I was getting along very well here. Dr. Hart, former superintendent, was letting me go out on passes for the day once a month into town where I spent the day in the homes of various friends, etc. Then when Dr. Conway came all of the attendants were worried saying Dr. Conway was trying to send me to Florence when I was still under the death sentence. So I ran away, went before the Grand Jury (the First session in 20 years since I went before it in 20 years ago) and the Grand Jury got me a commutation of sentence. Mr. Hoffmann of the Pardon Board came to see me in Sept 1952 and told me I had to go back to Florence before anything more could be done. As late as March 16, 1953, Dr. Wolfe medical director here told me I had to go back to Florence but on April 29, 1953 Dr. Conway told me I tried to send you to Florence but found out I can't. Someone has more power than I do. I asked who, the governor? He said no and refuses to tell me more. I cannot understand who. It can't be the Pardon Board for in Sept. they insisted I have to go back to Florence. I have an attorney, Mr. Harold Whitney. He is very young and is not fully acquainted with details in my case. The hospital doctors here told me I had to get a sanity hearing from the outside. So, I put every cent I had from Dr. Judd when he died into this sanity hearing. Psychiatrists and Psychologists from town say that I am sane but the hospital doctors say that I am crazy. Dr. Judd always told me someday a supt. would come who thought enough of me they would do something for me and several former doctors here have told me when the Board commuted my sentence they would come fight for me. I want a jury trial and things are being fought out over whether I have a jury hearing or just a judge. I was sent here by a jury not a judge – as most patients. Too many judges are going to think of votes. I'm afraid. A member of years ago, Governor Jones and Dr. Saxe were attacked over my operating a beauty parlor without a license. A great many politicians came to see me and told me things, some as friends, some threatening me. I do not forget one of them, what they said pro and con and into what political group they represent. Recently, some influential persons of two groups have sent me word they are for me. That I cannot understand. I figure very few persons, save my intimate friends are for me except only as they have their own axe to grind. The business manager here recently told me he had more to say than any other person probably in the state as to whether I get a sanity hearing or not. That whatever political pull I might have ever had 10 or 20 years ago is cut off, is gone. I've never said I had any kind of a pull. My husband and all his family were Republican – any persons 20 years ago who helped me did it out of sympathy because I was destitute and utterly helpless. I never realized any politicians were interested in me or my case until I was attacked over doing hair without a license and all that stir up – But for my sanity hearing now to have any hearing on this new business manager's statements, I cannot understand. I'm sane and no one can sentence a person to an insane asylum for life. I was sent here until I regain my sanity and several psychiatrists who have known me for years say I'm sane. as I stated my attorney is young, not thoroughly acquainted with my case. Many Phoenix attorneys have gone to him lately offering to assist him, help any way they can. I recognize certain of these attorneys as men who years ago were interested in me years ago only from a political stand point. They are smart men and certainly just because I happened to remember they were against me many years ago, I'm not going to cut off my nose to spite my face if they can be of help to me now. I did nothing to cause them to take their stand many years ago against me, (They had their axe to grind and if they still have their axe to grind) I'm not going to turn down help offered me. They do not know I know what I do of transactions many years ago if I say nothing. I've never even told my attorney. All I know is I need help now – The Powers that be are apparently against me, although this hospital and its Board of Control are supposed to have been taken out of politics. In summary, various attorneys I could never afford to engage have offered to help my

17

attorney in my case and I've only stated appreciation to my attorney. For these reasons I do not want you to turn all the legal papers which Judge Richardson has in his possession in a safety deposit box over to my attorney Mr. Whitney at this time. For I do not care for certain attorneys whom I'm accepting as a friend in need since they've offered to help to know all my business. Since the powers that be are against me, I cannot afford to let any previous circumstances influence me now to cut off my nose to spite my face. I can only be blissfully ignorant and strung along until something is done for me. I wish you would come see me so I could talk to you frankly and not in this round about fashion. My letters are censored here. I try to say as much as I can so you will understand. Yet say nothing definite those who read my letters can seize upon. The business manager throws up to me portions of my letters he reads. I'm sure I don't know what business he has reading my letters. He's no psychiatrist. Please come and see me yourself so I can explain more definitely. It is very important at this time. I could see you in my attorney's presence but I definitely do not wish all my legal papers turned over to his office in view of assisting attorneys helping until I've check all papers and material. Hoping to see you soon. Sincerely, Ruth Judd."[10]

1953, July 26
Ruth writes a letter to Reverend Walter Hofmann. She states that it has been almost a year since he came to see her. She requests that he come again soon. He had told her she would probably have to go back to Florence. She wanted to know what happened between March 16 and April 28 that caused the doctors at the hospital to first say that she had to go back to Florence and now they said they couldn't. She wanted to know, "Who is the power that is playing chess with my case?" When Judge LaPrade and Dr. Hendricks told her that they were her friends, she replied, "Oh, no, as far as you men are concerned, I'm dead." She stated when she had been here a few months, William Randolph Hearst had phoned offering his private plane to take her head attorney and his staff reporter to Washington, and he promised to back her financially to appeal my case to the US Supreme Court.[20] She stated that Dr. Conway stated to the grand jury that, "There is no reason I'm not perfectly safe to be walking the streets of Phoenix." He told her that nothing was wrong with her intelligence or her memory, but that she had no conscience.[20] She also stated that the health of her mother was critical and that she would like to have her with her.[20]

1953, September 27
Ruth writes another letter to Fern Richardson, wife of HG Richardson. She writes, "For some reason or another I do not know why unless someone with real money has got to him, my attorney Mr. Harold Whitney seems to be just stringing me along. Several Psychiatrists were out here in March and stated that I am not insane. My attorney promised my hearing would be in June or July and I have not seen or heard from him for over 3 months. I'm getting a very prominent attorney from the coast and I want all the papers you have on my case at once- So will you bring everything Mr. Richardson had of mine in the safety deposit box –He told me that in case anything ever happened to him he had instructed you to give them to me. I need them now and since you are not an attorney they can be of no value to you. Should anything happen to you I could not get them- I do not want you to turn any of my papers over to Dr. Conway or anyone but me. Will you please get them on your very next trip to Phoenix and bring them straight to me. Visiting days are everyday but Mondays & Friday. This is most urgent. Thanking you. Sincerely Ruth Judd."[25]

1953, November 5
W L Niswonger wrote to Mrs. Fern Richardson (wife of HG Richardson) to hand over "all of the papers she handed to you for safekeeping concerning her case". She asked to have them sent to Elizabeth Harvey instead of forwarding them to the State Hospital in fear that they would end up in the wrong hands. This was found with the confession letter that Ruth wrote in April of 1933. It seems as though she was trying to get this back. The letter came from Attica, Indiana. (Carrie McKinnell's family?) The letter stated that Ruth wanted to keep her interests, but she felt the odds so against her.[26]

1953, November 8
Carrie McKinnell dies at the Arizona State Hospital of chronic myocarditis at 6 AM. She also has an address listed as 1328 E Moreland (as did her husband). She is listed as a housewife and a widow. She is buried at Inglewood Cemetery in California. Her death certificate is signed by MW Conway who stated he knew her for 15 years. She is listed as living in Arizona for 22 years.[27,28]

1953, November 22
Ruth writes another letter to Mrs. Richardson, wife of HG Richardson:

"Dear Mrs. Richardson: I'm only allowed to write 3 letters a week and I have many letters right now I should acknowledge but it is most urgent you should understand, since Dr. Conway will not let me keep my papers myself, but must let him put them in the safe, that you do not bring them out to these grounds at all November 28. I've written and asked my brother to get in touch with you and come and get them for me. I do not want my guardian to handle these papers for she has before given articles to the hospital. I told her not to because they asked her to since two important letters I received in the mail were stolen from me by the attendant trusted to care for my belongings. And one letter I wrote my attorney through the office was given the business manager to read. It was about him and he came over and told me about it. So I want my brother to come get my papers. No one else. Sincerely, Ruth Judd."[10]

1953, December 15
Samuel Wick becomes acting head of the Arizona State Hospital.[1]

1954
Ernest McFarland is elected governor of Arizona. Winnie Ruth Judd writes him a 37-page letter stating that she will give him no trouble while he is governor. And in fact, she did not try to escape while he was in office. He stated that this letter convinced him even further that she had a "streak of insanity."[29]

1954, March 19
Dr. Samuel Wick becomes the superintendent of the Arizona State Hospital.[1]

1955, April 24
Abel Marie, Hedvig's mother dies of cancer of the colon that spread to the liver and lungs.[30]

1955, April 27
Marie is buried next to Anders and Sammy at Crystal Lake Cemetery.[30]

1955-1959
Fulbright visits Winnie Ruth Judd sometime in-between 1955-1959, getting permission from Dr.Wick. He stated that she was then in a secure ward with women who were not of high mentality who seemed

to adore her. He was taken to her bedroom where they could talk. The cell had a small glass window. She stated that now that Mac was Governor, that parole would be worked out for her. Fulbright stated that it was not up to Mac, but that it would still have to be worked out by the board of pardons and parole. He said that she had filled out; but that her complexion was still good and she had few wrinkles. She seemed well adjusted and in good physical condition. She talked freely and intelligently. She stated she had become a beautician and a lab technician. She said sometimes she also worked as a file clerk for the records, but that once she became adept at something they "jerk me off of it and place me on another." She also stated, "I can get out of here now any time I want to." And she explained how she could do it, but finished with, "What's the use? They always bring me back, and I have returned voluntarily a time or two because of the difficulties of living and keeping my identity concealed." She stated that she wanted to go to South America and live out her days by helping in the leper colony in Asuncion Paraguay, operated by her church. Fulbright thought at the time, that this might be a good solution for her and for the state of Arizona.[31]

1957, April 8
Hy Gardner of the New York Herald Tribune writes to Dr. Wick at the Arizona State Hospital. He asked a verification of something he received. He wanted to know if Winnie Ruth Judd had written a book of poems that is in the hands of an agent. The letter was unanswered.[32]

1957, August 25
Samuel Samuelson's (Sammy's brother) personal plane crashes in Tofte, Minnesota killing all the passengers including himself, his sons Gary and Paul and his friend Laurence Eidem. Winnie Ruth Judd reads of this incident in the paper. Years later in 1970 when she is denied parole (one of the reasons being she lacked remorse) was that "about two years ago in the paper I read an article where Sammy, the other girl in the tragedy where a younger brother in medical school, where we all lived in the duplex, had been killed with his small son in an aeroplane crash. I was sick for I suffered with the family that more sadness befalls the family. It was cruel of them to say I showed no remorse. I am sure the doctors never said such a thing. Actions speak louder than a few muttered words." I've died a thousand deaths of grief and agony over this regrettable unforeseen tragedy. It is the furthest thing I would

ever do, make money off of this tragedy where I have seen articles in the paper of sadness happening in the families of the two girls in this tragedy. One of the girl's baby brother became a doctor, two years ago. I saw where he and his small son crashed in their private plane and I was as grieved for the family as if it had been my own family that another sorrow had come into their lives."[33] She might have known about this when it happened. It was covered by both the Phoenix Gazette and the Arizona Republic. The headline from the Phoenix Gazette was, "Plane Crash Kills Winnie Judd Victim's Brother" and the Arizona Republic, "Judd Victim's Brother Killed."[34, 35]

August 29, 1957
Sam and his sons are buried next to Anders, Marie, and Sammy at Crystal Lake Cemetery.[30]

1959
MN Bunker publishes one of his books on Handwriting analysis. (Not the first time he has thoughts about Ruth's handwriting.) In the two samples he analyzes, he states that clear thinking is indicated in the writing of Winnie Ruth Judd. He states that two types of thinking can be seen in one of her samples. Her writing says that she was mentally busy. Penetrating thinkers must have something to occupy their minds. It may be associated with people, work they like, hobbies, anything to keep their active minds employed. Her initial strokes in another sample indicate resentment; that she wanted out of prison. Winnie Ruth went along for weeks and months; becoming bored, resentful. She was not planning to run away. All she wanted was out. The initial strokes indicate that the writer is suffering an urgent desire to get away. She clearly resents her conditions.[36] Another interpretation of her handwriting of an unknown period of time was performed by Shirley Spencer of the American Guild of Graphologists. She stated that from her signature: The exaggerated terminal on the capital R in combination with the very heavy pen pressure throughout the writing reveal an extremely materialistic person with strong appetites and passions. The T-bar pictures insufficient will to control these tendencies. Desire for attention and praise and a stubborn nature are marked characteristics. There is an utter lack of sensitiveness and fine feeling. This woman is quite capable of cold-blooded execution of the crime of which she is accused. In there no signs of insanity to excuse such a crime, but the uneven baseline and drooping signature are

evidences of a disturbed mental condition and despondency. Emotional shock and her present predicament naturally account for such a mental state. Unusual physical strength and endurance are shown.[37]

1. Arizona. State Hospital Phoenix. [from old catalog], *Milestones; a history of seventy-five years of progress at the Arizona State Hospital, Phoenix, Arizona, 1887-1962*. 1962, [Phoenix,. 150 p.
2. Judd, Winnie Ruth, *Letter of Winnie Ruth Judd written at the state hospital some 20 years after she arrived there. This may be the letter she wrote to Governor Pyle on January 25, 1953?*, in *Collection of Jerry Lewkowitz*. January 25, 1951?: Phoenix, Arizona. 1-12, 13, 21-22, incomplete.
3. *Freedom Dash From Hospital*, in *Arizona Republic*. February 3, 1952: Phoenix, AZ.
4. Judd, Winnie Ruth, *Letter from Winnie Ruth Judd to Governor Pyle*. December 21, 1952: Phoenix.
5. Judd, Winnie Ruth, *Letter from Winnie Ruth Judd to her niece Carolyn*. August 24, 1952: Phoenix.
6. *Killer Gives up Last Night*, in *Kentucky New Era*. February 8, 1952: Hopkinsville, KY.
7. Whitney, Rex E., *Memo to Willis H Bower Director regarding Winnie Ruth Judd. from Rex E Whitney, Assistant to the director*, in *Pineal County Historical Museum*. August 15, 1969: Florence, AZ.
8. Dobkins, J.D. and R. J. Hendricks, *Winnie Ruth Judd: The Trunk Murders*. 1973, New York: Grosset & Dunlap.
9. Judd, Winnie Ruth, *Letter from Ruth Judd to her brother Burton McKinnell*. March 20, 1952: Phoenix.
10. Judd, Winnie Ruth, *Letter from Ruth Judd to Mrs. Richardson*. June 21, 1953: Phoenix.
11. Judd, Winnie Ruth, *Notes Ruth Judd tried to slip to her Guardian; Enclosure of the letter of MW Conway to Governor Pyle on February 7, 1953*. Febrary 4, 1953: Phoenix.
12. *I've Been Locked Up Long Enough, Pleads Notorious Murderess*, in *Arizona Republic*. December 1, 1952: Phoenix, Arizona.
13. *State Hospital Faces Probe*, in *Tucson Daily Citizen*. December 1, 1952: Tucson.
14. Conway, MW, *Letter to Howard Pyle*, in *Arizona State University Library*. December 10, 1952: Tempe. 1.

15. *Gov. Pyle favors special insane ward*, in *Tucson Daily Citizen*. December 15, 1952: Tucson.

16. Pyle, Howad, *Letter from Governor Pyle to Ruth Judd*. March 3, 1933: Phoenix.

17. Conway, MW, *Letter from Dr. MW Conway to Governor Pyle*. April 25, 1953: Phoenix.

18. Pyle, Howard, *Memo from Governor Pyle to MW Conway*. March 3, 1953: Phoenix.

19. *Petition by Elizabeth Harvey, Guardian*, in *State Vs Judd: Arizona State Archives and Public Records*. March 14, 1953: Phoenix, AZ.

20. Judd, Winnie Ruth, *Letter from Ruth Judd to Walter Hoffmann; later forwarded to Governor Williams in 1971*. July 26, 1953: Phoenix.

21. *Superior Court Letter*, in *State vs Judd: Arizona State Archives and Public Records*. March 27, 1953: Phoenix, AZ.

22. Childs, Marian A, *Letter from Marian A Childs, President of the Woman's Humane Club of Southern California to Governor Pyle*. April 21, 1953: Pasadena, CA.

23. Judd, Winnie Ruth, *Letter of Ruth Judd to Mrs. Richardson*. June 7, 1953: Phoenix.

24. Judd, Winnie Ruth, *Letter to Mrs. Richardson by Winnie Ruth Judd (continuation of June 7th letter?)*. 1953: Phoenix.

25. Judd, Winnie Ruth, *Letter from Ruth Judd to Fern Richardson*. September 27, 1953: Phoenix.

26. Niswonger, W. L., *Letter from W. L. Niswonger to Mrs. Fern Richardson*. November 5, 1953, Arizona Historical Society, Tucson: Attica, Indiana.

27. Arizona State Department of Health, *Carrie B. McKinnell Death Certificate*, in *Arizona Vital Records*. November 8, 1953: Phoenix. http://genealogy.az.gov

28. Inglewood Park Cemetery, *Inglewood Park Cemetery Database*,. 2007. http://www.inglewoodparkcemetery.com/search_db.html

29. McFarland, Ernest William, *Mac : the autobiography of Ernest W. McFarland*. 1979, [s.l.]: McFarland. ix, 342 p.

30. Peterson, Phyllis, *Anders Severin Samuelson*. August 23, 1998: Carpinteria, CA.

31. Fulbright, Tom, *Cow-country counselor*. [1st ed. 1968, New York,: Exposition Press. 196 p.

32. Gardner, Hy, *Letter from Hy Gardner of the New York Herald Tribune to Dr. Samuel Wick*. April 8, 1957: New York.

33. Judd, Winnie Ruth, *Series of Letters written to Melvin Belli*, in *Pineal County Museum*. May, 1970: Florence, AZ.
34. *Plane Crash Kills Winnie Judd Victim's Brother*, in *Phoenix Gazette*. August 27, 1957: Phoenix.
35. *Judd Victim's Brother Killed*, in *Arizona Republic*. August 27, 1957: Phoenix.
36. Bunker, M. N., *Handwriting analysis; the art and science of reading character by grapho analysis*. 1959, Chicago,: Nelson-Hall. 256 p.
37. Spencer, Shirley, *Handwriting Analysis by Shirley Spencer, Director of the American Guild of Graphologists*, in *Unknown source from the Collection of Jerry Lewkowitz*. unknown, ?

Section 7

1960-1969

1962

Ruth escapes from the state hospital for the last time. Fulbright stated that there was a minimum exertion by the law enforcement agencies to find her. The public didn't care at this time either. Fulbright thought that she probably went to Mexico.[1] A doctor said, "We are not looking for her. She's not dangerous. The police are not looking for her and we're not either."[2] Ruth had called up a friend in Phoenix and they hid her at a church. This man was distantly related. He hid her and brought her food every day. The people in the church sent her a hot meal every day. This party hid her. Then her niece's husband came over in a car and got her and took her to California.[2]

1962, October 10

Samuel Wick of the Arizona State Hospital stated that number 1438 (Ruth Judd) has unauthorized absence.[3]

1963, December 6

A Marie Halloran passes away, wife of Jack Halloran. She was 74. Rosary was said for her on December 7. She died at her home. Requiem high mass was sung on December 8 at St. Mary's Catholic Church, 231 N Third St. She was buried in St. Francis Cemetery. She was born in LA and came to Phoenix in 1915. She was survived by her husband Jack, two daughters, Mrs. Henry Margaret Running of Phoenix and Mother Marie St John RSHN of Santa Barbara, Ca. She has six grandchildren and two great grandchildren.[4]

1964, June 26

The Brill Street Apartment at 1130 Brill is torn down to make room for a parking lot. This article states she had three parties the week of the murders. Salvage crews removed usable lumber from the building.[5]

1965

Ruth starts working for Mrs. Nichols sometime in 1965.[6] Ruth stated that she went to bed every night with my cookbooks. She would make out a menu and what she had to do. Ruth was always there. She took Thursdays off and every other Sunday. Mrs. Nichols insisted that they have a day off. Ruth went over to San Francisco and the Golden Gate Park. She would go through the de Young Museum. She liked the Steinhart Aquarium. She would go through the Wildlife Museum. She would walk through the Japanese Garden.[2] Ruth stated Henry died in April and she went to work for Mrs. Nichols in September. She said she worked for Mrs. Nichols for about 6.5 years though...[2]

1966

Langan Swent moves to San Francisco where the Homestake Mining Companies corporate offices were located. He moved to Piedmont where his father was living at 59 Lincoln Avenue. Langan moved to the house along King Avenue overlooking 40 Lincoln Avenue where Winnie Ruth Judd was living using the name Marian Lane. Marian was friendly with Mr. Swent's housekeeper, Nilene Peak. Marian occasionally brought the two little dogs over on leashes. They were quite well trained. She said her son had taken them to a school and had them trained. She would demonstrate how well trained they were. She used to babysit for many people in the neighborhood, but never baby-sat for Langan who had 4 children at the time.[7]

1966, January 25

County Attorney Robert Corbin writes to the Clerk of the Superior Court, Alma Jennings. "This office is attempting to determine under what judicial decrees Winnie Ruth Judd was committed to the Arizona State Hospital. The files in the office of the clerk of the Maricopa County Superior Court fail to contain this information. The Arizona State Hospital records indicate that she was committed from Pinal County on April 24, 1933, having been adjudged insane in your county five days before she was to have been executed. Would you please search your files for any documents supporting her commitment, and furnish our office with copies of such documents. Your aid and cooperation in this matter will be greatly appreciated, as it is necessary for us to determine the manner of her commitment in the event we find it necessary to commence extradition proceedings for her."[8] Did they know where she was?

2

1966, February 1
Carolyn (McKinnell) Keiser sues Robert J. Keiser for divorce. In it she
stated "that on occasion defendant has struck plaintiff and has recently
threatened to strike her; that plaintiff fears defendant will do her bodily
harm unless defendant is engaged? and restrained by the court from
access to the family home."[9] Alma Jennings responds by writing N
Warner Lee a letter: "On April 12, 1933, a petition supported by an
affidavit signed by AG Walker, acting superintendent of the Arizona
State Prison was filed requesting that the sanity of Winnie Ruth Judd be
inquired into. The matter was tried before a jury and on April 22, 1933,
a verdict was rendered finding Winnie Ruth Judd Insane. The minutes
of this trial are recorded in Minute Book 13, p. 315. Enclosed is a
certified copy of the judgement and order signed by Hon E. L. Green
committing Winnie Ruth Judd at the Arizona State Prison.[10]

1967
Mrs. Nichols died in 1967.[6] She leaves Marian a $10,000 bequest. She
kept living in the house while it was going through the estate
proceedings.[7] Burton visited Ruth in Piedmont in 1967.[11] (I bet this is
the time he brought Kirk, his son, to meet her as well). Ruth takes a jet
to St. Louis and takes a bus to complete visits with relatives in Illinois
and Indiana. She said she wanted to go back to Greenville and see the
old school and church she attended years ago. She telephoned ahead to
relatives to make sure she was welcome.[11]

1968, January 19
James Swent dies in Alameda County. On the day of his funeral, Ruth
walks back and forth along the house in the street. She knew that
Evelyn was there and wanted to see her again. Langan and Eleanor
lived next door. She wanted to speak to them but was too afraid of
being recognized.[2]

1968, September 30
Carolyn (McKinnell) Keiser files for a restraining order against Bob
Keiser stating, "Plaintiff alleges that within recent days, Plaintiff and
defendant have engaged in violent arguments and plaintiff is
exceedingly frightened of the conduct of the defendant toward her
physically. Plaintiff requests that defendant be restricted from going
near her place of residence and from harbor?, antagonize, molesting or
in any way interfering with her."[12]

3

1968, December 24

Carolyn Keiser and Bob Keiser were scheduled to appear in court. It seems it was delayed until April.[12]

1969, March 21

Bob Keiser makes a claim for psychiatric services from his insurance company. The claim was for psychiatric services between 12/18/68 and 3/31/69 for $1320. His policy was dropped and his claim denied.[13]

1969, April 25

Carolyn Keiser and Bob Keiser appear in divorce court. This seems to be the final divorce hearing before a divorce was granted.[12] Final filing was in October.

1969, April 28

In Alamo, a suburb of Oakland, a mother of two died of extensive head injuries suffered under unexplained circumstances at her home. The woman's name was Mrs. Z Alexander Aarons, 49 of 2750 Laverock Lane. Her husband was a psychiatrist with offices at his home and also at John Muir Hospital in Walnut Creek. The husband told deputies that it was her habit to take their two teenage children to school in the morning, returning to their home about 8:30 am. He thought she had followed the same routine. He got up about 8:45 and was preparing to leave for the hospital when he looked out the window and found her unconscious in a pool of blood on the patio. She underwent emergency surgery at John Muir, but died at 9 AM the following day. Doctors said that she had multiple skull fractures plus other head wounds which they described as the results of "blows" to the head, a fall or possible gunshot wounds.[14] Anna had left at 7:30 with the children and had dropped them off at 7:45. Vicky stated that she was a little late that day and left about 7:40. She indicated no plans of going anywhere else. It takes about 10-15 minutes to arrive back at the house. So, she probably arrived back at 8 or a bit later. John thought she would have arrived home about 8:15. The police report stated that Z. Alexander Aarons found her about 9:20. He got up that day about 8:45. He stated the door was open. He administered first aid and found Anna was having difficulty breathing. He called an ambulance and put a pillow under her head. She was supine with her arms extended. Her keys were near her hands. Nothing was missing from her purse. She was 5-6 feet from the front door. Her head was 2 feet from a planter. Her head was

4

pointed towards the residence and her feet towards the entrance gate. He cancelled all of his appointments and notified his answering service. He went to John Muir Hospital where they took Anna. The fire truck arrived at 9:32. The firemen cleaned the area of blood. No weapon was found at the scene. Dr. Danzig stated that the weapon used on Anna Aarons appeared to have been made by a semi blunt instrument and the appearance of possibly a double pronged instrument with one blow.[15] Another statement about the weapon was that it was between 1 and 1.5 inches in diameter (by Dr. Hauer and Dr. Danzig.)[15]

1969, April 30
An autopsy on Mrs. Z Alexander Aarons revealed that she died of a massive brain hemorrhage. The police declared it a homicide according to Contra Costa County Sheriff, Lt. Robert Sang.[16]

1969, May
Winnie Ruth Judd graduates from the program from the Oakland College of Medical Technicians. [17] As a routine part of the case of Anna Aarons, Sgt. Gardella was placed in charge of the investigation. As a part of this, he had been staking out day and night at the Aarons home, where the psychiatrist had offices in addition to those at John Muir Hospital. They stated this was because they asked for the doctor's records. He wouldn't give them to the police because they were personal, confidential information.[7] Sgt. Gardella wrote down license numbers on cars of patients who called. The investigation led him to a Ford Sedan, which was later revealed had been driven to the doctor's office by the nephew of Winnie Ruth Judd.[18] He said that he wanted to check out each of Dr. Aarons' patients but because of professional ethics, the doctor could not give out the names of the patients.[19]

1969, May 14
Police go and visit Marion Joan Lane (WRJ) at 40 Lincoln Ave. She is the owner of a 1968 Ford XPX376 which appeared at the Aarons residence on May 12, 1969. She stated that her car is being driven by her nephew Robert Keiser of 212 Pine St. Apt 13, Concord 689-7249. She stated that he was employed at the Phillips 66 Oil company and also works from 3AM to 6AM at another job. She stated that he had been a patient of Dr. Aarons for a short time. She said he was having marital problems, and he and his wife had separated. She stated that

the wife had custody of 4 small children and that he is going to Dr. Aarons for help.[15] The police went to call on Marion Lane to find out about the car. During the course of the conversation the policeman got very suspicious that she was somewhat evasive. He managed to get her fingerprints on something. He went back to the police station and checked. He began to think that she might be Winnie Ruth Judd. He investigated it and he got records from Arizona. The fingerprints confirmed it.[7]

1969, May 15
Police go and talk to Bob Keiser at Phillips 66 Oil Company at Avon. He stated that he had been a patient of Dr. Aaron's since December 18, 1968. He stated that before the death of Mrs. Aarons he had an appointment at 1:30 PM Monday through Friday and with a change sometimes on Thursdays at 6:20. He stated he didn't notice or hear anything of a suspicious nature while at the Aaron's office. He said he didn't know the Aarons family although he had seen a woman in a small blue car at times. He said at times he doubted that Dr. Aarons was married. He didn't know that he had children. He said since her death his appointments were now 1:10 pm on Mondays, 12:10 PM Tues-Fri and 6:20 on Thursdays at times. He stated he had nothing to say regarding the investigation.[15]

1969, May 29
Doctors get together to discuss the weapon and the autopsy report in the death of Anna Aarons. X-rays showed extensive damage to the left side of the head by two separate blows. The blow was flush with the side of the head crushing the skull in both areas. One blow was approximately 2 inches long. This was the one just in the hairline and a second one in the hair area. This blow was approximately 3 inches long. The two blows were apparently done in rapid succession cracking the skull completely around. The blows caused shattered bones from the skull to be embedded in the brain. The lacerations in the skin were very irregular. This type of damage was done by a great deal of extensive force. (According to Dr. Liu, neurologist) They said it could not have happened from a fall. Two of the Doctors thought that it could have been a tire iron to something possibly the size of a baseball bat and believes the instrument was fairly short possibly 18" in length. They thought that the two blows were in rapid succession indicating the subject had tremendous force and power. They thought

6

it had to have been a man. One of the doctors stated that the guy who did this was at least 4 inches taller or more than Anna Aarons. The blows were flush against the head.[15]

1969, June 26
Ruth states that Bob Keiser came to her and said he had to have $5000. He wanted to give her a second note. Ruth said that she couldn't do that. Bob insists. He said that he had to buy a new car – one in his own name. "I finally gave him $2000.", she stated. The next day she was arrested.[11]

1969, June 27
Winnie Ruth Judd is arrested in Danville, California by Robert Sang and Sgt. Joseph Walsh of the Contra Costa county Sheriff's office. She is arrested at 2 pm. She stated that she had only lived there since Monday, but Sang believed that she had been there longer.[20] She is identified by fingerprints and a scar on her left index finger. She is living at 1583 Green Valley Road, Danville. She is located because there was a crime in the neighborhood; Anna Aarons who was found beaten unconscious on the patio of her home at 2750 Laverock Lane on April 28. Anna died an hour later. Police took license plates from the neighborhood. A car registered in the name of Marion Lane, 40 Lincoln Avenue Piedmont is identified. Sang went to interview Marion Lane and reported back that "something is wrong". Marion moved to 1583 Green Valley Road in the meantime, home of the Blemers who were vacationing in Europe at the time. She moved because she was staying in the Nichols house until the estate was settled. Ruth's nephew was the one driving the car that was parked at the office of a psychiatrist, Dr. Z Alexander whose wife was killed. He kept an office at his home. As she was entering the jail, she told reporters "I don't know what this is about." She was wearing a brown and tan linen dress and appeared calm and smiled throughout the time she was awaiting admittance to the jail. She had brought two poodles with her to the Sheriff's office since she refused to leave them behind. The sheriff turned them over to friends. "She was always so nice and sweet, said Mrs. Patmont, who lived at 35 Lincoln Avenue just across the street from the Henry D. Nichols home. "We all liked her very much," said Dr. Albert H Rowe, 79 and still an active physician who lived at 1 Crocker Avenue just across the street on the Crocker side of the Nichols' house. He stated that when Mrs. Nichols had a stroke in 1967,

7

Miss Lane took the best care of Mrs. Nichols and was wonderful to her. "She took very good care of Grandma," stated Mrs. Lois Nichols Lippincott of 642 Creekside Road, Pleasant Hill. "She took wonderful care of the home and was always sweet and considerate" "I used to ride around with her in the car", said Clara Perrin, Dr. Howe's cook. "We used to go to the store. You mean she's a murderer?" "I can't praise the woman enough, said Herman D. Nichols of 62 Inverieth Terrace, Piedmont, and son of the late Mrs. Nichols. She was a wonderful friend of Mrs. Nichols and a very good housekeeper. I just can't believe this, he said. Mrs. Nichols died in 1967, so Ruth worked for her since sometime in 1965. Dr. Rowe also stated that she was very outgoing. She talked to everyone. She was very friendly.[6] Langan and his family were out at Lake Tahoe. He was glad they were gone. The press came around and questioned everybody in the neighborhood about her. He thought they would have looked very stupid in questions saying, "Yes, I used to know her forty years ago." He never recognized her even though he lived in the back of the Nichol's house and could look down at the house. He did not recognize her when one time she came to him and stated that she knew him as a child. She stated that she was a friend of Mrs. Swent. When Langan asked her where she knew her. She said, "I knew her back when she lived in Mexico." She stated that she had visited her in Tayoltita. She didn't mention a date and Langan was perplexed about it.[7] She was held at the contra costa jail. Sang stated that she was only being held as a fugitive, not a suspect.[20]

1969, late June
Melvin Belli is contacted by Winnie Ruth Judd. In his book he writes: Naturally, I, a celebrated lawyer, would also get the Winnie Ruth Judd case. Mrs. Judd was a notorious trunk murderess convicted in 1932, who used to escape regularly from the Arizona State Hospital in Phoenix and then finally disappeared in 1962. She showed up in 1969 as a plump, matronly cook, housekeeper and companion for the well-to do working under an assumed name in the San Francisco Bay area. When the California authorities found her, they clapped her into prison. I got a phone call from her in the middle of the night. "You know who this is." It was a statement, not a question. Groggily, I said, "Yeah." and waited. 'Winnie." "Winnie Churchill?" I said."No. "Winnie Ruth Judd." Through law school and beyond, WRJ had been a standing joke. She was over the wall more than Babe Ruth. "Oh,

shit," I said. "Now I've heard everything." But in the morning I sent one of my younger attorneys over to the jail in Contra Costa County.He came back and announced, "Mel, it's she and she look like Mother C., everybody's grandmother, Barbara Fritchie and Florence Nightingale." I took the case, even when she was extradited to Arizona. I thought that the thirty-odd years she'd spent behind bars and locked gates was enough – convicted murderers only spent nine or ten-and that her record for the past eight years was proof that she wasn't dangerous. I made some labyrinthine detours through a maze of Arizona politics, and had some hearings before a parole board that looked like a Grant Wood painting. All the board members had stiff, celluloid collars, high water pants, white cotton socks, Ben Franklin glasses and hair slicked down with shoe polish. Finally, after a long personal conference with Arizona's governor, Jack Williams (who impressed my son Caesar more than he impressed me), I got her sentence commuted to time served She now lives within fifteen miles of me.[21]

1969, June 30
Bail was set at $125,000 in Mt Diablo Municipal Court for a woman who claims to be Marian Joan Lane of Danville. Ruth denies that she is Winnie Ruth Judd. There is a court hearing set for July 14th to establish her identity. Melvin Belli represented her. He carefully only referred to her as "my client" and "the woman in custody" during the hearing. Belli asked that she should be released since she has held responsible jobs in the area for the past 6 years. He noted that 6 of the 7 escapes Ruth made from the hospital, she returned on her own.[22]

1969, July 2
Police contact the director of personnel at Avon for the Phillips 66 regarding Robert Jame Keiser. G. K Spradling, Keiser's immediate supervisorstated that Keiser usually left at lunchtime for his 1:20 appointment. However, there were no records of his comings and goings. He stated that he also had an allergy problem which made him come in late on occasion. No records of when he came in late were available. He stated that Keiser was a quiet individual who doesn't appear to blow. He was born on 10/10/28, social security 383-24-2405. He is a white male 6 foot 175 pounds. He has blonde hair and blue eyes. He had a Bachelor of Science degree from UCLA. He had been employed by Phillips for a salary of $1065 monthly.[15] They also talked to Lois Lippincott. She stated that she had no information regarding Marion

9

Lane or why Mrs. Aarons had stopped taking her children to her husband for dental work.[15] They met that afternoon with Dr. Aarons. At this time, Dr. Aarons stated that Keiser had had a peyote experience at one time and that he had recurrent flashbacks. He stated that he had advised the doctor on the first appointment after the homicide that this was something he could have done while he was in one of his flashbacks. [15]

1969, July 3
Police went to see Carolyn Keiser 2515 Cranbrook, in Concord. Her date of birth was 7/12/34. She stated that Robert called her on 4/28/1969 between 10:30 and 11:00 AM saying that Dr. Aarons had called cancelling his appointment, but that he would take off anyhow, and they would have lunch. She stated that on the following day Robert called the answering service and was advised that the appointments were cancelled due to a grave family problem. He did not know until the following Wednesday of the death of Anna. She said that Robert told her that on his first visit after the homicide the doctor was very normal, calm, etc. Carolyn stated that Robert thinks Dr. Aarons is the "Great White Father," the nearest thing to God, and that Robert was at her house on the morning of 4/28/69 after he was done delivering papers. She stated that Robert was at her house on the morning of 4/28/69 by 8 since the boy had to be in school early that morning and that this could be verified. The investigator stated that she appears to resent the relationship between Robert and Dr. Aarons and stated that she and her father had told Robert that Marian Lane was responsible for the homicide, since she felt that the doctor was really responsible and she was scared the doctor was coming after her if they didn't advise Robert differently. She stated that Robert tells the doctor everything that is said at the house. She stated that Robert has been going to Dr. Aarons on the advice of a marriage counselor, also that he is not getting any outside financial help except for Marian Lane, and that he has borrowed and has income from a title loan, also, that he works three jobs.[15] They also made contact with Mr. Mahler, the San Francisco Chronicle dealer who had employed Robert Keiser. He stated that Bob had a 3 AM to 6:30 AM paper route near the park and shop complex in Concord, CA. There were no complaints about the route on April 28th. He stated that Robert was always done by 7 or 7:30 AM.[15]

10

1969, July 8

Police contact Mr. Nichols at his offices at 211 Bush St. He stated that Richard was Richard Peak and that he did not know if his mother was paying for medical treatment for Peak. (?) However, he stated that it was not impossible. He stated that Heidi Brosch terminated employment on 1/15/68 and he believed that she was working for the William Olivers on Hazel Lane in Piedmont. He stated regarding Marion Lane that on 4/27/69 at approximately 10:30 PM Marian had called regarding people looking at the house at 40 Lincoln Way. Marian referred to Carolyn Keiser as "my baby" at times, "my daughter" He stated that she had purchased a 1959 or 1960 Lincoln for $400 from the estate. He stated that she had apparently given the car to her brother (Burton) and that she had discussed purchasing another car for her son- in- law, which was Robert Keiser. He stated that he had never seen Marian Lane drive a vehicle since her employment with his mother. Also she had mentioned that when she went out to the country to live with the Blemers in Danville she would probably have to learn to drive a car as there was no public transportation.[15]

1969, July 10

A conference was held again with Dr. Aarons. He stated again that Robert Keiser suffered blackouts quite often and it was possible that he might have killed his wife when he was in one of his blackout stages.[15] When checking with Carolyn and Robert Keiser, they both denied that Bob had ever had any black out spells.[15]

1969, July 14

Ruth admits in court to Judge Hall that her legal name is Ruth Judd. She said they called her Winnie, but that wasn't her real name. Judge Hall ordered her held without bail until an amended extradition could be received from Arizona. August 4th was the scheduled hearing with Ronald Reagan. He had sent a request back to Arizona stating that it was incomplete. Melvin Belli stated that he might not fight extradition but that he hoped "our most liberal governor will see fit not to extradite her." He stated that her life in California was one that she could be proud of. The newspaper stated that she had been cleared of any involvement with the Aarons' case. After the court hearing Ruth and Belli conducted a press conference in a small hot jury room before several television cameras and a dozen microphones. She said she expected to be declared legally sane at a hearing and then wanted to

11

join friends in Paraguay where she would be working with children. She stated that she felt that she had paid her debt to society. She stated in the leper colony she could take care of the children and do their hair, and be a medical assistant. She stated that she shot Hedvig Samuelson and Agnes Anne LeRoi in self-defense after a quarrel. She stated that she had never been allowed to take the stand. She stated that a psychiatrist, (?) now dead helped her dismember the bodies and stuff them in a trunk. She said his death was a suicide. She said that many knew her identity in the Bay area at the Oakland school for medical and dental assisting. She had requested that they keep it secret. She stated she never felt like a fugitive. She tried hard to block out the past and live for the future.[23] Winnie Ruth Judd does an interview from the Contra Costa Jail with Joe Patrick from Phoenix. It is made into a half hour TV special.[24]

1969, July 17
Police do a check on Robert James Keiser. They checked his employment application, and his background. Each was negative. They were doing an extensive background check on him since he was the nephew in law of Winnie Ruth Judd. They discovered on this date that part of the jack equipment was missing from the trunk of his car. On this date police also contacted Mrs. Allen Lippincott, Mr. Herman Nichols in order to obtain background information but received little factual information.[15] Drs. Liu, Hauer, and Danzig believed the skin was broken and not cut and the instrument which inflicted the damage was 1 to 1.5 inches in circumference on Mrs. Aarons.[15]

1969, July 18
Police go to the apartment of Bob Keiser at 121 Pine Street in Concord. They examine a 1969 Ford with California license number XTX-376. They examined stains which they thought might be blood stains. They examined the automobiles interior, exterior, and trunk. No stains or items having an evidentiary value were observed.[15] On this same date the lab examines a four-way lug wrench, one tire tool lug wrench, and a ball peen hammer. It seems reasonable that it is from this same car. The findings were negative including microscopic examination failed to reveal any material of significance. Presumptive chemical tests for blood performed on extracts from the submitted items were negative.[15]

1969, July 22

Police dispatched to the Los Angeles area to contact several people including Burton McKinnell. Burton is listed at 640 Weymouth, Cambria. They contacted him at his home. He stated that he was the brother of Winnie Ruth Judd who is currently incarcerated in Contra Costa County and that he could give no factual information regarding any connection between her and the Anna Aarons homicide. Burton stated that he had prepared a critique on his series regarding the Aarons homicide since his son- in- law had been a patient of the murdered woman's husband. A copy of the critique was attached to the report. (Not available in what I have). Burton stated that he would fully cooperate with Contra Costa County in any way in which he could possibly assist in the investigation of the Aarons homicide. Subsequent contacts were made with him in the Concord Martinez area, so far with no factual information.[15] They also tried to find a Climort Ray Butner, but they were unable to locate him. Contact had been attempted with Mr. Buttner as a possible person who had mailed a card to Mrs. Judd at the County jail. The card was addressed to a Mr. Eddie Miller at the traveler's hotel in Martinez. He (who?) denied any knowledge of the Judd woman or the man who signed himself as Clem (must be Eddie Miller). The card was in evidence and a Photostat was attached to the report (do not have).[15]

1969, July 23

A polygraph test was performed on Bob Keiser and Carolyn Keiser at the request of the Contra County Sheriff's office. They did not show sufficient responses to indicate that either was involved in the homicide. The report state that further investigation was being conducted.

Some notes: As a result of the subsequent Sheriff's investigation, it was determined that Robert James Keiser was a patient of Dr. Aarons, a psychiatrist. Robert Keiser's wife was Carolyn Keiser, niece of Winnie Ruth Judd. It was reported that Winnie Ruth Judd had been in hiding following her escape from a mental institution with the knowledge of Mr. and Mrs. Keiser. It was not established that Winnie Ruth Judd had anything to do with the murder of Anna Aarons; however, polygraph examinations were requested on Mr. And Mrs. Keiser in an attempt to determine if they were implicated or had any knowledge regarding Mrs. Aarons' death. Both subjects reportedly readily agreed to the polygraph examination.

13

Subject Robert Keiser was introduced to the reporting agent at 11:48 by Sgt. Ginsburg who then left the room. Keiser was then advised of his rights to which he stated he understood and would talk and take the test. He stated he did not need nor did he want an attorney. That he wanted to prove that he was not involved in any way in the death of Mrs. Aarons. During the pretest interview, he denied ever knowing Mrs. Aarons and was not even sure that he had seen her. He acknowledged that he might have seen her during his consultations with Dr. Aarons at the latter's office which was near his residence. He stated that if he suspected anyone, he would suspect Winnie Ruth Judd, his aunt- in- law, whom he reportedly had helped harbor since her escape from Arizona. He also expressed his belief that she was not guilty of her original crime for which she was convicted in Arizona. He was quick to add that he had no real reason to suspect her regarding the death of Mrs. Aarons except that she mentioned or described the Aarons' residential area. He stated that he told Lt. Sang about this. Following the tracing Keiser stated that he was told by his wife, Carolyn, that Winnie had described the area leading to Aarons' house and that statement was not made directly to him by his Aunt-in- Law. There was a slight response to the question, "On April 28th were you at Aarons' residence between 7:30 and 9:30 AM. To which he answered no. (Tracing 3) In tracing 4 there was slight response to the question, "To your knowledge did Dr. Aarons kill his wife" to which he answered no. There was slight response to the question, "Do you actually know who killed Anna Aarons?" To which he answered no. Carolyn Keiser was introduced to the reporting agents at 1:04 by Sgt. Ginsburg who then left the room. During the pretest interview she denied having anything to do with Mrs. Aarons' death and denied having any knowledge of who committed the act. She added that she never thought her aunt, Winnie Ruth Judd, had anything to do with Mrs. Aarons' death before but now is not sure. She added that she has no reason for this. That she just has been wondering about it. She stated she is now in the process of divorcing Robert. With reference to the information that she had told Robert that Winnie had described the area near Dr. Aarons' residence she stated that it was her father who told her that Winnie had telephoned him and told him about the "cow lane leading down to the Aarons' place." She stated that it was her father who told her about this and that she had told Robert in turn. Details: In tracing 3 there was slight response to the question, "On

14

April 28th between 7:30 and 9:30 were you at Dr. Aarons' residence. To which she answered no. There was also slight response to the question, "Did you kill Anna Aarons?" to which she answered No. Following the test, Mrs. Keiser continued to deny implication in the death of Anna Aarons. They ended the interview at 2:40.

The general report summary states that the polygraph showed no guilty knowledge of the Aarons' homicide in Robert's case.[15]

At 2:00, there was a meeting at Dr. Aarons' residence. During this interview, Dr. Aarons stated that Robert Keiser was a dupe of Marion Lane's and that he was sure that Marion Lane was responsible. He made no mention of Robert Keiser committing the homicide. [15] At 3:15 they were informed that Carolyn Keiser's polygraph was negative.[15]

1969, July 25

Police talk to Mrs. Long of 1534 38th Ave, Apt 6 in Oakland. She had met Marian Lane when she first obtained employment "at the residence" She stated that she had been introduced to Carolyn Keiser as Marion's daughter, stated that she had never seen Marion drive an automobile, that they usually went out using public transportation, that Marion had stated she had bought the car and given it to her son-in-law and that when she moved out to the country she would have to take driving lessons and learn how to operate the vehicle since there was no public transportation available.[15]

1969, August 9

Winnie Ruth Judd appears in court trembling and sobbing at her extradition hearing. She stated that she never tried to hurt anyone who threatened her during the seven years since her escape from the Arizona State Hospital. Richard Turner, Governor Reagan's assistant of legal affairs conducted the one-hour hearing to determine whether Ruth should be returned to Arizona as a fugitive. Melvin Belli tried to guide her during the hearing, but she often cut him off. She rattled on unrelated facts at random, her voice occasionally trailing off into a quivering sob. She said she returned to the hospital 5 of the 7 times she escaped. She stated she only left to help her case. She never explained this. She talked about doing hair in the hospital as many as 150 a week. Afterwards, she took care of children. She talked about taking care of a blind woman in Oakland, but left on the fear that she would die and they would ask her questions. They had offered her $3000 to stay. Belli pleaded that Ruth was "as much rehabilitated as any human being can be. If not. Rehabilitation is a mockery."[25]

1969, August 14
Ronald Reagan issues a statement that ordered Winnie Ruth Judd to return to Arizona. He stated, "There are certain legal defenses to extradition, none of which have been raised in this case." He also said, "The proper forum in which to consider matters such as Mrs. Judd's rehabilitation, her mental condition, and questions of parole is Arizona, the state in which the crime was committed and where Mrs. Judd was convicted and sentenced."[26]

1969, August 15
Rex E. Whitney writes a report on Winnie Ruth Judd to Willis H. Bower who is the director at the Arizona State Hospital. He relates a history of her time at the State Hospital.[27]

1969, August 19
Dr. Eugene R Almer writes the following analysis of Ruth Judd for Larry Debus. "This is a 64-year-old widow who is of high school education. She was seen at the Maricopa County Jail at the request of yourself as her attorney for the purpose of psychiatric evaluation. She had just recently been extradited from California. On meeting her, I found her to be in fairly reasonable spirits. The last time she left the Arizona State Hospital was in 1962 at which time she went to the San Francisco area. She took a job taking care of a blind, arthritic lady and remained with this work for about 10 months. After that she took a job as a housekeeper to an extremely wealthy family and there she planned all the meals and did all the shopping and was in charge of a 23 room home of a very wealthy man. She kept this job until she was brought back to Phoenix just recently. During the last few months she was there, a relative of hers was giving her a great deal of trouble and obtaining money from her. Because of complications with the relative her identity was discovered. Mental status examination reveals that she appears her stated age, is about 5 ½ feet tall, weighs about 150 pounds. She had reddish brown hair. She is well orientated as to time, place, and person. Her mood and spirits are reasonably good. She relates in a free, open and easy manner. Thought content is as given above. There is no evidence of delusions or hallucinations or any other type of psychotic ideation. Thought processes reveal that she speaks with an even flow and tempo. There is no evidence of blocking. She does tend

16

to go into a great deal of detail but her narrations have continuity and the details which she presents are quite relevant and fit into the points that she conveys. There is no evidence of a primary thinking disorder. Intellection functions are intact. General knowledge is quite good. Mathematical ability is below average. Abstract thinking ability is quite intact. Past medical history reveals that she had two pregnancies, both of which miscarried. She was in a TB sanitarium in California at the age of 22 for the treatment of tuberculosis. She had had hypertension since her early 60s. Over the last six months she has had difficulty with empyema and asthma. Her heart is quite enlarged. On examination of this woman, I find no evidence of any psychotic illness. Her record for the last several years and also while she was at the State Hospital would indicate that she had been rehabilitated herself. Further psychiatric treatment is not indicated. Eugene R. Almer, MD, Arizona State Hospital, Psychiatric Examination."[28]

1969, August 20
Ruth is ordered back to the Arizona State Hospital. Ronald Reagan extradited her to Arizona. They read the judgement to her and handed her over to Arizona authorities. She was wearing a blue dress with matching shoes. She stated that she didn't want to go back to Arizona a prisoner. She asked why she could not go back to Arizona like other patients. She stated she was being treated like a criminal rather than a mental patient. She stated her escape was not a felony. She stated, "It's not a felony when the door is open and the fence is down."[29] She complained about being questioned in the death of Anna Aarons. Her nephew had been identified as one of his patients. She said, "I don't want to be questioned about something that I don't know anything about. I haven't done anything they asked me about".[29] An interview by her stated, "However, bitterness crept into her voice as she spoke of her niece's husband. "He just used me," she said. She would not name the husband because, she said, she didn't want to hurt her niece. She said he was the person who took her from Phoenix to Oakland following her last escape and he had received money from her since."[30] She was in court with David Kogus who worked with Melvin Belli. Ruth told the judge she wished to have her freedom and go to Paraguay and work in a leper colony.[29] Noran Menendez makes the following observations regarding Ruth Judd: "The patient is a 64-year-old Caucasian female who looks her stated age. She is appropriately and well dressed and well groomed. The patient is alert, cooperative,

17

and orientated in all three spheres. The patient appears to be mildly tense and dejected which I would consider appropriate under the circumstances. The patients affect is mildly depressed. However, her affect is appropriate to her content of thought and she modulates well. She is able to laugh and joke appropriately with this examiner. The patient's stream of conversation is mildly discursive. However, at no time does she lose her point or train of thought. There is no formal thinking defect or loosening of associations. The patient's thinking is goal directed and reality oriented. When left on her own, the content centers mainly on her adjustment in California and the good impression she had made on people. However, when this examiner interjects other ideas or thoughts, she is able to pick up on them and deal with these. No delusions, leads of reference, nor somatic preoccupations were noted. The patient denies hallucination, auditory or visual. She denies any suicidal ideation or gestures. The patient's fund of information appears adequate. She did serial sevens and serial presidents well. There is no history of states of derealization or depersonalization elicited. There was no abnormality in the rate or flow of speech or in psychomotor activity. In describing how she lived after her unauthorized absence from here, she gave every indication of being able to fend for herself, and to realistically manage her own affairs. Impression: There is no sign of any overt psychotic disorder. On this basis of examination, it is my opinion that there is no indication for any ongoing psychiatric treatment or hospitalization, and that the patient is competent to manage her own affairs, legal, financial and otherwise."[31]

1969, August 22
Rex E Whitney writes his analysis in a memo to Willis H Bower. He states, "She is in good contact, is orientated as to time and place, and there is no evidence of any thought disorder. If allowed to talk freely, she tells about her various employers in California and how well she was liked, but if interrupted by a question she answers promptly and relevantly. Her emotional response is appropriate and she seems well adjusted at this time. When speaking of visiting the grave of her husband, who died many years ago while she was here in the Hospital, she had some tears in her eyes, and again when she spoke of the efforts to obtain her release when she was here before. This probably indicates some underlying depression but this would seem to be a normal reaction to her present situation. I find no evidence of psychosis at this time and no indication for any psychiatric treatment."[32] Arnold

Dendall MD also writes an analysis of Ruth Judd, "For more detailed information regarding this patient's background, the reader is referred to the hospital chart. Mental status description: The patient is a well groomed, cheerful and matron-like appearing female who entered the interview situation readily and without reservation. She indicated at the outset that she will cooperate to the fullest and making the point that she has nothing to hide. Her manner, voice and posture are in keeping with her coherently and spontaneously and otherwise very conversant. The psychomotor activity and emotional reactions are essentially appropriate to the situation. With regard to her escape, she indicates that she had left the hospital on impulse because of her feeling of being let down here in Arizona. After all, 31 years of hospitalization finally gets to you. In discussing her whereabouts in California, she reiterated that she worked very hard at her rehabilitation, taking care of a rather large household, and that her employer was entirely satisfied with her performance. She did most of the planning and marketing as part of her household duties. She described this period perhaps the happiest years of her life. Content of through association: she is able to maintain a fair continuity of ideas and a relatively orderly transition of one group of thoughts to another with very little circumstantivity, if any. There is no evidence of overt thought disturbances. Special preoccupations: relate primarily to her case, recent and past, with particular emphasis on the last seven years and her good functioning in California, her conversation suggests a heroine like image, a need to prove to the world that she is in fact a good person. Affect: appropriate, although more of a matter of fact with some evidence of outward display rather than actual feeling. Insight and judgement: good in the testing situation. She recognizes that she was emotionally ill in the past and that her former attitude and thinking was part of her illness. Formulation: On the basis of my mental examination which has revealed no abnormality in thought process and content, I would recommend that this patient is no longer in need of further psychiatric hospitalization and treatment."[33]

1969, August 25
Court decided that Ruth Judd is sane. "Opinion of the undersigned that the conditions justifying hospitalization of the said Winnie Ruth Judd in this hospital no longer obtain, and she is sufficiently restored to reason that she may be returned to the Arizona State Prison."[34]

1969, September 29
Robert Keiser sues his insurance company for them dropping his policy
and failing to pay for psychiatric services. He lost. He incurred a bill
of $4380 through September 17th. It did not state if Dr. Aarons had
been paid or not.[13]

1969, December 11
An appraisal filed in superior court in Oakland revealed that Mrs.
Aarons who was found beaten on the patio of her home at 2750
Laverock Lane and died had left behind an estate. No arrests have been
made in the case. The home which was valued at $75000 was in Mrs.
Aarons' name. Other items listed included $10,000 worth of art objects,
two automobiles, jewelry and other furnishings for a total of $95,113.
Mrs. Aarons' will specifies that her estate is to be put into trust for her
two children, Victoria, 16, and John David who is 11. Dr. Aarons will
receive $5000 a year from that trust.[35]

1.   Fulbright, Tom, *Cow-country counselor*. [1st ed. 1968, New York,:
        Exposition Press. 196 p.
2.   Swent, Eleanor, *Marian Lane: Mine Doctor's Wife in Mexico*.
        Western Mining in the Twentieth Century Oral History Services.
        1996, Berkeley. 121.
3.   *Letter from Dr. Samuel Wick to the superior Court*, in *State Vs Judd:
        Arizona State Archives and Public Records*. October 10, 1962:
        Phoenix, AZ.
4.   *A Marie Halloran*, in *Unknown newspaper clippings of Jerry
        Leukowtiz*. December 7, 1963: Phoenix.
5.   Haney, John, *Judd Murder Site Doomed*, in *Arizona Republic*. June
        26, 1964: Phoenix, AZ.
6.   Suttliff, Curt, et al., *Trunk Murderess Winnie Judd Held in Eastbay*, in
        Oakland Tribune. June 28, 1969.
7.   Swent, Langan W., et al., *Working for safety and health in
        underground mines : San Luis and Homestake mining companies,
        1946-1988*. Western mining in the twentieth century oral history
        series. 1995. xix, 1007.
8.   *Letter to Mrs. Alma Jennings of the superior court from Robert
        Corbin, County Attorney*, in *State vs Judd: Arizona State Archives
        and Public Records*. January 25, 1966: Phoenix, AZ.

SECTION SEVEN 1960-1969

9.   *Carolyn Keiser Vs Robert J Keiser.* 2/1/1966, 1966, Contra Costa County.

10.   *Letter from Alma Jennings, clerk of the superior court to Mr. N. Warner Lee,* in *State Vs Judd: Arizona State Archives and Public Records.* February 1, 1966: Phoenix, AZ.

11.   Williams, Bryan, *Dilemma for the State of Arizona: Should Winnie Ruth Judd Be Given Her Freedom?,* in *Master Detective.* April, 1970.

12.   *Carolyn Keiser vs Robert J Keiser.* 4/25/1969, 1968, Contra Costa County. C111839.

13.   *Robert J Keiser Vs Insurance Company.* 9/29/1969, 1969, Contra Costa County. C116736.

14.   *Mother of 2 Dies in Home Mystery,* in *San Francisco Examiner.* April 29, 1969: San Francisco.

15.   Contra Costa County Sheriff's Department, *Police Report regarding the Homicide of Anna Aarons.* 1969: Alamo.

16.   *Beating Killed Her,* in *San Francisco Examiner.* April 30, 1969: San Francisco.

17.   Bendheim, Otto L, *Psychiatric Exmination at the request of Attorney Larry L Debus.* January 21, 1971, Camelback Professional Building: Phoenix.

18.   *A Nagging Feeling Led to Judd Arrest,* in *San Francisco Examiner.* June 28, 1969: San Francisco.

19.   *Winnie Ruth Again,* in *San Francisco Chronicle.* June 28, 1969: San Francisco.

20.   *Winnie Ruth Judd in Custody Again,* in *Daytona Beach Sunday News Journal.* June 28, 1969: Daytona Beach, FL.

21.   Belli, Melvin M and Robert Blair Kaiser, *Melvin Belli : My Life on Trial : An Aautobiography* 1976, New York: Morrow.

22.   *Winnie Judd Bail Set at $125,000,* in *Morning News Gazette.* July 1, 1969: Martinez, CA.

23.   *Winnie Judd Admits Her Identity in Court,* in *Morning News Gazette.* July 15, 1969: Martinez, CA.

24.   *Winnie Ruth Judd: Then and Now.* July 1969, 1969, KTAR Broadcasting: Phoenix, Arizona. 30 minutes.
       http://www.youtube.com/watch?v=lA4dtH0tqxw

25.   *Winnie Says Nobody Hurt,* in *Morning News Gazette.* August 9, 1969: Martinez, CA.

26.   *Reagan Orders Judd Returned to Arizona,* in *Morning News Gazette.* August 15, 1969: Martinez, CA.

27.   Whitney, Rex E., *Memo to Willis H Bower Director regarding Winnie Ruth Judd. from Rex E Whitney, Assistant to the director*, in *Pineal County Historical Museum*. August 15, 1969: Florence, AZ.

28.   *Letter of examination findings of Ruth Judd by Dr. Eugene Almer MD to Larry Debus*, in *State Vs Judd: Arizona State Library and Public Records*. August 19, 1969: Phoenix, AZ.

29.   *Winnie Ruth Judd is sent back to State Hospital*, in *Lodi News Sentinel*. August 20, 1969: Lodi, CA.

30.   Mckechnie, Logan, *Winnie tried to forget: Trunk murderess claims she's not insane*, in *Arizona Republic*. August 20, 1969.

31.   *Examination of Ruth Judd By Noran Menendez*, in *State Vs Judd: Arizona State Archives and Public Records*. August 20, 1969: Phoenix, AZ.

32.   *Letter to Willis H Bower from Rext E Whitney*, in *State Vs Judd: Arizona State Archives and Public Records*. August 22, 1969: Phoenix, AZ.

33.   *Report of Arnold Dendall, MD on Ruth Judd*, in *State Vs Judd: Arizona State Archives and Public Records*. August 22, 1969: Phoenix, AZ.

34.   *Sanity Ruling Regarding Ruth Judd*, in *State Vs Judd: Arizona State Archives and Public Records*. August 25, 1969: Phoenix, AZ.

35.   *Murdered Wife Leaves $95,000*, in *Oakland Tribune*. December 11, 1969: Oakland, CA.

Section 8

1970-2001

1970, May 1
Ruth wrote this letter to her attorney Melvin Belli in California. Some of the excerpts were: "I have never driven a car in my life. In Mexico Dr. Judd had to have a chauffeur who was also a mechanic. There are no garages there as here in the USA. He couldn't be in the surgery half a day and change tires on those rough mountain roads. Here in Phoenix when he was ill and I had to work, we were too poor to own a car." "For 6.5 years my nieces' husband was trying to sell a story on my case. He brought me a clipping from the Oakland Tribune once, where he said she had been approached twice about doing a film on my case and he was considering it one night when he phoned me about selling a story to Truman Capote and talked about Susan Hayward doing the movie. I said please leave me alone. I do not want any money. All I want is to be left alone. I love my work and am happy here. I just want peace and quiet. Mrs. Nichols, we had 6 phones was listening in on part of the conversation from her room phone. I was crying and she came into the kitchen very distressed and said, what is it, are you in trouble of some kind, tell me so I can help you. I said no, someone is just trying to sell something and I may have to go back East. Mrs. Nichols told her daughter Mrs. Blemer about it. Mrs. Blemer remembers as long as my niece was married to Robert Keiser he didn't dare sell a story or turn me in, but then she sued for a divorce. I was the pawn First he induced me to buy him that Ford Galaxy as he was having to rent a car to get to work and earn a living for their 4 children. My niece drove that car 7 months. I didn't know where. He drove it to a doctor's office, whose wife had been killed 10 days before fifty miles from where I lived and I

1

had never heard of those people. I wasn't being evasive. I was nervous at the hearing and had been told to be brief. If I ever go again I will probably talk so much they will think I am crazy wandering from one subject to another, trying to tell them to explain everything. As to selling any story, I have never in 38 years. To me, it would be very repugnant to think of selling any story. I don't know what kind of morbid people would read such things. This was an unforeseen tragedy, which I have suffered years of agony over. The doctors at the hospital kept telling me you can't live in the past, only an unhealthy mind lives in the past."[1] Ruth during the period this story occurred stated that "My nieces and nephews and other relatives finally put a stop to it."[2] She also stated that Bob Keiser was demanding, but never threatening. In fact, he was quite polite about it. Ruth referred to Bob as a well salaried individual always ready for supplemental cash handouts.[2]

1971, January 21
Otto L Bendheim of the Camelback profession building wrote a psychiatric report of Winnie Ruth Judd as requested by her lawyer Larry Debus. He described her as a well preserved, jolly, clean, well groomed, elderly white person with grayish hair, a pink complexion, slightly chubby, well developed, and outwardly at least, without signs of physical illness." Throughout the conversation, interview evaluation and examination, Mrs. Judd displayed an excellent sense of humor, a friendly, courteous and sociable manner and behaved herself like a lady. Despite very thorough searching I found absolutely no evidence of delusions or hallucinations. A slight degree of anxiety was present but in no way more than one would expect under the circumstances, namely, a psychiatric evaluation performed in a prison environment. The intelligence is normal or above normal. Her way to express herself is adequate. The mood was appropriate for the circumstances. I found neither depression, elation nor any degree of violence or tendency toward vehemence, disturbed behavior or other psychopathology. The orientation is excellent; her fund of general knowledge is good. She was spontaneous, appropriate and alert in all her productions. His

conclusions were: 1. This person is sound, sane and absolutely harmless. 2. She presents no danger whatever to society or to herself. 3. There are no suicidal, homicidal or violent tendencies. 4. She has a potential for constructive and meaningful contribution to society. 5. Her motivation is excellent and her character at this time does not display any psychopathological or antisocial tendencies. His final words were, society is further damaged by unnecessary expense of keeping this harmless person behind prison walls. [3]

1971, October 21
Walter Hoffmann writes a letter to Governor Williams. He stated that it had been 18 months since he had visited Ruth at the State Prison in Florence. She sent word that she needed his help in her appearance before the parole board. He stated that as long as she was represented by an attorney that he did not want to be involved. She also asked if Reverend Hoffmann would appear on her behalf if she discharged her attorney. Ruth decided to keep her attorney and let him present her case before the board.[4] He stated that he had been in a car wreck and broke his right leg plus a broken left shoulder. He feels like he cannot get to Florence from his home at 4022 East Devonshire, Phoenix. He stated he hoped the Governor had a good trip to Spain.[4] He sent along this letter that he received in 1953.[5]

1971, October 28
Winnie Ruth Judd made the statement that a nephew drove her to California after her last escape and later forced her to give him most of the $30,000 that was left her by a former employer. She agreed not to sell her life story to newspapers or motion picture companies. John and Ethyl Blemer stated they would accept responsibility of her on her release. They looked forward to her return.[6]

1971, November 24
Governor Jack Williams returns the 1953 letter from Ruth Judd to Reverend Hofmann.[7]

1971, November 30
In a newspaper article talking about her possible upcoming release said,

3

"A nephew phoned her, she said, 'and told me I would never have to work again' if he could sell her story." A board member described the nephew's approach as "almost blackmail." She and her attorney promised that she would not profit financially from any story and agreed that any profits should go to charity." She also said when asked on Monday about efforts by speculators to capitalize on her memories, Mrs. Judd said she had been approached in prison by a man "high up in politics" who "caused me trouble years ago." The man, whom she did not identify, "showed me pictures and told me how executions looked almost as a veiled threat." She said she left word she didn't want to see him again. This was the only reason apparently that they were still holding her at Florence.[8]

1975, August
Dr. ZA Aarons publishes a paper about the effect of his relocation had on his patients. He relocated sometime in 1974 and his address is listed as 1025 Ardmore Ave, Portland, Oregon. He discusses 3 case studies specifically and some other patients in general. He makes some interesting statements.

"That the analyst himself is affected must be self-evident by the very nature of his role. His countertransference reactions, among which may be feelings of guilt over abandoning his children and love ones, being a bad or irresponsible parent, must, of course, be immediately recognized and surmounted by self- analysis, so that he will be able to distinguish the heightened transference reactions of his patients and not succumb to his own projection (which may happen when faced with a patient's reproaches.)"

"I could anticipate angry protests from one such patient with paranoid tendencies. He demanded to know what my reasons were for relocating, saying that he could not understand why a successful psychiatrist would want to move away. To analyze this reaction in terms of his mother's abandonment of him was, I thought, to miss the crucial point, namely his fear that when on his own, he would give in to his destructive impulses, either by again being harmful to loved ones, or becoming self-destructive, as he had been in the past, motivated by unconscious homosexual wishes, and allowing himself to be

4

'used'. Among his protests was the accusation that I had taken him on as a patient for my own benefit. I do not yet know whether my emphasis upon his main resistance (to be 'used', a cover-up for homosexual wishes) will have brought about an appreciable change in his relationships."

"Another more overtly paranoid patient, whose delusions were often impervious to correction by experience and reason, presented another predictable reaction. Given to projection, he believed that it was I who had the insuperable problems that made it necessary to me to relocate elsewhere. To a neurotic patient, an effective interpretation would be that seeking to find my problems would serve as a distraction from the pursuit of resolving his. My paranoid patient, however, fell into a delusional cause and effect relationship in his thinking, seeking to blame his not being 'cured' on my leaving, which would forever prevent him from solving his problems. This delusional attitude was not a means of assuaging the pain of his disappointment, as might be expected from a neurotic patient; rather it immediately enabled him to indulge and justify his anger (release aggression against me), also revealing a classic paranoid effort to turn love (of a threatening homosexual nature) into hate.

"A patient with unconscious homosexual inclinations, but not paranoid, welcomes the termination with a kind of hypomanic reaction, wishing to believe that if I could terminate his treatment, his problems were solved, and he transiently ceased serious work during his sessions. This patient had returned to his analysis three times. He had interrupted it (each time with good rationalization-money difficulty or a job change) to avoid a deeper confrontation of homosexual feelings towards me, yet each time he returned it was because he felt he could no longer function without me. 'His elated reaction to the termination as an expression of the wish not to have to need me any more (to appropriate my potency). During the last period of his analysis, foreseeing the inevitable (that he would have to forego reliance upon me), when told that he had created for himself in his relationship with me a false sense of potency and masculinity, he again fell into a depression which had originally broken out when his father died, leaving him bereft of the resources upon which he depended. His

5

depression ushered in an acute transference reaction, furthering the resolution of his latent homosexual problem."
"One aspect of the relocation problem for both patient and analyst is the question of how much it is necessary for the patient to know about the details of the analyst's move (where he is going and why); and what the analyst's motives are in offering an explanation for the move. That the patient would be curious and the analyst might feel obligated to respond to the patient's request (on the surface legitimate) is universally manifest. Due regard, however, for avoiding a disruption of the transference may place the analyst on guard against readily answering question posed by the patient. A possible exception is the patient reared in the tradition of the 'child is to be seen and not heard', who therefore feels that he has no right to know (and all that it implies in regard to what goes on during the primal scene). At the opposite extreme is the patient who belligerently asserts his right to know; and to the extent to which this makes the analyst feel guilt, such a patient may be intimidating. Grated that an explanation is in order, it is the timing that must determine when it is forthcoming. I believe the difficulties of the complication resented by the 'special event' may be lessened if the analyst is economical in the initial announcement of his intention to move away. When a patient revealed more apprehension that I had anticipated, it was necessary to assure her that an explanation would be forthcoming I reminded the patient that she had a choice of whether to have her questions answered or analyzed and, as she knew, if she adhered to our analytic role (far from arbitrary), she would gain by it.

As a general rule, 'not to know why' in regard to anything personal about the analyst does not increase the degree of anxiety in the patient. If it does, however, the patient may sharpen his wits in exploring the fantasy behind his need to know, thereby contributing to a heightening of the transference reactions (which no doubt directly or indirectly will be found to bear on crucial infantile complexes- loss of love object, primal scene, fear of helplessness and abandonment etc.).[9]

1976, July 6

Jack Halloran died the previous Monday at the age of 89. He had been in the lumber business in the valley 40 years until retiring in 1955 and was a former member of the Phoenix Country Club board of directors. He had been grand knight of the Knights of Columbus, a past president of the Southwest Golf Association, and a life member of the Arizona Club and Elks Lodge. He graduated from St. Mary's College, Moraga California in 1905 and came to Phoenix in 1915. He had been director of the Phoenix Chamber of Commerce. Survivors include his daughters. Margaret Running and Sister St. John Halloran. He had 6 grandchildren and 13 great grandchildren. Rosary for him was said on this date at Sacred Heart Home Chapel, 1110 N 16th Street (where he was a resident). Funeral mass was there as well. Arrangements were handled by Arcadia Funeral Home.[10]

1982, June 29

Marian J Lane makes a claim for $40,572.00 against the estate of Ethel Blemer for her work from May 1979 to 1982. She claimed that she worked 13 hours per day and so with overtime, the Blemer's owed her $9,795 for 1979 (this is just not for overtime) Apparently, they paid her $2965 for this period. In 1980 they owed her $12,639.50 while she was paid $4868.50. In 1981, they owed her $13, 519.50. In 1982, they owed her $4618. She did not claim wages before 1979. Her entire claim was for $4,875,000.00. Her attorney was Richard C. Bennett. Her address is listed as PO box 308 Diablo, California 94528. The 4 million included 225,000 for fair market value of domestic services from 1971 to the time of her death; $150,000 for the fair market value of all oral contracts entered into between decedent and claimant pertaining to a promised life estate in the duplex in Diablo, CA.; $1,500,000 for personal and emotional injuries sustained by claimant on an ongoing basis from 1971 to the decedents death. $2,000,000 for violations of claimants federally guaranteed civil and personal individual's rights stemming from involuntary servitude by claimant at the hands of the decedent; $2,000,000 claims for damages for fraud, misrepresentation, both negligently and intentionally, deceit and conversion of

7

claimant's personal property, assets and money for use by decedent. The inventory for the entire estate of Ethel Blemer was $1,856,304.11.[11]

1982, October 27
Lois Lippincott (Blemer) files a petition for approval of compromise and settlement of claims made against the estate for the distribution of assets in trust to provide monthly payments for claimant's lifetime. It stated that the petitioner has compromised and settled the claims. Lois received 7000 shares of Standard Oil Company stock to do the following. She would pay Marian J. Lane for the rest of her life on the first day of each month following her vacating 950 Blemer Road $1,250. Any leftover stock would become a part of the principal of the trust estate. On the death of Marian Lane, the money should be given to John Whitney Blemer; then Lois Ann Lippincott, and then those specified by Marian J Lane. She also got $50,000 to vacate Green Valley Farm. Marian Lane agrees to drop any claims, liens, demands, and causes of action, obligation, damages and liabilities. It was signed by Lois on October 26th.[11]

1987
Ruth returns to Darlington IN to visit.[12]

1993
Ruth visits Darlington IN.[12]

1995
Ruth visits Darlington IN.[12]

1998, October 23
Marion Lane (Ruth Judd) passes away in Phoenix. She is buried at Inglewood Cemetery in Los Angeles. She is located in the Cypress Mausoleum A Center Crypt, lot number 39[13] She said, "I had purchased a plot for my parents and myself. My brother didn't have much when he died. He didn't have a plot for himself. I buried him in my plot which is close to my parents. I brought another plot for myself near my parents. I paid $600 for my brother's plot and $1500 for one for myself.

I couldn't sell it for $500. I could be buried next to my husband. I would go there every other Sunday to San Bruno where my husband was buried." She didn't know where she wanted to be buried. She stated that her husband was cremated and that she did not want to be cremated. She stated that she would have to buy a coffin (this info from the oral tape only, not the transcript).[14]

2001, August
A confession letter written and dated by Winnie Ruth Judd to HG Richardson was anonymously donated to the Arizona Historical Society in Tucson. It was processed collection that same month.[15]

1. Judd, Winnie Ruth, *Series of Letters written to Melvin Belli*, in *Pineal County Museum*. May, 1970: Florence, AZ.
2. Williams, Bryan, *Dilemma for the State of Arizona: Should Winnie Ruth Judd Be Given Her Freedom?*, in *Master Detective*. April, 1970.
3. Bendheim, Otto L, *Psychiatric Exmination at the request of Attorney Larry L Debus*. January 21, 1971, Camelback Professional Building: Phoenix.
4. Hoffmann, Walter, *Letter to Governor Jack Williams from Walter Hoffmann*. October 21, 1971: Phoenix.
5. Judd, Winnie Ruth, *Letter from Ruth Judd to Walter Hoffmann; later forwarded to Governor Williams in 1971*. July 26, 1953: Phoenix.
6. Gould, Lee, *Winnie Judd Promised Job if Released from Life Term*, in *Oakland Tribune*. October 28, 1971: Oakland, CA.
7. Williams, Jack, *Letter from Governor Jack Williams to Reverend Walter Hofmann*. November 24, 1971: Phoenix.
8. *Tiger Woman Release May Unveil Old Mystery*, in *Bakersfield Californian*. November 30, 1971.
9. Aarons, Z. A., *The analyst's relocation: its effect on the transference- -parameter or catalyst*. Int J Psychoanal, 1975. 56(3): p. 303-19.
10. *Obituary: John J. Halloran*, in *Arizona Republic*. July 6, 1976: Phoenix. 11.
11. *Ethel Blemer Probate*. 1982, Contra Costa County. 07-16765.
12. *Strange Story of Winnie Ruth Judd Closes*, in *Journal Review Weekend*. November 7, 1998: Darlington?, IN.

13.   Inglewood Park Cemetery, *Inglewood Park Cemetery Database,.*
2007. http://www.inglewoodparkcemetery.com/search_db.html
14.   Swent, Eleanor, *Marian Lane: Mine Doctor's Wife in Mexico.*
Western Mining in the Twentieth Century Oral History Services.
1996, Berkeley. 121.
15.   Judd, Winnie Ruth, *Confession Letter of Winnie Ruth Judd: Letter to
HG Richardson.*, in *Winnie Ruth Judd, Arizona Historical Society.*
April 6, 8, 1933: Tuscon.

ABOUT THE AUTHOR

SUNNY LYNN WOREL worked independently as a Medical Information Specialist starting in 2002. She specialized in online data literature searches of biomedical data bases. She earned her B.S. degrees in Biochemistry and Microbiology from the University of Minnesota in 1990 She received her Masters of Library and Information Science in 1996 from Dominican University/College of St. Catherine and was a senior member of the Academy of Health Information Professionals (AHIP). She belonged to the Medical Library Association (MLA) and the Association of Independent Information Professionals (AIIP). She successfully combined her work over the last 15 years of her life with her passion for her search for Hedvig (Sammy) Samuelson, her great aunt. Sunny died in 2014. Her mother, Janet V. Worel, published this timeline on her behalf.

Made in the USA
Las Vegas, NV
27 October 2024

10540688R00308